# Fiscal Deficits in the Pacific Region

Nations of the Pacific region had, until recently, a reputation for prudent running of their economies with minimal fiscal imbalances and debt. This reputation has become tarnished of late thanks to some financial crises that have brought about real debt management problems for several economies in this area.

This book analyses a selection of these economies paying specific attention to their fiscal policies and structures. The impressive contributions cover a range of countries seeking to provide evidence that can be applied in future policy decisions.

A wide range of experts from across the globe have come together in this useful book. They have produced a work that will be recommended reading for students and academics involved in the areas of international finance, money and banking and Asia Pacific studies. The policy lessons that can be learned from this book will also need to be taken on board by policy-makers the world over.

**Akira Kohsaka** is Professor at the Osaka School of International Public Policy, Osaka University, Japan.

## Routledge Studies in the Modern World Economy

**1 Interest Rates and Budget Deficits**
A study of the advanced economies
*Kanhaya L. Gupta and Bakhtiar Moazzami*

**2 World Trade after the Uruguay Round**
Prospects and policy options for the twenty-first century
*Edited by Harald Sander and András Inotai*

**3 The Flow Analysis of Labour Markets**
*Edited by Ronald Schettkat*

**4 Inflation and Unemployment**
Contributions to a new macroeconomic approach
*Edited by Alvaro Cencini and Mauro Baranzini*

**5 Macroeconomic Dimensions of Public Finance**
Essays in honour of Vito Tanzi
*Edited by Mario I. Blejer and Teresa M. Ter-Minassian*

**6 Fiscal Policy and Economic Reforms**
Essays in honour of Vito Tanzi
*Edited by Mario I. Blejer and Teresa M. Ter-Minassian*

**7 Competition Policy in the Global Economy**
Modalities for co-operation
*Edited by Leonard Waverman, William S. Comanor and Akira Goto*

**8 Working in the Macro Economy**
A study of the US labor market
*Martin F.J. Prachowny*

**9 How Does Privatization Work?**
*Edited by Anthony Bennett*

**10 The Economics and Politics of International Trade**
Freedom and trade: Volume II
*Edited by Gary Cook*

**11 The Legal and Moral Aspects of International Trade**
Freedom and trade: Volume III
*Edited by Asif Qureshi, Hillel Steiner and Geraint Parry*

**12 Capital Markets and Corporate Governance in Japan, Germany and the United States**
Organizational response to market inefficiencies
*Helmut M. Dietl*

**13 Competition and Trade Policies**
Coherence or conflict
*Edited by Einar Hope*

**14 Rice**
The primary commodity
*A.J.H. Latham*

**15 Trade, Theory and Econometrics**
Essays in honour of John S. Chipman
*Edited by James C. Moore, Raymond Riezman and James R. Melvin*

**16 Who benefits from Privatisation?**
*Edited by Moazzem Hossain and Justin Malbon*

**17 Towards a Fair Global Labour Market**
Avoiding the new slave trade
*Ozay Mehmet, Errol Mendes and Robert Sinding*

**18 Models of Futures Markets**
*Edited by Barry Goss*

**19 Venture Capital Investment**
An agency analysis of UK practice
*Gavin C. Reid*

**20 Macroeconomic Forecasting**
A sociological appraisal
*Robert Evans*

**21 Multimedia and Regional Economic Restructuring**
*Edited by Hans-Joachim Braczyk, Gerhard Fuchs and Hans-Georg Wolf*

**22 The New Industrial Geography**
Regions, regulation and institutions
*Edited by Trevor J. Barnes and Meric S. Gertler*

**23 The Employment Impact of Innovation**
Evidence and policy
*Edited by Marco Vivarelli and Mario Pianta*

**24 International Health Care Reform**
A legal, economic and political analysis
*Colleen Flood*

**25 Competition Policy Analysis**
*Edited by Einar Hope*

**26 Culture and Enterprise**
The development, representation and morality of business
*Don Lavoie and Emily Chamlee-Wright*

**27 Global Financial Crises and Reforms**
Cases and caveats
*B.N. Ghosh*

**28 Geography of Production and Economic Integration**
*Miroslav N. Jovanović*

**29 Technology, Trade and Growth in OECD Countries**
Does specialisation matter?
*Valentina Meliciani*

**30 Post-Industrial Labour Markets**
Profiles of North America and Scandinavia
*Edited by Thomas P. Boje and Bengt Furaker*

**31 Capital Flows without Crisis**
Reconciling capital mobility and economic stability
*Edited by Dipak Dasgupta, Marc Uzan and Dominic Wilson*

**32 International Trade and National Welfare**
*Murray C. Kemp*

**33 Global Trading Systems at Crossroads**
A post-Seattle perspective
*Dilip K. Das*

**34 The Economics and Management of Technological Diversification**
*Edited by John Cantwell, Alfonso Gambardella and Ove Granstrand*

**35 Before and Beyond EMU**
Historical lessons and future prospects
*Edited by Patrick Crowley*

**36 Fiscal Decentralization**
*Ehtisham Ahmad and Vito Tanzi*

**37 Regionalisation of Globalised Innovation**
Locations for advanced industrial development and disparities in participation
*Edited by Ulrich Hilpert*

**38 Gold and the Modern World Economy**
*Edited by MoonJoong Tcha*

**39 Global Economic Institutions**
*Willem Molle*

**40 Global Governance and Financial Crises**
*Edited by Meghnad Desai and Yahia Said*

**41 Linking Local and Global Economies**
The ties that bind
*Edited by Carlo Pietrobelli and Arni Sverrisson*

**42 Tax Systems and Tax Reforms in Europe**
*Edited by Luigi Bernardi and Paola Profeta*

**43 Trade Liberalization and APEC**
*Edited by Jiro Okamoto*

**44 Fiscal Deficits in the Pacific Region**
*Edited by Akira Kohsaka*

# Fiscal Deficits in the Pacific Region

Edited by Akira Kohsaka

LONDON AND NEW YORK

First published 2004
by Routledge
2 Park Square, Milton Park, Abingdon, Oxfordshire OX14 4RN

Simultaneously published in the USA and Canada
by Routledge
711 Third Avenue, New York, NY 10017

*Routledge is an imprint of the Taylor & Francis Group*

First issued in paperback 2012



Typeset in Galliard by Wearset Ltd, Boldon, Tyne and Wear



*British Library Cataloguing in Publication Data*
A catalogue record for this book is available from the British Library

*Library of Congress Cataloging in Publication Data*
A catalog record for this book has been requested

ISBN 13: 978-0-415-32491-5 (hbk)
ISBN 13: 978-0-415-65485-2 (pbk)

# Contents

# Figures

# Tables

# Contributors

**Gustavo Arteta,** Academic Director, Development Research Corporation (CORDES), Ecuador.

**Kazumi Asako,** Professor of Economics, The Institute of Economic Research, Hitotsubashi University, Japan.

**Sang-Kun Bae,** Research Fellow, Center for Macroeconomic Studies/Center for Finance and Tax Director, Center for Information and Computing Services, Korea Economic Research Institute (KERI), Korea.

**Cheng-Mount Cheng,** Assistant Research Fellow, Taiwan Institute of Economic Research (TIER), Taiwan.

**Robert Dekle,** Associate Professor, Department of Economics, University of Southern California, USA.

**Peter Gardiner,** Economist, New Zealand Institute of Economic Research (NZIER), New Zealand.

**Tan Khee Giap,** Head, Econometric Modeling Unit, and Associate Professor of Banking and Finance, Nanyang Technological University, Singapore.

**Rafael E. Gómez-Tagle M.,** Coordinator, Credit Risk Infrastructure, BANAMEX, Mexico.

**Ronald Kneebone,** Professor, Department of Economics, University of Calgary, Canada.

**Akira Kohsaka,** Professor of Economics, Osaka School of International Public Policy, Osaka University, Japan.

**Ari Kuncoro,** Lecturer, Faculty of Economics, University of Indonesia, Indonesia.

**Li Jinshan,** Research Fellow, the Research Institute of Fiscal Science, the Ministry of Finance, People's Republic of China.

**Dongsoon Lim,** Research Associate, Interdisciplinary Institute for Environmental Economics, Department of Economics, University of Heidelberg, Germany.

**Luis Ignacio Lozano,** Director of the Public Finance Office, Department of Economic Studies, Central Bank of Colombia, Colombia.

**Sergio A. Luna,** Senior Vice President, BANAMEX, Mexico.

**Tony Makin,** Reader, Associate Professor, School of Economics, University of Queensland, Australia.

**Eduardo Moreno,** Economist, Central Reserve Bank of Peru, Peru.

**Suresh Narayanan,** Professor of Economics, School of Social Sciences, Universiti Sains Malaysia, Malaysia.

**Viet Lan Nguyen,** United Nations Development Programme, Vietnam.

**Jeffrey B. Nugent,** Professor, Department of Economics, University of Southern California, USA.

**Cayetano W. Paderanga, Jr.,** Professor, School of Economics, University of the Philippines, and Chairman, Institute for Development and Econometric Analysis, the Philippines.

**Jose L. Pereyra,** Economist, Central Reserve Bank of Peru, Peru.

**Douglas Steel,** Senior Research Economist, New Zealand Institute of Economic Research (NZIER), New Zealand.

**Hitoshi Suzuki,** Senior Researcher, Economic Research Department, Daiwa Institute of Research Ltd, Japan.

**Kim Chung Tran,** Principal Researcher, Central Institute for Economic Management, Vietnam.

**Masao Tsuri,** Research Fellow, the Japan Society for the Promotion of Science, Japan.

**Wang Xiaoguang,** Associate Research Fellow, the Research Institute of Fiscal Science, the Ministry of Finance, People's Republic of China.

**Soon Lee Ying,** Associate Professor of Applied Economics, Nanyang Business School, Nanyang Technological University, Singapore.

# Preface

This book is based on the study conducted by the Pacific Economic Outlook (PEO) Structure, one of the Task Forces under the Pacific Economic Cooperation Council (PECC). The aim of this book is to analyze recent developments in fiscal balances and government debt in the Pacific region and to draw policy implications from the analyses for immediate and future fiscal policy management issues.

A decade ago, the North American and European countries were said to have made only limited progress in getting their ratios of public debt-to-GDP right (IMF 1996). Also at that time, the Latin American countries had to contain their fiscal imbalances, as well as scale down the level of state intervention in the economy. In contrast, the East Asian economies were known to be rather prudent in government housekeeping with minimal fiscal imbalances and debt.

Ten years later, however, the fiscal picture in the economies of the world is very different. Particularly in the Pacific region, the advanced economies (with the exception of Japan) have made a great leap forward and the Latin American economies have taken important steps toward regaining fiscal health. In contrast, several economies in East Asia may face government debt management problems as a result of their heavy reliance on fiscal stimulus in the process of recovery from the Asian economic crisis.

As a matter of fact, it is claimed that, since the early 1990s, many countries, particularly the advanced economies, are said to have significantly improved their fiscal positions (IMF 2001). Can we find a similar trend in the Pacific region? If yes, how? If no, why not? The recent fiscal adjustment has also been characterized primarily by expenditure restraint and by widespread reforms aimed at strengthening institutional fiscal frameworks, both with less government involvement. Can we draw similar lessons from the Pacific experiences in their fiscal adjustment? Without doubt, the impact of recent currency crises in emerging markets has negatively affected the fiscal consolidation efforts of these countries. How can we assess the impact in the short and long run? Finally, we are not certain whether this trend of fiscal improvement is robust and that it will not be reversed by probable cyclical downturns. Today, with the test of a cyclical downturn literally in front of us, what can we tell about the future based on our experiences in the Pacific region?

In trying to answer these questions above, the authors scrutinize and compare the experiences of fiscal adjustment and consolidation efforts in the context of individual countries and address future policy concerns and options. In so doing, we examine the following points:

- How different are the Pacific economies in terms of fiscal structures?
- How did fiscal balances and government debt develop in the past several decades and what caused this development?
- At more disaggregated levels, what items in revenues and expenditures play relatively important roles in developments in aggregate fiscal positions?
- What factor has caused the contrasting patterns of fiscal developments among the Pacific economies and in what way and how much did fiscal policies affect these developments?
- What are the immediate as well as longer-run challenges for fiscal policy management and what can we say about these from what we have learned from our international comparison efforts?

From the chapters in this book, we can summarize five findings and/or policy implications:

1 Diversity in fiscal structure. The degree of centralization, size and organization of government, composition of fiscal revenue and expenditure, and institutional arrangements are all very different across the economies in the region.
2 There are distinct patterns in fiscal management between developed and developing economies with fiscal management that is stabilization-oriented in the former and development-oriented in the latter.
3 Successful fiscal consolidation that is characterized both by expenditure restraint and by economic growth. Reduction in expenditure along with strengthening of the fiscal framework has been highlighted as an effective approach for fiscal consolidation recently. Noting the close linkage between business cycles and fiscal development, however, strengthening revenue bases through economic recovery is also indispensable, especially for consolidation in recession.
4 Fiscal consolidation in emerging markets endangered by currency crises. The subsequent financial sector distress and severe currency depreciation hit those economies with relatively high debt-to-GDP ratios particularly hard. We need to reconcile the short-run accommodative fiscal adjustment with long-run consolidation.
5 Ever-increasing fiscal needs created by globalization and an aging society. We need not to simply cut expenditures, but to keep on rationalizing both the revenue and expenditure sides of the budget in terms of both size and composition.

These findings and policy implications, as well as the detailed analyses and many examples throughout this book, will hopefully help us and policy-makers establish sound and well-balanced fiscal management policies and frameworks in the context of individual economies in the Pacific region and elsewhere as well and thus promote their economic development and cooperation.

Finally, let us touch upon the background of this study. The study has been conducted by specialists from member economies of the PECC under the coordination of Akira Kohsaka. In the process of this study the PEO Structure held two international specialists meetings in September 2000 and March 2001 in Osaka, Japan, hosted by the Japan Committee for Pacific Economic Outlook. The committee has been housed in the Kansai Economic Research Center (now changed to the Kansai Institute for Social and Economic Research, KISER) and sponsored by the Ministry of Foreign Affairs of Japan and the business communities in the Kansai region. Since then, the outcome was reported twice, i.e., at the Concurrent Session of the PECC XIV General Meeting, Hong Kong, 29 November 2001, and at the APEC Finance and Central Bank Deputies Meeting, 9th APEC Finance Ministers' Process, Mexican Cultural Institute, Washington, DC, USA, 22 April 2002.

This book is the revised and updated outcome of these series of studies. It was made possible by the secretariat of Japan Committee for PEO, particularly Shinichi Numata and Tomoyuki Suga, Deputy Executive Directors (then and present, respectively), and Machiko Fujita, Program Officer. We owe them a great deal for all of their secretarial and management work. Janis Kea also supported the completion of this book with her economics background and professional editorial skills. Book design, editing and production were coordinated by Robert Langham, Routledge.

Akira Kohsaka
Editor

## References

International Monetary Fund (1996) *World Economic Outlook*, May, Washington, DC: International Monetary Fund.

International Monetary Fund (2001) *World Economic Outlook*, May, Washington, DC: International Monetary Fund.

# 1 Overview of fiscal policy issues

*Akira Kohsaka*

## Introduction

Almost ten years ago, the North American and European countries were considered to have made only limited progress in getting their ratios of public debt-to-GDP right (IMF 1996). Also then, the Latin American countries had to contain their fiscal imbalances, as well as scale down the level of state intervention in the economy. In contrast, the East Asian economies were considered rather prudent in government housekeeping with minimal fiscal imbalances and debt.

Now, however, the fiscal picture in the economies of the world is very different. Particularly in the Pacific region, the advanced economies (with the exception of Japan) have made a great progress and the Latin American economies have taken important steps toward regaining fiscal health (see Table 1.1). In contrast, several economies in East Asia face government debt management problems as a result of their heavy reliance on fiscal stimulus in the recovery process from the Asian economic crisis.

Looking at these past developments, it is high time to review the past, as well as look into future issues for fiscal policy from both the macroeconomic and microeconomic perspectives. The former covers issues of macroeconomic stability and sustainability, and the latter those of efficiency and consolidation. A basic dilemma between short-run demand management and long-run debt dynamics will be considered in the former, while renewed adequate division of labor between the public and private sectors will be discussed in the latter.

Given the long-shared policy principles for fiscal discipline among policy authorities, what has brought about the contrasting performance in the region as noted above? In this volume, the authors scrutinize and compare the experiences of their respective economies in terms of the fiscal policy issues and address future policy options.

This chapter provides an overview of fiscal policy issues in the Pacific region across economies and from the perspective of international comparison. In the next section, selected aspects of fiscal structures and their development in the Pacific region are reviewed and summarized. Reflecting the variety of structural differences and development stages, the diversity across the economies is highlighted. Brief observation of fiscal development in the past three decades across the economies of the region is summarily depicted. Resulting debt dynamics imply the

*Table 1.1* Fiscal deficit and government debt of PECC economies, 1996–2000 (as a % of GDP)

| *Fiscal deficit*[a] | *1996* | *1997* | *1998* | *1999* | *2000* | *Gov't debt* | *1996* | *1997* | *1998* | *1999* | *2000* |
|---|---|---|---|---|---|---|---|---|---|---|---|
| Advanced economies | | | | | | Advanced economies | | | | | |
| Australia | −1.3 | 0.1 | 0.2 | −1.9 | −1.9 | Australia (GG net) | 23.2 | 21.2 | 16.8 | 13.9 | 9.7 |
| Canada | −1.8 | 0.8 | 0.9 | 2.2 | 3.4 | Canada (GG net) | 69.8 | 65.2 | 61.9 | 75.3 | 66.7 |
| Japan | −4.7 | −3.8 | −6.1 | −7.4 | na | Japan (GG net) | 22.4 | 28.5 | 39.0 | 43.6 | na |
| New Zealand (CG) | 3.6 | 2.0 | 2.6 | 1.8 | 1.4 | New Zealand (CG net) | 31.0 | 26.4 | 24.5 | 21.7 | 20.4 |
| United States | −2.2 | −0.9 | 0.3 | 1.0 | 2.2 | United States (TG) | 67.4 | 65.6 | 63.4 | 61.7 | 57.0 |
| Asian newly industrialized economies (ANIEs) | | | | | | Asian newly industrialized economies (ANIEs) | | | | | |
| Hong Kong, China | −0.3 | 2.2 | 6.6 | −1.8 | 0.8 | Hong Kong, China | na | na | na | na | na |
| Korea | 0.3 | −1.5 | −4.2 | −2.7 | na | Korea (CG) | 8.8 | 11.1 | 16.1 | 18.6 | na |
| Singapore | 10.6 | 11.7 | 1.7 | 4.2 | na | Singapore | na | na | na | na | na |
| Chinese Taipei | −3.1 | −2.1 | 0.7 | −0.5 | −3.3 | Chinese Taipei | 10.2 | 11.3 | 11.1 | 10.4 | na |
| ASEAN and other Asia | | | | | | ASEAN and other Asia | | | | | |
| Indonesia (CG) | −2.0 | −2.5 | −5.7 | −3.9 | na | Indonesia (CG) | 23.9 | 72.5 | 53.3 | 44.4 | na |
| Malaysia (CG) | 0.8 | 2.5 | −1.9 | −3.4 | na | Malaysia (CG) | 37.1 | 33.7 | 38.3 | 40.1 | na |
| The Philippines (CG) | 0.3 | 0.1 | −1.9 | −3.7 | −4.1 | The Philippines (PS) | 98.9 | 105.6 | 104.8 | 116.2 | na |
| Thailand (CG) | 2.6 | −1.3 | −0.9 | −3.6 | −2.4 | Thailand (PS) | 14.9 | 47.5 | 59.6 | 66.2 | 65.5 |
| China | −0.8 | −0.8 | −1.2 | −2.1 | na | China | 7.3 | 8.2 | 10.9 | 13.8 | na |
| Vietnam (CG) | −0.2 | −0.8 | −0.8 | −0.9 | na | Vietnam | na | na | na | na | na |
| Latin America | | | | | | Latin America | | | | | |
| Chile (CG) | 2.3 | 2.0 | 0.4 | −1.5 | na | Chile (CG) | 16.7 | 14.5 | 13.9 | 15.1 | na |
| Colombia | −1.7 | −2.8 | −3.6 | −4.3 | −4.3 | Colombia (NFPS) | 24.7 | 29.0 | 33.4 | 41.1 | 46.2 |
| Ecuador | −3.1 | −2.6 | −6.0 | −5.9 | 0.4 | Ecuador (NFPS) | 75.6 | 72.1 | 81.3 | 123.9 | 100.9 |
| Mexico | −0.1 | −0.6 | −1.2 | −1.1 | −1.0 | Mexico (GG) | 30.5 | 25.4 | 27.5 | 24.5 | 24.0 |
| Peru | −1.1 | −0.4 | −0.6 | −3.1 | −2.6 | Peru (PS) | 36.5 | 33.9 | 36.1 | 39.9 | na |

Sources: Papers submitted to the Japan Committee for Pacific Economic Outlook; World Bank (2001); International Monetary Fund (2001).

Notes

na = Not available.

a Fiscal deficit refers to the deficit of the general government, unless otherwise noted. GG = general government, NFPS = nonfinancial public sector, PS = public sector, TG = total government and CG = central government. Government debt is gross, unless otherwise noted.

difficulties and challenges that the policy authorities have faced thus far and are going to face in the future. Subsequently, the next section provides a closer examination of more recent fiscal developments, and focuses on the impact of the Asian economic crisis. It appears that we have been witnessing new fiscal pictures in the region. More detailed scrutiny is then presented, by looking at disaggregated expenditure and revenue items to identify the causes and/or factors that have affected the process of fiscal consolidation. Challenges to future fiscal management and consolidation are later discussed. Finally, a summary and conclusions are given at the end of the chapter.

## Fiscal structure

### *Definition of government*

The concept of government that we are concerned with, i.e., general government (GG), goes beyond the central government (CG). General government is the consolidated account of the central government, provincial and other local governments, plus other government entities including social security funds. Nonfinancial government enterprises are sometimes included as part of general government, where the treatment differs across economies. Statistical information on general governments, however, is not always easily available or reliable, and the coverage of general government is being revised over time and across economies. As a consequence, the readers should note that the data on general government may not always be comparable across economies.

Given these limitations of the data on general government, we nevertheless choose to use the broader concept because the coverage of central government has declined in advanced economies and is likely to do so in developing economies in the near future. As such, focusing only on CG would not be enough to grasp the whole gamut of transactions between the private and nonprivate sectors.

### *Fiscal decentralization*

The Pacific economies are diverse in their fiscal structure that often consists of several layers of governments. Some economies adopt a federal government structure and are relatively decentralized, while others centralize both the revenue and expenditure side of government activities. One way to see to what extent a fiscal structure is decentralized is to look at the size of the central government relative to general government in terms of revenue and expenditure (Figure 1.1).

Apart from two city economies—namely, Hong Kong, China and Singapore, both of which are naturally centralized—provincial and/or local governments play significant roles. The provincial/local governments play a larger role in Canada, China, Colombia, Japan, Chinese Taipei and the United States than in Australia, Ecuador, Indonesia, Korea, Malaysia, Mexico, New Zealand, Peru, the Philippines and Thailand (and probably Vietnam).

We note, however, that the apparent decentralization in the former economies does not necessarily imply proportionately greater autonomy of local governments.

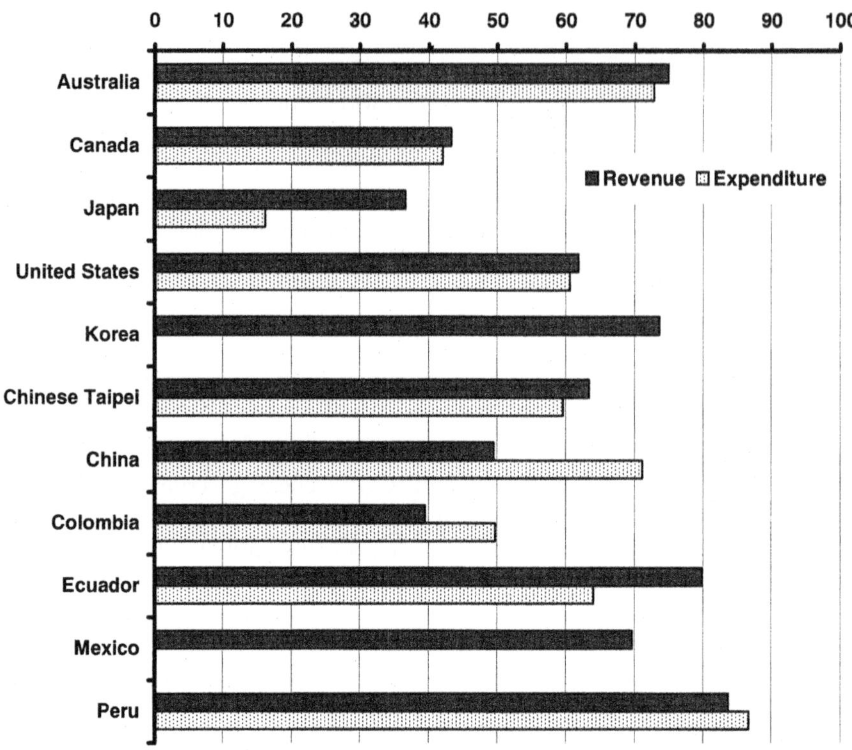


*Figure 1.1* Fiscal centralization, 1998 (%).

Note
Ratio of central government to general government.

In fact, various forms of intragovernmental transfers to local governments have often been used by the central government as an instrument to control the fiscal behavior of local governments.[1]

### *Size of government*

The size of government relative to the level of economic activity, as defined by the ratio of revenue and expenditure to GDP, is distributed from less than 15 percent to more than 45 percent across the Pacific economies (Figure 1.2). Canada is the largest and China is the smallest. Generally, the advanced economies tend to have larger governments—this is the case for Canada, New Zealand, Australia, the United States and Japan—though the governments in Korea, Colombia and Singapore are also relatively large. Governments in developing economies are significantly smaller in terms of GG activities (and in CG activities as well).

If we look at the counterpart data for central governments, however, we see a very different picture, particularly in terms of their relative size, because central governments tend to shrink along with decentralization (Table 1.2). This is appar-

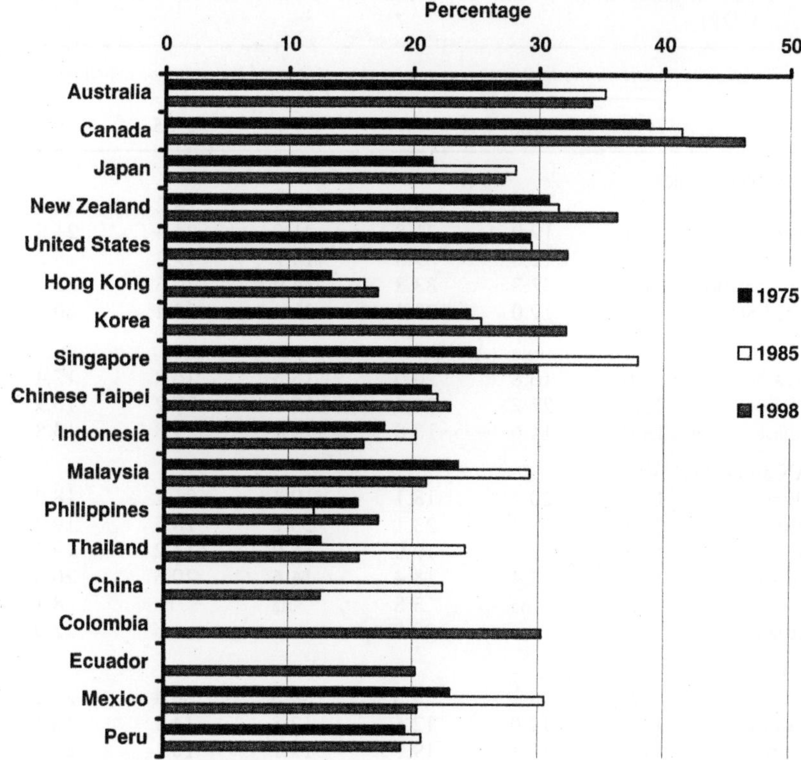


*Figure 1.2* Size of government as measured by general government revenue (as a % of GDP).

ent from the data for Canada, Japan and the United States. In terms of central government revenue in 1997, for instance, Canada and the United States were ranked 6th and 7th instead of 1st and 4th as in general government, respectively. The change in Japan was extreme, falling to a rank of 18th instead of 8th. In this respect, China is in a distinctive position; in other words, China has tried hard to centralize fiscal decisions as well as resources since the early 1990s. In fact, its CG revenue increased from 5.3 percent of GDP in 1990 to 6.2 percent in 1998, while its GG revenue decreased from 15.8 percent to 12.6 percent (the data are not reported in Table 1.2 but were taken from World Bank (2001) and papers prepared for the Japan Committee for Pacific Economic Outlook).

### *Revenue structure*

The fiscal structure depends heavily on the level of economic development or level of per capita income. While size is one thing and intragovernmental relationships are another, the structure of fiscal revenue and expenditure also reflects differences in fiscal needs due to different levels of economic development. For international comparison, we use World Bank's *World Development Indicators 2001*.[2]

*Table 1.2* Size of government by central government revenue and expenditure (as a % of GDP)

| | *Central government revenue* | | | *Central government expenditure* | | |
|---|---|---|---|---|---|---|
| | *1975* | *1985* | *1997* | *1975* | *1985* | *1997* |
| Advanced economies | | | | | | |
| Australia | 19.8 | 23.8 | 23.6 | 19.8 | 26.2 | 24.7 |
| Canada | 20.4 | 19.0 | 21.8 | 21.0 | 24.5 | 21.5 |
| Japan | 9.8 | 12.5 | 9.5 | 14.7 | 17.2 | 5.7 |
| New Zealand | 31.5 | 37.3 | 33.8 | 34.9 | 40.5 | 32.1 |
| United States | 18.0 | 19.0 | 20.2 | 20.6 | 23.4 | 20.6 |
| Asian newly industrialized economies (ANIEs) | | | | | | |
| Korea | 15.0 | 16.8 | 20.0 | 15.6 | 16.3 | 17.4 |
| Singapore | 23.4 | 27.7 | 24.6 | 17.9 | 27.2 | 16.9 |
| Chinese Taipei | 13.9 | 14.6 | 13.8 | 12.7 | 14.3 | 13.8 |
| ASEAN and other Asia | | | | | | |
| Indonesia | 17.2 | 20.7 | 18.1 | 19.4 | 21.1 | 18.0 |
| Malaysia | 21.3 | 29.4 | 23.1 | 25.2 | 28.5 | 19.7 |
| The Philippines | 15.4 | 12.0 | 19.0 | 16.0 | 11.2 | 19.3 |
| Thailand | 12.6 | 15.4 | 18.4 | 14.6 | 20.5 | 20.3 |
| China | na | na | 5.8 | na | na | 8.1 |
| Vietnam | na | na | 20.0 | na | na | 22.0 |
| Latin America | | | | | | |
| Chile | 31.9 | 28.1 | 23.3 | 34.3 | 30.4 | 21.2 |
| Colombia | 11.9 | 12.0 | 12.6 | 12.5 | 14.1 | 16.1 |
| Ecuador | 11.5 | 17.1 | 19.8 | 12.1 | 15.1 | 20.5 |
| Mexico | 12.2 | 15.4 | 14.7 | 14.7 | 23.5 | 16.3 |
| Peru | 13.4 | 14.8 | 17.6 | 16.1 | 17.4 | 17.3 |

Sources: World Bank (2001); papers submitted to the Japan Committee for Pacific Economic Outlook.

Note
na = Not available.

On the revenue side (Table 1.3), social security taxes are an important source in the United States, Canada, Japan (data are not reported in the table) and Korea. One conspicuous fact among developing economies is that those in Latin America tend to rely more on social security taxes than in Asia. A relative reliance on either the income tax or the goods/services tax is diverse in the Pacific region. Advanced economies such as New Zealand, Australia, Canada and the United States tend to rely on the former, while developing economies tend to rely on the latter. Distinctive differences are also found in the relative reliance on income and custom taxes between advanced and developing economies. Developing economies have generally shown poor performance in income tax collection partly due to low income levels or small tax bases as well as inefficient tax systems. By contrast, these economies—particularly, Vietnam, the Philippines, Malaysia and Thailand—have depended more heavily on custom duties. This suggests that they are still in the mid-process of trade liberalization, although their reliance on custom duties for revenue is becoming smaller in the process.

*Table 1.3* Central government revenue by item (as a % of GDP)

| | *Social security taxes* | *Goods and services taxes* | *Income taxes* | *Custom taxes* | *Nontax revenue* |
|---|---|---|---|---|---|
| Advanced economies | | | | | |
| Australia | | | | | |
| 1975 | 0.0 | 3.8 | 12.8 | 1.1 | 2.0 |
| 1985 | 0.0 | 5.8 | 14.2 | 1.2 | 2.5 |
| 1997 | 0.0 | 4.9 | 16.0 | 0.6 | 1.6 |
| Canada | | | | | |
| 1975 | 2.0 | 3.0 | 11.1 | 1.7 | 2.3 |
| 1985 | 2.8 | 3.5 | 9.4 | 0.9 | 2.5 |
| 1997 | 4.1 | 3.7 | 11.7 | 0.3 | 2.0 |
| Japan | | | | | |
| 1975 | na | 2.1 | 6.6 | 0.3 | 0.1 |
| 1985 | na | 2.4 | 8.4 | 0.2 | 0.6 |
| 1997 | na | na | na | na | na |
| New Zealand | | | | | |
| 1975 | 0.0 | 6.1 | 20.7 | 1.1 | 2.8 |
| 1985 | 0.0 | 6.5 | 23.1 | 1.3 | 5.7 |
| 1997 | 0.0 | 9.0 | 20.6 | 0.9 | 2.7 |
| United States | | | | | |
| 1975 | 5.1 | 1.0 | 10.1 | 0.3 | 1.3 |
| 1985 | 6.2 | 0.9 | 9.5 | 0.3 | 1.9 |
| 1997 | 6.5 | 0.7 | 11.2 | 0.2 | 1.4 |
| Asian newly industrialized economies (ANIEs) | | | | | |
| Korea | | | | | |
| 1975 | 0.1 | 7.0 | 3.4 | 2.0 | 1.3 |
| 1985 | 0.3 | 7.3 | 4.3 | 2.4 | 2.0 |
| 1997 | 1.9 | 6.8 | 5.4 | 1.3 | 2.7 |
| Singapore | | | | | |
| 1975 | 0.0 | 3.4 | 8.6 | 1.8 | 6.5 |
| 1985 | 0.0 | 3.8 | 7.5 | 1.0 | 11.2 |
| 1997 | 0.0 | 4.8 | 6.8 | 0.3 | 8.4 |
| ASEAN and other Asia | | | | | |
| Indonesia | | | | | |
| 1975 | na | 2.2 | 11.3 | 1.8 | 1.5 |
| 1985 | na | 3.3 | 13.7 | 0.7 | 2.6 |
| 1997 | 0.5 | 5.1 | 10.3 | 0.5 | 1.6 |
| Malaysia | | | | | |
| 1975 | 0.1 | 4.5 | 8.1 | 6.0 | 2.3 |
| 1985 | 0.2 | 4.8 | 11.2 | 5.8 | 6.9 |
| 1997 | 0.3 | 6.1 | 8.4 | 2.9 | 4.1 |
| The Philippines | | | | | |
| 1975 | 0.0 | 3.7 | 3.0 | 6.2 | 2.1 |
| 1985 | 0.0 | 4.4 | 3.2 | 2.8 | 1.3 |
| 1997 | 0.0 | 5.5 | 6.8 | 3.9 | 2.0 |

*continued*

*Table 1.3 continued*

| | *Social security taxes* | *Goods and services taxes* | *Income taxes* | *Custom taxes* | *Nontax revenue* |
|---|---|---|---|---|---|
| Thailand | | | | | |
| 1975 | 0.0 | 5.5 | 2.0 | 3.4 | na |
| 1985 | 0.0 | 7.0 | 3.2 | 3.2 | na |
| 1997 | 0.3 | 7.8 | 5.8 | 2.2 | na |
| China | | | | | |
| 1975 | na | na | na | na | na |
| 1985 | na | na | na | na | na |
| 1997 | 0.0 | 4.4 | 0.5 | 0.4 | 0.2 |
| Vietnam | | | | | |
| 1975 | na | na | na | na | na |
| 1985 | na | na | na | na | na |
| 1997 | 0.0 | 6.5 | 4.4 | 4.3 | 2.9 |
| Latin America | | | | | |
| Chile | | | | | |
| 1975 | 3.2 | 10.7 | 6.0 | 2.9 | 7.0 |
| 1985 | 2.1 | 11.2 | 3.2 | 3.1 | 6.6 |
| 1997 | 1.4 | 10.8 | 4.1 | 2.0 | 3.9 |
| Colombia | | | | | |
| 1975 | 1.5 | 2.3 | 4.3 | 2.2 | 0.7 |
| 1985 | 1.1 | 3.6 | 2.6 | 2.0 | 1.7 |
| 1997 | 0.0 | 5.4 | 4.4 | 1.0 | 1.8 |
| Ecuador | | | | | |
| 1975 | 0.0 | 2.2 | 2.9 | 5.2 | 0.9 |
| 1985 | 0.0 | 2.3 | 11.1 | 3.0 | 0.3 |
| 1997 | na | na | na | na | na |
| Mexico | | | | | |
| 1975 | 2.2 | 5.3 | 4.5 | 1.3 | 0.8 |
| 1985 | 1.6 | 11.0 | 4.0 | 0.7 | 0.7 |
| 1997 | 1.8 | 8.8 | 4.6 | 0.6 | 1.7 |
| Peru | | | | | |
| 1975 | 0.0 | 4.8 | 3.2 | 3.0 | 1.5 |
| 1985 | 0.0 | 8.2 | 1.4 | 3.3 | 1.7 |
| 1997 | 1.5 | 8.7 | 3.6 | 1.5 | 2.2 |

Source: World Bank (2001).

Note
na = Not available.

Finally, we note that nontax revenues are nonnegligible (though intermittently) in Chile, New Zealand, Malaysia, Singapore and Thailand, partly reflecting the privatization of government assets.

***Expenditure structure***

On the expenditure side (Table 1.4), the developing Pacific economies tend to have larger shares for wages/salaries, while the advanced economies spend distinctively larger amounts for subsidies/transfers, which is mainly related to social security needs. The developing economies in East Asia generally spend more on capital formation than the Latin American economies. Finally, the burden of interest payments impact heavy-debtor economies across the Pacific region, both advanced and developing economies. These economies—Canada, the Philippines, New Zealand, the United States, Malaysia, Mexico and Colombia—had interest payments of roughly more than 2 percent of GDP in the 1980s and 1990s. Thanks to unprecedented low interest rates, Japan escaped from large interest payments (2.2 percent of GDP) despite its recent skyrocketing debt burden.

While there are several common characteristics or patterns in fiscal structure, as pointed out above, the structures have never been stable and have not shown any convergence with each other. Rather, they have changed to a large extent and these changes have depended partly on endogenous responses and partly on discretionary policy choices. We will discuss these changes in relation to fiscal consolidation in the next section.

## Fiscal deficits and debt dynamics across business cycles

This section reviews long-run fiscal developments across business cycles over the past three decades in the Pacific economies to provide a general background for analyzing recent policy issues in a long-term and broad perspective. Before going into the individual cases, let us review the basic relationship among fiscal balances and debt accumulation.

Debt dynamics can be rather simple and mechanical. Fiscal deficits, if not monetized, must be financed by increased government liabilities, domestic or foreign. If we denote D, Y, PB and r to represent outstanding debt, nominal GDP, the primary balance and the nominal interest rate, respectively, the overall budget balance ($-dD$), which is defined as equal to the primary balance (PB) minus interest payments ($r^*D$), can be described by the following equation:

$$-dD = PB - r^*D \quad \text{or} \quad dD = r^*D - PB$$

Then, debt dynamics can be expressed as:

$$d\log(D/Y) = (r - (PB/Y)^*(Y/D)) - d\log Y$$

where $d\log X = dX/X$ is a percentage increase in variable X. This relationship implies that in order to stabilize (or decrease) the debt-to-GDP ratio or LHS = 0, nominal GDP growth ($d\log Y$) must be equal to (or larger than) the nominal interest rate plus the primary deficit-to-debt ratio. This equivalently means that, with the zero primary balance in the long run, *real GDP growth must be larger than or equal to the real interest rate* at least for a stable debt-to-GDP ratio.

*Table 1.4* Central government expenditure by item (as a % of GDP)

| | *Wages and salaries* | *Goods and services* | *Interest payments* | *Subsidies and transfers* | *Capital expenditure* |
|---|---|---|---|---|---|
| Advanced economies | | | | | |
| Australia | | | | | |
| 1975 | na | 4.9 | 1.1 | 11.2 | 2.6 |
| 1985 | 0.4 | 6.2 | 2.3 | 15.1 | 2.6 |
| 1997 | 0.7 | 6.4 | 1.7 | 15.2 | 1.4 |
| Canada | | | | | |
| 1975 | 2.6 | 5.0 | 1.7 | 13.7 | 0.7 |
| 1985 | 2.3 | 5.1 | 4.4 | 14.6 | 0.4 |
| 1997 | 2.1 | 3.6 | 3.6 | 14.0 | 0.3 |
| Japan | | | | | |
| 1975 | na | 2.4 | 0.8 | 8.6 | 3.0 |
| 1985 | na | 2.3 | 3.5 | 9.0 | 2.4 |
| 1997 | na | na | na | na | na |
| New Zealand | | | | | |
| 1975 | 7.3 | 9.9 | 2.4 | 19.0 | 3.6 |
| 1985 | 6.5 | 10.0 | 7.3 | 20.7 | 2.5 |
| 1997 | na | 15.8 | 3.2 | 12.3 | 0.9 |
| United States | | | | | |
| 1975 | 3.0 | 7.0 | 1.5 | 11.1 | 1.2 |
| 1985 | 2.4 | 7.1 | 3.7 | 11.5 | 1.1 |
| 1997 | 1.7 | 4.4 | 3.1 | 12.3 | 0.8 |
| Asian newly industrialized economies (ANIEs) | | | | | |
| Korea | | | | | |
| 1975 | 2.2 | 6.7 | 0.5 | 5.1 | 3.3 |
| 1985 | 2.3 | 6.6 | 0.2 | 6.3 | 2.2 |
| 1997 | 2.2 | 4.7 | 0.5 | 8.5 | 3.8 |
| Singapore | | | | | |
| 1975 | 6.2 | 11.9 | 1.6 | 1.4 | 2.5 |
| 1985 | 7.8 | 13.1 | 3.1 | 2.7 | 8.4 |
| 1997 | 4.9 | 9.7 | 0.7 | 1.4 | 5.1 |
| ASEAN and other Asia | | | | | |
| Indonesia | | | | | |
| 1975 | 3.1 | 7.7 | 0.3 | 3.4 | 8.0 |
| 1985 | 2.8 | 4.9 | 1.6 | 5.0 | 9.5 |
| 1997 | 1.8 | 4.2 | 1.7 | 6.5 | 5.5 |
| Malaysia | | | | | |
| 1975 | 5.9 | 11.1 | 2.5 | 7.2 | 4.8 |
| 1985 | 9.6 | 15.4 | 6.6 | 3.7 | 3.0 |
| 1997 | 5.1 | 8.2 | 2.4 | 4.6 | 4.5 |
| The Philippines | | | | | |
| 1975 | 4.2 | 8.4 | 0.9 | 1.5 | 2.4 |
| 1985 | 3.8 | 6.3 | 2.6 | 0.8 | 1.5 |
| 1997 | na | na | 3.2 | 3.4 | na |

| | *Wages and salaries* | *Goods and services* | *Interest payments* | *Subsidies and transfers* | *Capital expenditure* |
|---|---|---|---|---|---|
| Thailand | | | | | |
| 1975 | 3.8 | 7.6 | 1.2 | 2.5 | 3.1 |
| 1985 | 6.0 | 12.1 | 2.9 | 1.6 | 3.9 |
| 1997 | 5.5 | 9.6 | 0.3 | 1.3 | 9.0 |
| China | | | | | |
| 1975 | na | na | na | na | na |
| 1985 | na | na | na | na | na |
| 1997 | na | na | na | na | na |
| Vietnam | | | | | |
| 1975 | na | na | na | na | na |
| 1985 | na | na | na | na | na |
| 1997 | na | na | 0.6 | na | 5.8 |
| Latin America | | | | | |
| Chile | | | | | |
| 1975 | 8.6 | 12.8 | 3.5 | 11.2 | 6.8 |
| 1985 | 5.7 | 9.8 | 1.9 | 15.6 | 3.0 |
| 1997 | 4.2 | 6.2 | 0.4 | 11.1 | 3.5 |
| Colombia | | | | | |
| 1975 | na | na | na | na | 4.0 |
| 1985 | 2.8 | 4.0 | 0.8 | 6.7 | 2.6 |
| 1997 | 2.3 | 3.4 | 2.0 | 6.4 | 4.2 |
| Ecuador | | | | | |
| 1975 | na | na | na | na | na |
| 1985 | na | na | na | na | na |
| 1997 | na | na | na | na | na |
| Mexico | | | | | |
| 1975 | 4.3 | 5.9 | 1.3 | 4.1 | 3.5 |
| 1985 | 4.4 | 5.8 | 9.2 | 5.0 | 3.7 |
| 1997 | 2.3 | 3.7 | 2.2 | 8.4 | 1.9 |
| Peru | | | | | |
| 1975 | 4.8 | 8.0 | 1.7 | 2.6 | 3.9 |
| 1985 | na | 8.3 | 4.6 | 1.8 | 2.7 |
| 1997 | 3.1 | 6.6 | 1.8 | 6.2 | 2.8 |

Source: World Bank (2001).

Note
na = Not available.

Japan provides a good numerical example for understanding the above basic relationship. Japan's average growth rate was 4.0 percent in the 1980s and 1.3 percent in the 1990s. Suppose the real interest rate is 3 percent in the long run. It is easy to see that Japan turned from a successful case in fiscal consolidation in the 1980s into a heavy debtor in the 1990s. That is, in the 1990s, the Japanese government simply could not afford to create fiscal deficits (this is, of course, all in hindsight), if it was to keep fiscal prudence.

Now let us turn to the actual developments in the Pacific region, in the context of an international comparison.

### *Advanced economies*

All of the advanced Pacific economies have suffered and/or are still suffering from government debt burden in the past three decades (Figure 1.3). Australia's central government debt peaked at 20 percent of GDP in fiscal year 1995/96 (FY95/96);

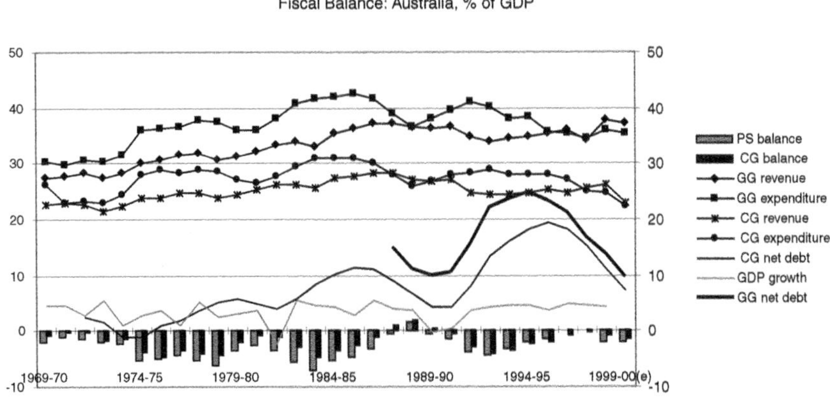


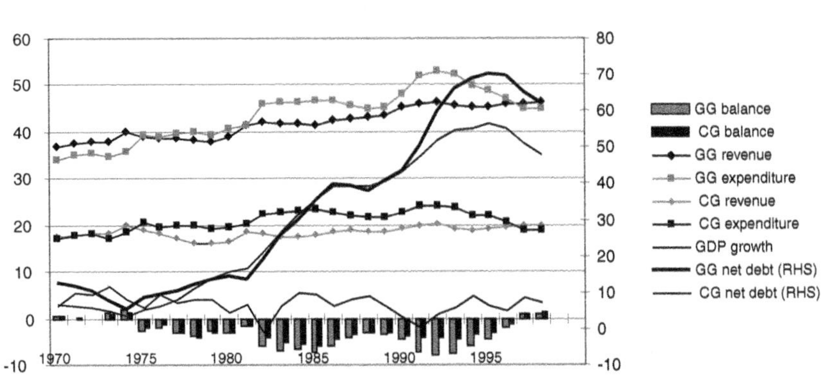


*Figure 1.3* Fiscal balance: percentage of GDP, Australia, Canada, Japan, New Zealand and the United States.

Source: Fiscal indicators are from country papers submitted to Japan Committee for Pacific Economic Outlook (PEO) and GDP growth data from World Bank, *World Development Indicators*, CD-Rom, 2001 (WDI).

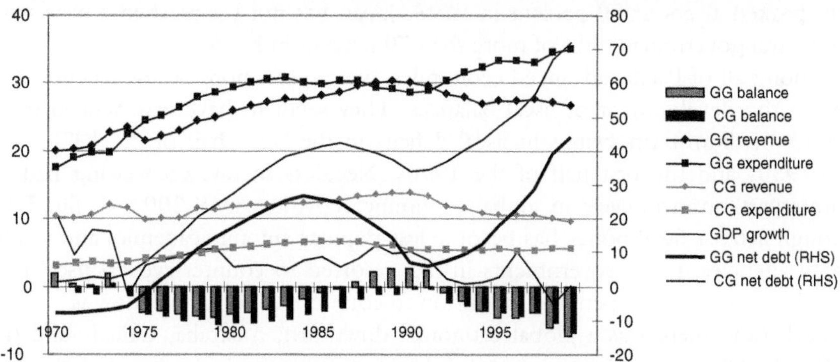


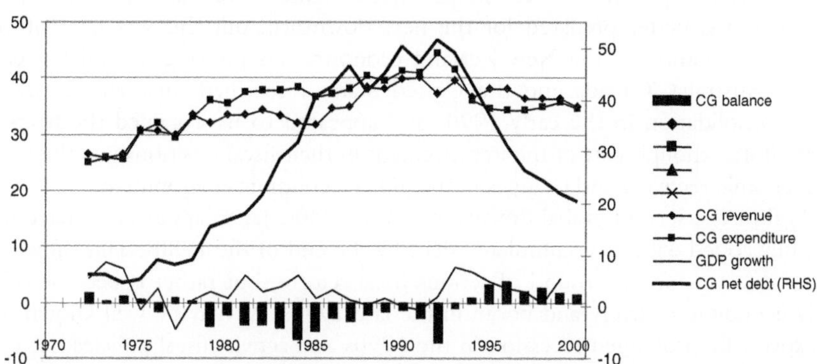


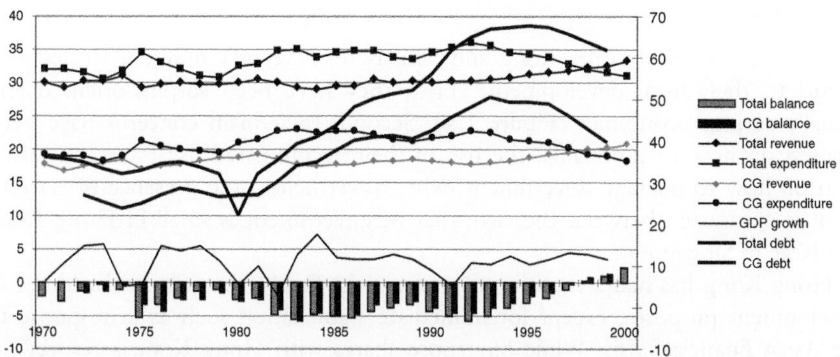


Note

GG: general government = consolidated account of central, provincial, and other local governments, social security funds and other government entities excluding public enterprises.

PS and NFPS: non-financial public sector = consolidated account of GC + non-financial public enterprises.

for Canada, debt peaked at more than 55 percent in FY95; New Zealand debt peaked at more than 560 percent in FY02; and in the United States, government debt peaked at about 50 percent in FY93. Japan has not yet reached a peak with net central government debt of more than 70 percent in FY99.

Among all of Pacific advanced economies, we can see more or less synchronization in the development of fiscal balances. They seem to have experienced three distinct medium-term swings in fiscal deficits in the latter half of the 1970s, the mid-1980s and the first half of the 1990s. Needless to say, each swing had its counterpart business cycle in global economic activities (IMF 2001: 3, fig. 1.1). Though activist fiscal policy has become less popular among academics and multilateral agencies, these governments in fact resorted to counter-cyclical fiscal policies, i.e., tax cuts and spending expansion to counter economic slowdowns.

Each time there was a global economic downturn, Australia, Canada and the United States took an expansionary fiscal stance and started and restarted to accumulate government debt. New Zealand began serious fiscal reforms earlier than the others, beginning with the second downturn in the 1980s, and as a result, the economy was better prepared for the next downturn; but this was not without costs as stagnation in the New Zealand economy was prolonged until the early 1990s. Australia, Canada and the United States intensified their efforts toward fiscal consolidation in the early 1990s and appeared to have gained the fruits of their efforts, though part of the improvement in their fiscal positions was the result of economic recovery and changes in the global economic environment.

Against the second global downturn in the 1980s, Japan appeared to have successfully coped with its accumulated debt by the end of the 1980s. This, however, is not due to a second round of serious fiscal reform, but rather is because of an early economic recovery and boom in the late 1990s. As may be well known, the unexpectedly prolonged recession in the 1990s and activist fiscal policies not only resumed increases in debt, but it aggravated the explosive accumulation of debt.

### *Asian NIEs*

Two city economies, Hong Kong and Singapore, have very different stories with regard to their fiscal developments. First, they have been surplus-oriented and actually surplus economies (Figure 1.4). Second, their main concerns have been focused on how to rationalize the use of their accumulated fiscal surplus, rather than on how to manage government debt. Nevertheless, the presence of government is contrasted between the two; that is, government is small in Hong Kong and large in Singapore.

Hong Kong has had a tradition of non-activist fiscal management for long-run development purposes, except for immediate stabilization such as in response to the Asian financial crisis. While Singapore shares with Hong Kong a respect for fiscal discipline and prudence, Singapore has never been afraid of having a large government. A huge government surplus has been transferred to statutory boards or other semi-governmental entities and put to use for various developmental purposes, although transactions between and within them are not clear. In fact, as far as the central government is concerned, its debt is more than 80 percent of GDP,

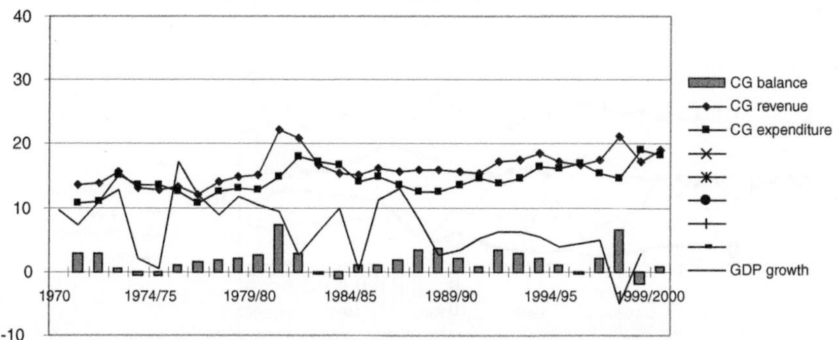
Fiscal Balance: Hong Kong, % of GDP
40
30
20
10
0
-10
1970
1974/75
1979/80
1984/85
1989/90
1994/95
1999/2000
CG balance
CG revenue
CG expenditure
GDP growth

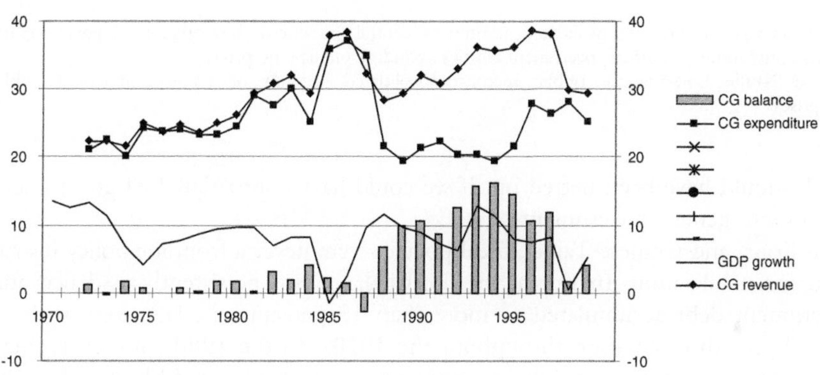
Fiscal Balance: Singapore, % of GDP
40
30
20
10
0
-10
1970
1975
1980
1985
1990
1995
CG balance
CG expenditure
GDP growth
CG revenue

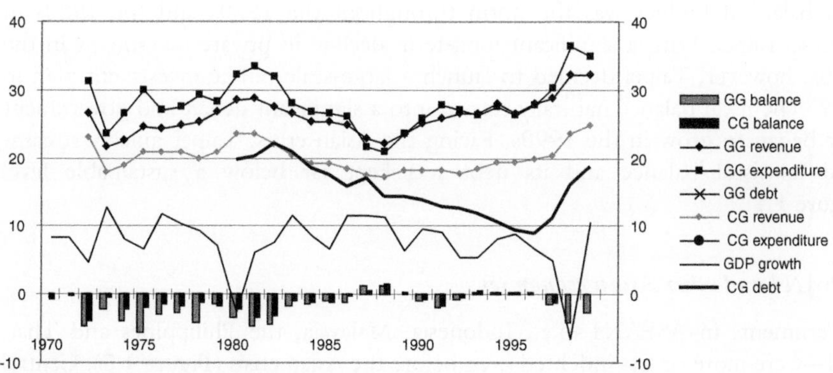
Fiscal Balance: Korea, % of GDP
40
30
20
10
0
-10
1970
1975
1980
1985
1990
1995
GG balance
CG balance
GG revenue
GG expenditure
GG debt
CG revenue
CG expenditure
GDP growth
CG debt

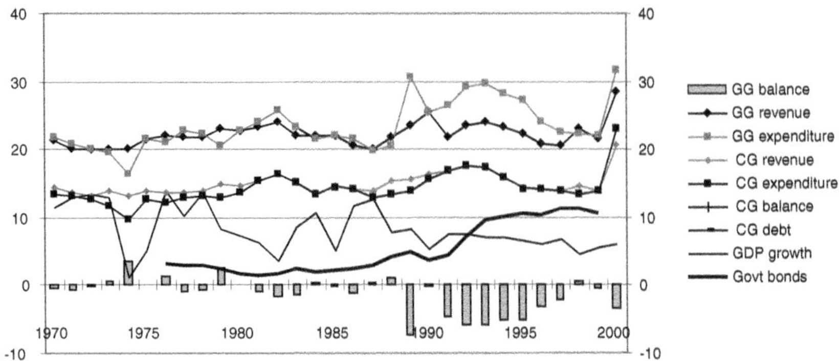


*Figure 1.4* Fiscal balance: percentage of GDP, Hong Kong, Singapore, Korea and Chinese Taipei.

Source: CG balance for Korea from World Bank (2001) *World Development Indicators*, CD-Rom.

Note
GG: general government = consolidated account of central, provincial, and other local governments, social security funds and other government entities excluding public enterprises.
PS and NFPS: non-financial public sector = consolidated account of GC + non-financial public enterprises.

which should have been netted out if we could have consolidated all government entities into general government.

In Korea and Chinese Taipei, fiscal policies were never a frontline policy instrument for stabilization. In Korea, the fiscal balance was persistently in deficit and government debt accumulated to more than 15 percent of GDP along with its general growth orientation throughout the 1970s. In the 1980s, however, there was a policy shift toward a stability orientation so that a balanced budget became the new norm until the Asian economic crisis in 1997. In the recovery process out of the crisis, fiscal stimulus, in turn, played a significant role. Thanks to past fiscal prudence, fiscal deficits and resulting debt increases do not appear to have reached an unsustainable level thus far (Figure 1.4).

A balanced budget was the norm throughout the 1970s and the 1980s in Chinese Taipei. With a significant long-term decline in private investment in the 1980s, however, Taipei decided to launch a large-scale public investment plan in 1989. The fiscal balance naturally turned into a significant deficit and government debt began to grow in the 1990s. Facing the Asian crisis, Taipei quickly streamlined its fiscal balance and its debt was kept far below a sustainable level (Figure 1.4).

### *ASEAN4 and other Asian economies*

Governments in ASEAN4—i.e., Indonesia, Malaysia, the Philippines and Thailand—were more or less indebted even before the Asian crisis (Figure 1.5). Central government debt peaked at more than 50 percent of GDP in Indonesia (1988), more than 100 percent in Malaysia (1986), 60 percent in the Philippines (1993) and 37 percent in Thailand (1986). Except for the Philippines, however, the ASEAN economies succeeded in reducing their debts significantly before the crisis in 1997. In fact, their debt-to-GDP ratios in 1996 were 25 percent for Indonesia, less than 40 percent for Malaysia, and less than 5 percent for Thailand. In other words, these ASEAN3 were successful in regaining overall fiscal health.

Fiscal reform was one of the most important pillars for the wide-ranging economic reforms that were initiated in 1984 in Indonesia, where the primary balance has been maintained in surplus since then. During the global recession in the early 1980s, Malaysia launched an ambitious development strategy with large-scale public investment, resulting in enlarged fiscal deficits and debt accumulation. However, this strategy was given up quickly and more than a balanced budget had been maintained since the mid-1980s up to the 1997 crisis. The Thai government had persistently spent more than its revenue since the first oil crisis through the mid-1980s. Government debt peaked in 1986, and fiscal tightening started to improve the budget balance. Subsequently, rapid economic growth helped to keep the primary balance in surplus until the crisis.

Then came the currency and financial crisis in 1997. After the immediate currency turmoil was over, all of the ASEAN3 economies resorted to fiscal expansion both to rescue and rehabilitate the collapsed financial system and to boost dried-up domestic demand. This resulted in plunging fiscal imbalances, on one hand, and skyrocketing government debt, on the other, due to rescue funds to address the financial distress and the free fall in currency values. Central government debt-to-GDP ratios jumped from 20 to 70 percent in Indonesia and from 5 to 20 percent in Thailand. However, public debt was estimated to be far larger than these figures. For example, in 1999, public debt was 96 percent in Indonesia, 56 percent in Malaysia, 74 percent in the Philippines and 56 percent in Thailand (Table 1.5).

The Philippines has suffered from debt burden since its economic crisis in the early 1980s up to the present, i.e., long before the 1997 crisis (Figure 1.5). Ambitious development plans generated fiscal deficits along with debt accumulation in the latter half of the 1970s and the early 1980s. The economic crisis in the early 1980s aggravated the fiscal imbalances through recession and devaluation, both of which seriously damaged the Philippines' fiscal situation. Although its primary balance turned into surplus as early as 1984 through severe belt tightening, its fiscal situation and debt burden did not show any significant improvement despite a continuous primary surplus. The 1997 crisis subsequently eroded the barely attained budget balance into deficit again.

The transition economies in Asia—China and Vietnam—face very different fiscal challenges than do the other Pacific economies (Figure 1.6). This is because the fiscal system lies at the heart of another key issue: how to reconcile an old centrally planned system with a new market-oriented one. China quickly reduced the size of government from 30 percent of GDP in 1979 to 10 percent in 1995 on one hand, and gradually strengthened the central government as opposed to provincial governments, on the other. In contrast, Vietnam maintained both government size (at

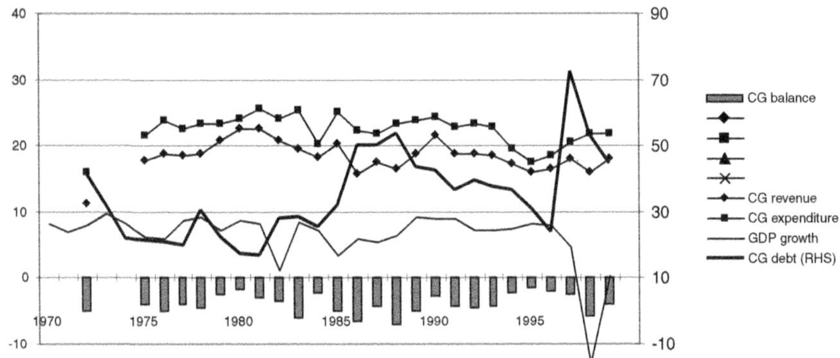
Fiscal Balance: Indonesia, % of GDP
40
30
20
10
0
-10
90
70
50
30
10
-10
1970
1975
1980
1985
1990
1995
CG balance
CG revenue
CG expenditure
GDP growth
CG debt (RHS)

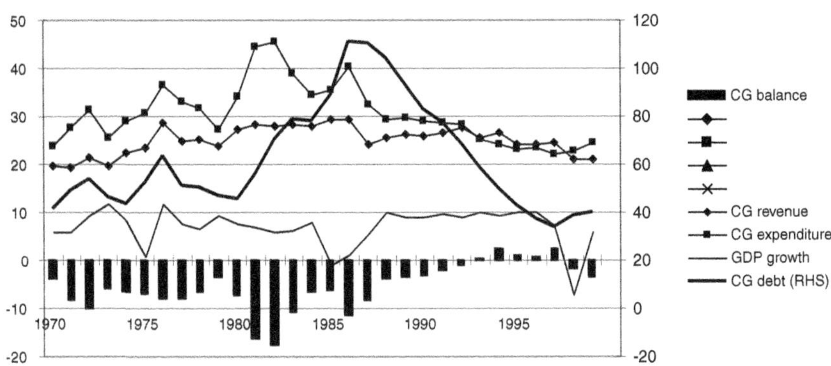
Fiscal Balance: Malaysia, % of GDP
50
40
30
20
10
0
-10
-20
120
100
80
60
40
20
0
-20
1970
1975
1980
1985
1990
1995
CG balance
CG revenue
CG expenditure
GDP growth
CG debt (RHS)

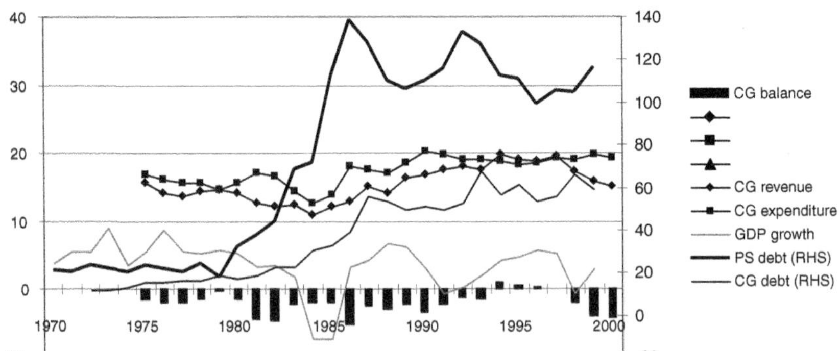
Fiscal Balance: The Philippines, % of GNP
40
30
20
10
0
-10
140
120
100
80
60
40
20
0
-20
1970
1975
1980
1985
1990
1995
2000
CG balance
CG revenue
CG expenditure
GDP growth
PS debt (RHS)
CG debt (RHS)

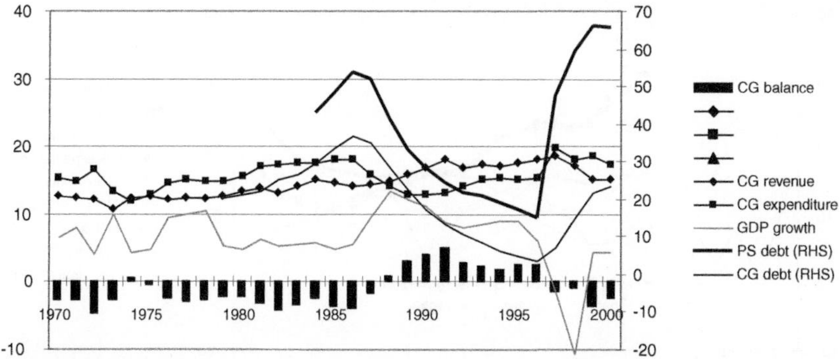


*Figure 1.5* Fiscal balance: percentage of GDP, Indonesia, Malaysia, the Philippines and Thailand.

Source: Fiscal indicators are from country papers submitted to Japan Committee for Pacific Economic Outlook (PEO) and GDP growth data from World Bank, *World Development Indicators*, CD-Rom, 2001 (WDI).

Note
GG: general government = consolidated account of central, provincial, and other local governments, social security funds and other government entities excluding public enterprises.
PS and NFPS: non-financial public sector = consolidated account of GC + non-financial public enterprises.

15 to 25 percent of GDP) and a centralized system. In both cases, however, the countries could not escape from the impact of the regional economic slowdown due to the 1997 crisis, which in turn affected their fiscal positions.

Since the opening up of the economy in 1979, China has taken a conservative attitude toward fiscal management. Even in the earlier period with the prevalence of soft budgets in state entities, the public sector as a whole kept budgets roughly

*Table 1.5* Public debt and financial sector restructuring in Asian economies, 1996–99 (as a % of GDP)

| | *1996* | *1997* | *1998* | *1999* |
|---|---|---|---|---|
| Indonesia | 24.5 | 106.4 | 103.4 | 96.0 |
| Financial restructuring | na | 39.9 | 55.3 | 60.1 |
| Korea | 8.8 | 12.7 | 24.4 | 29.6 |
| Financial restructuring | na | 1.5 | 8.5 | 12.9 |
| Malaysia | 47.7 | 49.0 | 53.5 | 56.4 |
| The Philippines | 68.2 | 66.4 | 72.9 | 74.4 |
| Thailand | 14.5 | 31.1 | 49.5 | 56.3 |
| Financial restructuring | 1.2 | 13.8 | 28.9 | 31.0 |

Source: International Monetary Fund (2000: 83, Table 2.6).

Note
na = Not available.

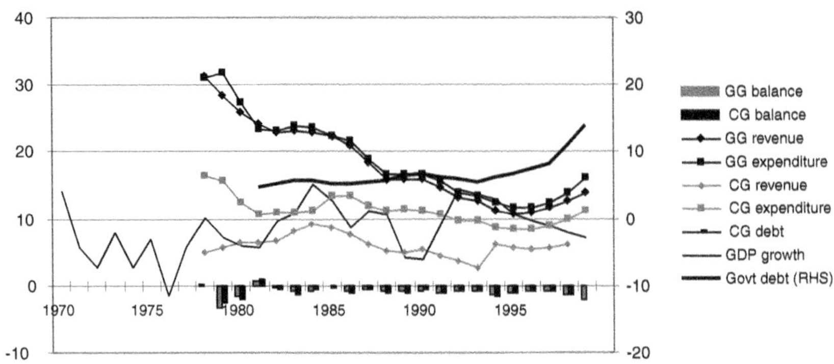


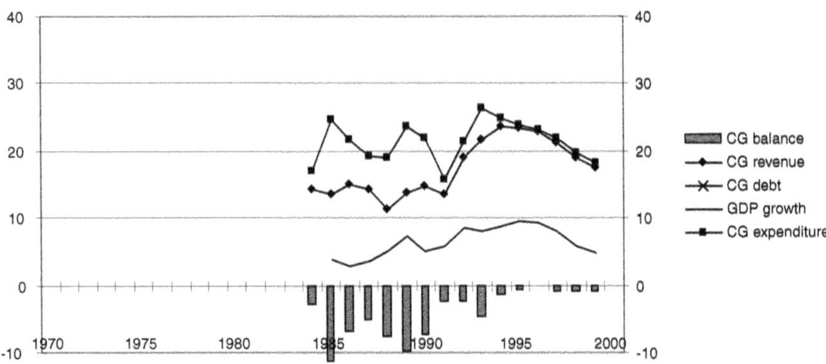


*Figure 1.6* Fiscal balance: percentage of GDP, China and Vietnam.

Source: Fiscal indicators are from country papers submitted to Japan Committee for Pacific Economic Outlook (PEO) and GDP growth data from World Bank, *World Development Indicators*, CD-Rom, 2001 (WDI).

Note
GG: general government = consolidated account of central, provincial, and other local governments, social security funds and other government entities excluding public enterprises.
PS and NFPS: non-financial public sector = consolidated account of GC + non-financial public enterprises.

in balance and the authorities rarely resorted to money- or bond-financing of fiscal deficits. Consequently, while there had been few inflationary episodes, there was no persistent inflation nor heavy government debt burdens, though one can point out the potential risks associated with the doubtful quality of public assets. In that sense, activist fiscal management unexpectedly appeared on the center stage because of the Asian economic crisis.

In Vietnam, with macroeconomic stability attained by the early 1990s, economic growth and fiscal improvement proceeded hand in hand until the Asian economic crisis. Thanks to the boom, tax revenue increased and the primary balance turned into surplus in 1995.

### *Latin America*

Except for Colombia, the Latin American economies—i.e., Chile, Ecuador, Mexico and Peru—muddled through a similar dismal tunnel, as did the Philippines in the 1980s, as the global financial crisis in 1982 eroded their fiscal positions (Figure 1.7). Colombia was also hit by the crisis, but thanks to their conservative fiscal management at that time, its fiscal imbalance was short-lived and there was no debt accumulation.

In its crisis management, Chile implemented serious fiscal retrenchment and attained overall budget surplus as early as 1987. Since then, Chile has maintained its overall balance in surplus and continued to reduce its debt-to-GDP ratio up until the Asian crisis. Both in Ecuador and Peru, by contrast, since fiscal retrenchment was half-hearted or almost absent and economic instability and/or stagnation was prolonged and pervasive, cumulative government debt put an increasingly heavier burden on their fiscal positions toward the end of the 1980s.

Mexico, the point of origin of the 1982 crisis, paid enormous costs to reduce its persistent fiscal deficits and then to eventually attain fiscal balance in 1991 for the first time in the past few decades. Aside from fiscal discipline issues, a combination of a heavy reliance on foreign borrowing and currency depreciation helped snowball these costs. Mexico has kept its primary balance positive since 1983, while its overall balance turned to surplus only in 1991 (see Figure 1.7). During this period, the government continued to pay interest burdens, which meant astronomical income transfers from the government or opportunity costs lost on the society.

## Fiscal development and consolidation in the 1990s

In this section, we focus on the recent experiences of fiscal management and look into what factors can explain either the successful or unsuccessful fiscal consolidation in the Pacific region.

### *Advanced economies*

As was pointed out at the outset, in the beginning of the 1990s, the level of government debt was high and increasing in Canada, New Zealand and the United States, while it was low in Australia, and fairly high but decreasing in Japan. In the subsequent ten years, the situation has changed dramatically, and Canada, New Zealand and the United States could realize rather persistent fiscal surplus (Figure 1.7). Why is this so? The IMF (2001) implies that it was mainly because these economies significantly reduced their expenditure from their peaks by as much as 8 percent, 10 percent and 5 percent of GDP, respectively. Australia also shared the same pattern with moderate debt accumulation in the 1990s. Of course, economic recovery contributed to regaining of the fiscal balance by increasing government revenue, but it appeared to be more or less secondary in each case.

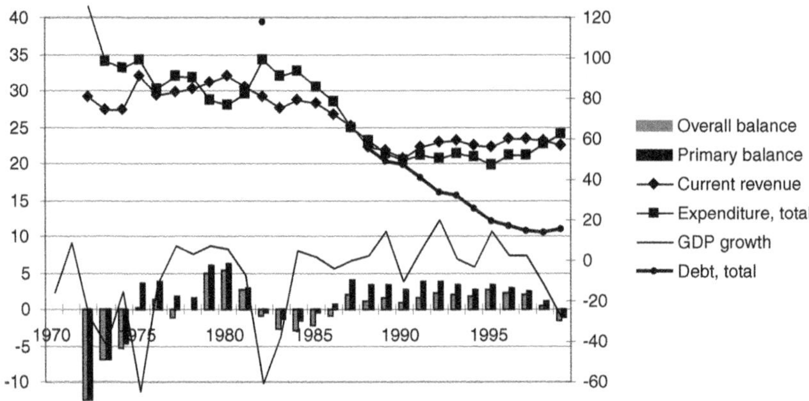
Fiscal balance: Chile, % of GDP
Overall balance
Primary balance
Current revenue
Expenditure, total
GDP growth
Debt, total
1970
1975
1980
1985
1990
1995

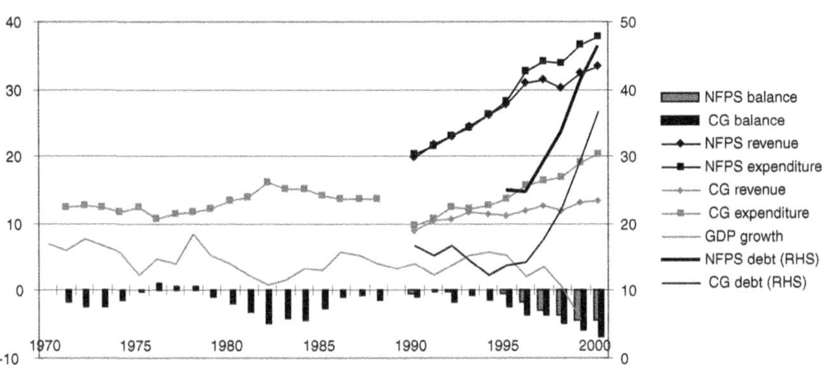
Fiscal Balance: Colombia, % of GDP
NFPS balance
CG balance
NFPS revenue
NFPS expenditure
CG revenue
CG expenditure
GDP growth
NFPS debt (RHS)
CG debt (RHS)
1970
1975
1980
1985
1990
1995
2000

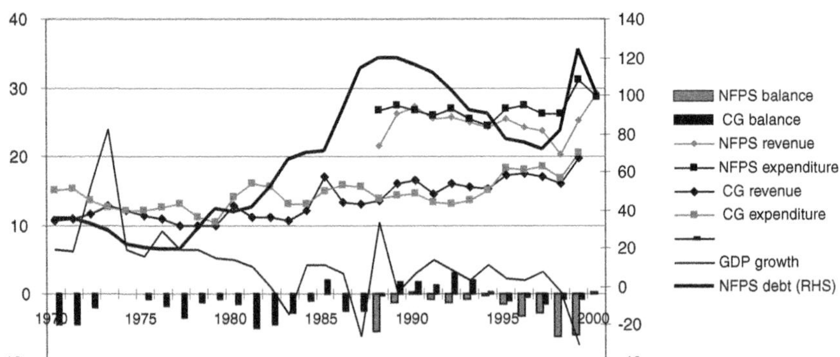
Fiscal Balance: Ecuador, % of GDP
NFPS balance
CG balance
NFPS revenue
NFPS expenditure
CG revenue
CG expenditure
GDP growth
NFPS debt (RHS)
1970
1975
1980
1985
1990
1995
2000

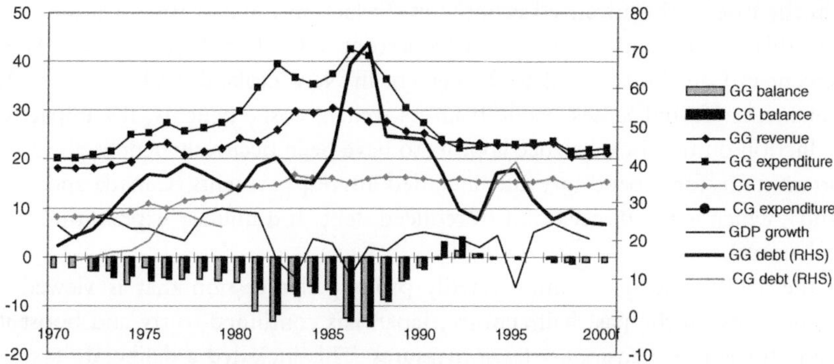


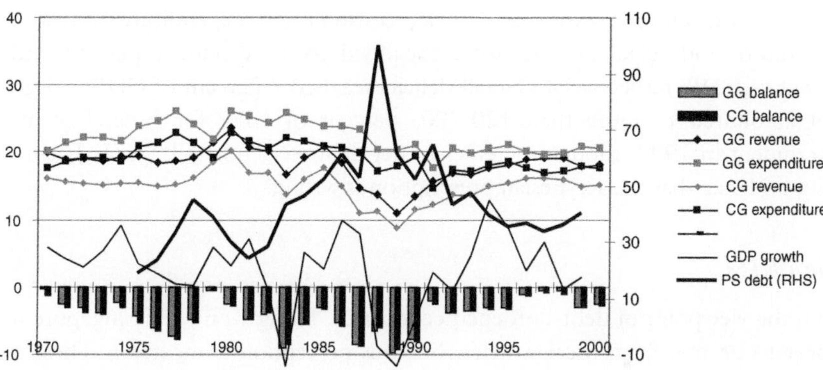


*Figure 1.7* Fiscal balance: percentage of GDP, Chile, Colombia, Ecuador, Mexico and Peru.

Source: CG balance and debt for Mexico, PS debt for Peru from World Bank (2001) *World Development Indicators*, CD-Rom. Fiscal indicators are from country papers submitted to Japan Committee for Pacific Economic Outlook (PEO) and GDP growth data fro World Bank, *World Development Indicators*, CD-Rom, 2001 (WDI).

Note
GG: general government = consolidated account of central, provincial, and other local governments, social security funds and other government entities excluding public enterprises.
PS and NFPS: non-financial public sector = consolidated account of GC + non-financial public enterprises.

What expenditure item was targeted for reduction? Subsidies and transfer payments are the most dominant and the most significantly increasing expenditure item in the case of the advanced economies. In fact, in the past three decades, the share of this item expanded from 10 to 15 percent of GDP in Australia, from 13 to 17 percent in Canada, from 12 to 28 percent in New Zealand, and from 9 to 12 percent in the United States. Aside from its welfare costs/benefits, the impact of the reduction on the fiscal balance appears to have been decisively beneficial. Other important items for expenditure cuts included interest payments (Canada and New Zealand), which is the direct result of reduced debt, and military expenditure (the United States).

In the 1990s, facing an unexpectedly prolonged recession that is viewed as being the worst in the past half-century, Japan has continued to try and boost its economy through expansionary fiscal measures. This included a deliberate tax cut on the revenue side and expansion of current and capital expenditure on the expenditure side. Both the tax cuts and the prolonged recession hit direct tax revenue hard; as a percentage of GDP, direct tax revenue declined from 14 percent to 8 percent. On the expenditure side, consumption expenditure, investment expenditure and social benefits were expanded to 1 percent, 1 percent and 4 percent of GDP, respectively. Overall deficits reached 7 percent of GDP and gross debt amounted to more than 120 (90) percent of GDP for general (central) government in 1999, though increases in net debt were not as large. Is Japan the living evidence that the Keynesian prescription is wrong?

### *Asian NIEs*

From the viewpoint of debt-burdened economies, Hong Kong and Singapore may appear to be free from fiscal worries, but this perception is incorrect. These two very small open economies must be alert to external changes and shocks, and take good care in maintaining their business and investment environments so as to be prepared for adverse climate changes. Fiscal surplus, which resulted from a relative increase in revenue in Hong Kong and from a declining trend in expenditure in Singapore, plays the role of insurance fees or buffers against unexpected shocks (Figure 1.4).

The relative presence of governments is, however, very different between these two economies. The size of the central government in Singapore is 50 percent larger than that of Hong Kong in terms of revenue and expenditure (as ratios to GDP) even without adding up other government entities (which would make the government in Singapore even larger).

Governments in both economies have been generally neutral against business cycles, but occasionally or in emergencies, the government has resorted to fiscal expansion for stability, as in the case of the 1997 crisis. Low income tax rates have been the norm in Hong Kong and are becoming so in Singapore, which implies that these economies need to invent another stable source of government revenue. In fact, although tax revenue appears to have stagnated, nontax revenue such as receipts from land sales (Hong Kong and Singapore) and investment income (Singapore) have compensated for conventional fiscal sources.

As more sizable economies, Korea and Chinese Taipei have used fiscal policies not as counter-cyclical instruments but rather for development purposes. With increasing revenue, Korea has reduced its debt ratios since the 1980s through a policy shift to a balanced budget principle, and Chinese Taipei invested in physical and human capital, resulting in fiscal deficits and debt increase in the 1990s through a policy shift out of balanced budgets (Figure 1.4). While Korea is compelled to resort to fiscal expansion in order to counter the crisis-led slowdown and to pay for remedies, its debt ratio is still at manageable levels, at least for the time being. In contrast, less seriously crisis-hit Taipei appears to have returned to a neutral position and is constraining expenditure.

### *ASEAN4 and other Asian economies*

Prudent fiscal management with persistently positive primary balances since the latter half of the 1980s does not appear to have been able to provide much breathing space against compelled fiscal expansion for economic recovery from the 1997 crisis in the ASEAN4 economies. In fact, a primary surplus was generated in these economies through a persistent fall in expenditure (Indonesia and Malaysia) or a continuous rise in revenue (the Philippines and Thailand) (Figure 1.5). Fiscal needs to boost the domestic economy and to rescue the fragile financial system forced these economies to be set back for at least several years in terms of fiscal and debt management. In the years ahead, increasing interest payments cannot but help crowd out other expenditure items. Moreover, while currency appreciation tends to help lighten debt service burdens in terms of domestic currency, monetary policy may face a dilemma. The heavier the debt burden, the more serious the social costs. This suggests that, aside from the costs due to their own political turmoil, Indonesia and the Philippines will suffer more seriously and longer than the other two ASEAN4 economies.

Against the crisis-driven slowdown, China appeared to be more active than Vietnam in fiscal policy (Figure 1.6). With a halt in the decreasing trend in government size in 1995, Chinese central government began to expand its resource base. As was the case in the other crisis-hit economies, fiscal expansion constituted one of the two vehicles to help keep up aggregate demand in China (the other was export growth). Naturally, this increased the fiscal deficit and initiated debt accumulation. The debt-to-GDP ratio remains below 20 percent so that it is too early to worry about its sustainability, but once it gives up the balanced budget, China may need new rules of conduct for fiscal discipline.

Since the early 1990s, Vietnam has adhered to a balanced budget, so that its expenditure is constrained by its revenue. While the crisis-driven regional economic downturn hit the economy severely, Vietnam made serious attempts to tighten its belt and has avoided deterioration in its fiscal balance thus far.

### *Latin America*

The degrees of fiscal consolidation at the outset of the Asian crisis generated contrasting developments for fiscal balances thereafter in the Latin American economies (Figure 1.7). While both Chile and Mexico as moderate debtors had some room for discretionary fiscal policy, Chile adopted a counter-cyclical policy with a worsening fiscal balance. In contrast, Mexico tried to be rather neutral. In both cases, there was a halt in the decline in the government debt ratio, but not a rebound.

In Colombia, loss of fiscal control on expenditure since the early 1990s appears to have aggravated the economic difficulty in facing the economic downturn, resulting in a sharp increase in government and public debt from its initial low level. In Ecuador, retrenchment of the fiscal balance since the late 1980s was halted in the mid-1990s with its debt ratio at nearly 80 percent; thereafter, its fiscal balance plunged into a shaky situation again along with the recent recession. Within a context of wide-ranging economic reforms, fiscal reforms have brought down the fiscal deficit and debt burden in Peru since 1990. However, here, too, the recent recession urged the authorities to take counter-cyclical measures, thereby expanding the fiscal deficit once again.

## Anatomy of fiscal consolidation

The Anglo-phonic economies in the Pacific region appear to have been successful in reducing their government debt in the 1990s, where their debt-to-GDP ratios peaked out in the first half of the 1990s, although their levels remain high in Canada and the United States. In Asia, Indonesia, Korea, Malaysia and Thailand generally piled up government debt in the 1980s, but they also successfully reduced the debt by the time the Asian crisis hit. In Latin America, Chile, Mexico and Peru succeeded in cutting their enormous debt-to-output ratios of the 1980s down to manageable levels by the mid-1990s, though with some turbulence in Mexico in 1994–95.

At the beginning of the 1990s, Japan looked as if it had completely escaped from debt accumulation through fiscal consolidation efforts during the 1980s, but it did not. Was Japan exceptional? In fact, it appeared that toward the end of the 1980s, Australia, Canada, New Zealand and even the United States were improving in terms of fiscal health, but this turned out not to be true. What then can we learn from these past experiences? Was there any significant difference in the success or failure of their fiscal consolidation efforts or between the 1980s and the 1990s? Or could the apparent successes in the Anglo-phonic economies turn out to be failures?

In order to answer these questions, let us examine the developments of each item of fiscal expenditure and revenue by looking at some fiscal consolidation episodes since the 1980s. Table 1.6 shows changes in the proportion of expenditure and revenue to GDP over the selected periods of fiscal consolidation for each economy: 1984–90 and 1993–98 for Australia, 1983–87 and 1993–97 for Canada, and so forth. We basically identify the periods by noting the troughs and peaks of the primary balances of the central governments. Accordingly, figures for the primary balances in Table 1.6 show the wide swings of these balances from the very negative to the very positive. For example, the primary balance of Australia swung from −1.6 percent of GDP in 1984 to 3.8 percent in 1990, a 5.5 percentage point increase over the period. Other expenditure and revenue items are also calculated in the same manner.

Since fiscal consolidation can be realized through either a reduction in expenditure or an increase in revenue or both, let us first focus on the relative contribution of these two. Both contributed more or less evenly in the 1980s and 1990s in Australia, and for the 1980s in Canada and Japan. Expenditure reduction played a dominant role in the 1980s in the United States and in the 1990s in Canada and New Zealand, and a major role in the 1990s in the United States, while revenue increase was a dominant factor in the 1980s in New Zealand. Note that the IMF (2001) has pointed out that expenditure reduction instead of revenue increase played a major role in fiscal consolidation in the 1990s as compared to the 1980s in the advanced economies.

In other economies in the Pacific region, expenditure reduction was dominant in fiscal consolidation in both the 1980s and 1990s in Indonesia, and in the 1980s in Korea, Malaysia, Chile and Mexico, while it was a major factor in the 1980s in Thailand and Colombia, and in the 1990s in Malaysia. Meanwhile, revenue increase contributed dominantly in the 1980s and 1990s in the Philippines and in the 1990s in Korea and Peru.

Now let us look at disaggregated levels, i.e., individual expenditure and revenue items. In the case of the advanced economies, dominant in expenditure reduction was subsidies/transfers. This item was dominant in seven out of nine episodes, among which the notable cases are Australia, Canada, Japan and the United States in the 1980s, and Canada and New Zealand in the 1990s. Among other important items were a cut in capital expenditure in Japan (1980s) and Australia (1990s), and in goods/services in Canada and the United States (1990s), and in wages/salaries and interest payments in New Zealand (1990s).

On the revenue side, an increase in income taxes almost always strongly contributed to fiscal consolidation. In fact, it was the largest contributor in Australia (1990s), Japan (1980s) and the United States (1990s). Exceptionally, increases in goods/service taxes and nontax revenue were the major items in New Zealand in the 1980s.

In other economies, major contributors to fiscal consolidation on the expenditure side are varied and are very different from the advanced economies. Reduction in capital expenditure was either a dominant or major factor in seven out of thirteen episodes. Expenditure cuts in wages/salaries, goods/services, subsidies/transfers, and interest payments were also sometimes important. On the revenue side, increases in income taxes were the most important contributor to fiscal consolidation as was the case in the advanced economies. Other revenue items also contributed such as social security taxes in Korea and Peru in the 1990s, goods/service taxes in Korea, Malaysia and Peru in the 1990s, and nontax revenue in Malaysia and Thailand in the 1980s.

We can summarize our findings as follows. In the advanced economies, successful fiscal consolidation generally involved an expenditure cut in subsidies/transfers

*Table 1.6* Contribution to fiscal consolidation by item[a] (change over the period, as a % of GDP)

| | *Australia* | | *Canada* | | *Japan* | *New Zealand* | | *United States* | |
|---|---|---|---|---|---|---|---|---|---|
| | *1984–90* | *1993–98* | *1983–87* | *1993–97* | *1981–90* | *1983–87* | *1992–96* | *1983–89* | *1992–99* |
| Overall balance | 5.54 | 5.97 | 3.66 | 6.40 | 4.95 | 10.25 | 7.44 | 3.14 | 5.96 |
| Primary balance | 5.48 | 6.21 | 4.38 | 6.03 | 5.22 | 12.50 | 5.40 | 3.38 | 5.14 |
| Expenditure, total | **−2.20** | **−1.88** | **−1.27** | **−5.26** | **−2.76** | 4.63 | **−6.12** | **−2.10** | **−3.58** |
| Wages and salaries | 0.47 | 0.07 | −0.07 | −0.67 | 0.00 | −0.20 | **−4.14** | −0.28 | −0.57 |
| Goods and services | 0.81 | −0.30 | −0.37 | **−1.20** | −0.15 | 1.72 | 0.56 | −0.68 | **−2.06** |
| Interest payments | −0.06 | 0.24 | 0.71 | −0.37 | 0.28 | 2.24 | **−2.04** | 0.24 | −0.82 |
| Subsidies and transfers | **−3.26** | **−0.85** | **−1.56** | **−3.47** | **−1.49** | 0.83 | **−4.19** | **−1.77** | −0.66 |
| Capital expenditure | 0.31 | **−0.97** | −0.05 | −0.21 | **−1.40** | −0.16 | −0.45 | 0.05 | 0.00 |
| Current revenue | **2.49** | **1.86** | **1.20** | **0.99** | **2.24** | **9.51** | **0.72** | **0.58** | **2.44** |
| Social security taxes | 0.00 | 0.00 | 0.21 | −0.11 | 0.00 | 0.00 | 0.00 | **0.68** | 0.11 |
| Goods and services taxes | −0.34 | 0.47 | −0.02 | −0.10 | 0.03 | **3.81** | −0.14 | −0.39 | 0.03 |
| Income taxes | **3.01** | **1.79** | **1.51** | **2.01** | **1.90** | 0.65 | **2.16** | **0.79** | **2.41** |
| Custom taxes | −0.06 | −0.15 | −0.12 | −0.19 | −0.08 | 0.16 | 0.15 | 0.06 | −0.07 |
| Other taxes | 0.28 | 0.23 | 0.00 | 0.00 | 0.27 | 0.51 | −0.32 | −0.01 | 0.12 |
| Nontax revenue | −0.39 | −0.49 | −0.40 | −0.62 | 0.02 | **4.38** | −1.12 | −0.54 | −0.17 |

| | *Indonesia* | | *Korea* | | *Malaysia* | | *The Philippines* | | *Thailand* |
|---|---|---|---|---|---|---|---|---|---|
| | *1986–90* | *1992–96* | *1981–88* | *1991–96* | *1982–88* | *1988–94* | *1981–89* | *1989–94* | *1982–90* |
| Overall balance | 3.75 | 1.55 | 4.85 | 1.72 | 13.74 | 6.36 | 2.20 | 3.08 | 10.91 |
| Primary balance | 3.78 | 0.85 | 4.53 | 1.61 | 16.34 | 3.04 | 7.25 | 1.84 | 10.78 |
| Expenditure, total | **−4.76** | **−3.85** | **−2.28** | 0.90 | **−8.01** | **−4.18** | 4.15 | 0.40 | **−6.10** |
| Wages and salaries | −0.50 | −0.48 | −0.78 | 0.14 | −1.14 | **−2.09** | 1.86 | −0.39 | −0.90 |
| Goods and services | **−1.07** | 0.03 | **−2.14** | **−0.90** | −0.51 | **−2.22** | 0.74 | −0.45 | **−3.42** |
| Interest payments | 0.04 | −0.70 | −0.32 | −0.11 | 2.60 | **−3.33** | 5.05 | **−1.24** | −0.13 |
| Subsidies and transfers | **−1.21** | 0.67 | 0.49 | 0.59 | **−2.91** | 0.32 | 0.34 | 1.83 | −0.54 |
| Capital expenditure | **−2.52** | **−3.52** | −0.30 | 1.32 | **−7.21** | 0.93 | **−1.97** | 0.26 | **−1.99** |

| | | | | | | | | | |
|---|---|---|---|---|---|---|---|---|---|
| Current revenue | −1.08 | −0.98 | −0.97 | **3.22** | −0.79 | **2.40** | **3.24** | **2.21** | **4.47** |
| Social security taxes | 0.00 | 0.46 | 0.47 | **0.94** | 0.04 | 0.11 | 0.00 | 0.00 | 0.00 |
| Goods and services taxes | −0.17 | 0.38 | −1.69 | **1.04** | 0.24 | **1.62** | −0.46 | 0.08 | 1.01 |
| Income taxes | **3.59** | −1.14 | **1.04** | 0.58 | −1.78 | **1.18** | **1.27** | **1.43** | **1.57** |
| Custom taxes | 0.23 | −0.40 | −0.12 | −0.25 | −2.10 | −0.66 | **1.13** | 0.63 | 1.28 |
| Other taxes | 0.19 | −0.36 | 0.16 | 0.82 | 0.08 | 0.87 | 0.13 | 0.66 | 0.53 |
| Nontax revenue | −4.88 | 0.09 | −0.83 | 0.80 | **2.74** | −0.72 | **1.16** | −0.58 | **6.01** |

| | *Chile* | *Columbia* | *Mexico* | *Peru* |
|---|---|---|---|---|
| | *1987–84* | *1987–82* | *1992–83* | *1994–89* |
| Overall balance | 4.87 | 4.04 | 16.09 | 9.38 |
| Primary balance | 5.53 | 4.61 | 15.21 | 10.41 |
| Expenditure, total | **−7.70** | **−2.30** | **−12.42** | 2.25 |
| Wages and salaries | **−2.28** | −0.28 | −1.44 | 2.97 |
| Goods and services | **−3.09** | −0.54 | −1.32 | **−1.62** |
| Interest payments | 0.67 | 0.57 | −0.88 | 1.03 |
| Subsidies and transfers | **−5.13** | **−1.11** | **−7.91** | 2.40 |
| Capital expenditure | −0.14 | **−1.35** | **−3.52** | 0.45 |
| Current revenue | −3.53 | **1.53** | **0.05** | **7.35** |
| Social security taxes | −0.55 | 0.22 | 0.22 | **1.53** |
| Goods and services taxes | −0.61 | 0.29 | −1.16 | **3.41** |
| Income taxes | −0.64 | 0.86 | 0.85 | 1.04 |
| Custom taxes | −0.18 | 0.65 | 0.37 | 0.04 |
| Other taxes | −0.44 | −0.04 | 0.12 | −0.78 |
| Nontax revenue | −0.62 | −0.45 | 0.17 | 1.51 |

Note

a The data refer to the difference in each item, as a ratio of GDP, between the beginning and the end of the designated period. Figures in boldface suggest a relatively large contribution to fiscal consolidation.

and a revenue increase in income taxes. The former might be a natural choice, because this item is the largest and most rapidly increasing among others in these economies, so that there may be relatively large room for discretion. Wages/salaries, goods/services and capital expenditure could also be reduced. Revenue increase in income taxes at least partially reflects a close linkage between fiscal balances and business cycles, implying that tax buoyancy remains important for fiscal health. Yet, the recent trend toward less progressive taxation than before tends to weaken this traditional built-in stabilizer mechanism and help put consolidation burdens solely on discretionary spending cuts. However, contrary to the claim made by the IMF (2001), we could not see any change in the pattern of fiscal consolidation between episodes in the 1980s and the 1990s, at least in the Pacific region.

In other economies, however, fiscal consolidation has been pursued through various channels. One reason is, of course, the diversity of their expenditure structures. Another factor is that, relatively, these economies are small in terms of government size, have low per capita income levels, and are weak in terms of tax and other revenue-raising capacity. Potential problems with past consolidation experiences were that adjustment or consolidation burdens tend to be borne by politically weakly supported, but potentially growth-enhancing sectors. Infrastructure, education and technocracy are likely to be targeted via capital expenditure, goods/services and wages/salaries, respectively, and this may be what happened and is happening in some developing economies in the region.

## Challenges to fiscal consolidation

### *Advanced economies*

In addition to the Asian economic crisis, we are now facing a global economic slowdown led by the United States. Although the advanced economies, except Japan, appeared to have succeeded in improving their fiscal positions toward the end of the twentieth century, the reality is that they have barely begun to reduce their old debt. As we have seen, fiscal positions are significantly affected by business cycles. A good example is the case of the United States, where the economy was able to reap the full benefit of the peace dividend and of an unprecedented New Economy boom. Once it is over, however, things may return to a starting point that is much like the early 1990s.

At the same time, however, discretionary restraints on some expenditure items such as subsidies/transfers contributed significantly to fiscal consolidation in our experiences of the 1980s and 1990s. A new trend in fiscal consolidation is to strengthen the fiscal framework. Measures such as debt ceilings, deficit targeting, expenditure rules, transparency in fiscal management, etc. have been advocated and implemented in advanced economies including Australia (as reflected in the Charter for Budget Honesty, 1998), Canada and New Zealand (as reflected in the Fiscal Responsibility Act, 1994), and the United States (as reflected in the 1990 Budget Enforcement Act). The fiscal framework is supposed to strengthen fiscal discipline through more accountable and transparent budgetary processes and rules (IMF 2001: 101–2, Box 3.4).

Becoming rich and old is the key factor that determines medium-run future developments of the fiscal positions in these economies. Quantitative restraint on social security cannot be an ultimate solution. We need to optimize fiscal expenditures as well as strengthen the resource base for revenue through tax reform or other alternative measures. As for the former, government employment, medical care and pension plans may have to be restructured, while for the latter, the present tax administration and tax structures themselves may have to be restructured. All of these possible remedies, including the fiscal framework, would also apply to ailing Japan.

### *Other economies*

Government intervention, which constrains the market mechanism, has become unpopular and its downsizing has been encouraged. Despite this general trend, it seems paradoxical that the Asian economic crisis possibly widened the role and scope of government. In fact, necessary macroeconomic adjustment after the crisis made activist fiscal actions inevitable and a large amount of private debt, with or without public guarantees, was acquired by government to cope with the systemic crisis of the financial and corporate sectors. In fact, those debts literally became contingent liabilities of government.

The crisis led to increasing fiscal deficits. One reason was a decline in tax revenue due to the business slowdown. In addition, currency depreciation expanded external debt service burdens, thereby increasing fiscal expenditure. Some governments rushed to expand budgets in order to maintain domestic demand, resulting in increasing fiscal deficits even further. Cyclical deficits will disappear along with business recovery, but the public debt will remain.

Contingent liabilities such as rescue funds for financial sectors constituted an additional burden on government. As public debt ratios multiplied, interest payments automatically increased. Indeed, interest burdens amounted to 15–30 percent of the total budget in the crisis-hit economies, which could possibly be more than half in Indonesia and the Philippines in a few years (Table 1.7). To cope with this, the authorities may wish to restrain total expenditure by cutting social expenditure related to education and public health, and wages and salaries of civil servants. Under the situation where the social safety net must be strengthened, however, it is apparent that these economies cannot manage just by restraining expenditure.

In order to keep their debt levels from going out of control, the crisis-hit economies have no choice but to improve their primary balances, as simple debt dynamics implies. As was shown above, in order to stabilize the debt-to-GDP ratio, GDP growth must be equal to or larger than the real interest rate plus the primary deficit-to-debt ratio. Since at present primary deficits are estimated to be 0.5–2.5 percent of GDP, income growth must be larger than the real interest rate by an equal percentage, or with GDP growth equivalent to the real interest rate, the primary deficit must be wiped out (Table 1.8). Otherwise the governments will not be able to restrain debt increases.

Developing economies have had relatively small governments, but the general trend toward globalization and greater market orientation, and moreover, economic development itself is placing pressure for changes in the status quo. The first

*Table 1.7* Public debt and interest payments of selected Asian economies (as a % of GDP)

| | *1996* | *1999* |
|---|---|---|
| China | 19.0 | 29.0 |
| Domestic debt | 6.0 | 14.0 |
| Foreign debt | 13.0 | 15.0 |
| Interest payments | 0.7 | 2.0 |
| Indonesia | 22.9 | 91.5 |
| Domestic debt | 0.0 | 52.5 |
| Foreign debt | 22.9 | 39.0 |
| Interest payments | 0.0 | 3.9 |
| Korea | 8.8 | 29.5 |
| Domestic debt | 7.6 | 22.2 |
| Foreign debt | 1.2 | 7.3 |
| Interest payments | 0.4 | 2.6 |
| Malaysia | 36.0 | 52.0 |
| Domestic debt | 31.8 | 44.0 |
| Foreign debt | 4.2 | 8.0 |
| Interest payments | 2.7 | 3.2 |
| The Philippines | 105.1 | 105.0 |
| Domestic debt | 72.5 | 59.6 |
| Foreign debt | 32.6 | 45.4 |
| Interest payments | 4.7 | 6.8 |
| Thailand | 15.7 | 50.3 |
| Domestic debt | 7.0 | 31.3 |
| Foreign debt | 8.7 | 19.0 |
| Interest payments | 0.9 | 2.3 |

Source: World Bank (2001: 98, Table 5.1).

*Table 1.8* Overall and primary balance of selected Asian economies (as a % of GDP)

| | *1994–96* | *1999* | *1999* |
|---|---|---|---|
| | *Average* | *Overall* | *Primary* |
| China | -1.0 | -2.5 | -2.4 |
| Indonesia | 1.0 | -1.1 | -1.0 |
| Korea | 0.9 | -2.6 | -2.2 |
| Malaysia | 4.0 | -2.3 | -0.6 |
| The Philippines | 4.1 | 1.7 | 1.8 |
| Thailand | 1.2 | -4.8 | -2.2 |

Source: World Bank (2001: 99, Table 5.2).

change is the increasing need for a social safety net. Public employment plans, rural development programs, social security funds and income guarantee mechanisms are being established to protect workers from enhanced global market competition. The second is enhanced need for education and related investment to cope with the greater orientation toward a knowledge economy and accelerated technological progress. The third change relates to the need to strengthen the industrial infrastructure in order to catch up with globalization and international competition, where transportation, communication and urban infrastructure are targeted.

Finally, insofar as fiscal consolidation involves fiscal contraction, it is important to know the impact of fiscal consolidation on the level of economic activity. Fiscal consolidation reduces aggregate demand, while it also lowers the real interest rate. Thus, it is not clear whether the consolidation leads consumers to anticipate smaller future tax burdens and thus increase their demand. If this holds true, even if deflationary expectations prevailed, the consolidation may enhance growth by breaking these expectations.

Unfortunately, we do not have solid evidence that shows definitely whether the impact of the consolidation on short-run output is positive or negative. In New Zealand in the 1980s, we saw a combination of consolidation and economic slowdown, and in Japan in 1997, the consolidation efforts brought about a severe recession. On the other hand, the experiences of Australia, Canada and the United States in the 1990s appear to suggest the opposite positive effect on output. Of course, simple correlation cannot tell us much, but sophisticated empirical results that control for other relevant variables have not yet reached any decisive conclusion (Alesina *et al.* 1998). This means that we should be cautious on the speed and sequence of fiscal consolidation, especially when it is launched under deflationary situations.

## Conclusion

Our main conclusions can be summarized as follows. The Pacific economies are quite diverse in fiscal structure. The degree of centralization, size and organization of government, composition of fiscal revenue and expenditure, and institutional arrangements are all very different across the economies. Canada, China, Colombia, Japan and the United States are more decentralized than the others. General governments in Australia, Canada and New Zealand are the largest, and they are the smallest in China, Hong Kong, the Philippines and Thailand. As for the composition of central government revenue and expenditure, income taxes are a major revenue item in advanced economies, while goods/service taxes and custom duties are significant in developing economies. Subsidies/transfers are a major expenditure item in advanced economies, while goods/services and capital expenditure are also significant in developing economies.

In the past three decades, the advanced and developing economies in the region have shown some distinct patterns in fiscal development across global business cycles. Counter-cyclical fiscal management has occasionally led to debt cycles in both the advanced and developing economies, while the latter appear to have also alternated with a developmental-expansion phase with fiscal deficits and an adjustment-consolidation phase with fiscal surplus. Two transition economies have recently become entangled with these processes in addition to their own agenda for intrinsic needs for fiscal reform as part of economic reform as a whole.

Reduction in expenditure on subsidies/transfers along with a strengthening of the fiscal framework has been highlighted as an effective approach for fiscal consolidation in recent years. Noting the close linkage between business cycles and fiscal development, however, strengthening the revenue base is also indispensable, especially for consolidation under recession, which is the current situation in many economies. Since we are not certain whether fiscal consolidation will stimulate or repress demand in the short run, caution should be followed in terms of the speed and sequencing of implementation. Among the advanced economies, fiscal consolidation is most needed in Japan. However, Canada and the United States are not yet completely free from potential risks with their high debt-to-GDP ratios. Australia and New Zealand seem to have gotten over the problem thus far, but not without costs.

Since the 1980s, the developing economies in the Pacific region have made significant progress in fiscal consolidation. Nevertheless, the Asian economic crisis with the subsequent financial sector distress and severe currency depreciation hit East Asia and other developing economies hard, particularly those with relatively high debt-to-GDP ratios. It appears that these economies will have to suffer an additional round of fiscal consolidation in the future. At issue is how to reconcile the short-run accommodative fiscal policy with longer-run consolidation. Colombia, Ecuador, Indonesia, Peru, the Philippines and Thailand are facing these challenges, while Chile and Mexico paid high costs in the 1980s. China, Korea and Chinese Taipei appear to have maintained their fiscal health thus far.

In many areas, including provision of an adequate social safety net, development of infrastructure and education, the fiscal needs are ever increasing along with the general trend in globalization and demographic changes. In order to meet these needs, we need to keep on rationalizing and optimizing both the revenue and expenditure sides of the budget in terms of both size and composition. This is applicable not only to the developing economies that are relatively lacking in fiscal resources (for example, China and Vietnam), but is also relevant for all member economies in the Pacific region, including the advanced economies, as well as surplus economies like Hong Kong and Singapore.

## Notes

1 As will be discussed in the chapter on Japan (Chapter 8), central government revenue share does not tell much about the autonomy of local government and the further decentralization of fiscal resources is one of the recent emergent policy issues in Japan.

2 This source lacks disaggregated data for Japan after 1994, for Ecuador after 1995 and data for Hong Kong and Chinese Taipei.

## References

Alesina, A., Perotti, R. and Tavares, J. (1998) "The political economy of fiscal adjustment," *Brookings Papers on Economic Activity*, 1: 197–266.

International Monetary Fund (1996) *World Economic Outlook*, May, Washington, DC: International Monetary Fund.

International Monetary Fund (2000) *World Economic Outlook*, May, Washington, DC: International Monetary Fund.

International Monetary Fund (2001) *World Economic Outlook*, May, Washington, DC: International Monetary Fund.

World Bank (2000) *East Asia: Recovery and Beyond*, Washington, DC: World Bank.

World Bank (2001) *World Development Indicators*, CD-Rom, Washington, DC: World Bank.

# 2 Australia

*Tony Makin*

## Introduction

The Australian government has actively used fiscal policy over recent decades to stabilize the business cycle. Fiscal policy was expansionary in the early 1980s and again in the early 1990s to counter recessions. In addition, external factors have influenced the stance of fiscal policy. For instance, in the late 1980s, fiscal policy was tightened as a means of reducing Australia's persistent current account deficit on the balance of payments.

Since the mid-1990s, raising national savings through higher public savings and reducing the net public debt to GDP ratio have motivated the federal budget strategy. Australia is now in a relatively strong fiscal position by international standards with the entire government sector's net debt having fallen from a peak of around 25 percent of GDP in 1995 to an expected 7.5 percent of GDP in 2001.

## Public sector activity

Since the 1950s, the relative size of the government sector in the Australian economy and many other industrialized economies has grown markedly. Government spending in the OECD region as a whole rose from around 25 percent of GDP in 1960 to over 40 percent in 1996. A major reason for this rise was the more widespread public provision of social welfare and the fact that over the course of numerous business cycles, fiscal policy had not been applied symmetrically. Governments usually increased public spending during economic downswings, but did not fully scale spending back during upswings.

In relation to other advanced economies, however, the size of Australia's government sector as a percentage of GDP remains at the lower end of the scale for OECD countries, and is of a similar order to that of the United States and Japan. Cross-country comparisons of public sector involvement in developed economies should be treated with caution, however, as interpretations and measurement of public sector activity can differ.

Government entities in Australia provide nonmarket goods and services, maintain law and order, regulate economic activity and redistribute income through transfer payments. Under the federal political system, there is a division of economic power between the central and state governments, the latter also being responsible for the local government sector.

In addition, publicly owned corporations produce a variety of goods and services (including transport, communications and financial services) that are sold to consumers to cover costs through the market process. However, as the federal government accounts for the bulk of public spending and revenue-raising in Australia, its fiscal activity is the main focus of the discussion that follows. The commercially oriented activity of corporations that are fully or partially government-owned is not addressed in this chapter.

### *Outlays and revenue*

The general government sector (comprising the federal, state and local governments) accounts for over a third of total national spending and raises revenue equivalent to around a third of national income. Figure 2.1 shows the trend in public sector outlays and revenue at the federal and state/local levels. Historically, the federal government has collected some 70 percent of total taxes, though it has spent less than 50 percent of total outlays. This implies a degree of so-called vertical fiscal imbalance that is high by the standards of other federations, including the United States, Canada and Mexico.

To manage this imbalance, the federal government transfers funds to the states, which are also largely responsible for the local government sector. These financial transfers are made in the form of general-purpose payments and specific-purpose payments, each accounting for around one-half of total intergovernmental transfers. General-purpose funds are used at the economic discretion of the states, whereas specific-purpose funds are tied to a specific spending area, for instance, health and education. An independent statutory body called the Commonwealth Grants Commission provides recommendations on the distribution of funds to the states, taking into account individual states' revenue-raising capacity and the cost of providing services.

For the most part, the federal budget balance has been in deficit since the early 1970s with the exception of surpluses recorded in the late 1980s and from the late 1990s onwards. Figure 2.2 reveals a cyclical pattern of federal imbalances and also that the state and local governments' budget balances have been relatively more stable than federal imbalances over past decades.

The composition of federal revenue and outlays is shown in greater detail in Figure 2.3. A noteworthy aspect of this figure is that the direct tax base (i.e., income tax and company tax) accounts for the bulk of revenue. The main indirect tax in Australia, which took effect in July 2000, is the goods and services tax (to be discussed) that replaced a host of existing sales and other indirect taxes. It provides revenue for the states and hence is not shown in Figure 2.3.

On the other side of the federal budget, the most notable feature is that government transfers in the form of social security and other welfare payments comprise the single largest component of outlays. Other significant items are expenditure on health care, education and training, defense and public debt interest.

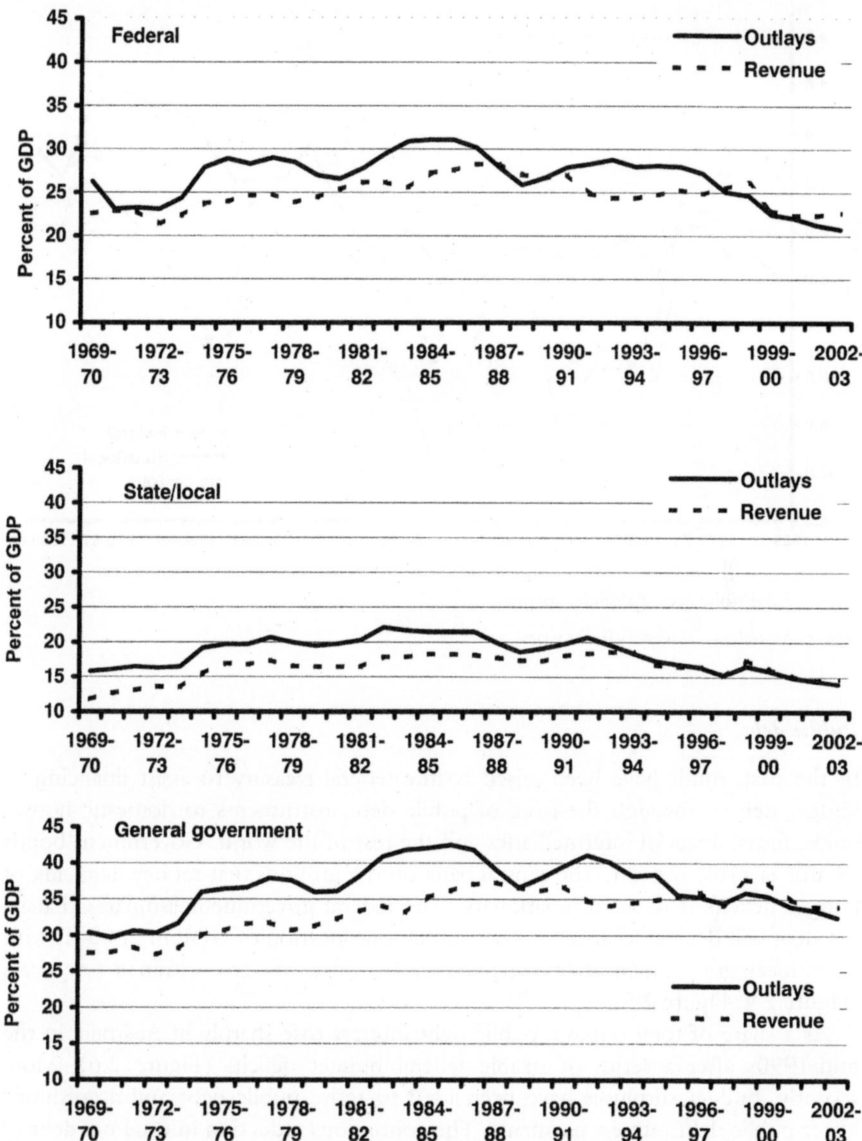


*Figure 2.1* Outlays and revenue of Australian federal, state and local governments.

Source: Australian Treasury (various years).

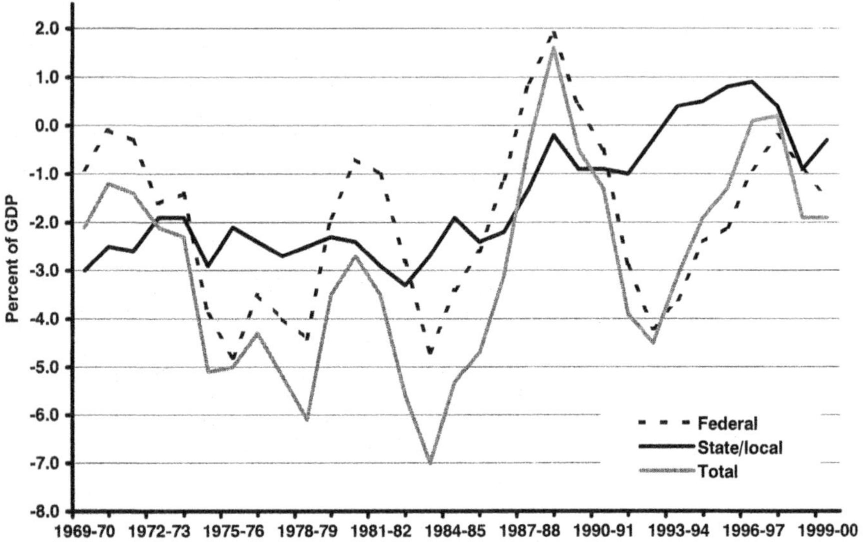


*Figure 2.2* Public sector deficit/surplus.

Source: Australian Treasury (various years).

### *Public debt*

In the past, funds have been raised by the federal treasury to assist financing of budget deficits through the issue of public debt instruments to domestic households, firms, financial intermediaries and the rest of the world. Government bonds are not as a rule issued to the central bank on the grounds that money financing of budget deficits is deemed inflationary. The federal government estimates that its net debt will decline to around 7 percent as a proportion of GDP in 2000–1, with state/local government debt expected to be close to zero within a few years (Figure 2.4, Figure 2.5).

As a share of total outlays, public debt interest rose sharply in Australia in the mid-1990s after a series of sizable federal budget deficits (Figure 2.6). More recently, budget surpluses have been used to retire public debt and accordingly lower public debt interest payments. The continuous reduction in total net debt of the consolidated public sector partly reflects the use of the proceeds of privatized assets to retire debt at the federal and state/local levels. The privatization of public assets in the areas of transport, financial services and utilities has provided a major alternative source of revenue, and public asset sales have been a frequent feature of federal and state budgets over the past decade.

The absolute size of the budget deficit or surplus is often taken as a summary indicator of the government's fiscal stance. However, adjustments can be made to official figures to account for the distortionary effect of domestic inflation. This is necessary because under inflationary conditions, interest payments on the public

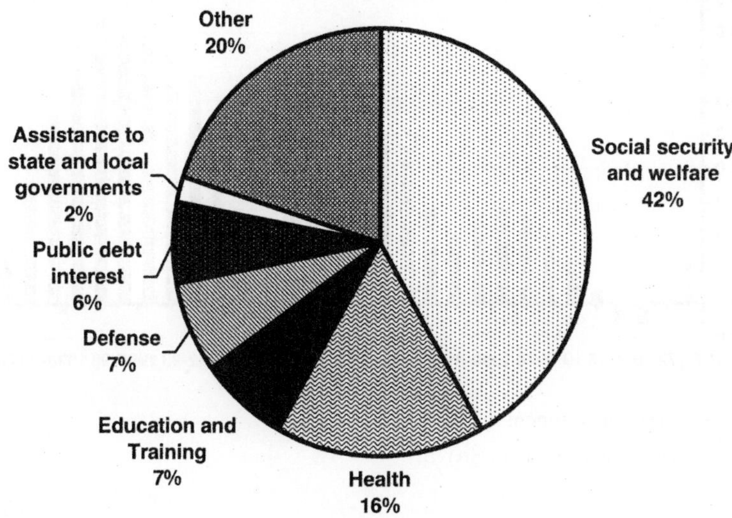


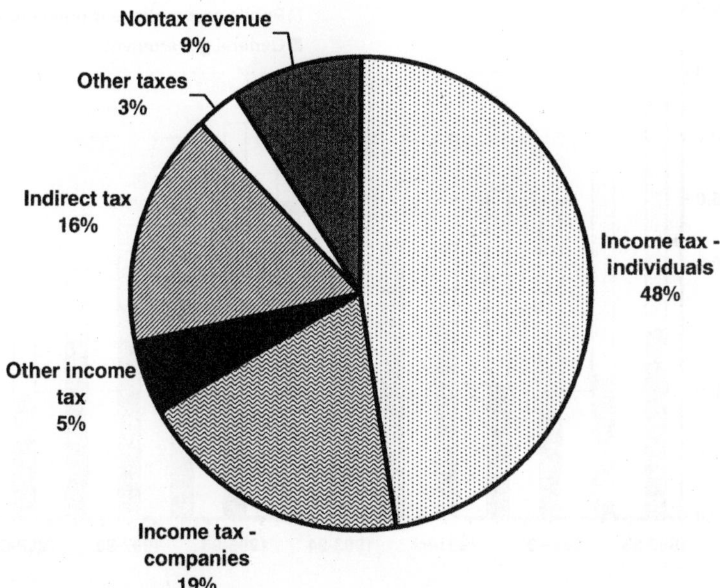


*Figure 2.3* Major categories of federal government expenses and revenues, 2000–01.

Source: Australian Treasury (2000–01).

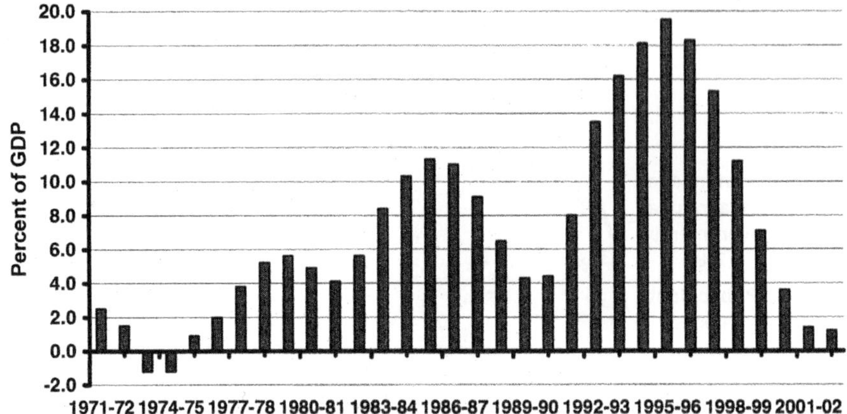


*Figure 2.4* Federal government net debt.

Source: Australian Treasury (various years).

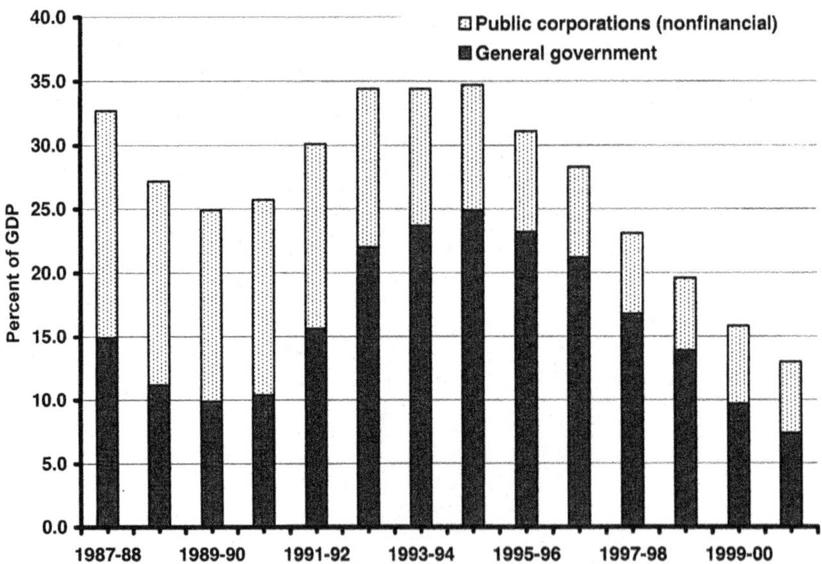


*Figure 2.5* Public sector net debt, nonfinancial.

Source: Australian Treasury (2000–01).

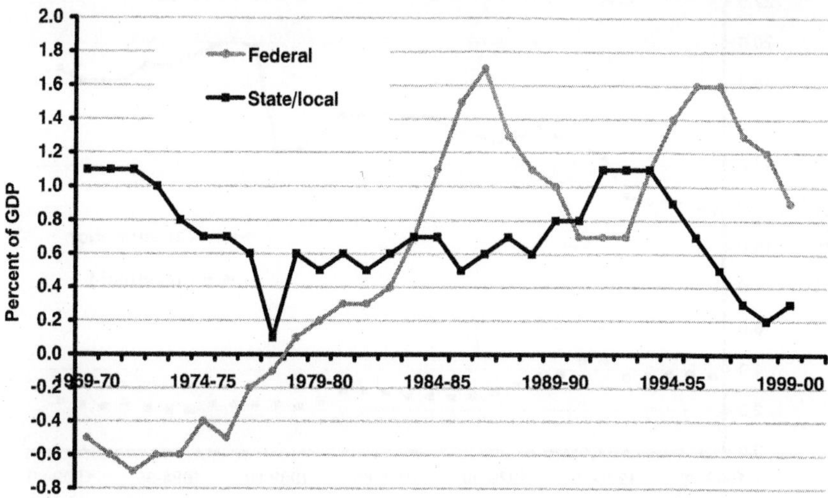


*Figure 2.6* Public debt interest (net).

Source: Australian Treasury (various years).

debt should arguably be included as part of total outlays.[1] Inflation-adjusted measures of budget deficits may still be misleading, however, to the extent that the state of the economy itself may affect budget outcomes. This is mainly because government revenue, especially income taxes, naturally increase in line with the level of domestic economic activity and the business cycle. This suggests that budget balances may be further adjusted when the economy is operating at less than its natural rate of unemployment to allow for cyclical influences, although no standard measure of the "full employment budget balance" for Australia is available.

In Australia's case, it is noteworthy that significant changes in the share of public consumption are often associated with opposite changes in the share of private investment. For instance, the sharp rise in the share of public consumption in the 1970s coincided with a fall in private investment that adversely affected the economy's growth performance. Figure 2.7 shows the relative shares of public consumption and investment by all levels of government as a percentage of GDP.

## Fiscal policy and the economy: traditional views

The standard Keynesian view that fiscal activism can stabilize macroeconomic activity remains influential in economic policy circles. This perspective has given successive Australian governments a rationale for using fiscal policy as an instrument for achieving the goals of internal and external balance. However, there are several well-known arguments that suggest that attempts at fiscal stabilization may not be effective.

These arguments are essentially based on the offsetting behavior of households and firms to fiscal shocks, as they are eventually reflected in private spending,

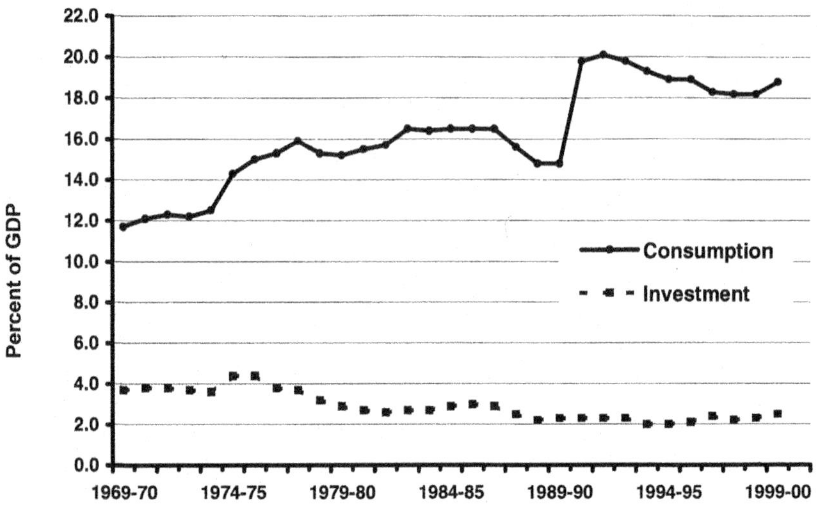


*Figure 2.7* Public consumption and investment[a].

Source: Australian Bureau of Statistics (various years).

Note

a The public consumption series from 1989–90 includes university expenditures.

interest rates and exchange rates. In one way or another, numerous perspectives predict that an increase in public spending will be offset by a fall in private sector spending, implying that higher public spending has no lasting effect on the size of national income. As a rule, these arguments imply that government spending is more appropriately seen as a substitute for, rather than a complement to, private sector spending.

### *Ricardian equivalence*

First, there is the Ricardian equivalence proposition that proposes that households are forward-looking and expect that a rise in public debt will, at some point in the future, have to be repaid. This means that taxes will eventually have to rise. If so, private saving rates would tend to rise and consumption would tend to fall in anticipation of future tax obligations. In its strict form, Ricardian equivalence asserts that private savings will increase to the same extent as the increase in the government spending that caused the budget deficit and the stock of public debt to rise. Empirical evidence for a range of advanced economies suggests, however, that such offsetting spending behavior by households has been partial at most, such that an extra dollar of public spending is matched by much less than a dollar of increased private savings.[2]

### *Crowding out*

Second, there is the standard "crowding out" argument. This asserts that because higher government spending raises the public sector borrowing requirement, other things equal, it pushes up interest rates and thereby "crowds out" private sector investment spending. Hence the pattern of expenditure shifts away from private investment toward government consumption. Because the rate of real domestic capital accumulation falls, fiscal expansion therefore delivers lower economic growth. Yet, like the basic Keynesian model against which it was originally set, the crowding out argument is somewhat limited by its closed economy assumptions.

### *International linkages*

The scale of international transactions for many economies has grown to such an extent that it is no longer appropriate to think about macroeconomic linkages without explicitly taking into account international factors such as foreign investment flows, current account deficits and exchange rates. The most widely accepted theoretical approach to examining the impact of fiscal policy in the open economy is the model proposed by Mundell (1963) and Fleming (1962). This approach predicts that if capital funds are highly mobile across borders and if the exchange rate floats, then a rise in government spending will crowd out net exports by lowering exports and raising imports.

In other words, in an open economy, fiscal policy is ineffective as an income stabilization tool under floating exchange rates, irrespective of the stage of the business cycle. According to this model, higher public spending initially pushes up the domestic interest rate; this induces foreign capital inflow, strengthens the nominal and real exchange rate, and worsens competitiveness. The loss of competitiveness, in turn, lowers exports and raises imports, in the process also providing a theoretical rationale for the "twin deficits" hypothesis (to be discussed further).

Hence, as with the other arguments outlined above, fiscal policy is rendered impotent as a stabilization tool because any rise in public spending simply offsets expenditure elsewhere, in this case, on net exports. However, a major empirical problem of the Mundell–Fleming analysis is that the exchange rates of advanced economies have generally tended to appreciate rather than depreciate after periods of fiscal consolidation. In addition, a fault of the Mundell–Fleming model is its presumption that aggregate production is essentially determined by total expenditure in the economy.

In other words, it is a demand-side model, with aggregate supply adjusting endogenously. International macroeconomic accounting dictates, however, that trade and current account deficits can only arise, in principle, when aggregate output and aggregate expenditure are unequal, or what amounts to the same thing, when domestic savings and investment differ.

## Savings, investment and fiscal activity

Alternatively, the basic linkages between fiscal activity and the economy can be considered with reference to domestic savings, investment, the external accounts and national income.

### *The effects of fiscal consolidation*

The causal links between domestic fiscal activity, the external accounts and the macroeconomy can be analyzed in the first instance using a savings and investment framework. Private sector savings is equal to national disposable income less private consumption. That is:

$$S_p = (Y_d - T - C_p)$$

where $Y_d$ is national disposable income, T is income taxes net of transfer (including welfare) payments, and $C_p$ is private sector consumption. Public sector savings is the difference between taxes raised from the private sector less public consumption, $S_g = (T - C_g)$, where $C_g$ is public consumption. Total domestic savings is the sum of private savings and public savings:

$$S = S_p + S_g = (Y_d - T - C_p) + (T - C_g).$$

Domestic savings is shown by the vertical savings schedule in Figure 2.8. Consistent with modern theories of consumption and saving behavior, the supply of national savings does not respond directly to the domestic interest rate. Total savings are fixed, given the level of national income and consumption. On the investment side of the economy, again there is an increased demand for available funds whenever firms invest by purchasing capital equipment, the cost of which is measured by the real interest rate, $r$. For an open economy with unlimited access to world capital markets, this interest rate is the same as the world interest rate, $r^*$. Total domestic investment is simply the sum of private investment, $I_p$, plus public investment, $I_g$.

Now consider the effects of fiscal consolidation on the external accounts by means of reduced public consumption spending. A fall in $C_g$ implies a rightward shift of the total savings schedule in Figure 2.8. If public consumption falls, the budget deficit will decrease and domestic savings will rise, other things being the same. This reduces the external financing requirement for the economy. With more domestic savings, there will be less demand for foreign funds to finance available domestic investment opportunities; income paid abroad will fall and national income will rise. At the same time, any foreign debt-related risk premium factored into domestic interest rates will fall as foreign debt levels are wound back. This would provide a further boost to domestic investment, reinforcing the positive effect of the fiscal consolidation on national income.[3]

In summary, this analysis shows how fiscal consolidation can be potentially expansionary if it contracts public consumption expenditure in open economies that are experiencing high current account deficits and significant levels of foreign debt. Reduced public consumption, easily the largest component of total public spending in most economies, lowers expenditure relative to output, or raises domestic savings relative to domestic investment, and hence lowers an economy's external borrowing requirement.[4]

Other things being unchanged, this reduces income paid abroad and raises national income, as well as lowers domestic interest rates to the extent that it mini-

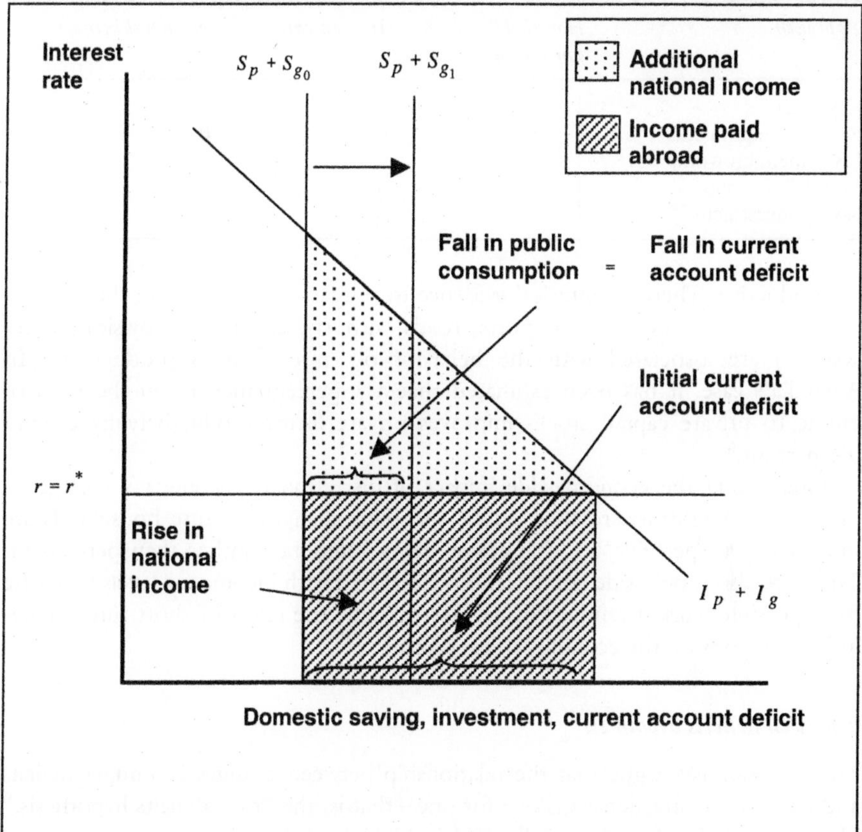


*Figure 2.8* Effects of fiscal consolidation.

mizes any foreign debt-related risk premium. In turn, the lower interest rates stimulate increased private domestic investment and subsequently spur higher economic growth, consistent with the macroeconomic behavior patterns of many open economies that have experienced episodes of fiscal consolidation over recent decades.

Table 2.1 summarizes the effects of reducing public consumption on private household consumption, interest rates and national income for each of the models presented. The Australian economy has behaved in a manner consistent with this model as shown by periods following the fiscal consolidation episodes in the late 1980s and mid-1990s. In both instances, lower interest rates, stronger-than-expected private investment and higher economic growth followed fiscal consolidation that was achieved by posting budget surpluses on the back of reduced government spending.

Fiscal policy involving increased public investment may still be expansionary, provided foreign investors deem the additional public investment expenditure to

*Table 2.1* Effects of reducing public consumption

| *Approach* | *Household consumption* | *Interest rate* | *National income* |
|---|---|---|---|
| Keynesian | ↓ | ↓ | ↓ |
| Ricardian equivalence | ↑ | 0 | 0 |
| Investment crowding out | ↑ | ↓ | ↑ |
| Mundell–Fleming | ↓ | 0 | 0 |
| Saving-investment | ↑ | ↓ | ↑ |

be productive. There is empirical evidence to suggest that changes in the stock of public infrastructure (such as ports, roads, airports, electricity provision, water systems) are associated with the behavior of an economy's productivity. In Australia's case, it has been estimated that a 1 percent increase in the ratio of public to private capital stocks improves private factor productivity by around 0.4 percent.[5]

Interpreting the economywide impact of discretionary income tax changes is much less straightforward than public spending changes because households are more likely to perceive tax changes as being temporary rather than permanent. There are also supply-side complications associated with income tax levels that arise from possible work incentive effects. Accordingly, the effect of short-run changes in income taxes on the economy is less certain.

### *The twin deficits hypothesis*

Many economists argue that the relationship between changes in budget deficits and current account deficits is one for one—that is, the "twin deficits hypothesis." However, empirical studies of the "twin deficits hypothesis" are not supportive of the proposal that the two deficits are identically twinned. One reason for this is that the business cycle itself may cause measured public and current account imbalances to move in opposite directions.

For instance, during recessions, a slump in private investment may lower the current account deficit but raise the budget deficit as tax revenue falls and unemployment benefits increase government outlays. Another is that foreign investors will react negatively to growing budget deficits and public debt levels, causing exchange rate depreciations that will improve competitiveness and reverse external deficits.

## Recent fiscal developments

### *Introduction of the Goods and Services Tax*

The most significant fiscal initiative in Australia in recent years has been the introduction of the goods and services tax (GST) that took effect in fiscal year 2000–01. The GST, which is applied to the sale of most goods and services with the notable exception of basic food items, replaced a wholesale tax that had been levied on a shrinking manufactured goods base. Revenue from the GST is transferred to the state and territory governments for the funding of essential services such as schools, hospitals and roads, and has allowed these governments to abolish numerous business and financial sector-specific taxes. Other benefits of this major reform of the taxation system include the removal of an indirect tax burden on business input costs and also on exporters.

### *The Charter of Budget Honesty*

Another noteworthy change that has occurred in Australia in recent years has been the establishment of a new institutional framework to improve the conduct of fiscal policy. In particular, the federal government has established the Charter of Budget Honesty aimed at strengthening the formulation and reporting of the federal budgetary position. The Charter of Budget Honesty Act 1998 ensures greater discipline, transparency and accountability for fiscal policy by specifically ensuring that governments maintain public debt at prudent levels, bearing in mind the intergenerational impact of higher public indebtedness.

The Charter aims to ensure that fiscal policy contributes to adequate national savings and, when necessary, to the dampening of cyclical fluctuations allowing for economic risks facing the economy. Governments are also required to provide comprehensive fiscal information before general elections and detail the means by which they will reverse temporary fiscal measures that are implemented to counter economic downturns. The Act also includes several reporting provisions. Prior to its first budget, the government must release a fiscal strategy statement that is evaluated and updated as part of the annual budget process. The fiscal authorities are also required to prepare annual reports on budget strategy, the economic outlook and budget outcomes.

In addition to these regular reports, an intergenerational report is to be released around every five years. Its purpose is to assess the long-term sustainability of current government policies over a 40-year time horizon, taking into account the financial implications of demographic change. The first of these reports is due in 2002–03 and is supposed to provide a long-term planning horizon for the government.

The Act also requires the public release of a pre-election economic and fiscal outlook before national elections. This document updates federal budget and general government activity for the current year and provides forward estimates for the next three financial years. It includes the economic and other assumptions relating to current positions and forward estimates, with discussion of the sensitivity of the outcomes to the assumptions and other possible risks that may influence fiscal outcomes.

Governments are also required to detail the means by which they will reverse temporary fiscal measures implemented to counter economic downturns. The pre-election economic and fiscal outlook, together with the cost of election policy commitments made by the government and opposition before polling day, aims to ensure that the fiscal intentions of the major political parties are open to public scrutiny.

## Conclusion

Fiscal policy has been used to achieve different macroeconomic objectives in Australia over recent decades. During periods of economic downturn, the fiscal stance has been relaxed as a means of stabilizing the business cycle. However, whether higher government spending and sizable budget deficits successfully achieved this goal remains open to question.

This is not to deny that fiscal policy involving increased public investment may still be expansionary. Additional public investment may improve output-generating capacity without adverse interest rate and exchange rate effects, provided foreign investors deem the additional public investment expenditure is productive. Empirical evidence suggests that changes in the stock of public infrastructure (such as ports, roads, airports, electricity provision and water systems) can improve an economy's productivity.

There have also been some notable fiscal consolidation episodes in Australia over recent decades, such as during the late 1980s and mid-1990s, when fiscal policy was directed at reducing both public and external debt levels. These consolidation episodes were largely achieved by posting budget surpluses on the back of reduced government consumption spending. As a consequence, interest rates tended to fall, asset prices strengthened, and investment and economic growth improved.

## Notes

1 See Makin (1990) for further discussion.
2 See Seater (1993) for a useful survey.
3 See also McDermott and Westcott (1996).
4 Makin (2000) contains an extended discussion of these issues.
5 Otto and Voss (1994) obtain results for Australia that are similar to Aschauer's (1989) results for the US.

## References


Aschauer, D. (1989) "Is public expenditure productive?," *Journal of Monetary Economics* 23(2): 177–200.

Australian Bureau of Statistics (various years) *Australian Economic Indicators*, Canberra: Australian Bureau of Statistics.

Australian Treasury (various years) *Budget Statements*, Canberra: Australian Government Publishing Service.

Fleming, J. (1962) "Domestic financial policy under fixed and floating exchange rates," *IMF Staff Papers* 9(3): 369–79.

International Monetary Fund (1996) *World Economic Outlook*, Chapters 3, 4, and 5, Washington, DC: International Monetary Fund.

McDermott, C. and Westcott, R. (1996) "Fiscal reforms that work," in *Economic Issues* 4, Washington, DC: International Monetary Fund.

Makin, A. (1990) "The real federal budget imbalance," *The Economic Record* 66(4): 249–53.

Makin, A. (2000) *Global Finance and the Macroeconomy*, London and New York: Palgrave.

Mundell, R. (1963) "Capital mobility and stabilization policy under fixed and flexible exchange rates," *Canadian Journal of Economics and Political Science* 29(4): 475–85.

Otto, G. and Voss, G. (1994) "Public capital and private sector productivity," *The Economic Record* 70(2): 121–32.

Reserve Bank of Australia (1996) *Australian Economic Statistics 1949–50 to 1994–95*, Occasional Paper No. 8, Sydney: Reserve Bank of Australia.

Seater, J. (1993) "Ricardian equivalence," *Journal of Economic Literature* 31(1): 142–90.

# 3 Canada

*Ronald Kneebone*

## Introduction

In reviewing recent trends in Canadian fiscal variables, this chapter also discusses how these trends relate to some key fiscal policy issues. The next section begins with an overview of the Canadian fiscal system, where Canadian fiscal policy is shown to operate within a federal system in which the fiscal policy tools are shared between levels of government. In this section, it will also be shown that fiscal policy operates within a national economy made up of regional economies that are subject to nonsynchronized business cycles. The chapter proceeds with an examination of the policy choices that have dominated Canadian fiscal policy in the past decade. It then speculates as to the emergent issues for Canadian fiscal policy and concluding remarks.

## Overview of the Canadian economy and fiscal system

This section provides a brief overview of the Canadian fiscal system and identifies those features of the Canadian economy that most seriously impact upon fiscal policy choices.

### *A federal fiscal structure*

Canada has a federal government structure; this means that government activities take place at several levels: national (or federal), provincial, territorial and local. The British North America (BNA) Act of 1867, Canada's constitution, sets out the taxing and spending responsibilities of the federal and provincial governments. While the BNA Act has been amended several times, most recently in 1982, the federalist structure of government in Canada has remained intact and indeed is one of the defining features of the country. An independent central bank (the Bank of Canada) determines the monetary and exchange rate policy under which the fiscal authorities must operate.

The federal government is responsible for matters of national interest including national defense and foreign policy, international trade, competition policy, criminal law, and money and banking. The federal government is responsible for the delivery of some of Canada's social programs (unemployment insurance, for example) but often shares this responsibility with the provinces. The federal government is also responsible for a public pension plan (the Canada Pension Plan), but the budget for this program is separate from the rest of the federal government. To all intents and purposes, the federal government has unlimited taxing powers, as it is able to employ any system or mode of taxation it deems necessary.

On the other hand, the provinces are responsible for programs in the areas of health care, education and welfare. The provinces have extensive taxing powers, although they are somewhat more limited than the federal government in the sense that they do not have access to money finance. Nevertheless, compared with most other federations, Canadian provinces have a great deal of power and fiscal autonomy. Indeed, the provinces account for about one-half of the activities undertaken by the public sector in Canada; thus, in the aggregate, the provinces are as important as the federal government. Local governments—i.e., cities, towns and municipalities—are creatures of the provinces, and receive all of their spending and taxing authority from the provinces.

An important aspect of the federal form of government in Canada is the role of transfers from the federal government to the provinces. Although the federal government is not directly responsible for programs related to health care, education and welfare, it has been able to exercise substantial influence over the provinces in these areas through "the power of the purse." The most important transfer program is the Canada Health and Social Transfer (CHST). Although the CHST is ostensibly to be used to finance provincial programs related to health, welfare and postsecondary education, it is, in fact, a block grant that goes to general provincial revenues and may be used as the provincial governments see fit. The CHST was introduced in 1996 to replace transfers under the Established Program Financing (EPF) program for hospitals and postsecondary education, and the Canada Assistance Plan (CAP) for welfare. Both the EPF and CAP were conditional grants that had to be spent in their respective areas.

Another important feature of the Canadian federation is the role of equalization payments. Under this program, the federal government provides unconditional transfers to the "have-not" provinces so that they may provide government services that are roughly comparable in quality to the services provided by the "have" provinces. The provinces of Alberta and Ontario are currently the only two "have" provinces—i.e., provinces that do not receive equalization payments.[1] The remaining eight provinces receive various amounts of equalization payments, depending upon need. The federal government funds the equalization program.

Table 3.1 presents data on the major revenue sources and the major spending responsibilities of the federal and provincial governments for fiscal year 1998/99 (FY98/99). The data show that in virtually all major tax fields and areas of spending, both the federal and provincial levels of government play substantial roles. The size of the debt service component shows that both levels of government have made extensive use of deficits to finance their expenditures in the past. More recently, governments at both levels have significantly reduced or eliminated their annual deficits. We will return to this issue below.

Not fully appreciated from looking at the data in Table 3.1 is the degree of interdependence of government budgets. There are two sources of interdependence. First, cost and revenue sharing, intergovernmental grants and equalization

*Table 3.1* Federal and provincial government revenue and expenditure, FY98/99 (as a % of GDP)

| | *Provincial* | *Federal* |
|---|---|---|
| Revenue | | |
| Personal income tax | 5.5 | 8.7 |
| Corporate income tax | 1.3 | 2.4 |
| Consumption taxes | 4.7 | 3.8 |
| Contributions to social insurance plans | 0.7 | 2.2 |
| Federal–provincial transfers | 3.1 | — |
| Total | 20.1 | 18.6 |
| Expenditure | | |
| Health | 6.1 | 0.2 |
| Social services | 3.6 | 5.4 |
| Education | 4.7 | 0.5 |
| Debt service | 3.1 | 4.9 |
| Federal–provincial transfers | — | 3.1 |
| Total | 21.5 | 18.4 |

Source: Statistics Canada, CANSIM database.

Note
Not applicable.

transfers are all reasons why the budgetary decisions made by one level of government have a direct impact upon the budget of the other.[2] But there is another indirect source of budgetary interdependence that is due to the fact that the two levels of government spend and collect revenues from the same private sector. Thus, any fiscal policy change by one level of government must, by affecting the tax base, interest rates and inflation, gives rise to what the other level of government sees as an exogenous shock to its budget position. The way this second level of government responds to the budget disturbance must feed back into the private sector and thereby into the budget of the first level of government. In this way, an interesting dynamic arises from the interdependence of budgets that complicates any attempt to forecast the economic impact of fiscal policy changes.

Some appreciation of the importance of this interdependency between federal and provincial budgets in Canada can be had from Wilson *et al.* (1994) who use the FOCUS macroeconometric model to simulate the effects of fiscal policy changes. In one simulation, they report that over the 1989–91 period, several federal tax increases had the effect of reducing the federal deficit by \$4.25 billion while simultaneously increasing the deficit of the provincial government sector by \$1.48 billion—an amount equal to 35 percent of the federal deficit reduction. Using the same model, Dungan and Wilson (1985) examine alternative fiscal policies under alternative monetary policy regimes. Although the degree of budgetary independence varies with the combination of fiscal and monetary policies chosen, in every case, improvements in the federal budget come at the price of disadvantages in the budgets of the provinces.

The latter set of simulations suggests that another important player in determining the impacts of fiscal policies is the Bank of Canada. The role of the bank is crucial, for it controls the levers of monetary policy. In a small open economy that has adopted a flexible exchange rate, like Canada, monetary policy is the pre-eminent tool of macroeconomic policy. By influencing the rate of economic growth, the bank thus exerts a powerful influence on tax revenue and the income-sensitive expenditure of fiscal authorities. Moreover, by influencing the level of interest rates, it directly affects the size of debt-servicing costs. In 2002, the federal Department of Finance estimated that a 1 percent increase in real output would improve the financial position of the federal government by $2.6 billion per year after two years, an amount equal to 1.8 percent of federal program expenditures. A sustained 100 basis point reduction in nominal interest rates is estimated to improve the federal government's fiscal position by $1.4 billion per year after two years. Since real output and nominal interest rates tend to move in opposite directions in response to monetary policy shocks, these estimates indicate that Bank of Canada policies can have substantial impacts on federal finances.

### *A regional economy*

Just as control over fiscal variables is fragmented in the Canadian economy, so too the economy is itself "fragmented." Table 3.2 shows the correlation of changes in real per capita GDP between each of the provinces and between each province and the national economy over the period 1961–95. It is evident that movements in output are not always highly correlated across the provinces. The province of Alberta stands out in particular, with changes in output negatively correlated with five of the other provinces, including Ontario and Québec, and low positive correlations with the other provinces, except Saskatchewan. Moreover, it is evident that changes in the provincial economies are correlated to varying degrees with movements in the national economy.

In such circumstances, monetary policy may be usefully supplemented by regionally differentiated fiscal policy. That is, a stabilization policy that is based upon fluctuations in national output may not be appropriate for all regions and a monetary policy that is appropriate for some provinces will be inappropriate for others. For this reason, fiscal policy in Canada plays an important function in offsetting what might be, for a particular region, the effects of a less-than-appropriate monetary policy. Automatic stabilizers associated with either federal or provincial budgets can provide this service so long as they are not constrained to allowing their budget balances to fluctuate as necessary as the economy moves through the business cycle.

### *A small open economy*

Canada is a small open economy whose exports are heavily weighted toward commodities. For the most part, commodity prices are determined in world markets in which the supply of Canadian commodities has relatively little influence on price. Thus fluctuations in world commodity prices are very important for determining

*Table 3.2* Correlation between changes in real per capita GDP, 1961–95

| | *NL* | *PEI* | *NS* | *NB* | *QU* | *ON* | *MA* | *SA* | *AB* | *BC* | *Canada* |
|---|---|---|---|---|---|---|---|---|---|---|---|
| NL | 1.00 | | | | | | | | | | |
| PEI | 0.50 | 1.00 | | | | | | | | | |
| NS | 0.34 | 0.41 | 1.00 | | | | | | | | |
| NB | 0.72 | 0.63 | 0.64 | 1.00 | | | | | | | |
| QU | 0.34 | 0.39 | 0.34 | 0.47 | 1.00 | | | | | | |
| ON | 0.42 | 0.43 | 0.44 | 0.57 | 0.87 | 1.00 | | | | | |
| MA | 0.43 | 0.36 | 0.40 | 0.44 | 0.63 | 0.70 | 1.00 | | | | |
| SA | 0.08 | 0.10 | −0.21 | −0.13 | 0.05 | 0.05 | 0.39 | 1.00 | | | |
| AB | 0.04 | −0.16 | −0.24 | −0.25 | −0.01 | −0.09 | 0.37 | 0.64 | 1.00 | | |
| BC | 0.36 | 0.44 | 0.12 | 0.33 | 0.58 | 0.59 | 0.62 | 0.36 | 0.33 | 1.00 | |
| Canada | 0.45 | 0.41 | 0.33 | 0.47 | 0.84 | 0.88 | 0.84 | 0.38 | 0.35 | 0.80 | 1.00 |

Note
Provinces
NL = Newfoundland    PEI = Prince Edward Island
NS = Nova Scotia    NB = New Brunswick
QU = Québec    ON = Ontario
MN = Manitoba    SK = Saskatchewan
AB = Alberta    BC = British Columbia.

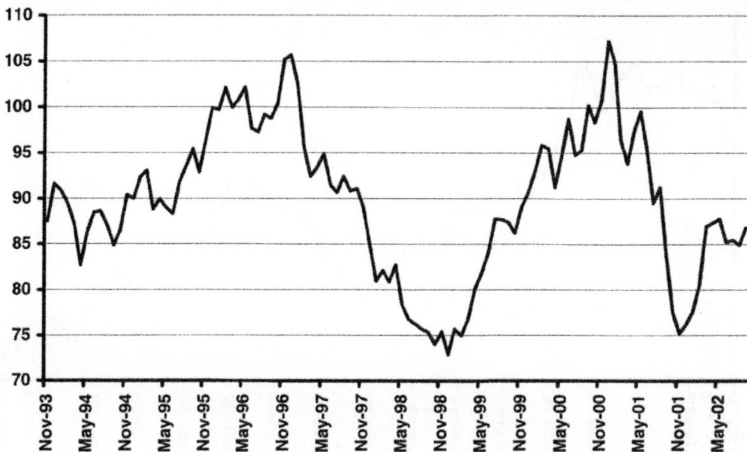


*Figure 3.1* Commodity price index, 1993–2002.

Source: Royal Bank of Canada (various years).

the health of the Canadian economy and are beyond the control of Canadian producers.

Figure 3.1 plots an index of a large number of commodity prices weighted by the share of each commodity in Canada's exports (index = 100 in 1996). The volatility of this index indicates that over the past ten years, international commodity prices have played havoc with producers' revenues. Many commodity-exporting industries are regionally based—oil and natural gas in Alberta, grain in Saskatchewan, and lumber in British Columbia—so that fluctuations in international commodity prices tend to have economic effects that hit some regions far harder than others. This also has implications for provincial government revenues. The government of the province of Alberta, for example, saw its revenues fall by over 40 percent following a crash in the price of oil in 1986. More recently, the same province was witness to an unexpected $6.5 billion gain in revenue (equal to 34 percent of planned total revenue) due to unexpectedly higher energy prices.

McCallum (1998) argues that over the long term, these fluctuations also play havoc with the value of the Canadian dollar. Figure 3.2 shows that the Canadian dollar has suffered a substantial fall in value against the US dollar since 1970. McCallum estimates that changes in commodity prices are responsible for about one-third of the drop in the value of the dollar *vis-à-vis* the US dollar since 1973.

### *The elephant and the mouse*

The United States is the largest economic power in the world and is by far and away Canada's largest trading partner. Canada is also the largest trading partner of the US. The Canadian economy is, however, only one-tenth the size of the US

*Figure 3.2* The Canada–US exchange rate.

Source: Statistics Canada, CANSIM series B3400.

economy. As a consequence, how the US economy performs has enormous impact on the health of the Canadian economy.

Canada has benefited a great deal from the impressive growth in the US economy over the past decade. Figure 3.3 plots real growth rates of GDP for Canada and the US since 1970. The high correlation between these series attests to the close integration of these two economies.

Figure 3.4 plots data on Canada's exports and imports with the world and with the US. Two things are apparent from Figure 3.4: (i) the shares of exports and imports in the Canadian economy have grown rapidly since the signing of free trade agreements with the US and Mexico; and (ii) most of the growth in trade has been with the US.[3]

## Recent fiscal policy problems and policies

The fiscal policies of Canada's federal and provincial governments have been dominated for the past decade by two related events: the realization that it was necessary to take strong action to control the accumulation of government debt and the monetary policy choices of the Bank of Canada.

### *Monetary policy*

In 1988, the Governor of the Bank of Canada announced the central bank's decision to pursue a monetary policy rule. The rule would be a simple one: the central bank would conduct monetary policy in a way that is consistent with a target of zero inflation. (This policy was subsequently redefined as maintaining a rate of inflation between 1 and 3 percent.) This decision marked the second time

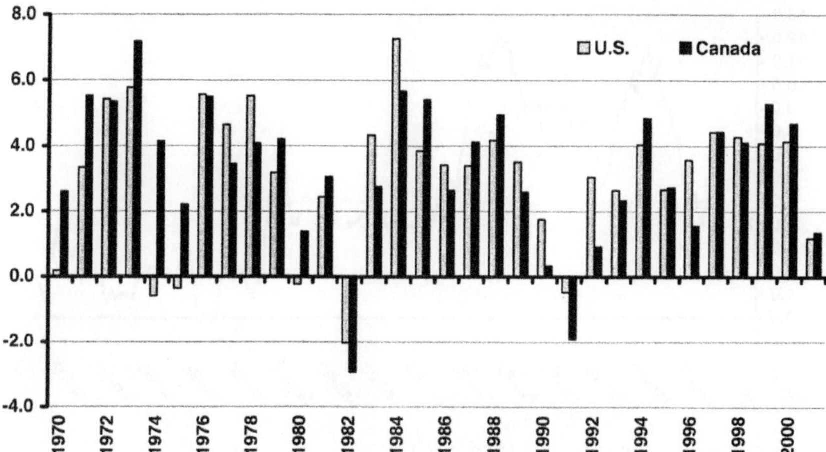


*Figure 3.3* Annual growth in real GDP of Canada and the US (%).

Source: Statistics Canada, CANSIM series D100525, D369476.

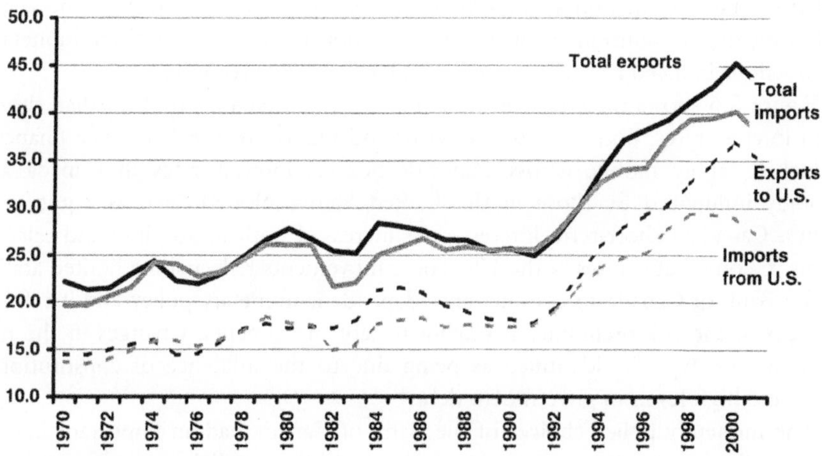


*Figure 3.4* Exports and imports of goods and services, total and with the US (as a % of GDP).

Source: Statistics Canada, CANSIM series D58001, D58017, D58101, D58117, D22435.

since 1970 that the central bank had embarked on a concerted effort to reduce the rate of inflation. The first effort was in the early 1980s when, in tandem with the US Federal Reserve, the Bank of Canada imposed what Laidler and Robson (1993) describe as an "excruciatingly" contractionary monetary policy. The announcement in 1988 would lead to another period of monetary contraction that began in late 1989 and another successful reduction in the rate of inflation.

Figure 3.5 which plots the rate of CPI inflation since 1970 shows the dramatic

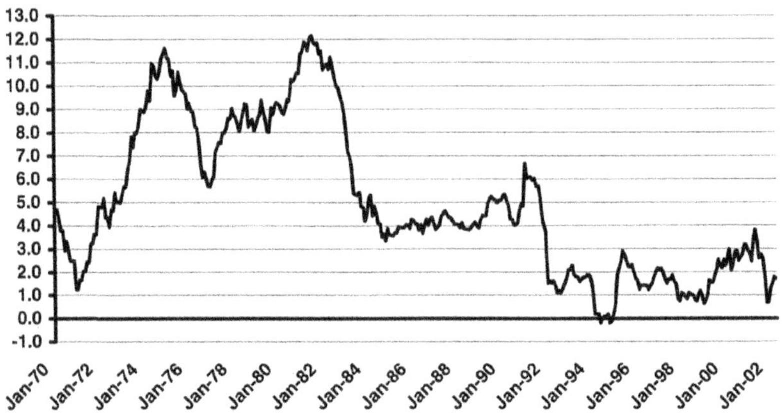


*Figure 3.5* Canadian inflation rate, 1970–2002 (% change in CPI).

Source: Statistics Canada, CANSIM series P100000.

fall in the rate of inflation at the time of the first monetary contraction and again following the announcement of the zero inflation target. Each of these monetary contractions induced a serious recession and a prolonged recovery.

Figure 3.6 shows the effect of these monetary contractions on Canadian short-term interest rates, both in absolute terms and relative to the US. Since financial capital is highly mobile across Canada's border, interest rates in Canada are strongly influenced by those in the United States. Nonetheless, as Figure 3.6 shows, Canadian short-term interest rates increased both in absolute and relative terms to comparable rates in the US. These movements reflect some limited ability of the Bank of Canada to conduct an independent monetary policy and it reflects changes in the risk premium on Canadian debt instruments. Changes in the risk premium are typically identified as being due to the influence of constitutional crises and high levels of government debt.[4]

The monetary policy choices of the Bank of Canada had an important impact on Canadian fiscal policy choices. Not only would these policies cause a temporary reduction in output and thus an increase in budget deficits, but also by pushing up interest rates, they would dramatically increase debt-servicing costs. Thus while in the 1970s the federal government's interest payments on its debt averaged 2.2 percent of GDP, in the 1980s, this increased to 4.7 percent and in the 1990s, it increased to 5.8 percent. Many of the provinces faced similar jumps in their debt-servicing costs.

### *Deficit reduction*

Soon after the Bank of Canada's adoption of a zero inflation target, it became apparent to the provincial governments that they would need to take strong meas-

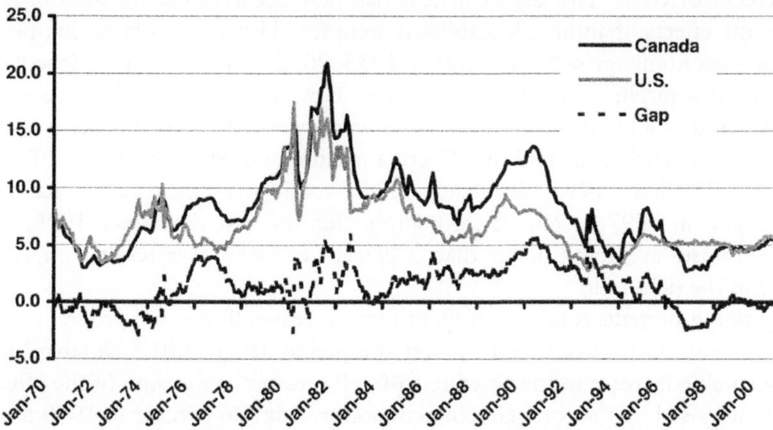


*Figure 3.6* Short-term interest rates.

Source: Statistics Canada, CANSIM series B14060, B54409.

ures to offset their growing debt-service payments. This would require that they eliminate their deficits and begin to reduce their debt loads. While this realization was undoubtedly encouraged by the run-up of interest rates that accompanied the bank's monetary contraction, it is also fair to say that the provinces had for many years fought a battle against their deficits (Kneebone 1998).

By the early 1990s, however, stronger action was deemed necessary. For many provincial governments, this stronger action came in the form of a policy rule. New Brunswick was the first province to act when it introduced legislation in 1993 that restricted the size of its deficit. Since 1995, Alberta has passed a number of pieces of legislation designed to establish a schedule for deficit and debt reduction. Manitoba, in 1995, passed legislation with an especially interesting rule; it established financial penalties for provincial cabinet ministers in the event of a deficit.

Although it was readily apparent to most economic observers, the federal government was much slower to come to the realization that steps had to be taken to reduce its deficit. Indeed, it seemed to understand the requisite to take seriously the need for deficit reduction only after an international credit-rating agency downgraded the federal government's debt in the spring of 1995.[5] Whereas many of the provinces have adopted formal rules with respect to deficit reduction, the federal government has been reluctant to do so. Rather than introduce legislation limiting the scope for deficits and debt accumulation, the federal government has relied more on promises to meet deficit targets "come hell or high water."[6]

Figure 3.7 presents the annual deficit and accumulated debt (both expressed as a percentage of GDP) for the total government sector since 1970.[7] It shows that prior to 1975, surpluses were not uncommon with the result that the ratio of net debt to GDP (hereafter referred to as the debt ratio) was falling. From 1975 to 1996, however, government deficits were consistently positive and large, averaging

4.5 percent of GDP. The largest deficits naturally occurred during years of recession as the effects of automatic stabilizers were felt. However, even during periods of strong economic growth, particularly 1985–90, deficits never approached zero, never mind a surplus. Figure 3.7 also shows how these consistently large deficits have resulted in a rapid accumulation of government debt over this period—from 15 percent of GDP at the end of 1974 to a maximum of 89 percent of GDP at the end of 1995. Since 1993, the deficit of the total government sector has fallen rapidly, and in 1997, it moved into surplus for the first time since 1975. Since 1999 surpluses averaging better than 2 percent of GDP have resulted in a rapid decline in the debt ratio.

Figure 3.8 presents total government revenue, expenditure and program spending, all measured relative to GDP, over the period 1970–2001.[8] Notable here is the inexorable increase in the revenue-to-GDP measure, a measure of the effective tax rate imposed by the total government sector, from 36 percent in 1970 to over 43 percent in 2001. The fact that the effective tax rate continued to rise even during the course of serious recessions beginning in 1982 and again in 1991 indicates that governments were choosing to impose procyclical tax policies in an effort to halt the growth in debt. Notable too is the rapid reduction in program expenditure as a fraction of GDP since 1993. This reflects two factors. First, the end of the recession that began in 1990 reduced income-sensitive expenditure. Second, governments at all levels, but especially at the provincial level, introduced large cuts in education, social services and health care spending as a way of reducing their deficits. In conjunction with the high and steady ratio of revenue to GDP, this reduction in program expenditure as a fraction of GDP explains the rapid reduction in the deficit observed in Figure 3.7. Although the total government sector has been in a primary surplus over this whole period, it is only since 1997 that it has been in overall surplus.

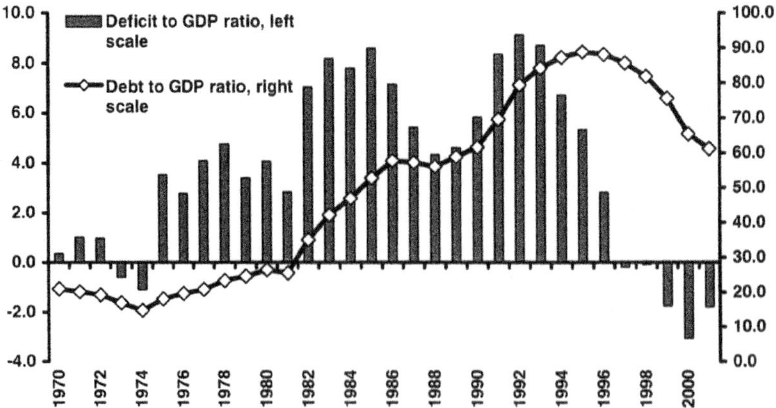


*Figure 3.7* Total government sector deficit and debt, at end of calendar year (as a % of GDP).

Sources: Department of Finance (2002); Statistics Canada, CANSIM series D162171, D162241, D162591, D162661, D22435.

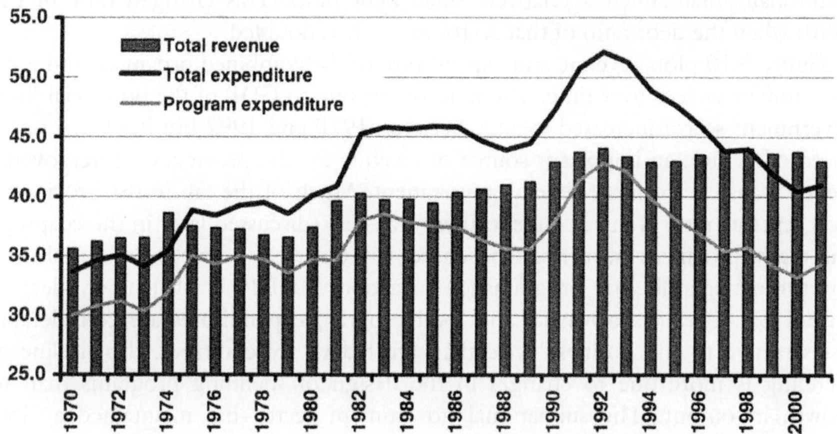


*Figure 3.8* Total government revenue and expenditure, at end of calendar year (as a % of GDP).

Sources: Department of Finance (2002); Statistics Canada, CANSIM series D22435.

Looking at budgetary data for the total government sector can be misleading due to the federal nature of the Canadian government sector. In Figure 3.9, debt ratios are plotted by level of government. Removing public pension plan assets increases the net debt of what remains of the government sector; namely, the federal government, the provinces and local governments. This ratio peaked at 96 percent in 1995 and fell to 68 percent by the end of 2001. It is apparent from Figure 3.8 that federal government debt is the main driving force behind the accumulation of total government debt. The provincial and local governments have

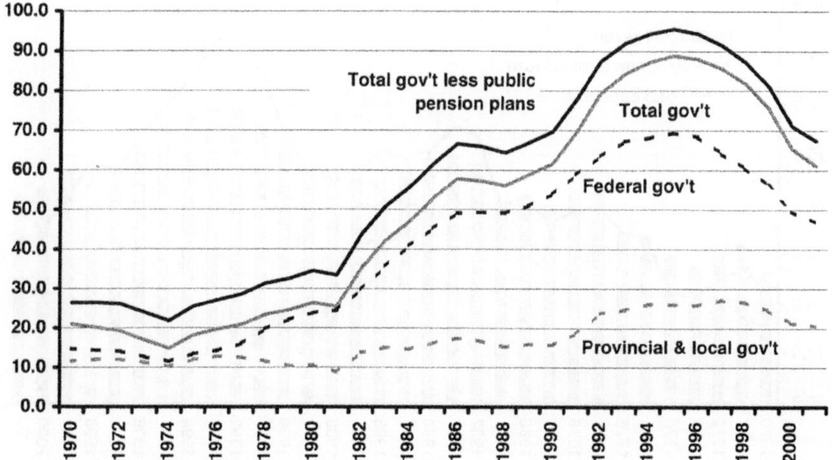


*Figure 3.9* Net debt ratios by level of government (as a % of output).

Source: Statistics Canada, CANSIM series D162171, D162241, D162591, D162661, D22435.

traditionally maintained a relatively small debt ratio. This changed only in the 1990s when the debt ratio of that sector more than doubled.

Figure 3.10 plots revenue and expenditure of the combined provincial and local government sectors over time. The ratio of revenue to GDP of the provincial-local government sector increased steadily between 1970 and 1992 but has fallen since. As noted earlier, an important source of revenue for the provinces is intergovernmental transfers from the federal government. Much of the fall in the provincial-local revenue ratio is due to cuts in these transfers (discussed later in the chapter), but many provinces have also chosen to cut tax rates as well. Provincial-local government spending on programs (as a fraction of GDP) has fallen considerably since 1992. Because provincial and local program expenditures are considerably less sensitive to the business cycle than are federal expenditures, this decline in spending is more due to changes in the design of spending programs than to growth in output. The subnational government sector has maintained a close balance between total revenue and total expenditure, and has been in a sizable primary surplus in every year since 1970.

The clear implication of Figures 3.8, 3.9 and 3.10 is that the culprit behind the rapid accumulation of debt in Canada has been the federal government. Figure 3.11 plots time-series data of federal government revenue and expenditure ratios to GDP. Whereas the subnational governments maintained a rough balance between revenue and total expenditure, here we see a consistently negative and often large total deficit for the federal government (identified by the vertical distance between the lines denoting total expenditure and total revenue). In every year between 1974 and 1997, the federal government was in an overall deficit that averaged over 4 percent of GDP. The federal government had a primary surplus off and on between 1970 and 1993, but has produced large primary surpluses since. The sizable primary surpluses since 1993 have been mainly the result

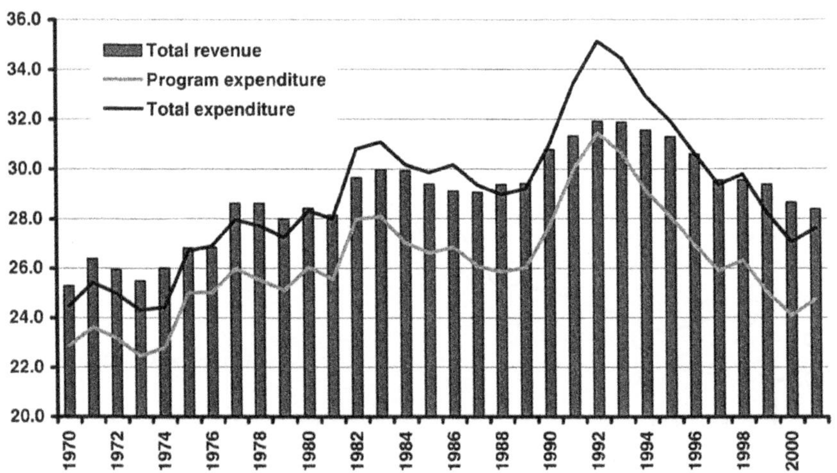


*Figure 3.10* Provincial and local government revenue and expenditure (as a % of GDP).

Sources: Department of Finance (2002); Statistics Canada, CANSIM series D22435.

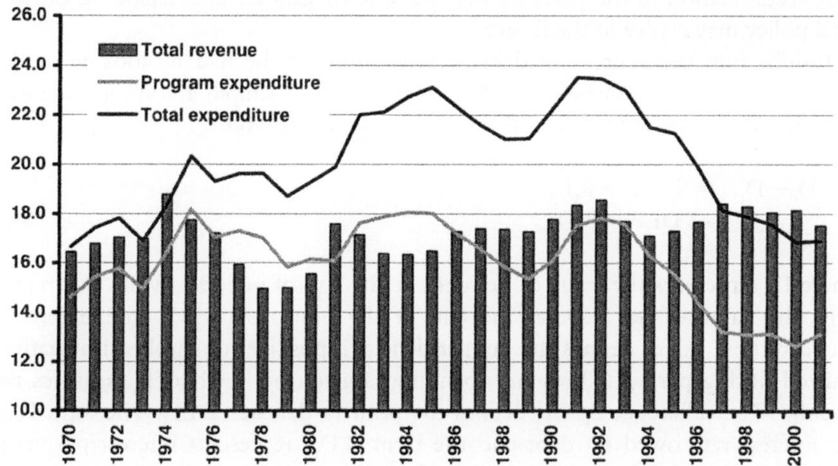


*Figure 3.11* Federal government revenue and expenditure (as a % of GDP).

Source: Department of Finance (2002); Statistics Canada, CANSIM series D22435.

of a fall in the ratio of program expenditures to GDP. Federal program spending is considerably more sensitive to the cycle than is provincial or local government spending and much of this decline in the spending ratio can be attributed to economic growth.

Another important source of the decline in federal spending has been cuts to intergovernmental transfers to the provinces. As a result, the federal government has been accused of "off-loading" its deficit onto the provinces. The federal government moved into overall surplus in 1997.

## Fiscal policy issues on the horizon

At the beginning of the new century, there is reason to be optimistic about the Canadian economy. In the eyes of most observers, the economy is operating at or near full capacity. The unemployment rate, at 7.1 percent in November 2002, is low by Canadian standards; real GDP has grown strongly for the past five years and is expected to continue to do so; and inflation remains subdued despite strong economic growth. Despite this rosy picture, at least two serious issues pertaining to fiscal policy will need to be addressed.

### *Budget policy*

Canadian governments have dramatically increased their debt ratios since 1975. The federal government has produced the great majority of this debt. The aim in this section is to provide some perspective on the future direction of fiscal policy by looking backwards at the reasons why the federal government accumulated so much debt over the 1975–96 period (Table 3.3). By understanding the reasons for debt accumulation in the past, we may be able to gain an understanding of how fiscal policy may evolve in the future.[9]

Insight into the sources of debt accumulation can be had by looking at the government budget constraint (GBC). The GBC is a simple accounting identity that can be represented by the following algebraic expression:

$$\begin{aligned} D_t - D_{t-1} &= S_t - T_t + R_t D_{t-1} \\ &= PDEF_t + R_t D_{t-1} \end{aligned} \tag{3.1}$$

where $D_t$ represents the value of net debt at the end of period t, while $D_{t-1}$ represents the value of net debt at the end of the previous period. The difference between these values defines the budget deficit (if positive) or surplus (if negative) realized during period t. Program spending is given by $S_t$ while $T_t$ measures tax revenue. The difference $S_t - T_t$ defines the primary deficit, $PDEF_t$. The term $R_t$ is the interest rate owed on debt and the term $R_t D_{t-1}$ represents interest payments made in period t on the net debt inherited from period $t-1$.

Judging whether a debt is large or small depends on one's income. For this reason, it is useful to evaluate the size of a government's debt by measuring it relative to collective national income. Similarly, whether the amount of tax revenue governments collect and the amount of spending governments choose to do is large or small depend on the size of national income. Thus, it is useful to express all components of the government's budget constraint relative to national income. Some manipulation of equation (3.1) allows one to rewrite the GBC as an expression describing the sources of change in the debt ratio:

$$D_t/Y_t - D_{t-1}/Y_{t-1} = PDEF_t/Y_t + (R_t - G_t)D_{t-1}/Y_t \tag{3.2}$$

*Table 3.3* Explaining the accumulation of debt[a]

| | *1974–95* | *1995–98* |
|---|---|---|
| Federal government | | |
| Change in debt-to-output ratio | 60.9 | −9.3 |
| Structural component | 19.0 | −14.4 |
| Cyclical component | 15.5 | 2.3 |
| Rate component | 23.1 | 4.8 |
| Data reconciliation[b] | 3.9 | −2.0 |
| Provincial/local government sector | | |
| Change in debt-to-output ratio | 13.6 | −1.3 |
| Structural component | 1.1 | −6.7 |
| Cyclical component | 30.9 | 3.9 |
| Rate component | −20.1 | 0.5 |
| Data reconciliation[b] | 2.0 | 0.9 |

Notes

a In these calculations, debt is measured relative to GDP at factor cost. This inflates the value of the debt-to-output ratio relative to what it would be if GDP at market prices were used.

b Problems with the data required construction of a fourth component. Essentially this component measures increases in the debt-to-output ratio that cannot be allocated to the other components. See Kneebone and Leach (2000) for details.

where $Y_t$ represents the level of national income at the end of period t, $G_t$ represents the rate of growth in national income and $D_t/Y_t$ represents the debt ratio.

To gain some understanding as to the source of debt accumulation, this identity can be adjusted slightly so it becomes:

$$\frac{D_t}{Y_t} - \frac{D_{t-1}}{Y_{t-1}} = \frac{PDEF^*_t}{Y^*_t} + \left(\frac{PDEF_t}{Y_t} - \frac{PDEF^*_t}{Y^*_t}\right) + (R_t - G_t)\frac{D_{t-1}}{Y_t} \quad (3.3)$$

where $PDEF_t^*$ and $Y_t^*$ are the structural, or cyclically adjusted, primary deficit and potential output in period t, respectively. The structural primary deficit measures what the primary deficit would be if actual output was equal to potential output.

The primary deficit changes with the structure of the government's programs (i.e., changes in tax rates and the design of spending programs), but it also changes with the level of output. This is so because some components of program spending (such as unemployment insurance payments) and tax revenue (such as income taxes) rise and fall as the level of output rises and falls. In other words, the primary deficit is influenced by both the business cycle and fiscal policy choices. The manipulation of the GBC presented in equation (3.3) separates these two influences on the primary deficit.

Equation (3.3) now identifies three sources of change in the debt ratio. The first term on the right-hand side, $PDEF^*/Y^*$, will be zero if the government designed its tax and spending programs in such a way as to produce a zero primary deficit at potential output. A positive value will result if these settings are such that a primary deficit results at $Y^*$. In this case, fiscal choices are producing a structural deficit with the result that the debt ratio increases even at full employment. A negative value indicates a structural surplus indicating that the debt ratio will fall when the economy is operating at full employment. Since changes in the debt ratio due to this term arises because of structural deficits and surpluses, this component is referred to as the structural component.

The second term on the right-hand side of equation (3.3) is the cyclical component. It measures the increase in the debt ratio that results from the economy operating at more or less than potential output. The cyclical component measures the influence the business cycle has on the amount of debt accumulated in the current period.

The third term on the right-hand side of equation (3.3) is the rate component. If the primary deficit were zero, the debt ratio would change only if the interest rate on net debt ($R_t$) were different from the rate of income growth ($G_t$). The debt ratio would rise if $R_t$ were greater than $G_t$ and it would fall if $R_t$ were smaller than $G_t$. The rate component measures the increase in the debt ratio that occurs because there is a gap between these two rates and because of pre-existing net debt.

An evaluation of these components requires estimates of potential output for each province and for Canada as well as estimates of the structural deficit. The method by which this is done follows the approach taken by the OECD.[12] With these estimates, equation (3.3) generates measures of the contribution of the structural, cyclical and rate components to the annual change in the debt ratio. Figure

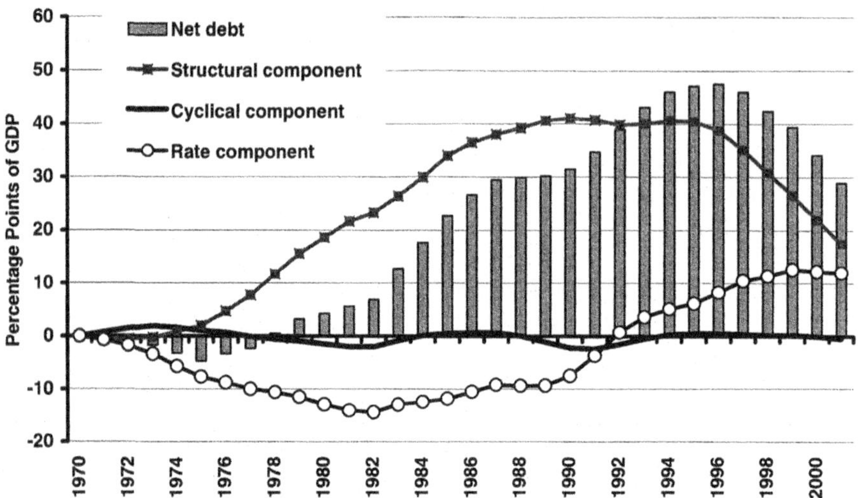


*Figure 3.12* Cumulative contributions to the federal debt ratio.

3.12 shows the cumulative effects of the cyclical, rate and structural components on the federal government's debt ratio in 1970–2001. The bars show the cumulative increase in the debt ratio since 1970.

The cumulative cyclical component rises and falls with contractions and expansions. Over the 32-year period of our sample, the cyclical component contributed little to the growth in the federal debt ratio as the effects of expansions on debt have more or less cancelled the effects of contractions.

The early part of our sample period, i.e., 1970–82, was one of high growth rates and relatively low interest rates with the result that the rate component was contributing to reductions in the debt ratio. By 1982, the rate component had contributed to a 15 percentage point reduction in the federal debt ratio. After 1982, the relative sizes of the growth rate and the interest rate reversed so that the rate component contributed to increases in the debt ratio. This turnaround can be attributed to the combined effects of the slowdown in the rate of growth of income experienced by most western economies in the mid- to late 1970s and to the monetary policy choices of the US Federal Reserve and the Bank of Canada that pushed up interest rates in the early 1980s in an effort to fight inflation. When, in 1989, the Bank of Canada again tightened monetary policy as part of its zero inflation goal, this, combined with slower rates of economic growth in Canada, the US and elsewhere, produced large, positive rate components that had the effect of producing large annual contributions to the debt ratio. By 1992, the cumulative effects of the rate component had turned positive and in the nine years between 1989 and 1996, it added 18 percentage points to the debt ratio. Over the entire 32-year period from 1970 to 2001, the rate component contributed 12 percentage points to the federal debt ratio.

Taken together, the cyclical and rate components added 9 percentage points to the federal debt ratio between 1970 and 1996. The remaining 39 percentage points of national income by which the debt ratio increased from 1970 to 1996 were due to the structural component. Thus, the vast majority of the debt accumulated by the federal government between 1970 and 1996 was the result of a mismatch between revenues and expenditures that would result in large deficits even under conditions of full employment.

What is striking about the calculations presented in Figure 3.12 is how persistent the structural deficit was. From 1972–90 inclusive, the federal government produced budgets that would yield a deficit even at full employment. Kneebone and Chung (2003) describe the years from 1971–76 to be crucial ones for federal debt accumulation. This was a period of oil price shocks, high inflation and rising unemployment rates mixed with minority governments and policy-makers trained to believe in the efficacy of discretionary fiscal policy, a veritable witches' brew of ingredients designed to conjure up budget deficits! Perry's (1989) description of the budget presentations of this period indicates that increases in the structural deficit were motivated by attempts at counter-cyclical stabilization policy. Tax cuts, accelerated depreciation allowances, investment tax credits, new spending on capital projects, and job training programs highlighted the budgets of the period. This aggressive attack on unemployment using both tax cuts and spending increases moved the structural deficit from near zero to nearly 3 percent of potential output by 1976. Into this mix was thrown a policy to index income tax brackets for inflation beginning in January 1974. This reform would prove very costly as the rate of inflation increased. By 1979, the structural deficit had widened to almost 4 percent of potential output and despite the efforts to attack it with discretionary fiscal policy, the unemployment rate (7.5 percent) was higher than what it was in 1972 (6.2 percent).

Despite large structural deficits and all sorts of economic turmoil, the 1970s ended with a federal debt ratio that was not very much higher than it was at the beginning of the decade. The reason for this was the favorable rate component. An unfortunate by-product of this favorable rate component was that it hid from view a very large structural deficit. At the beginning of the 1980s, the average voter could hardly have thought that the federal government was in serious financial difficulties. As a result, the political conditions that were required for an attack on structural deficits were not ripe. Yet if economic conditions changed to slower growth rates and/or higher interest rates, the federal budget was set to produce a rapidly growing debt ratio. At the end of the 1970s, the federal finances were in serious trouble even if it was not readily apparent from looking at the debt ratio.

The turnaround in the rate component coincided with the deepest recession in Canada since the 1930s. This recession, the worst recession in fifty years, was not the best time, either politically or economically, to begin to raise revenues and cut spending in an effort to close a structural deficit. Thus when, in 1982, the rate component changed from contributing to reductions in the debt ratio to contributing to increases in the ratio, the government was slow to react. The observed debt ratio grew quickly as both the rate and the structural components contributed to its growth.

By 1994, it had become apparent to politicians and voters that structural surpluses were required to keep control of the debt ratio. Unfortunately by 1994, the structural deficits of the early 1970s and the slow response that did not see them disappear until 1990 had caused the net debt ratio to increase by 41 percentage points. Paying interest on the debt was now by far the largest expenditure item in the federal budget. The economic pain and dislocation occasioned by the large spending cuts and tax increases that the federal government introduced after 1994 are from this perspective in large part due to a failed attempt at discretionary stabilization policy twenty years earlier.

Between 1996 and 2001, the federal debt ratio fell rapidly. While the rate component added a further 6 percentage points to the debt ratio in this period, interest rates were falling and the growth rate was increasing so that by 2000, the rate component was no longer contributing to the debt ratio. However, the structural component contributed a 23 percentage point reduction in the debt ratio over the period 1996–2001. Some 70 percent of this reduction was due to a fall in spending relative to potential output, while 30 percent was due to an increase in revenue relative to potential output. In terms of the fall in spending relative to potential output, 40 percent of the decline came in the form of cuts to provincial transfers and 25 percent came in the form of cuts to the unemployment insurance program. In Canada, the federal government finances unemployment insurance while the provinces finance welfare programs. Since cuts to unemployment insurance often force former unemployment insurance recipients on to the welfare rolls, it is fair to say that between 40 and 65 percent of federal efforts at expenditure reduction over the period 1996–2001 were enjoyed at the expense of provincial budgets. In other words, "deficit off-loading" onto the provinces played an important role in the federal debt reduction strategy.

The federal government has been responsible for the majority of the government debt accumulated in Canada and is thus mainly responsible for the attendant problems typically associated with high levels of government debt—higher interest rates, slower economic growth and falling living standards, in particular. The costs of the recent reduction in the federal debt ratio has, on the other hand, been shared (unwillingly) by the provinces as the federal government has to a significant degree "solved" its deficit problem by making worse the deficit problems faced by provincial governments. The provinces, in turn, have responded with significant cuts to program expenditures. By 2002, most governments in Canada, but particularly the federal government, had settled into reasonably secure budget surpluses.

What does this experience imply for the future of fiscal policy in Canada? To a large extent, the answer to this question remains up in the air. While the declining federal debt ratio is welcome, the temptation for the federal government is to ease up on the reins and begin to increase spending and, in so doing, slow or halt the fall in the debt ratio. Indeed, there is evidence of this beginning to happen. In 2001, federal program expenditures increased by 7 percent, more than double the rate of inflation. The temptation to ease up is made greater by the fact that the rate component is no longer contributing to increases in the debt ratio. In the past, this has been associated with increases in the structural deficit. It is also important to stress that the battle the federal government has fought to regain control of its finances has seriously impacted federal-provincial relations. The so-called "power of the purse" by which the federal government exerts influence over provincial spending choices has been greatly diminished by cuts to intergovernmental grants. Provincial governments are increasingly setting the agenda for change in key areas of public spending. This is particularly so in the area of health care. With a greatly diminished role in the financing of health care, the federal government is finding it difficult to stand in the way of provincial government initiatives to allow a greater role for private over public health care provision. Eliminating its deficit and reducing its debt ratio may, therefore, prove to be a Pyrrhic victory for the federal government as it comes at the cost of losing control over public spending programs to the provinces. For the taxpayer, this shuffling of responsibilities between the various levels of government might be less important than the fall in the debt ratio of the aggregate government sector, something that is already associated with falling interest rates. If this can be translated into improved living standards, Canadian taxpayers may yet conclude that the battle against government debt was worthwhile.

### *Falling living standards*

A useful summary measure of the effectiveness of Canadian macroeconomic policy over the past thirty years is to compare real per capita disposable incomes in Canada versus the United States. Disposable income measures what is left from earned income after all taxes have been paid and after all government transfers have been received. Changes in this measure reflect changes in taxes, government transfers and changes in earned income. Figure 3.13 presents these measures, along with a measure of the gap between them.

Figure 3.13 shows that real per capita disposable income in Canada has increased less quickly than that in the US since 1974 and particularly since 1981. As a result, the gap between these two series (both of which are measured in 1997 Canadian dollars measured PPP) has widened over time from $3,200 in 1970 to $9,300 in 2001.

What explains this rather dramatic change in living standards in Canada relative to that of the US? One possibility is that there has been a fall in the relative productivity of Canadian industry leading to a fall in real earned income and hence in disposable income. On the face of it, this explanation seems to have some merit. The productivity of Canadian manufacturing *vis-à-vis* that of the US has fallen quite substantially in the past twenty years.[11]

One problem with looking at an aggregate measure of productivity is that it may hide important information at the industry level. In a careful analysis of industry-level data in Canada and the US, Sharpe (1999) shows that almost all of Canada's productivity woes come from two industries: the electrical and electronic products industry and the industrial and commercial machinery industry. Over the period 1989–97, the US lead in the average annual rate of growth in manufacturing productivity (2.90 percent versus Canada's 2.35 percent) disappears when these two industries are removed. Indeed, with that adjustment, the annual rate of growth in Canadian manufacturing exceeds that of the US by 2.21 percent to just 0.20 percent! While Sharpe stresses caution that more work needs to be done to refine the data, his analysis nonetheless shows that over the 1989–97 period, Canadian productivity growth exceeded that of the US in fifteen out of nineteen industries.

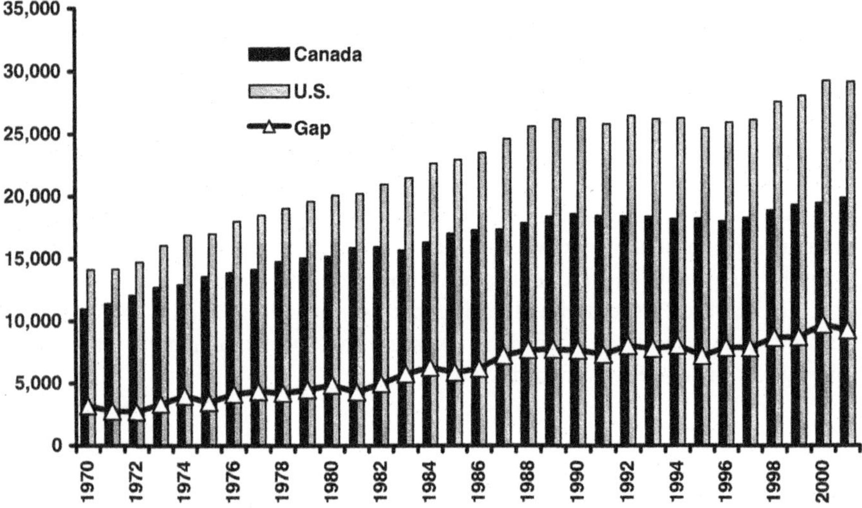


*Figure 3.13* Real per capita disposable income, Canada and the US (in 1997 Canadian dollars at PPP).

Sources: Statistics Canada, CANSIM series D22435, B51230, D100525, D369455; OECD online database; US Office of the President (2000).

Unless the data on Canadian and US productivity are totally and dramatically misleading, it is difficult to discount the conclusion that there is no "across-the-board" productivity crisis.

If falling productivity does not seem to be a wholly convincing explanation for the relative fall in Canadian real per capita disposable income, then this suggests that fiscal policy choices affecting taxes and government transfers, rather than a fall in earned income, is a contributing factor. The inexorable increase in the ratio of government revenue to national income and the more recent reductions in program spending, both highlighted in Figure 3.8, give credence to this view. The double whammy of rising taxes and cuts to social programs, together with somewhat slower aggregate productivity growth in Canada, have seemingly combined to drive down per capita disposable income in Canada *vis-à-vis* the United States. If this speculation is correct, then both absolutely and relative to its major trading partner, Canadian macroeconomic policy has produced a rather poor outcome over the period. Reversing these trends must become the focus of Canadian fiscal policy.

## Conclusion

In the past fifteen years, Canadian policy-makers have introduced three key macroeconomic policies that are capable of reversing the trend observed in Figure 3.13: free trade, a monetary policy aimed at low inflation, and a goal to reduce government debt levels. All three of these policies have the characteristic of imposing what economists like to refer to as "short-term pain for long-term gain." The adoption of free trade required a substantial adjustment of Canadian industry and created "winners" and "losers" among industries, categories of workers and even regions of the country. It takes time for these transition costs to be absorbed and for the full benefits of the reorientation to free trade to be realized. Similarly, adjusting to the zero inflation target required a period of transition during which interest rates increased and output slowed. Finally, the reduction in government debt levels requires a transition period wherein taxes remain high relative to program spending. All three of these new policies would, in other words, inflict short-term pain on the economy.

Figure 3.14, which plots indexes of real per capita GDP for Canada and the US, illustrates this concept. Figure 3.14 shows that the adoption of the zero inflation target and the signing of free trade agreements in the late 1980s, along with government cutbacks to spending and increases in taxes in the 1990s, combined to shift Canadian per capita GDP downward relative to that of the US. Since the mid-1990s, however, per capita GDP in the two countries has grown more or less at the same rate. The still-growing gap in real per capita disposable income is due to the still-growing gap between taxes in Canada and the US (largely unchanged in Canada over the past decade but down in the US). Faced with large and reasonably secure budget surpluses, Canadian governments, particularly the federal government, have an opportunity to narrow the gap in living standards with the US by introducing substantial tax cuts. If this can be done, and the temptation to increase government involvement in the economy can be avoided, then what has been a prolonged period of rather discouraging macroeconomic outcomes may be coming to an end. While this is certainly not guaranteed, the difficult choices have

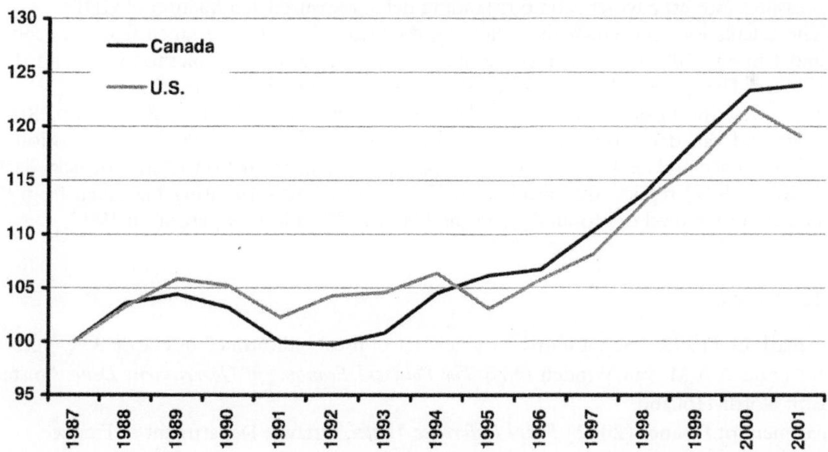


*Figure 3.14* Real per capita GDP in Canada and the US.

Sources: Statistics Canada, CANSIM series D22435, B51230, D100525, D369455; OECD online database; US Office of the President (2000).

Note
1997 dollars, 1987 = 100.

been made and the short-run transition costs have been paid. What remains is for the federal government to allow these hard-fought-for potential gains to be realized.

## Notes

1 The province of British Columbia, a "have" province since 1962, recently slipped into "have-not" status.

2 Until quite recently, provincial personal income tax rates were defined as a percentage of the federal rate. Thus, changes in the federal tax rate had a direct effect on provincial revenues and this provided another important way in which the budgets of the two levels of government were linked. Since 2001, provinces have been able to set income tax rates independent of the federal rate and most have chosen to do so. The province of Québec has always set its personal income tax rate independently of the federal rate.

3 Canada signed a free trade agreement (CUSTA) with the United States in 1988, and this agreement came into effect in 1989. The North American Free Trade Agreement (NAFTA) between Canada, the United States and Mexico was signed in 1993.

4 Fillion (1996) suggests that up to two-thirds of the differential between Canadian and US interest rates may be due to the accumulation of Canadian government debt.

5 In April 1995, Moody's, a bond-rating agency, downgraded federal Canadian dollar-denominated debt from AAA to AA1. Federal foreign currency-denominated debt was downgraded from AA1 to AA2.

6 This quotation is attributed to federal Finance Minister Paul Martin. It was an oft-quoted remark during the years of severe budget cuts in the mid-1990s.

7 The total government sector is comprised of the federal government, the provincial and territorial governments, local governments, public hospitals and public pension plans. In the rest of the paper, the small amounts associated with public hospitals are subsumed within the provincial government sector.

8 Program spending is defined as total expenditure minus interest payments on outstanding debt. The vertical distance between the lines denoting total and program spending measures interest payments on outstanding debt (measured as a fraction of GDP).

9 The calculations on which the following discussion is based are taken from Kneebone and Chung (2003). The reader should refer to this source for methodology and data sources. That paper relies on Fortin (1998) for suggesting this approach.

10 For a description of the approach taken by the OECD, see Giorno, Richardson, Roseveare and van den Noord (1995). See Kneebone and Chung (2003) for discussion of this approach and details on how it was applied to Canadian national and provincial data.

11 Sharpe (1999) reports that productivity in Canadian manufacturing has fallen from 90 percent of the level of productivity in the US in 1977 to just 74 percent in 1997.

## References

Blanchard, O. (1993) "Suggestions for a new set of fiscal indicators," in Harrie A.A. Verbon and Frans A.A.M. van Winden (eds) *The Political Economy of Government Debt*, Amsterdam: North-Holland.

Department of Finance (2002) *Fiscal Reference Tables*, Ottawa: Department of Finance.

Dungan, P. and Wilson, T. (1985) "Altering the fiscal-monetary policy mix: credible policies to reduce the federal deficit," *Canadian Tax Journal* 33: 304–18.

Fillion, J.F. (1996) "L'endettement du Canada et ses effets sur les taux d'intérêt reels de long terme," Bank of Canada Working Paper 96-14, Ottawa: Bank of Canada.

Fortin, P. (1998) "The Canadian fiscal problem: the macroeconomic connection," in Pierre

Fortin and Lars Osberg (eds) *Hard Money, Hard Times: Why Zero Inflation Hurts Canadians*, Toronto: Lorimer Press.

Giorno, C., Richardson, P., Roseveare, D. and van den Noord, P. (1995) "Potential output, output gaps and structural balances," *OECD Economic Studies* 24 (Spring).

Kneebone, R. (1998) "Four decades of deficit and debt," in Pierre Fortin and Lars Osberg (eds) *Hard Money, Hard Times: Why Zero Inflation Hurts Canadians*, Toronto: Lorimer Press.

Kneebone, R. and Chung, J. (2003) "Where Did the Debt Come From?" in Christopher Ragan and William Watson (eds) *Is the Debt War Over?*, Montreal: Institute for Research in Public Policy.

Kneebone, R. and McKenzie, K. (1999) *Past (In)Discretions: Canadian Federal and Provincial Fiscal Policy*, University of Toronto Monograph Series on Public Policy and Public Administration, Toronto.

Laidler, D. and Robson, W. (1993) *The Great Canadian Disinflaton*, Policy Study 19, C.D. Howe Institute, Toronto.

McCallum, J. (1998) "Government debt and the Canadian dollar," *Current Analysis* (Sept.), Royal Bank of Canada.

McDermott, C.J. and Westcott, R.F. (1996) "An empirical analysis of fiscal adjustments," IMF Working Paper WP/96/59, Washington, DC.

Organisation for Economic Co-operation and Development (OECD). *National Accounts, Main Aggregates*, vol. 1. Paris: OECD. Online at www.oecd.org.

Perry, J. (1989) "A fiscal history of Canada," Canadian Tax Paper No. 85, Canadian Tax Foundation.

Royal Bank of Canada (various years) *Commodity Price Monitor*, various issues, RBC Financial Group, Economics Department.

Sharpe, A. (1999) *New Estimates of Manufacturing Productivity Growth for Canada and the United States*, Ottawa: Centre for the Study of Living Standards.

Statistics Canada, CANSIM Division, CANSIM database, Ottawa: Statistics Canada.

Statistics Canada (1992) *Public Finance Historical Data 1965/66–1991/92*, Catalogue No. 68-512, Ottawa: Statistics Canada.

United States, Office of the President (2000) *Economic Report of the President 2000*, Washington, DC: US Government Printing Office.

Wilson, T., Dungan, P. and Murphy, S. (1994) "The sources of the recession in Canada: 1989–1992," *Canadian Business Economics* 2(2): 3–15.

# 4 China

*Li Jinshan and Wang Xiaoguang*

## Introduction

In the three decades from 1950 to the end of the 1970s, the financial system in China experienced frequent changes that reflected either fiscal centralization or decentralization. Since the economic reform in 1978, the trend of fiscal decentralization has continued and by most conventional measures, China's economic reform has been astonishingly successful. In this period, especially from 1978 to 1996, real GDP grew on average by nearly 10 percent. Ironically, during this period of prosperity, the Chinese government struggled to raise enough revenue to sustain itself as growth in government budget revenue relative to GDP fell from almost 31 percent to less than 11 percent. The situation was particularly difficult for the central government, whose share of total budget revenue fell from around two-thirds on the eve of the reform to one-third in 1993. In real terms, the economy grew more than fivefold during this period, but total government revenue only doubled and central government revenue was barely held constant at 1978 levels.[1]

For the central government, the fiscal issue of most concern was and is the low "two ratios," i.e., the share of government revenue to GDP and the share of central government revenue to total government revenue. It is interesting to see how the Chinese government dealt with the problem of limited revenue in the context of a rapidly developing economy. In this chapter, we first discuss the issue of revenue and expenditure. Then the issue of deficit and debt management in central government is considered. In the third section, we analyze the fiscal relationship between the central and local governments, and it is in this section that institutional changes, especially in the 1994 fiscal system, are analyzed. This reform can be seen as a means to improve the two ratios; more importantly, it serves to deal with an improved central–local fiscal relationship by law. All of the discussion and analyses presented are for the period starting from 1978 up to the present. The year 1978 is used as the beginning because this is when the economic reform began and it is often viewed as the watershed year for the PRC. Finally, we draw some concluding remarks from the discussions and analyses.

## Revenue and expenditure: changes led by policies

### *Government revenue*

#### *Definitions*

In most countries, government revenue is synonymous with budget revenue. However in China, the concept of government revenue is different from what people understand it to be in other countries. In fact, in China there are three levels of the concept of revenue: government revenue, budget revenue and fiscal revenue.

Government revenue includes fiscal revenue, bond issuing revenue, extrabudget funds, and other off-budget revenue which is taken out of the extrabudget funds management system. This last revenue item is completely beyond the control of the budget, but is in the hands of various government agencies that are able to create revenue generally through the use of service charges and fees. Budget revenues are composed of fiscal revenue and bond-issuing revenue.[2] Fiscal revenue consists of tax revenue, SOE loss subsidies and other revenue. To avoid confusion, we use the term "fiscal revenue" rather than conventional government or budget revenue in this chapter, because all of the statistics for revenue and expenditure of the budget in the statistical yearbooks of China do not include debt services.

With respect to revenue, we should clarify some points that are indeed exclusively very Chinese:

- Subsidies to SOEs. In most countries, budget subsidies are represented on the expenditure side; in China, however, they are dealt with on the revenue side by subtracting the subsidies from SOEs' remitted revenues. While this accounting method does not affect the budget result, it does result in a shrinking in the size of the budget revenue/spending.
- Most social security funds do not appear in the budget. In 1995, these funds amounted to 236.13 billion yuan. If they were included in the budget, the size of the budget would certainly be larger.
- Extrabudget funds refer to funds that are in the hands of various government agencies but are not managed by the budget. However, there are rules that govern the basis and use of funds. In 1995, according to the new definition, the funds accounted for 384.3 billion yuan or 61.6 percent of fiscal revenue.
- Other off-budget revenues are different from extrabudget funds which are defined in scope, charges and fee standard. Management of off-budget revenues is, in fact, in a mess.[3] It was estimated that, in 1995, off-budget revenues amounted to about 200 billion yuan, accounting for nearly 30 percent of budgetary revenues. Some observations indicate that off-budget revenues accounted for 5 percent of GDP (Liu 1999).

Of the above four categories of revenue, the latter three are not included in the budget, and the accounting method of the first revenue item shrinks the size of the budget. The last two items of revenue, which are not included and not even represented in the budget, are beyond the control and supervision of the legislature.

Although they constitute the citizens' tax burden, the use of these funds is in anarchy. If we count only fiscal revenue as government revenue, it appears that the tax burden in China is much lower than in developed countries, and is even lower than in most developing countries. However, according to unofficial estimates, government revenue in 1996 amounted to 25 percent of GDP, while another estimate was as high as 30 percent of GDP. This is in contrast to the value of registered tax revenue which was only about 10 percent of GDP (in 1996, budget revenue = fiscal revenue + bond-issuing revenue = 736.61 + 1967.42 = 933.40 billion yuan; tax revenue amounted to 690.14, i.e., 73.94 percent of budget revenue). No doubt, there exists a large gap between the share of fiscal or budget revenue to GDP and the citizens' tax plus other burden. It is this gap that leaves the management of revenue in a mess, and is an important institutional cause of corruption.

As discussed above, the real tax burden in China is not as low as it appears. However, disposable revenue for the budget of the government is much less than the real tax burden people shoulder. Furthermore, for the sake of convenience of analysis, and because of availability of statistics, we use fiscal revenue as government revenue in the discussion and analyses, unless otherwise specified.

### *Declining trend of the two ratios*

The share of government revenue to GDP, as well as the share of expenditure to GDP, has steadily declined since 1978. Figure 4.1 shows that both the share of government revenue and the share of government spending relative to GDP have decreased over time, as GDP grew quickly.

The reasons for the decline in government revenues include pro-business tax policies, a decline in the profitability of state enterprises, and tax evasions. Prior to 1978, government revenues were heavily dependent on profits from state enterprises, which were required to turn in all of their profits to the state. Major fiscal

*Figure 4.1* General government revenue and spending in China.

Sources: State Statistical Bureau of the People's Republic of China (various years).

reforms have occurred since 1979. The government lowered taxes and allowed state enterprises to retain a part of their profits to expand production and to issue bonuses and awards to employees. Further fiscal reform occurred in 1983 with state enterprises becoming subject to income taxes, called "substituting taxes for profit" (*ligaishui*). Furthermore, the contract responsibility system was introduced in 1986. Under this tax system, enterprises were contracted to pay income taxes on a specific level of profit. If they did not achieve that level of profit, they were supposed to make up the taxes from their own resources. If they exceeded that level of profit, they paid taxes at a lower rate on the additional profit. Since the contracted profits were not set to grow at a sufficiently high rate, growth in government revenue from enterprise contracts did not keep pace with general economic growth. In fact, the contract responsibility system has been identified as the main factor behind the lower share of government revenue in output. The 1994 tax reform, the tax sharing system or tax assignment system (*fenshuizhi*) increased the share of central government revenues to total revenue, but failed to increase the share of total government revenues to GDP. In addition, the decline in the profitability of state enterprises reduced taxable income. Moreover, the current tax reform has not covered many new economic activities while tax evasions are widespread. It has been estimated that 30 percent of state enterprises, 60 percent of joint ventures, 80 percent of private enterprises, and 100 percent of individual street vendors evade taxes. Table 4.1 shows the declining trend in the ratios of government revenue to GDP and government expenditure to GDP.

With respect to the second ratio, the share of central government revenue to total government revenue is now much larger than it was in 1978. In 1978, the share of fiscal revenues collected by the central government was 15.5 percent; it reached 40.5 percent in 1984, decreased to 22.0 percent in 1993, jumped back to 55.7 percent in 1994, and fell to 49.5 percent in 1998 (Table 4.1, Figure 4.2).

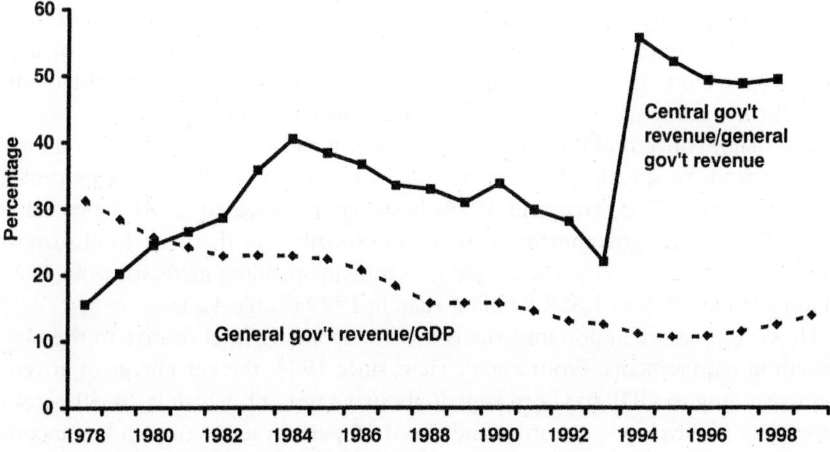


*Figure 4.2* The two ratios of government revenue, 1978–99.

Sources: State Statistical Bureau of the People's Republic of China (various years).

*Table 4.1* Indices of revenue in China, 1978–2001

| *Year* | *General government revenue* | | | *Central government revenue/general government revenue (%)* |
|---|---|---|---|---|
| | *Amount (bn yuan)* | *Growth (%)* | *As a % of GDP* | |
| 1978 | 113.23 | 29.5 | 31.2 | 15.5 |
| 1979 | 114.64 | 1.2 | 28.4 | 20.2 |
| 1980 | 115.99 | 1.2 | 25.7 | 24.5 |
| 1981 | 117.58 | 1.4 | 24.2 | 26.5 |
| 1982 | 121.23 | 3.1 | 22.9 | 28.6 |
| 1983 | 136.70 | 12.8 | 23.0 | 35.8 |
| 1984 | 164.29 | 20.2 | 22.9 | 40.5 |
| 1985 | 200.48 | 22.0 | 22.4 | 38.4 |
| 1986 | 212.20 | 5.8 | 20.8 | 36.7 |
| 1987 | 219.94 | 3.6 | 18.4 | 33.5 |
| 1988 | 235.72 | 7.2 | 15.8 | 32.9 |
| 1989 | 266.49 | 13.1 | 15.8 | 30.9 |
| 1990 | 293.71 | 10.2 | 15.8 | 33.8 |
| 1991 | 314.95 | 7.2 | 14.6 | 29.8 |
| 1992 | 348.34 | 10.6 | 13.1 | 28.1 |
| 1993 | 434.90 | 24.8 | 12.6 | 22.0 |
| 1994 | 521.81 | 20.0 | 11.2 | 55.7 |
| 1995 | 624.22 | 19.6 | 10.7 | 52.2 |
| 1996 | 740.80 | 18.7 | 10.9 | 49.4 |
| 1997 | 865.11 | 16.8 | 11.6 | 48.9 |
| 1998 | 987.60 | 14.2 | 12.6 | 49.5 |
| 1999 | 1,144.41 | 15.9 | 14.0 | 51.1 |
| 2000 | 1,339.52 | 17.0 | 15.0 | 52.2 |
| 2001 | 1,638.60 | 22.3 | 17.1 | 52.4 |

Sources: State Statistical Bureau of the People's Republic of China (various years).

Before 1978, although there were several changes in the allocation of fiscal resources, the central government had final control over the allocation of fiscal revenue; therefore, it did not matter who collected revenues. (We will discuss this point further in the section on the central–local fiscal relationship.)

The major concern of the central government is the share of central spending to total government spending. The share was 59.0 percent in 1970, 47.4 percent in 1978, and only 27.1 percent in 1996; however, it increased to 31.5 percent in 1999. The central government spent proportionally less than the local government, although the level of the central government spending increased from 112.2 billion yuan in 1978 to 1,318.8 billion yuan in 1999 (Table 4.2).

However, a more important issue is the low spending level relative to the rapid growth in requirements. From a static view, since 1994, the percentage of government spending to GDP has been kept at about 12 percent, which is 20–30 percent lower than in developed countries and about 10 percent lower than in low-income countries where the average was 21 percent. Even if extrabudget expenditures are included (amounting to about 4 percent to GDP), the spending level in China is still lower than in most countries (Lei 1997; Zhao 1998).

*Table 4.2* Indices of expenditure in China, 1978–2001

| *Year* | *General government spending* | | | *Central government spending/general government spending (%)* |
|---|---|---|---|---|
| | *Amount (bn yuan)* | *Growth (%)* | *As a % of GDP* | |
| 1978 | 112.2 | 33.0 | 31.0 | 47.4 |
| 1979 | 128.2 | 14.2 | 31.7 | 51.1 |
| 1980 | 122.9 | −0.04 | 27.2 | 54.3 |
| 1981 | 113.8 | −0.07 | 23.4 | 55.0 |
| 1982 | 123.0 | 0.08 | 23.2 | 53.0 |
| 1983 | 141.0 | 14.6 | 23.8 | 53.9 |
| 1984 | 170.1 | 20.7 | 23.7 | 52.5 |
| 1985 | 200.4 | 17.8 | 22.4 | 39.7 |
| 1986 | 220.5 | 10.0 | 21.6 | 37.9 |
| 1987 | 226.2 | 2.6 | 18.9 | 37.4 |
| 1988 | 249.1 | 10.1 | 16.7 | 33.9 |
| 1989 | 282.4 | 13.3 | 16.7 | 31.5 |
| 1990 | 308.4 | 9.0 | 16.6 | 32.6 |
| 1991 | 338.7 | 9.8 | 15.7 | 32.2 |
| 1992 | 374.2 | 10.5 | 14.0 | 31.3 |
| 1993 | 464.2 | 24.0 | 13.4 | 28.3 |
| 1994 | 579.3 | 24.8 | 12.4 | 30.3 |
| 1995 | 682.4 | 17.8 | 11.7 | 29.2 |
| 1996 | 793.8 | 16.3 | 11.7 | 27.1 |
| 1997 | 923.4 | 16.3 | 12.4 | 27.4 |
| 1998 | 1,079.8 | 16.9 | 13.8 | 28.9 |
| 1999 | 1,318.8 | 22.1 | 16.1 | 31.5 |
| 2000 | 1,588.7 | 20.5 | 17.8 | 34.7 |
| 2001 | 1,890.3 | 19.0 | 19.7 | 30.5 |

Sources: State Statistical Bureau of the People's Republic of China (various years).

From a dynamic perspective, from 1980, and especially from 1990, the share of government expenditure to GDP almost decreased 1 percent every year (Table 4.1). If we compare the period 1986–95 during which the average growth of nominal per capita GNP was 18.95 percent per year, this decline appears even more paradoxical since the historical experiences of other countries show that growth in government spending accompanied rapid economic growth.

The elasticity of government spending to GNP, $E_G$, better describes this lower ratio of government spending in China.[4] Calculations based on 1986–95 data from the *1996 China Statistical Yearbook* show that the elasticity of government spending, $E_G$, was only 0.657; that is, $E_G$ had very low elasticity or, in other words, growth in government spending was much lower than that of GNP. The inelastic $E_G$ was correlated to the marginal government spending propensity, MGP.[5] MGP per year in this same period was 0.108; this means that for each 1 yuan increase in GNP, the increase in government spending was only 0.108 yuan.

The low ratio of government spending to GNP can be explained by two reasons. One is the institutional changes that took place during this period. In the past, because of the planned and centralized economic system, the government spending ratio was very high. The economic reform that started in 1978 was, in fact, a process of decentralization, and less government spending in this process had its rationale *per se*. However, since the 1990s, institutional reform has not had such a close relation with the declining ratio in government spending, and reform is not enough to explain this paradoxical phenomenon.

Another important reason for the low ratio of government spending is the taxation bound. The ratio of tax revenue to GDP between 1986–95 was decreasing by about 1 percent a year. This ratio was 10.36 percent in 1995, which is one-quarter the average of developed countries. The average elasticity of tax revenue and the average marginal propensity of tax revenue to GDP in the same decade were 0.527 and 0.076, respectively. Such an inelastic tax mechanism means that the growth in tax revenue was much slower than economic growth.

### *Extrabudget revenue*

One important feature of the Chinese economy is that there is a large amount of extrabudget revenues and expenditures. Extrabudget revenue is the nontax revenue that is collected by various levels of government and government agencies by using the administrative authorities, but these funds are not included in the government budget. Extrabudget revenue includes revenue from the services provided by government agencies, administrative fees (license fees, for instance), and revenue from businesses run by colleges, high schools and primary schools. Extrabudget revenue is used for investments in fixed assets, for city maintenance, for welfare, for encouragement and awards, for administrative and business activities, etc. By 1978, extrabudget revenue represented 30.65 percent of total budget revenues, and by 1992, this percentage had risen to 110.66 percent (Table 4.3) (State Statistical Bureau of the People's Republic of China, various years).

One of the major aims of the changes in the fiscal system was to provide lower levels of government with the incentive to increase revenue and improve fiscal efficiency, thereby reducing the number of governmental units operating with a budget deficit. Combined with market reforms and increasing freedom for enterprises to determine production and pricing in their own interests, however, the effects of the reforms as a whole have been to reduce government revenues at all levels. Enterprise profits declined, and thus government income was reduced. For the nation as a whole, budget income declined as a proportion of national income.

The size and growth of these funds for almost thirty years before 1978 are summarized in Table 4.4. Overall, Deng *et al.* (1990) estimated that around 60 percent of the total extrabudget funds between 1953 and 1978 were generated within enterprises and their ministerial systems. Furthermore, the bulk of these funds were used for investment. Over the 20 years from 1958 to 1977, they accounted for an average of 16.0 percent of basic investment each year and 67.4 percent of investment in technical improvement (Deng *et al.* 1990: 16–18).

The existence of extrabudget funds is thus not a new creation of the reform period. Nevertheless, as the above discussion has shown, before 1978 the size of these funds was small and the constraints of the economic environment imposed limits on the way these funds were used. The absence of markets and the require-

*Table 4.3* Extrabudget funds, 1978–2000[a]

| *Year* | *Extrabudget funds (bn yuan)* | *Budget revenue (bn yuan)* | *Extrabudget funds/ budget revenue (%)* |
|---|---|---|---|
| 1978 | 34.71 | 113.23 | 30.7 |
| 1979 | 45.29 | 114.64 | 39.5 |
| 1980 | 55.74 | 115.99 | 48.1 |
| 1981 | 60.11 | 117.58 | 51.1 |
| 1982 | 80.27 | 121.23 | 66.2 |
| 1983 | 96.77 | 136.70 | 70.8 |
| 1984 | 118.85 | 164.29 | 72.3 |
| 1985 | 153.00 | 200.48 | 76.3 |
| 1986 | 173.73 | 212.20 | 81.9 |
| 1987 | 202.88 | 219.94 | 92.2 |
| 1988 | 236.08 | 235.72 | 100.2 |
| 1989 | 265.88 | 266.49 | 99.8 |
| 1990 | 270.86 | 293.71 | 92.2 |
| 1991 | 324.33 | 314.95 | 102.0 |
| 1992 | 385.49 | 348.34 | 110.7 |
| 1993 | 143.25 | 434.90 | 33.0 |
| 1994 | 186.25 | 521.81 | 35.7 |
| 1995 | 240.65 | 624.22 | 38.6 |
| 1996 | 389.33 | 740.80 | 52.6 |
| 1997 | 282.60 | 865.11 | 32.7 |
| 1998 | 308.23 | 987.60 | 31.2 |
| 1999 | 338.52 | 1,144.41 | 29.6 |
| 2000 | 382.64 | 1,339.52 | 28.6 |

Sources: Lou (2000: 206); State Statistical Bureau of the People's Republic of China, 2002 issue (various years).

Note

a The scope of extrabudget funds was adjusted between 1993–95 and 1996, and is not comparable with previous years. Since 1997, extrabudget revenue has not included those funds (fees) that have been brought into budgetary management, which is not consistent with previous years. Each year's growth rate was calculated using constant figures.

ments of the plan system limited the opportunities for local governments, ministries and enterprises to use the funds to pursue their own economic interests. As a whole, therefore, the operation of the budget system and the constraints on the use of extrabudget funds ensured the reasonably steady central direction of the flow of investment funds.

The introduction of fiscal contracting was accompanied by an explosive growth of extrabudget funds which grew more than elevenfold from 34.7 billion yuan to 385.5 billion yuan between 1978 and 1992; this growth is much higher than the growth of budget income and national income. As a result, extrabudget funds during the years 1988–92 were about equivalent to budget income, and by 1992, it had risen to 110.66 percent (Table 4.3). Furthermore, this growth was accompanied by further intensification of the proportion controlled by SOEs and their controlling departments.

The main reason for this trend has been the various reforms to reduce state intervention in enterprises and to increase the proportion of income retained at the

*Table 4.4* Extrabudget funds, 1953–77

| *Period* | *Extrabudget funds (bn yuan)* | *Budget revenue (bn yuan)* | *Extrabudget funds/budget revenue (%)* | *Average growth of extrabudget funds (%)* |
|---|---|---|---|---|
| 1953–57 | 8.79 | 131.85 | 6.67 | 14.1 |
| 1958–62 | 39.14 | 211.66 | 18.49 | 19.3 |
| 1963–65 | 19.33 | 121.51 | 15.91 | 5.9 |
| 1966–70 | 43.05 | 252.89 | 17.02 | 6.0 |
| 1971–75 | 91.53 | 391.97 | 23.35 | 20.0 |
| 1976 | 27.53 | 77.66 | 35.50 | 35.5 |
| 1977 | 31.13 | 87.45 | 35.50 | 35.6 |

Source: Lou (2000).

enterprise level. The introduction of budget contracting has not, therefore, led to growth in extrabudget funds at the local government level. Those funds remain with local enterprises. However, the fact that local governments own these enterprises means that the funds are also within the local system. This has led to incentives for local government to intervene in the management of enterprises, and this has, in turn, affected the efficiency of local governments. Local governments have attempted to tax extrabudget funds, shift their own spending responsibilities onto enterprises, and evade taxes by concealing the revenue as extrabudget funds.

It is worth noting that in Table 4.5, from 1993, the scope of extrabudget funds was adjusted and is therefore not comparable with previous years. Since 1997, extrabudget revenue has not included funds (fees) that have been brought into budgetary management, which were not accounted for in previous years. The revenues retained by SOEs and their managing ministries or government agencies were considered as those institutions' discretionary funds, and were no longer monitored by the budget system. If these funds were included in the statistics, the data in Table 4.5 after 1993 would be much larger. It is common sense that the size should be larger than budget revenue.

In terms of expenditure, there has also been a small shift in the use of extrabudget funds, with a slight drop in the proportion going to investment in production. According to Deng *et al.* (1990), during most of the 1980s, about 47 percent of these funds was used for technical improvement, repairs, working capital and R&D; 14 percent for capital investment; 15 percent for welfare and bonuses; and the remainder for administration. These funds thus were a major source of the rapid inflation in incentives and bonuses paid to enterprise workers, and also contributed to the overheating of the economy that occurred as a result of the surge in investment at local levels.

The growth of extrabudget funds—one of the results of fiscal contracting—is the consequence of the central government losing much of the direct control it once had over capital investment. In national terms, state budget expenditure on capital construction investment dropped from 83 percent of the total in 1978 to 39 percent in 1985, with the extrabudget investment funds coming from lower levels of government, administrative departments and the production units them-

*Table 4.5* Indicators of government borrowing, 1981–2000

| *Year* | *Government borrowing*[a] | | *Accumulated debt* | |
|---|---|---|---|---|
| | *Billion of yuan* | *Growth rate* | *Billion of yuan* | *As a % of GDP* |
| 1981 | 14.79 | — | 22.82 | — |
| 1982 | 8.42 | −43.10 | 27.24 | 19.37 |
| 1983 | 9.32 | 10.69 | 33.83 | 24.19 |
| 1984 | 7.70 | −17.38 | 39.86 | 17.82 |
| 1985 | 9.05 | 17.53 | 46.36 | 16.31 |
| 1986 | 11.37 | 25.64 | 52.45 | 13.14 |
| 1987 | 18.58 | 63.41 | 63.88 | 21.79 |
| 1988 | 21.78 | 17.22 | 82.27 | 28.79 |
| 1989 | 24.46 | 12.30 | 108.17 | 31.48 |
| 1990 | 21.15 | −13.53 | 120.87 | 11.74 |
| 1991 | 29.91 | 41.42 | 133.78 | 10.68 |
| 1992 | 47.91 | 60.18 | 154.55 | 15.53 |
| 1993 | 44.70 | −6.70 | 184.47 | 19.36 |
| 1994 | 117.41 | 162.66 | 283.28 | 53.56 |
| 1995 | 154.98 | 32.01 | 382.94 | 35.18 |
| 1996 | 196.80 | 26.98 | 494.57 | 29.10 |
| 1997 | 247.71 | 25.87 | 607.44 | 22.68 |
| 1998 | 389.10 | 57.08 | 852.56 | 40.35 |
| 1999 | 401.50 | 3.19 | 1,128.76 | 32.39 |
| 2000[b] | 501.50 | | | |

Sources: State Statistical Bureau of the People's Republic of China (various years); Department of Bond and Finance, Ministry of Finance (2000).

Notes

a Government borrowing consists of national bond and foreign debt.

b Estimate, foreign debt is not included.

selves (Ma 1982: 409–11). The changes have also generated friction between the various levels of administration, as each level has tried to increase the range of its autonomy, maximize the proportion of funds transferred downwards and minimize the amount of revenue controlled within the contract.

## *Deficit and debt management*

### *Evolution of budget deficits and government borrowing*[6]

One point that should be noted is that in China, local governments are not allowed to have deficits. Thus, theoretically, deficits of the central government should be equal to or less than the national deficit. In reality, however, as Table 4.6 shows, the national deficit was often larger than those of the central government. This means that some local governments were not able to make ends meet and had to borrow from banks.

The situation from the start of the economic reform up to the present is quite similar to what German economist Adolph Wagner observed in the nineteenth century in Europe when the state began to expand its activities both quantitatively

*Table 4.6* Indicators of fiscal balance and debt service, 1979–2000 (billion yuan)

| *Year* | *Primary balance* | | *Debt services* | | *Payment of interest and principal* |
|---|---|---|---|---|---|
| | *Total* | *Central government* | *Domestic* | *Foreign* | |
| 1979 | −13.54 | −9.81 | | 7.05 | |
| 1980 | −6.89 | −8.69 | | 7.30 | |
| 1981 | +3.74 | +5.10 | 4.87 | 9.92 | — |
| 1982 | −1.77 | −3.46 | 4.42 | 4.00 | — |
| 1983 | −4.26 | −8.31 | 4.17 | 5.15 | — |
| 1984 | −5.82 | −4.36 | 4.22 | 3.48 | — |
| 1985 | +0.06 | −2.02 | 6.13 | 2.92 | — |
| 1986 | −8.29 | −10.65 | 6.23 | 5.14 | 0.67 |
| 1987 | −6.28 | −8.00 | 11.66 | 6.92 | 1.84 |
| 1988 | −13.40 | −16.19 | 18.84 | 2.94 | 2.17 |
| 1989 | −15.89 | −17.64 | 22.61 | 1.85 | 1.32 |
| 1990 | −14.65 | −11.51 | 19.72 | 1.43 | 7.62 |
| 1991 | −23.71 | −21.70 | 28.08 | 1.83 | 11.16 |
| 1992 | −25.88 | −22.88 | 46.08 | 1.83 | 23.81 |
| 1993 | −29.34 | −29.89 | 38.13 | 6.57 | 12.33 |
| 1994 | −57.45 | −66.70 | 102.83 | 14.58 | 28.26 |
| 1995 | −58.15 | −66.28 | 151.09 | 3.89 | 49.70 |
| 1996 | −52.96 | −60.88 | 184.85 | 11.95 | 78.66 |
| 1997 | −58.24 | −55.85 | 241.18 | 6.53 | — |
| 1998 | −92.22 | −95.80 | 380.88[a] | 8.22 | — |
| 1999 | −179.7 | na | 401.50 | 0.00 | — |
| 2000 | −149.93[b] | −259.82 | 418.01 | 0.00 | — |

Sources: Lou (2000: 29), State Statistical Bureau of the People's Republic of China (various years), Department of Bond and Finance, Ministry of Finance (various years).

Notes

na = Not available.

a Bond issues in 1998 include 58 billion yuan to local governments, but 270 billion of special bonds are not included. The special bonds were used for capitalizing bad loans of state-owned commercial banks.

b The huge deficit in 2000 mainly resulted from the change in accounting method whereby the interest payment is included in current spending. The real deficit of 2000 was 155 billion, less than that in 1999.

and qualitatively (for example, the development of infrastructure, provision of health services, support of industrialization, etc.). As a result, tax income could hardly keep up with expenditure needs, and a growing public deficit and debt were the inevitable consequence (Sturm and Muller 1999: 9).

As shown in Table 4.6, the deficits since 1979 have increased markedly. The evolution of the change in the deficit can be divided into four phases:

1 Between 1979 and 1985, deficits were an accidental phenomenon, and in 1985, China even had a minor surplus.
2 A moderate increase occurred in the period 1986–93.
3 The deficit increased sharply in 1994 and this was related to the fiscal reform announced that year. The central government had to compensate the vested

interests of local governments in order to make the reform take off smoothly. We will discuss this reform in the next section on the central–local fiscal relationship.

4 Expansionary fiscal policy occurred beginning in 1997. As a result, budget deficits jumped again and reached more than 90 billion yuan in 1997. Real deficits in that year were 58.3 billion, but because of the Asian financial crisis and a natural catastrophe of flood in the country, the central government issued 100 billion bonds after September to maintain and stimulate economic activities that were seriously affected by both the external and internal storm. This amount of 100 billion bonds was accounted into the budgets of 1997 and 1998, and made the deficit for 1997 reach more than 90 billion yuan. If the expansionary fiscal policy adopted in 1997–98 was a response to the external and internal storm, then the quick increase in the deficit in 1999 could explain two facts: (i) after two years of experiment, the Chinese government found that expansionary fiscal policy was not so harmful, but rather was a useful tool for a developing economy; and (ii) China was facing a recession and an anti-cyclical measure became a necessity. The 230 billion yuan deficit in 2000 is another story. In this year, China changed its budget accounting method so that interest payments were now included in current spending. Taking this into account, we can say that the real deficit for 2000 was 155 billion yuan, which is less than that in 1999 (Minister of Finance 2000).

With regard to debt, the central government issued two kinds of bonds in the 1950s for the purpose of restoring and developing the economy. Meanwhile, the government also engaged in some foreign borrowing. By 1968, all debts had been paid off and from that point on, China had no debt for a decade until 1981.

Table 4.6, which shows the evolution of government borrowing from 1981 to 1999, demonstrates that the debt increased sharply from 14.79 billion yuan in 1981 to 401.50 billion yuan in 1999, i.e., growth of twenty-sevenfold. Among government debt, the percentage of treasury bonds increased faster than that of foreign debt. Issuing of bonds in 1988 and 1994 exceeded 20 and 100 billion yuan and in 1997, 1998, and 1999, it topped 200, 300, and 400 billion yuan, respectively. In fact, 1999 witnessed 100 percent growth.

There is a close relationship between growth in government debt and the budget deficit since the economic reform (with the exception of 1985). On the one hand, each year's budget deficit and its growth determined the growth of debt, and on the other hand, successive deficits forced the government to pay off the due debt with new issuance that, in turn, led to an increase in the next fiscal year's debt.

Another reason for the exponential increase in government debt is the policy change of deficit covering. Before 1988, the budget deficit was financed from two sources: (i) treasury bonds issued in the current fiscal year; and (ii) overdraft or borrowing from the central bank. In the statistics on government debt, these two sources were not included in the figures during that period. In order to stabilize finance, and reduce and stop the overdraft, the government issued 4 billion yuan in finance bonds to national financial institutions in 1988. This represented 30.14 percent of revenue of debt issuing that year and led to the first jump in government debt. The government stopped overdrafts from the central bank in 1994, and the deficit could thus only be covered by issuing debt which crumbled to 102.83 billion in 1994 or 2.7 times over the previous year. This represents the second jump. In 1988, the expansionary fiscal policy led to another jump in government debt. Given that debt is the only source for covering the deficit, the annual issuing of debt is determined by two factors: one is the scale of the deficit, and the other is the payment of interest and principal.

### *Indebtedness*

Since the beginning of the 1980s, government debt in China has seen rapid expansion, especially after the government adopted Keynesian policy from 1997. Our discussion here focuses on the relationship between growth of debt and revenue, the debt dependency ratio, and the percentage of debt to GDP.

Let us first examine the relationship between growth of debt and growth of revenue (Figure 4.3). From Table 4.6, we can see that the growth of debt proceeded at a rapid pace. The years 1985, 1988, 1990, 1994, 1997, 1998 and 1999 are crucial years in which government debt increased significantly; in other words, during the 1990s, government debt in China grew tremendously. However, there is no relevance between growth of debt and growth in government revenue; rather, growth of debt is mainly determined by the financial needs of the government (i.e., deficits) and redemption of interest and principal.

Comparing the data in Table 4.1 and Table 4.6, we can see that the average annual growth of debt is far higher than that of revenue. Between 1995 and 1999, government debt increased annually by 35 percent, but growth in government

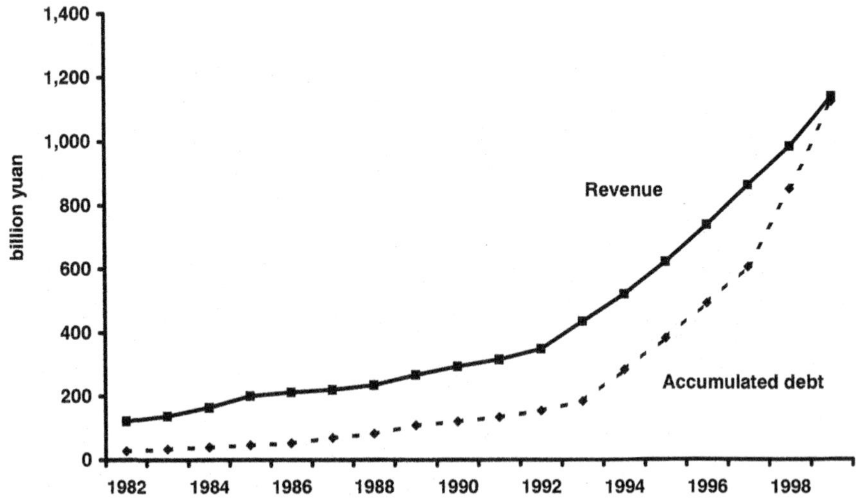


*Figure 4.3* Growth of government revenue and accumulated debt, 1982–99.

revenue was only 14.7 percent, meaning that the growth of debt did not improve the financial embarrassment of the Chinese government, although the economy continued to grow rapidly.

With regard to the debt dependency ratio, we list here the outlays of the entire country and that of the central government; but it must be pointed out that in China, local governments *must* balance their budget. The international alert line for the debt dependency ratio is about 20 percent. Table 4.7 suggests that during the 1990s, China stepped into the alert area. Even when we take total expenditure as the base, the ratio is more than 20 percent and becomes increasingly higher.

The debt-to-GDP ratio indicates not only the national burden in a certain period, but also the relationship between increasing debt and economic growth. The conventional point of view is that this percentage should be controlled under 60 percent. In developed countries, government revenue generally represents 40–50 percent of GNP, whereas in China, it is only about 20 percent (including off-budget revenue). This explains the paradox between the low debt-to-GDP ratio and the high debt-to-spending ratio in China.

The problem with debt is not necessarily its absolute figure, but its growth rate, which started to accelerate in the early 1990s. Regarding the deficit and government debt, the most important issues for discussion, apart from economic concerns, are ethical and political. Ethical concerns refer to the burden of excessive spending today which will fall upon future generations. If the present government is convinced that public borrowing is necessary, then it should arrange the repayment of the accumulated debt within the lifetime of one generation. While this argument may be plausible for consumption expenditures, it is illogical in the case

*Table 4.7* Indicators of government indebtedness

| *Year* | *GDP* | *Current government spending* | | *Debt to spending (%)* | | *Debt to GDP (%)* |
|---|---|---|---|---|---|---|
| | | *Total (bn yuan)* | *Central (bn yuan)* | *Total* | *Central* | |
| 1985 | 896.4 | 200.43 | 83.48 | 4.51 | 10.84 | 5.17 |
| 1990 | 1,854.8 | 308.36 | 119.45 | 6.85 | 17.70 | 6.51 |
| 1995 | 5,847.8 | 682.37 | 287.84 | 22.71 | 53.84 | 6.54 |
| 1996 | 6,788.4 | 793.96 | 350.63 | 24.79 | 56.12 | 7.28 |
| 1997 | 7,446.2 | 923.36 | 427.09 | 26.82 | 57.99 | 8.15 |
| 1998 | 7,939.5 | 1,079.82 | 548.35 | 36.03 | 70.95 | 10.7 |
| 1999 | 8,205.4 | 1,313.6 | 600.93 | 30.56 | 66.81 | 13.7 |
| 2000 | 8,940.4 | 1,588.7 | na | na | na | na |
| 2001 | 9,593.3 | 1,890.3 | na | na | na | na |

Sources: State Statistical Bureau of the People's Republic of China (various years), Department of Bond and Finance, Ministry of Finance (various years).

Notes

na = Not available.

a Gross financial liabilities as a % of government expenditures and of GDP. The total debt dependency ratio is the percentage between current government borrowing to total government spending. The central debt dependency ratio is the percentage between current government borrowing to central government spending.

of investments (for example, expenditure on highways and railways). Requiring a government to adhere to strict time limits for the repayment of debt caused by spending on consumption is further complicated by the fact that not all public expenditures can be easily classified as consumption or investment expenditures, including most spending on social policies.

### *Debt management in perspective*

Political concerns are also brought forward. The Chinese political tradition with regard to finances is "balance" and the culture did not permit spending over revenue. Foreign debt was especially unwelcome. This political sentiment could be explained by the bitter experience of borrowing from the Soviet Union in the early days of the Republic. This is also the reason why China had no government debt between 1968 and 1981. Although popular opinion can accept a certain amount of debt, the "balanced" tradition for either the whole country or a family cannot be forgotten in one day. Suspicion over the sustainability of Keynesian policy always exists. A characteristic regarding national debt in China is that the government has no need to take into account the vote, but it need only justify to itself the necessity of borrowing; in contrast, in developed countries, the government must take into consideration the popular vote (Sturm and Muller 1999). Another political concern on debt is more "realistic." That is, it is a fact that a rising burden of interest narrows the room for maneuvering in budgeting. It is indeed the case that interest payments on the national debt have become one of the biggest items of the central government budget.

## The central–local fiscal relationship

### *The fiscal arrangement before 1978*

The fiscal arrangements in China have acted as a substitute for the capital market. The main source of investment funds in China from the early 1950s to the 1980s was the budget system. In its purest form, central planning implied that the revenue from taxes at all levels and the income of all state-owned enterprises should be handed over to the central government, which would then disburse expenditure through its budget, including allocations for capital investment. The banks provided additional capital through their supply of credit, and also acted as the mechanism for the distribution of funds that were allocated through the budget. At the central level, the collection of revenues and the management of the budget were handled by the Ministry of Finance. This ministry controlled central income and expenditure, and administered the balances remitted between different levels of government, especially between the center and provinces. The central budget played a role of general distributor of national resources in the economy in this period for about thirty years.

In the early 1980s, central expenditure accounted for some 50 percent of all budget expenditures, and the remainder was handled through provincial and county budgets. Revenue from the surplus provinces was also used by the central government to support the budgets of poorer provinces.[7] Government revenue consisted primarily of tax income and profits from SOEs, the latter accounting for the largest proportion. By the early 1980s, enterprise taxes and profits accounted for some 85 percent of total budget income (Ma 1982: 446). Taxes managed by the local governments included agricultural taxes that they collected themselves, but the items that could be taxed and the rates that were applied were fixed by the central government.

Commonly the largest single line of expenditure in the budget was for "economic construction," i.e., investment in SOEs and infrastructure. This expenditure was given as interest-free grants to the projects concerned. The remainder included defense, education, social services and administration. Outlays for capital projects, national defense and so on were the responsibility of the central government, while spending on agriculture, urban construction, education, health and administration was the responsibility of local governments. This means that local governments had responsibility for managing the funds, but the policies, regulations and objectives of their expenditure programs were laid down by the central government.

The published budgets were conservative and aimed to achieve surpluses, though deficits were not uncommon. As Wong (1992: 197–227) explains, this system had other important incentive effects. Local governments had little incentive to either collect revenues or to be responsible in their expenditures. Shortfalls in revenue were passed back to the central government and had little effect on local spending. As is explained later, reforms designed to offset these incentives created a new set of side effects.

### *The 1978–94 reforms: fiscal contracting*

With the economic reform that started in 1978, the fiscal system was replaced by a new one in which each level of government agreed with the next level above it to meet certain income and expenditure targets. If an administrative level was able to generate additional revenue, this was shared with its next superior level according to an agreed ratio set out in the fiscal contract. The contract also stipulated any expenditure subsidy to be provided to the lower level, regardless of changes in its revenue during the contract period. The surplus income retained at the lower level could be used to cover new investment or other expenditures at its own discretion.

There were five different sets of arrangements of the contracting system:

1. 1980–82: provinces were assigned to each of the categories according to the nature of their economies and financial resources and set the contracts.
2. 1982–83: a more standardized arrangement was established in an attempt to increase the size of remittances to the center, and the arrangements set the tax sharing and subsidy levels for up to five years.
3. 1983: tax-for-profit reform in SOEs that were to be freed from handing over their profits to the state and were instead to be governed by a new set of tax payments.
4. 1984: introduction of enterprise management contract for a guaranteed profit hand-over.

5 1988: reaffirmation of a straightforward contract between the center and provinces, an agreed payment (subsidy) between two levels was negotiated and fixed for a number of years.

The consequence of these changes was that provincial levels retained greater freedom in managing local taxation and their financial strength continued to be dependent on their local economic development. Despite the fact that the contract was not unified for all local governments—better or not, the terms of the contract depended on the bargaining ability of local governments—local governments were now allowed to keep most of the income from enterprises under their control and no longer had to share a proportion with the central government. This system is commonly known in Chinese as "eating from separate kitchens." This change had a very important consequence. The financial well-being of government, at the provincial and county levels, was now closely linked with the strength of the local economy.

There are some key differences between the contracting system and the prereform system. Before the reforms, local governments were given revenue targets but were also supposed to hand over all of the revenue earned from particular taxes. After the reforms, local governments were given a fixed revenue target from particular taxes and allowed to retain any excess over the target. However, the central government continued to determine the tax base and tax rates.

Such a fiscal arrangement no doubt stimulated local governments' initiative for collecting fiscal revenue and developing the local economy, but at the same time, it led to various inefficiencies, especially the rise in local protectionism.[8] It has also been argued that the strategy of encouraging local growth to generate revenue for governments contributed to the macroeconomic imbalances in the 1980s in China.

### *The 1994 fiscal reform*

The massive decline in the two ratios enfeebled the government's ability to exercise macro adjustments. The 1994 reform was an attempt to replace the old, discretion-based system of revenue sharing with a new rule-based system of revenue sharing, to clarify the central–local fiscal relationship and to guarantee the revenues of the central government. The new system was called the tax assignment system (*fenshuizhi*).

#### *Key elements of the reform*

The 1994 reform led to a fundamental shift in the way revenue was shared between the central and provincial governments. Rather than a negotiated percentage of locally collected revenues being remitted to the central government, taxes were now divided into three distinct categories: central, local and shared. Central taxes would go into the central government's coffers and local taxes into the local budget. As for shared taxes, they were to be divided between the central government and provincial governments according to established formulas. For instance, 75 percent of the revenue from VAT belonged to the central government and the remaining 25 percent to the provincial governments. These ratios were fixed and applied to all provinces, and were not subject to negotiation. The rule-based method was expected to reduce bargaining costs.

In addition, the tax structure was simplified and tax rates were standardized. For instance, a universal tax rate of 33 percent was imposed on all enterprises whether they were state-owned, collective, private, or foreign-funded. By improving transparency, these two measures were expected to help monitor the behavior of both taxpayers and tax collectors, and plug important loopholes in tax collection.

Local governments were now no longer allowed to grant tax breaks. The discretion to grant privileges of "reduced taxes and tax exemption" had been a big loophole in the old system that local governments often used to channel budget funds into extrabudget funds, thus reducing the revenues to be shared with the center. With the reform, the central government reclaimed this authority.

The most important institutional design of the 1994 reform was that of tax administration. There were now two parallel systems of tax administration with separate chains of command: a national system for central taxes and a local system for local taxes. Shared taxes were collected by the national system first, and were then split between the central and local governments according to the formulas mentioned above. The separation of the national tax service from the local one was crucial for rule enforcement. In the past, when tax collection lay solely within the purview of local governments, they often abused the upward-sharing mechanism by strategically lowering their tax effort or recategorizing revenues in ways that the center could not share, thus reducing their remittance to the center. Replacing upward-sharing with downward-sharing, the new system was designed to deprive local governments of their ability to play such a game against the central government.

### *Central arrangement for local vested interests*

The adoption of the tax assignment system in 1994 marked a paradigm shift in China's fiscal reform that was sure to affect the interests of every province. Conflicts of interest were unavoidable in the course of such a radical change. To ensure a relatively smooth transition to the new system, the center had to make concessions to the provinces.

The first concession was to guarantee that the level of each province's revenue after 1993 would not be lower than that in 1993. Originally, 1992 had been selected as the base year by the Standing Committee of the politburo. However, due to great pressure from coastal provinces, especially Guangdong, the center was forced to replace 1992 with 1993 as the base year, a change that represented a major concession to the southeastern provinces (Zhou 1994: 5–17). Under this concession, each province's net loss in accepting the new system was calculated, and the center promised to compensate the province for what it would have to sacrifice to the new system.

Furthermore, no province would be happy merely to maintain its 1993 income level. Thus, the center had to make another concession: starting from 1994, central compensation to the provinces would increase by 30 percent of the average growth rate of total VAT and the consumption tax (a central tax) collection in the nation as a whole. However, in August 1994, under growing pressure from some provinces, this rule was changed so that central compensation to a province would grow by 30 percent of the average growth rate of total VAT and consumption tax collection in that particular province, instead of in the nation as a whole.

The third concession was to allow a two-year "transitional period" (1994–95) in which tax breaks and tax exemptions authorized by provincial governments in the years prior to the introduction of the 1994 system would continue to be effective, and lower corporate income tax rates (27 and 18 percent, respectively) might be applicable to enterprises with low profitability.

Finally, the center made a pledge that, once its share of total government revenues reached 60 percent, at least one-third of its revenue would be used as a fiscal transfer to narrow regional disparities between rich and poor provinces.

Without such concessions, the new system would not have been able to garner much support from the provinces. The first two concessions were obviously geared to the needs of rich provinces. Because those provinces had a vested interest in the status quo and were capable of blocking institutional change, the center had no choice but to guarantee that their interests would not be damaged, at least for the time being. Otherwise, the reform might never have had a chance in getting off the ground. The third concession was a lure for all provinces, and the last a response to the pressing needs of poor provinces. Collectively, the poor provinces were large in number, and their support for the new system was indispensable.

### *Assessment of the 1994 system*

Compared to the old systems, the rules of the game were much clearer, the enforcement mechanisms were much more reliable, and the discretionary powers of both the central and local governments were much smaller than before. All of these changes were expected to produce positive results but there were still many institutional defects that were left unaddressed. The most obvious one was the vestiges of the old system. For example, the revenue-sharing contracts negotiated under the old system were allowed to remain effective. The provinces were still supposed to remit a specified amount of locally collected revenue to, or receive a certain amount of subsidies from, the central government, according to the deals cut with Beijing before 1993. As a result, transfer arrangements between the center and provinces were extremely complicated. The center and provinces first collected taxes and divided revenues according to the new rules; then, the center returned revenue compensation to the provinces according to the formulas discussed above; finally, the provinces handed over remittances or received subsidies from the center according to the old revenue-sharing contracts. In the end, no one knew what constituted real central revenue or local revenue.

Prior to 1994, China had made an effort to amend and improve central–local fiscal relations, but none were able to halt the free fall of the "two ratios." The 1994 reform was the most fundamental and daring reform in the fiscal institution. However, the 1994 system was by no means perfect, and we may expect further improvements in the performance of China's fiscal system.

*Table 4.8* Fiscal indicators, 1992–2001

| *Year* | *General gov't revenue (bn yuan)* | *Growth of general gov't revenue (%)* | *Central gov't revenue* | *Local gov't revenue* | *Local remittances* | *Central refunds* |
|---|---|---|---|---|---|---|
| 1992 | 348.34 | 100 | 28.1 | 71.9 | 55.86 | 59.65 |
| 1993 | 434.90 | 125 | 22.0 | 78.0 | 60.03 | 54.46 |
| 1994 | 521.81 | 150 | 55.7 | 44.3 | 57.01 | 238.91 |
| 1995 | 624.22 | 180 | 52.2 | 47.8 | 61.00 | 253.41 |
| 1996 | 740.80 | 213 | 49.4 | 50.6 | 60.39 | 272.25 |
| 1997 | 865.11 | 248 | 48.9 | 51.1 | 60.38 | 285.67 |
| 1998 | 987.60 | 284 | 49.5 | 50.5 | 59.71 | 332.15 |
| 1999 | 1,144.41 | 329 | 51.1 | 48.9 | 59.81 | 408.66 |
| 2000 | 1,339.52 | 385 | 52.2 | 47.8 | 59.91 | 466.53 |
| 2001 | 1,638.60 | 470 | 52.4 | 47.6 | na | na |

Sources: State Statistical Bureau of the People's Republic of China (various years); Lou (2000).

Note
na = Not available.

From Table 4.8, we can see that total government revenue has increased at a much faster pace since the reform. Before 1993, the annual increase had normally been in the 20–30 billion yuan range, but the 1994 increase was 85 billion yuan and this grew to 740 billion in 1996 and 1,144 billion yuan in 1999. The central government's share of total government revenue is also on the rise, going up from one-third to about one-half. When viewed in relation to GDP, the annual increase in total government revenue is disappointing. Even after the 1994 reform, revenue growth continued to lag behind economic growth. As a result, the ratio of total government revenue to GDP has continued its declining trend of the 1980s, though the situation in 1999 was much improved (Table 4.1).

It is also unclear whether the rising share of central government revenue to total government revenue is real or illusory. Given the complexity of the 1994 system, one may come up with three different definitions of the central government's share. The first is the central collection of taxes. As Table 4.9 shows, the proportion of central collection has increased from less than 30 percent to around 50 percent, which by any measure is a great improvement. The second definition includes not only central collection, but also that part of locally collected revenues that local governments are obliged to remit to the central government. If we use this definition, the central government's share reached around two-thirds of total government revenue, comparable to the ratio observed in many countries. However, the central government could not use such combined funds at will because it had to compensate, through refunds, the provinces' loss in agreeing to accepting the new system. Such refunds were in a sense the provinces' entitlements. The central government was also not free to decide whether to withhold or reduce the refunds; it had to make them if it did not want the system to be derailed. Subtracting the refunds the center was obliged to transfer to the

*Table 4.9* Central government's share of total revenue according to the three definitions

| *Year* | *Definition 1* | | *Definition 2* | | *Definition 3* | |
|---|---|---|---|---|---|---|
| | *Bn yuan* | *(%)* | *Bn yuan* | *(%)* | *Bn yuan* | *(%)* |
| 1993 | 95.751 | 22.0 | 155.782 | 35.8 | | |
| 1994 | 290.650 | 55.7 | 347.655 | 66.6 | 135.855 | 26.0 |
| 1995 | 325.662 | 52.2 | 384.513 | 62.1 | 186.863 | 30.2 |
| 1996 | 366.107 | 49.4 | 425.226 | 57.7 | 153.598 | 20.9 |
| 1997 | 422.692 | 48.9 | 475.384 | 56.6 | 184.880 | 22.0 |
| 1998 | 489.200 | 49.5 | 548.913 | 55.6 | — | — |
| 1999 | 584.921 | 51.1 | — | — | — | — |
| 2000 | 698.917 | 52.2 | — | — | — | — |
| 2001 | 858.274 | 52.4 | — | — | | |

Sources: State Statistical Bureau of the People's Republic of China (various years); Lou (2000: 48).

provinces, the central share accounted for only 20–30 percent of total government revenue, a share that is lower than the levels through 1993 (definition 3 in Table 4.9).

### *System to be improved*

Strictly speaking, what China's 1994 reform introduced was not a real tax assignment system. While some taxes were designated as "local," the central government still dictated the rates and the base of all taxes, including local taxes. Local governments had no control over the rates and the base of their assigned taxes and hence could not determine automatically the size of their budgets. Since the introduction of the 1994 fiscal reform, many Chinese officials and scholars have called for independent taxing power for local governments. They have complained that the revenues from the assigned local taxes fell far short of local expenditure needs, and have thus demanded formal autonomy for local governments to make changes concerning local tax base and rates, and even to levy new local taxes (Xiang 1994; Yang and Jia 1994).

In fact, it makes perfect sense for the center to confer a degree of autonomous taxation power to local governments, as long as such power does not distort the allocation of resources in the economy or fragment the common market (Agarwala 1995). Devolution of this power could enhance efficiency of the fiscal system, because decentralized decision-making would better suit the preferences of local residents and make the incentives of local governments compatible with the center's, thus reducing enforcement costs. Some form of transfer between the center and provinces will always be needed to fill vertical and horizontal fiscal gaps. The 1994 reform, however, did not adequately address this issue. Fiscal transfers played a minimal role at best in the new system.

Developing a formula-based system of intergovernment transfer is an urgent task from not only an economic but also a political standpoint. The current baseline figure method (*jishufa*) in determining budgetary allocation to the provinces, which favors provinces that had greater revenue-generating capacity, has become increasingly unacceptable to poor provinces. To give these provinces incentives to stick to the tax assignment system, the center had to adopt the factor analysis method (*yinsufa*) for determining central transfers.

Finally, the 1994 reform did not touch extrabudget funds. Just before announcing its decision in July 1993 to introduce the system, the central government redefined the concept of extrabudget funds to exclude funds retained by SOEs. However, even according to the new much narrower definition, extrabudget revenue still amounted to 186.3 billion yuan in 1994, equivalent to 35.68 percent of total budget revenue, or about 4 percent of GDP for that year (Table 4.3). Such an important source of government resources was beyond central budgetary control. Until extrabudget funds are incorporated into the formal system of budgetary accounting, local governments will continue to possess great discretionary power over an enormous amount of fiscal resources.

The discussion in this paper examined how the new system has overcome the old institutional drawbacks. However, while the 1994 reform represented a notable move away from the old bargaining system, the new one is not truly rule-based. The central as well as provincial governments retained some key discretionary powers that allowed them to continue acting opportunistically, although to a lesser degree. Consequently, the reform's initial results have been mixed at best. Unless these discretionary powers are removed, it is not certain whether the current system will fare much better in the long run than previous systems. Although the drawbacks of the 1994 system were well known by scholars and authorities, further reform is seen as a must; however, vested interests are a huge obstacle to overcome.

## Acknowledgment

The authors gratefully acknowledge the helpful discussion with Deputy Director Su Ming.

## Notes

1 Wang (1997) provides an interesting discussion on this point.
2 It is worth noting here that fiscal indicators that have appeared in official statistics do not correspond well with these concepts. When government revenue (spending) or budget revenue (spending) are quoted from the *China Statistical Yearbook*, they are not comparable to the concept used in most other countries.
3 Other off-budget revenues include various fees, fines and funds raised. Many government agencies, educational institutes and local governments have off-budget revenues that are referred to as "the little golden box" or "third source of finance."
4 $E_G = G_g/GNP_g$, where $E_G$ is government spending elasticity, $G_g$ is growth in government spending, and $GNP_g$ refers to growth of GNP.
5 $MGP = \Delta G/\Delta GNP$, where $\Delta G$ is the increase in government spending and $\Delta GNP$ is the increase in GNP.
6 The main references for this section are as follows: working reports of Directorate of Debts of Ministry of Finance, Jia and Wang (2000), and Yang (1998).
7 For a discussion of the significance of these transfers and their implications for the ability of the central government to maintain macroeconomic control, see Lardy (1978).
8 With regard to how local governments protect their investment by denying raw material supplies to competitor processors and leading commodity wars, see Zang (2000) and Findley (1992).

## References

Agarwala, Ramgopal (1995) *China: Intergovernmental Fiscal Relations*, World Bank Discussion Paper, no. 178, Washington, DC: World Bank.

Deng Yingtao, Yao Gang, Xu Xiaobo and Xie Yuwei (1990) *Zhongguo Yusuanwai Zijin Fenxi* [an analysis of extra-budget funds in China], Beijing: Zhongguo Renmin Daxue Chubanshe.

Department of Bond and Finance, Ministry of Finance (2000) *Report to the National People's Congress*, March6, Beijing: Ministry of Finance.

Department of Bond and Finance, Ministry of Finance (various years) *Working Reports*, Beijing: Ministry of Finance.

Findlay, Christopher (ed.) (1992) *Challenges of Economic Reform and Industrial Growth: China's Wool War*, Sydney: Allen and Unwin.

Jia Kang and Wang Xiaoguang (2000) "A case study on our country's treasury bonds," *Xiandai Caijing* [Modern finance and economics], 10: 3–6.

Lardy, Nicholas R. (1978) *Economic Growth and Distribution in China*, New York: Cambridge University Press.

Lei Hailiang (1997) *Caizheng zhichu zengzhang yu kongzhi yuanjiu* [Growing government spending and its control], Shanghai: Shanghai Financial University Press.

Liu Rongcang (ed.) (1999) *Zhongguo caizheng lilun qianyan* [Theories of public finance in China], Beijing: Shehui Kexue Wenxian Chubanshe (Social Sciences Documentation Press).

Lou Jiwei (2000) *Xin Zhongguo 50 nian caizheng tongji* [New China fifty years' government finance statistics], Beijing: Jingji Kexue Chubanshe (Economic Science Press).

Ma Hong (1982) *Xiandai Zhongguo Jingji Shidian* [An encyclopedia of the contemporary Chinese economy], Beijing: Zhongguo Shehui Kexue Chubanshe.

Ministry of Finance (2000) *Report to the National People's Congress*, March 6, Beijing: Ministry of Finance.

State Statistical Bureau of the People's Republic of China (various years) *China Statistical Yearbook*, Beijing: China Statistical Information and Consultancy Service Centre.

Sturm, Roland and Muller, Markus M. (1999) *Public Deficits: A Comparative Study of their Economic and Political Consequences in Britain, Canada, Germany and the United States*, London: Longman.

Wang Shaoguang (1997) "China's 1994 fiscal reform," *Asian Survey* 37(9): 801–17.

Wong, Christine P.W. (1992) "Fiscal reform and local industrialization," *Modern China* 18(2): 18–23.

Xiang Zhi (1994) "Caizheng zhengce yu caizheng tizhi guanxi gaishu" [Fiscal policy and fiscal system), *Shanghai caizheng* [Shanghai finance], 6: 25–7.

Yang Canmin and Jia Wenjun (1994) "Dui zhongyang he difang caizheng fenpei guanxi de chongxin sikao" [Rethinking central–local fiscal relations], *Journal of Central South Financial University* 3: 3–5.

Yang Liangchu (1998) "Analysis of government debt: scale and recommendation," *Guanli Shijie* [Management world], 6: 68–75.

Zang Yaogu (2000) "Guanyu dapo difang shichang fenge wenti de yanjiu" [An analysis of breaking-down the separation of local markets], *Gaige* [reform], 6: 13–16.

Zhao Zhiyun (1998) "Lun caizheng zhichu guimo de zengzhang qushi" [Growing trend of government spending], *Caimao Jingji* [finance and trade economics], 12: 41–3.

Zhou Xiaochuan *et al.* (1994) "1994 nian zhongguo shuizhi gaige: chengji yu wenti" [The 1994 fiscal reform: achievement and problems], *Gaige* [reform], 5: 23–5.

# 5 Colombia

*Luis Ignacio Lozano*

## Introduction

At the beginning of the 1990s, a diversity of economic reforms were designed and implemented to reduce the size of Colombia's public sector with the objective of making it more efficient. Despite the reforms, ten years later, the Colombian public sector is 80 percent larger and the financial sustainability of the government presents serious problems. In 1999, GDP growth of Colombia was −4.3 percent and the unemployment rate had reached 20 percent. This drop in economic activity has been accompanied by imbalances in the macroeconomic accounts, particularly in the public sector.

This chapter provides a general description of Colombia's economic trends in the past few years, and closely examines the factors that have undermined the country's public finances. The next section contains an overview of the fiscal imbalances registered as of the 1960s, and their relationship with both the real business cycle and the country's tax policy. This is followed by a synthesis of the main economic reforms that were introduced in the early 1990s, and compares the size of the Colombian public sector with those of several neighboring countries. Next, the key issues involved in the country's recent fiscal imbalance are reviewed and the dynamics of the public debt and the question of its sustainability are analyzed. The closing section outlines the policies for economic adjustment and reactivation that are currently debated in Colombia.

## Historical overview

### *Trends of fiscal imbalance*

The Colombian public sector has registered two major fiscal imbalances since the 1960s. The first fiscal imbalance occurred at the beginning of the 1980s, when both the central government and the decentralized agencies recorded large cash deficits. The nonfinancial public sector (NFPS) deficit reached 7.6 percent of GDP in both 1982 and 1983, with half of the deficit explained by the financial operations of the central government. Three years later, the NFPS deficit was adjusted thanks to an effective economic program.

The second major fiscal imbalance began in the mid-1990s and attained its critical point in 1999. By then, the consolidated fiscal accounts had reached a cash deficit of 4.3 percent of GDP, due entirely to the financial transactions of the central government.[1] Even though the size of the last deficit is smaller than the first one, its adjustment could be more complicated because it depends completely on the central government's operations. In fact, the central government is currently facing serious obstacles to making successful fiscal adjustments because of the narrow margins of its expenditure policy as well as the modest revenue increases gathered from several tax reforms.

Apart from these two fiscal crises, the fiscal data indicate that in the 1960s, macroeconomic management of Colombian public finances did not pose any problems. For instance, in the 1960s, the government fiscal deficit was, on average, 0.6 percent of GDP, while the consolidated public deficit was 1.8 percent. At this time, the government's fiscal results stemmed from a simple fiscal framework: on the revenue side, income and imports were heavily taxed, while on the expenditure side, investment was mostly geared toward building infrastructure. The budget destined for the public payrolls was negligible.

In the 1970s, the public deficit followed very similar trends. The government's fiscal deficit averaged 0.7 percent of GDP and the overall public deficit was 2.2 percent. Although throughout the 1970s the government's spending framework remained the same, by the mid-1970s, significant changes had been introduced to the taxation scheme: both income tax rates and the capital gains tax for corporations were increased. These reforms, as well as increases in the international coffee prices, registered as of 1976, rendered additional resources to the public treasury. Therefore, between 1976 and 1978, the government attained a cash surplus of 0.5 percent of GDP.

There is no question that the composition of the public deficit began to change in the 1990s. As will be shown, both the introduction of major economic reforms and the new rules imposed by the 1991 Political Constitution had a strong impact in shaping public finances. Until 1990, the central government's deficit had always been below the consolidated one. For instance, in the 1960s and 1970s, the government deficit was, on average, one-third of the consolidated fiscal result. By the 1980s, this deficit had increased to two-thirds, and by 1990, the size of the government's fiscal imbalance was larger than the total public deficit. This implies that throughout this period, the remaining public agencies experienced cash surpluses in their financial operations. This was particularly true in the oil and social security sectors.

### *Fiscal balance and the real business cycle*

Figure 5.1(a) shows the aforementioned fiscal trends as well as the close relationship between the public fiscal imbalance and the real business cycle. Times of crisis in public finances go hand in hand with periods of severe economic recession. The inverse relationship between the fiscal deficit and economic growth can be explained by the fiscal automatic stabilizers theory. These stabilizers "smooth" the size of economic cycles by stimulating economic activity in periods of recession, or by decelerating it in times of high growth. Fiscal policy and the level of economic openness as well as the composition of public revenues and expenditures determine the effectiveness of these self-regulatory tools.

(a)

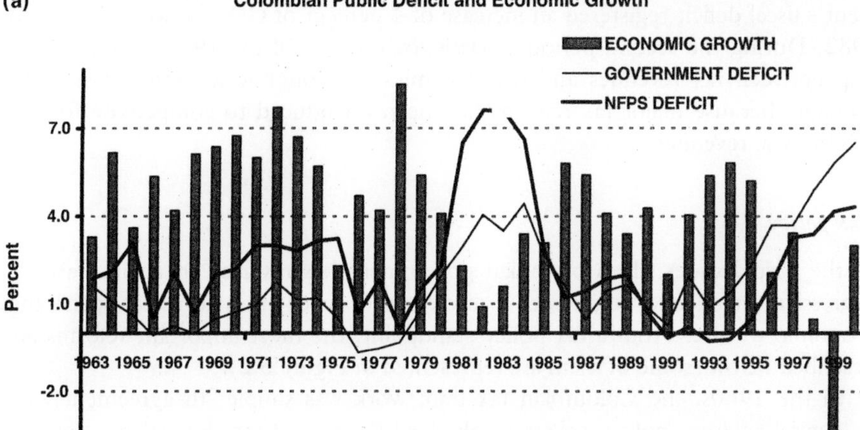


(b)

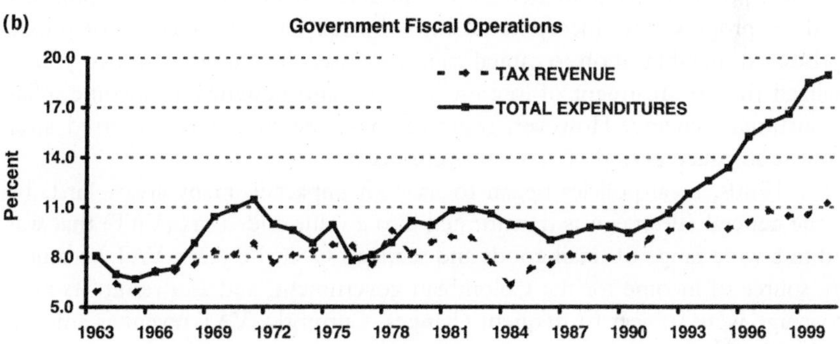


*Figure 5.1* Public deficit and economic growth of Colombia, and government fiscal operations (as a % of GDP).

Source: Banco de la República.

The average size of automatic stabilizers in the European Community countries is 0.5. For developed, yet more closed, economies such as the United States and Japan, the average size is near 0.3. In the Latin American countries (LAC), the size of automatic stabilizers ranges from 0.25 in Brazil to 0.10 in Ecuador, Venezuela and Mexico. In Argentina, the automatic stabilizer is 0.17, while in Chile and Colombia, it is 0.19 (Martner 2000). That is in Colombia, a contraction of 2 percent in the gap of the economic growth rate, with an automatic stabilizer of 0.19, will lead to an increase in the fiscal deficit of 0.38 percent of GDP.

Figure 5.1(a) and (b) show the expected relationships between economic growth, government tax revenues and the fiscal deficit for Colombia. It is clear that as a consequence of the economic crises of the early 1980s, government revenues decreased from an average level of 9 percent of GDP (between 1978 and

1981) to 7 percent (between 1982 and 1983). Not surprisingly, the government's fiscal deficit registered an increase of 4 percent of GDP between 1979 and 1982. During the second period of crisis, by the end of the 1990s, the relationship between tax revenues and the dynamics of economic growth is less clear, probably because major tax reforms had been introduced to compensate for the loss in fiscal revenues.

### *Tax policy*

In the past decades, the Colombian government has resorted to an increasingly aggressive set of fiscal reforms as a discretionary mechanism to foster social and economic welfare. From a tax policy standpoint, the most important reforms are described below (some of them are represented in Figure 5.2).

In the 1960s, the Colombian tax framework was simple. In agreement with influential advisers, policy-makers emphasized the role of taxation as an automatic stabilizer.[2] In the 1970s, less emphasis was placed on the stabilizing effects of fiscal policy and greater emphasis was given to the inequities and distortions that result from an unindexed income tax.

The major reforms implemented by the mid-1970s increased the income tax rate and its progressivity; incorporated into the tax base the income of public enterprises; extended taxation to capital gains (on assets held more than two years); rationalized the tax treatment of interest incomes; and designed an income inflation adjustment scheme. However, some of these measures were reversed after 1975 in the so-called period of "counter-reforms."

In the 1980s, fiscal policies began to have an impact in many areas. First, by 1983, the general sales tax was transformed into a value added tax (VAT) that was applied to a wide range of retail goods and services. Over the years, VAT became a leading source of income for the Colombian government, and as a result, its rates and coverage were subject to frequent changes. Currently, VAT revenues amount to nearly 40 percent of the government's total tax revenues. Next, by the mid-1980s, policy-makers began to favor fiscal decentralization as well as the strengthening of regional and local budgets through transfers made from the central government. In addition, in 1986, a major income tax reform took place to stimulate savings and investment as well as to recover the original neutrality and simplicity of the country's tax system. This reform ended double taxation on return assets, reduced personal income tax rates, leveled the rates on corporation profits, and simplified tax administration mechanisms in general.

During the 1990s, Colombia endured an unprecedented number of tax reforms that were not based on a single set of guiding principles. Some of these reforms were directly associated with structural reforms that were implemented in other economic areas. Still other reforms were simply designed to help bridge the increasing gap between the government's expenditures and revenues. Between 1990 and 2000, there were at least eight national tax reforms, including an executive decree that established a temporary tax on financial transactions. Figure 5.2 illustrates the common feature of all of these reforms—that is, the constant changes to the VAT coverage and rates.

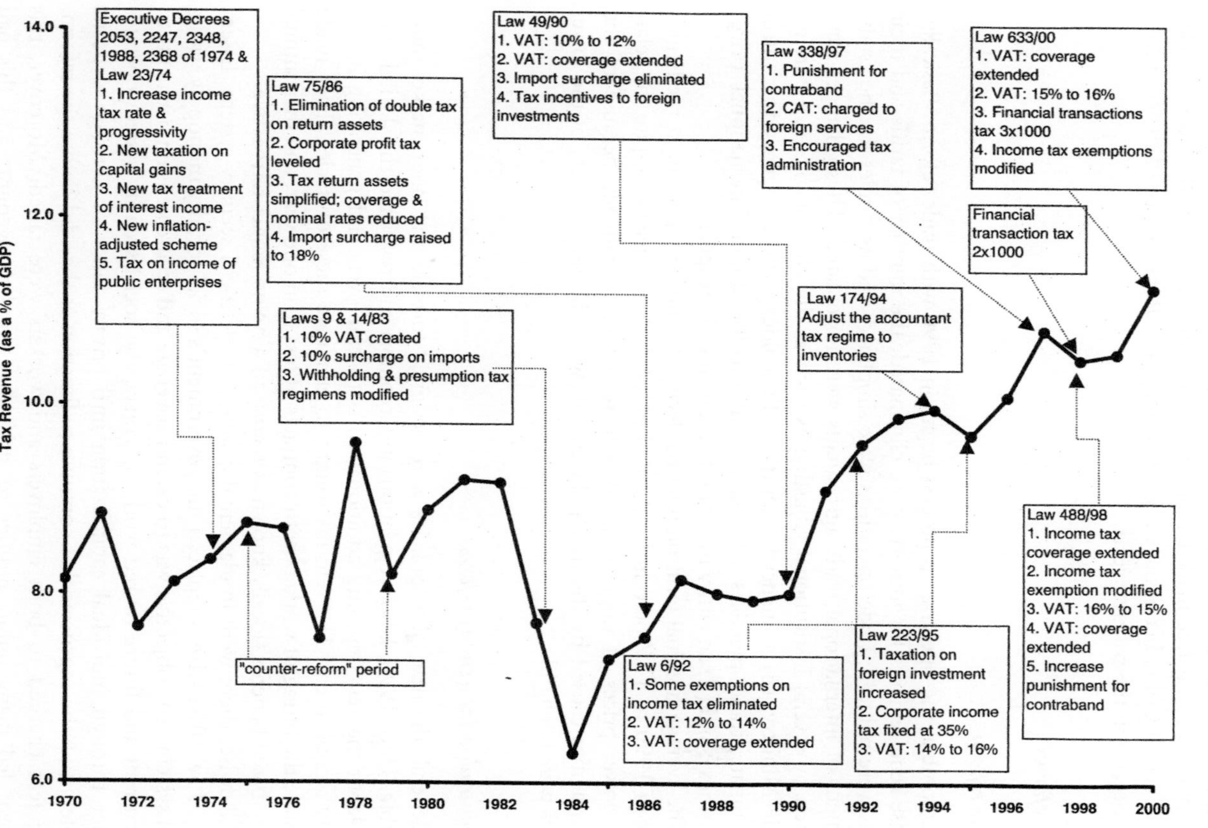


*Figure 5.2* Main reforms to government's tax revenue.

## Structural reforms and the size of the state in the 1990s

In 1991, the new Political Constitution prompted fiscal decentralization as well as a variety of financial, exchange and social security reforms that were akin to the country's emerging free-market policies.[3] A brief description of the main policies introduced in Colombia in the early 1990s maps out the behavior of the country's public sector in the past ten years.

### *The reforms*

#### *Trade reform*

In Colombia, the opening-up process began in 1990 with trade reform. Basically, license requirements for imports were eliminated; the number of tariffs and their levels were reduced; trade operations were simplified; and new rules for the establishment of international trade agreements were formulated. These changes were backed by several institutional adjustments such as the creation of: (i) a Foreign Trade Ministry; (ii) a financial institution (Bancoldex); (iii) an agency to control illegitimate trade practices and supply information about international prices (Incomex); and (d) an entity to promote exporting (Proexport).

The average nominal tariff on imports declined from 49.4 percent at the beginning of 1990 to 11.7 percent by the end of 1991. Nonetheless, despite the relatively lower prices of imports, imports increased only gradually because of the uncertainties caused by the new policies. Likewise, the fiscal effects of the lower tariffs were negligible.

#### *Labor and social security reforms*

In general, the new labor policies were designed to make the labor market more flexible. Until 1990, labor regulations in Colombia had restricted the flexibility of the labor market, imposing additional costs to employers and generating uncertainty among them. The reforms sought to eliminate these obstacles. They made possible the hiring of workers with contracts of less than one year, and their annual salary-based benefits (locally known as *cesantías*) were no longer retroactive.

Likewise, there were fundamental changes in the social security system. Essentially, Law 100 of 1993 replaced the government's social security monopoly with a dual system. The objective was to extend coverage and secure pension payments to all current and future retired workers. Today, the social security system operates either through individual capitalization into private funds or through deposits made into public agencies that continue to function as they did before the reform. The fees charged to both employers and workers were raised. Moreover, this reform led many public entities to straighten up their accounts and this had important fiscal effects.

### *Financial system reform*

Colombia's Political Constitution of 1991 established an autonomous central bank (CB) that was responsible for maintaining the purchasing power of the currency (Law 31 of 1992). To meet this objective, the board of the CB draws and implements the country's monetary, exchange rate and financial policies. The main fiscal effect of the new CB is its inability to make direct loans to the government. The CB can offer direct credits to the government only if all of its board of directors unanimously approve such a decision. Nevertheless, this has never been the case since the reform took place in 1992. In addition, the law requires that as of January 1999, all of the CB's open market operations must be carried out exclusively with government securities negotiated in the secondary market.

The financial reforms also ended the CB's practice of subsidizing loans to specific sectors, and drew the legal and economic conditions under which commercial banks could become multibank institutions rather than specialized banks (Law 35 of 1993). Likewise, the new regulations eliminated obligatory investments for the banking system and decreased the banks' required reserves in the CB. Last but not least, the financial system was opened to foreign investment.

### *Exchange reform*

Under the new regulations, the CB no longer has a monopoly on trade of foreign currencies. Market forces determine the exchange rate as well as the allocation of foreign trade resources. The exchange control mechanisms have been modified and the financial institutions became more involved. Anyone can now hold foreign currencies or assets, though in limited quantities (Law 9 of 1991). With the introduction of these reforms, Law 444 of 1967 on exchange transactions, which had been enforced for the past twenty-five years, was revoked.

Between 1991 and 1994, there was a transition period toward a system of exchange rate bands, which was finally established in February 1994. Throughout these years, the exchange authorities continued to announce on a daily basis the "official exchange rates" according to the crawling peg system.[4] However, the band system was dismantled in September 1999, partly as a result of the speculative attacks associated with the high vulnerability of the Latin American capital markets to the Asian crisis. Subsequently, a free-floating exchange system was adopted.

### ***The size of the public sector***

In clear opposition to the goals established by Colombian policy-makers, the size of the Colombian public sector increased considerably throughout the 1990s. The nonfinancial levels of the Colombian public sector comprise the central government, the social security system, a variety of decentralized entities, a number of enterprises, and the provincial and local governments. As Table 5.1 illustrates, total public expenditure between 1990 and 2001 increased from 20.4 percent of GDP to 38.9 percent; that is, the size of the state almost doubled in this period.

*Table 5.1* Total expenditures of the nonfinancial public sector in Colombia (as a % of GDP)

| | *Central gov't (CG)* | *Social security system (SSS)* | *Decentralized entities and enterprises (DE&E)* | *Provincial and local gov'ts (P&LG)* | *Total* |
|---|---|---|---|---|---|
| 1990 | 5.4 | 2.6 | 6.7 | 5.6 | 20.4 |
| 1991 | 6.4 | 2.7 | 6.9 | 5.7 | 21.6 |
| 1992 | 7.5 | 2.7 | 7.1 | 5.8 | 23.1 |
| 1993 | 6.6 | 3.3 | 8.0 | 6.5 | 24.3 |
| 1994 | 6.6 | 3.9 | 8.6 | 7.0 | 26.1 |
| 1995 | 6.8 | 4.7 | 9.3 | 7.2 | 28.1 |
| 1996 | 7.7 | 5.6 | 10.1 | 9.3 | 32.7 |
| 1997 | 8.2 | 6.1 | 10.7 | 9.1 | 34.1 |
| 1998 | 8.2 | 6.8 | 9.5 | 9.4 | 33.9 |
| 1999 | 8.9 | 7.7 | 8.7 | 11.3 | 36.6 |
| 2000 | 11.1 | 6.7 | 9.3 | 10.8 | 37.9 |
| 2001 | 12.0 | 6.9 | 10.3 | 9.7 | 38.9 |

Sources: DNP; CONFIS; BR.

The fiscal decentralization process requires the transfer of an increasing share of the central government's current revenue to the provincial governments. Therefore, the provincial and local governments must carry out expenditures. Between 1990 and 2000, provincial and local expenditures in Colombia increased from 5.6 percent to 10.8 percent of GDP (Figure 5.3). Likewise, the central government transferred a significant amount of resources to the social security system. Through these resources, the social security institutions increased their reserves and their spending rose from 2.6 percent to 7.7 percent of GDP between 1990 and 1999. Interestingly enough, expenditures of the central government that are not related to transfers increased from 5.4 percent to 12 percent between 1990 and 2001, which contradicts the expected results under a decentralization scheme. To sum up, presently Colombia's public sector is much larger than the average for the Latin American region.

Unfortunately, fiscal statistics for the year 2001 are not available for all of the Latin American countries. However, Figure 5.4 illustrates the sharp increase in the size of the Colombian public sector between 1990 and 2000, which is the same period when neighboring countries were decreasing their own public expenditures. In 1990, public expenditure in Colombia accounted for 20.4 percent of GDP, a figure that is substantially below the regional average of 28 percent. However, ten years later, Colombia's public expenditure was 8 points above the regional average.

## The main issues in public finance

Colombia's fiscal imbalance of the last few years can be explained through a set of nine issues that are closely related to public spending and revenue. The first six issues have to do with the finances of the central government, and the last three with the consolidated results of the public sector at large.

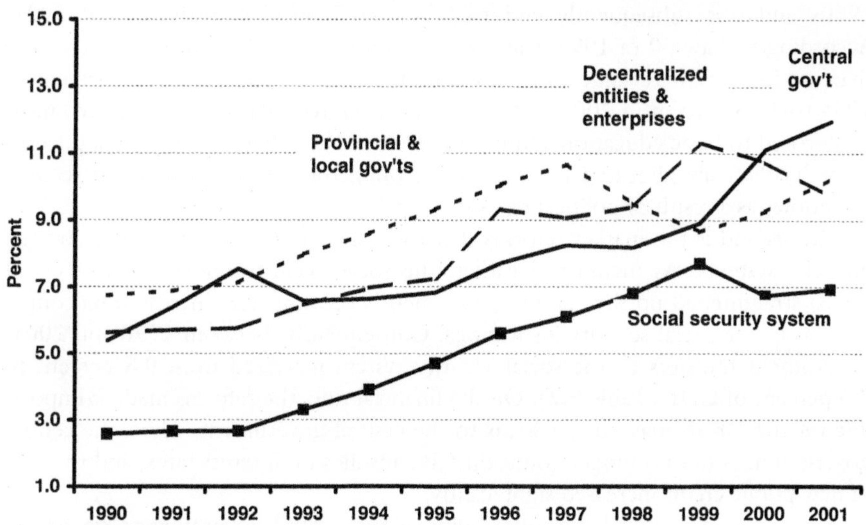


*Figure 5.3* Total expenditures of the nonfinancial public sector (as a % of GDP).

Source: DNP; CONFIS; BR.

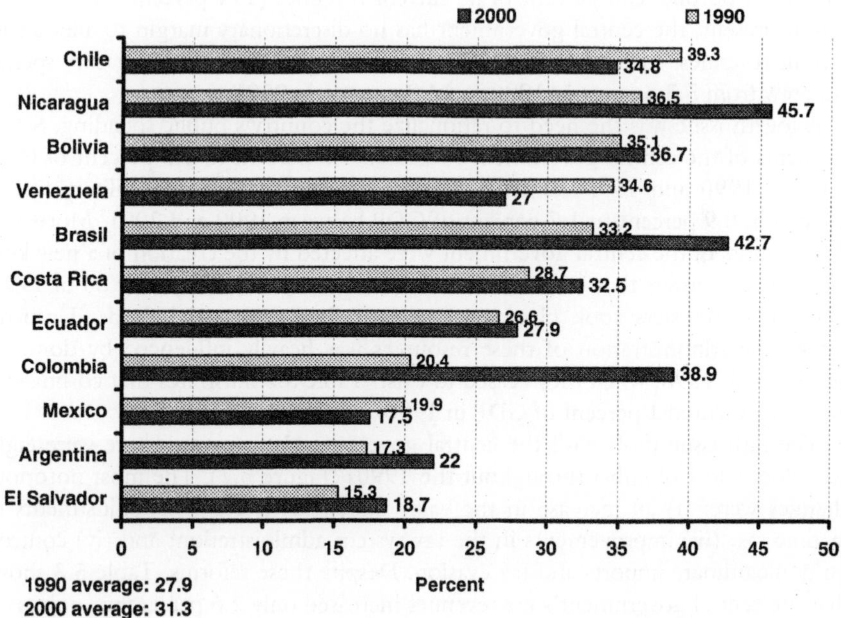


*Figure 5.4* Total expenditures of the nonfinancial public sector in Latin American countries, 1999–2000 (as a % of GDP).

Source: BID.

The first issue involves the decentralization process that had begun by the mid-1980s and was subsequently endorsed by the Political Constitution of 1991. According to Law 60 of 1993, the central government must transfer an increasing share of its current revenue to the provincial governments (from 38.0 percent in 1994 to 46.5 percent in 2001). Most of these resources (close to 80 percent) must be devoted to basic education and health services. Nonetheless, the central government has actually allocated more than the obligatory resources to these sectors, sometimes as a result of political pressures.

The second is the market reforms that took place in the social security and the financial systems. As mentioned earlier, the social security reforms (Law 100 of 1993) straightened up the central government's accounts and increased its contributions to the social security institutions. Consequently, between 1990 and 2001, government transfers to the social security system increased from 0.8 percent to 2.5 percent of GDP (Table 5.2). On the financial side, the reforms made it impossible for the CB to make direct loans to the central government. Thus, the central government could no longer count on CB subsidies on interest rates, and the cost of new public credit increased significantly.

A third issue involved the inflexibility of the central government's obligatory spending, which is comprised of transfers to the social security system and to the provincial governments, as well as the payment of interest on the public debt. As shown in Table 5.2, this spending amounted to 64 percent of the government's current revenues in 1990. In 2001, the central government's obligatory expenditures went beyond 100 percent of its current revenues (114 percent). This means that at present, the central government has no discretionary margin to allocate its current revenues. In relation to GDP, the central government's obligatory spending grew from 5.3 percent in 1990 to 14.9 percent in 2001.

A fourth issue was the need to rationalize the country's public spending. Salary payments of the central government rose from 1.6 percent to 2.5 percent of GDP between 1990 and 1995. Other expenditures, mainly related to military forces, grew from 0.9 percent to 1.7 percent of GDP between 1990 and 2001. Moreover, the accounts of the central government were affected by the creation of a new kind of regional transfers that were different from the ones created by Law 60 of 1993. These new transfers took place through so-called co-financial funds. Unfortunately, the administration of these resources was heavily influenced by domestic politics until 1998, when they ceased to exist. Table 5.3 illustrates that co-financial funds represented 1 percent of GDP in 1996.

The fifth issue deals with the central government's revenue. There were eight tax reforms in Colombia throughout the 1990s (Figure 5.2). The most notorious changes were: (i) an increase in the value added tax (VAT); (ii) adjustments to income tax; (iii) improvements in the tax system administration; and (iv) controls on nonlegitimate imports and tax evasion. Despite these reforms, Table 5.3 shows that the central government's tax revenues increased only 2.6 percentage points (as a percentage of GDP) between 1990 and 1999. It is clear, then, that these policies had only a short-term impact. However, the central government gathered additional resources from profits coming from the central bank and public enterprises such as Ecopetrol (the public oil company). Additional sources of income for the

*Table 5.2* Central government expenditure, 1990–2001

| | *1990* | *1991* | *1992* | *1993* | *1994* | *1995* | *1996* | *1997* | *1998* | *1999* | *2000* | *2001* |
|---|---|---|---|---|---|---|---|---|---|---|---|---|
| As a % of GDP | | | | | | | | | | | | |
| Interest | 1.1 | 1.2 | 1.0 | 1.1 | 1.2 | 1.2 | 1.9 | 2.0 | 2.9 | 3.3 | 3.8 | 3.9 |
| Internal | 0.3 | 0.3 | 0.3 | 0.5 | 0.6 | 0.8 | 1.4 | 1.5 | 2.2 | 2.3 | 2.5 | 2.3 |
| External | 0.8 | 0.9 | 0.7 | 0.7 | 0.6 | 0.5 | 0.5 | 0.6 | 0.7 | 1.0 | 1.3 | 1.6 |
| Transfers | 4.2 | 4.2 | 4.9 | 5.7 | 6.1 | 6.8 | 8.0 | 8.0 | 8.7 | 10.2 | 10.0 | 11.0 |
| Law 60/93 | 2.4 | 2.6 | 3.2 | 3.4 | 3.5 | 3.4 | 4.2 | 4.0 | 4.1 | 5.0 | 4.0 | 5.0 |
| Social security | 0.8 | 0.8 | 0.9 | 1.0 | 1.2 | 1.3 | 1.6 | 1.7 | 1.8 | 2.0 | 2.2 | 2.5 |
| Other | 1.0 | 0.8 | 0.8 | 1.3 | 1.5 | 2.0 | 2.2 | 2.3 | 2.8 | 3.1 | 3.8 | 3.5 |
| Obligatory expenditures | 5.3 | 5.4 | 6.0 | 6.9 | 7.3 | 8.0 | 9.8 | 10.1 | 11.6 | 13.5 | 13.8 | 14.9 |
| Repayments on debt | 1.4 | 2.8 | 2.6 | 1.8 | 3.1 | 1.6 | 2.8 | 3.5 | 3.4 | 5.4 | 4.4 | 6.1 |
| Obligatory exp. + repayments on debt | 6.8 | 8.2 | 8.5 | 8.6 | 10.4 | 9.6 | 12.6 | 13.5 | 15.0 | 18.9 | 18.2 | 21.1 |
| As a % of gov't current revenue | | | | | | | | | | | | |
| Interest | 13.3 | 12.8 | 10.5 | 11.1 | 11.4 | 12.2 | 17.7 | 18.2 | 26.9 | 30.6 | 32.9 | 29.8 |
| Internal | 3.3 | 3.4 | 3.3 | 4.6 | 5.9 | 7.7 | 13.3 | 13.3 | 20.0 | 21.1 | 21.7 | 17.4 |
| External | 10.0 | 9.3 | 7.2 | 6.4 | 5.5 | 4.5 | 4.4 | 4.9 | 6.8 | 9.5 | 11.2 | 12.4 |
| Transfers | 50.6 | 45.1 | 49.5 | 55.5 | 60.4 | 67.4 | 75.7 | 71.5 | 80.6 | 94.2 | 86.5 | 84.1 |
| Law 60/93 | 28.7 | 27.8 | 32.1 | 32.7 | 34.1 | 34.3 | 39.5 | 36.1 | 38.0 | 46.5 | 34.9 | 38.3 |
| Social security | 9.4 | 8.9 | 9.4 | 9.9 | 11.4 | 13.4 | 15.4 | 14.8 | 16.8 | 18.7 | 18.8 | 18.9 |
| Other | 12.4 | 8.4 | 8.0 | 12.9 | 14.9 | 19.8 | 20.9 | 20.6 | 25.8 | 29.0 | 32.8 | 26.9 |
| Obligatory expenditures | 63.9 | 57.9 | 60.1 | 66.6 | 71.8 | 79.7 | 93.4 | 89.7 | 107.5 | 124.8 | 119.4 | 113.9 |
| Repayments on debt | 16.8 | 29.4 | 26.1 | 17.2 | 30.2 | 16.3 | 26.6 | 30.8 | 31.0 | 49.6 | 37.6 | 46.7 |
| Obligatory exp. + repayments on debt | 80.6 | 87.3 | 86.2 | 83.8 | 102.0 | 96.0 | 120.1 | 120.5 | 138.4 | 174.4 | 157.0 | 160.7 |

*Table 5.3* Central government indicators, 1990–2001

| | *1990* | *1991* | *1992* | *1993* | *1994* | *1995* | *1996* | *1997* | *1998* | *1999* | *2000* | *2001* |
|---|---|---|---|---|---|---|---|---|---|---|---|---|
| In billions of Colombian pesos | | | | | | | | | | | | |
| Total revenue | 2,088 | 3,164 | 4,208 | 5,908 | 7,701 | 9,600 | 12,140 | 15,238 | 16,880 | 20,164 | 23,197 | 28,942 |
| Tax revenue | 1,886 | 2,768 | 3,747 | 5,051 | 6,731 | 8,185 | 10,172 | 13,148 | 14,825 | 16,067 | 19,644 | 24,802 |
| Other | 202 | 396 | 461 | 856 | 969 | 1,415 | 1,969 | 2,089 | 2,055 | 4,098 | 3,553 | 4,140 |
| Total expenditure | 2,269 | 3,232 | 4,858 | 6,284 | 8,628 | 11,462 | 15,783 | 19,787 | 23,821 | 29,033 | 33,591 | 40,111 |
| Interest | 262 | 365 | 407 | 582 | 780 | 1,036 | 1,879 | 2,485 | 4,090 | 5,026 | 6,630 | 7,497 |
| Personal services | 385 | 566 | 789 | 1,166 | 1,628 | 2,072 | 2,295 | 2,848 | 3,548 | 4,106 | 4,675 | 5,280 |
| Transfers | 998 | 1,289 | 1,917 | 2,923 | 4,146 | 5,704 | 8,021 | 9,753 | 12,259 | 15,472 | 17,400 | 21,186 |
| Capital expenditure | 408 | 610 | 797 | 973 | 1,339 | 1,746 | 2,316 | 3,169 | 2,280 | 2,255 | 2,679 | 2,904 |
| Other | 215 | 402 | 948 | 639 | 734 | 904 | 1,273 | 1,532 | 1,644 | 2,174 | 2,207 | 3,245 |
| Surplus/deficit | −180 | −68 | −650 | −376 | −927 | −1,862 | −3,643 | −4,549 | −6,941 | −8,868 | −10,395 | −11,170 |
| Total debt | 3,971 | 4,622 | 6,498 | 7,477 | 8,320 | 11,560 | 14,452 | 21,778 | 31,232 | 45,592 | 66,157 | 84,412 |
| Domestic debt | 980 | 1,077 | 2,270 | 2,905 | 3,453 | 5,272 | 7,176 | 11,351 | 15,559 | 22,950 | 34,222 | 42,742 |
| External debt | 2,991 | 3,545 | 4,227 | 4,572 | 4,867 | 6,288 | 7,276 | 10,427 | 15,673 | 22,642 | 31,935 | 41,671 |
| Co-financial funds | na | na | na | na | 520 | 738 | 979 | 809 | 537 | na | na | na |
| As a % of GDP | | | | | | | | | | | | |
| Total revenue | 8.9 | 10.4 | 10.8 | 11.6 | 11.4 | 11.4 | 12.1 | 12.5 | 12.0 | 13.3 | 13.4 | 15.1 |
| Tax revenue | 8.0 | 9.1 | 9.6 | 9.9 | 10.0 | 9.7 | 10.1 | 10.8 | 10.6 | 10.6 | 11.3 | 12.9 |
| Other | 0.9 | 1.3 | 1.2 | 1.7 | 1.4 | 1.7 | 2.0 | 1.7 | 1.5 | 2.7 | 2.0 | 2.2 |
| Total expenditure | 9.6 | 10.6 | 12.4 | 12.3 | 12.8 | 13.6 | 15.7 | 16.3 | 17.0 | 19.2 | 19.3 | 20.9 |
| Interest | 1.1 | 1.2 | 1.0 | 1.1 | 1.2 | 1.2 | 1.9 | 2.0 | 2.9 | 3.3 | 3.8 | 3.9 |
| Personal services | 1.6 | 1.9 | 2.0 | 2.3 | 2.4 | 2.5 | 2.3 | 2.3 | 2.5 | 2.7 | 2.7 | 2.8 |
| Transfers | 4.2 | 4.2 | 4.9 | 5.7 | 6.1 | 6.8 | 8.0 | 8.0 | 8.7 | 10.2 | 10.0 | 11.0 |
| Capital expenditure | 1.7 | 2.0 | 2.0 | 1.9 | 2.0 | 2.1 | 2.3 | 2.6 | 1.6 | 1.5 | 1.5 | 1.5 |
| Other | 0.9 | 1.3 | 2.4 | 1.3 | 1.1 | 1.1 | 1.3 | 1.3 | 1.2 | 1.4 | 1.3 | 1.7 |

|  |  |  |  |  |  |  |  |  |  |  |  |  |
|---|---|---|---|---|---|---|---|---|---|---|---|---|
| Surplus/deficit | −0.8 | −0.2 | −1.7 | −0.7 | −1.4 | −2.2 | −3.6 | −3.7 | −4.9 | −5.9 | −6.0 | −5.8 |
| Total debt | 16.9 | 15.2 | 16.6 | 14.6 | 12.3 | 13.7 | 14.4 | 17.9 | 22.2 | 30.1 | 38.1 | 44.0 |
| Domestic debt | 4.2 | 3.5 | 5.8 | 5.7 | 5.1 | 6.2 | 7.1 | 9.3 | 11.1 | 15.1 | 19.7 | 22.3 |
| External debt | 12.7 | 11.7 | 10.8 | 8.9 | 7.2 | 7.4 | 7.2 | 8.6 | 11.2 | 14.9 | 18.4 | 21.7 |
| Co-financial funds | na | na | na | na | 0.8 | 0.9 | 1.0 | 0.7 | 0.4 | na | na | na |
| Gross domestic product | 23,560 | 30,407 | 39,035 | 51,129 | 67,533 | 84,439 | 100,711 | 121,708 | 140,483 | 151,565 | 173,730 | 191,863 |

Sources: CONFIS; DANE.

Note
na = Not available.

central government were privatizations (mainly in the banking and electricity sectors) and concessions (mainly in the telecommunications sector). In 1994, the central government obtained revenues equivalent to 2.1 percent of GDP from concessions, while in 1996 and 1997, revenues amounting to 0.7 and 0.4 percent of GDP, respectively, came from privatizations.

The sixth issue involves the central government's raising of credit requirements. The large gap between the central government's expenditures and revenues led to the swift development of a deep fiscal deficit that rose from 0.8 percent of GDP in 1990 to 6 percent in 2000. The financing of this deficit as well as the repayments on the public debt led to the central government's increasing demand for new credit. The sustainability of such an accelerated increase in the level of public debt became a serious problem for the country's government as will be analyzed in greater detail in the next section.

Another issue surrounded provincial and local finances. From the early 1990s, regional public spending expanded notoriously. As shown in Table 5.4, total regional spending increased by 5.7 percentage points (as a percentage of GDP) between 1990 and 1999, while regional tax revenue increased by only 0.9 percent. Between 1991 and 1999, regional expenditures on salaries increased from 3.0 percent to 4.6 percent of GDP. Moreover, by the mid-1990s, transfer funds began to be used as a kind of collateral for banking credits. By December 1999, the debt of regional governments with the domestic financial system had grown to 2.1 percent of GDP. In that same year, the fiscal deficits of the provincial and local governments together amounted to 1.1 percent of GDP.

The eighth issue deals with the social security surplus. After the reform of the social security system, Colombia's leading public social security institution—Instituto de los Seguros Sociales (ISS), which covers nearly 62 percent of the country's insured workers—increased its resources from 1.8 percent of GDP in 1993 to 2.9 percent in 1998 (Table 5.5). This surplus was invested in central government securities. By the end of 1999, the ISS held $6.2 billion (4.1 percent of GDP) in TES B, which are the most important securities of the central government (this amount represented approximately 30 percent of the total TES B issued). From a fiscal point of view, the social security sector reached a cash surplus of 1.6 percent of GDP between 1994 and 1997, which compensated for the deficit of the central government.

The ninth and final issue involves fiscal revenues coming from specific public enterprises. In the 1970s and 1980s, Colombian public finances were heavily influenced by the international prices of coffee. Coffee prices under the international agreement of producers had been steadily high. When the agreement ended in the late 1980s, coffee prices plummeted and so did coffee's contribution to the country's public finances. In the 1990s, Colombia turned to its oil reserves and embarked on several exploration projects, led by the public oil enterprise (Ecopetrol), as well as various transnational companies. The high international prices of petroleum in the last couple of years have provided Ecopetrol with substantial revenues that have contributed toward neutralizing the central government's unbalanced accounts. In 1999, Ecopetrol's cash surplus amounted to 0.73 percent of GDP.

*Table 5.4* Indicators of Colombian provincial and local governments, 1990–2001

| | *1990* | *1991* | *1992* | *1993* | *1994* | *1995* | *1996* | *1997* | *1998* | *1999* | *2000* | *2001* |
|---|---|---|---|---|---|---|---|---|---|---|---|---|
| In billions of Colombian pesos | | | | | | | | | | | | |
| Total revenue | 1,267 | 1,635 | 2,179 | 3,035 | 4,333 | 5,998 | 8,520 | 10,138 | 12,492 | 15,458 | 16,582 | 17,709 |
| Tax revenue | 504 | 653 | 850 | 1,149 | 1,616 | 2,042 | 2,621 | 3,211 | 3,776 | 4,493 | 4,854 | 5,076 |
| Other | 763 | 982 | 1,329 | 1,886 | 2,717 | 3,956 | 5,899 | 6,926 | 8,716 | 10,965 | 11,728 | 12,633 |
| Total expenditure | 1,327 | 1,735 | 2,249 | 3,299 | 4,706 | 6,120 | 9,388 | 11,042 | 13,220 | 17,174 | 18,680 | 18,657 |
| Interest | 57 | 82 | 108 | 141 | 256 | 450 | 601 | 704 | 913 | 926 | 831 | 638 |
| Personal services | 703 | 899 | 1,214 | 1,596 | 2,179 | 2,816 | 3,712 | 3,760 | 5,826 | 6,987 | 8,218 | 9,146 |
| Transfers | 64 | 91 | 106 | 144 | 182 | 263 | 373 | 512 | 605 | 619 | 780 | 664 |
| Capital expenditure | 273 | 374 | 455 | 790 | 1,129 | 1,264 | 2,137 | 3,348 | 2,335 | 3,353 | 3,635 | 2,474 |
| Other | 231 | 291 | 367 | 627 | 959 | 1,328 | 2,565 | 2,718 | 3,541 | 5,289 | 5,215 | 5,735 |
| Surplus/deficit | −60 | −101 | −70 | −264 | −373 | −122 | −868 | −904 | −728 | −1,716 | −2,098 | −949 |
| As a % of GDP | | | | | | | | | | | | |
| Total revenue | 5.4 | 5.4 | 5.6 | 5.9 | 6.4 | 7.1 | 8.5 | 8.3 | 8.9 | 10.2 | 9.5 | 9.2 |
| Tax revenue | 2.1 | 2.1 | 2.2 | 2.2 | 2.4 | 2.4 | 2.6 | 2.6 | 2.7 | 3.0 | 2.8 | 2.6 |
| Other | 3.2 | 3.2 | 3.4 | 3.7 | 4.0 | 4.7 | 5.9 | 5.7 | 6.2 | 7.2 | 6.8 | 6.6 |
| Total expenditure | 5.6 | 5.7 | 5.8 | 6.5 | 7.0 | 7.2 | 9.3 | 9.1 | 9.4 | 11.3 | 10.8 | 9.7 |
| Interest | 0.2 | 0.3 | 0.3 | 0.3 | 0.4 | 0.5 | 0.6 | 0.6 | 0.7 | 0.6 | 0.5 | 0.3 |
| Personal services | 3.0 | 3.0 | 3.1 | 3.1 | 3.2 | 3.3 | 3.7 | 3.1 | 4.1 | 4.6 | 4.7 | 4.8 |
| Transfers | 0.3 | 0.3 | 0.3 | 0.3 | 0.3 | 0.3 | 0.4 | 0.4 | 0.4 | 0.4 | 0.4 | 0.3 |
| Capital expenditure | 1.2 | 1.2 | 1.2 | 1.5 | 1.7 | 1.5 | 2.1 | 2.8 | 1.7 | 2.2 | 2.1 | 1.3 |
| Other | 1.0 | 1.0 | 0.9 | 1.2 | 1.4 | 1.6 | 2.5 | 2.2 | 2.5 | 3.5 | 3.0 | 3.0 |
| Surplus/deficit | −0.3 | −0.3 | −0.2 | −0.5 | −0.6 | −0.1 | −0.9 | −0.7 | −0.5 | −1.1 | −1.2 | −0.5 |
| Gross domestic product | 23,560 | 30,407 | 39,035 | 51,129 | 67,533 | 84,439 | 100,711 | 121,708 | 140,483 | 151,565 | 173,730 | 191,863 |

Source: Banco de la República.

Note
na = Not available.

Overall, the nine issues described above indicate that the fiscal imbalance of the NFPS in Colombia has increased sharply, particularly after 1995. Table 5.5 shows a relative financial equilibrium in the first half of the 1990s as well as an increasing deficit in the second half of the decade (from 0.3 percent of GDP in 1995 to 4.3 percent in 2000). As a result of this fiscal trend, the public sector at large has widely increased the size of its domestic and foreign debt.

## The dynamics of public debt and the question of its sustainability

This section begins with a brief description of Colombia's accelerated process of public indebtedness in the last five years (which is most evident in the case of the central government); it also provides an analysis of the debt's sustainability as well as of the country's vulnerability to external shocks.

### *Public indebtedness*

#### *Indebtedness of the nonfinancial public sector*

Beginning in 1995, Colombia's public debt skyrocketed. Between 1995 and 2002, the consolidated public debt of the NFPS climbed from 25 percent of GDP to 58 percent, not including the central government's social security liabilities (Table 5.6). The total of such an increase was explained by the central government's indebtedness.

In the first half of the 1990s, the ratio of public debt to GDP went down as a result of economic growth and the public sector's decreasing need for new credit. As has already been mentioned, the public sector gathered substantial resources from the sale of assets and the concession of licenses, which were used to make prepayments of the external debt. Between 1992 and 1994, the central government along with other national entities, made prepayments of US$3.193 million. By that time, the value of the foreign debt was US$10.089 million. Not surprisingly, the ratio of external public debt to GDP dropped from 26 percent to 16 percent between those two years.

Between 1997 and 2000, public indebtedness levels reached a critical point. Foreign public debt rose from 14 percent of GDP to 24 percent, while domestic public debt increased from 15 percent to 22.4 percent. The central government's indebtedness accounted for 80 percent of the increase in total debt. Likewise, the rest of the NFPS foreign indebtedness was on the rise, and between 1996 and 1999, it climbed from 5.6 percent to 6.2 percent. We will now examine the central government's indebtedness, because of its predominance, and because of the limited information available on the structure of provincial and local debt.

#### *Indebtedness of the central government*

Between 1995 and 2002, the central government's indebtedness rose from 13.6 percent to 49.5 percent of GDP (Table 5.6). By the end of the 1990s, the foreign

*Table 5.5* Indicators of the nonfinancial public sector[a], 1990–2001 (as a % of GDP)

| | *1990* | *1991* | *1992* | *1993* | *1994* | *1995* | *1996* | *1997* | *1998* | *1999* | *2000* | *2001* |
|---|---|---|---|---|---|---|---|---|---|---|---|---|
| Total expenditures[a] | 20.35 | 21.64 | 23.09 | 24.30 | 26.10 | 28.10 | 32.70 | 34.10 | 33.90 | 36.60 | 37.91 | 38.91 |
| Central government | 5.39 | 6.39 | 7.53 | 6.57 | 6.64 | 6.82 | 7.71 | 8.24 | 8.18 | 8.91 | 11.13 | 11.98 |
| National social security system | 2.58 | 2.66 | 2.66 | 3.30 | 3.90 | 4.70 | 5.60 | 6.10 | 6.80 | 7.70 | 6.74 | 6.93 |
| National decentralized entities and nonfinancial public enterprises | 6.74 | 6.88 | 7.13 | 7.98 | 8.60 | 9.33 | 10.07 | 10.68 | 9.51 | 8.66 | 9.29 | 10.28 |
| Departments and municipalities[b] | 5.63 | 5.71 | 5.76 | 6.45 | 6.97 | 7.25 | 9.32 | 9.07 | 9.41 | 11.33 | 10.75 | 9.72 |
| NFPS surplus/deficit | −0.59 | 0.03 | −0.22 | 0.25 | 0.12 | −0.31 | −1.70 | −3.28 | −3.67 | −4.08 | −4.22 | −4.25 |
| Central government | −0.76 | −0.22 | −1.67 | −0.74 | −1.37 | −2.21 | −3.62 | −3.74 | −4.94 | −5.85 | −5.98 | −5.82 |
| National social security system | −0.12 | −0.05 | 0.12 | 0.52 | 1.06 | 1.92 | 2.04 | 1.15 | 1.20 | 0.90 | 1.80 | 0.49 |
| National decentralized entities and nonfinancial public enterprises | 0.31 | 0.29 | 1.36 | −0.08 | 0.75 | −0.20 | 0.17 | −0.13 | 0.33 | 0.70 | 1.24 | 0.78 |
| Departments and municipalities[b] | −0.02 | 0.02 | −0.03 | 0.54 | −0.32 | 0.18 | −0.29 | −0.56 | −0.26 | 0.17 | −1.28 | 0.30 |
| Privatizations | 0.00 | 0.00 | 0.00 | 0.00 | 2.24 | 0.25 | 0.83 | 3.26 | 0.53 | 0.34 | 0.37 | 0.00 |
| NFPS surplus/deficit, net of privatizations | −0.59 | 0.03 | −0.22 | 0.25 | 2.36 | −0.06 | −0.87 | −0.02 | −3.14 | −3.74 | −3.85 | −4.25 |
| Revenue of ISS | 1.46 | 1.49 | 1.58 | 1.78 | 2.25 | 2.81 | 2.91 | 2.59 | 2.90 | 2.52 | 2.71 | 2.72 |

Source: DNP – UMACRO.

Notes

a Net of transfers.

b Includes local government and local enterprises.

*Table 5.6* Stock of public debt (as a % of GDP)

| | *External* | | | *Domestic* | | | *Total* | | |
|---|---|---|---|---|---|---|---|---|---|
| | *Non-financial public sector* | *Central government* | *Rest of the NFPS* | *Non-financial public sector* | *Central government* | *Rest of the NFPS* | *Non-financial public sector* | *Central government* | *Rest of the NFPS* |
| 1995 | 7.4 | 6.8 | 14.2 | 6.2 | 5.5 | 11.8 | 13.6 | 12.3 | 26.0 |
| 1996 | 7.2 | 5.6 | 12.8 | 7.1 | 5.5 | 12.6 | 14.3 | 11.1 | 25.4 |
| 1997 | 8.6 | 5.6 | 14.2 | 9.3 | 6.1 | 15.4 | 17.9 | 11.7 | 29.6 |
| 1998 | 11.2 | 5.9 | 17.1 | 11.1 | 6.0 | 17.0 | 22.3 | 11.9 | 34.1 |
| 1999 | 14.9 | 6.3 | 21.2 | 15.1 | 5.1 | 20.2 | 30.0 | 11.4 | 41.4 |
| 2000 | 18.4 | 5.3 | 23.7 | 19.7 | 4.6 | 24.3 | 38.1 | 9.9 | 48.0 |
| 2001 | 22.0 | 4.5 | 26.5 | 22.6 | 4.2 | 26.7 | 44.6 | 8.7 | 53.2 |
| 2002 (Sept.)[a] | 24.8 | 4.9 | 29.7 | 24.7 | 3.9 | 28.6 | 49.5 | 8.8 | 58.3 |

Sources: SGEE; Banco de la República.

Note
a Preliminary.

and domestic debts were almost similar in size (50.4 percent vs. 49.6 percent, respectively). At the end of 2000, foreign liabilities had reached US$14,325 billion and were represented as follows: 54 percent in bonds; 30 percent from the multilateral credit system; 14 percent from the commercial banks; and the remaining balance, in credits with foreign governments and other agencies. Foreign indebtedness was usually negotiated in the medium and long terms. Regarding the currencies used, 82 percent were negotiated in American dollars; 8.2 percent in Euro; 1.2 percent in yen; and the rest, in other currencies.

The indebtedness strategy followed by the central government after 1992 consisted of substituting external debt with domestic indebtedness. The main instrument employed was the so-called TES B bonds which the treasury issued for the first time in 1992, when the domestic debt accounted for 33 percent of the total indebtedness. By the end of 2000, these leading government securities represented 88 percent of total internal debt. Currently, the central government counts with other securities, yet the TES B continues to be paramount. Some decentralized government agencies, such as the Agricultural Development Bank (Finagro) and the Deposit Insurance Fund (Fogafin), have placed their own bonds. By the end of 2000, these entities' share in the public debt bond market was 20 percent.

Although financial reforms were aimed at allocating resources through market mechanisms, large portions of the central government's securities were placed by other means. As some studies point out, perhaps the strongest restriction to the placement of the government's securities is the segmentation and thinness of the Colombian public bonds market (Correa 2000). These market characteristics led the central government to attract liquidity from some public agencies (particularly, national enterprises and social security institutions), and from the banking system.

Policy-makers designed three mechanisms to attract resources through the TES B: (i) direct transaction with the treasury (*inversiones forzosas*), in which the bonds (as collateral) cannot be traded in the secondary market; (ii) transactions with the ISS (main social security agency), in which the ISS is capable of buying TES B directly from the treasury, or in the secondary market (*inversiones convenidas*); and (iii) auctions, which are explicit market mechanisms. It is clear that the first two strategies are institutional agreements rather than market mechanisms.

Figure 5.5 illustrates the composition of TES B investments, as related to these three mechanisms, during the second half of the 1990s. Forced investments declined from 24 percent in 1995 to 18 percent in 1998; arranged investments increased from 40 percent in 1995 to 98 percent in 2000; the auction mechanism kept its participation at around 24 percent until 1999, and then its share decreased to 1.1 percent. Consequently, the arranged investments were the most dynamic channel.

From a bondholder standpoint, Table 5.7 displays the main TES B holders up to September 2002. The public sector (including the CB) holds 39.3 percent of these securities, the financial sector holds 25.5 percent, and the private sector, 35.1 percent. As far as the public agencies are concerned, the social security system holds 40.6 percent of the TES B and the enterprises, 11.5 percent. Therefore, public entities have kept the majority of these securities

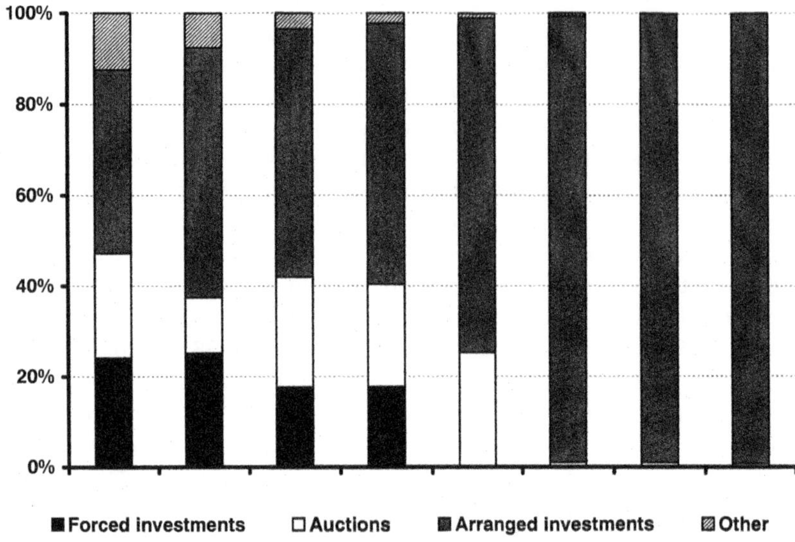


*Figure 5.5* Composition of TES B (main government securities).

Source: Banco de la República.

The interest payments made by the central government on new credits have increased since 1995. This is another trait of the indebtedness process of the central government. For new external credits, the average-weighted interest rate grew from 4.7 percent in 1995 to 10.0 percent in 1999 (Table 5.8). Furthermore, the Colombian spreads in the foreign capital market began to rise in November 1997 as a consequence of the international financial crisis (Figure 5.6). Up to October 1997, Colombian spreads, on average, were about 200 basic points; eight months later, they had climbed to 600 basic points. In addition, the Colombian

*Table 5.7* Holders of TES B and TRD, as of September 2002

| | *Billions of Colombian pesos* | *(%)* |
|---|---|---|
| Total | 43,831.8 | 100.0 |
| Public sector | 15,131.9 | 34.5 |
| Social security[a] | 6,144.1 | 40.6 |
| Enterprises[b] | 1,734.3 | 11.5 |
| Others[c] | 7,253.5 | 47.9 |
| Central Bank | 2,124.9 | 4.8 |
| Financial sector | 11,175.6 | 25.5 |
| Private sector | 15,399.4 | 35.1 |

Source: Banco de la República.

Notes

a Includes ISS, Cajanal, Caprecom and others.

b Includes Ecopetrol, Telecom, Isagen, Sena and others.

c Includes TGR, ICBF, Bogotá, FNC and others.

*Table 5.8* Interest rates, 1993–2000

| | *Domestic debt, effective* | | *External debt* | | | *Market, end of period* | |
|---|---|---|---|---|---|---|---|
| | *Nominal* | *Real* | *Effective* | *Devaluation* | *New debt* | *Nominal* | *Real* |
| 1993 | 29.0 | 5.2 | 7.5 | 9.0 | — | 26.7 | 3.3 |
| 1994 | 25.0 | 2.0 | 8.0 | 3.4 | 7.3 | 38.7 | 13.1 |
| 1995 | 25.4 | 5.0 | 6.4 | 18.8 | 4.7 | 33.1 | 11.4 |
| 1996 | 27.1 | 7.9 | 7.3 | 1.8 | 7.8 | 28.0 | 5.2 |
| 1997 | 25.3 | 8.4 | 7.2 | 28.7 | 7.9 | 24.4 | 5.7 |
| 1998 | 26.6 | 11.2 | 8.4 | 19.2 | 8.2 | 34.3 | 15.1 |
| 1999 | 22.1 | 13.2 | 8.2 | 21.5 | 10.0 | 15.8 | 6.0 |
| 2000 | 23.9 | 13.9 | 8.4 | 19.0 | na | 13.4 | 4.2 |

Note
na = Not available.

peso has depreciated in the last three years. The real exchange rate index rose approximately 30 points between June 1997 and December 1999. Hence, the cost of foreign debt went up from 0.5 percent in 1995 to 1.6 percent of GDP in 2001 (Table 5.2).

The interest rate on central government debt also began to increase after 1996. Table 5.8 shows that the effective real interest rate grew from 5.0 percent in 1995 to 13.9 percent in 2000 (9.7 percent above the real market interest rate). The cost of government securities depends upon the interest rates negotiated. By the end of 1999, 74 percent of the domestic debt in TES B were negotiated at a fixed rate,

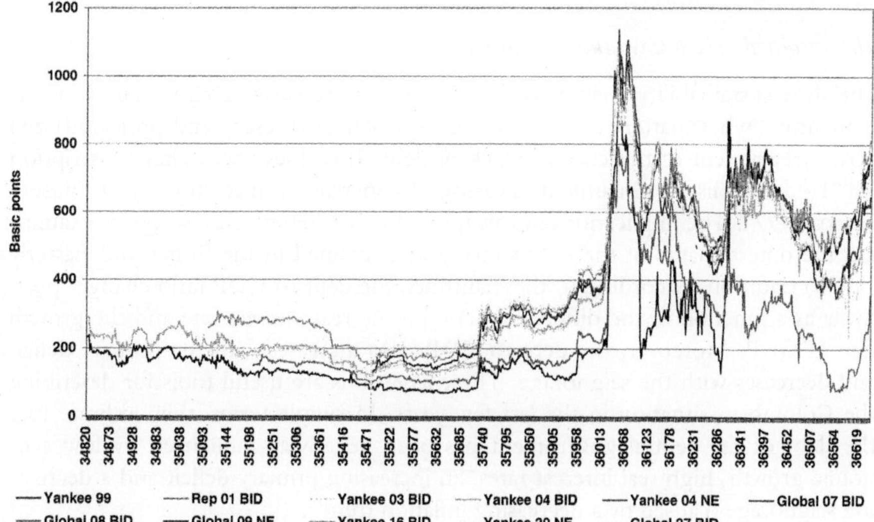


*Figure 5.6* Colombian spreads.

Source: Finance Minister.

while the rest was settled with a floating interest rate. Thus, the domestic interest payments of the central government's debt went up from 0.6 percent to 2.5 percent of GDP between 1994 and 2000.

To sum up, high interest rates as well as the government's accelerated process of indebtedness increased the government's interest payments from 1.2 percent of the GDP in 1995 to 3.9 percent by 2001. However, the main cause of the increase was the indebtedness policy itself. Table 5.9 shows that, by the end of 1999, the accumulation of the primary deficit explained 50 percent of the total interest payments; of this, 43 percent was related to the domestic debt. The remainder is explained by the capitalization of the initial stock of debt (Hernández *et al.* 2000).

## *Debt sustainability*

Our analysis of Colombia's fiscal sustainability starts by understanding that:

> debt sustainability is an integral element of macroeconomic stability. Interactions between different policy variables (such as debt, fiscal and interest rate policies), and outcome variables (such as GDP and exports growth), as well as international economics conditions (international interest rates) jointly define if the country is on a sustainable debt path.
>
> (Ghani and Hyoungsoo 1995)

An accurate forecast of the debt's path must then be based on reliable information on all of these variables. However, most empirical studies on fiscal sustainability are accomplished through two simple yet useful approaches.

### *The standard debt sustainability approach*

The debt sustainability analysis is, in essence, a fiscal sustainability analysis. Consequently, "what matters is whether the fiscal stance (present and projected) will permit repayment of the current stock of debt. If it does not, policy prescription will focus on fiscal adjustment measures to increase future primary surpluses" (Perry 1997). The implications of this quotation are better understood by examining the determinants of the debt's changes, as defined in the Fisher and Easterly (1990) tradition. According to these authors, the debt to GDP ratio changes positively as a function of the difference between the real interest rate and the growth rate of GDP. Moreover, the debt to GDP ratio increases with the primary deficit and decreases with the seignorage. These assertions are useful tools for describing the Colombian situation in the last few years. In simple terms, they indicate that the debt of the central government has been negatively influenced by low economic growth, high real interest rates, an increasing primary deficit and a decreasing seignorage (caused by a decreasing inflation trend).

Figure 5.7 illustrates some of these developments. It compares the dynamics of the government's debt with primary deficit trends since 1990. At the beginning of the decade, the government's finances had a primary surplus of 1 percent of GDP.

*Table 5.9* Determinants of interest payments on central government debt (%)

| | *Domestic interest payments* | | | | *External interest payments* | | | |
|---|---|---|---|---|---|---|---|---|
| | *Primary deficit (t−1)* | *Primary deficit accumulation (before t−1)* | *Initial stock of debt (capitalization)* | *Subtotal* | *Primary deficit (t−1)* | *Primary deficit accumulation (before t−1)* | *Initial stock of debt (capitalization)* | *Subtotal* |
| 1994 | — | — | 51.90 | 51.90 | — | — | 48.10 | 48.10 |
| 1995 | 13.310 | — | 49.68 | 62.99 | −0.33 | — | 37.33 | 37.00 |
| 1996 | 21.630 | 11.31 | 42.20 | 75.14 | −0.22 | −0.22 | 25.31 | 24.87 |
| 1997 | 7.100 | 28.84 | 36.95 | 72.89 | 1.52 | −0.46 | 26.04 | 27.10 |
| 1998 | 13.420 | 30.13 | 30.97 | 74.52 | 0.96 | 0.96 | 23.56 | 25.48 |
| 1999 | 6.420 | 36.55 | 26.00 | 68.97 | 4.36 | 2.01 | 24.66 | 31.03 |

Source: Hernández *et al.* (2000).

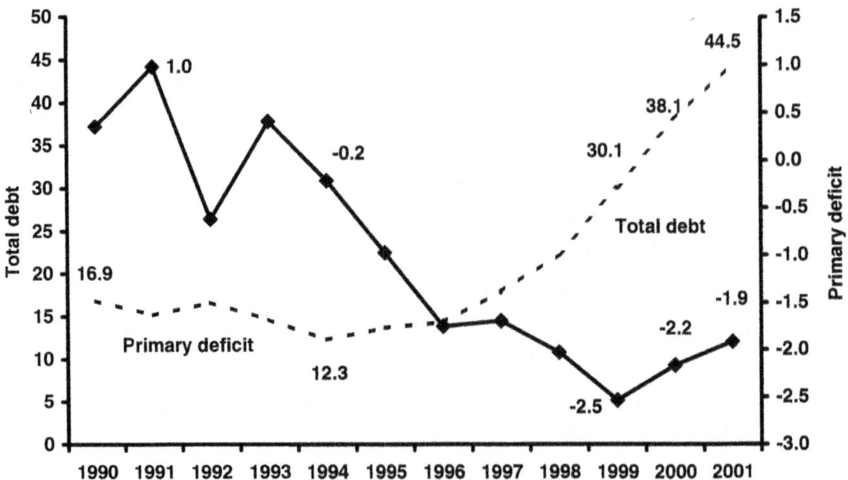


*Figure 5.7* Primary deficit and total debt of the central government (as a % of GDP).

Source: BR; CONFIS.

This primary fiscal imbalance increased to 2.5 percent of GDP by 1999 and, subsequently, it decreased slightly.

Figure 5.8 illustrates the dynamics of both the real interest rate and the rate of economic growth. The large gap between these two variables during the second half of the 1990s led to the further expansion of government debt. Moreover, a decreasing inflation trend in the past twelve years has led to a shrinking of the seignorage (Figure 5.9). For example, in 1992, seignorage amounted to 2.9 percent of the GDP (on M1); by 1999, it amounted to 0.4 percent (Posada 1999).

If Fisher and Easterly's equation is used to calculate the level of the government's primary surplus, two aspects must be considered in an exercise to keep constant the government's debt level for the year 2000. First, the new liabilities of the government, and second, the variables included in the exercise. Between 1999 and 2000, the central government faced a deep crisis in the financial system, which was particularly related to the financing of housing. To solve this crisis, the government issued a new type of bond (locally known as Law 546 and TRDs). Moreover, the government was forced to close some public entities. By the end of 2000, the new liabilities of the Colombian government amounted to 6.7 percent of GDP.

The second aspect is the set of variables included in the sustainability exercise. From a long-term perspective (1980–2000), the real interest rate was 7.5 percent and real economic growth was 4.5 percent. Furthermore, the inflation forecast is below 10 percent, which is compatible with a seignorage of 0.4 percent. Within this context, in the upcoming years, the central government will generate a primary surplus of about 1.1 percent of GDP.

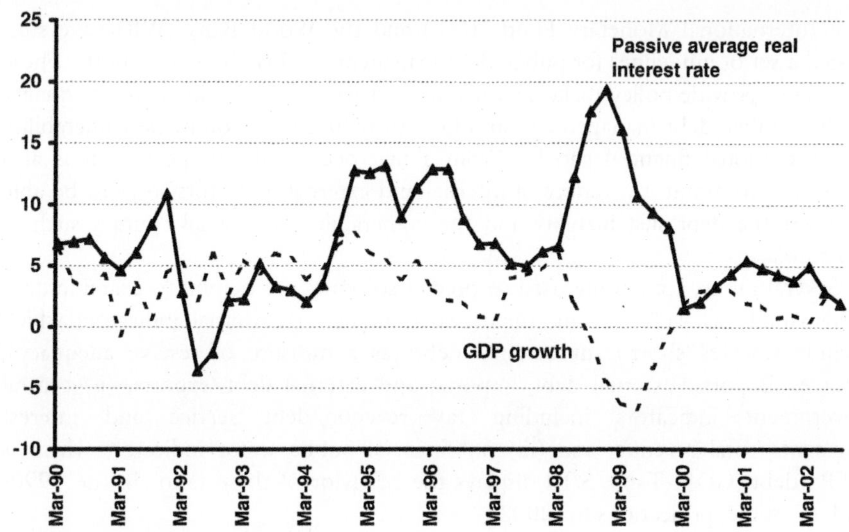


*Figure 5.8* Real interest rates and economic growth, March 1990–March 2002.

Sources: BR; CONFIS.

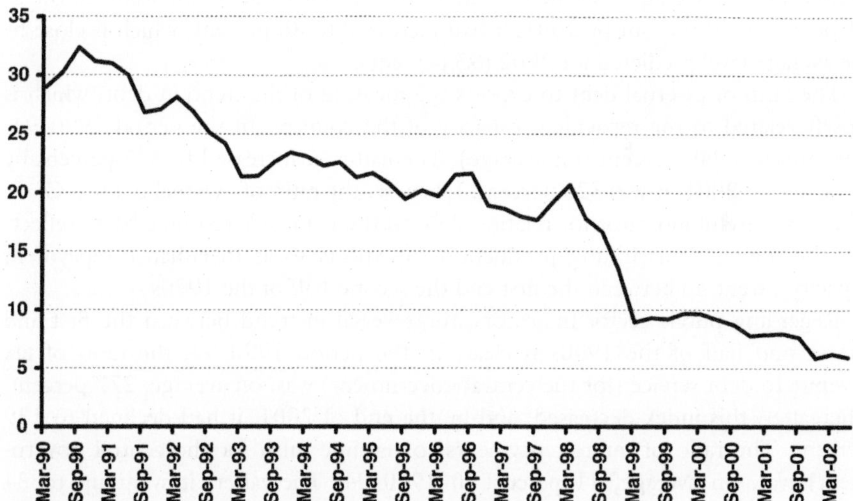


*Figure 5.9* Inflation rates, March 1990–March 2002.

Sources: BR; CONFIS.

*Financial institutions approach*

The International Monetary Fund (IMF) and the World Bank (WB) have suggested a set of guidelines for public debt management (IMF and WB 2000). These guidelines provide policy-makers with sound advice on how to improve the quality of their public debt management, and how to reduce their countries' vulnerability to international financial shocks. From a macroeconomic perspective, it is also important to monitor a variety of internal and external indicators so as to be able to assess the debt sustainability and the vulnerability of a small country such as Colombia.

Several ratios, commonly used to predict solvency, are helpful to examine debt sustainability as well. Among them, we examine: (i) external indicators which include reserves/short-term external debt (as a measure of reserve adequacy); reserves/imports; external debt/imports; and external debt/exports; (ii) central government indicators including tax revenue/debt service and interest payments/total revenue; and (iii) nonfinancial public sector indicators which is NFPS debt/GDP. Table 5.10 displays the behavior of these ratios in the 1990s and, for some, projections for 2002.

The erosion of Colombia's main economic variables since the mid-1990s is evident from the data. Regarding the vulnerability indicators, the ratio of reserves to short-term debt went up from an average of 250 percent in the period 1990–94 to 273 percent in 2001. If official predictions are accurate, by the end of 2002, this ratio will reach 229 percent. The ratio of reserves to imports (a measure of reserve needs) was, on average, 104 percent in 1990–94. Subsequently, it went as low as 64 percent in 1998, but by 2001, it had increased to 86 percent, which is close to the average level predicted for 2002 (95 percent).

The ratio of external debt to exports is a measure of the trend in debt, which is closely related to the repayment capacity of the country. In the period 1990–94, this ratio was 249 percent (on average). Thereafter, it increased to 335 percent by 1998 and in 2001, it was 326 percent. Likewise, the ratio of external debt to GDP, which is a useful indicator for relating debt to the country's resource base (reflecting the potential of shifting production to exports so as to enhance repayment capacity), went up between the first and the second half of the 1990s.

Regarding public sector indicators, the reversal in trend between the first and the second half of the 1990s is clear. In the period 1990–94, the ratio of tax revenue to debt service (for the central government) was, on average, 277 percent. Thereafter, this index decreased, and by the end of 2001, it had declined to 129 percent. The ratio of interest payments to revenue (also for the central government) was, on average, 11 percent in 1990–94. Thereafter, it went up to 34 percent by 2000. In the last few years, the high cost of the central government's debt, along with its dwindling tax revenues, have become increasingly evident.

## Conclusion

Since the mid-1990s, the Colombian economy has endured a pattern of slow growth and expanding economic imbalance, particularly in its fiscal accounts. As

*Table 5.10* Selected economic indicators for Colombia

| | *1990–94* | *1995* | *1996* | *1997* | *1998* | *1999* | *2000* | *2001* | *2002 (projection)* |
|---|---|---|---|---|---|---|---|---|---|
| General indicators | | | | | | | | | |
| GDP (MM$) | 42,332.8 | 84,439.1 | 100,711.4 | 121,707.5 | 140,483.3 | 151,565.0 | 173,729.8 | 189,525.3 | 203,475.3 |
| GDP (US$ m) | 59,806.9 | 92,507.3 | 97,160.1 | 106,659.5 | 98,443.7 | 86,186.2 | 83,226.9 | 82,410.6 | 80,520.7 |
| Growth of GDP (%) | 4.3 | 5.2 | 2.1 | 3.4 | 0.6 | −4.2 | 2.7 | 1.4 | 1.6 |
| Exports[a] (US$ m) | 7,565.0 | 10,155.4 | 10,539.0 | 11,534.3 | 10,930.2 | 11,563.4 | 13,098.8 | 12,219.5 | 12,085.5 |
| Imports[a] (US$ m) | 7,168.6 | 12,894.3 | 12,749.8 | 14,302.1 | 13,616.3 | 9,899.3 | 10,654.6 | 11,826.0 | 11,294.3 |
| Reserves (US$ m) | 6,945.0 | 8,446.4 | 9,933.0 | 9,905.2 | 8,739.6 | 8,102.0 | 9,004.1 | 10,192.2 | 10,677.0 |
| Fiscal indicators | | | | | | | | | |
| NFPS fiscal deficit (%) | −0.1 | −0.3 | −1.7 | −2.8 | −3.7 | −4.1 | −4.2 | −4.3 | −4.4 |
| NFPS expenditures[b] (US$ b) | 10,091.5 | 23,723.5 | 32,898.0 | 41,535.0 | 48,052.3 | 57,521.0 | 65,888.1 | 73,762.3 | 79,984.0 |
| NFPS revenues[b] (US$ b) | 10,135.1 | 23,460.6 | 31,190.1 | 38,110.6 | 42,895.7 | 51,337.9 | 58,556.0 | 65,604.0 | 71,107.0 |
| NFPS debt (US$ b) | na | 21,946.4 | 25,698.2 | 36,518.5 | 48,667.5 | 63,486.9 | 84,054.6 | 101,404.0 | 110,088.5 |
| Short-term public debt[c] (US$ b) | 681.6 | 1,568.7 | 1,300.7 | 1,211.1 | 1,505.1 | 1,259.7 | 443.6 | 733.9 | 1,266.5 |
| NFPS interest payments (US$ b) | 1,423.9 | 2,777.1 | 3,908.2 | 4,531.9 | 6,439.0 | 5,662.0 | 7,898.5 | 9,372.3 | 10,218.0 |
| Indicators of sustainability/vulnerability (%) | | | | | | | | | |
| Reserves/short-term external debt | 250 | 153 | 224 | 224 | 221 | 269 | 311 | 273 | 229 |
| External debt/imports[d] | 287 | 204 | 244 | 241 | 269 | 370 | 342 | 336 | 335 |
| External debt/exports[d] | 249 | 259 | 295 | 298 | 335 | 317 | 278 | 326 | 313 |
| Reserves/imports | 104 | 66 | 78 | 69 | 64 | 82 | 85 | 86 | 95 |
| External debt/GDP | 32 | 28 | 32 | 32 | 37 | 43 | 44 | 48 | 47 |
| Central gov't tax revenue/debt-service | 277 | 339 | 216 | 196 | 168 | 122 | 138 | 129 | 128 |
| Central gov't interest payments/revenue | 11 | 13 | 18 | 19 | 28 | 31 | 34 | 30 | 32 |
| NFPS interest payments/revenue | 14 | 12 | 13 | 12 | 15 | 11 | 13 | 14 | 14 |
| NFPS debt/GDP | na | 26 | 26 | 30 | 35 | 42 | 48 | 54 | 54 |

Source: CGR.

Notes

na = Not available.

a Exports and imports data correspond to the balance of payments. Since 1994, a methodological change took place (see Manual V of the IMF).

b Net of transfers.

c Includes the Central Bank, decentralization entities, the central government, banks and other financial corporations.

d Since 1994, the external debt stock includes leasing and titularization.

discussed in this chapter, these trends are related to unsustainable fiscal policies, external shocks, as well as the country's internal political turmoil (which was not mentioned explicitly). In December 1999, Colombia signed a three-year agreement with the IMF to restore long-term economic growth, reduce inflation even further, and achieve an external sustainable position. This agreement would have required strong fiscal adjustment through a tight wage policy, a tax reform, a redesign of the transfer's policy, reforms in the pension system, and a downsizing of the public sector through privatization.

Some of these reforms were approved by congress throughout this period. However, they were insufficient to attain the expected fiscal adjustment. The NFPS cash deficit was 4.2 percent of GDP in 2001, a little larger than in 1999. At the beginning of 2003, the new Colombian authorities again signed a two-year agreement with the IMF (standby agreement) to carry on with the fiscal adjustment. They expect to reduce the deficit of the public sector at large down to 2.5 percent of GDP in 2003.

## Acknowledgments

The views expressed in the chapter are those of the authors and are not necessarily those of the Banco de la República. The authors wish to thank Dr Akira Kohsaka and Dr José Dario Uribe for comments and A. Samper, N. Espinosa, J. Berthel and M. Gómez for their valuable cooperation.

## Notes

1 If we add accrue basis operations, which are important in Colombia in the last few years, the public fiscal deficit reaches 6.3 percent of GDP in 1999.
2 See Joint Tax Program of the Organization of American States and the Inter-American Development Bank: Fiscal Mission to Colombia (1965) and Musgrave and Gilles (1971).
3 Details of this can be found in Hommes *et al.* (1994).
4 For further details on Colombia's exchange rate policy throughout this transition period, see Villar and Rincón (2000).

## References

Correa, P. (2000) "Public debt, public debt market and monetary policy in Colombia," *Borradores de Economía*, 147.

Fisher, S. and Easterley, W. (1990) "The economics of the government budget constraint," *The World Bank Research Observer*, 5.

Ghani, E. and Hyoungsoo, Z. (1995) *Is Ethiopia's Debt Sustainable?*, Policy Research Working Paper no. 1525, Washington, DC: World Bank.

Hernández, A., Lozano, I. and Misas, M. (2000) "La disyuntiva de la deuda pública: pagar o sisar," *Economía Institucional, Universidad Externado de Colombia*, 3.

Hommes, R., Montenegro, A. and Roda, P. (1994) "Una apertura hacia el futuro, Balance Económico 1990–1994," Bogotá: MHCP, DNP, FONADE.

International Monetary Fund (IMF) and World Bank (WB) (2000) *Draft Guidelines for Public Debt Management*, Washington, DC: IMF and WB.

Joint Tax Program of the Organization of American States and the Inter-American Development Bank: Fiscal Mission to Colombia (1965) *Fiscal Survey of Colombia*, Baltimore, MD: Johns Hopkins Press.

Martner, R. (2000) *Gestión pública y programación plurianual: Desafíos y experiencias recientes*, Bogotá: CEPAL ECLAC, UN.

Musgrave, R. and Gilles, M. (1971) *Fiscal Reform for Colombia: The Final Report and Staff Papers of the Colombian Commission on Tax Reform*, Cambridge, MA: Harvard University International Tax Program.

Perry, G. (1997) "Debt and fiscal sustainability: déjà vu?," unpublished manuscript, Washington, DC: World Bank.

Posada, C. (1999) "Señoraje, impuesto inflacionario y utilidades (brutas) del emisor: definiciones y medidas del caso colombiano reciente," *Borradores de Economía*, 140.

Villar, L. and Rincón, H. (2000) "The Colombian economy in the nineties: capital flows and foreign exchange regimes," *Borradores de Economía*, 149.

# 6 Ecuador

*Gustavo Arteta*

## Introduction

For decades, the Ecuadorian government has mismanaged public accounts, and this has led to generations of continuous deficits and accumulation of significant public debt, which has been defaulted three times since 1980. Meanwhile, the country's huge oil reserves have remained untapped and reforms have been held back, leaving natural phenomena and the price of oil to determine economic performance and fiscal finances.

The government has had fiscal deficits in twenty-one of the last thirty years as a result of structural deficiencies that have been unable to establish a core tax revenue base to complement the volatile revenues from petroleum exports. The ups and downs of oil prices have led to boom and bust cycles in government coffers that have, in turn, resulted in a systematic source of debt accumulation with a bias toward increasing expenditures during oil upswings and not reducing them in downtimes, leading to a structural deficit. Despite various reforms that sought to increase nonpetroleum revenues and that managed to decrease the share of oil revenues in total central government revenues from 71 percent in the 1970s to about 35 percent by 1999, successive governments have failed to fully address the heart of the country's fiscal problems.

The fiscal disarray, along with low economic growth, provided for a tendency to finance deficits through money creation that, in turn, resulted in chronic high inflation for years. The country suffered repeated currency and debt crises. In 1999 and 2000, these were pushed to the limit by a major financial crisis that strained government finances, generating a severe acceleration of inflation and devaluation. As a result, and in the midst of repeated political crises, Ecuador opted to abandon its currency and control of its monetary policy by adopting, in March 2000, the US dollar as the legal tender. This radical policy may well alter the past structural and institutional mechanisms that created a sort of "unpleasant monetarist arithmetic" where an almost permanent disorder of fiscal accounts handcuffed the central bank into printing money and generating inflation. At the same time, the monetary regime will demand stricter fiscal discipline in the future. Without the option of monetizing the deficits and in light of a highly indebted public sector with low creditworthiness, the government faces strict financing constraints that will almost eliminate the possibility of running deficits (at least in the near future).

This could help to place Ecuador on track toward fiscal sustainability. However, it will also challenge policy-makers and society as a whole into adopting the necessary fiscal policies that may, more responsibly, avoid possible costly real sector economic adjustments to external shocks.

This chapter seeks to present an overview of the conditions for sustainability of fiscal deficits and the consolidation of fiscal revenues and expenditures for sound fiscal management for the future. For this task, the next section presents an overview of the fiscal systems in Ecuador. This is followed by a section that summarizes the trends in revenues and expenditures in the past thirty years, focusing on the generation of deficits and growth in public debt. Subsequently, the chapter discusses fiscal sustainability issues for the future, and presents some concluding remarks.

## Overview of fiscal systems

The structure of the Ecuadorian public sector is based on a centralized budgetary system that governs most of the public sector finances, except for autonomous (off-budget) agencies and enterprises and local governments. The National Accounting Office of the Ministry of Economy and Finance (Dirección Nacional de Contabilidad de Ministerio de Economía y Finanzas) prepares on an annual basis the nonfinancial public sector (NFPS) balance; this NFPS balance consolidates the accounts based on the different government levels and agencies that comprise the NFPS. Fiscal statistics are presented for the "central government," the "rest of public administration" and "public enterprises." Table 6.1 presents the consolidation process through which the NFPS is obtained.

Annually, the president presents a budget to congress that comprises the revenues and expenditures for centralized public administration.[1] This budget is the focus of a great deal of public attention. Yet, for most macroeconomic evaluations and International Monetary Fund programs, the consolidated NFPS receives most of the attention. Over the years, the share of the central government in the NFPS has grown from about 50 percent in the 1980s to 73 percent in the late 1990s. In

*Table 6.1* Consolidation of the nonfinancial public sector

| *Public entities* |
|---|
| 1 Budgetary central government and state entities |
| a Central government |
| b National treasury |
| c Decentralized entities |
| 2 Rest of public administration |
| a Ecuadorian Social Security Institute (IESS) |
| b Autonomous entities |
| c Local government |
| d Provincial councils |
| e Municipal councils |
| f Other local government entities |
| 3 Public enterprises (operational balance) |

large part, this is because of a decline in central government transfers to local governments, which have been the casualties of the adjustment and austerity programs that have demanded cuts in public spending.

In terms of data, there are readily available statistics for the central government accounts reported on a cash basis. However, data since 1986 on an accrual basis are only available. Meanwhile, data since 1988 for the consolidated NFPS are only available. This situation forces the discussion to focus on the central government in the 1970s and 1980s in particular. For the last decade, the analysis concentrates on the NFPS but also makes references to the central government, when historical comparisons are called for.

## Trends in fiscal development

Since Ecuador began producing oil in the early 1970s, economic growth has largely tracked the performance of this sector (Figure 6.1). Between 1970 and 1979, GDP grew at an annual average rate of about 9 percent, when large-scale exploitation of oil commenced. In the 1980s, as the OPEC boom ended and prices fell, the economy stagnated and barely surpassed population growth at 2.3 percent annually. In the 1990s, because of the continued large world supply of oil, oil prices continued to be depressed along with economic growth, which averaged 1.9 percent per year.

The transformation of the economy by the large-scale exploitation, however, also produced a "Dutch disease" in the government accounts. Petroleum earnings as a share of total central government revenues climbed from 8 percent in 1970 to an average of 80 percent during the 1970s. Under a series of military dictatorships during the decade, tax collection gave way to OPEC-fueled revenues and 121 percent real growth in central government expenditures. In US dollar terms (at a

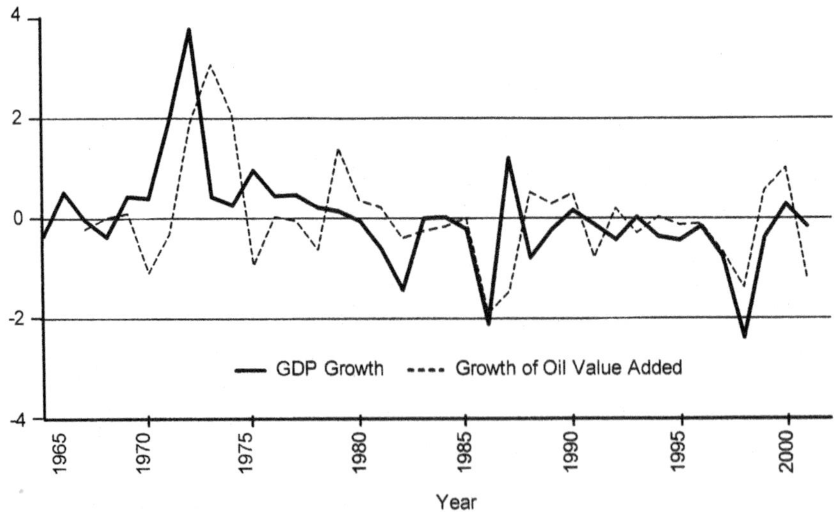


*Figure 6.1* Growth in GDP and the oil sector in Ecuador.

fixed exchange rate that prevailed during the decade), central government expenditures grew from US$256 million in 1970 to US$1.6 billion in 1980. The country lost the sense of "tax-paying" at the national and local levels and that, in turn, created a fatal dependence on oil revenue. Once the boom ended in 1980, the country found itself with growing fiscal deficits, ballooning foreign debt, an aversion to tax paying and collecting, as well as deficient fiscal institutions and policies.

In the 1980s and 1990s, various attempts at structural reform were made. However, these created a vicious cycle of austerity packages, devaluations and public protests that were followed by a slackening of fiscal policy and accelerating inflation. As a result, Ecuador defaulted or fell into debt arrears three times, inflation averaged 40 percent annually, and the country devalued its currency 88,900 percent in 20 years.

This dismal history notwithstanding, a glimmer of light has been shed in the last three years as a result of a few trend-breaking reforms that have transformed the tax collection agency and have given the country, for the first time, a chance to stabilize its fiscal accounts.

### *The 1970s*

The oil boom of the 1970s allowed the government to expand by 121 percent between 1970 and 1980 (in terms of constant sucres). Moreover, even though revenues grew by 183 percent, the fiscal deficit (on a cash basis) of the central government averaged −1.8 percent annually during the 1970s and accumulated US$653 million in deficit spending in ten years (or 17.8 percent of GDP). These data are similar to those typically presented for government statistics by the International Monetary Fund, which only covers the central government for Ecuador.

As remarkable as these figures are, however, they mask total growth of the state. Off-budget ancillary government agencies and public enterprises ballooned and multiplied. While in 1965 there were 36 public sector agencies, by 1976 these had increased to 163. A consolidated balance could capture the impact of this increase in government size, but unfortunately, this information is not available. Nevertheless, the growth in government debt during this period provides a proxy for the size of the accumulated deficits of the entire government. Total public debt grew between 1970 and 1979, and by the end of the decade, public debt was almost 40 percent of GDP (Table 6.2).

### *The 1980s*

The growth in revenues and potential revenues from expected oil reserves also stimulated private sector indebtedness to finance imports and the flourishing of an inefficient domestic industry under heavy protection from foreign competition. But all of this came to an abrupt end when the oil prices collapsed and commercial bank credit lines dried up in the early 1980s. Table 6.3 gives a summary of central government finances.

Coming into the 1980s, the large capital inflows from petroleum and a fixed

*Table 6.2* Key economic indicators for Ecuador

| | *1970* | *1975* | *1980* | *1985* | *1990* | *1996* | *1998* | *1999* | *2000* |
|---|---|---|---|---|---|---|---|---|---|
| GDP at market prices (S/. bn) | 35 | 108 | 293 | 1,110 | 8,204 | 60,727 | 107,421 | 161,350 | 312,422 |
| GDP (US$ m) | 1,629 | 4,310 | 11,733 | 11,890 | 10,569 | 19,157 | 19,710 | 13,769 | 12,498 |
| Real GDP growth (%) | 6.5 | 5.6 | 4.9 | 4.3 | 3.0 | 2.0 | 0.4 | −7.3 | 0.9 |
| Consumer price inflation (avg.; %) | 9.1 | 10.0 | 9.2 | 24.4 | 48.2 | 24.3 | 36.1 | 52.2 | 99.1 |
| Consumer price inflation (end of period; %) | na | na | na | 28.0 | 49.5 | 25.4 | 43.4 | 60.7 | 85.1 |
| Exchange rate (avg.; S/. per $)[a] | 21 | 25 | 25 | 93 | 776 | 3,189 | 5,442 | 11,828 | 24,997 |
| Population (million) | 5.9 | 7.0 | 8.1 | 9.1 | 10.3 | 11.7 | 12.2 | 12.4 | 12.6 |
| Population growth (%) | 3.3 | 3.1 | 2.9 | 2.6 | 2.3 | 2.1 | 2.0 | 1.9 | 1.9 |
| Merchandise exports (US$ m) | na | na | na | na | 2,714 | 4,900 | 4,203 | 4,451 | 5,014 |
| Merchandise imports (US$ m) | 190 | 974 | 2,481 | 2,905 | 1,862 | 3,680 | 5,198 | 2,786 | 3,082 |
| Current account (US$ m) | 274 | 987 | 2,253 | 1,767 | −360 | 111 | −2,169 | 955 | 640 |
| Reserves (US$ m) | −113 | −220 | −642 | 76 | 603 | 1,831 | 1,276 | 1,068 | 1,238 |
| Petroleum exports | na | na | na | na | 1,418 | 1,776 | 923 | 1,480 | 2,431 |
| | | | | | | | | | |
| Central gov't total revenue | 10.6 | 11.5 | 12.8 | 17.1 | 16.5 | 14.7 | 16.2 | 19.8 | 22.4 |
| Central gov't total expenditure | 15.0 | 12.1 | 14.2 | 15.1 | 14.7 | 18.0 | 16.8 | 20.5 | 22.5 |
| Central government balance | −4.4 | −0.6 | −1.4 | 2.0 | 1.8 | −0.5 | −0.7 | −0.7 | −0.1 |
| NFPS total revenue | na | na | na | na | 27.1 | 24.4 | 20.3 | 25.3 | 29.1 |
| NFPS total expenditure | na | na | na | na | 26.6 | 27.5 | 26.3 | 31.2 | 28.7 |
| NFPS balance | na | na | na | na | 0.5 | −3.1 | −6.0 | −5.9 | 0.4 |
| Total public debt | 35.7 | 20.3 | 38.8 | 71.1 | 97.4 | 75.6 | 82.3 | 115.5 | 96.1 |
| | | | | | | | | | |
| Oil exports/fiscal revenue | na | na | 22.9 | 15.9 | 35.7 | 20.2 | 6.2 | 21.2 | 28.9 |

Sources: Central Bank of Ecuador (1993, 1997, various years a, various years b); Ministerio de Economía y Finanzas (2003).

Note

na = Not available.

*Table 6.3* Summary of central government finances (as a % of GDP)

| | *1970–99* | *1970–79* | *1980–89* | *1990–99* | *1990–94* | *1995–99* |
|---|---|---|---|---|---|---|
| Deficit (–)/surplus (+) | −1.0 | −1.8 | −1.5 | 0.4 | 1.7 | −0.9 |
| Total current and capital revenues | 13.6 | 11.1 | 13.2 | 16.7 | 15.7 | 17.6 |
| Total current and capital expenditures (excluding Amt) | 14.6 | 12.9 | 14.7 | 16.3 | 14.0 | 18.5 |
| Deficit financing | 1.0 | 1.8 | 1.5 | −0.4 | −1.7 | 0.9 |
| Net foreign financing | −0.3 | 0.1 | 0.3 | −1.4 | −2.0 | −0.7 |
| Net domestic financing | 1.3 | 1.7 | 1.2 | 1.0 | 0.3 | 1.6 |
| Memo: | | | | | | |
| Interest payments | 1.5 | 0.0 | 1.0 | 3.4 | 2.6 | 4.1 |
| Primary balance | 0.5 | −1.8 | −0.4 | 3.8 | 4.3 | 3.2 |
| Total disbursements (foreign + domestic) | 2.9 | 1.8 | 2.7 | 4.2 | 1.3 | 7.1 |
| Total amortization (foreign + domestic) | 1.9 | 0.0 | 1.1 | 4.5 | 2.4 | 6.5 |
| Budgetary balance | 0.1 | 0.0 | 0.1 | 0.2 | 0.6 | −0.2 |
| Deficit (on an accrual basis) | na | na | na | −0.9 | 1.0 | −2.8 |

Sources: Banco Central del Ecuador (1993, 1997, various issues a, various issues b).

Note
na = Not available.

exchange rate that had kept inflation at an average 12 percent during the 1970s caused a significant appreciation of the currency that further deteriorated the fiscal accounts when world interest rates surged. The growing burden of interest payments for private and public external debt and the curtailment of capital flows, as other developing countries began facing the incipience of the 1980s' debt crisis, brought a balance-of-payments crisis for Ecuador. The government was forced to devalue for the first time in over a decade, leading the private sector debt to be at risk of default. In a controversial policy, the government at that time assumed about US$3 billion of the private external debt, increasing total public debt from 39 percent of GDP in 1980 to 70 percent in 1984. Initially the debt was exchanged with domestic sucre-denominated debt at market terms, but in an exemplary case of time inconsistency in government policy, a few years later, interest and the indexing norms were abolished, such that with the high inflation and devaluation, the debt was effectively repudiated. Meanwhile, the fiscal accounts deteriorated as debt payments ballooned and oil prices fell. The inward-looking economy fell into a recession. Between 1981 and 1986, GDP only grew 2.1 percent annually on average, and was not even near the rate of population growth.

The hard times got worse in 1987, when earthquakes ruptured the main oil pipeline, forcing the suspension of petroleum exports for about half the year.

Revenues from oil fell by 2.3 percentage points of GDP and the recession also led to a decline in tax revenues. The inflexibility of expenditures due to the high and growing interest burden, together with the widespread use of earmarking, caused the nonfinancial sector balance to reach −10 percent of GDP. With such a high deficit, despite falling into significant arrears, the government had to resort to central bank financing. Consequently, inflation rose rapidly. During this period, the ratio of public debt to GDP rose above 110 percent in 1988.

A new government in 1988 proceeded to implement strong adjustment measures to bring down inflation from 90 percent, reduce the fiscal deficit and build up international reserves which were in the red. Tax increases and reductions in tax loopholes, as well as subsidy reductions, helped to bring down the NFPS deficit to 5.3 percent. In 1989, expenditures were further cut and aided by a slight increase in oil prices (from about US$12 per barrel to US$16.2 per barrel) that helped the government to reduce the deficit to around 1.2 percent. By 1990, the economy grew by 3 percent and by 1991, growth was 5 percent. However inflation was only brought down to 60 percent (at year end) and debt arrears continued to accumulate as only partial payments were being made to commercial banks and on the bilateral debt. The adjustment process was derailed and the IMF program was not completed. The government faced stiff opposition in congress and the public was less acquiescent to further squeezing of subsidies and hikes in the rates of public services.

### *The 1990s*

A new government in 1992 attempted to introduce a far-reaching reform program of economic liberalization and privatization. However, political opposition, divisions within the government itself and a string of external shocks halted other reforms and the planned privatization program. The fiscal accounts were kept in control averaging −1.3 percent of GDP per year for the NFPS, while the central government ran a 0.2 percent surplus.

Economic stabilization and moderate deregulation, as well as debt renegotiations and clean-up of arrears with the Paris Club and private creditors (in a Brady deal), made Ecuador more attractive for foreign investment and restoration of credit lines gave way to important capital inflows (though small by Asian standards) and to a credit boom (Arteta 2000). Expansion of credit (especially dollar-denominated credit), rising consumer demand and expectations of growth continued to bolster consumer confidence and financial services. The downside to this was a deterioration in the current account balance, as the overvalued exchange rate induced import growth.

A series of external shocks and increased political instability brought an abrupt end to this nascent boom in 1995. The costs of the short border conflict with Peru strained the public sector budget, and imports of armaments contributed to a widening of the current account deficit. Political uncertainty increased and as capital flows reversed, the Central Bank of Ecuador raised interest rates to prevent capital from leaving the country.[2] The NFPS deficit reached 6 percent of GDP in 1998 as world oil prices fell to less than US$7 per barrel and the recession depressed tax revenues.

The steady increase in financing needs was covered by domestic debt, which grew from US$776 million in 1996 to US$3.3 billion in the first quarter of 2000. As a result, the government's borrowing crowded out the private sector and contributed to the rise in interest rates. At the same time, the Central Bank's efforts to contain the pressure on the sucre through interest rate hikes only aggravated the financial sector's problems. As both the exchange rate and interest rates rose, debtors' problems were compounded and finally led to an escalation of a series of bank collapses.[3] An unprecedented "bank holiday" followed by a year-long emergency freeze on bank deposits wiped out domestic demand. GDP contracted by 7.3 percent in 1999.

The severe bank crises ran up a fiscal tab, estimated at over 22 percent of GDP, that was paid by domestic debt and central bank financing. Domestic debt climbed from 8.4 percent of GDP at the end of 1997 to 24 percent of GDP in 1999. Toward the end of 1999, the government faced stiff cash flow deficits that resulted in the decision to curtail servicing of the Brady and Eurobond debt. This worsened the condition of the private sector, which saw its external credit lines close as Ecuador's country risk went up and its creditworthiness nose-dived.

The large money creation used to bail out some banks and to pay the deposit guarantee contributed to acceleration of inflation and devaluation. These factors outweighed the impact of the huge contraction in domestic demand and the bank deposit freeze, leading inflation to rise to 61 percent by the end of 1999 and the exchange rate, which was freed early in 1999, to be devalued 200 percent.

In the first few days of 2000, a 25 percent fall in the sucre was the final straw. In January 2000, President Mahuad was forced out of office and the post was assumed by then-Vice President, Gustavo Noboa. However, Mr Noboa put in place his predecessor's proposal to adopt the US dollar as the country's legal tender. Following the dollarization announcement, consumer prices raced to reach a par with purchasing power parity levels and inflation peaked at 108 percent before it started to come down at the end of 2000. The government secured an IMF Standby Program (the first in five years). Throughout the year, fiscal finances were greatly helped by the booming oil price and a remarkable effort in tax collection, which allowed a fiscal surplus at the central government and NFPS levels.

### *Structure of revenues and expenditures*

The nonfinancial public sector has averaged 24.5 percent of GDP in total revenues. About 32 percent of this revenue comes from nontax (petroleum) revenues, 58 percent from tax revenues and the remainder from the operating surplus of public enterprises. The average 1988–99 is shown in Table 6.4.

Oil revenues come mostly from the export sales of petroleum by the national petroleum enterprise, PETROECUADOR. About 15 percent of revenues are generated by the sale of domestic consumption fuels and royalties paid by foreign oil firms that have concessions to exploit some oil fields.

The expenditure side has averaged 26.8 percent of GDP between 1988 and 1999 (Table 6.5), 76 percent of which are current expenditures and 24 percent

*Table 6.4* Consolidated nonfinancial public sector revenue (on an accrual basis; as a % of GDP)

| *Revenue* | *Average 1988–99* |
|---|---|
| NFPS total revenue | 24.54 |
| Total current revenue | 24.54 |
| Tax revenue | 14.30 |
| Direct taxes (income) | 1.55 |
| Indirect taxes | 12.76 |
| On international trade | 1.95 |
| Value added tax | 3.33 |
| Capital transactions tax | 0.20 |
| Other (including nontax fees) | 7.28 |
| Nontax revenue | 8.10 |
| Oil exports | 5.57 |
| Domestic fuel sales | 2.53 |
| Other | 0.00 |
| Surplus of public enterprises | 2.14 |

Sources: Banco Central del Ecuador (1993, 1997, various issues a, various issues b).

*Table 6.5* Consolidated nonfinancial public sector expenditure (on an accrual basis; as a % of GDP)

| *Expenditure* | *Average 1988–99* |
|---|---|
| Total expenditure | 26.84 |
| Current expenditure | 20.06 |
| Wages and salaries | 7.74 |
| Goods and services | 2.56 |
| Transfers (social security) | 0.00 |
| Interest payments | 5.61 |
| External debt | 4.65 |
| Internal debt | 0.97 |
| Others | 4.14 |
| Total capital expenditures | 6.78 |
| Fixed investment | 6.33 |
| Central government | 1.68 |
| Public enterprises | 2.47 |
| Rest of the central government | 2.19 |
| Other capital expenditures | 0.45 |
| Overall balance (– = deficit) | –2.30 |
| Primary balance (– = deficit) | 3.32 |

Sources: Banco Central del Ecuador (1993, 1997, various issues a, various issues b).

capital expenditures. Wages and salaries account for 28 percent of total expenditures or 38 percent of current expenditures. Interest payments represent one-third of current expenditures and the line labeled "other" which corresponds to transfers is 20 percent of current expenditures.

This structure of government finances does not suggest a "bloated" state compared to international averages (International Monetary Fund, various years). The same is true for the central government, which averaged 17.6 percent of GDP. For the period for which data are available, i.e., 1986–2001, the NFPS reported an average primary surplus of 4.7 percent of GDP, which shows that every year the state makes a considerable effort to service its debt. Despite this, the average interest bill of 6 percent of GDP has strained the government and made it at times unsustainable.

## Debt dynamics

From 36 percent of GDP in 1970, the debt stock climbed to an average of 87 percent of GDP in the 1980s and 1990s, of which 80 percent are foreign obligations (Table 6.6). The off and on reform efforts, excessive dependence on volatile oil revenues led Ecuador to default or fall into debt arrears thrice in twenty years. It is evident from Figure 6.2, which marks the periods of debt defaults, that these defaults have come after episodes of explosive growth of the debt-to-GDP series. The last two defaults came at the point when the ratio had surpassed 100 percent of GDP. The experience suggests that Ecuador's debt servicing difficulties reflect severe unresolved structural troubles that become unsustainable debt-financed fiscal deficits.

The debt problems that began in the early 1980s were on bilateral debt and these extended to commercial bank debt in the mid-1980s. As a result of several restructurings during most of the 1990s, Ecuador's external public debt declined gradually as a proportion of GDP. In 1994, Ecuador adopted the Brady Plan proposal by converting old commercial bank debt into a Brady Bond package. Under

*Table 6.6* Public debt, 1970–2002

| | *Total public debt* | | *External debt* | | *Domestic debt* | |
|---|---|---|---|---|---|---|
| | *% of GDP* | *US$ m* | *% of GDP* | *US$ m* | *% of GDP* | *US$ m* |
| 1970 | 35.7 | 581 | 13.1 | 213 | 22.6 | 368 |
| 1975 | 20.3 | 874 | 9.5 | 410 | 10.8 | 464 |
| 1980 | 38.8 | 4,553 | 30.3 | 3,554 | 8.5 | 999 |
| 1985 | 71.1 | 8,456 | 63.9 | 7,596 | 7.2 | 860 |
| 1990 | 116.0 | 12,265 | 114.0 | 12,052 | 2.0 | 213 |
| 1994 | 90.0 | 15,193 | 81.5 | 13,758 | 8.5 | 1,435 |
| 1995 | 77.0 | 13,857 | 68.7 | 12,379 | 8.2 | 1,478 |
| 1999 | 121.1 | 16,676 | 97.1 | 13,372 | 24.0 | 3,304 |
| 2002 | 68.6 | 14,106 | 55.1 | 11,337 | 13.5 | 2,769 |

Sources: Banco Central del Ecuador (1993, 1997, various years a, various years b).

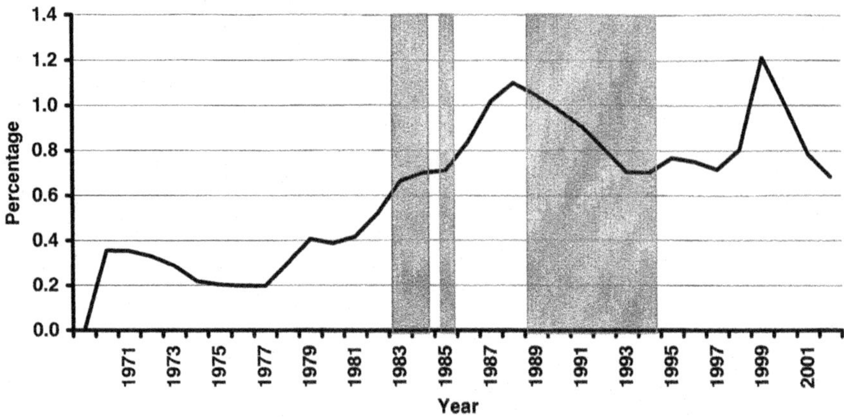


*Figure 6.2* Total public debt-to-GDP ratio and periods of default.

Note
Shaded areas represent periods of default.

this agreement with creditors, to which many countries adhered, most of the debt burden was postponed for five years whence service would be restarted. The plan assumed that the economy would grow at a faster rate than external interest rates as a result of an aggressive modernization plan geared to transform the state and to enhance productivity. However, political barriers prevented the reforms from taking place and domestic public debt grew at an alarming pace to finance growing deficits. The crisis that ensued in 1999 pushed the fiscal accounts into dire cash flow difficulties forcing the government, in November 1999, to declare another moratorium on its service of Brady and Eurobond debt.

Ecuador's debt defaults are indicative of the violation of the basic long-run intertemporal requirement that the real growth rate of the economy must be greater than the real interest rate paid on the debt. Between 1990 and 2000, Ecuador paid an average implicit real interest rate of 3.4 percent, while the average annual real growth rate of GDP was 1.9 percent. From Figure 6.3, it is evident that the real interest rate was greater than economic growth from 1995 onward. Weighing in the fact that the stock of debt during the period was very high, the difference in the rates for five straight years resulted in the last default. Clearly, these trends suggest that the future fiscal sustainability of the country will depend on policies and economic conditions that reverse them.

By 2000, and following the bond restructuring, the external debt stock was reduced from US$13.4 billion to US$10.9 billion. As a share of GDP, it fell from 97 percent to 80 percent. Subsequently, three consecutive years of fiscal surpluses and economic recovery have reduced total public debt as a share of GDP from 121 percent of GDP in 1999 to 68.6 percent in 2002. At least in this respect, the straitjacket that dollarization implies for fiscal policy has been binding. In the future, all expectations are for continuous surpluses that should gradually reduce the debt burden. However, the structure of the amortization profile in the coming

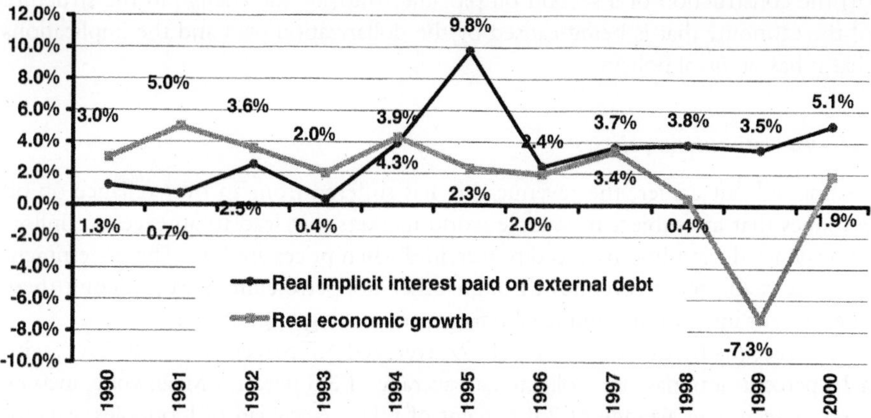


*Figure 6.3* Real GDP growth and the real implicit interest rate paid on debt.

years suggests that additional restructurings will be needed. To this end, the current government is seeking from Paris Club countries an exchange of bilateral debt for social projects. In addition, a debt repayment fund has been set up to use new oil revenues that will be forthcoming from the new oil pipeline that will begin operations in 2003.

## Fiscal sustainability and consolidation: future challenges

Arteta and Samaniego (2001) estimate that the government has a substantial positive net worth[4] to use if the government could capitalize on existing oil reserves. The excess of the present value of government assets over that of current and contingent liabilities suggests a possibility for long-term sustainability. If the government could approach world capital markets, it could solve the short-term problems. However, as capital markets are not perfect and Ecuador's access to them is limited, the government faces the short-run challenge of realizing its assets to pay its current liabilities. Consequently, the degree of solvency will depend on the government's short-run liquidity. This brings to bear the reform requirements in revenue generation and expenditure structure and control.

The institutional, legal and implementation deficiencies of fiscal policies that are carried over from the past require much work ahead in order for the government to change the running deficits. The austere–expansionary–austere cycle of policies has not sustained a long-term outlook that is needed to set the tone for economic stability and growth. Tackling these problems will be key for the economy's future. In the long run, the country can tap into its assets to pay for its existing current and contingent liabilities. However, in the short and medium term, it must take the necessary actions to avoid problems from the past by raising revenues, cutting expenditure or a combination of the two.

These notwithstanding, three issues are particularly important and are worthy of highlight: (i) the recent remarkable turnaround in tax administration and collections;

(ii) the construction of a second oil pipeline; and (iii) the change in the structure of the economy that is being caused by the dollarization plan and the implications that it has on fiscal policy.

### *Revenue-enhancing policies*

As pointed out earlier, the revenue side has suffered from an over-reliance on oil revenues that are subject to volatile world markets that lead to an excessive inflow of revenues during booms and dire scarcities when prices are low. The government needs to stabilize its revenues through other nonpetroleum sources. Along these lines, recent institutional and legal reforms are making huge strides.

Tax receipts between 1993 and 1997 averaged 6.7 percent of GDP. VAT, with a 10 percent nominal rate, collected an average of 3.5 percent. Meanwhile, income taxes collected an average of 2.0 percent of GDP. A myriad of loopholes, exemptions, and occurrences of sophisticated evasion prevailed in the tax system. Corrupt bureaucrats were in control of the tax collections department of the Ministry of Finance, and this ministry had never established a tax accounting system. Forms for filing taxes were outdated, and the ministry did not have an information cross-checking system. In short, the country did not have a modern, functioning tax administration entity. This weak legal and institutional structure was a major obstacle to any sort of tax policy.

Extraordinarily, in the midst of the worst economic crisis on the century, Ecuador made significant progress in tax reform and institutional building. In 1997, the Servicio de Rentas Internas (SRI, Internal Revenue Service) was created as an autonomous agency. The first year was dedicated to organizing and cleaning up the disarray that was inherited from the old tax collection department of the Ministry of Finance, and in 1998 the SRI began changing the government's poor track record in tax collection. The institution was strengthened through tax reforms in 1998, 1999 and 2000 that gave the SRI more power and instruments to collect more effectively and penalize tax evaders. The number of registered taxpayers has increased from 150,000 at the end of 1998 to over 3 million and the ministry is on its way toward consolidating the information-crossing systems to clamp down on evasion. Its campaigns have been helped by notorious sanctions given out to businesses and the arrest and incarceration of one of the wealthiest businessmen in the country for tax fraud.

After 1997, and especially after 1999, tax collection underwent a transformation. By 2001, total collections had almost doubled to 13.2 percent of GDP. Income taxes grew 64 percent, reaching record levels in 2001. Excise taxes grew 46 percent in relation to GDP, and other taxes improved by 39 percent (Table 6.7).

The most striking outcome was the significant improvement in VAT collection. From its 1993–97 average (3.5 percent of GDP), VAT collection grew 137 percent to 8.2 percent of GDP in 2001. This implies an efficiency improvement from an average of 35 percent for 1993–97 to 68 percent in 2001, the highest among the Latin American countries.

In the coming years, the government has plans to tackle problems in customs,

*Table 6.7* Tax collections by SRI, 1997–2001 (as a % of GDP)

| | *Avg. 1993–97* | *1998* | *1999* | *2000* | *2001* | *Difference from average* | *% change* |
|---|---|---|---|---|---|---|---|
| Total tax collection | 6.7 | 7.4 | 10.0 | 12.3 | 13.2 | 6.5 | 98 |
| Income tax (personal + corporate) | 2.0 | 2.1 | 0.7 | 2.0 | 3.2 | 1.3 | 64 |
| Value-added tax | 3.5 | 4.2 | 4.5 | 6.8 | 8.2 | 4.7 | 137 |
| Excise consumption taxes | 0.7 | 0.6 | 0.6 | 0.7 | 1.0 | 0.3 | 46 |
| Other[a] | 0.5 | 0.6 | 4.3 | 2.9 | 0.7 | 0.2 | 39 |
| Nominal VAT rate (%) | 10 | 10 | 10 | 12 | 12 | 0.02 | 20 |

Sources: Banco Central del Ecuador (various years b); Servicio de Rentas Internas (2003).

Note

a Excludes social security contributions and other local taxes not collected by Servicio de Rentas Internas.

where evasion and corruption remain rampant. In this connection, it has presented a bill to Congress that would call for the SRI to take over the administration of the customs with which it expects to obtain between 2–4 percent of GDP of duties and taxes that are annually being evaded.

By the end of 2002, the government will also begin to receive the benefits of granting a private consortium of firms the rights to build a second oil pipeline. Ecuador has been hampered by a transportation bottleneck for years while political debates killed various plans. In 2001, the contract was signed with a company that will, at their own risk, build the pipeline in 25 months. The new pipeline will more that double transport capacity from 390,000 barrels per day to 900,000 barrels per day and should gradually provide an additional 2–4 percent of GDP in oil fiscal revenues.

Summed together, the above actions are on track to provide between 3 to 8 percentage points of GDP in additional revenues compared to the average of the last decade. The most uncertain reforms are those pertaining to customs. But even without the latter, one could expect that as long as expenditure growth is controlled, the fiscal imbalances of the past could be gradually eliminated. Of course, not increasing expenditures is likely to be a challenge in a weak political system, which could be tempted to spend all of the new resources.

### *Expenditure controls and targeting*

At the same time that revenues have been volatile, expenditures have been particularly rigid because of the widespread use of earmarked items and the burden of debt service that ranges from 40 to 55 percent of total NFPS expenditures from year to year. Overall, about 92 percent of fiscal revenues are either earmarked or pre-committed to servicing public debt and entitlements. This situation clearly makes it very difficult for a government to implement fiscal policy in any significant sense. The interest burden will be somewhat alleviated following the renegotiation of the global bonds. However, the Paris Club debt has not been restructured and the current proposal to transform external debt obligations into domestic social obligations would not change the total expenditure level. If this bilateral debt can be swapped with social projects, the funds that are now destined to debt service could be used in domestic projects that are aimed at health, education and other social targets.

With regard to earmarking, the IMF and World Bank have pressed Ecuador to reduce or eliminate the practice, but these efforts have proven futile against political opposition. In the second semester of 2002, the government plans to introduce a reform proposal to reduce earmarking. Early indications of the political scene, however, point toward a tug of interest between group powers that may allow the elimination of some earmarking but not far-reaching reform.

### *Policy challenges under dollarization*

Implementation of the radical step to do away with the domestic currency and to adopt the US dollar as the legal tender poses various policy challenges. By losing monetary and exchange rate policy instruments to counter exogenous shocks, fiscal policy has become all the more important. In particular, fiscal policy must allow greater stability of revenues and flexibility of expenditures.

Dollarization has already borne out some results. Inflation has declined rapidly. After peaking at 108 percent in September 2000, it fell to 9.4 percent in December 2002. Producer price inflation reached −5.6 percent year-on-year in April 2001, compared to 300 percent just 12 months earlier. In addition, fiscal revenues have benefited from the disappearing potential for firms and individuals to evade tax obligations by exaggerating exchange rate and monetary adjustments to balance sheets. Without an exchange rate effect on businesses' balance sheets, the reported profits are more accurate. As a result, profits are more transparent, which increases the taxable base and transparency. This will almost certainly allow for improved tax collections in the future.

Dollarization will also help government cash flows related to the exchange rate loss in interest payments. Since almost close to 99 percent of foreign debt is denominated in US dollars and over 65 percent of domestic debt was dollar-denominated (before the dollarization), devaluations tended to increase the interest bill in sucres. Considering that interest payments represent about 35 percent of total expenditures, the exchange rate effect was significant. Therefore, the dollarization of the economy will alleviate the additional burden that devaluations had on the fiscal balance.

On the negative side, the change in regime also leads to a loss of about 2 percent of GDP in seignorage annually, according to central bank estimates. These helped to finance the government deficits over the years and will need to be substituted from other sources. Also, dollarization has taken away the nominal adjustment mechanisms to external shocks. Fiscal policy is the only instrument left, and as was pointed out earlier, the expenditure side lacks the desirable flexibility to accommodate any economic fluctuation, in particular that coming from oil prices.

In 2002, Congress passed the Fiscal Responsibility Law that establishes various spending growth rules and an oil stabilization and debt repayment fund. The rules should help control the growth of expenditures and reduction in the non-oil deficit (of about 5 percent). The oil fund earmarks the windfalls from the new pipeline to paying off the debt and accumulation of a fiscal stabilization fund. While the legislation still contains some wrinkles that need to be taken care of, it has elements that should contribute to fiscal sustainability.

In the middle of the debate, the role, if there is one, for the Central Bank of Ecuador in the dollar-system is being analyzed. On this, there seems to be a gap in the academic literature on dollarization. Most of the studies limit the analysis to portraying the Panama system as compared to a currency board—like Argentina—system, while rekindling the ageless merits and vices of flexible versus fixed exchange rates.[5] Regardless, Ecuador is experimenting with a system that does not have any clear prior examples, and, while not all implications may have been identified, it is clear that the only traditional policy instrument left with wide scope is fiscal policy. It is quite possible that the steps taken by the government in the future may well determine the fate of the dollarization plan.

## Conclusion: policy issues and future prospects

This chapter has described the development of fiscal accounts since 1970. It identifies that the revenue and spending structures have been insufficient to provide a sustainable fiscal situation. The volatility of oil revenues together with inflexibility on the spending side has generated continuous fiscal deficits and the build-up of public debt. Since for extended periods the real growth rate of the economy has been less than the real interest rate, the debt surpassed 100 percent of GDP on various occasions and this resulted in debt defaults.

Fiscal sustainability in the future will depend on the government's ability to provide more stable revenue sources and to create budgeting flexibility on the expenditure side. For the first challenge, the government must continue the process of strengthening the revenue base through the tax system. The construction of the second pipeline will also help to cash in on the country's vast oil reserves. However, unless these revenues are channeled responsibly through a stabilization fund, they will likely create the same boom–bust cycle experienced in the past. Expenditure cuts and the elimination of earmarking will also be necessary but this will face political difficulties.

The adoption of the US dollar as the country's currency poses various policy challenges. While it will help to stabilize prices, by losing monetary and exchange rate policy instruments to counter exogenous shocks, fiscal policy will become all the more important. At the same time, the loss of central bank financing will force the government to balance its accounts.

## Notes

1 The consolidation excludes the financial public sector, which includes the Central Bank and other public lending institutions.

2 Since 1995, producers and the financial sector have struggled against lower liquidity, rising interest rates and bad debts. The export sector was unable to compensate fully for these difficulties, with major products such as bananas, oil, coffee and prawns facing poor international trading conditions or domestic production problems. GDP growth rates have been low and declining. Only in 1997 did economic growth exceed the rate of population growth. In 1998 and 1999, the El Niño climatic pattern devastated key export crops and destroyed road infrastructure, and, in turn, depressed the economy. The NFPS deficit in mid-1998 was projected at over 10 percent of GDP as world oil prices fell to less than US$7 per barrel, but drastic measures by the government toward the end of the year were able to cut the deficit in half.

3 In August 1998, there were forty-one private banks and one public commercial bank operating. By December 1999, there were twenty-seven banks operating, of which four were in state hands. In terms of bank assets, over 70 percent of the system had either failed or had been bailed out by the state.

4 They estimate that without considering the existence of what they call "social debt," the government has a positive net worth of almost 90 percent of GDP.

5 See, for example, Hausman (1999), Schuler (1999), McKinnon (2000) and Frankel (1999).

## References

Arteta, Gustavo (2000) "Uso, destino, y consecuencias del capital extranjero en El Ecuador en los 1990," Nota Técnica, Dirección General de Estudios, Quito: Banco Central del Ecuador.

Arteta, Gustavo and Samaniego, P. (2001) "Government net worth and fiscal sustainability in Ecuador," in World Bank, *Government Net Worth in Andean Countries*, Washington, DC: World Bank.

Banco Central del Ecuador [Central Bank of Ecuador] (1993) *Deuda Externa Ecuatoriana 1970–1991*, Quito: Banco Central del Ecuador.

Banco Central del Ecuador [Central Bank of Ecuador] (1997) *Setenta Años de Información Estadística*, various issues, Quito: Banco Central del Ecuador.

Banco Central del Ecuador [Central Bank of Ecuador] (various years a) *Boletín Anual*, various issues, 1980–2000, Quito: Banco Central del Ecuador.

Banco Central del Ecuador [Central Bank of Ecuador] (various years b) *Información Estadística Mensual*, various issues, 1992–2003, Quito: Banco Central del Ecuador.

Calvo, Guillermo (1999) "Fixed versus flexible exchange rates: preliminaries of a turn-of-millennium rematch," mimeo, available at: www.bsoso.unmd.edu/econ/.

Frankel, Jeffrey (1999) "No single currency regime is right for all countries or at all times," *Essays in International Finance*, 215.

Hausman, Ricardo (1999) "The exchange rate debate," in R. Hausman (ed.) *Latin American Economic Policies*, vol. 7, Washington, DC: Inter-American Development Bank.

McKinnon, Ronald (2000) "Mundell, the euro, and optimum currency areas," mimeo.

Ministerio de Economía y Finanzas [Ministry of Economy and Finance] (2003) available at: www.sigov.gov.ec.

Schuler, Kurt (1999) "Basics of dollarization," *Joint Committee Staff Report*, July, available at: www.senate.gob/jec/basics.htm.

Servicio de Rentas Internas (SRI) (2003) available at: www.sri.gov.ec.

# 7 Indonesia

*Ari Kuncoro*

## Introduction

The history of fiscal policy started in the late 1960s when the New Order government, under the leadership of Soeharto, took over from the first president Soekarno. In Soekarno's era, the budget deficit was financed by money creation which ultimately fueled hyperinflation in the mid-1960s. This policy was drastically changed in the Soeharto era. To control inflation, the size of the government deficit was reduced and in contrast to the policy of the Old Order government, the deficit was financed only by foreign aid and loans. The policy of a balanced budget was pursued every fiscal year and this became the hallmark of the New Order economic policy. The economic stabilization program brought positive impacts to the country with inflation being brought under control to around 10–30 percent per annum.

The oil boom in the 1970s greatly eased the government budget constraint. Proceeds from oil revenues greatly improved the "domestic" revenue side of the government budget and led to a further increase in government savings. This enabled a larger portion of development expenditure to be financed by government savings instead of foreign aid. The downside of the oil boom was that it made efforts to collect non-oil tax revenues less urgent. Reliance of the government budget on oil tax revenues continued to increase such that by 1980, non-oil tax revenues accounted for less than 30 percent of total tax revenues and only 25 percent of total budgetary revenue.

The fall in the oil price in 1982 and again in 1986 brought a new impetus to the country's development strategy. It was acknowledged that export revenues from oil and primary commodities were unreliable and there was a sense of urgency to develop and to diversify non-oil sectors in the economy, particularly manufacturing and agriculture. As a first step in this direction, the government announced banking deregulation in 1983, which was followed by the overhaul of the taxation system. The first part of this chapter discusses the budgetary trend before and after the 1984 tax reform. Thereafter, the chapter focuses on the implication of the 1998 currency crisis and the enactment of the law of regional decentralization.

## Trend in government revenues

### *The overhaul of the tax system*

Before the 1984 tax reform, the inadequacy of the tax system in Indonesia was reflected in the low and declining non-oil tax revenues (NOTR) as a percentage of total tax revenue (Table 7.1). In 1969, NOTR still occupied 58.4 percent of total revenue, but this ratio continued to decline substantially until it reached 29.4 percent in 1981. The declining share of NOTR also reflected the impact of an external event, namely, the rise in the price of oil. In the aftermath of the 1973 Arab-Israeli War and the Iraq-Iran war, the oil price almost quadrupled from less than US$10 per barrel to around US$30 per barrel in 1982. As a result, revenue from oil rose from 1.8 percent of GDP in 1969 to around 10 percent in 1976 (Table 7.2).

On the positive side, the oil boom provided the government with fresh money to finance economic development. However, it also made the effort to intensify the

*Table 7.1* Indicators of revenue reliance, 1969–99

| *Fiscal year* | *Non-oil tax as a % of total tax revenues* | *Non-oil tax as a % of total expenditures* | *Foreign aid/ borrowing as a % of dev't expenditures* |
|---|---|---|---|
| 1969 | 58.36 | 58.32 | 77.17 |
| 1972 | 41.52 | 42.22 | 52.95 |
| 1975 | 45.69 | 45.74 | 35.17 |
| 1976 | 44.27 | 34.92 | 38.16 |
| 1977 | 44.88 | 36.85 | 35.86 |
| 1978 | 45.88 | 36.94 | 40.53 |
| 1979 | 36.39 | 32.59 | 39.69 |
| 1980 | 31.36 | 29.16 | 27.41 |
| 1981 | 29.35 | 26.04 | 25.04 |
| 1982 | 34.21 | 29.49 | 26.08 |
| 1983 | 27.80 | 26.17 | 45.37 |
| 1984 | 34.42 | 30.79 | 41.53 |
| 1985 | 42.12 | 33.72 | 30.43 |
| 1986 | 60.73 | 42.98 | 63.26 |
| 1987 | 53.60 | 42.97 | 56.87 |
| 1988 | 59.27 | 41.74 | 82.20 |
| 1989 | 57.53 | 45.62 | 54.11 |
| 1990 | 57.96 | 51.62 | 45.93 |
| 1991 | 64.61 | 52.78 | 43.23 |
| 1992 | 68.62 | 55.41 | 41.25 |
| 1993 | 77.72 | 63.46 | 37.83 |
| 1994 | 79.62 | 70.73 | 32.05 |
| 1995 | 78.01 | 71.90 | 31.30 |
| 1996 | 77.02 | 68.51 | 33.10 |
| 1997 | 72.78 | 63.86 | 37.50 |
| 1998 | 74.04 | 54.57 | 82.84 |
| 1999 | 72.10 | 59.30 | 55.72 |

Sources: Bank Pembangunan Indonesia, Unit Riset (various years).

*Table 7.2* Revenues and expenditures in Indonesia, 1969–99 (as a % of GDP)

| *Year* | *Non-oil revenues* | *Oil and gas revenues* | *Total revenues* | *Total expenditures* | *Budget deficit* | *Foreign aid/ borrowing* |
|---|---|---|---|---|---|---|
| 1969 | 7.19 | 1.78 | 8.97 | 12.33 | −3.36 | 3.35 |
| 1972 | 6.81 | 4.36 | 11.17 | 16.13 | −4.96 | 3.46 |
| 1975 | 9.88 | 7.85 | 17.73 | 21.60 | −3.87 | 3.89 |
| 1976 | 8.33 | 10.48 | 18.81 | 23.85 | −5.04 | 5.07 |
| 1977 | 8.35 | 10.25 | 18.60 | 22.65 | −4.05 | 4.07 |
| 1978 | 8.61 | 10.15 | 18.76 | 23.30 | −4.54 | 4.55 |
| 1979 | 7.61 | 13.30 | 20.91 | 23.35 | −2.44 | 4.31 |
| 1980 | 7.06 | 15.45 | 22.50 | 24.20 | −1.70 | 3.29 |
| 1981 | 6.64 | 15.97 | 22.60 | 25.49 | −2.88 | 3.16 |
| 1982 | 7.12 | 13.70 | 20.82 | 24.16 | −3.34 | 3.25 |
| 1983 | 6.67 | 12.92 | 19.58 | 25.47 | −5.89 | 5.27 |
| 1984 | 6.29 | 11.98 | 18.27 | 20.43 | −2.15 | 4.00 |
| 1985 | 8.45 | 11.77 | 20.22 | 25.07 | −4.85 | 3.77 |
| 1986 | 9.56 | 6.18 | 15.74 | 22.24 | −6.50 | 5.61 |
| 1987 | 9.33 | 8.08 | 17.41 | 21.72 | −4.31 | 4.45 |
| 1988 | 9.77 | 6.71 | 16.48 | 23.40 | −6.92 | 7.12 |
| 1989 | 10.84 | 8.00 | 18.84 | 23.76 | −4.92 | 4.98 |
| 1990 | 12.50 | 9.07 | 21.57 | 24.22 | −2.65 | 4.29 |
| 1991 | 12.10 | 6.63 | 18.72 | 22.92 | −4.20 | 4.39 |
| 1992 | 12.90 | 5.90 | 18.80 | 23.28 | −4.48 | 4.27 |
| 1993 | 14.44 | 4.14 | 18.58 | 22.75 | −4.17 | 3.56 |
| 1994 | 13.84 | 3.54 | 17.38 | 19.56 | −2.18 | 2.57 |
| 1995 | 12.53 | 3.53 | 16.06 | 17.43 | −1.36 | 1.98 |
| 1996 | 12.67 | 3.78 | 16.45 | 18.50 | −2.04 | 2.23 |
| 1997 | 13.06 | 4.89 | 17.95 | 20.46 | −2.51 | 2.30 |
| 1998 | 11.89 | 4.17 | 16.06 | 21.78 | −5.73 | 5.68 |
| 1999 | 12.99 | 5.03 | 18.02 | 21.90 | −3.89 | 3.90 |

Sources: Bank Pembangunan Indonesia, Unit Riset (various years).

collection of non-oil taxes lower on the priority list. Before 1969, NOTR was dominated by taxes on international trade such as import duties, export duties and sales taxes on imports. The role of oil revenues only became dominant after 1973. Since that year, oil revenues have contributed to more than half of government domestic revenues.

In 1984, Indonesia overhauled its tax system. The primary objective of the overhaul was to increase the ratio of NOTR to GDP, and the secondary objective was to reduce the complexities and ambiguities in the tax laws, regulations and procedures. As reflected in Table 7.2, this objective was achieved in a relatively short time period; the ratio of NOTR to GDP rose from 6.3 percent in 1984 to 8.5 percent in 1985. This ratio continued to improve thereafter such that by 1989, it had reached 10.8 percent. Meanwhile, the share of NOTR within total tax revenues rose from 28.2 percent in 1984 to 35.1 percent in 1985.

In the short term, the main instrument for achieving the first objective—i.e., to increase the ratio of NOTR to GDP—was the VAT package. In the medium term, improvement in the administration of the income tax and the land and building tax also contributed to a further increase in the ratio. In achieving the second objective, effort had been made to simplify the tax system of ambiguity. For example, the tax base is now defined broadly, while exemptions and exclusions are minimized. The new system also adopts a self-assessment system to replace the old official assessment system.

It is interesting to examine the impact of the 1984 tax reform on the collection of income tax. The share of income tax within NOTR actually started to rise in 1982 (40.18 percent of NOTR) before the introduction of the reform (Table 7.3). In subsequent years, the number fluctuates rather erratically below and over 30 percent of NOTR. However, if we look at the ratio of income tax to GDP, the impact of the reform only appeared from 1988 onward. After showing disappointing performance for almost four years, for the first time, the income tax share began to improve in 1988 when the ratio of income tax to GDP was above 3 percent. Why was the impact felt so late? One possible reason was that the enactment of the new tax law did not immediately improve the quality of the tax machinery. Another possible reason was that the rate of compliance was as low as in the pre-reform period. Whatever the reason, after 1990 during the economic boom, receipts from income tax managed to stay above 4 percent of GDP.

*Table 7.3* Structure of non-oil and gas revenues, 1976–99 (as a % of total non-oil and gas revenues)

| *Year* | *Income tax* | *Sales tax/ VAT* | *Import duties* | *Excise duties* | *Export tax* | *Other taxes* | *Land and bldg. tax* | *Nontax receipts* |
|---|---|---|---|---|---|---|---|---|
| 1976 | 16.43 | 20.56 | 20.01 | 10.16 | 4.80 | 0.83 | 3.28 | 9.21 |
| 1977 | 17.27 | 20.04 | 18.08 | 11.46 | 5.12 | 0.79 | 3.31 | 9.05 |
| 1978 | 17.81 | 17.71 | 15.09 | 12.92 | 8.49 | 0.89 | 3.22 | 9.78 |
| 1979 | 18.27 | 13.52 | 12.99 | 13.39 | 15.97 | 0.76 | 2.93 | 7.69 |
| 1980 | 19.07 | 14.36 | 13.97 | 13.65 | 9.51 | 0.92 | 2.72 | 9.84 |
| 1981 | 21.38 | 14.90 | 14.96 | 15.18 | 3.58 | 0.92 | 2.64 | 9.38 |
| 1982 | 40.18 | 16.67 | 12.29 | 14.60 | 1.93 | 1.62 | 2.47 | 10.24 |
| 1983 | 48.14 | 20.71 | 13.88 | 19.26 | 2.59 | 1.62 | 3.29 | 12.93 |
| 1984 | 38.74 | 16.04 | 9.68 | 15.95 | 1.66 | 2.52 | 2.87 | 12.55 |
| 1985 | 28.53 | 27.47 | 7.49 | 11.64 | 0.63 | 2.55 | 2.06 | 18.40 |
| 1986 | 23.17 | 29.58 | 9.79 | 10.77 | 0.81 | 1.94 | 1.94 | 11.70 |
| 1987 | 24.69 | 32.85 | 12.38 | 9.50 | 1.55 | 2.48 | 1.82 | 14.74 |
| 1988 | 31.94 | 31.47 | 9.91 | 10.16 | 1.02 | 1.84 | 2.61 | 11.05 |
| 1989 | 31.76 | 33.03 | 10.44 | 8.18 | 0.95 | 1.05 | 3.34 | 11.25 |
| 1990 | 33.74 | 33.20 | 11.45 | 7.36 | 0.16 | 0.88 | 3.21 | 9.99 |
| 1991 | 35.36 | 33.24 | 10.44 | 6.96 | 0.06 | 1.09 | 3.43 | 9.42 |
| 1992 | 37.33 | 32.04 | 9.61 | 6.69 | 0.03 | 0.75 | 3.30 | 10.26 |
| 1993 | 33.84 | 31.97 | 8.15 | 6.02 | 0.03 | 0.65 | 3.40 | 13.54 |
| 1994 | 35.48 | 31.29 | 7.38 | 5.96 | 0.25 | 0.57 | 3.11 | 12.17 |
| 1995 | 36.18 | 32.36 | 5.73 | 6.47 | 0.35 | 0.90 | 3.39 | 13.76 |
| 1996 | 39.27 | 31.41 | 4.32 | 6.50 | 0.11 | 0.88 | 3.51 | 14.00 |
| 1997 | 39.78 | 33.61 | 4.54 | 6.06 | 0.14 | 0.86 | 3.42 | 11.24 |
| 1998 | 25.95 | 29.06 | 5.52 | 7.79 | 0.95 | 0.54 | 3.43 | 26.77 |
| 1999 | 37.79 | 22.69 | 2.58 | 7.15 | 0.57 | 0.39 | 2.51 | 26.32 |

Sources: Bank Indonesia (various years).

*Table 7.4* Non-oil and gas revenues, 1976–99 (as a % of GDP)

| *Year* | *Income tax* | *Sales tax/ VAT* | *Import duties* | *Excise duties* | *Export tax* | *Other taxes* | *Land and bldg. tax* | *Nontax receipts* |
|---|---|---|---|---|---|---|---|---|
| 1976 | 1.37 | 1.71 | 1.67 | 0.85 | 0.40 | 0.069 | 0.27 | 0.77 |
| 1977 | 1.44 | 1.67 | 1.51 | 0.96 | 0.43 | 0.066 | 0.28 | 0.76 |
| 1978 | 1.53 | 1.52 | 1.30 | 1.11 | 0.73 | 0.076 | 0.28 | 0.84 |
| 1979 | 1.39 | 1.03 | 0.99 | 1.02 | 1.21 | 0.058 | 0.22 | 0.58 |
| 1980 | 1.35 | 1.01 | 0.99 | 0.96 | 0.67 | 0.065 | 0.19 | 0.69 |
| 1981 | 1.42 | 0.99 | 0.99 | 1.01 | 0.24 | 0.061 | 0.17 | 0.62 |
| 1982 | 2.86 | 1.19 | 0.88 | 1.04 | 0.14 | 0.116 | 0.18 | 0.73 |
| 1983 | 2.62 | 1.13 | 0.76 | 1.05 | 0.14 | 0.088 | 0.18 | 0.70 |
| 1984 | 2.44 | 1.01 | 0.61 | 1.00 | 0.10 | 0.159 | 0.18 | 0.79 |
| 1985 | 2.44 | 2.35 | 0.64 | 1.00 | 0.05 | 0.219 | 0.18 | 1.58 |
| 1986 | 2.21 | 2.83 | 0.94 | 1.03 | 0.08 | 0.185 | 0.19 | 1.12 |
| 1987 | 2.30 | 3.07 | 1.16 | 0.89 | 0.14 | 0.232 | 0.17 | 1.38 |
| 1988 | 3.12 | 3.07 | 0.97 | 0.99 | 0.10 | 0.180 | 0.25 | 1.08 |
| 1989 | 3.44 | 3.58 | 1.13 | 0.89 | 0.10 | 0.114 | 0.36 | 1.22 |
| 1990 | 4.22 | 4.15 | 1.43 | 0.92 | 0.02 | 0.110 | 0.40 | 1.25 |
| 1991 | 4.28 | 4.02 | 1.26 | 0.84 | 0.01 | 0.131 | 0.42 | 1.14 |
| 1992 | 4.82 | 4.13 | 1.24 | 0.86 | 0.00 | 0.097 | 0.43 | 1.32 |
| 1993 | 4.89 | 4.62 | 1.18 | 0.87 | 0.00 | 0.094 | 0.49 | 1.95 |
| 1994 | 4.91 | 4.33 | 1.02 | 0.82 | 0.03 | 0.079 | 0.43 | 1.68 |
| 1995 | 4.51 | 4.04 | 0.71 | 0.81 | 0.04 | 0.112 | 0.42 | 1.72 |
| 1996 | 4.79 | 3.83 | 0.53 | 0.79 | 0.01 | 0.107 | 0.43 | 1.71 |
| 1997 | 5.50 | 4.03 | 0.48 | 0.82 | 0.02 | 0.076 | 0.42 | 1.72 |
| 1998 | 5.62 | 3.23 | 0.25 | 0.91 | 0.52 | 0.053 | 0.36 | 2.46 |
| 1999 | 5.41 | 3.25 | 0.37 | 1.02 | 0.08 | 0.056 | 0.36 | 3.77 |

Sources: Bank Pembangunan Indonesia, Unit Riset (various years).

However, this ratio began to turn around at the time of Asian crisis. At this time, the share of income tax in total non-oil and gas revenues plunged again to 25.95 percent; however, income tax as a percentage of GDP was not affected because of the severe contraction in the economy (Table 7.4).

The impact of the 1984 tax reform on the collection of NOTR was more immediate than its impact on the income tax (Table 7.3, Table 7.4). The introduction of the VAT package in April 1985 was intended to replace the old system of indirect taxes, primarily sales taxes. After the reform, the contribution of VAT to NOTR jumped to 27.47 percent in 1985, after it managed to reach around 20 percent in previous years. Relative to GDP, VAT recorded 2.35 percent in 1985 as compared to 1.01 percent in 1984. The economic boom in the early 1990s provided another boost for VAT. From 1990 to 1995, the ratio never fell below 4 percent of GDP. The economic crisis also exacted a substantial toll on VAT, and it dropped to 3.23 percent of GDP in 1998. In comparison to the impact of the economic crisis on the collection of income tax, VAT fared better.

The land and building tax is designed to replace the old property tax system. Looking at the figures, one can judge that the land and building taxes have never been too important in NOTR, and it never exceeded 4 percent of NOTR (Table 7.3). The land and building tax, however, has an important regional dimension.

Various levels of governments share the tax revenues, but most of the land and building tax revenue is received by the municipal government. Thus, the land and building tax provided additional revenues for often cash-strapped municipal governments.

Other revenue items in the category of NOTR—i.e., excise taxes, import duties and export taxes—have not been touched by the 1984 tax reform. The share of excise taxes and import duties in NOTR as a proportion of GDP has declined (Table 7.4), reflecting the fact that Indonesia has moved away from nontariff barriers to tariffs. Although the contribution of excise duties to NOTR has become less important, it is still an important item in comparison to import duties and the export tax. This reflects the importance of the tobacco excise tax levied on cigarette manufacturers.

### *External financing and development revenues*

Foreign aid is a rather sensitive issue in Indonesia. This was perhaps the best reason why the New Order government has never used the term "foreign aid" in its annual budget, and has instead recorded foreign aid as development revenues, a practice that continues until the present day. By placing foreign aid in the category of development revenues, it is obvious that foreign aid is restricted for investment expenditures or capital expenditures.[1] Moreover, foreign aid is supposed to only provide partial financing for development expenditures, and the rest of the financing would come from government savings, namely, the surplus of domestic revenues over routine expenditures.

The notion that foreign aid provided only partial financing to development expenditures can be observed from Table 7.1. In 1969, the ratio of foreign aid to development expenditures was among the highest in Indonesia's history, amounting to 77.2 percent. The reason was simple; after years of neglect, the program of economic reconstruction had just started and Indonesia was short of cash. In subsequent years, foreign aid as a ratio of development expenditures behaves rather erratically. However, anyone familiar with Indonesian economic history would observe that this trend was dictated by developments in the oil market and the domestic need for economic restructuring.

The first round of oil price increases in 1973 provided ample opportunity for the government to reduce its dependence on foreign aid. As shown in Table 7.1, the ratio of foreign aid fell from 53 percent in 1972 to 35.2 percent and 38.2 percent in 1975 and 1976, respectively. The second round of oil price increase in 1979 provided another opportunity, and the ratio of foreign aid to development expenditures fell from 39.7 percent in 1979 to 27.4 percent in 1980. The momentum continued until a historical low of 25 percent was reached in 1981.

The fall in the oil price in 1982 and again in 1986 signaled to Indonesian economic planners that the days of the oil boom had finally come to an end. Efforts were made to restructure the economy away from its dependence on oil toward a more diversified economy based on non-oil sectors. The combination of the drop in oil revenues and the need for economic restructuring led to a jump in the ratio of foreign aid to development expenditure, with the ratio rising from 26.1 percent in 1982 to 45.4 percent in 1983. The economic restructuring that began in 1986 had an immediate impact on raising the ratio, which reached its historical peak of 82.2 percent in 1988.

The 1986 economic restructuring succeeded in boosting economic growth. Economic growth resumed in the early 1990s and lasted until 1997. This boom in the domestic economy made it possible for the government to increase its tax collection from non-oil sources. This was also possible due to the functioning of the tax system that had been enacted by the 1984 tax reform. The government was, thus, able once again to reduce its dependence on foreign aid. Looking at Table 7.1, the ratio of foreign aid to development expenditures fell from 54.1 percent in 1989 to 37.5 percent in 1997.

The last row in Table 7.1 documents the negative impact of the economic crisis on domestic revenues. The ratio of foreign aid to development expenditures rose to an unprecedented figure of 82.84 percent, and revenues fell due to contraction of the domestic economy. At the same time, expenditures tended to increase as a result of providing a social safety net or some kind of subsidies to protect the poor from the worst impacts. The result is that foreign aid is used not only for financing development expenditures, but also for routine expenditures.

## Trends in government expenditure

There is little change in the ratio of total expenditures to GDP. The most visible impact of an external event took place in 1975 in the aftermath of the oil price increase. The ratio of total expenditures to GDP increased from 18.41 percent in 1974 to 21.60 percent in 1975 (Table 7.5). Thereafter, the ratio continued to be higher, albeit it has never exceeded 26 percent.

To some, the period 1994–96 is known as the period of fiscal austerity. This was the only time where the government used its budget for demand management. In this period, Indonesia was in the middle of an economic boom. The inflation rate had begun to rise and the current account continued to worsen in three successive years. The government opted to put the brakes on the economy before it became too overheated. Some concern has been raised regarding whether the Indonesian government in this respect was too conservative with regard to its expenditure policy. The policy of fiscal austerity, however, was to no avail since the current account continued to deteriorate, which eventually triggered the worst economic crisis in Indonesia's history. In 1998, the ratio of total expenditure to GDP seemed to be on the increase again. To a certain extent, this was caused by the contraction of GDP, but the government also made a conscious effort to stimulate the economy through its social safety net and public work programs so that it appeared to be higher than usual.

### *Routine expenditures*

In 1969, routine expenditures made up of 64.64 percent of total expenditure (Table 7.6) or roughly 8 percent of GDP (Table 7.5). In the early period of the New Order government, the priority was to improve government bureaucracy that

*Table 7.5* Actual government expenditures and public savings, 1969–99 (as a % of GDP)

| *Year* | *Receipts* | *Operating expenditures* | *Public savings* | *Foreign aid* | *Dev't expenditures* | *Deficit* | *Total receipts and foreign aid* | *Total expenditures* |
|---|---|---|---|---|---|---|---|---|
| 1969 | 8.98 | 7.98 | 0.99 | 3.35 | 4.34 | −0.99 | 12.33 | 12.33 |
| 1970 | 10.33 | 8.62 | 1.71 | 3.59 | 5.09 | −1.50 | 13.92 | 13.71 |
| 1971 | 11.66 | 9.50 | 2.15 | 3.70 | 5.34 | −1.63 | 15.36 | 14.84 |
| 1972 | 12.95 | 9.60 | 3.35 | 3.46 | 6.53 | −3.07 | 16.41 | 16.13 |
| 1973 | 14.33 | 10.56 | 3.78 | 3.02 | 6.68 | −3.66 | 17.35 | 17.24 |
| 1974 | 16.54 | 9.21 | 7.33 | 1.93 | 9.20 | −7.27 | 18.47 | 18.41 |
| 1975 | 17.73 | 10.54 | 7.19 | 3.88 | 11.06 | −7.17 | 21.62 | 21.60 |
| 1976 | 18.81 | 10.55 | 8.26 | 5.08 | 13.30 | −8.22 | 23.89 | 23.85 |
| 1977 | 18.59 | 11.30 | 7.29 | 4.07 | 11.35 | −7.28 | 22.66 | 22.65 |
| 1978 | 18.75 | 12.06 | 6.69 | 4.55 | 11.23 | −6.68 | 23.31 | 23.30 |
| 1979 | 21.02 | 12.49 | 8.54 | 2.42 | 10.87 | −8.45 | 23.44 | 23.35 |
| 1980 | 22.50 | 12.21 | 10.29 | 3.29 | 11.99 | −8.71 | 25.79 | 24.20 |
| 1981 | 22.51 | 12.85 | 9.66 | 2.89 | 12.63 | −9.75 | 25.40 | 25.49 |
| 1982 | 20.75 | 11.68 | 9.07 | 3.36 | 12.48 | −9.11 | 24.11 | 24.16 |
| 1983 | 22.21 | 13.86 | 8.35 | 3.45 | 11.61 | −8.16 | 25.66 | 25.47 |
| 1984 | 18.30 | 10.80 | 7.50 | 2.05 | 9.62 | −7.57 | 20.35 | 20.43 |
| 1985 | 22.11 | 12.68 | 9.43 | 2.99 | 12.39 | −9.41 | 25.09 | 25.07 |
| 1986 | 16.95 | 13.38 | 3.58 | 5.38 | 8.87 | −3.49 | 22.33 | 22.24 |
| 1987 | 17.41 | 13.89 | 3.52 | 4.45 | 7.83 | −3.38 | 21.86 | 21.72 |
| 1988 | 16.48 | 14.73 | 1.74 | 7.12 | 8.67 | −1.54 | 23.60 | 23.40 |
| 1989 | 18.84 | 14.56 | 4.29 | 4.98 | 9.21 | −4.23 | 23.83 | 23.76 |
| 1990 | 21.57 | 14.89 | 6.68 | 4.29 | 9.33 | −5.05 | 25.86 | 24.22 |
| 1991 | 18.72 | 12.77 | 5.95 | 4.39 | 10.15 | −5.76 | 23.11 | 22.92 |
| 1992 | 18.80 | 12.93 | 5.87 | 4.27 | 10.35 | −6.08 | 23.07 | 23.28 |
| 1993 | 18.58 | 13.34 | 5.24 | 3.56 | 9.41 | −5.85 | 22.14 | 22.75 |
| 1994 | 17.38 | 11.53 | 5.85 | 2.57 | 8.03 | −5.46 | 19.95 | 19.56 |
| 1995 | 16.06 | 11.10 | 4.97 | 1.98 | 6.33 | −4.35 | 18.05 | 17.43 |
| 1996 | 16.45 | 11.75 | 4.71 | 2.23 | 6.75 | −4.52 | 18.69 | 18.50 |
| 1997 | 17.30 | 14.33 | 2.97 | 2.30 | 6.13 | −3.83 | 20.25 | 20.46 |
| 1998 | 15.09 | 14.93 | 0.16 | 5.68 | 6.86 | −1.18 | 21.74 | 21.78 |
| 1999 | 18.02 | 14.91 | 3.11 | 3.90 | 7.00 | −3.10 | 21.92 | 21.90 |

Sources: Bank Pembangunan Indonesia, Unit Riset (various years).

was directly involved in subsidizing several basic food items, so there was not much left for capital expenditures. The oil boom and foreign aid greatly eased the government budget constraint such that in 1975–77 and again in 1982 and 1983, the share of development expenditures within total expenditures exceeded routine expenditures. Starting in the mid-1980s, however, the burden of servicing the foreign debt began to eat away at the budget so that the share of routine expenditures went back to the 1969 level, i.e., more than 60 percent of total annual expenditures.

Although the ratio of total expenditure to GDP has been relatively unchanged, things look different with respect to the composition of expenditures (Table 7.6). As a percentage of total expenditures, debt servicing jumped dra-

*Table 7.6* Composition of routine expenditures, 1969–99 (as a % of total expenditures)

| *Year* | *Personnel expenditures* | *Material expenditures* | *Subsidies to local gov't* | *Debt servicing* | *Other* | *Total routine expenditures* |
|---|---|---|---|---|---|---|
| 1969 | 31.00 | 15.01 | 13.17 | 4.31 | 1.15 | 64.64 |
| 1972 | 27.23 | 12.96 | 11.40 | 7.39 | 0.68 | 59.52 |
| 1975 | 21.75 | 11.16 | 10.42 | 2.87 | 2.59 | 48.79 |
| 1976 | 17.28 | 9.22 | 8.50 | 5.14 | 4.10 | 44.24 |
| 1977 | 20.74 | 8.75 | 11.11 | 5.30 | 4.00 | 49.90 |
| 1978 | 18.90 | 7.92 | 9.86 | 10.09 | 5.02 | 51.78 |
| 1979 | 18.99 | 7.61 | 8.96 | 9.15 | 9.61 | 54.31 |
| 1980 | 18.39 | 6.10 | 8.87 | 7.13 | 12.23 | 52.73 |
| 1981 | 16.54 | 6.70 | 8.78 | 6.76 | 11.89 | 50.68 |
| 1982 | 16.78 | 7.23 | 9.13 | 8.50 | 6.92 | 48.56 |
| 1983 | 14.69 | 5.63 | 8.24 | 11.20 | 5.05 | 44.81 |
| 1984 | 17.14 | 6.65 | 10.59 | 15.61 | 3.04 | 53.03 |
| 1985 | 16.92 | 5.76 | 10.48 | 13.99 | 3.18 | 50.33 |
| 1986 | 18.90 | 5.99 | 11.61 | 22.18 | 0.76 | 59.45 |
| 1987 | 17.03 | 4.90 | 10.38 | 30.26 | 1.90 | 64.48 |
| 1988 | 16.51 | 3.69 | 9.06 | 33.20 | 0.51 | 62.96 |
| 1989 | 15.62 | 4.29 | 9.00 | 30.01 | 2.33 | 61.25 |
| 1990 | 14.96 | 3.89 | 8.21 | 27.05 | 7.36 | 61.47 |
| 1991 | 15.67 | 4.47 | 8.39 | 24.63 | 2.57 | 55.73 |
| 1992 | 15.79 | 4.84 | 8.90 | 24.00 | 2.01 | 55.54 |
| 1993 | 16.22 | 4.41 | 10.05 | 24.98 | 2.97 | 58.63 |
| 1994 | 16.85 | 5.78 | 9.73 | 24.61 | 1.98 | 58.95 |
| 1995 | 16.41 | 6.53 | 10.39 | 27.91 | 2.43 | 63.67 |
| 1996 | 14.67 | 8.23 | 9.50 | 27.83 | 3.20 | 63.51 |
| 1997 | 13.49 | 7.03 | 8.64 | 24.31 | 16.54 | 70.02 |
| 1998 | 11.36 | 5.13 | 6.58 | 25.88 | 19.57 | 68.52 |
| 1999 | 13.71 | 4.43 | 7.82 | 16.31 | 25.79 | 68.06 |

Sources: Bank Pembangunan Indonesia, Unit Riset (various years).

matically from 7.13 percent in 1980 to 33.20 percent in 1988. One consequence of the debt-servicing burden was that the percentage of nondebt routine expenditures, which consisted mainly of salaries and wages, continued to decline. From a high level in 1969 (60.3 percent of total expenditures), nondebt routine expenditures in the 1980s appeared to stabilize at around 30 percent (Table 7.7). The impact of the *de facto* squeeze of nondebt routine expenditures was borne mainly by government employees. This brought about unseen effects, namely, the widespread perception of corruption at almost all levels of government. The base pay of government employees is so low that salaries have to be supplemented from the development budget. This scheme results in a complex series of allowances that are not related to performance. Since allowances are also based on the discretion of the worker's superior, what emerges is a network of patronage and personal loyalty, which is prone to corruption and abuse of power.

It is interesting to examine the impact of rising debt-servicing charges on other components of routine expenditures. Personnel expenditures fell from 31 percent

*Table 7.7* Composition of total expenditures, 1969–99 (as a % of total expenditures)

| *Year* | *Nondebt routine expenditures* | *Debt servicing* | *Total routine expenditures* | *Total dev't expenditures* |
|---|---|---|---|---|
| 1969 | 60.3 | 4.31 | 64.64 | 35.36 |
| 1972 | 52.1 | 7.39 | 59.52 | 40.48 |
| 1975 | 45.9 | 2.87 | 48.79 | 51.21 |
| 1976 | 39.1 | 5.14 | 44.24 | 55.76 |
| 1977 | 44.6 | 5.30 | 49.90 | 50.10 |
| 1978 | 41.7 | 10.09 | 51.78 | 48.22 |
| 1979 | 45.2 | 9.15 | 54.31 | 45.69 |
| 1980 | 45.6 | 7.13 | 52.73 | 47.27 |
| 1981 | 43.9 | 6.76 | 50.68 | 49.32 |
| 1982 | 40.1 | 8.50 | 48.56 | 51.44 |
| 1983 | 33.6 | 11.20 | 44.81 | 55.19 |
| 1984 | 37.4 | 15.61 | 53.03 | 46.97 |
| 1985 | 36.3 | 13.99 | 50.33 | 49.67 |
| 1986 | 37.3 | 22.18 | 59.45 | 40.55 |
| 1987 | 34.2 | 30.26 | 64.48 | 35.52 |
| 1988 | 29.8 | 33.20 | 62.96 | 37.04 |
| 1989 | 31.2 | 30.01 | 61.25 | 38.75 |
| 1990 | 34.4 | 27.05 | 61.47 | 38.53 |
| 1991 | 31.1 | 24.63 | 55.73 | 44.27 |
| 1992 | 31.5 | 24.00 | 55.54 | 44.46 |
| 1993 | 33.7 | 24.98 | 58.63 | 41.37 |
| 1994 | 34.3 | 24.61 | 58.95 | 41.05 |
| 1995 | 35.8 | 27.91 | 63.67 | 36.33 |
| 1996 | 35.7 | 27.83 | 63.51 | 36.49 |
| 1997 | 45.7 | 24.31 | 70.02 | 29.98 |
| 1998 | 42.6 | 25.88 | 68.52 | 31.48 |
| 1999 | 51.8 | 16.31 | 68.06 | 31.94 |

Sources: Bank Pembangunan Indonesia, Unit Riset (various years).

of total expenditures in 1969 to 17.03 percent in 1987 (Table 7.6). In subsequent years, the share of personnel expenditures has never exceeded 17 percent. Material expenditures also experienced a similar fate although the decline was less dramatic, decreasing from around 15 percent of total expenditure in 1969 to its lowest figure of 3.69 percent in 1988. It later recovered in 1995–97 at the time of economic boom.

One component that seems to have escaped a drastic decline is subsidies to local government. Subsidies to local government are mainly meant to pay for civil servant salaries in the provincial and lower governments and also for material expenditures. For this reason, the figure seems fairly constant from year to year, except for 1998 when it dropped to 6.6 percent. Since it is impossible to cut salaries, severe cuts were made mainly in material expenditures.

Another component of expenditures that had to yield to the ever-increasing debt burden was non-aid development expenditures. These included capital expenditures by departments, central government transfers to regions for the purpose of carrying out development projects (INPRES allocation[2]), and some subsidies including those on fertilizer and government equity participation in public enter-

*Table 7.8* Major components of central government expenditure, 1969–99 (as a % of total expenditures)

| *Year* | *Nondebt routine expenditures* | *Debt servicing* | *Dev't expenditures excl. project aid* | *Dev't expenditures financed by aid* | *Total subsidies* |
|---|---|---|---|---|---|
| 1969 | 60.33 | 4.31 | 27.67 | 27.18 | — |
| 1972 | 52.13 | 7.39 | 32.02 | 21.44 | — |
| 1975 | 45.92 | 2.87 | 33.93 | 18.00 | — |
| 1976 | 39.10 | 5.14 | 34.76 | 21.28 | 22.39 |
| 1977 | 44.60 | 5.30 | 32.96 | 17.96 | 22.08 |
| 1978 | 41.69 | 10.09 | 29.58 | 19.54 | 23.77 |
| 1979 | 45.16 | 9.15 | 28.93 | 18.47 | 25.30 |
| 1980 | 45.59 | 7.13 | 36.55 | 13.58 | 29.44 |
| 1981 | 43.91 | 6.76 | 37.49 | 12.41 | 30.25 |
| 1982 | 40.06 | 8.50 | 38.28 | 13.47 | 29.06 |
| 1983 | 33.61 | 11.20 | 24.98 | 20.68 | 32.11 |
| 1984 | 37.42 | 15.61 | 27.93 | 19.56 | 27.76 |
| 1985 | 36.33 | 13.99 | 34.69 | 15.04 | 21.24 |
| 1986 | 37.27 | 22.18 | 23.22 | 25.21 | 20.69 |
| 1987 | 34.22 | 30.26 | 18.07 | 20.49 | 22.28 |
| 1988 | 29.76 | 33.20 | 14.61 | 30.45 | 15.31 |
| 1989 | 31.24 | 30.01 | 20.21 | 20.97 | 20.20 |
| 1990 | 34.42 | 27.05 | 23.68 | 17.69 | 20.79 |
| 1991 | 31.11 | 24.63 | 27.79 | 19.14 | 16.75 |
| 1992 | 31.53 | 24.00 | 26.98 | 18.34 | 16.66 |
| 1993 | 33.65 | 24.98 | 25.72 | 15.65 | 18.39 |
| 1994 | 34.33 | 24.61 | 27.89 | 13.16 | 24.54 |
| 1995 | 35.76 | 27.91 | 24.96 | 11.37 | 22.50 |
| 1996 | 35.67 | 27.83 | 24.42 | 12.08 | — |
| 1997 | 41.35 | 22.58 | 18.73 | 11.24 | — |
| 1998 | 39.78 | 25.10 | 19.46 | 26.08 | — |
| 1999 | 51.80 | 16.31 | 24.49 | 17.80 | — |

Sources: Bank Pembangunan Indonesia, Unit Riset (various years).

prises (Table 7.8). In this respect, development expenditures excluding aid fell from its highest in 1982 (38.28 percent) to as low as 14.61 percent in 1988. Thereafter, the percentage of non-aid development expenditures has never exceeded 30 percent.

The same trend is seen if one looks at the ratio of various categories of expenditures to GDP. In 1988, debt-servicing expenditures soared to almost 8 percent of GDP, while among the other components, nondebt routine and non-aid development expenditures fell further relative to GDP.

### *Development expenditures*

Development expenditures consist of two categories: non-aid development expenditures and foreign aid. From the point of view of aggregate demand creation, foreign aid has very little impact since it is immediately spent in the donor country. Therefore, it enters the country mainly in the form of goods, usually capital goods, which adds to the production capacity of the economy. Non-aid development expenditure, on the other hand, is denominated in the domestic currency and spent domestically. Thus, in addition to increasing the production capacity of the economy, it will also expand aggregate demand.

From 1969 to 1999, the amount of foreign aid ranges from 3 to 7 percent of GDP (Table 7.2). In terms of its ratio to total expenditures, in the same period, it made up 11 to 30 percent of total expenditures (Table 7.8). There is no clear pattern regarding whether the portion of non-aid development expenditures within development expenditures is larger or smaller than foreign aid. However, under normal conditions, non-aid development expenditure is expected to be larger than foreign aid since the latter is only meant to be a complementary source of financing for development expenditures and not a primary source. During the 1969–91 period, non-aid development expenditures ranged from a low of 3.41 percent of GDP in 1988 to a high of 9.55 percent of GDP in 1981 (Table 7.9).

*Table 7.9* Major components of central government expenditure, 1969–99 (as a % of GDP)

| *Year* | *Nondebt routine expenditures* | *Debt servicing* | *Dev't expenditures excl. project aid* | *Dev't expenditures financed by aid* | *Total subsidies* |
|---|---|---|---|---|---|
| 1969 | 7.44 | 0.53 | 3.41 | 3.35 | — |
| 1972 | 8.41 | 1.19 | 5.16 | 3.46 | — |
| 1975 | 9.92 | 0.62 | 7.33 | 3.89 | — |
| 1976 | 9.32 | 1.23 | 8.29 | 5.07 | 5.34 |
| 1977 | 10.10 | 1.20 | 7.47 | 4.07 | 5.00 |
| 1978 | 9.71 | 2.35 | 6.89 | 4.55 | 5.54 |
| 1979 | 10.55 | 2.14 | 6.76 | 4.31 | 5.91 |
| 1980 | 11.04 | 1.73 | 8.85 | 3.29 | 7.13 |
| 1981 | 11.19 | 1.72 | 9.55 | 3.16 | 7.71 |
| 1982 | 9.68 | 2.05 | 9.25 | 3.25 | 7.02 |
| 1983 | 8.56 | 2.85 | 6.36 | 5.27 | 8.18 |
| 1984 | 7.64 | 3.19 | 5.70 | 4.00 | 5.67 |
| 1985 | 9.11 | 3.51 | 8.70 | 3.77 | 5.32 |
| 1986 | 8.29 | 4.93 | 5.17 | 5.61 | 4.60 |
| 1987 | 7.43 | 6.57 | 3.92 | 4.45 | 4.84 |
| 1988 | 6.96 | 7.77 | 3.42 | 7.12 | 3.58 |
| 1989 | 7.42 | 7.13 | 4.80 | 4.98 | 4.80 |
| 1990 | 8.34 | 6.55 | 5.73 | 4.29 | 5.04 |
| 1991 | 7.13 | 5.64 | 6.37 | 4.39 | 3.84 |
| 1992 | 7.34 | 5.59 | 6.28 | 4.27 | 3.88 |
| 1993 | 7.66 | 5.68 | 5.85 | 3.56 | 4.18 |
| 1994 | 6.72 | 4.81 | 5.46 | 2.57 | 4.80 |
| 1995 | 6.23 | 4.86 | 4.35 | 1.98 | 3.92 |
| 1996 | 6.60 | 5.15 | 4.52 | 2.23 | — |
| 1997 | 9.35 | 4.97 | 3.83 | 2.30 | — |
| 1998 | 9.29 | 5.64 | 4.24 | 5.68 | — |
| 1999 | 11.33 | 3.57 | 5.36 | 3.90 | — |

Sources: Bank Pembangunan Indonesia, Unit Riset (various years).

*Table 7.10* Major components of non-aid development expenditures, 1969–99 (as a % of total expenditures)

| *Year* | *Institution/ department* | *Regional grants* | *Road infra-structure* | *Reforest-ation* | *Fertilizer subsidy* | *Gov't equity partici-pation* | *School children* |
|---|---|---|---|---|---|---|---|
| 1969 | 23.80 | 1.64 | na | na | na | na | — |
| 1972 | 20.39 | 7.85 | na | na | na | 3.06 | — |
| 1975 | 14.09 | 6.19 | na | na | na | 3.98 | — |
| 1976 | 16.04 | 4.04 | 0.00 | 0.43 | 2.91 | 5.91 | 0.00 |
| 1977 | 17.29 | 4.02 | 0.00 | 0.57 | 0.74 | 3.88 | 0.00 |
| 1978 | 16.06 | 3.54 | 0.00 | 0.08 | 1.56 | 2.42 | 0.00 |
| 1979 | 19.79 | 2.93 | 0.17 | 0.55 | 1.67 | 3.38 | 0.00 |
| 1980 | 23.03 | 3.06 | 0.24 | 0.44 | 2.58 | 4.33 | 0.00 |
| 1981 | 19.79 | 3.26 | 0.40 | 0.51 | 2.70 | 3.49 | 0.00 |
| 1982 | 22.63 | 3.71 | 0.29 | 0.34 | 2.92 | 2.34 | 0.00 |
| 1983 | 17.15 | 2.87 | 0.35 | 0.31 | 1.73 | 3.15 | 0.00 |
| 1984 | 19.54 | 3.04 | 0.57 | 0.34 | 4.12 | 1.89 | 0.00 |
| 1985 | 18.81 | 2.42 | 0.29 | 0.18 | 2.01 | 1.73 | 0.00 |
| 1986 | 8.78 | 2.49 | 0.33 | 0.14 | 2.05 | 0.38 | 0.00 |
| 1987 | 5.11 | 2.42 | 0.60 | 0.06 | 2.79 | 0.21 | 0.00 |
| 1988 | 7.11 | 2.40 | 0.53 | 0.05 | 0.60 | 0.53 | 0.00 |
| 1989 | 7.94 | 1.81 | 0.69 | 0.04 | 2.89 | 2.24 | 0.00 |
| 1990 | 10.84 | 2.24 | 1.40 | 0.07 | 0.56 | 1.36 | 0.00 |
| 1991 | 14.36 | 2.71 | 1.88 | 0.14 | 0.58 | 1.90 | 0.00 |
| 1992 | 17.08 | 3.02 | 1.93 | 0.16 | 0.29 | 0.23 | 0.00 |
| 1993 | 15.89 | 2.98 | 1.58 | 0.16 | 0.25 | 0.55 | 0.00 |
| 1994 | 15.03 | 6.31 | 0.00 | 0.00 | 1.09 | 0.57 | 0.00 |
| 1995 | 13.86 | 5.88 | 0.00 | 0.00 | 0.18 | 0.48 | 0.00 |
| 1996 | 12.34 | 5.40 | 0.00 | 0.00 | 0.19 | 0.84 | 0.00 |
| 1997 | 9.43 | 4.69 | 0.00 | 0.00 | 0.55 | 0.30 | 0.04 |
| 1998 | 6.22 | 2.85 | 0.00 | 0.00 | 0.99 | 0.91 | 0.05 |
| 1999 | 4.94 | 3.92 | 0.00 | 0.00 | 0.00 | 0.00 | 0.00 |

Sources: Bank Pembangunan Indonesia, Unit Riset (various years).

Note
na = Not available.

Within non-aid development expenditures, capital expenditures for department/ institutions make up the largest share (Table 7.10). In 1969, for example, department capital expenditures amounted to almost 24 percent of total expenditures. As debt-serving charges soared, these numbers fell dramatically, sometimes as low as 5.11 percent as in 1987. In the 1990s, the share of departmental capital expenditures managed to get back to above 10 percent, but in 1998, the figure once again dropped sharply as the government's priority shifted once again to routine expenditures. Looking into details of this type of expenditures, one can observe that development or capital expenditure is a flexible term. It is possible to find many items that should be more appropriately put in the routine category, for example, salaries for government employees involved in certain projects. But as mentioned earlier, without taking from the development budget to supplement their low salaries, it is almost impossible for civil servants to live decently. This practice eventually exerts a negative cultural impact on the government bureaucracy as a whole. The allocation of some part of development expenditures is not based on any clear criteria, but is based solely on the discretion of upper-echelon officials who often also act as "project managers." In the process, many unnecessary projects are created, with the real purpose being only to spend money from the development budget.

The second-largest chunk of non-aid development expenditures goes to regional aid in the form of capital expenditure transfers to provincial and municipal governments and even in the late 1990s, to the village level. The transfer is intended for basic infrastructure development in backward regions, so that development across regions will be more or less equal. After reaching its peak in 1972, the share of regional aid fluctuates around 3 to 6 percent of total expenditures. Although the figure seems rather small in comparison with departmental expenditures, regional aid is a very important tool for the central government in intervening in regional development in Indonesia, particularly in rural areas.

Development expenditures allocated to the development of basic infrastructure as a part of the central government transfer to provinces and municipalities consists of several development grants for primary schools, health clinics, markets and road development. The share continues to decline such that in 1995–97 it only amounted to around 1 percent of total expenditures (Table 7.11, Table 7.15). In the earlier years, the percentage figures for these several grants were higher, particularly after the oil boom in 1974 which continued until 1986 when the oil price fell for the second time in the decade. The percentage of development expenditures allocated to basic infrastructure development recovered somewhat in the early 1990s. Improved prospects for both growth and the balance of payments persuaded the government to adopt a more expansionary budget. After 1993, basic infrastructure expenditures resumed its downward trend although the decline was not as drastic as departmental development expenditures.

There are several reasons why the ratio of infrastructure development to total expenditures continued to decline. The first reason is, of course, budget stringency which is usually dictated by general economic conditions, domestic as well as external. But perhaps the most important reason is that most projects have already been completed and the funds are now allocated for maintenance instead of building new facilities. Other components of non-aid development expenditures such as government equity participation, fertilizer subsidies and reforestation also showed a declining trend albeit for different reasons. For example, the allocation to reforestation was cut due to perceived ineffectiveness of this program.

The inclusion of government equity participation in capital expenditures is a controversial one, since it is mostly in the form of subsidies to state-owned enterprises that lose money. The reservation has some merit since the subsidies are often used to support operating expenses; there is very little capital stock, if any, created in the process. In any case, the share of government equity participation in total expenditures has never exceeded 6 percent of total expenditures, and the highest figures were reached in the early years of the New Order government. The almost

*Table 7.11* Major components of non-aid development expenditures, 1969–99 (as a % of GDP)

| *Year* | *Institution/department* | *Regional grants* | *Road infrastructure* | *Reforestation* | *Fertilizer subsidy* | *Gov't equity participation* |
|---|---|---|---|---|---|---|
| 1969 | 2.93 | 0.20 | na | na | na | na |
| 1972 | 3.29 | 1.27 | na | na | na | 0.49 |
| 1975 | 3.04 | 1.34 | na | na | na | 0.86 |
| 1976 | 3.83 | 0.96 | 0.00 | 0.10 | 0.69 | 1.41 |
| 1977 | 3.92 | 0.91 | 0.00 | 0.13 | 0.17 | 0.88 |
| 1978 | 3.74 | 0.82 | 0.00 | 0.02 | 0.36 | 0.56 |
| 1979 | 4.62 | 0.68 | 0.04 | 0.13 | 0.39 | 0.79 |
| 1980 | 5.57 | 0.74 | 0.06 | 0.11 | 0.62 | 1.05 |
| 1981 | 5.04 | 0.83 | 0.10 | 0.13 | 0.69 | 0.89 |
| 1982 | 5.47 | 0.90 | 0.07 | 0.08 | 0.70 | 0.57 |
| 1983 | 4.37 | 0.73 | 0.09 | 0.08 | 0.44 | 0.80 |
| 1984 | 3.99 | 0.62 | 0.12 | 0.07 | 0.84 | 0.39 |
| 1985 | 4.72 | 0.61 | 0.07 | 0.05 | 0.50 | 0.43 |
| 1986 | 1.95 | 0.55 | 0.07 | 0.03 | 0.46 | 0.08 |
| 1987 | 1.11 | 0.53 | 0.13 | 0.01 | 0.61 | 0.05 |
| 1988 | 1.66 | 0.56 | 0.12 | 0.01 | 0.14 | 0.12 |
| 1989 | 1.89 | 0.43 | 0.16 | 0.01 | 0.69 | 0.53 |
| 1990 | 2.62 | 0.54 | 0.34 | 0.02 | 0.14 | 0.33 |
| 1991 | 3.29 | 0.62 | 0.43 | 0.03 | 0.13 | 0.43 |
| 1992 | 3.98 | 0.70 | 0.45 | 0.04 | 0.07 | 0.05 |
| 1993 | 3.61 | 0.68 | 0.36 | 0.04 | 0.06 | 0.13 |
| 1994 | 2.94 | 1.23 | 0.00 | 0.00 | 0.21 | 0.11 |
| 1995 | 2.42 | 1.02 | 0.00 | 0.00 | 0.03 | 0.08 |
| 1996 | 2.28 | 1.00 | 0.00 | 0.00 | 0.03 | 0.16 |
| 1997 | 1.93 | 0.96 | 0.00 | 0.00 | 0.11 | 0.06 |
| 1998 | 1.53 | 0.62 | 0.00 | 0.00 | 0.24 | 0.22 |
| 1999 | 1.19 | 0.86 | 0.00 | 0.00 | 0.00 | 0.00 |

Sources: Bank Pembangunan Indonesia, Unit Riset (various years).

Note
na = Not available.

nonexistence of the private sector in the Indonesian economy necessitated the government to set up various enterprises in many sectors including food, medicine, transportation, and so on. However, as the economy progresses to maturity, its importance in the daily life of ordinary people is declining. Since 1993, the share of government equity participation has fallen below 1 percent of total expenditures. Their functions are now replaced by private enterprises as many state-owned entities are not healthy financially and could not meet the competitive pressure from private enterprises.

The fertilizer subsidy showed the same pattern as government equity participation. It was more important in the early years of the New Order government since in order to reach self-sufficiency in rice, procurement was the top priority at least until 1988. The drive for rice self-sufficiency has become less pressing as the economy has matured. Moreover, self-sufficiency in rice production is achieved at the cost of underdevelopment of nonrice commodities of which many have good export potential. For these reasons, the share of the fertilizer subsidy has decreased to less than 1 percent of total expenditures since 1990 as the government has reduced the amount of subsidy and allowed the price of fertilizer to be closer to its market equilibrium.

## Fiscal management: the impact of the economic crisis

The most pronounced impact of the economic crisis on the fiscal balance is a dramatic increase in public indebtedness.[3] In June 1997, just before the currency crisis, the Indonesian external debt stood at a comfortable level of 24 percent of GDP. The need for external finance to stabilize the currency, finance the domestic budget deficit and provide a social safety net forced the government to borrow heavily from the IMF. As a result, by the end of 1998, the ratio of public indebtedness to GDP rose to 60 percent.

The banking restructuring program that was started in 1998 necessitated the government to issue bonds; as a consequence, by the end of 1999, public indebtedness had reached a staggering 102 percent of GDP. Sixteen percentage points of this increase was a result of the currency depreciation and the impact of inflation on GDP (World Bank 1999); 11 percent was from the increase in government borrowing from official sources; and the rest was a consequence of the issuance of domestic bonds.

In the face of the economic crisis, the government had no choice but to increase its indebtedness. A large budget deficit was needed to provide fiscal stimulus to the crisis-stricken domestic economy. The biggest constraint was the government budget. Despite efforts to raise taxes and improve tax administration, a decline in economic activity caused non-oil revenues to drop from 13.06 percent of GDP in 1997 to 11.89 percent in 1998 (Table 7.2). On the other hand, budget expenditures reached 21.78 percent of GDP, implying a deficit of 5.73 percent of GDP. This level of expenditure reflects the government's concerns with protecting the poor, maintaining investment in human capital, and pursuing bank restructuring. Under the IMF program, the bank restructuring was a first priority so as to avoid a systemic collapse of the banking system, and this restructuring program required injection of a large amount of public capital into the banking system which had to be financed by the issuance of government bonds.

To avoid inflation, the budget deficit had to be financed by inflows of official capital from abroad. In the immediate future, the pressing problem for the government is how to service this higher public debt. This will exacerbate pressures on the government budget which has already been weakened by declining tax revenues, high interest payments and large energy subsidies. Fortunately, external factors such as declining interest rates and higher oil prices provide some reprieve.

Budgetary pressure is expected to continue in fiscal year 2001–2 as the entire stock of restructuring bonds will have been issued. To remedy the problem, a range of pre-emptive budget actions are being taken. These actions include: (i) acceleration of the asset recovery program by the Indonesian Banking Restructuring Agency (IBRA); (ii) increasing the pace of privatization; (iii) raising tax revenues especially from the removal of VAT exemptions, better tax and customs administration, and reduction in tax incentives; and (iv) cutting expenditures on untargeted subsidies like energy and interest rate subsidies.

### *Fiscal sustainability*

At a time of economic crisis, an increase in the government budget deficit is inevitable. The question is then whether the deficit can be sustained. It is true that there is no consensus of what constitutes a sustainable fiscal policy. However, it seems to be acceptable that fiscal policy is not sustainable if the present and prospective fiscal stance results in a persistent and rapid increase in the ratio of public debt to GDP. From the experiences of many countries, it is evident that persistent high debt-to-GDP ratios are costly because it places pressure on real interest rates and increases the portion of debt repayment in the budget deficit, and hence, reduces room for fiscal flexibility. In addition, the unsustainable fiscal policy will affect the financial market expectation as the credibility of present policies are in doubt and need to be revised.

Mahi *et al.* (2000) estimated a fiscal sustainability model for Indonesia. The model defines the sustainable operational deficit as the one that is consistent with a level of domestic and foreign financing that keeps the debt-to-output ratio constant and with the monetization revenues calculated at a target inflation and output growth rate. The estimating equation basically says that the excess of non-interest expenditures plus interest payments on domestic and foreign components of public debt over domestic revenue must necessarily be financed through a change in the real value of domestic debt or foreign debt or by a change in the real value of the monetary base. A negative figure for the left-hand side of the equation means that the budget is in surplus, while a positive figure refers to a deficit.

Mahi *et al.* (2000) found that the level of actual operational deficit as a percentage of GDP during 1990–98 was lower or at the same level of sustainable operational deficit with 1990 as the exception. This means that the required deficit reduction must be close to zero. One can thus conclude that during those years, the government successfully achieved a sustainable level of foreign public debt. One special case is in 1998 where the actual operational deficit jumped to 8.6 percent while the sustainable level required no more than 5 percent of GDP. This is not surprising since in 1998 the economic crisis was at its worst. In that year, the nominal value of the rupiah against the US dollar plummeted by 250 percent, which meant that the value of foreign debt, interest payment and imported inputs soared, and eventually brought the economy to a standstill.

The dominance of official capital inflows as a means to finance the government budget deficit makes it susceptible to volatility in the exchange rate. Therefore, maintaining exchange rate stability is very important in dealing with the issue of fiscal sustainability. At present, the movement of the exchange rate is beyond the economic fundamentals. Non-economic factors such as the political situation and social unrest seem to exert a dominant influence on the exchange rate movement. As a result, maintaining political stability and social order are necessary conditions for the government to avoid an insolvency problem.

## Central and local governments relationship

At least before 2000, for about thirty years, Indonesia was known for its highly centralized fiscal system. The proportion of total revenues raised by local governments was very low by international standards. Using the 1982–83 fiscal years as an illustration, the transfer from the central government was more than 60 percent of provincial government routine revenues. Meanwhile, within the development budget, the largest contribution came from the central government's capital transfer, which accounted for around 40 percent of the provinces' development revenues. A similar pattern can be observed for district governments (*kabupaten* and *kotamadya*) where about 50 percent of their routine budgets and 39 percent of their development budgets were provided by the central government. In 1998, on average district-own revenue accounted for 9.55 percent of total revenue, while transfers from the central government constituted 74 percent (Alisjahbana 2000).

With regard to the central–regional fiscal balance, there were two types of grants and subsidies in Indonesia. The first type was allocated for regional government routine expenditures such as government employee salaries and wages. The second is an investment type allocation. As it became common in the New Order (Soeharto) era, the second type was authorized by the president and was thus called the INPRES grant. The INPRES grant was very important for regional economic growth, since it was supposed to increase the regions' capital stock (for example, to build roads, health facilities, rural markets and other facilities related to the regions' productive capability). The INPRES grant can be distinguished into two categories: specific grants and block grants. Specific grants were intended to be used for specific purposes dictated by the central government such as to build schools and health facilities. The regional governments did not have the authority to use the grant for other purposes. In the case of block grants, regional governments have a high degree of freedom to allocate the funds according to the region's needs.

The oil boom in 1974–82 provided more room to increase development expenditures (Table 7.8, Table 7.9), and most of the capital investment was not conducted by the central government. In terms of the composition of regional grants, there was a decline in capital transfers in favor of grants for routine/operational expenditures. The portion of capital transfers received by regional governments fell from 32.21 percent in 1976 to below 30 percent thereafter (Table 7.12). Only in 1994 did the share of capital transfers go up again to above 30 percent and it has remained above 30 percent. The picture suggested even before the launching of the Law of Regional Autonomy in 2001 is that there was a trend toward increasing the active role of regional governments in capital accumulation. This trend was confirmed by the strong shift toward block grants within capital transfers.

The fall in the oil price in 1982 and 1986 brought another decline in capital transfers. In absolute terms, regional capital grants fell continuously from its peak of 1.91 percent of GDP in 1981 to 0.73 percent of GDP in 1989 (Table 7.13) or about 3.07 percent of total expenditures (Table 7.14). The decline in capital transfers was due to the sharp reduction in the primary school building program (Table

*Table 7.12* Composition of grants to regions, 1976–99

| *Year* | *Routine expenditures* | *Capital expenditures* |
|---|---|---|
| 1976 | 67.79 | 32.21 |
| 1977 | 73.42 | 26.58 |
| 1978 | 73.58 | 26.42 |
| 1979 | 75.38 | 24.62 |
| 1980 | 74.35 | 25.65 |
| 1981 | 72.96 | 27.04 |
| 1982 | 71.08 | 28.92 |
| 1983 | 74.16 | 25.84 |
| 1984 | 77.68 | 22.32 |
| 1985 | 81.23 | 18.77 |
| 1986 | 82.34 | 17.66 |
| 1987 | 81.10 | 18.90 |
| 1988 | 79.05 | 20.95 |
| 1989 | 83.22 | 16.78 |
| 1990 | 78.53 | 21.47 |
| 1991 | 75.58 | 24.42 |
| 1992 | 74.65 | 25.35 |
| 1993 | 77.13 | 22.87 |
| 1994 | 60.64 | 39.36 |
| 1995 | 63.86 | 36.14 |
| 1996 | 63.77 | 36.23 |
| 1997 | 64.84 | 35.16 |
| 1998 | 69.76 | 30.24 |
| 1999 | 66.63 | 33.37 |

Sources: Bank Pembangunan Indonesia, Unit Riset (various years).

7.15, Table 7.16). Although a tightening of the budget was also responsible for this decline, another reason was the decline in demand for construction of new schools since the primary school enrollment had risen to over 90 percent for the 7–12 age groups in most parts of the country by 1985. The allocations for reforestation and construction of markets were scaled back mainly because of the perceived failure of these programs. The only items that showed improvement was road development.

In 1990, an improved outlook for both growth and the balance of payments persuaded the government to pursue a more expansionary budget, with non-aid development expenditures almost doubling as a proportion of total expenditures. Development expenditures channeled through the government capital transfer program or INPRES began to improve once again. INPRES as a share of total expenditure rose to 6.24 percent in 1991 or about 1.43 percent of GDP (Table 7.13, Table 7.14). This upward trend persisted until reaching its peak in 1994; thereafter, it began to decline and the Asian crisis in 1997 accelerated the downward trend further. In 1998 and 1999, funds allocated to the INPRES program were only 3.70 and 3.92 percent of GDP, respectively.

Starting January 1, 2001, Indonesia has implemented two laws that govern the financial relationship between the central and regional governments: Law No. 22/1999 and Law No. 25/1999. Law No. 22/1999 basically governs regional

*Table 7.13* Composition of grants to regions, 1976–99 (as a % of GDP)

| *Year* | *Routine expenditures* | *Capital expenditures* | | | *Total regional grants* |
|---|---|---|---|---|---|
| | | *Sectoral/ specific grants* | *Block grants* | *Total capital expenditures* | |
| 1976 | 2.03 | 0.61 | 0.96 | 1.57 | 3.60 |
| 1977 | 2.52 | 0.72 | 0.91 | 1.63 | 4.15 |
| 1978 | 2.30 | 0.64 | 0.82 | 1.46 | 3.76 |
| 1979 | 2.09 | 0.79 | 0.68 | 1.47 | 3.56 |
| 1980 | 2.15 | 0.83 | 0.74 | 1.57 | 3.72 |
| 1981 | 2.24 | 1.08 | 0.83 | 1.91 | 4.15 |
| 1982 | 2.21 | 0.74 | 0.90 | 1.64 | 3.85 |
| 1983 | 2.10 | 1.05 | 0.73 | 1.78 | 3.88 |
| 1984 | 2.16 | 0.95 | 0.62 | 1.57 | 3.73 |
| 1985 | 2.63 | 0.80 | 0.61 | 1.40 | 4.03 |
| 1986 | 2.58 | 0.70 | 0.55 | 1.26 | 3.84 |
| 1987 | 2.26 | 0.36 | 0.53 | 0.89 | 3.14 |
| 1988 | 2.12 | 0.29 | 0.56 | 0.85 | 2.97 |
| 1989 | 2.14 | 0.30 | 0.43 | 0.73 | 2.87 |
| 1990 | 1.99 | 0.64 | 0.54 | 1.18 | 3.17 |
| 1991 | 1.92 | 0.81 | 0.62 | 1.43 | 3.35 |
| 1992 | 2.07 | 0.86 | 0.70 | 1.56 | 3.63 |
| 1993 | 2.29 | 0.71 | 0.68 | 1.38 | 3.67 |
| 1994 | 1.90 | 0.25 | 1.23 | 1.48 | 3.39 |
| 1995 | 1.81 | 0.18 | 1.02 | 1.21 | 3.02 |
| 1996 | 1.76 | 0.22 | 1.00 | 1.22 | 2.97 |
| 1997 | 1.77 | 0.24 | 0.96 | 1.20 | 2.97 |
| 1998 | 1.43 | 0.18 | 0.62 | 0.81 | 2.24 |
| 1999 | 1.71 | 0.00 | 0.86 | 0.86 | 2.57 |

Sources: Bank Pembangunan Indonesia, Unit Riset (various years).

autonomy, while Law No. 25/1999 or the Fiscal Balance Law, focuses on fiscal decentralization. Law No. 22/1999 regulates the devolution of both fiscal/taxing and project implementation power to whatever level of government is deemed more suitable. In addition, it regulated the transfer of financing, personnel and assets.

The main difference between the Old Law and the New Law is that more block transfers will be offered to regional governments; hence, the regions can use the transfers in accordance with its own needs. According to Law No. 25/1999, total block grant transfers or DAU is calculated as 25 percent of national domestic revenues in the respective year (Mahi *et al.* 2000). DAU is used specifically to finance basic services at the regional level. In addition, DAU is designed to balance the financial capacity of regional governments across the country. In 2001, the estimate of DAU is around Rp. 50 trillion, which will be allocated to all regional governments. The central government has an obligation to meet the rule of 25 percent of domestic revenue. The primary weakness of this rigid rule is that in trying to accommodate fiscal decentralization, it may threaten the sustainability of the national budget.

*Table 7.14* Composition of grants to regions, 1976–99 (as a % of total expenditure)

| *Year* | *Routine expenditures* | *Capital expenditures* | | | *Total regional grants* |
|---|---|---|---|---|---|
| | | *Sectoral/ specific grants* | *Block grants* | *Total capital expenditures* | |
| 1976 | 8.50 | 2.55 | 4.04 | 6.59 | 15.09 |
| 1977 | 11.11 | 3.18 | 4.02 | 7.20 | 18.31 |
| 1978 | 9.86 | 2.73 | 3.54 | 6.27 | 16.12 |
| 1979 | 8.96 | 3.37 | 2.93 | 6.29 | 15.25 |
| 1980 | 8.87 | 3.43 | 3.06 | 6.49 | 15.36 |
| 1981 | 8.78 | 4.25 | 3.26 | 7.50 | 16.28 |
| 1982 | 9.13 | 3.07 | 3.71 | 6.79 | 15.92 |
| 1983 | 8.24 | 4.11 | 2.87 | 6.98 | 15.22 |
| 1984 | 10.59 | 4.63 | 3.04 | 7.68 | 18.27 |
| 1985 | 10.48 | 3.18 | 2.42 | 5.60 | 16.08 |
| 1986 | 11.61 | 3.16 | 2.49 | 5.65 | 17.27 |
| 1987 | 10.38 | 1.66 | 2.42 | 4.08 | 14.46 |
| 1988 | 9.06 | 1.25 | 2.40 | 3.64 | 12.70 |
| 1989 | 9.00 | 1.26 | 1.81 | 3.07 | 12.07 |
| 1990 | 8.21 | 2.64 | 2.24 | 4.88 | 13.09 |
| 1991 | 8.39 | 3.53 | 2.71 | 6.24 | 14.64 |
| 1992 | 8.90 | 3.68 | 3.02 | 6.70 | 15.59 |
| 1993 | 10.05 | 3.10 | 2.98 | 6.09 | 16.14 |
| 1994 | 9.73 | 1.27 | 6.31 | 7.58 | 17.31 |
| 1995 | 10.39 | 1.05 | 5.88 | 6.93 | 17.31 |
| 1996 | 9.50 | 1.17 | 5.40 | 6.57 | 16.07 |
| 1997 | 8.64 | 1.18 | 4.69 | 5.87 | 14.51 |
| 1998 | 6.58 | 0.85 | 2.85 | 3.70 | 10.29 |
| 1999 | 7.82 | 0.00 | 3.92 | 3.92 | 11.73 |

Sources: Bank Pembangunan Indonesia, Unit Riset (various years).

From the point of view of local-revenue mobilization, aside from local taxes and user charges, the new law provides regional governments with greater flexibility in determining their potential own-revenue sources. The concern is that exercising too much local taxing power may result in overtaxing at the local level, and hence will undermine the health of the region's economy. It is argued, however, that in a competitive setting, the temptation to overtax will be balanced by the concern to maintain a region's competitiveness relative to others in such a way that the setting of local tax rates should not drive investors away from the region. In a limited sense, it is also possible for a region to offer incentives to potential investors in the form of concessionary tax rates.

## Conclusion

Throughout the era of the New Order government and up to the present, the Indonesian government has continued to run a balanced budget policy. The balanced budget policy is deceiving, however, since it does not meet the standard accounting criteria of a balanced budget; rather, the balanced budget is defined

*Table 7.15* Regional sectoral and specific grants, 1976–99 (as a % of total expenditure)

| *Year* | *Primary schools* | *Health clinics* | *Markets* | *Reforestation* | *Road development* | *Total* |
|---|---|---|---|---|---|---|
| 1976 | 1.56 | 0.56 | 0.00 | 0.43 | 0.00 | 2.55 |
| 1977 | 1.97 | 0.61 | 0.03 | 0.57 | 0.00 | 3.18 |
| 1978 | 2.11 | 0.51 | 0.02 | 0.08 | 0.00 | 2.73 |
| 1979 | 2.08 | 0.40 | 0.17 | 0.55 | 0.17 | 3.37 |
| 1980 | 2.27 | 0.46 | 0.02 | 0.44 | 0.24 | 3.43 |
| 1981 | 2.72 | 0.57 | 0.04 | 0.51 | 0.40 | 4.25 |
| 1982 | 1.85 | 0.56 | 0.03 | 0.34 | 0.29 | 3.07 |
| 1983 | 2.92 | 0.46 | 0.06 | 0.31 | 0.35 | 4.11 |
| 1984 | 3.22 | 0.37 | 0.14 | 0.34 | 0.57 | 4.63 |
| 1985 | 2.22 | 0.47 | 0.02 | 0.18 | 0.29 | 3.18 |
| 1986 | 2.17 | 0.47 | 0.05 | 0.14 | 0.33 | 3.16 |
| 1987 | 0.71 | 0.27 | 0.01 | 0.06 | 0.60 | 1.66 |
| 1988 | 0.39 | 0.27 | 0.01 | 0.05 | 0.53 | 1.25 |
| 1989 | 0.25 | 0.25 | 0.02 | 0.04 | 0.69 | 1.26 |
| 1990 | 0.78 | 0.37 | 0.03 | 0.07 | 1.40 | 2.64 |
| 1991 | 0.99 | 0.51 | 0.01 | 0.14 | 1.88 | 3.53 |
| 1992 | 1.07 | 0.52 | 0.00 | 0.16 | 1.93 | 3.68 |
| 1993 | 0.87 | 0.49 | 0.00 | 0.16 | 1.58 | 3.10 |
| 1994 | 0.72 | 0.55 | 0.00 | 0.00 | 0.00 | 1.27 |
| 1995 | 0.62 | 0.43 | 0.00 | 0.00 | 0.00 | 1.05 |
| 1996 | 0.60 | 0.57 | 0.00 | 0.00 | 0.00 | 1.17 |
| 1997 | 0.51 | 0.67 | 0.00 | 0.00 | 0.00 | 1.18 |
| 1998 | 0.27 | 0.58 | 0.00 | 0.00 | 0.00 | 0.85 |
| 1999 | 0.00 | 0.00 | 0.00 | 0.00 | 0.00 | 0.00 |

Sources: Bank Pembangunan Indonesia, Unit Riset (various years).

such that total government receipts from all sources, including foreign borrowing, equals total expenditures. In other words, items elsewhere classified as a means of financing the budget deficit have been classified as receipts in Indonesia. The purpose of the balanced budget policy is to impose fiscal discipline and to avoid the 1960 experience of budget-induced hyperinflation.

From the beginning, it was obvious that the prospect of using fiscal policy for demand management is very limited in Indonesia. Given this limitation, the government focused on using the budget as a tool of allocation. As the burden of debt servicing continues to increase, the government's ability to use the budget as an allocation tool is further eroded. Capital expenditures, which are crucial in boosting economic growth and in lessening inequality across regions, must yield to make room for debt-servicing expenditures. Thus, a rapid increase in debt expenditures will result in a lower growth potential and at the same time, greater inequality.

With regard to fiscal management, the increase in government debt is inevitable at a time of economic crisis. The need for fiscal stimulus to Indonesia's crisis-stricken economy required a large budget deficit, which had to be financed in a non-inflationary way by inflows of official capital from abroad. The need to avoid total collapse of the banking system also required a large injection of public capital

*Table 7.16* Regional sectoral and specific grants, 1976–99 (as a % of GDP)

| *Year* | *Primary schools* | *Health clinics* | *Markets* | *Reforestation* | *Road development* | *Total* |
|---|---|---|---|---|---|---|
| 1976 | 0.37 | 0.13 | 0.00 | 0.10 | 0.00 | 0.61 |
| 1977 | 0.45 | 0.14 | 0.01 | 0.13 | 0.00 | 0.72 |
| 1978 | 0.49 | 0.12 | 0.01 | 0.02 | 0.00 | 0.64 |
| 1979 | 0.49 | 0.09 | 0.04 | 0.13 | 0.04 | 0.79 |
| 1980 | 0.55 | 0.11 | 0.01 | 0.11 | 0.06 | 0.83 |
| 1981 | 0.69 | 0.15 | 0.01 | 0.13 | 0.10 | 1.08 |
| 1982 | 0.45 | 0.13 | 0.01 | 0.08 | 0.07 | 0.74 |
| 1983 | 0.74 | 0.12 | 0.01 | 0.08 | 0.09 | 1.05 |
| 1984 | 0.66 | 0.07 | 0.03 | 0.07 | 0.12 | 0.95 |
| 1985 | 0.56 | 0.12 | 0.00 | 0.05 | 0.07 | 0.80 |
| 1986 | 0.48 | 0.10 | 0.01 | 0.03 | 0.07 | 0.70 |
| 1987 | 0.15 | 0.06 | 0.00 | 0.01 | 0.13 | 0.36 |
| 1988 | 0.09 | 0.06 | 0.00 | 0.01 | 0.12 | 0.29 |
| 1989 | 0.06 | 0.06 | 0.00 | 0.01 | 0.16 | 0.30 |
| 1990 | 0.19 | 0.09 | 0.01 | 0.02 | 0.34 | 0.64 |
| 1991 | 0.23 | 0.12 | 0.00 | 0.03 | 0.43 | 0.81 |
| 1992 | 0.25 | 0.12 | 0.00 | 0.04 | 0.45 | 0.86 |
| 1993 | 0.20 | 0.11 | 0.00 | 0.04 | 0.36 | 0.71 |
| 1994 | 0.14 | 0.11 | 0.00 | 0.00 | 0.00 | 0.25 |
| 1995 | 0.11 | 0.07 | 0.00 | 0.00 | 0.00 | 0.18 |
| 1996 | 0.11 | 0.11 | 0.00 | 0.00 | 0.00 | 0.22 |
| 1997 | 0.11 | 0.14 | 0.00 | 0.00 | 0.00 | 0.24 |
| 1998 | 0.06 | 0.13 | 0.00 | 0.00 | 0.00 | 0.18 |
| 1999 | 0.00 | 0.00 | 0.00 | 0.00 | 0.00 | 0.00 |

Sources: Bank Pembangunan Indonesia, Unit Riset (various years).

into the banking system financed through government bonds. Although much of the new borrowing has been from concessional official sources, the cost of servicing the new debt will place pressure on economic growth and the balance of payments in the future. This could mean a slower recovery and a lower level of sustained growth for the economy.

Responding to the question of fiscal sustainability, during the 1990–98 period, the government successfully achieved a sustainable level of foreign public debt. Except for 1990, the level of actual operational deficit as a percentage of GDP during 1990–98 is lower or at the same level with the level of sustainable operational deficit. This means that the required deficit reduction is close to zero. The dominance of foreign borrowing as a means to finance the government budget deficit has made fiscal sustainability susceptible to fluctuations in the exchange rate. Therefore, maintaining exchange rate stability is very important in dealing with the issue of fiscal sustainability. At present, movement of the exchange rate is influenced by many non-economic factors such as the political situation and social unrest, both of which seem to exert significant influence on the exchange rate. Therefore, maintaining political stability and social order are necessary conditions for the Indonesian government to avoid an insolvency problem.

On the issue of regional finance, the demand for greater regional autonomy has prompted the government and the legislative body to design a new law of regional autonomy that regulates the transfer of fiscal authority and responsibility from the central government to the provincial and municipal levels. However, this means that without alternative revenue sources or cutting expenditures, i.e., potential revenue for the central government, the budget deficit cannot be sustained for too long. The positive side is that if done correctly, decentralization not only gives people the freedom to shape their own lives, but it can also enhance a nation's political cohesion and economic competitiveness. On the other hand, if it is done poorly, it can mean macro instability, more rather than less corruption, a worsening of the investment climate, over-exploitation of natural resources and even disintegration of the nation.

## Notes

1 In the strictest sense, some development expenditure items actually cannot be categorized into capital expenditures.
2 INPRES is the acronym for Instruksi Presiden (presidential instruction).
3 Public external debt is defined as the external debt of government, state-owned enterprises and state banks.

## References

Alisjahbana, A.S. (2000) "Local government on revenue mobilization," paper presented at the Indonesian Economic Recovery in Changing Environment Conference, September, Jakarta, Indonesia.

Asher, G. Mukul and Booth, A. (1995) "Fiscal policy," in A. Booth (ed.) *The Oil Boom and After: Indonesian Economic Policy and Performance in the Soeharto Era*, Singapore: Oxford University Press.

Asian Development Bank (1999) "Country economic review: Indonesia," unpublished report, Manila: ADB.

Bank Indonesia, Urusan Ekonomi and Statistik (various years) *Indonesian Financial Statistics*, various issues, Jakarta: Bank Indonesia.

Bank Pembangunan Indonesia, Unit Riset (various years) *Economic Indicators Indonesia*, various issues, Jakarta: Bank Pembangunan Indonesia, Unit Riset.

Bardhan, P. and Mookherjee, D. (1998) "Expenditure decentralization and the delivery of public services in developing countries," mimeo, Department of Economics, University of California, Berkeley.

Basri, M.C. and Kuncoro, A. (1998) "Indonesian quarterly review," *Economics and Finance in Indonesia* 46(2): 147–71.

Bawazier, Fuad (1989) "Keuangan Daerah," paper presented to the Conference on Regional Economic Development, May, Jakarta, Indonesia.

Brueckner, J. (1999) "Fiscal decentralization in LDCs: the effects of local corruption and tax evasion," mimeo, Department of Economics, University of Illinois at Urbana-Champaign.

Huther, J. and Shah, A. (1998) *Applying a Simple Measure of Good Governance to the Debate on Fiscal Decentralization*, World Bank Policy Research Working Paper, no. 1894, Washington, DC: World Bank.

Mahi, R. and Jasmina, T. (2000) "The impact of regional autonomy on the central government fiscal sustainability," paper presented at the Indonesian Economic Recovery in Changing Environment Conference, September, Jakarta, Indonesia.

Mahi, R., Winoto, A. and Damayanti, A. (2000) "Fiscal sustainability: the case of Indonesia 1990–1999," paper presented at the Indonesian Economic Recovery in Changing Environment Conference, September, Jakarta, Indonesia.

Omura, K. (1996) "Less depending on the official development assistance," in D. Kuntjoro-Jakti and K. Omura (eds) *Indonesian Economy toward the Twenty-First Century*, Tokyo: Institute of Developing Economics.

Ravallion, Martin (1988) "INPRES inequality: a distributional perspective on the center's regional disbursements," *Bulletin of Indonesian Economic Studies* 24(3): 53–72.

Shleifer, A. and Vishny, R. (1993) "Corruption," *Quarterly Journal of Economics* 108: 599–617.

Tiebout, C. (1956) "A pure theory of local expenditures," *Journal of Political Economy* 64: 416–24.

Treisman, D. (2000) "The causes of corruption: a cross-national study," *Journal of Public Economics* 76: 399–457.

Wade, R. (1997) "How infrastructure agencies motivate staff: canal irrigation and the republic of Korea," in Ashoka Mofy (ed.) *Infrastructure Strategies in East Asia*, Washington, DC: World Bank.

World Bank (1998) "Indonesia in crisis: a macroeconomic update," unpublished report, Washington, DC: World Bank.

World Bank (1999) "Indonesia: from crisis to opportunity," unpublished report, Washington, DC: World Bank.

# 8 Japan

*Kazumi Asako, Hitoshi Suzuki and Masao Tsuri*

## Introduction

It was not so long ago that Japan was praised for its superb macroeconomic performances and its underlying and well-functioning social as well as economic systems and institutions. Today, however, Japan is being criticized for and suffering from a slow transition from an old to a new economic system. This transition was inevitable partly because of the intruding globalization of economic activities across nations as well as basic organizational changes that are rapidly taking place in the structure of Japanese society. Fiscal issues in Japan are a typical area where structural reform is urgently needed as the conditions on which most fiscal issues were designed have been changed, drastically in some areas and unnoticeably but steadily in others.

This chapter consists of two parts. The first section is devoted to summarizing and presenting compactly the underlying data with which one can understand the institutions, history and present condition of fiscal issues in Japan. In this chapter, we also attempt to spotlight the Japanese case by comparing it with other nations around the world.

In the second section, we explain why Japan has a history of rising and falling fiscal deficits over the period 1965–2000. In so doing, we pay special attention to whether the rise and fall of deficits are intended or unintended. Naturally intended deficits are under the control of government, whereas unintended deficits are thought to be either beyond the government's control or due to incessant unanticipated shocks.

## Government budget of Japan: institutional structure and the current situation

### *Institutional structure of the government budget*

#### *Types of budgets*

The government budget in Japan can broadly be categorized into a general account and special accounts. The general account is the nation's core budget. Revenues recorded in the general account include tax revenues and revenues from the issue of public bonds. Expenditure entries include outlays for social security, public works projects, education and science, and defense as well as funds disbursed to local governments and the national debt service. The general account can be said to express the fiscal stance and current situation of the government.

In contrast, special accounts are established when budget accounting needs to be kept separate from the general account, such as when the government engages in specified activities and makes use of specified funds. There are currently thirty-two special accounts. Each special account has its own independent source of revenues, and the flow of funds between the general account and special accounts is complex.

In the system of national accounts (SNA), a series of secondary statistics, the general account and special accounts are categorized as the accounts of the central government, social security funds and public corporations. Since the complex and overlapping flow of funds between accounts is offset in this process, SNA provides an effective means of understanding the situation for the government budget.

As another way of categorizing the budget, the budget developed through a process lasting about a year is called the regular annual budget or initial budget (we later refer to this as a "plan"). In contrast, budgets drawn up during the fiscal year in response to disasters and changes in government policy are known as supplementary budgets (we refer to these as a "revised plan"). The accounting year of the government budget is from 1 April to 31 March of the following year.

### *The budget process*

The cabinet has the responsibility and authority for preparing and submitting a budget to the Diet. Japan has a parliamentary system of government, meaning that the governing party/parties hold a majority in the Diet, and the budget prepared and submitted by the cabinet composed of the governing party/parties is usually passed by the Diet with few, if any, changes.

Below the cabinet level, the Ministry of Finance (MOF) has the authority to plan the fiscal system and to prepare each year's budget (Box 8.1). We will discuss the budget cycle in detail later.

**Box 8.1 Reorganization of central government ministries and budget compilation**

Central government ministries and agencies were extensively reorganized in January 2001, the first major reorganization to take place since immediately after World War II. Following this restructuring, the MOF became responsible for preparing each year's budget (as was the case before). On the other hand, the Cabinet Office, which was founded to support cabinet activities as they relate to major policies, is responsible for developing basic principles for budget management and basic guidelines for budget compilation. With these goals in mind, the Council on Economic and Fiscal Policy was established, which, at the request of the Prime Minister, examines basic guidelines for managing the entire economy, managing the budget, and budget compilation.

*The budget and the macroeconomy*

From the view of economic policies, the overall size of the government budget is all but decided in the previous summer through the "Guidelines for Budget Requests." As a result, fiscal policies may prove to be inadequate due to unpredicted changes in the economy. For this reason, it has become a common practice to prepare supplementary budgets during the fiscal year, so as to allocate additional funds for public works projects. The size of supplementary budgets has grown tremendously in recent years (Figure 8.1). In the 1990s, supplementary budgets were frequently used to provide fiscal stimulus to the economy. It has therefore become increasingly difficult to ignore supplementary budgets in debating the relationship between the macroeconomy and public finances.

Government budgets are prepared for each accounting year, and expenditures of a given fiscal year must be covered by revenues of the same year. In actuality, expenditures, such as public works spending, are often carried forward to the following fiscal year, subject to approval of the Diet. The increasing size of supplementary budgets is beginning to have an effect on the macroeconomy unrelated to accounting years.

## The general account and Japanese government bonds (JGBs)

### *Construction bonds and deficit-financing bonds*

Two classes of bonds are issued under the general account: construction bonds and deficit-financing bonds (deficit bonds). While the Public Finance Law forbids

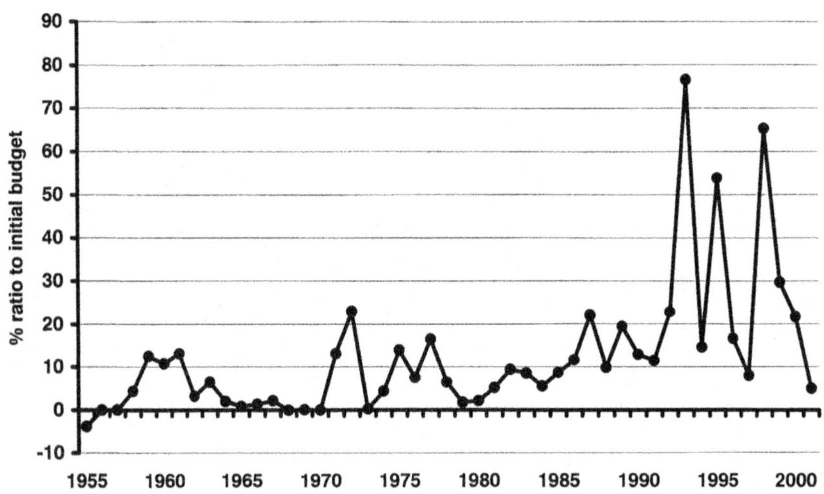


*Figure 8.1* Public works spending allocated in supplementary budgets in Japan.

Sources: Ministry of Finance; Daiwa Institute of Research.

Notes

a Based on central government general account.

b Negative values are cases where the initial budget was reduced through supplementary budget drawing.

borrowings, including the flotation of public bonds, an exception is made for such borrowings that finance public works projects and other investment expenditures. These bonds are known as construction bonds. It is not difficult to imagine tax revenues alone being insufficient to finance social overhead capital used across generations. Using government bonds to spread the benefits and costs of social overhead capital over several generations is therefore extremely rational. Although the flotation of deficit-financing bonds is not sanctioned by the Public Finance Law, a special law is passed each fiscal year to permit the issue of these bonds when tax revenues fail to cover current (non-investment) expenditures.

### *History of the general account*

After experiencing a period of economic confusion following World War II, Japan adhered to a balanced budget policy until the mid-1960s, in part supported by a high-growth economy. The flotation of government bonds was authorized for the first time in the post-war period in the FY65 supplementary budget to finance a revenue shortfall, and since FY66, construction bonds have been issued to fund budget expenditures. In subsequent years—such as during the economic downturn following the yen's revaluation in 1971, the outbreak of inflation accompanying the first oil crisis in 1973, and the first post-war economic contraction in FY74—the government sought to control the level of budget expenditures to stabilize the economy.

The next turning point occurred in FY75. Expansion of the social security system in the first half of the 1970s and sluggish growth of tax revenues ensuing from the transition to stable rather than high economic growth led to the issue of deficit-financing bonds in the FY75 supplementary budget. As Figure 8.2 illustrates, the dependency on debt, the share of Japanese government bond (JGB) issuance in total revenues, grew rapidly in the second half of the 1970s. It peaked at 34.7 percent in FY79, when the second oil crisis coincided with mounting calls from abroad for Japan to bolster domestic demand.

In the 1980s, efforts were made to restore healthy public finances; these efforts included reducing expenditures through administrative reform. Dependency on debt gradually declined and no deficit-financing bonds were issued in FY90. This picture changed with the economic downturn that began in 1991. Starting in FY91, tax revenues in the general account decreased for four straight years. Substantial cuts in personal income tax since 1994 have compelled the government to issue deficit-financing bonds in FY94 and subsequent years. Moreover, to respond to the weak economy in the 1990s, the government instituted ten stimulus packages over the period FY92–FY00, consisting of supplementary budgets that were to fund additional public works spending, in an effort to stimulate the economy from the expenditure side; this led to large flotations of construction bonds, and the dependency on debt turned upward. In 1997, the Fiscal Structural Reform Act was passed and some effort was made at fiscal reform, but the law's provisions are currently under suspension.[1] Japan's dependency on debt in FY03 is estimated to be 44.6 percent (initial budget basis).

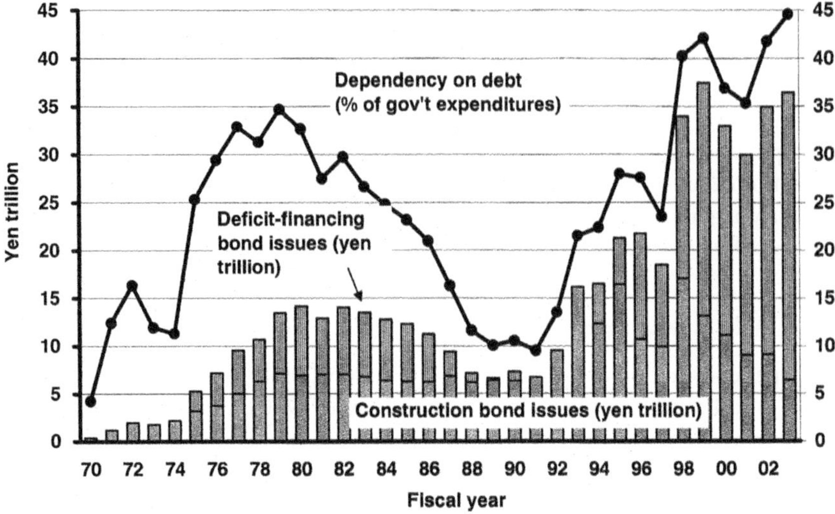


*Figure 8.2* New JGB issues and dependency on debt.[a]

Source: Ministry of Finance.

Note

a Through FY01, closing account; FY02, supplementary budget; FY03, initial budget. Issue of deficit-financing bonds in FY90 was an exceptional case.

### *Redemption system and JGB outstanding*

Under the redemption system for JGB, 1.6 percent (about one-sixtieth) of JGB outstanding at the start of the previous fiscal year are transferred from the general account to the special account for the Government Debt Consolidation Fund to enable bonds to be redeemed over a period of about sixty years (Box 8.2). Such a systematic redemption can be commended for increasing the certainty of repayment.

As a result of flotations and redemptions occurring through yearly budget activities, JGB outstanding is forecast to total Y450 trillion at end-FY03, or 90.4 percent of nominal GDP. Of this amount, deficit-financing bonds are expected to total Y207 trillion, whose issue has grown rapidly since the second half of the 1990s (Figure 8.3).

## Intra-government relationship: local governments and social security funds

### *Local government budgets*

There are about 3,300 prefectural and municipal governments in Japan, each having a legislature and budget. The shape and implementation of these budgets largely conform with those of the central government. Local government budgets,

**Box 8.2 Sixty-year redemption rule**

Government bonds are under the control of the sixty-year redemption rule in Japan. For example, when ten-year government bonds reach maturity, 10/60 of the original issue amount is redeemed through the Government Debt Consolidation Fund, and the remainder is refinanced through the issue of refunding bonds. Once this process (10/60 redemption of the original amount and the issue of refunding bonds for the rest every ten years) is repeated six times, the original bonds will be fully redeemed after sixty years.

This rule assumes that assets for which construction bonds are issued have an average useful life of sixty years. Questions, however, have been raised on the appropriateness of having a uniform standard for social overhead capital whose useful life can vary considerably and on whether the standard is too long. Another problem that has been noted is that deficit-financing bonds without corresponding assets are treated in the same manner as construction bonds.

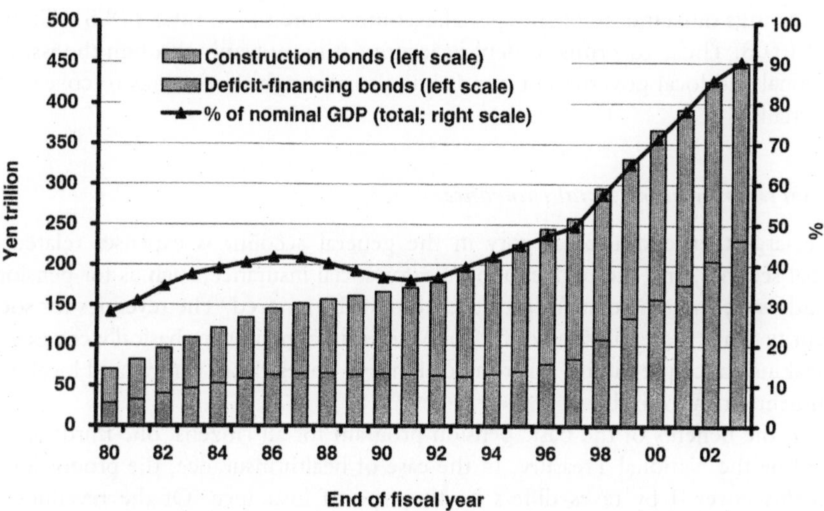


*Figure 8.3* JGB outstanding.[a]

Sources: Ministry of Finance; CAO of Japan.

Note

a FY80–FY01, actual; FY02–FY03, government estimate.

however, have two distinguishing features. Fiscal transfers from the central government make up a large portion of local government budgets, and local governments have major fiscal restrictions in the areas of taxation and local government bond issuance.

Important components of transfers to local governments are the local allocation tax (LAT) and national government disbursements. LAT has the purpose of equalizing sources of funds for government expenditures between localities, and a fixed percentage of national taxes are transferred to local governments with no restrictions on their use. In contrast, national government disbursements are transfers whose use is specified. In FY03, revenues in the budget plans of local governments are estimated to be Y86.2 trillion (including Y15.1 trillion from the issue of local government bonds). Of this total, 21.0 percent was LAT, 14.2 percent was national government disbursements, and 37.3 percent was local tax revenues.

As a matter of fact, LAT is directly related to the problem of budget deficits. LAT calculated as a fixed percentage of national taxes is a general account expenditure that is recorded as revenue in the special account for the Allotment of Local Allocation Tax and Local Transfer Tax. In contrast, the amount of LAT disbursed as expenditure from this special account is determined by the revenue shortages of local governments. Accordingly, there is no guarantee that the shortfall in the revenues of local governments will correspond exactly with the fixed percentage of national taxes. In recent years, this difference has been covered by the special account borrowings from the MOF Trust Fund Bureau (TFB; which was replaced with the Fiscal Loan Fund) and financial markets. The borrowings outstanding of the special account is forecast to total Y48.5 trillion at end-FY03. Thus, government debt is accumulating not only through the issue of national and local government bonds but also through borrowings to cover LAT shortfalls.

### *Social security funds: social insurance*

The largest expenditure category in the general account is expenses related to social security, and the budget allocated for social insurance, such as for pensions, health care, and employment measures, cannot be ignored. The revenues for social security funds (revenue sources for social security benefits) are basically covered by social insurance premiums, but related transfers (taxes) from central and local governments are also sizable.

Of the benefits of the basic pension program for all citizens, one-third[2] is supplied by the National Treasury. In the case of health insurance, the proportion of benefits covered by taxes differs by the type of insurance. Of the revenues for national health expenditure, the share of public payments in the combined total of insurance premiums and public payments (central and local governments) was 37.7 percent in FY00.

### *Transfers between government budgets*

Figure 8.4 portrays an estimate of transfers occurring within general government. According to this estimate, current transfers from the central government to local governments have held at approximately 5–6.5 percent of nominal GDP since the second half of the 1970s. Current transfers to social security funds have been more than 2 percent of GDP for the central government since the 1980s (except for FY90 and FY91), and the corresponding percentage for local governments has trended gradually upward. Net capital transfers from the central government to

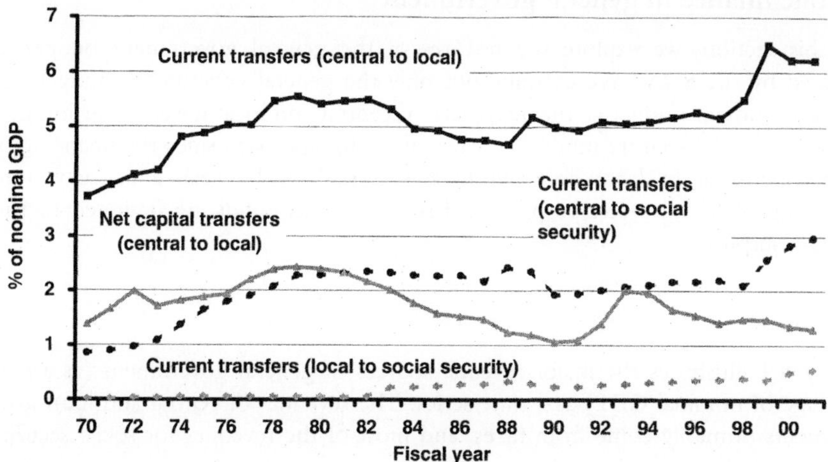


*Figure 8.4* Intra-governmental transfers.[a]

Sources: CAO of Japan; Daiwa Institute of Research.

Note
a FY70–FY89 based on SNA68; FY90–FY01 based on SNA93.

local governments fell during the 1980s, rose in the 1990s owing to a series of stimulus measures, and have edged downward in recent years.

The argument has been made that the substantial transfer of funds between central and local governments makes it difficult to understand the relationship between the benefit and costs of public finances, that is to say, the relationship between administrative services and their costs. Local governments depend on central government transfers for a large portion of their revenues, and the central government entrusts local governments with the implementation of national policy. Under such conditions, local governments may not have the incentive to manage public finances efficiently.

In other words, fiscal problems in Japan have arisen mainly from difficulties in local government finances. Therefore, the move toward greater decentralization that is being promoted in Japan is worthy of attention since it has the potential of appropriately reallocating administrative authority and revenue sources between central and local governments, thereby increasing the efficiency of public finances overall.

The growth of fiscal transfers to social security funds can be viewed as a natural outcome of the aging of the Japanese society, and further increase of such transfers can be expected. With this in mind, the reform of public pensions and health insurance is being debated, and the argument is being made that it should be possible to increase the efficiency of both the funding and payments of these programs.

## Public finance in general government

In this section, we explore the features of the general government budget as defined by the SNA.[3] We examine not only the general government budget but the government budget as the aggregate of central and local government budgets excluding social security funds. We have taken this approach since the financing of public pensions in Japan is a hybrid system midway between a pay-as-you-go financing plan and a reserve plan, and social security funds are designed to run budget surpluses.

### *Revenues*

Table 8.1 illustrates the major revenue sources of general government (as a percentage of nominal GDP) as a time series. The revenues of central and local governments primarily come from taxes, and most of the revenues for social security funds come from social security contributions.

#### *Direct taxes and indirect taxes*

After bottoming in FY75, indirect taxes as a proportion of GDP have trended gradually upward. In FY89, Japan adopted a consumption tax, a form of a value-added tax, with a tax rate of 3 percent, which was raised to 5 percent in FY97. When compared with the corresponding ratio for direct taxes, however, that for indirect taxes has been stable over a long period of time. The proportion of direct taxes in GDP surpassed that for indirect taxes in FY67 and increased further in subsequent years. In the 1990s, however, this proportion fell rapidly, and in FY98 and FY99, it dropped below that of indirect taxes. The decrease in direct taxes can be explained by (i) the tax system's automatic stabilizing mechanism coming into play during the deep recession in the 1990s; and (ii) the government's discretionary reduction of direct taxes since FY94 to stimulate the economy. As such, these changes are in part the result of the government deliberately curtailing tax revenues.

Therefore, should Japan's economy expand steadily, the stabilizing mechanism is certain to bring an increase in direct taxes, but this mechanism did not work as well as it did in the 1980s. There are two reasons for this. First, due to the government lowering of direct taxes and raising of indirect taxes as a policy, the share of indirect taxes has increased, which is likely to have reduced the elasticity of taxes. Second, while the indirect tax burden has increased gradually, that of direct taxes has fallen sharply, and the overall taxpayer burden (i.e., the average tax rate at the macroeconomic level) has trended downward after peaking in FY89 (Table 8.1). In other words, as is widely known, Japan's taxpayer burden is considerably smaller relative to that of other nations (Table 8.2), and there is considerable room for increasing revenues and taxes. It should therefore be possible to explore avenues for raising the efficiency of tax collection, including a suitable combination of direct and indirect taxes, through restructuring of the overall tax system.

*Table 8.1* General government revenues in Japan, 1955–2001[a] (as a % of nominal GDP)

| *FY* | *Central and local governments* | | | *Central government* | | | *Local government* | | | *Social Security Fund*[b] |
|---|---|---|---|---|---|---|---|---|---|---|
| | *Indirect taxes* | *Direct taxes* | *Total* | *Indirect taxes* | *Direct taxes* | *Total* | *Indirect taxes* | *Direct taxes* | *Total* | |
| 1955 | 8.7 | 6.9 | 15.5 | | | | | | | 2.7 |
| 1956 | 8.9 | 7.2 | 16.2 | | | | | | | 2.7 |
| 1957 | 8.9 | 7.0 | 15.9 | | | | | | | 2.8 |
| 1958 | 8.8 | 6.2 | 15.0 | | | | | | | 2.9 |
| 1959 | 8.5 | 6.2 | 14.7 | | | | | | | 2.8 |
| 1960 | 8.5 | 7.0 | 15.5 | | | | | | | 2.9 |
| 1961 | 8.5 | 7.3 | 15.8 | | | | | | | 3.0 |
| 1962 | 8.1 | 7.7 | 15.8 | | | | | | | 3.2 |
| 1963 | 7.8 | 7.5 | 15.3 | | | | | | | 3.4 |
| 1964 | 7.7 | 7.6 | 15.3 | | | | | | | 3.5 |
| 1965 | 7.3 | 7.4 | 14.6 | | | | | | | 4.0 |
| 1966 | 7.0 | 7.0 | 14.0 | | | | | | | 4.1 |
| 1967 | 7.1 | 7.3 | 14.4 | | | | | | | 4.1 |
| 1968 | 7.2 | 7.6 | 14.7 | | | | | | | 4.1 |
| 1969 | 7.1 | 7.9 | 15.0 | | | | | | | 4.1 |
| 1970 | 7.2 | 8.5 | 15.6 | 3.6 | 6.8 | 10.4 | 3.6 | 1.7 | 5.2 | 4.4 |
| 1971 | 7.0 | 8.5 | 15.5 | 3.4 | 6.7 | 10.1 | 3.6 | 1.8 | 5.4 | 4.7 |
| 1972 | 7.0 | 9.0 | 16.0 | 3.5 | 7.1 | 10.6 | 3.5 | 1.9 | 5.4 | 4.7 |
| 1973 | 7.2 | 10.6 | 17.8 | 3.4 | 8.6 | 11.9 | 3.8 | 2.0 | 5.8 | 4.9 |
| 1974 | 6.8 | 11.0 | 17.8 | 3.0 | 8.6 | 11.6 | 3.9 | 2.3 | 6.2 | 5.7 |
| 1975 | 6.5 | 8.9 | 15.4 | 3.0 | 6.8 | 9.8 | 3.5 | 2.1 | 5.6 | 6.1 |
| 1976 | 6.8 | 9.1 | 15.8 | 3.2 | 6.8 | 10.0 | 3.5 | 2.3 | 5.8 | 6.4 |
| 1977 | 6.8 | 9.2 | 16.0 | 3.2 | 6.8 | 10.0 | 3.7 | 2.3 | 6.0 | 6.8 |
| 1978 | 7.1 | 10.4 | 17.5 | 3.5 | 7.9 | 11.4 | 3.6 | 2.4 | 6.1 | 7.0 |
| 1979 | 7.4 | 10.4 | 17.8 | 3.6 | 7.8 | 11.3 | 3.8 | 2.6 | 6.4 | 7.1 |
| 1980 | 7.4 | 11.1 | 18.5 | 3.4 | 8.4 | 11.8 | 4.0 | 2.7 | 6.7 | 7.4 |
| 1981 | 7.5 | 11.3 | 18.8 | 3.6 | 8.4 | 12.0 | 3.9 | 2.9 | 6.8 | 7.9 |
| 1982 | 7.5 | 11.6 | 19.1 | 3.5 | 8.6 | 12.1 | 4.0 | 3.0 | 7.0 | 8.0 |
| 1983 | 7.6 | 11.9 | 19.4 | 3.5 | 8.8 | 12.3 | 4.0 | 3.1 | 7.1 | 8.1 |
| 1984 | 7.6 | 12.0 | 19.6 | 3.5 | 8.9 | 12.4 | 4.1 | 3.1 | 7.2 | 8.1 |
| 1985 | 7.5 | 12.2 | 19.8 | 3.4 | 9.1 | 12.4 | 4.1 | 3.2 | 7.3 | 8.4 |
| 1986 | 7.7 | 12.4 | 20.1 | 3.5 | 9.2 | 12.7 | 4.2 | 3.2 | 7.4 | 8.5 |
| 1987 | 8.1 | 13.0 | 21.0 | 3.7 | 9.6 | 13.2 | 4.4 | 3.4 | 7.8 | 8.4 |
| 1988 | 8.3 | 13.3 | 21.6 | 3.8 | 9.8 | 13.6 | 4.6 | 3.5 | 8.1 | 8.4 |
| 1989 | 8.2 | 13.7 | 21.8 | 3.7 | 10.1 | 13.8 | 4.4 | 3.6 | 8.0 | 8.6 |
| 1990 | 7.7 | 13.5 | 21.2 | 3.7 | 10.0 | 13.7 | 4.1 | 3.5 | 7.6 | 8.3 |
| 1991 | 7.6 | 13.1 | 20.7 | 3.6 | 9.6 | 13.2 | 4.1 | 3.5 | 7.5 | 8.5 |
| 1992 | 7.6 | 11.6 | 19.1 | 3.6 | 8.2 | 11.8 | 3.9 | 3.3 | 7.3 | 8.6 |
| 1993 | 7.5 | 11.0 | 18.6 | 3.7 | 7.8 | 11.6 | 3.8 | 3.2 | 7.0 | 8.8 |
| 1994 | 7.7 | 9.8 | 17.5 | 3.8 | 7.0 | 10.8 | 3.9 | 2.9 | 6.7 | 9.0 |
| 1995 | 7.7 | 9.7 | 17.4 | 3.8 | 6.8 | 10.6 | 3.9 | 2.9 | 6.8 | 9.5 |
| 1996 | 7.8 | 9.6 | 17.4 | 3.7 | 6.8 | 10.5 | 4.1 | 2.8 | 6.9 | 9.5 |
| 1997 | 8.1 | 9.4 | 17.5 | 3.9 | 6.5 | 10.5 | 4.1 | 2.9 | 7.0 | 9.8 |
| 1998 | 8.5 | 8.4 | 16.9 | 4.0 | 5.9 | 10.0 | 4.4 | 2.5 | 6.9 | 9.9 |
| 1999 | 8.5 | 8.0 | 16.5 | 4.1 | 5.5 | 9.6 | 4.4 | 2.6 | 7.0 | 9.9 |
| 2000 | 8.3 | 9.0 | 17.2 | 4.0 | 6.3 | 10.3 | 4.3 | 2.7 | 7.0 | 9.8 |
| 2001 | 8.4 | 8.7 | 17.1 | 4.0 | 6.0 | 10.0 | 4.4 | 2.7 | 7.2 | 10.3 |

Source: CAO of Japan.

Notes

a FY55–FY89 based on SNA68; FY90–FY01 based on SNA93. SNA93 defines indirect taxes, direct taxes and social security contributions as "taxes on production and imports," "current taxes on income, wealth, and etc.," and "social contributions," respectively.

b Actual social contributions.

*Table 8.2* General government revenue, 2000 (as a % of nominal GDP)

| *Country* | *Revenue* | |
|---|---|---|
| | *Total* | *Excluding social security* |
| Sweden | 54.2 | 39.0 |
| Denmark | 48.8 | 46.5 |
| Finland | 46.9 | 34.9 |
| Belgium | 45.6 | 31.5 |
| France | 45.3 | 29.0 |
| Austria | 43.7 | 28.8 |
| Italy | 42.0 | 30.0 |
| Luxembourg | 41.7 | 31.0 |
| Netherlands | 41.4 | 25.3 |
| Norway | 40.3 | 31.2 |
| Czech Republic | 39.4 | 22.1 |
| Hungary | 39.1 | 27.6 |
| Germany | 37.9 | 23.1 |
| Greece | 37.8 | 26.4 |
| United Kingdom | 37.4 | 31.2 |
| Iceland | 37.3 | 34.4 |
| Canada | 35.8 | 30.7 |
| Slovak Republic | 35.8 | 21.0 |
| Switzerland | 35.7 | 23.7 |
| Spain | 35.2 | 22.8 |
| New Zealand | 35.1 | 35.1 |
| Portugal | 34.5 | 25.6 |
| Poland | 34.1 | 24.0 |
| Turkey | 33.4 | 27.7 |
| Australia | 31.5 | 31.5 |
| Ireland | 31.1 | 26.8 |
| United States | 29.6 | 22.7 |
| Japan | 27.1 | 17.2 |
| Korea | 26.1 | 21.8 |
| Mexico | 18.5 | 15.4 |

Source: OECD (2001).

### *Social security contributions*

Social security contributions, as a source of revenue for social insurance programs such as health, pension, and employment insurance, have been rising due to improvement of the social security system and the aging of the society (Table 8.1). Social security contributions were 10.3 percent of GDP in FY01, of which health insurance and pension insurance accounted for 3.3 percentage points and 5.9 percentage points, respectively. With the aging of the society further progressing, social security contributions are nearly certain to increase, and the complete overhaul of the social security system is being debated, including the idea of constraining the growth of social security contributions. In this context, the combined share of taxes and social security contributions (as a percentage of GDP), after peaking in FY89, has been decreasing. Therefore, one focus in the debate of the overhaul of social security is how to divide revenue sources between contributions and taxes.

### *Expenditures*

Table 8.3 lists the major expenditure categories of general government (as a percentage of nominal GDP).

#### *Government consumption expenditures*

A typical recurring expense of government is final consumption expenditures. In the past twenty-five years, the final consumption expenditures of government (particularly the series excluding fixed capital consumption[4]) have changed very little. This would suggest that general administrative costs have not been behind the growth of the budget deficit. The proportion of government consumption expenditures to GDP is not unusually large in Japan when compared with other nations (Table 8.4).

#### *Fixed capital formation*

The ratio of gross fixed capital formation to nominal GDP peaked at 6.3 percent in FY79, after which the ratio fell to 4.7 percent in FY85 and then surged to 6.3 percent in FY95. The trend of government investment in the 1990s reflected a fiscal policy where successive stimulus packages were implemented to maintain the growth of public works spending and to keep it at a high level. In the SNA, which is compiled according to sectors that are determined as making final payments, local government investments account for about 80 percent of total investments of general government, and changes in the investment of general government are basically determined by investments of local governments. In the second half of the 1990s, the decrease in investment expenditures of local governments was pronounced. Since the mid-1990s, worsening finances of local governments have prevented them from maintaining the level of investment desired by the central government. As a result, it is possible to say that unintended fiscal restructuring is progressing at the level of general government.

Although the amount of public works spending is decreasing, such spending remains high as a percentage of GDP when compared with other nations (Table 8.5). More recently, as part of the assessment of government policies, public works projects are required to undergo cost-benefit analyses, and explorations are under way toward increasing the efficiency and transparency of public works spending and reviewing the allocation of the budget for public works projects. Should these efforts bear fruit, it may be possible to curb the size of public works spending (Box 8.3).

*Table 8.3* Major expenditures of general government, 1955–2001[a] (as a % of nominal GDP)

| *FY* | *General government* | | | | | *Central government* | | | *Local government* | | | *Public corporations* |
|---|---|---|---|---|---|---|---|---|---|---|---|---|
| | *Final consumption expenditure* | *Excl. fixed capital consumption* | *Gross fixed capital formation* | *Interest payments* | *Social benefits* | *Final consumption expenditure* | *Gross fixed capital formation* | *Interest payments*[b] | *Final consumption expenditure* | *Gross fixed capital formation* | *Interest payments*[b] | *Gross fixed capital formation* |
| 1955 | 9.9 | 9.4 | 3.7 | 0.7 | 4.4 | | | | | | | 3.0 |
| 1956 | 9.1 | 8.5 | 3.6 | 0.7 | 4.0 | | | | | | | 3.1 |
| 1957 | 8.7 | 8.2 | 3.7 | 0.5 | 3.9 | | | | | | | 3.4 |
| 1958 | 8.8 | 8.2 | 3.9 | 0.6 | 4.1 | | | | | | | 3.6 |
| 1959 | 8.2 | 7.7 | 3.9 | 0.6 | 4.0 | | | | | | | 3.3 |
| 1960 | 7.9 | 7.5 | 3.9 | 0.5 | 3.6 | | | | | | | 3.1 |
| 1961 | 7.6 | 7.2 | 4.2 | 0.4 | 3.8 | | | | | | | 3.8 |
| 1962 | 8.2 | 7.7 | 4.8 | 0.4 | 4.0 | | | | | | | 4.3 |
| 1963 | 8.1 | 7.7 | 4.5 | 0.4 | 4.2 | | | | | | | 4.3 |
| 1964 | 8.0 | 7.6 | 4.5 | 0.4 | 4.4 | | | | | | | 3.8 |
| 1965 | 8.2 | 7.7 | 4.6 | 0.4 | 4.7 | | | | | | | 4.2 |
| 1966 | 7.9 | 7.4 | 4.6 | 0.5 | 4.6 | | | | | | | 4.2 |
| 1967 | 7.6 | 7.1 | 4.3 | 0.5 | 4.6 | | | | | | | 4.1 |
| 1968 | 7.4 | 6.9 | 4.4 | 0.6 | 4.5 | | | | | | | 3.9 |
| 1969 | 7.3 | 6.8 | 4.3 | 0.6 | 4.4 | | | | | | | 3.5 |
| 1970 | 7.5 | 7.1 | 4.6 | 0.6 | 4.7 | 2.0 | 0.8 | 0.4 | 5.4 | 3.7 | 0.3 | 3.6 |
| 1971 | 8.0 | 7.6 | 5.3 | 0.6 | 4.9 | 2.1 | 1.0 | 0.4 | 5.8 | 4.4 | 0.3 | 4.1 |
| 1972 | 8.1 | 7.6 | 5.7 | 0.8 | 5.2 | 2.1 | 1.0 | 0.5 | 5.9 | 4.7 | 0.3 | 4.1 |
| 1973 | 8.3 | 7.9 | 5.2 | 0.9 | 5.4 | 2.0 | 0.9 | 0.5 | 6.1 | 4.4 | 0.4 | 3.8 |
| 1974 | 9.5 | 9.1 | 5.4 | 1.0 | 6.6 | 2.2 | 0.9 | 0.6 | 7.1 | 4.5 | 0.4 | 3.8 |
| 1975 | 10.0 | 9.6 | 5.3 | 1.2 | 7.8 | 2.3 | 0.9 | 0.8 | 7.6 | 4.4 | 0.5 | 3.9 |
| 1976 | 9.8 | 9.4 | 5.2 | 1.6 | 8.5 | 2.3 | 0.9 | 1.0 | 7.4 | 4.3 | 0.6 | 3.5 |

| | | | | | | | | | | | | |
|---|---|---|---|---|---|---|---|---|---|---|---|---|
| 1977 | 9.8 | 9.3 | 5.7 | 2.0 | 8.9 | 2.3 | 0.9 | 1.3 | 7.3 | 4.8 | 0.7 | 3.6 |
| 1978 | 9.7 | 9.1 | 6.3 | 2.3 | 9.6 | 2.3 | 1.0 | 1.6 | 7.2 | 5.2 | 0.7 | 3.7 |
| 1979 | 9.7 | 9.2 | 6.3 | 2.7 | 9.8 | 2.3 | 1.0 | 1.9 | 7.3 | 5.3 | 0.8 | 3.5 |
| 1980 | 9.8 | 9.2 | 6.1 | 3.2 | 10.1 | 2.3 | 0.9 | 2.4 | 7.4 | 5.1 | 0.9 | 3.5 |
| 1981 | 10.0 | 9.3 | 6.0 | 3.6 | 10.6 | 2.3 | 0.9 | 2.7 | 7.5 | 5.1 | 0.9 | 3.3 |
| 1982 | 9.9 | 9.2 | 5.7 | 3.9 | 11.0 | 2.3 | 0.9 | 2.9 | 7.4 | 4.9 | 1.0 | 3.0 |
| 1983 | 9.9 | 9.2 | 5.4 | 4.3 | 11.2 | 2.3 | 0.8 | 3.3 | 7.4 | 4.5 | 1.1 | 2.8 |
| 1984 | 9.8 | 9.1 | 4.9 | 4.4 | 11.0 | 2.3 | 0.8 | 3.4 | 7.2 | 4.1 | 1.1 | 2.6 |
| 1985 | 9.6 | 8.9 | 4.7 | 4.5 | 11.0 | 2.3 | 0.8 | 3.4 | 7.1 | 3.9 | 1.1 | 1.9 |
| 1986 | 9.6 | 9.0 | 4.8 | 4.4 | 11.4 | 2.4 | 0.8 | 3.4 | 7.0 | 4.0 | 1.1 | 1.9 |
| 1987 | 9.3 | 8.7 | 5.2 | 4.3 | 11.5 | 2.2 | 0.9 | 3.3 | 6.9 | 4.2 | 1.0 | 1.7 |
| 1988 | 9.1 | 8.5 | 4.9 | 4.1 | 11.2 | 2.2 | 0.8 | 3.2 | 6.7 | 4.1 | 1.0 | 1.6 |
| 1989 | 9.0 | 8.4 | 5.0 | 3.9 | 11.1 | 2.2 | 0.8 | 3.1 | 6.7 | 4.2 | 0.9 | 1.5 |
| 1990 | 9.5 | 8.1 | 4.8 | 3.6 | 10.7 | 2.1 | 0.7 | 2.7 | 7.2 | 4.1 | 0.8 | 1.7 |
| 1991 | 9.5 | 8.1 | 5.0 | 3.5 | 10.8 | 2.1 | 0.7 | 2.6 | 7.3 | 4.2 | 0.8 | 1.7 |
| 1992 | 9.8 | 8.3 | 5.7 | 3.4 | 11.3 | 2.2 | 0.9 | 2.4 | 7.5 | 4.8 | 0.8 | 2.0 |
| 1993 | 10.1 | 8.5 | 6.2 | 3.4 | 11.8 | 2.2 | 1.0 | 2.4 | 7.7 | 5.2 | 0.9 | 2.2 |
| 1994 | 10.4 | 8.6 | 6.1 | 3.4 | 12.4 | 2.2 | 0.9 | 2.4 | 7.9 | 5.1 | 0.9 | 2.2 |
| 1995 | 10.5 | 8.7 | 6.3 | 3.4 | 12.9 | 2.3 | 1.0 | 2.3 | 8.0 | 5.3 | 1.0 | 2.3 |
| 1996 | 10.5 | 8.6 | 5.9 | 3.4 | 13.1 | 2.3 | 0.9 | 2.3 | 8.0 | 5.0 | 1.0 | 2.2 |
| 1997 | 10.7 | 8.8 | 5.5 | 3.4 | 13.3 | 2.3 | 0.9 | 2.2 | 8.2 | 4.6 | 1.0 | 2.1 |
| 1998 | 11.1 | 9.0 | 5.7 | 3.4 | 14.0 | 2.5 | 1.0 | 2.3 | 8.4 | 4.7 | 1.1 | 2.0 |
| 1999 | 11.5 | 9.2 | 5.6 | 3.4 | 14.6 | 2.6 | 1.1 | 2.2 | 8.7 | 4.5 | 1.0 | 1.9 |
| 2000 | 11.5 | 9.1 | 5.0 | 3.2 | 15.3 | 2.7 | 1.0 | 2.1 | 8.5 | 4.0 | 1.0 | 1.8 |
| 2001 | 11.8 | 9.3 | 4.8 | 3.1 | 16.3 | 2.7 | 1.0 | 2.0 | 8.8 | 3.8 | 1.0 | 1.7 |

Source: CAO of Japan.

Notes

a FY55–FY89 based on SNA68; FY90–FY01 based on SNA93. "Social benefits in kind" defined in SNA93 are excluded from final consumption expenditures. Under SNA93, the scope fixed capital consumption is expanded in Japan.

b Through FY89, "property income paid" substitutes for interest payments.

*Table 8.4* Government final consumption expenditure (as a % of GDP)

| *Country* | *Gov't final consumption expenditure* |
|---|---|
| Sweden (2001) | 26.7 |
| Denmark (2001) | 25.5 |
| Iceland (2000) | 23.5 |
| France (2001) | 23.3 |
| Netherlands (2000) | 22.7 |
| Hungary (2001) | 22.4 |
| Slovak Republic (1998) | 21.5 |
| Belgium (2001) | 21.5 |
| Finland (2001) | 21.2 |
| Portugal (2001) | 20.5 |
| Austria (2001) | 19.2 |
| United Kingdom (2001) | 19.2 |
| Germany (2001) | 19.1 |
| Norway (2000) | 19.0 |
| Czech Republic (2001) | 19.0 |
| Canada (2001) | 18.9 |
| Australia (2000) | 18.7 |
| New Zealand (1997) | 18.7 |
| Italy (2001) | 18.4 |
| Japan (2001) | 17.6 |
| Luxembourg (2001) | 17.4 |
| Spain (2000) | 17.4 |
| Poland (2000) | 15.5 |
| Greece (2000) | 15.5 |
| United States (2000) | 14.4 |
| Turkey[a] (2001) | 14.1 |
| Ireland (2001) | 13.7 |
| Switzerland[a] (1999) | 13.7 |
| Mexico (2000) | 11.1 |
| Korea (2000) | 10.1 |

Sources: OECD (2002b); CAO of Japan.

Note
a Based on SNA68.

### *Interest payments*

Interest payments (gross) began to increase from around FY75, when the first deficit-financing bonds were issued, reaching 4.5 percent of nominal GDP in FY85. Since then, this figure has trended downward to 3.1 percent in FY01. Taking the long view, the nominal long-term interest rate has decreased after peaking in FY79. The trend of interest payments is thought to reflect two factors working in tandem: (i) the accumulation of government debt; and (ii) the decline of interest rates after some delay. In the 1990s, the ratio of interest payments to GDP did not largely decrease, the consequence of the pace of declining interest rates matched by the accumulation of government debt.

*Table 8.5* Gross fixed capital formation by general government (as a % of GDP)

| *Country* | *GFCF by general gov't* |
|---|---|
| Korea (2000) | 5.8 |
| Japan (2001) | 4.8 |
| Luxembourg (2001) | 4.7 |
| Czech Republic (2001) | 4.5 |
| Ireland (2001) | 4.1 |
| Slovak Republic (1998) | 4.1 |
| Greece (2000) | 4.1 |
| Portugal (2001) | 4.1 |
| Iceland (2000) | 3.7 |
| Poland (2000) | 3.6 |
| Spain (1999) | 3.3 |
| France (2001) | 3.3 |
| Netherlands (2000) | 3.2 |
| Norway (2000) | 2.8 |
| Finland (2001) | 2.7 |
| Switzerland[a] (1999) | 2.6 |
| Sweden (2001) | 2.6 |
| New Zealand (1997) | 2.5 |
| Canada (2001) | 2.5 |
| Australia (2000) | 2.4 |
| Italy (2001) | 2.2 |
| United States[a] (1997) | 1.9 |
| Germany (2001) | 1.7 |
| Denmark (2001) | 1.7 |
| Mexico (2000) | 1.7 |
| Belgium (2001) | 1.5 |
| United Kingdom (2001) | 1.3 |
| Austria (2001) | 1.3 |

Sources: OECD (2002b); CAO of Japan.

Note

a Based on SNA68.

**Box 8.3 Investments by public corporations**

Another factor that should not be ignored in relation to public capital formation is the existence of public corporations. Although public corporations are not categorized under general government, the level of their investment before the 1970s corresponded to that of general government when social infrastructure was inadequate (far right of Table 8.5). In the 1980s, Japan National Railways, Nippon Telegraph and Telephone, etc. were privatized as part of an administrative reform program, and the investments by public corporations fell to around 2 percent of nominal GDP. Increasing the efficiency of these investments, such as through privatizations, will help reduce the investment subsidies of general government.

*Social security benefits*

Social security benefits and social assistance benefits (grants) have grown rapidly since FY73, the so-called First Year of High-level Social Welfare. In this year, public pension benefits were increased substantially and the coverage of health insurance was also expanded. In the 1980s, efforts were made to curb the growth of benefit payments, such as introducing patient copayments for some medical costs that had been free, and by fundamentally reforming the public pension program to restrain benefit payments. In the 1990s, various attempts were undertaken to reform health insurance and public pension programs but, with the aging of the society, social security expenditures have continued to increase.

## *Budget deficit*

Now that we have looked at major revenue and expenditure categories of the government budget, we will examine the budget deficit (Table 8.6). At the level of general government, the budget balance, which was in balance or in surplus prior to the first oil crisis, turned negative in FY74 and budget deficits continued to FY86. During the 1980s, efforts were initiated to restore the health of public finances, and the government ran budget surpluses of more than 2 percent of nominal GDP from FY88 to FY91, helped in part by economic expansion. In the 1990s, however, a serious recession was ushered in by a cyclical downturn combined with falling asset prices and financial system uncertainties, and Japan recorded substantial budget deficits (even by international standards).

The budget deficit of the general government after excluding social security funds, or the aggregate budget deficit of central and local governments, was 6.6 percent of GDP in FY01. The Cabinet Office estimates that the budget deficit will be 7.6 percent of GDP in FY02. Although its provisions are currently suspended, the target established under the Fiscal Structural Reform Act for the budget deficits of central and local governments was less than 3 percent of GDP by FY05. Since the government's net interest payments are nearly 3 percent of GDP, the target would nearly equilibrate the government's primary balance.

## *Government debt outstanding*

Table 8.7 lists the government's financial assets and liabilities. The outstanding financial liabilities (gross) of general government rose as a percentage of nominal GDP (except for FY70, FY73, and the FY88–FY91 period) and reached 152.5 percent at end-FY01. At the same time, financial assets have also accumulated, and net financial liabilities were 64.1 percent of nominal GDP at end-FY01. As such, a distinguishing feature of Japan is the substantial differential in outstanding financial liabilities of the government when viewed on a gross and net basis (Table 8.8). (However, in the period covered by Table 8.7, net government liabilities in recent years are the highest, and they are accumulating at a rapid pace.)

What exactly are the financial assets of government? The most pronounced are the financial assets of social security funds, which correspond to public pension

*Table 8.6* General government fiscal balances, 1955–2001 (as a % of nominal GDP)

| *FY* | *General government* | | | *Central and local governments* | | | *Central government* | | | *Local government* | | | *Social Security Fund* | | |
|---|---|---|---|---|---|---|---|---|---|---|---|---|---|---|---|
| | *Overall balance* | *Primary balance* | *Net interest payment*[a] | *Overall balance* | *Primary balance* | *Net interest payment*[a] | *Overall balance* | *Primary balance* | *Net interest payment*[a] | *Overall balance* | *Primary balance* | *Net interest payment*[a] | *Overall balance* | *Primary balance* | *Net interest payment*[a] |
| 1955 | −0.7 | −0.3 | −0.3 | | | | | | | | | | | | |
| 1956 | 1.4 | 1.7 | −0.3 | | | | | | | | | | | | |
| 1957 | 1.3 | 1.5 | −0.2 | | | | | | | | | | | | |
| 1958 | −0.1 | 0.0 | −0.1 | | | | | | | | | | | | |
| 1959 | 1.0 | 1.1 | −0.1 | | | | | | | | | | | | |
| 1960 | 2.2 | 2.3 | −0.0 | | | | | | | | | | | | |
| 1961 | 2.4 | 2.3 | 0.1 | | | | | | | | | | | | |
| 1962 | 1.3 | 1.1 | 0.2 | | | | | | | | | | | | |
| 1963 | 1.0 | 0.9 | 0.2 | | | | | | | | | | | | |
| 1964 | 1.0 | 0.7 | 0.4 | | | | | | | | | | | | |
| 1965 | 0.4 | 0.1 | 0.3 | | | | | | | | | | | | |
| 1966 | −0.4 | −0.6 | 0.3 | | | | | | | | | | | | |
| 1967 | 0.8 | 0.5 | 0.2 | | | | | | | | | | | | |
| 1968 | 1.2 | 1.0 | 0.2 | | | | | | | | | | | | |
| 1969 | 1.8 | 1.5 | 0.3 | | | | | | | | | | | | |
| 1970 | 1.8 | 1.5 | 0.3 | −0.4 | −0.1 | −0.3 | −0.0 | 0.2 | −0.2 | −0.4 | −0.3 | −0.1 | 2.2 | 1.6 | 0.6 |
| 1971 | 0.5 | 0.1 | 0.4 | −2.0 | −1.7 | −0.3 | −1.0 | −0.8 | −0.2 | −1.0 | −0.9 | −0.1 | 2.5 | 1.8 | 0.7 |
| 1972 | 0.2 | −0.1 | 0.3 | −2.2 | −1.8 | −0.5 | −1.1 | −0.8 | −0.3 | −1.1 | −1.0 | −0.1 | 2.4 | 1.7 | 0.7 |
| 1973 | 2.0 | 1.7 | 0.3 | −0.6 | −0.1 | −0.4 | 0.4 | 0.7 | −0.3 | −1.0 | −0.8 | −0.2 | 2.6 | 1.8 | 0.7 |
| 1974 | −0.0 | −0.3 | 0.3 | −2.7 | −2.2 | −0.5 | −1.4 | −1.1 | −0.3 | −1.3 | −1.0 | −0.2 | 2.6 | 1.9 | 0.8 |
| 1975 | −3.7 | −3.8 | 0.1 | −6.1 | −5.4 | −0.8 | −4.0 | −3.5 | −0.5 | −2.1 | −1.8 | −0.3 | 2.4 | 1.5 | 0.9 |
| 1976 | −3.6 | −3.3 | −0.2 | −5.9 | −4.7 | −1.2 | −4.3 | −3.5 | −0.8 | −1.6 | −1.2 | −0.4 | 2.3 | 1.4 | 0.9 |
| 1977 | −4.2 | −3.6 | −0.5 | −6.8 | −5.3 | −1.5 | −5.0 | −4.0 | −1.0 | −1.8 | −1.3 | −0.5 | 2.7 | 1.7 | 1.0 |
| 1978 | −4.2 | −3.4 | −0.8 | −6.6 | −4.8 | −1.8 | −4.8 | −3.6 | −1.3 | −1.7 | −1.2 | −0.5 | 2.4 | 1.3 | 1.0 |
| 1979 | −4.4 | −3.4 | −1.0 | −7.0 | −4.9 | −2.1 | −5.7 | −4.1 | −1.5 | −1.4 | −0.8 | −0.6 | 2.6 | 1.5 | 1.1 |
| 1980 | −4.0 | −2.8 | −1.3 | −6.7 | −4.2 | −2.5 | −5.4 | −3.5 | −1.9 | −1.3 | −0.7 | −0.6 | 2.6 | 1.4 | 1.2 |
| 1981 | −3.7 | −2.3 | −1.4 | −6.5 | −3.8 | −2.7 | −5.2 | −3.2 | −2.1 | −1.2 | −0.6 | −0.6 | 2.8 | 1.5 | 1.3 |
| 1982 | −3.4 | −1.8 | −1.6 | −6.1 | −3.1 | −3.0 | −5.2 | −2.9 | −2.3 | −0.9 | −0.2 | −0.7 | 2.7 | 1.3 | 1.4 |
| 1983 | −2.9 | −1.0 | −2.0 | −5.6 | −2.1 | −3.5 | −4.9 | −2.1 | −2.8 | −0.8 | 0.0 | −0.8 | 2.7 | 1.1 | 1.6 |

*continued*

*Table 8.6* Continued

| *FY* | *General government* | | | *Central and local governments* | | | *Central government* | | | *Local government* | | | *Social Security Fund* | | |
|---|---|---|---|---|---|---|---|---|---|---|---|---|---|---|---|
| | *Overall balance* | *Primary balance* | *Net interest payment*[a] | *Overall balance* | *Primary balance* | *Net interest payment*[a] | *Overall balance* | *Primary balance* | *Net interest payment*[a] | *Overall balance* | *Primary balance* | *Net interest payment*[a] | *Overall balance* | *Primary balance* | *Net interest payment*[a] |
| 1984 | −1.8 | 0.1 | −1.9 | −4.6 | −1.0 | −3.6 | −4.0 | −1.2 | −2.8 | −0.6 | 0.2 | −0.8 | 2.8 | 1.1 | 1.7 |
| 1985 | −0.8 | 1.1 | −1.9 | −3.9 | −0.3 | −3.7 | −3.6 | −0.7 | −2.9 | −0.3 | 0.5 | −0.8 | 3.1 | 1.3 | 1.8 |
| 1986 | −0.3 | 1.3 | −1.6 | −3.4 | 0.3 | −3.7 | −3.0 | −0.1 | −2.9 | −0.4 | 0.4 | −0.8 | 3.1 | 1.0 | 2.0 |
| 1987 | 0.7 | 2.1 | −1.4 | −2.1 | 1.3 | −3.4 | −1.9 | 0.8 | −2.7 | −0.2 | 0.6 | −0.7 | 2.8 | 0.8 | 2.0 |
| 1988 | 2.2 | 3.4 | −1.2 | −1.0 | 2.1 | −3.1 | −1.1 | 1.4 | −2.5 | 0.1 | 0.7 | −0.7 | 3.2 | 1.2 | 2.0 |
| 1989 | 2.6 | 3.6 | −1.0 | −0.6 | 2.3 | −2.9 | −1.2 | 1.1 | −2.3 | 0.6 | 1.1 | −0.6 | 3.2 | 1.3 | 1.9 |
| 1990 | 2.6 | 3.8 | −1.2 | 0.0 | 2.8 | −2.8 | −0.5 | 1.9 | −2.3 | 0.5 | 0.9 | −0.5 | 2.6 | 1.0 | 1.6 |
| 1991 | 2.4 | 3.5 | −1.0 | −0.3 | 2.4 | −2.7 | −0.4 | 1.9 | −2.3 | 0.1 | 0.5 | −0.4 | 2.7 | 1.1 | 1.6 |
| 1992 | −0.8 | 0.3 | −1.1 | −3.2 | −0.5 | −2.7 | −2.4 | −0.2 | −2.2 | −0.9 | −0.4 | −0.5 | 2.4 | 0.8 | 1.6 |
| 1993 | −2.7 | −1.6 | −1.2 | −4.9 | −2.1 | −2.8 | −3.5 | −1.4 | −2.1 | −1.4 | −0.7 | −0.7 | 2.2 | 0.5 | 1.6 |
| 1994 | −4.1 | −2.9 | −1.2 | −6.1 | −3.1 | −2.9 | −4.3 | −2.1 | −2.1 | −1.8 | −1.0 | −0.8 | 1.9 | 0.3 | 1.7 |
| 1995 | −4.9 | −3.5 | −1.3 | −6.7 | −3.8 | −2.9 | −4.3 | −2.3 | −2.0 | −2.4 | −1.5 | −0.9 | 1.9 | 0.3 | 1.6 |
| 1996 | −4.7 | −3.3 | −1.3 | −6.4 | −3.5 | −2.9 | −4.4 | −2.4 | −1.9 | −2.0 | −1.0 | −0.9 | 1.7 | 0.1 | 1.5 |
| 1997 | −3.9 | −2.5 | −1.3 | −5.6 | −2.8 | −2.8 | −3.9 | −2.0 | −1.8 | −1.7 | −0.8 | −1.0 | 1.7 | 0.2 | 1.5 |
| 1998 | −6.2 | −4.7 | −1.5 | −7.3 | −4.4 | −2.9 | −5.4 | −3.5 | −1.9 | −1.9 | −0.9 | −1.0 | 1.1 | −0.3 | 1.4 |
| 1999 | −7.6 | −6.2 | −1.5 | −8.6 | −5.8 | −2.8 | −7.7 | −5.8 | −1.8 | −0.9 | 0.1 | −1.0 | 1.0 | −0.4 | 1.4 |
| 2000 | −6.6 | −5.2 | −1.5 | −7.0 | −4.4 | −2.6 | −6.7 | −5.0 | −1.7 | −0.3 | 0.7 | −1.0 | 0.3 | −0.8 | 1.2 |
| 2001 | −6.6 | −5.2 | −1.4 | −6.6 | −4.1 | −2.5 | −6.2 | −4.7 | −1.5 | −0.3 | 0.6 | −1.0 | 0.0 | −1.1 | 1.0 |

Source: CAO of Japan.

Notes

a FY55–FY89 based on SNA68, FY90–FY01 based on SNA93. For FY55–FY89, "net property income paid" substitutes for net interest payments. Assumption by the central government of debts of the Japan National Railway Settlement Corporation and the National Forest Special Account are excluded.

b Negative figures represent cases when "interest paid" exceeds "interest received."

*Table 8.7* Government financial assets and liabilities, 1969–2001 (as a % of nominal GDP)

| *FY* | *General government* | | | *Central and local governments* | | | *Central government* | | | *Local government* | | | *Social Security Fund* | | |
|---|---|---|---|---|---|---|---|---|---|---|---|---|---|---|---|
| | *Assets (gross)* | *Liabilities (gross)* | *Net assets* | *Assets (gross)* | *Liabilities (gross)* | *Net assets* | *Assets (gross)* | *Liabilities (gross)* | *Net assets* | *Assets (gross)* | *Liabilities (gross)* | *Net assets* | *Assets (gross)* | *Liabilities (gross)* | *Net assets* |
| 1969 | 18.8 | 12.0 | 6.8 | 8.4 | 11.6 | −3.3 | 5.9 | 7.7 | −1.8 | 3.0 | 4.5 | −1.5 | 10.4 | 0.3 | 10.1 |
| 1970 | 20.1 | 11.9 | 8.1 | 8.9 | 11.5 | −2.6 | 6.4 | 7.6 | −1.1 | 3.1 | 4.6 | −1.5 | 11.2 | 0.4 | 10.8 |
| 1971 | 22.4 | 14.2 | 8.2 | 9.9 | 13.8 | −3.9 | 7.3 | 9.1 | −1.9 | 3.4 | 5.4 | −2.0 | 12.5 | 0.4 | 12.1 |
| 1972 | 25.9 | 18.4 | 7.5 | 12.6 | 17.9 | −5.3 | 9.8 | 12.5 | −2.7 | 3.6 | 6.3 | −2.7 | 13.3 | 0.5 | 12.8 |
| 1973 | 25.4 | 18.1 | 7.3 | 12.2 | 17.7 | −5.5 | 9.6 | 11.8 | −2.2 | 3.4 | 6.7 | −3.3 | 13.2 | 0.4 | 12.8 |
| 1974 | 24.9 | 18.9 | 6.1 | 11.0 | 18.5 | −7.5 | 8.5 | 12.2 | −3.7 | 3.3 | 7.1 | −3.8 | 14.0 | 0.4 | 13.5 |
| 1975 | 25.9 | 23.9 | 2.1 | 10.6 | 23.4 | −12.8 | 8.3 | 15.7 | −7.4 | 3.2 | 8.7 | −5.4 | 15.3 | 0.4 | 14.9 |
| 1976 | 27.4 | 29.1 | −1.6 | 11.4 | 28.6 | −17.2 | 8.9 | 19.9 | −11.0 | 3.5 | 9.7 | −6.2 | 16.0 | 0.5 | 15.6 |
| 1977 | 29.4 | 35.1 | −5.7 | 12.2 | 34.7 | −22.4 | 9.6 | 25.0 | −15.4 | 3.7 | 10.8 | −7.1 | 17.2 | 0.5 | 16.7 |
| 1978 | 30.9 | 41.7 | −10.8 | 12.8 | 41.2 | −28.4 | 10.0 | 30.5 | −20.5 | 4.0 | 12.0 | −8.0 | 18.1 | 0.5 | 17.6 |
| 1979 | 33.5 | 47.6 | −14.1 | 14.2 | 47.1 | −33.0 | 10.7 | 35.0 | −24.2 | 4.7 | 13.5 | −8.7 | 19.4 | 0.5 | 18.9 |
| 1980 | 35.8 | 52.9 | −17.1 | 15.4 | 52.5 | −37.1 | 12.3 | 40.0 | −27.6 | 4.5 | 13.9 | −9.4 | 20.4 | 0.5 | 20.0 |
| 1981 | 37.5 | 57.5 | −19.9 | 15.4 | 57.0 | −41.6 | 12.3 | 43.7 | −31.4 | 4.6 | 14.9 | −10.2 | 22.1 | 0.5 | 21.7 |
| 1982 | 38.9 | 61.3 | −22.4 | 15.0 | 60.9 | −45.9 | 12.0 | 47.0 | −35.0 | 4.6 | 15.5 | −10.9 | 23.9 | 0.5 | 23.5 |
| 1983 | 40.7 | 65.8 | −25.0 | 15.3 | 65.3 | −50.1 | 12.4 | 50.9 | −38.5 | 4.6 | 16.2 | −11.6 | 25.5 | 0.4 | 25.0 |
| 1984 | 41.0 | 67.5 | −26.5 | 15.3 | 67.0 | −51.7 | 12.5 | 52.5 | −40.1 | 4.7 | 16.3 | −11.6 | 25.7 | 0.4 | 25.2 |
| 1985 | 43.0 | 68.8 | −25.8 | 15.4 | 68.4 | −53.0 | 12.6 | 53.9 | −41.3 | 4.6 | 16.4 | −11.7 | 27.7 | 0.4 | 27.3 |
| 1986 | 48.5 | 73.1 | −24.6 | 18.7 | 72.6 | −53.9 | 15.5 | 58.1 | −42.6 | 5.1 | 16.4 | −11.4 | 29.8 | 0.4 | 29.4 |
| 1987 | 53.6 | 74.5 | −21.0 | 22.2 | 74.1 | −51.9 | 18.4 | 59.5 | −41.1 | 5.8 | 16.6 | −10.8 | 31.3 | 0.4 | 30.9 |
| 1988 | 55.7 | 73.2 | −17.5 | 23.7 | 72.8 | −49.1 | 19.2 | 58.4 | −39.3 | 6.6 | 16.4 | −9.8 | 31.9 | 0.4 | 31.6 |
| 1989 | 57.4 | 71.5 | −14.1 | 25.1 | 71.2 | −46.1 | 19.7 | 57.1 | −37.4 | 7.6 | 16.2 | −8.7 | 32.4 | 0.4 | 32.0 |
| 1990 | 56.6 | 68.4 | −11.8 | 27.4 | 66.1 | −38.8 | 16.4 | 49.7 | −33.4 | 11.0 | 16.4 | −5.4 | 29.3 | 2.2 | 27.0 |
| 1991 | 59.0 | 69.6 | −10.7 | 27.5 | 67.0 | −39.5 | 16.1 | 50.2 | −34.0 | 11.4 | 16.9 | −5.5 | 31.4 | 2.6 | 28.8 |
| 1992 | 61.0 | 73.6 | −12.6 | 27.2 | 70.4 | −43.3 | 15.9 | 52.1 | −36.2 | 11.2 | 18.3 | −7.1 | 33.8 | 3.2 | 30.7 |
| 1993 | 63.9 | 79.4 | −15.4 | 27.3 | 75.7 | −48.4 | 15.8 | 55.5 | −39.7 | 11.5 | 20.2 | −8.7 | 36.6 | 3.7 | 32.9 |

*continued*

*Table 8.7* Continued

| *FY* | *General government* | | | *Central and local governments* | | | *Central government* | | | *Local government* | | | *Social Security Fund* | | |
|---|---|---|---|---|---|---|---|---|---|---|---|---|---|---|---|
| | *Assets (gross)* | *Liabilities (gross)* | *Net assets* | *Assets (gross)* | *Liabilities (gross)* | *Net assets* | *Assets (gross)* | *Liabilities (gross)* | *Net assets* | *Assets (gross)* | *Liabilities (gross)* | *Net assets* | *Assets (gross)* | *Liabilities (gross)* | *Net assets* |
| 1994 | 65.9 | 85.6 | −19.7 | 27.7 | 81.5 | −53.8 | 15.9 | 59.2 | −43.4 | 11.8 | 22.2 | −10.4 | 38.2 | 4.1 | 34.1 |
| 1995 | 70.2 | 93.5 | −23.3 | 31.1 | 89.3 | −58.2 | 19.1 | 64.5 | −45.4 | 12.0 | 24.7 | −12.8 | 39.1 | 4.3 | 34.9 |
| 1996 | 71.8 | 101.0 | −29.2 | 31.7 | 96.8 | −65.0 | 19.8 | 69.8 | −49.9 | 11.9 | 27.0 | −15.1 | 40.1 | 4.3 | 35.8 |
| 1997 | 74.8 | 111.5 | −36.8 | 33.1 | 107.1 | −74.0 | 21.7 | 78.2 | −56.5 | 11.4 | 28.9 | −17.5 | 41.7 | 4.4 | 37.3 |
| 1998 | 74.8 | 121.8 | −47.0 | 30.7 | 117.1 | −86.5 | 19.0 | 85.9 | −66.9 | 11.7 | 31.2 | −19.5 | 44.2 | 4.7 | 39.4 |
| 1999 | 80.7 | 132.9 | −52.1 | 34.8 | 127.9 | −93.1 | 22.7 | 95.1 | −72.5 | 12.1 | 32.8 | −20.6 | 45.9 | 4.9 | 41.0 |
| 2000 | 84.1 | 142.9 | −58.8 | 38.7 | 137.9 | −99.1 | 26.1 | 104.5 | −78.4 | 12.6 | 33.4 | −20.8 | 45.3 | 5.0 | 40.3 |
| 2001 | 88.4 | 152.5 | −64.1 | 40.6 | 146.4 | −105.8 | 27.9 | 111.4 | −83.5 | 12.7 | 35.0 | −22.3 | 47.8 | 6.1 | 41.7 |

Source: CAO of Japan.

Note

a FY55–FY89 based on SNA68; FY90–FY01 based on SNA93.

*Table 8.8* General government financial liabilities, 2001 (as a % of GDP)

| | *Liabilities* | | *Assets* |
|---|---|---|---|
| | *Gross outstanding (A)* | *Net outstanding (B)* | *Gross outstanding (A–B)* |
| Australia | 20.9 | 5.1 | 15.8 |
| Austria | 63.2 | 50.3 | 12.9 |
| Belgium | 108.6 | 98.1 | 10.4 |
| Canada | 83.2 | 43.6 | 39.7 |
| Denmark | 46.1 | 22.7 | 23.4 |
| Finland | 51.5 | −42.0 | 93.4 |
| France | 65.0 | 37.7 | 27.2 |
| Germany | 60.2 | 44.3 | 15.9 |
| Greece | 107.0 | na | — |
| Iceland | 47.2 | 27.2 | 19.9 |
| Ireland | 36.4 | na | — |
| Italy | 109.8 | 97.5 | 12.3 |
| Japan | 132.6 | 58.4 | 74.3 |
| Korea | 17.2 | −32.7 | 50.0 |
| Luxembourg | 5.6 | na | — |
| Netherlands | 52.8 | 41.6 | 11.2 |
| New Zealand | 42.8 | 20.1 | 22.7 |
| Norway | 25.7 | −73.4 | 99.1 |
| Portugal | 55.4 | na | — |
| Spain | 68.4 | 41.5 | 26.9 |
| Sweden | 67.0 | −1.0 | 68.0 |
| United Kingdom | 50.7 | 29.0 | 21.6 |
| United States | 59.7 | 42.9 | 16.8 |

Source: OECD (2002a).

Note
na = Not available.

reserves that are set aside based on actuarial calculations spanning many years. The government has established the pension premium rates of working generations higher than if public pensions were funded strictly through a pay-as-you-go financing plan in order to accumulate net financial assets, which were 41.7 percent of nominal GDP at end-FY01. These reserves are intended to restrain the rise of pension premiums in the future. Therefore, viewing these reserves as funds offsetting government liabilities assumes that public pension benefits will be cut in the future and/or that alternate sources of funding will be found (for example, increasing pension premium rates and/or increasing transfers from other government sectors).

Central and local governments also hold some financial assets. For example, central and local governments have more than Y60 trillion in equities (as of end-FY01), which correspond to equity investments in public institutions, some of which are FILP-financed agencies (FILP will be discussed in greater detail below). Therefore, a certain case can be made for viewing government liabilities on a net basis. However, given concerns that some of the assets held by these public institutions may have turned out to be nonperforming, these equities will need to be valued suitably as assets. Of course, even if public institutions have unrecoverable assets on their books, it will not give rise to new government liabilities as long as doubtful assets are less than net worth of these corporations. Therefore, viewing government liabilities on a gross basis will mean viewing such liabilities conservatively without expressly allowing for the soundness of public corporations' assets.

As this analysis should make clear, there are several ways of understanding government liabilities. Moreover, it may be more important to offset government liabilities not with financial assets, but with real assets such as social overhead capital. The outlook for sustainability of budget deficits will differ depending on how government assets are understood.

## Fiscal investment and the loan program and its reform

### *The Fiscal Investment and Loan Program (FILP)*

Besides the narrow definition of public finances discussed above, the Fiscal Investment and Loan Program (FILP) plays a major role in Japan's fiscal policies. FILP is defined as fiscal policies employing financial methods. It is a program where the government grants credit to public corporations, known as FILP-financed agencies, through loans, investments, and guarantees, and these agencies, in turn, offer policy loans and invest in social infrastructure.

Figure 8.5 illustrates the broad flow of funds within FILP through end-FY00. The sources of funds for FILP are postal savings and postal life insurance premiums collected from the household sector, and by the government from the private sector for the national pension and employee pension programs. These funds were required to be deposited with the MOF Trust Fund Bureau (TFB) excluding the reserve for postal life insurance, and TFB undertook their long-term investment in view of fiscal policy. In other words, funds deposited with TFB were supplied to policy institutions such as government financial institutions, public corporations, and local governments in the form of loans and the underwriting of bonds, and these institutions invested in the development of social overhead capital and offered loans in accordance with policy goals. FILP as a whole can therefore be viewed as a public finance institution offering (super) long-term financing. The FILP plan balance was Y410 trillion (81.6 percent of nominal GDP) at end-FY01.

### *The changing role of FILP*

By using funds backed by the credit and institutions of the government, FILP made a significant contribution to the development of Japan's economy when investment funds were short and social and economic infrastructure was inadequate. FILP also provided support for financial and capital markets functioning in both qualitative and quantitative terms when such markets were still undeveloped.

However, once Japan's economy began to grow more slowly and funds were in abundant supply, the need for conventional FILP activities, such as policy loans and the development of social overhead capital, declined. In addition, an increasing

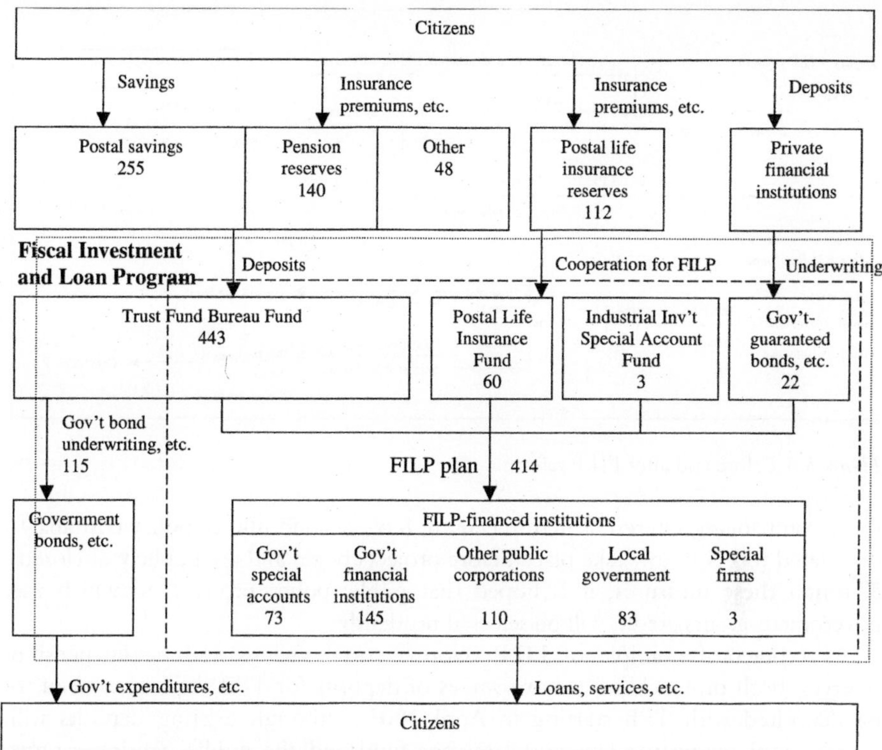


*Figure 8.5* Fiscal investment and loan program system[a] (pre-reform).

Source: Ministry of Finance (2001).

Note

a Numbers represent outstanding balances at the end of FY99, expressed in trillion yen.

amount of funds invested through FILP began to recycle through financial and capital markets and finance the budget deficit of the government sector.

How did such a situation for FILP come about? One of the reasons was that the funds being raised were unrelated to the demand for conventional FILP (TFB liabilities were passively decided). Questions also arose about the possibility that the enlarged overall FILP system was having adverse repercussions, such as weakening fiscal discipline and increasing inefficiency of government policies pursued through FILP. For this reason, debates arose on the restructuring of FILP in view of economic and social changes for a few years, and reform of the FILP system began extensively in April 2001.

### *FILP reform and its effect on government finance*

The FILP reform has two main features. First, market principles were introduced to the flow of funds, which was nearly limited within the government sector, and

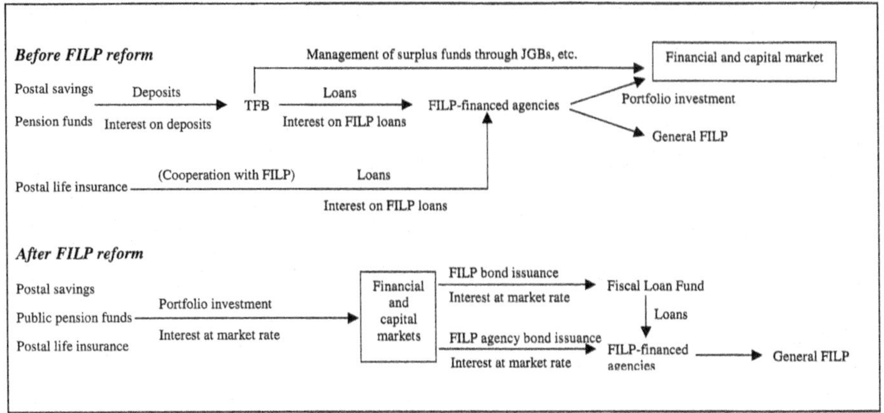


*Figure 8.6* Before and after FILP reform.

the accompanying interest structure (Figure 8.6). Second, future policy cost analyses related to FILP now take place before projects begin and are publicly disclosed. Through these measures, it is hoped that public policy projects, to which the government grants credit, will be selected prudently.

As a practical example of FILP reform, postal savings and public pension reserves, both of which are major sources of deposits for TFB, no longer need to be deposited with TFB starting in April 2001 (although existing deposits will remain until maturity). The postal savings fund and the public pension reserve fund invest their assets in financial and capital markets in accordance with their liabilities, and these funds behave as financial institutions and institutional investors. TFB was reorganized and a new account known as the Fiscal Loan Fund (FLF) was established. FLF raises funds needed for FILP through the issue of FILP bonds, which are lent to FILP-financed agencies following policy cost analyses. FILP-financed agencies (public institutions) not only borrow from the FLF but also issue FILP-agency bonds to raise funds directly from markets. FILP bonds have the same credit rating as government bonds since the issuer is the government, but FILP-agency bonds are issued by public corporations without being guaranteed by the government. Projects financed through the issue of FILP-agency bonds are not categorized as part of FILP since government credit is not involved.

The FILP reform will have a range of consequences. Since market principles are supposed to come into play to some degree on the management of projects undertaken by FILP and public institutions, there is reason to hope that these projects will be slimmed down and carried out more efficiently. If such a situation materializes, it would reduce the amount of transfers from government to public corporations, a favorable development for government finances. More importantly, however, is that the enormous amount of public financing will pass through financial and capital markets in the form of bonds. The introduction of FILP bonds and FILP-agency bonds may increase bond issuance. Although FILP reform may not, in principle, change the saving–investment balance of the public sector, what is certain is that the public sector's cost of funds (credit risk) will be exposed to a greater extent to market principles. The long-term interest rate could therefore bear a risk premium to reflect the government's fiscal situation. In the past, TFB was able to finance the government's budget deficit through its ample access to funds. This is no longer the case after the FILP reform since the FLF and FILP agencies are required to raise from markets only the amount of funds they need for FILP and for policy projects of public institutions.

## The rise and fall of fiscal deficits: 1975–2000

The post-war Japanese government had no debts until 1965, when a large unexpected shortfall in tax revenues left the country no choice but to issue construction bonds. Once issued, construction bonds were issued regularly in subsequent years. Then, another downturn that followed the first oil crisis made the Japanese government issue a new type of bonds in 1975. The new bonds are an "exception" to the rule in the sense that they are not based on the Public Finance Law and they are called "deficit-financing bonds," hereafter "deficit bonds."

Although it is not crystal clear how construction bonds and deficit bonds are distinguishable from one another from an accounting viewpoint, the distinction is legally and politically important. Moreover, the fiscal "stance" of the government is more obvious from the behavior of deficit bonds. Thus, in the subsequent discussion, we follow the legal tradition and center on the examination of deficit bonds. We also concentrate our discussion on the central (national) government general account.

## Historical observations

Since deficit bonds were issued as a temporary measure, the Japanese government aimed to restore balance in the government budget as soon as possible. As such, the government plan of January 1976 mentioned 1980 as a target date to eliminate the government "deficits" (as defined by the new issues of deficit bonds). However, by 1979, it became clear that it would be impossible to balance the budget by 1980. In fact, the deficit-to-GNP ratio had been rapidly increasing from 1975 to 1979. The revised plan of January 1979 stated that deficits would be eliminated by FY84. By 1983, the deficit-to-GNP ratio had begun to decline, but the level was still relatively high and the target date for elimination of deficits had to be pushed back once again. In August 1983, the government called for a gradual reduction of government deficits so that deficits would become zero by FY90. This revised schedule indeed was successful.

Thus the rise and fall of government deficit (defined as its ratio to the general account) completed a fifteen-year cycle in 1990, as shown in Figure 8.2. In this sense, FY90 marked an epoch in post-war fiscal policy in Japan, although there was an outstanding stock of government debt at the end of this cycle. Moreover, an old success story is only one part of the entire history and the completion of one cycle only brought the beginning of a new rise of government deficit.

Namely, the Japanese government restarted issuing deficit bonds in 1994 only to pave the way for continued accumulation of deficits bonds from Y64.2 trillion at end-FY94 to Y159 trillion in 2001. It is not clear when this new rise in deficits will turn into the corresponding fall and complete the second cycle.

The aim of this chapter is to examine the underlying driving forces of the history of deficits in Japan. In particular, we attempt to answer the question of whether the rises in deficits in 1975–79 and 1994–2000 were intended or were instead out of the control of the government? To be more specific, we try to answer the following questions: Was the rise of deficits in 1975–79 a result of intended fiscal stimuli *à la* Keynesian policy, possibly with a mistaken growth target? Was a successful drive toward elimination of deficits in 1980–90 achieved by enhancing revenues or by reducing expenditures? Why did deficits keep rising in 1994–2000?

### *The budget cycle*

As was briefly explained earlier, fiscal year T is defined as the period from April 1 of (calendar) year T to March 31 of the following year. A government budget for FY T starts from the budget guideline issued by the Ministry of Finance in July of calendar year T–1. The guideline includes the ceiling of the total budget for each ministry or government agency. According to this guideline, budget requests by ministries and agencies are submitted to the Minister of Finance by the end of August. Then, details of the budget plan are negotiated by the Ministry of Finance and other ministries and government agencies during the fall of year T–1. Sometime between the end of December (of year T–1) and the beginning of January (of year T), the cabinet approves a tentative government budget proposal. The proposal must be worked out, submitted to, and approved by the Diet. Although technical details may be modified by the Diet, the total size of the cabinet budget proposal almost always stays unchanged throughout the Diet discussion. The cabinet proposal incorporates a "government forecast" of economic growth and inflation for fiscal year T, announced usually at the end of December (of year T–1) or at the latest at the beginning of February (of year T). The Diet usually approves a cabinet plan around the beginning of the fiscal year T or April 1.

During the fiscal year, the budget may be revised to reflect evolving economic conditions. In the past, the budget was revised sometime in the fall or winter at least once, and in some years, the budget was revised twice or thrice. The first revised budget was approved as early as May (in FY95) and the second revised budget was approved as late as the last week of March (in FY89). The actual (ex post) government expenditures are determined on March 31.

In the following analysis, we exploit budget information and decision timing to infer what the government knew and what the government did not know. For example, we regard the "cabinet budget plan" for FY T as the government's intention with information as of January of year T. The difference between the plan (January of year T) and actual expenditures (March of year T+1) reflects the concurrent revision of government intentions during the budget period.

***Budget: plan, revision and final***

To quantify intended and unintended deficits, we take three avenues. First, the government budget revisions within the budget cycle are examined. Second, deviations between the budget plan and the final budget (expenditures) are compared with regard to bond issues and tax revenue. Third, the relationship between the budget and the (government) forecasts and the actual performance of economic growth are compared.

First, the government budget "plan," "revised plan" and "actual" budget (expenditures) are tabulated in Table 8.9 (as growth rates over the actual expenditure of the year before). Figure 8.7 shows the bond issues (planned and final) along with the deviations (final plan) in tax revenues.

Table 8.10 shows how the government sees the need for a change in the budget during the course of a fiscal year and how the government reacts to this need. The difference between actual and planned growth rates of the budget could be taken as unintended growth or contraction in the budget size.

## Intended and unintended deficits: the first cycle, 1975–90

In the 1960s, growth in the size of the budget was stable at around 15 percent. Deviations between the plan and the final expenditures were small (except FY68). However, during the first half of the 1970s, this budget stability ceased and the deviations became rather large especially at the time of the first oil crisis. For instance, the growth rate of FY74 budget, which was planned in the midst of the sharp inflation triggered by the first oil crisis, was set at 19.7 percent. However, the growth rate of the revised budget was increased to 25 percent, and the final budget to 29 percent. This was an unprecedented number of upward revisions during the fiscal year.

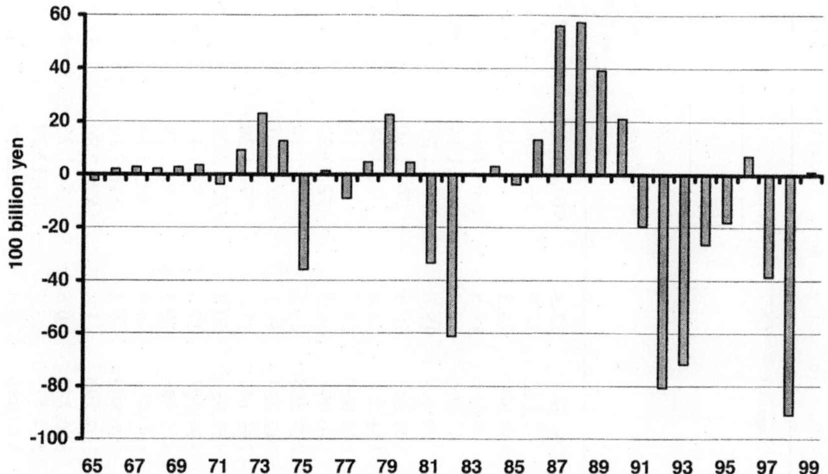


*Figure 8.7* Tax revenue: difference between actual and planned.

*Table 8.9* Plan, revision and actual budget, 1965–2001[a]

| *FY* | *Amount* | *T/(T–1)* | *Plan* | | | | *Actual* | | | | |
|---|---|---|---|---|---|---|---|---|---|---|---|
| | | | *Date* | | *Revision* | | | *Expenditure* | | *Revenue* | |
| | | | *Approval by the Cabinet* | *Decision by the House of Councilors* | *Amount* | *T/(T–1)* | *Date* | *Amount* | *T/(T–1)* | *Amount* | *T/(T–1)* |
| 1965 | 36,581 | 12.4 | 1964.12.28 | 1965.3.31 | 37,447 | 12.1 | 1965.12.27 | 37,230 | 12.4 | 37,730 | 9.5 |
| 1966 | 43,142 | 17.9 | 65.12.30 | 66.4.2 | 44,771 | 19.6 | 66.12.19 | 44,592 | 19.8 | 45,521 | 20.6 |
| 1967 | 49,509 | 14.8 | 67.2.28 | 67.4.1 | 52,034 | 16.2 | 67.12.21 | 51,130 | 14.7 | 52,994 | 16.4 |
| 1968 | 58,186 | 17.5 | 68.1.12 | 68.4.15 | 59,173 | 13.7 | 68.12.22 | 59,370 | 16.1 | 60,598 | 14.3 |
| 1969 | 67,396 | 15.8 | 69.1.14 | 69.4.1 | 69,308 | 17.1 | 70.3.4 | 69,178 | 16.5 | 71,092 | 17.3 |
| 1970 | 79,498 | 18.0 | 70.1.31 | 70.4.17 | 82,131 | 18.5 | 71.2.12 | 81,876 | 18.4 | 84,591 | 19.0 |
| 1971 | 94,143 | 18.4 | 70.12.30 | 71.3.29 | 96,590 | 17.6 | 71.11.9 | 95,611 | 16.8 | 99,708 | 17.9 |
| 1972 | 114,677 | 21.8 | 72.1.28 | 72.4.28 | 121,189 | 25.5 | 72.11.13 | 119,321 | 24.8 | 127,938 | 28.3 |
| 1973 | 142,840 | 24.6 | 73.1.15 | 73.4.11 | 152,726 | 26.0 | 73.12.14 | 147,783 | 23.9 | 167,619 | 31.0 |
| 1974 | 170,994 | 19.7 | 73.12.28 | 74.4.10 | 191,981 | 25.7 | 74.12.23 | 190,997 | 29.2 | 203,791 | 21.6 |
| 1975 | 212,888 | 24.5 | 75.1.10 | 75.4.2 | 208,371 | 8.5 | 75.11.7 | 208,608 | 9.2 | 214,734 | 5.4 |
| 1976 | 242,961 | 14.1 | 75.12.31 | 76.5.8 | 246,502 | 18.3 | 77.2.22 | 244,676 | 17.3 | 250,760 | 16.8 |
| 1977 | 285,142 | 17.4 | 77.1.20 | 77.4.16 | 287,843 | 16.8 | 78.1.31 | 293,466 | 19.9 | 294,336 | 17.4 |
| 1978 | 342,950 | 20.3 | 77.12.29 | 78.4.4 | 344,400 | 19.6 | 78.10.12 | 340,960 | 16.2 | 349,072 | 18.6 |
| 1979 | 386,001 | 12.6 | 79.1.11 | 79.4.3 | 396,675 | 15.2 | 80.2.14 | 387,898 | 13.8 | 397,792 | 14.0 |
| 1980 | 425,888 | 10.3 | 79.12.29 | 80.4.4 | 436,813 | 10.1 | 81.2.13 | 434,050 | 11.9 | 440,406 | 10.7 |
| 1981 | 467,881 | 9.9 | 80.12.29 | 81.4.2 | 471,253 | 7.9 | 82.2.17 | 469,211 | 8.1 | 474,433 | 7.7 |
| 1982 | 496,808 | 6.2 | 81.12.28 | 82.4.5 | 475,621 | 0.9 | 82.12.25 | 472,450 | 0.7 | 480,012 | 1.2 |
| 1983 | 503,796 | 1.4 | 82.12.30 | 83.4.4 | 508,394 | 6.9 | 84.2.24 | 506,353 | 7.2 | 516,529 | 7.6 |
| 1984 | 506,272 | 0.5 | 84.1.25 | 84.4.10 | 515,134 | 1.3 | 85.2.13 | 514,806 | 1.7 | 521,833 | 1.0 |
| 1985 | 524,996 | 3.7 | 84.12.29 | 85.4.5 | 532,228 | 3.3 | 86.2.15 | 530,045 | 3.0 | 539,925 | 3.5 |
| 1986 | 540,886 | 3.0 | 85.12.28 | 86.4.4 | 538,248 | 1.1 | 86.11.11 | 536,404 | 1.2 | 564,891 | 4.6 |

| | | | | | | | | | | |
|---|---|---|---|---|---|---|---|---|---|---|
| 1987 | 541,010 | 0.0 | 86.12.30 | 87.5.20 | 561,802 | 4.4 | 88.2.20 | 582,141 | 8.5 | 582,141 | 3.1 |
| 1988 | 566,997 | 4.8 | 87.12.28 | 88.4.7 | 618,517 | 10.1 | 89.3.7 | 614,710 | 5.6 | 646,074 | 11.0 |
| 1989 | 604,142 | 6.6 | 89.1.24 | 89.5.28 | 663,119 | 7.2 | 90.3.26 | 658,589 | 7.1 | 672,478 | 4.1 |
| 1990 | 662,368 | 9.6 | 89.12.29 | 90.6.7 | 696,511 | 5.0 | 91.3.6 | 692,686 | 5.2 | 717,034 | 6.6 |
| 1991 | 703,474 | 6.2 | 90.12.29 | 91.4.11 | 706,134 | 1.4 | 91.12.13 | 705,471 | 1.8 | 729905 | 1.8 |
| 1992 | 722,180 | 2.7 | 91.12.28 | 92.4.9 | 714,896 | 1.2 | 92.12.10 | 704,974 | −0.1 | 714,659 | −2.1 |
| 1993 | 723,548 | 0.2 | 92.12.26 | 93.3.31 | 774,375 | 8.3 | 94.2.23 | 751,024 | 6.5 | 777,311 | 8.8 |
| 1994 | 730,816 | 1.0 | 94.2.15 | 94.6.23 | 734,305 | −5.2 | 95.2.28 | 736,136 | −2.0 | 763,390 | −1.8 |
| 1995 | 709,871 | −2.9 | 94.12.25 | 95.3.22 | 780,340 | 6.3 | 96.2.16 | 759,385 | 3.2 | 805,572 | 5.5 |
| 1996 | 751,049 | 5.8 | 95.12.25 | 96.5.10 | 777,712 | −0.3 | 97.1.31 | 788,478 | 3.8 | 818,090 | 1.6 |
| 1997 | 773,900 | 3.0 | 96.12.25 | 97.3.28 | 785,332 | 1.0 | 98.2.4 | 784,703 | −0.5 | 801,704 | −2.0 |
| 1998 | 776,691 | 0.4 | 97.12.25 | 98.4.8 | 879,915 | 12.0 | 98.12.11 | 843,917 | 7.5 | 897,825 | 12.0 |
| 1999 | 818,601 | 5.4 | 98.12.25 | 99.3.17 | 890,189 | 1.2 | 99.12.9 | 890,374 | 5.5 | 943,753 | 5.1 |
| 2000 | 849,871 | 3.8 | 99.12.24 | 00.3.17 | 897,702 | 0.8 | 00.11.22 | | | | |
| 2001 | 826,524 | −2.7 | 00.12.24 | 01.3.26 | | | | | | | |

Note

a Amounts in 100 million yen; T/(T–1) in percent.

*Table 8.10* Growth of GNP: government forecast, estimate and actual (%), 1965–2000

| *FY* | *Government forecast* | | | *Estimate* | | | *Actual* | | | *Long-term planning* |
|---|---|---|---|---|---|---|---|---|---|---|
| | *Nominal (a)* | *Real (b)* | *(a) – (b)* | *Nominal (a)* | *Real (b)* | *(a) – (b)* | *Nominal (a)* | *Real (b)* | *(a) – (b)* | *Real* |
| 1965 | 11.0 | 7.5 | 3.5 | 10.1 | 4.3 | 5.8 | 11.1 | 6.2 | 4.9 | 8.1 |
| 1966 | 11.3 | 7.5 | 3.8 | 16.3 | 10.8 | 5.5 | 17.6 | 11.1 | 6.5 | 8.1 |
| 1967 | 13.4 | 9.0 | 4.4 | 18.0 | 13.2 | 4.8 | 17.0 | 11.0 | 6.0 | 8.2 |
| 1968 | 12.1 | 7.6 | 4.5 | 18.3 | 14.3 | 4.0 | 18.3 | 12.3 | 6.0 | 8.2 |
| 1969 | 14.4 | 9.8 | 4.6 | 18.8 | 13.0 | 5.8 | 18.4 | 12.0 | 6.4 | 8.2 |
| 1970 | 15.8 | 11.1 | 4.7 | 16.5 | 9.9 | 6.6 | 15.8 | 8.3 | 7.5 | 10.6 |
| 1971 | 15.1 | 10.1 | 5.0 | 10.5 | 5.7 | 4.8 | 10.2 | 5.1 | 5.1 | 10.6 |
| 1972 | 12.4 | 7.2 | 5.2 | 17.4 | 11.5 | 5.9 | 16.6 | 9.3 | 7.3 | 10.6 |
| 1973 | 16.4 | 10.7 | 5.7 | 23.0 | 5.4 | 17.6 | 20.9 | 5.0 | 15.9 | 9.4 |
| 1974 | 12.9 | 2.5 | 10.4 | 17.9 | −0.6 | 18.5 | 18.4 | −0.7 | 19.1 | 9.4 |
| 1975 | 15.9 | 4.3 | 11.6 | 9.4 | 3.1 | 6.3 | 10.2 | 4.1 | 6.1 | 9.4 |
| 1976 | 13.0 | 5.6 | 7.4 | 13.0 | 5.8 | 7.2 | 12.4 | 3.8 | 8.6 | 6.25 |
| 1977 | 13.7 | 6.7 | 7.0 | 11.3 | 5.4 | 5.9 | 11.0 | 4.6 | 6.4 | 6.25 |
| 1978 | 12.0 | 7.0 | 5.0 | 10.0 | 5.5 | 4.5 | 9.9 | 5.5 | 4.4 | 6.25 |
| 1979 | 9.5 | 6.3 | 3.2 | 7.4 | 6.1 | 1.3 | 8.0 | 5.1 | 2.9 | 5.70 |
| 1980 | 9.4 | 4.8 | 4.6 | 7.7 | 5.0 | 2.7 | 8.9 | 2.4 | 6.5 | 5.70 |
| 1981 | 9.1 | 5.3 | 3.8 | 5.2 | 2.7 | 2.5 | 6.1 | 2.9 | 3.2 | 5.70 |
| 1982 | 8.4 | 5.2 | 3.2 | 5.2 | 3.3 | 1.9 | 5.0 | 3.3 | 1.7 | 5.70 |
| 1983 | 5.6 | 3.4 | 2.2 | 4.1 | 3.7 | 0.4 | 4.6 | 2.6 | 2.0 | 4.00 |
| 1984 | 5.9 | 4.1 | 1.8 | 6.7 | 5.7 | 1.0 | 6.9 | 4.1 | 2.8 | 4.00 |
| 1985 | 6.1 | 4.6 | 1.5 | 5.9 | 4.2 | 1.7 | 6.5 | 4.3 | 2.2 | 4.00 |
| 1986 | 5.1 | 4.0 | 1.1 | 4.1 | 2.6 | 1.5 | 4.7 | 3.2 | 1.5 | 4.00 |
| 1987 | 4.6 | 3.5 | 1.1 | 4.8 | 4.9 | −0.1 | 5.0 | 5.0 | 0.0 | 4.00 |
| 1988 | 4.8 | 3.8 | 1.0 | 5.7 | 5.1 | 0.6 | 6.8 | 6.0 | 0.8 | 3.75 |

| | | | | | | | | | | |
|---|---|---|---|---|---|---|---|---|---|---|
| 1989 | 5.2 | 4.0 | 1.2 | 6.9 | 5.0 | 1.9 | 7.3 | 4.7 | 2.6 | 3.75 |
| 1990 | 5.2 | 4.0 | 1.2 | 7.2 | 5.2 | 2.0 | 7.7 | 5.3 | 2.4 | 3.75 |
| 1991 | 5.5 | 3.8 | 1.7 | 5.5 | 3.7 | 1.8 | 5.6 | 3.0 | 2.6 | 3.75 |
| 1992 | 5.0 | 3.5 | 1.5 | 3.0 | 1.6 | 1.4 | 2.2 | 0.7 | 1.5 | 3.50 |
| 1993 | 4.9 | 3.3 | 1.6 | 1.1 | 0.2 | 0.9 | 0.9 | 0.3 | 0.6 | 3.50 |
| 1994 | 4.0 | 2.6 | 1.4 | 1.9 | 1.7 | 0.2 | 0.4 | 0.6 | −0.2 | 3.50 |
| 1995 | 3.7 | 2.8 | 0.9 | 1.0 | 1.3 | −0.3 | 2.3 | 3.1 | −0.8 | 3.50 |
| 1996 | 2.8 | 2.5 | 0.3 | 2.8 | 2.8 | 0.0 | 3.3 | 4.7 | −1.4 | 3.00 |
| 1997 | 3.1 | 1.9 | 1.2 | 1.0 | 0.2 | 0.8 | 0.8 | 0.0 | 0.8 | 3.00 |
| 1998 | 2.4 | 2.0 | 0.4 | −1.9 | −1.9 | 0.0 | −2.0 | −1.9 | −0.1 | 3.00 |
| 1999 | 0.5 | 0.5 | 0.0 | −0.5 | 0.6 | −1.1 | −0.9 | 0.9 | −1.8 | 3.00 |
| 2000 | 0.9 | 1.2 | −0.3 | | | | | | | 2.00 |

Casual observation of Table 8.9 shows the following. The budget size was increased in FY72–FY74. Deficit bonds were issued in FY75 to finance an acute shortage in revenue, directly due to the recession after the first oil crisis. From FY76 to FY78, an increasing amount of deficit bonds was planned and intended. From FY79 to FY82, efforts were made to reduce the size of deficit bonds at the planning stage. However, a slowdown in 1981–82, partly due to the second oil crisis and partly due to a recession in the United States, necessitated increasing deficit bonds again. Since FY83, the budget size (growth rate) and deficit bond issues have been reduced gradually. Major positive surprises in tax revenues in FY88 and FY89 eliminated all but a trivial amount of the deficit.

### *Growth rate surprise*

To examine the source of the unexpected increase and decrease in tax revenue, we compare the government forecast and the actual outcome of the GNP growth rate. Forecasts (by the government every year) of economic growth rate, early estimates, and actual performances are listed in Table 8.10. The data in Table 8.10 illustrate how the government forecast and actual performance are compared with the target GNP growth of the long-term planning of the government. The long-term plan is designed by the Economic Planning Agency as a base for coordinating the economy for several years.

First, the deviation between the forecast and actual numbers was very large in both directions until FY75. After FY75, both the forecast and the actual growth rates fluctuate around the long-term target rate. However, the deviation of the actual rate from the long-term target exhibits a serial correlation coefficient of 0.55. The actual performance tended to outpace the long-term target during the 1960s, while it under-achieved in the 1970s.

It is clear from Table 8.10 that economic performances in FY73 and FY74 were clearly below the long-term target or the government's annual plan. This must have caused the shortage in tax revenue in FY75 (with a lag). The tax revenue shortages in FY81 and FY82 are also associated with forecast errors in growth rate, while tax surpluses in FY88 and FY89 are explained by a surprise increase in the growth rate. In summary, casual observations suggest that surprises in tax revenues are mostly due to forecast errors in the economic growth rate. We now examine this conjecture in greater detail.

### *The beginning*

According to conventional wisdom, government revenues plummeted in FY75 due to a recession in FY73–FY74 caused by the first oil crisis. In FY74, the growth rate of real GNP turned negative for the first time in post-war Japanese economic history, while the CPI inflation rate was as high as 30 percent per annum. It thus was an acute case of stagflation.

During the FY75 budget, there was a sudden shortfall in revenues, while expenditures of public construction and government employee salaries increased with inflation, although they were not formally indexed. As a result of this economic

**Box 8.4 Report of Fiscal Institution Committee, Strategic Subcommittee, October 1975**

In FY75, the shortage of revenues amounts to 3 trillion yen reflecting the recent economic conditions. In order to stimulate a stagnant economy, additional public works will be implemented, while the salary increase for government employees is mandated by the government employee agency. These additional expenditures necessitate additional revenue source. However, expenditure cuts or an increase of taxes are not appropriate under the current economic circumstances.

condition, deficit bond issues were recognized as being inevitable and they were recommended by the Fiscal Institution Committee, Strategic Subcommittee (Box 8.4).

The advice of the Committee could be a textbook statement written by some Keynesian macroeconomist. It seems appropriate to interpret that the "deficit bonds" started as a response to an unexpected downfall in revenues, caused by the first oil crisis. They were introduced as an emergency measure in the mid-year revision of the budget.

### *Snowballing, 1976–80*

Although the introduction of deficit bonds is due to a sharp, unexpected downfall of revenues, a real puzzle is the rapid increase in deficits in the second half of the 1970s. In this section, we examine several candidate hypotheses.

#### *Keynesian policy*

If the introduction of deficit bonds was an act of Keynesian policy, was the increase of deficit bonds a continuation of such a policy? One might hypothesize that the government did not realize for several years that the first oil crisis caused a rather permanent shift in the growth potential of the Japanese economy. In other words, a rapid increase in deficits was also caused by a series of unexpected shortfalls in revenues, which was a result of unexpected slow growth.

In fact, the government over-estimated the growth rate in its one-year forecast for eight consecutive years from FY76 to FY83 (see Table 8.10). This was quite unusual, especially compared to the constant under-estimation during the 1960s (with an exception of FY65). There, however, is contrary evidence. As Figure 8.7 shows, surprises in tax revenues during the fiscal year were minimal from FY76 to FY80. This means that the issuing of deficit bonds was intended in the initial plan of budgets. We cannot reconcile these pieces of evidence. On the one hand, the government continued to over-estimate the economy's growth potential, and on the other hand, revenue forecasts were basically correct.

### *The locomotive theory*

At the economic summit of 1978, Germany and Japan were urged by other western countries, notably the United States, to expand their economies to be a "locomotive" for the rest of the world. One hypothesis is that Japan undertook stimulative fiscal policy in order to keep this promise. However, FY78 was only slightly higher than FY77 in terms of the growth rate of the general budget. The budget growth rate dropped sharply in FY79, indicating that whatever the locomotive stimulus was, it lasted for only a short period.

### *The second oil crisis*

Just when the deficit reduction plan was put in place, the second oil crisis forced down the growth potential of the Japanese economy. As growth slowed, so did tax revenues. But this was not unique to the second oil crisis years. Hence, the second oil crisis cannot explain why deficits mushroomed so rapidly, even allowing for the effect of the second oil crisis causing an unexpectedly low growth rate in FY79–FY80.

From Figure 8.2, it seems that the dependency ratio on bonds was decreasing in FY78, but this was reversed in FY79–FY80. As the decreasing trend is evident from this dependency ratio on entering the 1980s, this temporal reversal was due to the second oil crisis. But obviously this hypothesis does not explain why deficit bonds were high and increased in FY76 and FY77.

### *Social welfare*

The year 1973 is usually referred to as the year new social security (welfare) programs were introduced. The share for the program increased automatically during the 1970s, since it was indexed to inflation, while other budget items are typically not indexed. This trend is clearly witnessed by the rapid rise in government social security burdens as seen in Table 8.1. According to this hypothesis, the introduction of social welfare unfortunately coincided with rapid inflation caused by the first oil crisis and a shift to low growth, so that the long-run revenue trend was miscalculated and deficit bonds became necessary.

### *Intended deficits with an expectation of introducing a new tax*

The last hypothesis is that deficits were intended, with an implicit understanding that a kind of value-added tax would be introduced in the near future. It was hoped during the second half of the 1970s that a new tax would be introduced to cover deficits created for whatever reasons. When an attempt to introduce such a tax by the Ohira government failed in 1980, deficits became a real problem, according to this hypothesis. Although this hypothesis does not explain why deficits occurred in the first place, it is consistent with evidence that deficit bonds from FY76 to FY80 were fully planned at the beginning of the fiscal years.

In evaluating these hypotheses, we recall that much of the deficits in the period of FY76–FY79 were "intended." That is, deficits were included in the budget plan, and there was only a small surprise in economic growth. In summary, the increase in deficits of the second half of the 1970s is due to a combination of several factors. First, the government misread the growth potential, which seemed to have had a kink in 1974–75. It took more than a few years before the government realized this. This is evident in the government forecasts of growth which underpredicted the actual outcome.

On the expenditure side, social security (welfare) programs and other items were not checked enough. It could have been true that some hope of introducing a new tax made the government lax about expenditure increases. The revenue gap was covered by deficit bonds, which were issued as an emergency measure in FY75, but fully planned, and increased in the revenue share from FY76 to FY80. When an attempt to introduce a new tax failed, the government became serious about dealing with the budget deficits. But this was at the time of the second oil crisis, and as a result, expenditure was kept relatively high to help a sagging economy.

### *A period of recovery: 1983–90*

A smooth reduction in deficit bonds did not start until FY83 when the "zero-ceiling" policy was introduced. Basically, this policy meant that no ministries were allowed to ask for an increase in the budget (for that ministry) over the previous year. (Civil servants' salaries, debt service, and transfers to local governments were under more lenient ceilings.) This was imposed on the nominal terms. Any increase in budget items in principle had to be accompanied by a matching decrease in others. On the revenue side, any technical corrections (reduction) of income and other taxes were deferred. (Tax brackets are not indexed in Japan.) Due to inflation and real income growth, taxpayers move up to a higher marginal tax bracket.

The "zero-ceiling" policy from FY83 to FY87 was a freeze on the expenditure and revenue rate schedules, but it was essentially a tax increase combined with an expenditure cut in *real* terms. This policy was very effective, and the increase in the general budget was held down (see Table 8.9). From FY82 to FY89, the deficit bonds' share of revenues declined constantly. This was basically achieved by rapid and more-than-intended increases in tax revenues.

To check the contribution of bracket creeps (in a broader sense, that is, to include effects of both inflation and real economic growth), Asako *et al.* (1991) decomposed the total changes in the effective tax rates into the contribution of tax reform (any institutional changes in tax code and tax rates) and bracket creeps, and concluded that almost all changes in the tax rates during the late 1980s were due to bracket creeps. The Ministry of Finance routinely gave a "tax break" in the 1970s to offset bracket creeps, and we refer to this as a technical correction. In the 1980s, as technical corrections were not applied, bracket creeps acted as tax increases by default.

Although it is not clear how the rise of deficits was allowed, the fall of deficits was undeniably achieved by a classic measure, a tax increase by default. It, however, was implemented in a politically acceptable manner—a nominal freeze on expenditures and a nominal freeze on tax brackets. Moreover, it is well known that there were some technical maneuvers introduced by the Ministry of Finance which transferred the deficits of the general account to those of other specific accounts and local governments. This mechanism is too complicated to write down in a few sentences, but Asako *et al.* (1991) point out that these so-called hidden deficits amounted at end-FY90 to as large as 50 trillion yen or as high as 70 percent of total bonds and 177 percent of deficits bonds.

## The second rise in deficits: 1994–2000

Although the completion of the budget deficit cycle in FY90 by itself sounds successful, the basic economic condition that brought about this success story became the very seeds of the second rise in deficits. Namely, on entering the 1990s, Japan fell into a more-than-decade long period of economic stagnation from the "Japan as number one" state of the latter half of the 1980s. However, long-term interest rates fell from a high in 1991 to less than 1 percent in 2003 (Figure 8.8).

The Plaza Accord of the G5 countries in 1985 obliged Japan to take expansionary macroeconomic policy to raise domestic demand and thereby imports, and decrease Japanese surpluses in the current account. As fiscal reforms to decrease budget deficits had been underway, Japan responded to the international agreement by taking a loose stance in its monetary policy. This easy monetary policy brought about booms in the assets market and the goods and services markets. In particular, the land and stock markets absorbed the "excess liquidity" only to invite bubbles in the formation of asset prices.

As was hinted at in the previous section, the booms in both the assets and goods and services markets were the main sources of the unexpectedly high tax revenues and helped to cease the new issue of deficit bonds in FY90. What became seeds to the later long-term stagnation was the huge pile of bank as well as nonbank loans that assumed high asset prices in evaluating the collateral values of loans. These loans

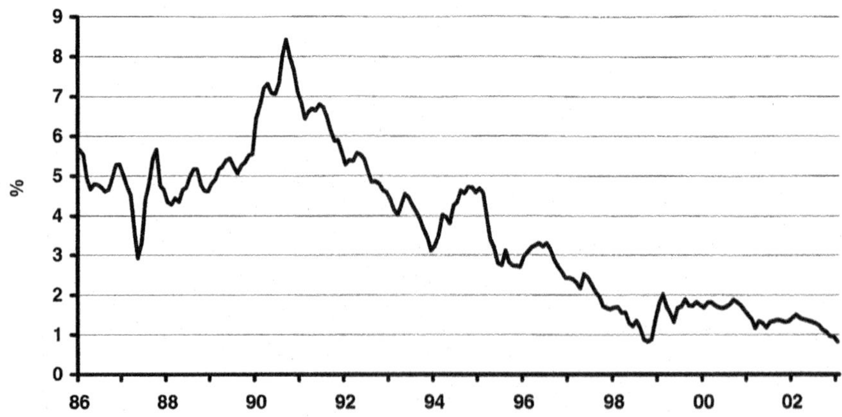


*Figure 8.8* Long-term interest rate, 1986–2002.

Source: Daiwa Institute of Research.

are deemed to become bad loans once asset prices and thereby the collateral values fall, which is what actually happened in Japan on entering the 1990s.

### *Unintended deficits*

In contrast to the intended or determined rises in deficits during the latter half of the 1970s, the second rises in deficits starting in FY94 were unintended. This is evident if only we look at Figure 8.7 in which unintended shortages of tax revenues are plotted throughout the 1990s since FY91 except for two opposite outcomes of FY96 and FY99. Moreover, note that the magnitude of tax shortages is rather significant, which explains why deficits grew so rapidly.

Figure 8.7 shows that, even before 1994, FY92 and FY93 suffered from large tax shortages. Why did this happen and how were the deficits maneuvered? In those years, construction bonds, rather than deficits bonds, were issued in large magnitude.

### *The long stagnation and Keynesian fiscal policy*

New issues of unintended construction bonds imply that there were mid-year budget revisions in those years and public works were the main expenditure item. This is what really happened in FY92 and FY93 (Figure 8.1). In fact, as was pointed out earlier, in the 1990s, supplementary budgets were frequently used to stimulate the stagnant macroeconomy *à la* Keynesian prescription.

Officially in the 1990s, the Japanese economy experienced two downturns (91:2–93:10 and 97:5–99:1) and three upturns (86:11–91:2, 93:10–97:5, 99:1–). However, regardless of such an official classification of business cycles, the Japanese economy was said to have been trapped by a long-term stagnation throughout the decade.

It is true that the Japanese economy had been in the transitional phase throughout the 1990s from the good-old-days or Japan-as-number-one type quasi-open economy to a competitive market full-open economy, or what is called a globalized economy. This transition forced the Japanese economy to adjust with pain in such a way as to abandon many of its old traditional institutions. However, not all Japanese public and government officials understood the necessary direction of restructuring and instead hoped Japan would revive shortly without changing the basic old structures.

Thus, the government policy has always been that of Keynesian demand management so as to stimulate the economy and wait for strong recovery by revitalizing private economic activities. However, this traditional channel has not worked sufficiently throughout the post-bubble period partly because the public's expectations of the future course of the economy have never been strong enough to revitalize the "animal spirits" and partly because the bad loan problem has prevented the economy from flexibly using its resources. The latter even invited systemic instability of the financial sectors as was typically exemplified by the bankruptcies of big banks and securities companies.

The pessimistic scenario of the Japanese economy stems from the very fact that asset markets have not absorbed enough money to sustain land and stock prices and allowed them to decrease to the record low levels since their bubbles crashed on entering the 1990s. If this is true, it is conceivable that the government took a rather optimistic scenario in the sense that once land and stock prices came back to higher levels, most problems of the Japanese economy would be cured and the old good days would return. Furthermore, because asset prices are often too volatile and uncertain, there has been some possibility of the optimistic view materializing and that the Japanese economy would revive with minimal costs.

The above has been what has been happening during most of the 1990s except for FY96–FY97 when the economy was enjoying a notable temporal upturn but was endangered by government failure or by misjudged premature introduction of budget and fiscal reforms. These explain the repeated biased over-estimates of economic growth over the actual rates seen during the 1990s. It thus also explains the repeated unintended shortage of tax revenues and rapid increases in unintended deficit bonds.

## Conclusion

This chapter has attempted to explain fiscal issues in Japan. In the first part of the chapter, the institutions, history and present condition of fiscal issues in Japan were succinctly reviewed. In the second section, we explained why Japan had the history of rising and falling fiscal deficits over the period 1975–2000.

Although with respect to many descriptions in the text we have not presented analytical and statistical details on which our views are derived, we hope that our figures and tables are sufficient for readers to understand the essence of Japanese fiscal issues. In separate future papers, we would develop our discussions in greater detail with the direct aid of analytical and statistical analyses.

## Notes

1 The initial budget for FY98 was prepared in conformance with the Fiscal Structural Reform Act, but public finances deteriorated with the passage of two major stimulus packages in the same year.
2 The government has been discussing whether this share should be increased to one-half by FY04.
3 We used SNA93 data as much as possible in preparing this chapter.
4 Under SNA93, the scope of social overhead capital estimated with regard to fixed capital consumption was expanded in Japan. This has had the effect of increasing government consumption expenditures since FY90 in Table 8.3.

## References

Asako, K., Ito, T. and Sakamoto, K. (1991) "The rise and fall of deficit in Japan, 1965–1990," *Journal of the Japanese and International Economics* 5(4): 451–72.
Cabinet Office, Japan (2003) *Annual Report on National Accounts, 2003*, Tokyo: CAO.
Daiwa Institute of Research.
Fukuda, S. and Teruyama, H. (1994) "The sustainability of budget deficits in Japan," *Hitotsubashi Journal of Economics* 35: 109–19.
Fund Operation Council (1999) *Summary of the Discussion Concerning Fundamental*

*Reform of the Fiscal Investment and Loan Program*, Tokyo: Ministry of Finance, available on: www.mof.go.jp/english/zaito/za054b.htm.

Homma, M. (1991) "Tax reform in Japan," in A.O. Krueger and T. Ito (eds) *Tax Reform in Asia*, National Bureau of Economic Research, Chicago: Chicago University Press.

Ishi, H. (1989) *The Japanese Tax System*, Oxford: Clarendon Press.

Ministry of Finance, Japan (1999) *Guide to Japanese Government Bonds*, Tokyo: MOF.

Ministry of Finance, Japan, Budget Bureau (2000) *The Japanese Budget in Brief, 2000*, Tokyo: MOF.

Ministry of Finance, Japan, Financial Bureau (2001) *FILP Report 2000*, Tokyo: MOF.

Noguchi, Y. (1987) "Public finance," in K. Yamamura and Y. Yasuda (eds) *The Political Economy of Japan*, Vol. 1, *The Domestic Transformation*, Stanford, CA: Stanford University Press.

Noguchi, Y. (1992) "Aging of population, social security and tax reform," in A.O. Krueger and T. Ito (eds) *Tax Reform in Asia*, National Bureau of Economic Research, Chicago: Chicago University Press.

OECD (2001) *Revenue Statistics of OECD Member Countries, 1965–2001*, Paris: OECD.

OECD (2002a) *Economic Outlook*, December, Paris: OECD.

OECD (2002b) *National Accounts of OECD Countries, 2002 edition*, Paris: OECD.

Suzuki, H., Kaku, K., Nagai, T. and Ono, K. (2001) "Zaisei no shinnin wo kaifuku surutameni saikenno tameno giron wo isogubeki" [We should hurry to discuss budget reform], *Daiwa Review* 1: 10–56.

# 9 Korea

*Sang-Kun Bae and Dongsoon Lim*

## Introduction

In December 1997, the (South) Korean economy was caught in the wave of turmoil of the foreign exchange crisis that eventually spread like wildfire throughout the Asian region. However, Korea has achieved a relatively quick and strong recovery from the financial crisis, thanks to supportive fiscal and monetary policies and progress in structural reform. Real GDP grew by 10.9 percent in 1999 and 9.3 percent in 2000. In 2001, however, the Korean economic recovery slowed down mainly due to the difficulty and delay in the restructuring process both in the public and private sectors.

In order to sustain the pace of economic recovery, Korea's monetary and fiscal policies need to play a fundamental role. In the context of the strong expansion, the newly independent Bank of Korea should ensure that its inflation target is achieved, while fiscal policy should meet the new goal of accelerating the achievement of a balanced budget and limiting public debt. Given the need to increase tax revenue to meet medium-term spending pressures associated with the aging of the population and cooperation with the North, it is important to restructure remaining distortions in the tax system and to pursue reforms in the pension system.

In short, having launched an ambitious program to transform its economic system, Korea needs to follow through on the implementation of these reforms. Such reforms, together with appropriate macroeconomic policies, will boost the supply potential of the country and reduce its vulnerability to shocks, thereby sustaining rapid economic growth in the future.

### *Fiscal systems*

As can be seen from Table 9.1, the ratio of foreign debt to nominal GDP from 1988 to 1993 has been stable at less than 20 percent. However, the ratio continuously increased to 31.4 percent in 1996, while the ratio of foreign reserves to GDP continuously decreased from 46.2 in 1993 to 20.3 percent in 1996. Therefore, Korea faced a shortage of liquidity at that time, and subsequently, the foreign exchange crisis happened at the end of 1997.

It was initially expected that Korea would emerge quickly from the foreign

*Table 9.1* Annual foreign debt and reserves in Korea, 1979–2001

| *Year* | *Nominal GDP* | *Foreign debt* | | *Foreign reserves* | |
|---|---|---|---|---|---|
| | *US$ million* | *US$ million* | *% of GDP* | *US$ million* | *% of debt* |
| 1979 | 61,900 | 20,287 | 32.8 | 5,708 | 28.1 |
| 1980 | 62,200 | 27,170 | 43.7 | 6,571 | 24.2 |
| 1981 | 69,600 | 32,433 | 46.6 | 6,891 | 21.2 |
| 1982 | 74,400 | 37,083 | 49.8 | 6,984 | 18.8 |
| 1983 | 82,300 | 40,378 | 49.1 | 6,910 | 17.1 |
| 1984 | 90,600 | 43,053 | 47.5 | 7,650 | 17.8 |
| 1985 | 93,400 | 46,762 | 50.1 | 7,749 | 16.6 |
| 1986 | 107,600 | 44,510 | 41.4 | 7,955 | 17.9 |
| 1987 | 135,200 | 35,568 | 26.3 | 9,193 | 25.8 |
| 1988 | 180,800 | 31,150 | 17.2 | 12,378 | 39.7 |
| 1989 | 220,700 | 29,372 | 13.3 | 15,245 | 51.9 |
| 1990 | 252,500 | 31,699 | 12.6 | 14,822 | 46.8 |
| 1991 | 295,100 | 39,135 | 13.3 | 13,733 | 35.1 |
| 1992 | 314,700 | 42,819 | 13.6 | 17,154 | 40.1 |
| 1993 | 345,700 | 43,870 | 12.7 | 20,262 | 46.2 |
| 1994 | 402,400 | 97,437 | 24.2 | 25,673 | 26.3 |
| 1995 | 489,400 | 127,491 | 26.1 | 32,712 | 25.7 |
| 1996 | 520,000 | 163,489 | 31.4 | 33,237 | 20.3 |
| 1997 | 476,600 | 159,237 | 33.4 | 20,405 | 12.8 |
| 1998 | 317,700 | 148,705 | 46.8 | 52,041 | 35.0 |
| 1999 | 405,800 | 137,069 | 33.8 | 74,055 | 54.0 |
| 2000 | 461,700 | 131,668 | 28.5 | 96,198 | 73.1 |
| 2001 | 422,200 | 117,652 | 27.9 | 102,821 | 87.4 |

Source: Bank of Korea (2003: national accounts database, balance of payments database).

exchange crisis since macroeconomic indices, barring the balance on the current account, were generally stable. However, Korea could not overcome the foreign exchange crisis, and instead, slipped into a serious economic crisis.

The recession in 1998 can be summarized as the worst economic disaster since the Korean War. The growth rate of real GDP in 1998 was −6.7 percent and the unemployment rate almost tripled. However, a recovery began in the second half of 1998, and then a remarkably rapid and strong economic upturn was achieved in 1999.

What led to the rapid recovery of the Korean economy? One of the many economic factors behind the rapid recovery is the contribution of fiscal policy in terms of structural reforms and welfare programs. Since the balanced budget principle kept the size of the government debt at a manageable level from 1982–96, the Korean government could plan massive fiscal support to troubled financial institutions and to expanded welfare programs for the poor and the unemployed. Moreover, there is not a great deal of concern about the rapid explosion of the budget deficit and public debt.

As the Korean economy is emerging from the economic crisis, it is worthwhile reviewing Korea's public expenditure and its role in different historical periods, in particular, in the period of the financial crisis. In the next section of this chapter, the past thirty years are divided into four periods in order to summarize the economic conditions and fiscal policies of Korea. A brief overview of the Korean budget process and taxation is presented in subsequent sections. The last section discusses the emerging issues on fiscal policy in Korea.

## Economic development and fiscal policy in Korea

Although Korea has experienced extreme political and social changes since the Korean War, its economy has grown rapidly. The foundations for rapid economic growth were laid by the promotion of industrialization and exports in the 1960s and 1970s, while price stabilization and adjustment of the industrial structure were implemented in the 1980s.

Before the economic crisis of 1997, the prospects for the Korean economy were bright and Korea was expected to soon reach a level of economic development that is comparable to developed countries. Although Korea slipped into serious financial crisis at the end of 1997, a strong recovery, with almost 11 percent economic growth, was achieved in 1999.

While there are many factors behind the rapid and outstanding economic development in Korea, fiscal policy also played an important role in forming the necessary infrastructure for economic development and in supporting key and strategic industries. Yet, compared with advanced countries, fiscal policy in Korea has been criticized for playing a passive role in the improvement of either income distribution or economic classes.

Nevertheless, generally speaking, Korean fiscal policy in the past thirty years has contributed a great deal to price stabilization and effective distribution of financial resources to support economic development, while at the same time, keeping true to prudent public finance principles.

### *Fiscal management in the 1970s*

The Korean government successfully employed development strategies for rapid economic growth in the 1970s. The government's strategy was intended to promote and sustain stable economic growth and it resulted in tremendous investment in the heavy and chemical industries. Large import substitution effects were induced to reduce the high dependency on foreign countries for raw materials and equipment, while at the same time, the strategy resulted in the necessity for a large amount of financial resources.

Mobilizing financial resources in the public sector and investing for social infrastructure became crucial when the main economic policy focused on rapid development of the industrial sector and export promotion. Thus, the structural transformations, including the fiscal and financial reforms, and fiscal policy in the 1970s can be credited with supporting rapid economic growth in Korea. However, this expansionary fiscal policy also led to high inflation.

As can be seen in Table 9.2 and Figure 9.1, it is clear that a relatively high growth rate of real GDP prevailed in the 1970s, while inflation rates (as measured by changes in the CPI) were above 10 percent except in 1973, which the first oil

*Table 9.2* Nominal and real GDP, inflation and the tax burden, 1971–2001

| *Year* | *Nominal GDP (billion won)* | *Growth of nominal GDP (%)* | *Growth of real GDP (%)* | *CPI inflation rate* | *Tax/GDP (%)* |
|---|---|---|---|---|---|
| 1971 | 3,379.1 | 24.0 | 8.6 | 13.5 | 4.6 |
| 1972 | 4,171.6 | 23.5 | 4.9 | 11.7 | 12.5 |
| 1973 | 5,378.3 | 28.9 | 12.3 | 3.2 | 12.1 |
| 1974 | 7,596.7 | 41.2 | 7.4 | 24.3 | 13.4 |
| 1975 | 10,228.1 | 34.6 | 6.5 | 25.2 | 15.2 |
| 1976 | 13,997.6 | 36.9 | 11.2 | 15.3 | 16.5 |
| 1977 | 17,945.5 | 28.2 | 10.0 | 10.1 | 16.5 |
| 1978 | 24,233.1 | 35.0 | 9.0 | 14.5 | 16.9 |
| 1979 | 31,035.8 | 28.1 | 7.1 | 18.3 | 17.3 |
| 1980 | 37,788.5 | 21.8 | −2.1 | 28.7 | 17.4 |
| 1981 | 47,382.6 | 25.4 | 6.5 | 21.4 | 17.2 |
| 1982 | 54,431.3 | 14.9 | 7.2 | 7.2 | 17.5 |
| 1983 | 63,857.5 | 17.3 | 10.7 | 3.4 | 17.9 |
| 1984 | 73,003.6 | 14.3 | 8.2 | 2.3 | 17.0 |
| 1985 | 81,312.3 | 11.4 | 6.5 | 2.5 | 16.6 |
| 1986 | 94,861.7 | 16.7 | 11.0 | 2.8 | 16.3 |
| 1987 | 111,197.7 | 17.2 | 11.0 | 3.0 | 16.7 |
| 1988 | 132,111.8 | 18.8 | 10.5 | 7.1 | 17.1 |
| 1989 | 148,197.0 | 12.2 | 6.1 | 5.7 | 17.7 |
| 1990 | 178,796.8 | 20.6 | 9.0 | 8.6 | 18.6 |
| 1991 | 216,510.9 | 21.1 | 9.2 | 9.3 | 17.7 |
| 1992 | 245,699.6 | 13.5 | 5.4 | 6.2 | 18.2 |
| 1993 | 277,496.5 | 12.9 | 5.5 | 4.8 | 18.1 |
| 1994 | 323,407.1 | 16.5 | 8.3 | 6.3 | 18.7 |
| 1995 | 377,349.8 | 16.7 | 8.9 | 4.5 | 19.1 |
| 1996 | 418,479.0 | 10.9 | 6.8 | 4.9 | 19.7 |
| 1997 | 453,276.4 | 8.3 | 5.0 | 4.5 | 19.5 |
| 1998 | 444,366.5 | −2.0 | −6.7 | 7.5 | 19.1 |
| 1999 | 482,744.2 | 8.6 | 10.9 | 0.8 | 19.5 |
| 2000 | 521,959.2 | 8.1 | 9.3 | 2.3 | 18.7 |
| 2001 | 545,013.3 | 4.4 | 3.0 | 4.1 | 20.7 |

Sources: Bank of Korea (2003: national accounts database); National Statistical Office (2003: price, consumer price index database); Ministry of Planning and Budget (2003: annual ratio of tax burden to GDP database).

shock occurred. Thus, the 1970s can be summarized as a period of rapid growth with high inflation.

Since an increase in government expenditure was necessary to support the economic development plan, special accounts were set up. These accounts refer to budgets that were established by law when the government needed to have a separate account from the general account in order to manage special projects. In addition, many other government funds were established during the 1970s.

Several characteristics of fiscal management in the 1970s are shown in Table 9.3 and Figure 9.2. At first, the relative size of public expenditure in the 1970s remained stable as its rate of growth was comparable to that of nominal GNP. Second, the size of local government's public expenditure expanded faster than

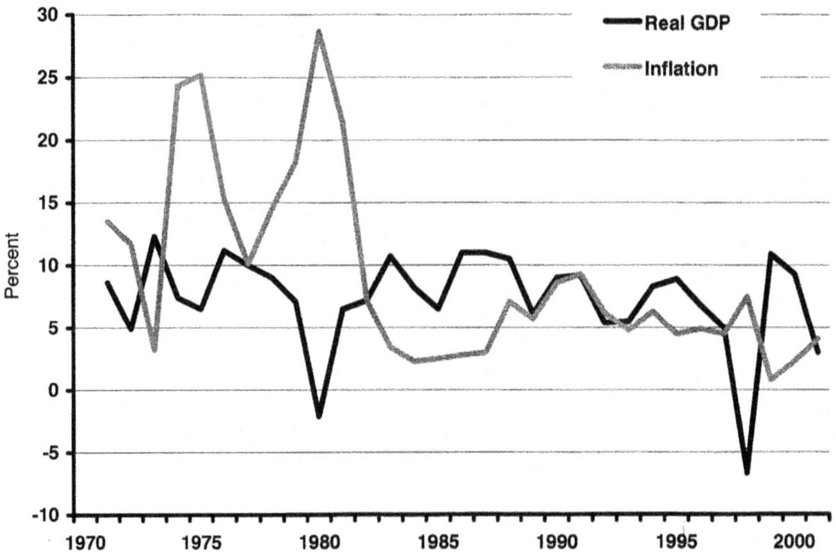


*Figure 9.1* GDP growth and inflation in Korea.

Sources: Bank of Korea (2003: national accounts database); National Statistical Office (2003: price, consumer price index database).

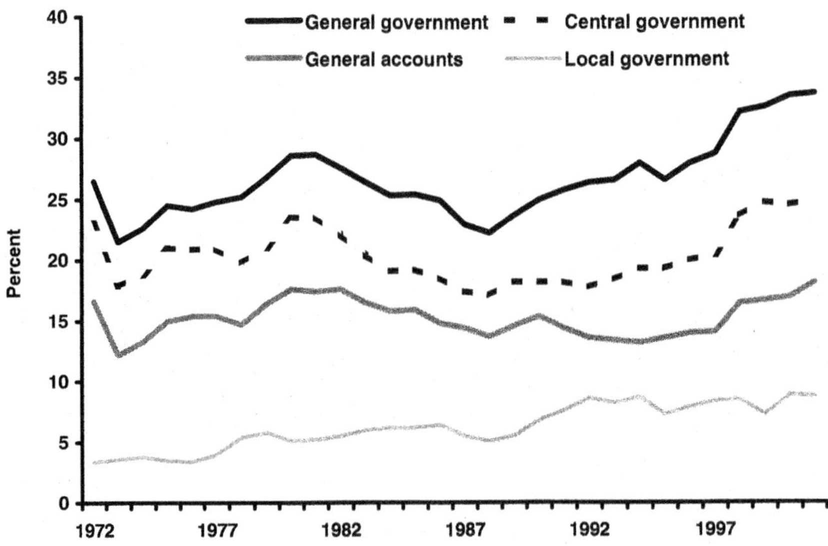


*Figure 9.2* Government budget (as a % of nominal GDP).

Source: Ministry of Planning and Budget (2003).

that of the central government. That is, the size of local government's expenditure increased from 3.4 percent of GNP in 1972 to 5.8 percent in 1979.

In terms of the components of expenditures in the general accounts of the central government, the data in Table 9.3 and Figure 9.3 show that national defense expenditures increased rapidly due to increased instability of national security after the end of the Vietnam War. Expenditure on economic development also increased from 16.5 percent of expenditures in general accounts in 1972 to 27.8 percent in 1979.

Thus, the need for expansion of fiscal investment to support economic development resulted in fiscal deficits. As can be seen in Table 9.3, the Korean government ran a persistent budget deficit in the 1970s and the deficit of the consolidated central government reached 5.5 percent of GNP in 1975.

### *Fiscal management in the 1980s*

Korea achieved outstanding real GDP growth in the 1970s through the maximization of the fiscal function in economic growth and development. As result of an expansionary fiscal policy, a fiscal deficit was accumulated and high inflation prevailed. Thus, it was felt that the role of fiscal policy should shift to economic stabilization with the introduction of the zero-base budgeting system and price level stability, and this became the fundamental direction of economic policy in the 1980s.

*Table 9.3* General government budget and expenditure in the 1970s

| | *1972* | *1973* | *1974* | *1975* | *1976* | *1977* | *1978* | *1979* |
|---|---|---|---|---|---|---|---|---|
| General government budget (% of GNP) | | | | | | | | |
| Total budget of general gov't | 26.5 | 21.5 | 22.6 | 24.5 | 24.2 | 24.8 | 25.2 | 26.8 |
| Central gov't budget | 23.1 | 17.9 | 18.8 | 21.0 | 20.9 | 20.9 | 19.8 | 21.0 |
| General accounts of central gov't | 16.6 | 12.2 | 13.3 | 15.0 | 15.4 | 15.4 | 14.7 | 16.4 |
| Local gov't budget | 3.4 | 3.6 | 3.8 | 3.5 | 3.4 | 4.0 | 5.4 | 5.8 |
| Consolidated budget balance | −4.7 | −2.1 | −3.9 | −5.5 | −2.8 | −2.6 | −4.0 | −1.5 |
| Composition of the general accounts (% of total general account) | | | | | | | | |
| Economic dev't expenditure | 16.5 | 20.2 | 18.6 | 25.3 | 25.2 | 22.8 | 20.5 | 27.8 |
| Social dev't expenditure | 20.3 | 23.2 | 20.7 | 19.8 | 20.8 | 21.2 | 22.4 | 22.7 |
| Nat'l defense expenditure | 25.9 | 29.3 | 30.0 | 29.4 | 33.6 | 34.7 | 37.0 | 30.8 |
| Education expenditure | 37.3 | 27.3 | 30.5 | 25.4 | 21.6 | 21.3 | 20.1 | 18.7 |

Source: Ministry of Planning and Budget (2003: budget of general government database, budget revenues database, budget expenditures database).

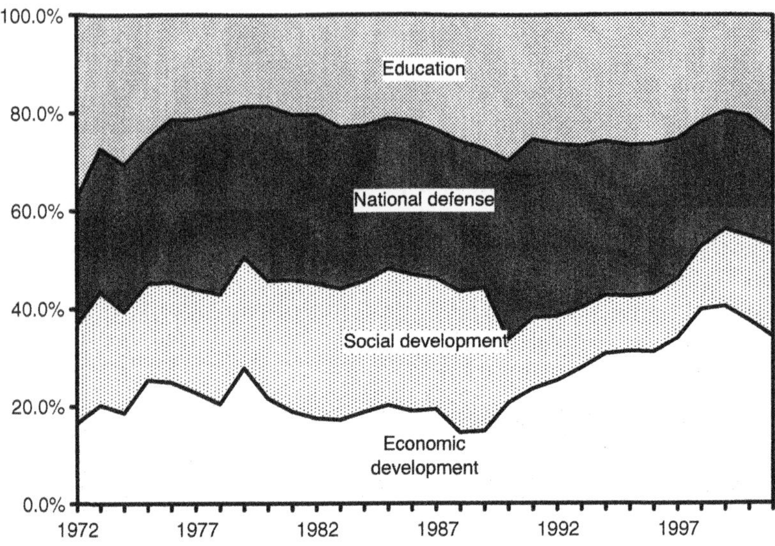


*Figure 9.3* Composition of the general accounts.

Source: Ministry of Planning and Budget (2003: budget of general government database, budget revenues database, budget expenditures database).

Fiscal policy during the 1980s can be characterized as a conservative operation through balanced budget principles. In 1984, the size of the budget was frozen in order to escape from government deficits in the general accounts and to achieve price stabilization. As can be seen from Table 9.4 and Figure 9.2, the ratio of the total budgets to GNP was reduced from 28.6 percent of GNP in 1980 to 23.7 percent in 1989.

Table 9.4 also shows the composition of government expenditures in the general accounts by functional classification. Both national defense and economic development expenditures fell from 35.6 percent and 21.6 percent in 1980 to 28.5 percent and 14.9 percent in 1989, respectively. The decrease in economic development expenditure caused the insufficiency problem of social overhead capital in the late 1980s, as shown in Figure 9.3.

A consistent fiscal policy stance for economic stability in the 1980s is presented in Table 9.5 and Figure 9.4. The deficits of the consolidated budget balances continued to decrease from 2,111 billion won in 1981 to 65 billion won in 1986, and the first surplus can be seen in 1987. That is, the ratio of the budget balance to the GDP began to change drastically from −4.4 percent in 1981 to 1.2 percent in 1988.

In sum, economic policy during the 1980s shifted toward achieving stability, efficiency and balance. The Korean economy could restructure the international competitiveness of its industries on the basis of efficiency and achieve price stability through tightened fiscal and monetary policy.

Therefore, the balanced budget principle was established in fiscal management

*Table 9.4* General government budget and expenditure in the 1980s

| | *1980* | *1981* | *1982* | *1983* | *1984* | *1985* | *1986* | *1987* | *1988* | *1989* |
|---|---|---|---|---|---|---|---|---|---|---|
| General government budget (% of GNP) | | | | | | | | | | |
| Total budget of general gov't | 28.6 | 28.7 | 27.6 | 26.4 | 25.3 | 25.4 | 24.9 | 22.9 | 22.2 | 23.7 |
| Central gov't budget | 23.5 | 23.5 | 22.1 | 20.4 | 19.1 | 19.2 | 18.5 | 17.4 | 17.1 | 18.2 |
| General accounts of central gov't | 17.6 | 17.4 | 17.6 | 16.5 | 15.8 | 15.9 | 14.8 | 14.4 | 13.7 | 14.6 |
| Local gov't budget | 5.1 | 5.2 | 5.5 | 6.0 | 6.2 | 6.2 | 6.4 | 5.5 | 5.1 | 5.5 |
| Consolidated budget balance | −3.5 | −4.6 | −4.4 | −1.6 | −1.4 | −1.0 | −0.1 | 0.2 | 1.3 | −0.0 |
| Composition of the general accounts (% of total general account) | | | | | | | | | | |
| Economic dev't expenditure | 21.6 | 18.9 | 17.5 | 17.2 | 18.8 | 20.2 | 19.0 | 19.4 | 14.6 | 14.9 |
| Social dev't expenditure | 24.1 | 27.0 | 27.6 | 26.9 | 26.9 | 28.0 | 28.0 | 26.8 | 28.9 | 29.3 |
| Nat'l defense expenditure | 35.6 | 33.8 | 34.6 | 33.0 | 31.7 | 30.7 | 31.4 | 30.4 | 30.7 | 28.5 |
| Other expenditures incl. general administrative expenditures | 18.7 | 20.3 | 20.3 | 22.9 | 22.6 | 21.1 | 21.6 | 23.4 | 25.8 | 27.3 |

Source: Ministry of Planning and Budget (2003: budget of general government database, budget revenues database, budget expenditures database).

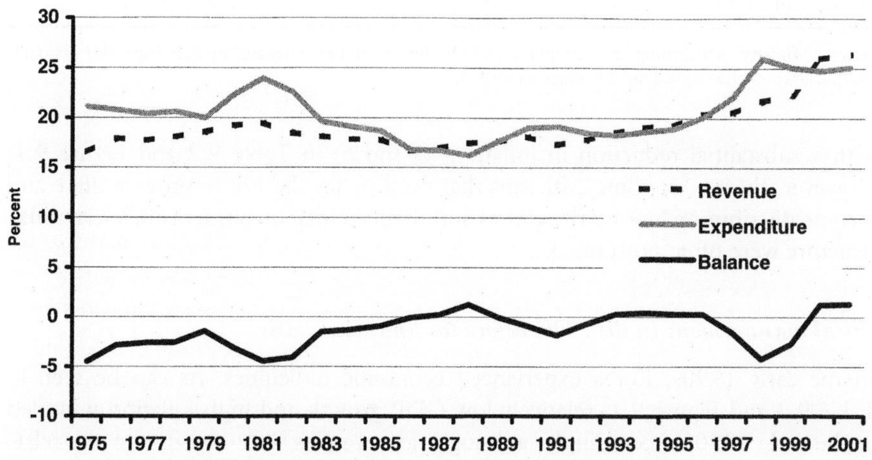


*Figure 9.4* Consolidated budget balance (as a % of nominal GDP).

Source: Ministry of Planning and Budget (2003).

*Table 9.5* Annual consolidated budget balance, 1975–2001

| | *Revenue* | | *Expenditure* | | *Balance* | |
|---|---|---|---|---|---|---|
| | *Billion won* | *Growth from prior year (%)* | *Billion won* | *Growth from prior year (%)* | *Billion won* | *As a % of GDP* |
| 1975 | 1,692.5 | — | 2,158.6 | — | −466.1 | −4.5 |
| 1976 | 2,511.4 | 48.4 | 2,909.7 | 34.8 | −398.3 | −2.8 |
| 1977 | 3,184.9 | 26.8 | 3,660.5 | 25.8 | −475.6 | −2.6 |
| 1978 | 4,385.2 | 37.7 | 5,001.1 | 36.6 | −615.8 | −2.5 |
| 1979 | 5,769.8 | 31.6 | 6,210.1 | 24.2 | −440.3 | −1.4 |
| 1980 | 7,280.8 | 26.2 | 8,454.5 | 36.1 | −1,173.7 | −3.1 |
| 1981 | 9,246.7 | 27.0 | 11,357.6 | 34.3 | −2,110.9 | −4.4 |
| 1982 | 10,074.3 | 9.0 | 12,296.4 | 8.3 | −2,222.1 | −4.1 |
| 1983 | 11,595.5 | 15.1 | 12,546.1 | 2.0 | −950.6 | −1.5 |
| 1984 | 13,039.6 | 12.5 | 13,962.5 | 11.3 | −922.9 | −1.3 |
| 1985 | 14,504.8 | 11.2 | 15,218.1 | 9.0 | −713.3 | −0.9 |
| 1986 | 15,855.6 | 9.3 | 15,920.5 | 4.6 | −64.9 | −0.1 |
| 1987 | 18,881.7 | 19.1 | 18,622.0 | 17.0 | 259.7 | 0.2 |
| 1988 | 23,100.9 | 22.3 | 21,458.2 | 15.2 | 1,642.7 | 1.2 |
| 1989 | 26,187.4 | 13.4 | 26,206.5 | 22.1 | −19.1 | −0.0 |
| 1990 | 32,457.2 | 23.9 | 34,035.4 | 29.9 | −1,578.2 | −0.9 |
| 1991 | 37,486.0 | 15.5 | 41,508.0 | 22.0 | −4,022.0 | −1.9 |
| 1992 | 43,766.7 | 16.8 | 45,469.6 | 9.5 | −1,702.9 | −0.7 |
| 1993 | 51,547.8 | 17.8 | 50,734.9 | 11.6 | 812.9 | 0.3 |
| 1994 | 61,741.0 | 19.8 | 60,356.7 | 19.0 | 1,384.3 | 0.4 |
| 1995 | 72,820.3 | 17.9 | 71,578.7 | 18.6 | 1,241.6 | 0.3 |
| 1996 | 85,528.3 | 17.5 | 84,429.3 | 18.0 | 1,099.0 | 0.3 |
| 1997 | 93,367.8 | 9.2 | 100,327.1 | 18.8 | −6,959.3 | −1.5 |
| 1998 | 96,672.9 | 3.5 | 115,403.2 | 15.0 | −18,757.3 | −4.2 |
| 1999 | 107,923.0 | 11.6 | 120,988.0 | 4.8 | −13,065.0 | −2.7 |
| 2000 | 135,811.0 | 25.8 | 129,284.0 | 6.9 | 6,527.0 | 1.3 |
| 2001 | 144,033.0 | 6.1 | 136,765.0 | 5.9 | 7,268.0 | 1.3 |

Source: Ministry of Planning and Budget (2003: budget revenues database, budget expenditures database, balance of the consolidated budget database).

with a substantial reduction in inflation, as shown in Table 9.2 and Figure 9.1. However, there were some criticisms that fiscal policy did not improve welfare and income distribution among the classes and that essential investments in social infrastructure were often postponed.

### *Fiscal management in the 1990s before the financial crisis*

In the early 1990s, Korea experienced economic difficulties. As can be seen in Table 9.2 and Figure 9.1, relatively low GDP growth and high inflation prevailed in the early 1990s. Accordingly, although tax revenues were low due to the relatively slow growth, public expenditure was needed to promote economic growth and to satisfy public demands on the country's welfare program.

As presented in Table 9.6 and Figure 9.2, the size of total public expenditure

*Table 9.6* General government budget and expenditure before the financial crisis

| | *1990* | *1991* | *1992* | *1993* | *1994* | *1995* | *1996* |
|---|---|---|---|---|---|---|---|
| General government budget (% of GDP) | | | | | | | |
| Total budget of general gov't | 25.0 | 25.8 | 26.4 | 26.6 | 28.0 | 26.6 | 28.0 |
| Central gov't budget | 18.2 | 18.2 | 17.8 | 18.4 | 19.3 | 19.3 | 20.0 |
| General accounts of central gov't | 15.4 | 14.4 | 13.6 | 13.4 | 13.2 | 13.6 | 14.0 |
| Local gov't budget | 6.8 | 7.6 | 8.6 | 8.2 | 8.7 | 7.3 | 7.9 |
| Consolidated budget balance | −0.9 | −1.9 | −0.7 | 0.3 | 0.4 | 0.3 | 0.3 |
| Composition of the general accounts (% of total general account) | | | | | | | |
| Economic dev't expenditure | 14.1 | 16.4 | 18.6 | 20.7 | 23.1 | 22.3 | 22.4 |
| Social dev't expenditure | 8.9 | 10.2 | 9.7 | 9.2 | 9.0 | 8.1 | 8.6 |
| Nat'l defense expenditure | 25.0 | 25.4 | 25.9 | 24.6 | 23.7 | 22.1 | 22.1 |
| Education expenditure | 20.4 | 17.7 | 19.4 | 19.8 | 19.3 | 18.9 | 18.9 |

Sources: Bank of Korea (2003: national account database); Ministry of Planning and Budget (2003: budget of general government database).

amounted to 25 percent of GDP in 1990 and 28 percent in 1996 in order to invest in social overhead capital and to improve social welfare. Moreover, the size of local government's public expenditure relative to GDP increased rapidly and continuously, rising from 6.8 percent in 1990 to 8.7 percent in 1994.

In terms of the components of expenditure in the general accounts (shown in Table 9.6 and Figure 9.3), national defense expenditures declined from 25 percent of the total general account in 1990 to 22.1 percent in 1996, while economic development expenditures increased sharply from 14.1 percent in 1990 to 22.4 percent in 1996. Interestingly, although the Korean government spent a lot of public money, the stable and sustained economic growth has been maintained along with a balanced budget.

As can be seen in Table 9.5 and Table 9.6 and Figure 9.4, after the fiscal deficit ratio reached its peak in 1991 (−1.9 percent), this turned to a fiscal surplus in 1993, and thereafter the fiscal surplus was sustained until right before the financial crisis. Thus, fiscal management before 1997 kept the balanced budget rule that public expenditure should be limited by the amount of tax revenue.

### *Fiscal management and the economic crisis*

Korea slipped into financial crisis in late 1997 (Table 9.2 and Table 9.7, Figure 9.1). Growth of real GDP fell −6.7 percent in 1998 and the unemployment rate almost tripled, rising from 2.6 percent in 1997 to 6.8 percent in 1998. In response to this, the Korean government launched a series of comprehensive economic reform measures to restructure the corporate and financial sectors, which are the fundamental structural weaknesses in the Korean economy, and to assist the poor and the unemployed. On the expenditure side, financial reform and social security net programs required a tremendous amount of fiscal expenditure.

*Table 9.7* General government budget and expenditure and main indicators, 1996–2001

| | *1996* | *1997* | *1998* | *1999* | *2000* | *2001* |
|---|---|---|---|---|---|---|
| General government budget (% of GDP) | | | | | | |
| Total budget of general gov't | 28.0 | 28.8 | 32.2 | 32.6 | 33.5 | 33.7 |
| Central gov't budget | 20.0 | 20.4 | 23.7 | 24.8 | 24.6 | 24.9 |
| General accounts of central gov't | 14.0 | 14.1 | 16.5 | 16.7 | 17.0 | 18.2 |
| Local gov't budget | 7.9 | 8.4 | 8.5 | 7.3 | 8.9 | 8.8 |
| Consolidated budget balance | 0.3 | −1.5 | −4.2 | −2.7 | 1.3 | 1.3 |
| Composition of the general accounts (% of total general account) | | | | | | |
| Economic dev't expenditure | 22.4 | 25.4 | 30.3 | 29.2 | 26.1 | 24.9 |
| Social dev't expenditure | 8.6 | 9.2 | 9.8 | 11.4 | 11.9 | 13.6 |
| Nat'l defense expenditure | 22.1 | 21.3 | 19.3 | 17.3 | 17.0 | 16.2 |
| Education expenditure | 18.9 | 18.9 | 16.6 | 14.2 | 14.3 | 17.9 |
| Main indicators | | | | | | |
| Real growth (%) | 6.8 | 5.0 | −6.7 | 10.9 | 9.3 | 3.0 |
| Unemployment rate (%) | 2.0 | 2.6 | 6.8 | 6.3 | 4.1 | 3.7 |
| Government debt (A) (trillion won) | 49.8 | 65.6 | 87.7 | 107.7 | 123.1 | 134.4 |
| Central government (trillion won) | 36.8 | 50.5 | 71.4 | 89.7 | 100.9 | 113.1 |
| Local government (trillion won) | 12.3 | 15.1 | 16.2 | 18.0 | 22.3 | 21.3 |
| Gov't guarantees (B) (trillion won) | 7.6 | 13.0 | 72.0 | 81.5 | 74.6 | 106.8 |
| Total A + B (trillion won) | 57.4 | 78.6 | 159.7 | 189.2 | 197.7 | 241.2 |
| Government debt (A) (% of GDP) | 11.9 | 14.5 | 19.7 | 22.3 | 23.6 | 24.2 |
| Central government (% of GDP) | 8.8 | 11.1 | 16.1 | 18.6 | 19.3 | 20.3 |
| Local government (% of GDP) | 3.1 | 3.4 | 3.6 | 3.7 | 4.3 | 3.9 |
| Gov't guarantees (B) (% of GDP) | 1.8 | 2.9 | 16.2 | 16.9 | 14.3 | 19.6 |
| Total A + B (% of GDP) | 13.7 | 17.4 | 35.9 | 39.2 | 37.9 | 43.8 |

Sources: Bank of Korea (2003: national account database); Ministry of Finance and Economy (2003); Ministry of Planning and Budget (2003: budget of general government database).

On the consolidated accounts,[1] the budget deficit recorded 18.8 trillion won in 1998 (Table 9.5).

One of the most urgent measures was liquidation of bad loans held by domestic financial institutions. The fiscal assistance to domestic financial institutions took the form of interest payments on bonds issued by two public corporations: the Korea Asset Management Corporation (KAMCO) and the Korea Deposit Insurance Corporation (KDIC). Another critical issue was the support for the unemployed in the form of unemployment insurance payments and other social safety net expenditures. Thus, public assistance to the poor and unemployed almost doubled after the crisis.

As can be seen in Table 9.2, Table 9.7 and Figure 9.1, a rapid economic recovery along with the government's measures was achieved in 1999, as the growth rate of real GDP rose to almost 11 percent, and this high growth was sustained in 2000. However, these measures also caused a rapid increase in government expenditures. As shown in Table 9.5, Table 9.7 and Figure 9.4, the easing of fiscal policy to restructure the unsound corporate and financial sectors and to assist the unemployed and small and medium-sized enterprises resulted in an increase in the consolidated central government deficits to −4.2 percent of GDP in 1998.

Fortunately, a strong economic recovery in 1999 resulted in the government deficit declining to 2.7 percent and the consolidated budget turned to surplus. Since Korea had adhered to balanced budget principles, the government was able to plan for massive fiscal support to the unsound financial and corporate sectors and to the unemployed through social welfare programs, as the unemployment rate fell from 6.8 percent in 1998 to 3.7 percent in 2001. The result was rapid economic recovery with tremendous government debt (this will be discussed in greater detail later in the chapter).

## The budget process and management of financial resources

In order to overcome the limitation of annual budgeting in improving efficiency and flexibility, Korea adopted pluri-annual budgeting in 1998. The government developed the Medium-Term Fiscal Plan, which lays out indicative targets for fiscal investment, sources of revenue, budget balance, etc. This plan is revised annually and is adjusted to accommodate the rapidly changing environment. In managing the plan, the government assesses competing requests for funds among agencies and projects by evaluating the effectiveness of long-term programs, policies and procedures.

A number of channels exist to incorporate a wide range of public opinion into the budget process, including special interest groups, experts from relevant fields and local communities. These channels of communication include: a system in which interest groups can assess the performance of their concerned ministry, public debates on budgetary policy for major spending areas, and budgetary conferences of mayors and province governors. Other sources of feedback to enhance budgetary efficiency include the National Assembly's account statements and reports by the Board of Audit and Inspection.

To make better use of taxpayers' money, an incentive system for budget saving was introduced in 1998. Early in 1999, nine organizations were rewarded with 4.2 billion won out of the 32.3 billion won they had saved through new budget-saving initiatives. On the other hand, the number of off-budget funds was reduced from 75 to 55.

The Ministry of Planning and Budget continually monitors the progress of major projects by government ministries and agencies. This is done through periodic on-site inspections, reviews of documents and computerized reviews of project accounts. The evaluation results are reflected in subsequent annual budgets.

## Taxation in Korea

Taxes in Korea are comprised of both national and local taxes. Currently, national taxes can be divided into internal taxes, custom duties, a transportation tax, an education tax and a special tax for rural development (Table 9.8).

*Table 9.8* Annual government tax revenue, 1970–2002 (as a % of total tax revenue)

| | *Total tax revenue (billion won)* | *Internal tax* | *Transportation tax* | *Custom duty* | *Defense duty* | *Education tax* | *Special tax for rural dev't* | *Monopoly profits* | *Local tax* |
|---|---|---|---|---|---|---|---|---|---|
| 1970 | 398 | 71.3 | | 12.8 | | | | 7.6 | 8.3 |
| 1971 | 493 | 72.1 | | 10.6 | | | | 9.2 | 8.1 |
| 1972 | 523 | 71.6 | | 11.3 | | | | 8.2 | 8.9 |
| 1973 | 653 | 67.3 | | 12.6 | | | | 8.7 | 11.4 |
| 1974 | 1,022 | 70.3 | | 12.4 | | | | 6.8 | 10.6 |
| 1975 | 1,550 | 65.3 | | 11.7 | 4.0 | | | 8.7 | 10.2 |
| 1976 | 2,313 | 59.2 | | 11.9 | 11.6 | | | 7.7 | 9.5 |
| 1977 | 2,959 | 56.6 | | 13.0 | 11.5 | | | 7.4 | 11.4 |
| 1978 | 4,096 | 55.0 | | 15.8 | 11.6 | | | 6.8 | 10.8 |
| 1979 | 5,361 | 56.7 | | 13.7 | 11.8 | | | 6.7 | 11.2 |
| 1980 | 6,575 | 55.9 | | 11.7 | 13.0 | | | 7.8 | 11.7 |
| 1981 | 8,172 | 56.2 | | 10.9 | 13.4 | | | 8.3 | 11.2 |
| 1982 | 9,516 | 55.2 | | 10.6 | 12.4 | 2.1 | | 8.0 | 11.8 |
| 1983 | 11,448 | 54.1 | | 12.8 | 11.4 | 2.3 | | 7.3 | 12.2 |
| 1984 | 12,408 | 53.2 | | 12.8 | 11.9 | 2.3 | | 6.8 | 12.2 |
| 1985 | 13,531 | 55.4 | | 11.6 | 12.3 | 2.4 | | 6.1 | 12.2 |
| 1986 | 15,416 | 54.9 | | 12.6 | 12.0 | 2.4 | | 6.4 | 11.7 |
| 1987 | 18,536 | 54.0 | | 14.5 | 12.5 | 2.2 | | 4.9 | 11.8 |
| 1988 | 22,583 | 55.5 | | 11.4 | 12.9 | 2.3 | | 4.2 | 13.7 |
| 1989 | 26,195 | 58.1 | | 8.1 | 13.3 | 1.6 | | 0.0 | 18.9 |
| 1990 | 33,215 | 57.6 | | 8.3 | 13.3 | 1.6 | | | 19.2 |
| 1991 | 38,355 | 62.8 | | 9.0 | 3.3 | 4.0 | | | 20.9 |
| 1992 | 44,681 | 67.3 | | 7.1 | 0.4 | 4.1 | | | 21.2 |
| 1993 | 50,287 | 68.0 | | 5.7 | 0.2 | 4.1 | | | 21.9 |
| 1994 | 60,493 | 63.6 | 4.1 | 5.7 | 0.1 | 4.2 | 0.5 | | 21.9 |
| 1995 | 72,091 | 61.6 | 4.7 | 6.4 | 0.1 | 4.2 | 1.8 | | 21.2 |
| 1996 | 82,355 | 59.7 | 5.9 | 6.4 | 0.0 | 5.0 | 1.8 | | 21.1 |
| 1997 | 88,333 | 59.0 | 6.3 | 6.6 | 0.0 | 6.1 | 1.2 | | 20.8 |
| 1998 | 84,947 | 60.3 | 7.7 | 4.5 | 0.0 | 6.1 | 1.2 | | 20.2 |
| 1999 | 94,244 | 59.8 | 7.7 | 5.0 | 0.0 | 5.6 | 2.1 | | 19.7 |
| 2000 | 98,177 | 59.2 | 9.6 | 4.9 | | 6.0 | 1.5 | | 18.8 |
| 2001 | 119,350 | 60.4 | 9.2 | 5.6 | | 3.0 | 2.0 | | 19.6 |
| 2002 | 129,810 | 62.3 | 7.8 | 5.6 | | 2.8 | 1.4 | | 20.2 |

Source: Ministry of Planning and Budget (2003).

A modern tax system was introduced in Korea in 1948. The government reorganized the tax structure of the Japanese colonial and the US military administration era and introduced several new taxes. After the Korean War period in which the Korean government had to adopt a wartime tax system, the government implemented major tax reforms in 1962 and 1967 with a focus on providing financial support for economic development. These tax reforms established important features of the current Korean tax system.

The Defense Tax law, one of the important changes in the tax system in the 1970s, was enacted to secure adequate funding for national defense in response to the communization of Vietnam in 1975. The defense tax was a temporary national tax for five years until 1980. However, as can be seen in Table 9.8, the tax remained in place until 1999.

The government introduced the value added tax and a special excise tax in 1976. This tax reform was mainly aimed at providing fiscal support for the economic development plan and the building of a modern tax system. However, the value added tax was criticized because it increased the tax burden (as shown in Table 9.2 and Figure 9.5).

In 1980, Korea experienced a sharp decline in economic growth, and the most urgent task for the economy was to recover from the recession. Fortunately, the Korean government maintained a stable tax system due to relatively low inflation after 1981.

One of the major changes in the tax system during the 1980s was the introduction of the education tax (1982) to provide financial support for improvement of the public education system. As can be seen in Table 9.8, the education tax was a temporary national tax for five years until 1986, but it was extended to 1991. After the revision of the education tax law, the education tax became a permanent national tax in 1991.

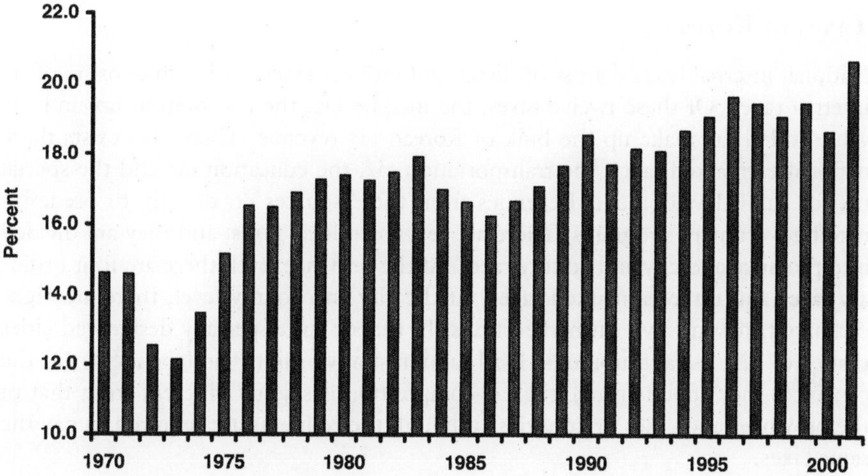


*Figure 9.5* Tax burden (as a % of GDP).

Source: Ministry of Planning and Budget (2003).

At the end of 1988, the prospects for the Korean economy seemed to be less promising than before. The major objectives of the tax reforms from 1989 to 1992 were to mitigate the tax burden of low-income earners, to improve tax burden equality across the income classes, and to provide financial support for local governments. As shown in Table 9.8, monopoly profits were transferred to a local tax.

The Korean government implemented the real-name financial transaction system in 1993. The aim of this system was to strengthen economic justice by enforcing the conduct of financial transactions under real names. Thus, the 1994 tax reform lowered the tax rate to assist the early establishment of the real-name system. And, as shown in Table 9.8, the transportation tax for social overhead capital investments was introduced in 1993.

The 1997 financial crisis forced the government to initiate a series of comprehensive economic reform measures and to assist the unemployed in the form of a social safety net. Due to the sharp decline in consumption and investment in 1998, the government revised several tax laws to promote tax incentives to firms and to stimulate private consumption.

As shown in Table 9.8, although the local tax has increased from 8.3 percent of total tax receipts in 1970 to 20.2 percent in 2002, local taxes are less than 70 percent of local government expenditures except in major cities. It is therefore necessary to transfer some of the national taxes to local taxes to support local government expenditures.

Meanwhile, tax burdens in Korea have risen to more than 20 percent of nominal GDP in 2001, which is similar to other developed countries (Table 9.2, Figure 9.5). However, Korea has numerous quasi-taxes including the national pension, bribes, rebates and monetary gifts to celebrations or funerals, etc. Thus, it is necessary to increase the transparency of the Korean economy and to change old and wasteful customs.

## Taxes in Korea

National internal taxes consist of direct and indirect taxes, and each consists of six internal taxes. Of these twelve taxes, the income tax, the corporation tax and the value added tax make up the bulk of Korean tax revenue. There also exists three national earmarked taxes: the transportation tax, the education tax and the special tax for rural development. Revenues from these sources go directly to predesignated government programs. There are seventeen local taxes, and they are divided into province and city and county taxes. At the province level, there are four ordinary taxes and three earmarked taxes. At the city and county level, there are eight ordinary taxes and two earmarked taxes. In the six large specially designated cities that are run as autonomous local administrative units (independent of the provinces they appertain to), the tax composition is slightly different from that of the provinces and cities or counties, although the residents are required to pay the same taxes.

A person is either a resident or a nonresident of Korea depending on residence or domicile. A resident is liable to income tax on items of income derived from sources both within and outside Korea. On the other hand, a nonresident is liable to income tax only on items of income derived from sources within Korea. Under the income tax law, income earned by both residents and nonresidents is subject to global and schedular taxation. Under global taxation, real estate rental income, business income, earned income, temporary property income and miscellaneous income attributed to a resident are aggregated and taxed progressively.

Interest and dividends are subject to tax withholding. Nonresidents are similarly taxed on income from Korean sources. The tax rates on individual income range from 10 to 40 percent. When a company is incorporated in Korea, it is deemed a domestic corporation and is liable to tax from worldwide income whereas a foreign corporation is liable to tax on Korean source income. The corporate income tax rates are 16 percent and 28 percent. A foreign corporation without a permanent establishment in Korea is subject to withholding tax.

### *Laws and regulations*

A presidential decree may be set in order to enforce tax laws. The Minister of Finance and Economy also enacts ministerial decrees to enforce the presidential decree, to make rulings and authoritative interpretations of the laws, and to enforce the decrees. In addition to the presidential and ministerial decrees, the Commissioner of the National Tax Service may issue administrative orders and rules to ensure the consistent application of the laws. The courts of justice have the final authority in interpreting the tax laws, and the rulings and interpretations by tax authorities are not binding. The constitution also provides for the principle of local autonomy. Under this principle, local governments are given the right to assess and collect local taxes. The Local Tax Law, the Presidential Enforcement Decree on Local Tax Law and the Ministerial Enforcement Decree on Local Tax Law are enacted under the constitution.

## Fiscal policy issues

### *The budget system*

The budget of the central government is controlled by the National Assembly and is comprised of one general account and various special accounts. On a consolidated basis, the central government budget includes, in addition to the general accounts and twenty-two special accounts, fifty-five funds in the fiscal year 2002 budget. Several problems related to the budget system are found.

The first serious problem is that the local government is not included in the Korean consolidated budget structure. Moreover, there are too many special accounts and funds (public funds and other funds). Special accounts and public funds are established when needed to achieve specific policy objectives and are abolished when no longer required. The difference between public funds and special accounts is that public funds do not require authorization from the National Assembly for their budget plans. Furthermore, since other funds are managed by the ministries, their operational plans do not even require authorization from the cabinet. But there is no clear-cut rule for classification between public and other funds. The biggest problem is the exclusion of other funds from the central government.

The Korean budget system can be characterized as a complex budget system. Thus, since this Korean budget system could impede the efficient and transparent management of public money, the number of special accounts and public and other funds should be reduced. It is also necessary to introduce evaluation processes before, during or after a project, since those evaluation studies should be overseen and sponsored by the budget authority rather than by ministries related to the projects; moreover, the project evaluations will enhance transparency of the budget.

### *The government deficits and debts*

The Korean government experienced persistent budget deficits and government debt during the 1970s. Fiscal policy in the 1970s that promoted heavy and chemical industries for rapid economic growth caused the consolidated budget deficit to rise to 3.1 percent of GDP in 1980 and the consolidated central government debt to reach 19.7 percent.

But the Korean government tried to reduce the government deficit and debt continuously in the 1980s (Table 9.5, Figure 9.4, Figure 9.6). As a result, the consolidated budget surplus was around 0.3 percent of nominal GDP over the period 1993–96 and the ratio of central government debt to nominal GDP was continuously decreased to 8.8 percent in 1996 (as shown in Table 9.7 and Figure 9.6). Moreover, although government debt guarantees were around 8 percent of GDP in the mid-1980s, it continuously declined to 1.8 percent in 1996 in response to the balanced budget. Thus, total government debt, including government debt guarantees, was only 13.7 percent of nominal GDP in 1996.

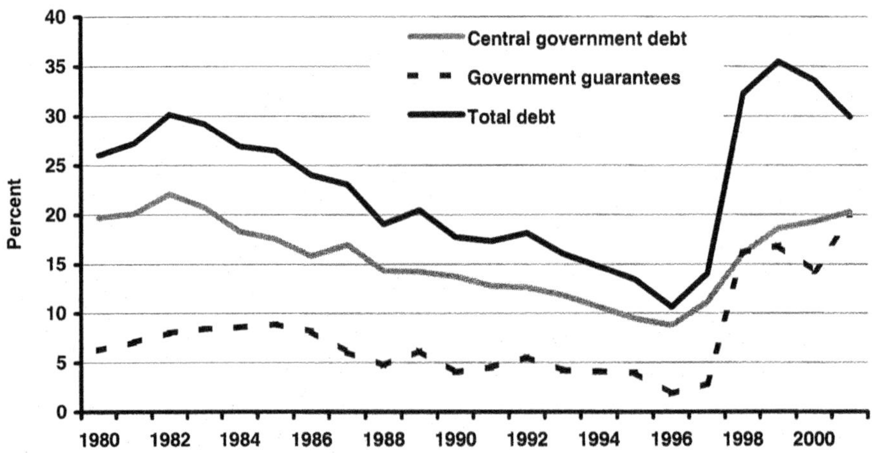


*Figure 9.6* Government debt (as a % of nominal GDP).

Source: Ministry of Planning and Budget (2003).

However, the tremendous fiscal expenditure to restructure the unsound corporate and financial sectors and to assist the unemployed and small and medium-sized enterprises caused the ratio of the consolidated budget deficit to GDP to increase to 4.2 percent in 1998 (Table 9.5, Table 9.7, Figure 9.4 and Figure 9.6). Moreover, the ratio of government debt to GDP increased from 11.9 percent in 1996 to 24.2 percent in 2001, and the central government debt to GDP ratio doubled from 8.8 percent in 1996 to 20.3 percent in 2001. Furthermore, government debt guarantees sharply increased from 1.8 percent of GDP in 1996 to 19.6 percent in 2001. Although government debt guarantees are excluded from the consolidated budget, in accordance with the 1986 IMF manual, if government debt guarantees are included, the total public burden was 43.8 percent of GDP at the end of 2001.

Korea has faced many difficulties such as: (i) the uncertain costs of economic cooperation with North Korea; (ii) the spending pressure for the social safety net including the public pension system and the Protection of Minimum Living Standards Act; and (iii) the financial support to stimulate the recent business downturn and to further resources for restructuring the unsound financial institutions.

While the sums committed to financial restructuring are extremely large, the final cost can be reduced substantially by sales of impaired assets on secondary markets. Thus, it is important that KAMCO press ahead with its program of asset sales, in which it hopes to recoup by 2003 most of the funds it has spent in acquiring bad loans. In addition, successful restructuring of the banks with large government ownership would reduce the final cost of the financial rehabilitation program by allowing the sale of government equity positions to private investors.

A second area where there is rising demand for increased expenditure is the social safety net, which is an essential part of a well-functioning market economy. Outlays in this area are likely to rise following the introduction in 2001 of the National Basic Livelihood Protection Law, which is based on the concept of "productive welfare" and makes social assistance a right for low-income citizens. The level of total assistance is to be set so as to ensure that the recipient's total income meets the minimum cost of living as calculated by the government. Therefore, the new role of fiscal policy in Korea should be to achieve a balanced budget, to limit public debt, to improve the efficiency of public money and to remove existing distortions in the tax system.

### *Public pension*

The public pension program is another area of rising outlays. With the maturation of the system, established in 1988, and the aging of the population, the number of beneficiaries is projected to increase by a factor of 12 over the next decade. Certain measures, such as lowering the replacement rate and raising of the retirement age, have recently been adopted to contain spending. Nevertheless, the contribution rate would have to double from the current 9 percent of wages to 18 percent in order to maintain the actuarial balance under the current program, and this would likely have adverse effects on Korea's growth potential.

Given the relatively young population and the still immature public pension program, Korea has a window of opportunity to adopt systemic reforms that would promote the long-run viability of the public pension system. One option that could be considered would be to transform the separation allowances that firms are required to provide for departing employees into an occupational pension system based on defined contributions that are managed by private institutions.

### *Tax reform for additional revenue*

In sum, the prospects for increased outlays on financial restructuring and the social safety net, as well as the uncertain cost of economic cooperation with North Korea, will necessitate higher tax revenues over the medium term. While a rationalization of spending in many areas would be welcome, it is unlikely to be sufficient.

A number of weaknesses, nevertheless, continue to undermine tax bases, efficiency and the fairness of the system. These include generous allowances and loopholes for individuals, large-scale and wide-ranging tax preferences for enterprises, and an inappropriate taxation of property. Moreover, there is a lack of strong and uniform tax enforcement, especially toward the self-employed.

It is also important to minimize existing tax-related distortions in order to avoid magnifying their negative effects. Korea has, in fact, made some progress over the past decades in reducing such distortions, in particular by broadening some tax bases and lowering tax rates along the lines followed in many other developed countries. It is imperative to continue this movement toward even more neutrality in the personal income tax system and to avoid excessive use of taxes as instruments of industrial policy. The priority should be to further broaden tax bases for the personal and corporate income tax systems, as well as the VAT system. Allowances and exemptions in the personal tax system should be reduced or at least consolidated into a simpler structure, perhaps initially by limiting indexation.

Any reduction in personal tax relief should be accompanied by stricter tax enforcement of the self-employed in order to avoid exacerbating the prevailing sense of unfairness among wage and salary earners. Enforcement could be improved through improved targeting of audits and more systematic sharing of information from other government bodies as well as from financial institutions. The number of audits and the penalties for tax evasion should also be increased. Regarding the corporate tax system, tax incentives should be substantially reduced, including those given to small and medium-sized enterprises, research and development, and overall investment. Finally, the VAT base should be expanded by eliminating the special tax regime, leaving only a minimum VAT-exempt threshold for very small retailers.

Equity could also be enhanced in several other areas. First, personal capital income should be taxed more evenly across sources, though not necessarily included in the progressive global income schedule. Second, a tax on fringe benefits should be introduced, perhaps at the company level to facilitate implementation. Third, public pension contribution rates should be equalized across sources of income and such payments should be excluded from taxable income. In addition, retirement income from all sources—public pensions, company separation allowances and private pension accounts—should be taxed as ordinary global income. Such a reform would improve equity across generations as well.

Efficiency of resource allocation should also be promoted through tax reform. In the area of property taxation, the tax mix should be changed so as to encourage development and more efficient use of land. This would require higher holding taxes, through valuation closer to market levels, and lower transaction taxes. The capital gains tax structure should be independent of the holding period in order to reduce lock-in effects. Ongoing restructuring in the corporate sector should be encouraged by introducing a consolidated tax treatment of holding companies and by making permanent the tax deferral offered in 1998 in the case of assets and equity swaps, mergers, acquisitions and divisions, subject to appropriate tests for continuation of business and ownership. Simplicity should be increased by streamlining the special consumption tax into a few excise taxes and by eliminating the various earmarked taxes and quasi-taxes.

## Note

1 The consolidated government accounts in Korea include the central government and non-financial public enterprises, excluding local governments.

## References

Bank of Korea (2003) Statistics database, available on: www.bok.or.kr.

Jun, Joosung (2002) "Fiscal policy during and after the crisis," paper presented at The Korean Economy: Beyond the Crisis Seminar, Research Center for International Finance, Seoul National University, Seoul, October 4.

Jun, Joosung and Hwang, Jinwoo (1998) "The fiscal costs of financial sector restructuring in Korea," paper presented to the Fiscal Affairs Department, International Monetary Fund, Washington DC, September 3.

Jun, Joosung, Hwang, Jinwoo and Koh, Youngsun (2000) "Financial section restructuring and fiscal adjustment," *Journal of Korean Economic Analysis* 6(1): 173–200.

Ministry of Finance and Economy (2003) Statistics database, available on: http://www.mofe.go.kr.

Ministry of Planning and Budget (2003) Statistics database, available on: http://www.mpb.go.kr.

National Statistics Office (2003) Statistical database, available on: http://www.nso.go.kr.

Park, Jongkyu (2002) *Reflections on Fiscal Policy Reactions to the Korean Economic Crisis*, Korea Institute of Finance Working Paper 2002-01, Seoul: Korea Institute of Finance.

Planning and Budget Commission (1999) *Summary of the Mid-Term Fiscal Plan 1999–2002*, Seoul: Planning and Budget Commission.

# 10 Malaysia

*Suresh Narayanan*

## Introduction

Malaysian fiscal policy did not go beyond the traditional role of generating revenues and providing expenditures to support basic infrastructure and maintaining law and order until the late 1960s (MIER 1987: 3). Post-independence growth had come largely from the private sector which was dominated by Chinese Malaysians and foreign interests, leaving out the politically dominant Malays from the economic mainstream. This triggered a violent backlash involving the Malays and Chinese in May 1969. The New Economic Policy (NEP) was announced in 1970 to address this imbalance. The NEP was a twenty-year plan meant to "eradicate poverty regardless of race" and "restructure the economy so that race was no longer identifiable with economic function" (Malaysia 1971). To achieve both functions, the government enlarged its role in the economy and in so doing, the form and function of fiscal policy changed dramatically.

## Malaysian fiscal policy

Malaysia has a federal system of government that is presided over by a strong central government. The fiscal structure is also highly centralized, with the federal government holding powers to levy and collect major taxes and other forms of revenue. Thus, state contributions to public sector revenue and expenditures were quite small and did not exceed 20 percent of public revenue and expenditures, respectively, during the period under review.

Malaysia's fiscal policy experience is conveniently analyzed by examining three periods: the NEP period (1970–90), the post-NEP period (1991–96) and the Asian financial crisis period (1997 and after). For the most part, fiscal policy was used primarily as a tool to serve the objectives of the NEP.

### *The NEP period, 1970–90*

In the initial period of the NEP (1970–79), the aim of poverty eradication was emphasized with most expenditure being channeled for rural and agricultural development. There was also a rapid expansion in basic health and education infrastructure. Concrete government attempts at restructuring the society took shape only in the ambitious Third and Fourth Malaysia Plans, implemented during 1976–80 and 1981–85, respectively.

Efforts to achieve the restructuring objective saw massive increases in public sector spending that enlarged the size of the public sector and opportunities within it, and this created well-endowed off-budget agencies (OBAs) that were charged with helping the Bumiputera (defined as Malays and other indigenous people) find a niche in urban, business activities. New opportunities were channeled to the Bumiputera through a system of quotas that favored them. Anticipating apathy from the existing indigenous Chinese business community toward creating a Bumiputera business class, the government also fostered an alliance with foreign capital. Liberal tax incentives were offered to foreign investors in return for reserved employment and equity shares.

Expansionary fiscal policy became a central tool in realizing the objectives of the NEP on two grounds. First, the expansionary fiscal policy was necessary to support the greater role that the government had assigned itself in reshaping the economy. Second, since a growing economy was seen as a critical prerequisite for the realization of the NEP, the government declared itself ready to adopt anti-cyclical measures if external fluctuations threatened the growth process.

This resolve was demonstrated during the brief economic downturn of 1974–75.[1] The slackening in real output growth in the industrial economies adversely affected external demand for Malaysia's primary commodity exports. This was compounded by the lack of domestic investment activity induced by fears surrounding the newly introduced Industrial Co-ordination Act (ICA) that threatened to dilute the ownership of Chinese-held enterprises that grew too large (Yong 1987: 165–6). Thus, real growth fell to 2.2 percent in 1975, well below the 7.1 percent average achieved in 1971–75 (Bank Negara Malaysia, various years a, 1976 issue: 21).

A concerted effort was made to counter the recessionary impact. Although revenues were stagnating, federal capital expenditure was increased by 8.5 percent in real terms in early 1975. Current expenditure was also raised by 11 percent in real terms (Bank Negara Malaysia, various years a, 1974 issue: 4). With the recovery of the export sector in 1976, GNP achieved 11.3 percent growth in real terms and fiscal policy appeared to have successfully countered the economic downturn.

Buoyed by this success, the same approach was used again in the face of another crisis, and initially, at least, it appeared to work. By the 1980s, although the OECD economies displayed signs of weakening, Malaysia was scarcely affected. An export boom and large public sector spending afforded some measure of protection. Between 1979 and 1981, federal government spending had risen from RM12.0 billion to RM24.8 billion (Table 10.1).

As the worldwide recession worsened, counter-cyclical spending was increased in earnest. The 1982 budget estimates saw a further 38 percent increase (to RM32 billion) in the allocation for government expenditure over the original allocation. The Finance Minister made it clear that public spending was being increased to stave off the recession evident elsewhere and to "ensure that Malaysia's economy will continue to expand . . . in order to achieve the socio-economic objectives of the New Economic Policy and the long-term perspective Plan" (Department of Information Services, 1982 Budget speech: 7).

*Table 10.1* Malaysian federal government revenue, expenditure and GNP, 1970–99 (RM million)

| *Year* | *Tax revenue* | *Total revenue* | *Nontax revenue/ total revenue* | *Expenditures* | *GNP*[a] |
|---|---|---|---|---|---|
| 1970 | 1,840 | 2,400 | 23.3 | 2,875 | 12,155 |
| 1971 | 1,917 | 2,418 | 20.7 | 3,468 | 12,501 |
| 1972 | 2,190 | 2,920 | 25.0 | 4,291 | 13,641 |
| 1973 | 2,807 | 3,399 | 17.4 | 4,448 | 17,443 |
| 1974 | 4,054 | 4,791 | 15.4 | 6,172 | 21,234 |
| 1975 | 4,256 | 5,117 | 16.8 | 6,618 | 21,684 |
| 1976 | 5,145 | 6,157 | 16.4 | 7,862 | 21,606 |
| 1977 | 6,661 | 7,760 | 14.2 | 10,236 | 31,074 |
| 1978 | 7,567 | 8,841 | 14.4 | 11,090 | 35,090 |
| 1979 | 8,997 | 10,505 | 14.4 | 12,040 | 44,354 |
| 1980 | 12,060 | 13,926 | 13.4 | 17,630 | 51,390 |
| 1981 | 12,594 | 15,806 | 20.3 | 24,821 | 55,602 |
| 1982 | 12,590 | 16,690 | 24.6 | 27,111 | 59,690 |
| 1983 | 15,263 | 18,608 | 18.0 | 25,541 | 65,530 |
| 1984 | 16,474 | 20,805 | 20.8 | 25,580 | 74,182 |
| 1985 | 16,700 | 21,115 | 20.9 | 25,522 | 72,039 |
| 1986 | 14,682 | 19,518 | 24.8 | 27,024 | 66,814 |
| 1987 | 12,474 | 18,143 | 31.2 | 24,296 | 74,679 |
| 1988 | 14,708 | 21,967 | 33.0 | 25,257 | 85,777 |
| 1989 | 16,674 | 25,273 | 34.0 | 28,683 | 96,631 |
| 1990 | 21,244 | 29,521 | 28.9 | 32,958 | 114,017 |
| 1991 | 25,830 | 34,053 | 24.1 | 36,693 | 128,324 |
| 1992 | 28,772 | 39,250 | 26.7 | 40,493 | 142,678 |
| 1993 | 31,900 | 41,691 | 23.5 | 41,337 | 163,928 |
| 1994 | 37,487 | 49,446 | 24.2 | 45,038 | 186,049 |
| 1995 | 41,670 | 50,952 | 18.2 | 49,093 | 212,095 |
| 1996 | 47,272 | 58,280 | 18.9 | 56,465 | 241,931 |
| 1997 | 53,627 | 65,736 | 18.4 | 59,110 | 266,699 |
| 1998 | 45,336 | 56,710 | 20.0 | 61,712 | 269,151 |
| 1999 | 45,346 | 58,675 | 22.7 | 68,162 | 279,461 |

Source: Bank Negara Malaysia (various years a, various years b).

Note

a Expressed in current prices. Data from 1980 onward are based on a new system of national accounts and may not be strictly comparable with data from previous periods.

However, this was not to be. Unlike the earlier attempt, the policy proved unsustainable and the fiscal initiative was soon in retreat. In early 1982, barely seven months after the announcement of the determined counter-cyclical spending, the government reversed its fiscal strategy. A 30 percent cutback of the 1982 budget expenditure allocation was announced, citing eroding revenues due to the impact of a recession that was refusing to abate. However, the actual cutback was only about 10 percent lower than the original allocation because it was feared that the NEP objectives would be compromised. By the end of 1982, total federal expenditure had peaked at 45 percent of GNP. Subsequent years saw restrained government expenditure, primarily in development spending. The effect of the sudden cutback in expenditure in the midst of a recession put the Keynesian idea of countercyclical spending on its head.

What motivated this reversal? The length and severity of the worldwide recession had remained unpredictable, forcing counter-cyclical spending to be sustained over a time horizon beyond what policy-makers were prepared for. Furthermore, since the private sector was largely crippled, the public sector had to shoulder the burden alone, but the public sector had already grown too large and the government could not marshal the additional resources required.

Public enterprises that spearheaded fiscal expansion had mushroomed rapidly growing from 109 to 656 between 1970 and 1980. The financial allocation for them grew in tandem, from one-third of the total development budget (RM1.4 billion) in 1966–70 to 48 percent (RM12 billion) in 1976–80 (Rugayah 1995: 66). In 1984, there were 46 public sector employees per thousand persons in Malaysia relative to 20 for Africa, 38 for Latin America, 30 for Asia, 8 for the OECD economies and 29 for developing nations as a whole. The cost of maintaining the large number of public sector employees was estimated at RM8.8 billion, or 46 percent of the operating budget (Yip 1987: 137–8).

Traditionally, current revenues covered operating expenditures; the size of the federal budget deficit thus coincided with the size of development expenditures. As development expenditures burgeoned because of the NEP targets in the Third Malaysia Plan and the anti-recessionary spending, federal tax revenue growth moderated to 2.1 percent per annum over 1980–82. This slower revenue growth was due to the cyclical downturn in the demand for export commodities. Nontax revenue, primarily from profits of the national petroleum company (PETRONAS), helped to keep revenue from actually falling. The federal budget deficit increased almost threefold, from RM3.7 billion in 1980 to RM10.4 billion by 1982[2] (Table 10.2).

As the recession took hold and incomes fell, internal sources of savings stagnated. The government turned increasingly to foreign borrowing, which increased from 10 percent to 22 percent of GNP between 1979 and 1982 (Table 10.3).

The balance of payments suffered as well. The fall in exports and export prices, due to the recession, created a merchandise account deficit that compounded the services account deficit (that had been present and growing since the 1970s). However, when the world economy showed signs of recovery in 1981–83, commodity prices, unlike on previous occasions, failed to respond due to excess supply and improved substitution possibilities (Thong 1987: 2). The current account deficit that surfaced in 1980 grew and hit its zenith in 1982 at RM8.3 billion, despite indications of recovery in the world economy.

Current account deficits of the past were ameliorated by net inflows of private investment. However, in the 1980s, net investment failed to offset the growing current account deficit and large external borrowings were relied upon instead. These, in turn, came back later to worsen the service account deficit as debt-servicing charges increased.

The enlarged public sector left two legacies by the end of 1982: the federal budget deficit was equivalent to 17.5 percent of GNP (Table 10.4), while the

*Table 10.2* Total revenue, expenditure and deficit (surplus) of the federal government, 1970–99 (RM million)

| *Year* | *Total revenue* | *Current expenditure* | *Development expenditure*[a] | *Deficit/surplus* |
|---|---|---|---|---|
| 1970 | 2,400 | 2,163 | 712 | −475 |
| 1971 | 2,418 | 2,398 | 1,070 | −1,050 |
| 1972 | 2,920 | 3,068 | 1,223 | −1,371 |
| 1973 | 3,399 | 3,342 | 1,106 | −1,049 |
| 1974 | 4,791 | 4,318 | 1,854 | −1,381 |
| 1975 | 5,117 | 4,500 | 2,118 | −1,901 |
| 1976 | 6,157 | 5,528 | 2,334 | −1,705 |
| 1977 | 7,760 | 7,098 | 3,138 | −2,476 |
| 1978 | 8,841 | 7,391 | 3,699 | −2,249 |
| 1979 | 10,505 | 7,890 | 4,150 | −1,535 |
| 1980 | 13,926 | 10,292 | 7,338 | −3,704 |
| 1981 | 15,806 | 13,686 | 11,135 | −9,015 |
| 1982 | 16,690 | 15,922 | 11,189 | −10,421 |
| 1983 | 18,608 | 16,124 | 9,417 | −6,933 |
| 1984 | 20,805 | 17,506 | 8,074 | −4,775 |
| 1985 | 21,115 | 18,766 | 6,756 | −4,407 |
| 1986 | 19,518 | 20,075 | 6,949 | −7,506 |
| 1987 | 18,143 | 20,185 | 4,111 | −6,153 |
| 1988 | 21,967 | 21,212 | 4,045 | −3,290 |
| 1989 | 25,273 | 22,982 | 5,701 | −3,410 |
| 1990 | 29,521 | 25,026 | 7,932 | −3,437 |
| 1991 | 34,053 | 28,296 | 8,397 | −2,640 |
| 1992 | 39,250 | 32,075 | 8,418 | −1,243 |
| 1993 | 41,691 | 32,217 | 9,120 | 354 |
| 1994 | 49,446 | 35,064 | 9,974 | 4,408 |
| 1995 | 50,952 | 36,573 | 12,520 | 1,859 |
| 1996 | 58,280 | 43,865 | 12,600 | 1,815 |
| 1997 | 65,736 | 44,665 | 14,445 | 6,626 |
| 1998 | 56,710 | 44,584 | 17,128 | −5,002 |
| 1999 | 58,675 | 46,699 | 21,463 | −9,487 |

Source: Bank Negara Malaysia (various years a, various years b).

Note
a Refers to net development expenditure.

current account deficit amounted to 14 percent of GNP. These deficits were 7.2 percent and 1.2 percent, respectively, in 1980. The sudden expenditure cuts, coupled with the inability of the private sector to take up the slack, caused real GDP growth to plunge from 7.8 percent in 1984 to a negative 1 percent in 1985. Malaysian fiscal policy was in disarray.

The fiscal thrust was overhauled under a new Finance Minister (July 1984–December 1990). While continuing to withdraw the public sector from economic activities, the private sector was encouraged to fill the gap. The number of off-budget agencies was reduced and the remaining agencies were placed under stricter supervision. Privatization was initiated to pass the burden of public economic entities into private hands. While the manner of the privatization exercises

*Table 10.3* Debt indicators, 1970–99

| *Year* | *Total debt/GNP* | *External debt/GNP* |
|---|---|---|
| 1970 | 41.3 | 6.1 |
| 1971 | 48.8 | 8.7 |
| 1972 | 53.6 | 10.2 |
| 1973 | 46.5 | 7.4 |
| 1974 | 43.3 | 7.1 |
| 1975 | 52.5 | 11.2 |
| 1976 | 63.4 | 14.2 |
| 1977 | 51.3 | 10.8 |
| 1978 | 50.3 | 11.0 |
| 1979 | 46.9 | 10.2 |
| 1980 | 45.6 | 9.5 |
| 1981 | 56.0 | 14.9 |
| 1982 | 70.1 | 22.0 |
| 1983 | 78.9 | 27.1 |
| 1984 | 78.1 | 28.1 |
| 1985 | 88.7 | 32.0 |
| 1986 | 110.8 | 42.4 |
| 1987 | 110.3 | 37.0 |
| 1988 | 103.8 | 30.2 |
| 1989 | 93.1 | 25.0 |
| 1990 | 83.1 | 21.7 |
| 1991 | 77.2 | 19.0 |
| 1992 | 68.0 | 14.7 |
| 1993 | 58.5 | 11.8 |
| 1994 | 50.0 | 8.0 |
| 1995 | 43.1 | 6.3 |
| 1996 | 37.1 | 4.3 |
| 1997 | 33.7 | 4.9 |
| 1998 | 38.3 | 5.5 |
| 1999 | 40.1 | 6.6 |

Source: Bank Negara Malaysia (various years a, various years b).

has been questioned (Adam and Cavendish 1995), about twenty-four major initiatives had been listed as government privatizations by 1990, although there were many smaller efforts as well.

Money-losing, state-run heavy industry projects were overhauled. In 1988, ailing enterprises in the gas, steel, shipyard engineering and cement industries had total accumulated losses of about RM1.3 billion (Bank Negara Malaysia, various years a, 1989 issue: 162). In a major revamp of their top management, control was handed over to foreign and local (Chinese) entrepreneurs.

Improvements in the federal budget after 1987 and better external conditions allowed the government to borrow cheaper domestic funds to refinance foreign loans. In 1987–89, RM13.6 billion was prepaid by both the private and government sectors. External debt as a proportion of GNP declined from 42 percent in 1986 to 25 percent by 1989 (Table 10.3).

Efforts to rehabilitate the private sector included allowing 100 percent foreign equity participation in certain export-oriented projects, liberalizing some controversial

*Table 10.4* Tax-to-GNP, expenditure-to-GNP, deficit (surplus)-to-GNP and tax revenue-to-expenditure ratios, 1970–99

| *Year* | *Tax revenue/ GNP* | *Expenditure/ GNP* | *Deficit (surplus)/ GNP* | *Tax revenue/ expenditure* |
|---|---|---|---|---|
| 1970 | 15.1 | 23.7 | −4.0 | 64.0 |
| 1971 | 15.2 | 27.7 | −8.0 | 44.7 |
| 1972 | 15.8 | 31.5 | −10.1 | 51.0 |
| 1973 | 15.6 | 25.5 | −6.0 | 63.1 |
| 1974 | 18.5 | 29.1 | −6.5 | 65.7 |
| 1975 | 19.7 | 30.5 | −8.8 | 64.3 |
| 1976 | 19.0 | 36.4 | −7.9 | 65.4 |
| 1977 | 21.4 | 32.9 | −8.0 | 65.1 |
| 1978 | 21.6 | 31.6 | −6.4 | 68.2 |
| 1979 | 22.1 | 27.1 | −3.5 | 74.7 |
| 1980 | 23.5 | 34.3 | −7.2 | 68.4 |
| 1981 | 22.7 | 44.6 | −16.2 | 50.7 |
| 1982 | 21.1 | 45.4 | −17.5 | 46.4 |
| 1983 | 23.3 | 39.0 | −10.6 | 59.8 |
| 1984 | 22.2 | 34.5 | −6.4 | 64.4 |
| 1985 | 23.2 | 35.4 | −6.1 | 65.4 |
| 1986 | 22.0 | 40.5 | −11.2 | 54.3 |
| 1987 | 16.7 | 32.5 | −8.2 | 51.3 |
| 1988 | 17.1 | 29.4 | −3.8 | 58.2 |
| 1989 | 17.2 | 29.7 | −3.5 | 58.1 |
| 1990 | 19.2 | 28.9 | −3.0 | 64.5 |
| 1991 | 20.6 | 28.6 | −2.1 | 70.4 |
| 1992 | 20.5 | 28.3 | −0.9 | 71.1 |
| 1993 | 20.3 | 25.2 | +0.2 | 77.2 |
| 1994 | 20.7 | 24.2 | +2.4 | 83.2 |
| 1995 | 20.0 | 23.1 | +0.9 | 84.9 |
| 1996 | 19.9 | 23.3 | +0.8 | 83.7 |
| 1997 | 19.9 | 22.2 | +2.5 | 90.7 |
| 1998 | 16.8 | 22.9 | −1.9 | 73.5 |
| 1999 | 16.2 | 24.4 | −3.4 | 66.5 |

Source: Computed based on Tables 11.1 and 11.2.

provisions of the ICA on licensing requirements, and income tax-based incentives under a newly announced Promotion of Investments Act of 1986 that replaced the Investment Incentive Act. Small-scale enterprises received a boost with automatic "pioneer" status for approved products and other tax concessions.

To strengthen domestic demand and to keep the corporate tax attractive *vis-à-vis* Malaysia's neighbors, the income tax schedule was revamped in the budget proposals of 1985. The top marginal tax rate for personal income was cut, the number of taxable income brackets was reduced, and the lowest threshold income (when personal income tax becomes payable) was raised. Similarly, the corporate tax was reduced while the development tax was abolished in stages.

These fiscal initiatives were aided by a favorable turn of external events but from which Malaysia benefited substantially. Commodity prices strengthened with the recovery of the US economy, and rising labor costs and appreciating national currencies led to the relocation of investments from Japan, Taiwan and Singapore. The Malaysian economy bounced back from negative growth in 1985 to 5.2 percent growth in GDP by 1987 and 9.7 percent by 1990. The twin deficits, too, were brought to manageable proportions with the federal budget deficit and the current account deficit at 3 percent and 4.2 percent of GNP, respectively.

However, fiscal reform ignored the tax system that was fraught with weaknesses, distortions and an impaired capacity to maximize revenue. The tax side of the fiscal strategy to revive the economy had focused on giving out liberal tax concessions to attract private investment. This was supplemented by reductions in the corporate and personal tax rates to keep Malaysia's investment climate competitive. These moves eroded the revenue potential of direct taxes. Consequently, greater reliance had to be placed on indirect taxes to generate revenues. Yet, indirect taxes had major deficiencies requiring attention (see subsequent discussion). While there was a suggestion of a major tax reform—especially of indirect taxes—in the budget of 1989 (Department of Information Services, 1989 Budget speech: 10), nothing came of it.

In 1991–97, the economy grew at rates in excess of 8 percent. The buoyant economy and good petroleum prices kept revenues high, masking the underlying flaws in the tax system and reducing the pressure for tax reform.

### *The Post–NEP period, 1990–96*

By 1991, the Governor of the Central Bank (Bank Negara) cautioned that the economy might be overheating: inflation was on the rise, the current account deficit in the balance of payments was widening and infrastructure bottlenecks were surfacing in key sectors. The bank recommended prudence and policy measures to moderate growth and followed it up with tighter monetary policies (Bank Negara Malaysia, various years a, 1993 issue: Governor's message). However, the thrust of fiscal policy seemed to be in the opposite direction. Major fiscal incentives since 1992 included further cuts in personal and corporate income taxes, and the lowering or abolition of import taxes on a large number of goods. Development spending of the federal government was increased and recorded double-digit growth since 1988 (Table 10.2). A number of multibillion ringgit projects, instigated by the public sector but executed by the private sector, also took center-stage.

As indicated earlier, although the need to rationalize the indirect system was mentioned as early as 1988, with the possibility of introducing a broad-based tax on consumption (Department of Information, 1989 Budget speech: 10), nothing came of it. Then in 1993, when measures to extend the service tax slightly were announced, there was a promise of a broader sales and service tax (SST) to come. However, the continually buoyant economy yielded enough revenues to turn around the public sector budget from being in deficit to a surplus and reduced the urgency for tax reform.

A period of rapid growth would have been the time to introduce the broad-based consumption tax that could "integrate the existing sales, service and excise taxes and derive economies in a single tax administration" (Bank Negara Malaysia, various years a, 1991 issue: 207). Such an exercise would have served several objectives. First, a streamlined indirect tax structure would have removed the distortions in the current system and simplified the tax machinery. Second, it would have helped moderate growth and curb inflationary pressures by reducing resources in private hands. Third, a solid foundation would have been laid to generate fiscal surpluses in the years of prosperity. More importantly, this could have been achieved without serious opposition to the new tax since incomes were rising. Unfortunately, this opportunity was allowed to slip.

### *The 1997 financial crisis and after*

The immediate cause of the 1997 economic slowdown was the speculative attacks against the Thai baht. When the Thai central bank abandoned efforts to defend the baht in July 1997, the markets panicked and triggered a massive outflow of short-term capital. The Malaysian ringgit depreciated and the stock market suffered a serious decapitalization. What began as a currency crisis soon affected the real sector as investor confidence shrank, domestic demand collapsed and real GDP contracted in 1998.

The handling of the 1997 crisis went through three phases. In the first phase, the problem was viewed as one caused by a weak financial sector, a growing current account deficit, excessive and unbalanced lending to certain sectors (like the property and stock markets) and capital flight (Narayanan *et al.* 1997). Accordingly, a tight monetary and fiscal stance was adopted. Various measures were announced to reduce the excess liquidity in the system, to raise interest rates, to cap credit growth, and to restrain further lending for real estate and stock market purchases. Attempts to limit private consumption came via allowance cuts in the public sector and wage restraints in the private sector. The underlying rationale was that financial prudence would stabilize the ringgit, restore market confidence, and attract foreign capital that, in turn, would form the basis for an economic recovery.

After more than a year of monetary and fiscal restraint, the results were less than satisfactory. GDP contracted by 2.8 percent over the first quarter of 1998 and GDP growth was negative for the first time in 13 years; manufacturing output declined by 5 percent for the first five months of 1998. Exports in US dollar terms declined by 10.3 percent, primarily because of a 22.5 percent fall in exports to ASEAN and Japan. This prompted a shift in strategy, which was to be the second phase of the policy mix aimed at handling the crisis. Parliament was told, on July 13, 1998:

> [T]he capacity of the private sector as the engine for economic growth is limited because of liquidity problems. The government has agreed to implement counter-cyclical measures including a fiscal stimulus to generate economic activities and contain the contractionary impact of the financial crisis.
>
> (*New Straits Times*, 14 July 1998: 12)

However, the measures announced came too late. Bank Negara (the central bank) reported at the end of August 1998 that GDP had declined by 6.8 percent in the second quarter of the year, and announced measures to slightly ease its monetary stance (*New Straits Times*, 28 August 1998: 1). Manufacturing and construction—two key sectors—had shrunk by 9.2 percent and 22 percent, respectively (*New Straits Times*, 31 August 1998: 23). It was widely expected that overall GDP growth for 1998 would be a negative figure, and this was later confirmed. The 1999 budget proposals had forecasted GDP contraction of 4.8 percent for 1998.

In the second phase of the policy, the primary focus was to inject life into the domestic sector via increased government spending. However, high interest rates were still maintained (despite growing dissatisfaction from some quarters), presumably to address the problems of the external sector.

The high interest rate policy of the first thirteen months will no doubt remain a point of debate and opponents of the policy will attribute the GDP contraction to this policy. Supporters, on the other hand, may argue that it was precisely the tight monetary policy in the early phase that contributed to stabilization of the exchange rate and opened the way for a more expansionary stance. Although the exchange rate had depreciated by about 40 percent since the crisis began, it had shown signs of stabilizing at RM4.20 to the US dollar by the end of August 1998. Indeed, with inflation contained and the current account balance improving, Bank Negara announced (on 3 August 1998) that the "fundamental trends provide Malaysia with room for a cautious easing of monetary policy to minimize the severity of the downturn in [the] domestic economy" (*New Straits Times*, 11 August 1998: 25).

The date 1 September 1998 marked the third phase. Despite signs of a lower but more stable exchange rate, the government opted for a fixed exchange rate. The ringgit was also no longer tradable in the foreign exchange market and capital account transactions were declared nonconvertible. These measures effectively severed the link between the exchange rate and domestic interest rates, allowing Bank Negara to have a virtually free hand to ease domestic credit. Policy-makers had moved on to a strategy of fiscal and monetary expansion. It also signaled that the primary focus was to revive domestic economic activity since the foreign exchange controls insulated the economy from the external sector.

The 1999 budget proposals gave concrete form to the expansionary fiscal policy. Learning from previous experience, the budget deficit was kept at a "sustainable" level not exceeding 6 percent of GNP. The fiscal stimulus was to be "disciplined and . . . manageable" (Bank Negara Malaysia, various years a, 1999 and 2000 issues: 87).

External developments lent a helping hand. The strong external demand for electronics coupled with the undervalued ringgit gave a significant boost to exports. The virtual collapse of imports, on the other hand, helped secure an unexpected surplus in the overall balance of payments. The projected decline in revenue also proved to be less serious than originally anticipated. All of these factors allowed the government to expand spending in 1999 while keeping the budget deficit well below the target of 6 percent of GNP. Total expenditure was increased from the budgeted RM65.1 billion to RM74.6 billion, the bulk of which was to go to the economic and social sectors that had minimum import requirements.

However, due to delays in disbursements of development expenditure, there was a shortfall in actual spending; only RM21.5 billion of the original allocation of RM25.8 billion was expended (Bank Negara Malaysia, various years a, 1999 and 2000 issue: 88).

Largely domestic funding of the increased expenditures was facilitated by two main factors: the small budget surpluses of previous years and the large current account surpluses in the overall balance of payments (in 1998 and 1999)[3] which injected ample liquidity into the system. The government borrowed via the domestic bond market, the EPF and insurance companies, and also drew down accumulated realizable assets. The 2000 budget (tabled on October 1999) and its revised version (tabled on February 2000) continued to be expansionary though the projected deficit was only 4.5 percent of GNP, well below the self-imposed limit of 6 percent.

While the major thrust of the expansionary fiscal policy was being initiated through increased government spending, some measures on the tax side were announced as well. These were aimed at rejuvenating activity in targeted areas such as export, import-substituting commodities and services, and the services sector.

More general tax measures aimed at stimulating domestic businesses include tax exemption on instruments that attract stamp duty for refinancing of loans for business and trade. In moving to change the income tax assessment method from one based on the income derived from the preceding year to the current year, beginning from the year 2000, income earned in 1999 was exempted from income tax. Furthermore, business losses in 1999 could be carried forward.

Revenue-generating changes in tax were, understandably, few. Excise duties on alcoholic beverages and tobacco were raised, along with the tax on gambling. A new levy on crude palm oil and crude palm kernel was announced to tap windfall gains.

The easy fiscal stance was supplemented by an easy monetary policy as well. This was a luxury that was afforded by the fixing of the exchange rate and a clamping of outflow of short-term capital for a year announced as part of the September 1998 package.

The easing of the tight monetary policy has come largely by way of reductions in the statutory reserve ratio (SRR) by the Bank Negara. The SRR has been lowered repeatedly from a high of 13.5 percent in February 1998 to 6 percent by 1 September 1998, when foreign exchange controls were announced. It was reduced further to 4 percent, with the possibility of it being reduced to 2 percent at some future date. Given that an estimated RM4 billion is released into the interbank market, for every percentage point reduction of the SRR, about RM38 billion was freed into the system.

The base lending rate (BLR) framework was also changed to allow for faster transmission of changes in monetary policy on interest rate levels. The calculation of the BLR is now based on the Bank Negara's three-month intervention rate rather than the KL Inter-Bank Offer Rate (Klibor). In August 1998, the benchmark three-month intervention rate was cut from 11 percent to 10.5 percent, and a series of rapid cuts brought it down to 5.5 percent by the end of 1999. The BLR declined from 12.27 percent from the end of June 1998 to 6.79 percent by the end of 1999. The administrative margins of financial institutions that are allowed in the BLR computation were reduced from 2.50 to 2.25 percentage points.

It was also stipulated that banking institutions must maintain a minimum annual loan growth of 8 percent for 1998. Tight restrictions on lending for transactions in the property sector and the stock market were eased and nonperforming loans (NPLs) were reclassified as loans not serviced for six rather than three months.

Alongside these measures, efforts are underway to restructure the banking system. Steps were in place to strengthen prudent regulatory and supervisory standards. Banks and financial institutions were encouraged to merge and consolidate their positions. Institutions such as Danaharta, Danamodal and the Corporate Debt Restructuring Committee were established to help strengthen the financial sector.[4]

In general, these measures have resulted in better-than-expected recovery. GDP growth (at current prices), which had recorded a negative 7.4 percent between 1997 and 1998, rose again to 6.1 percent in 1999 and posted 8.3 percent by 2000 (Bank Negara Malaysia, various years a, 2002 issue: table A.1).

## Fiscal policies: a mixed record

In the economic downturn of 1974–76, fiscal policy was used successfully as a tool of economic stabilization. Keynesian-style counter-cyclical spending helped the economy come out of a mild recession fairly quickly. The key to the successful effort lay in the fact that the downturn was relatively short and was primarily caused by weak external demand. Thus, the fiscal effort was needed only as an interim measure, and when demand abroad picked up, it provided a natural antidote to the sluggish local economy.

However, in the 1980s, fiscal policy became a major tool for economic restructuring. Consequently, it proved ineffective as a tool for economic stabilization. Fueled largely by ethnic nationalistic sentiment rather than economic reasoning, public sector spending in support of the NEP acquired a momentum and focus that were hard to check. This over-involvement of the public sector in economic activities[5] restricted its ability to act in a recessionary environment when counter-cyclical spending might genuinely have helped. Instead, public sector spending generated the typical "twin deficits" as suggested by conventional theory, although the sequence varied somewhat. Faced with resource constraints, the public sector had to adopt the unconventional action of slashing its spending in the midst of a recession. The economy nose-dived into negative growth as a result. The response to the new turn of events was to downsize public sector involvement and to fill the gap by measures to revive private sector activity. This was done with earnest, despite fears that it would undermine the gains made under the NEP. But for this belated pragmatism, the economy might have taken a longer period to recover.

The lessons from this experience are evident. Expansionary fiscal policies are burdensome and essentially short-term measures that must be well focused. They demand a considerable amount of public resources and frequently lead to borrowing. More importantly, fiscal stimulus must be part of a larger and more comprehensive policy aimed at reviving private sector initiatives—both domestic and foreign—particularly in an open economy. Any attempt by the public sector to "go it alone" on a large scale could "crowd out" the private sector and be counterproductive. In the good run of eight years of prosperity that followed, there was no attempt to maximize the fiscal surplus. Nor was there any attempt to overhaul the complex indirect tax system that had developed piecemeal over time. Instead generous tax breaks contributed to the "overheating" of the economy.

The final shape of the response to the crisis of 1997 is a policy mix consisting of both fiscal and monetary expansion targeted at reviving domestic economic activity. This was made possible by restrictions on short-term capital flight and a fixed exchange rate regime. In tandem with this, serious efforts are underway to strengthen and consolidate the badly battered financial sector.

The fiscal response to the latest crisis appears to be more coherent and better planned. The size of the budget deficit has been limited to 6 percent of GNP and definite attempts have been made to finance the deficit from domestic funds. The massive drawing of domestic funds by the public sector does not immediately raise the specter of "crowding out" of domestic private investment since excess liquidity in the system will ensure that the interest rate will remain low for some time. Additionally, the fear that increased government spending will reduce net exports is neutralized by the fixed exchange rate, the excess liquidity in the system and controls on capital flows.[6]

A deficit budget strategy led by increased government spending is a proper prescription in circumstances where the private sector cannot or will not be able to move the economy out of the doldrums (such as in situations of imperfect information or poor level of business confidence). In the initial stages of the economic crisis, this was indeed the case. A budget deficit strategy can be implemented by tax cuts or through increased public spending. The former yields more resources for increased private spending and investment to revive the economy, while the latter leaves the task to the public sector. Although the prevailing policy has elements of both, it is clearly driven by increased government spending.

However, it is essential to recognize that as the economy begins to gain momentum, the task of leading the recovery process is better left to the private sector. This is achieved through appropriate incentives to rejuvenate the private sector. When the private sector shoulders the burden of economic recovery, the public sector is free to focus on other important longer-term issues.

Malaysia has avoided a serious or sustained debt crisis primarily because sufficiently large domestic sources of funds have been available on reasonable and flexible terms. In general, the central bank has exercised strict supervision over both public and private institutions borrowing of funds from abroad. Hence, the exposure of Malaysian institutions in the foreign loan market was small when the 1997 crisis broke.

## Policy issues and future prospects

With the experience of a fiscal strategy that fell apart in the 1980s being well understood, it appears that the conduct of fiscal policy in Malaysia, at least in the short term, has become better managed. This is clearly indicated by the self-imposed restraint of the budget deficit to 6 percent of GNP. The fixed exchange rate regime and the initial curb on short-term capital outflows have enhanced the effectiveness of the fiscal initiatives. The debt situation also appears to be under control. Thus, economic growth has shown some signs of recovery.

However, there are at least three important issues that require attention. First, although the economy has gained a valuable breathing space, an essentially open economy like Malaysia cannot remain insulated by a fixed exchange rate system and capital controls. The capital controls have now been largely dismantled, but getting the exchange rate to reflect market forces is being postponed because there are no easy options. In fact, the options may become less attractive, the longer the exchange rate remains fixed (Ariff 1999).

Second, several factors can impair the recovery process. The health of economies such as the United States, Japan and Europe are a cause for concern since they are major markets for Malaysian exports; foreign investment inflows are critical and appear to have moderated; and domestic investment activity and confidence remain low. Already, the negative impact of the economic downturn in the US and the dampening demand for electronics globally have impacted the Malaysian economy in 2001 and reduced GDP growth to a mere 0.4 percent, down from the impressive 8.3 percent of the previous year (Bank Negara Malaysia, various years a, 2002 issue: table A.1). In fact, an RM3 billion stimulus package was introduced in March 2001, and this was followed by an additional RM4.3 billion at the end of the year, to keep the growth rate positive (*Star*, 8 January 2003). Unless improvements are forthcoming on all fronts, the public sector may end up shouldering the burden of recovery—a responsibility it cannot sustain indefinitely. A prolonged anti-cyclical effort will require recourse to foreign loans and a debt burden that is more difficult to contain.

Finally, there is a crying need to streamline and revitalize the indirect tax system to maximize revenue. Many taxes (like the sales, excise and import taxes) share a similar and narrow base. About 60 percent of imported and locally manufactured goods are outside the sales tax net, and over 60 percent of imports are spared the import tax (Bank Negara Malaysia, various years a, 1991 issue: 206). Additionally, the single-stage sales tax imposed on the manufacturer distorts behavior,[7] generates tax pyramiding[8] and has elements of tax cascading.[9] These features cause the effective tax rates to diverge from the statutory rates (Narayanan 1991). A well-designed broad-based consumption-type value added tax may be an alternative worthy of consideration.

## Notes

1 This and the subsequent sections are based largely on Narayanan (1996).

2 In contrast, the previous decade (1970–79) saw revenues growing at an average annual rate of 19 percent, thanks to receipts from increased exports of commodities that were also commanding high prices. New taxes such as the sales tax also boosted collections.

3 The surplus amounted to RM40.3 billion in 1998 due to the collapse in domestic demand. As import demand recovered and in the face of excess capacity, the surplus declined somewhat to RM17.8 billion in 1999. The surplus in 1999 caused the external

reserves of Bank Negara to increase to RM117.2 billion, which was sufficient to finance 5.9 months of retained imports (Bank Negara Malaysia, various years a, 1999 and 2000 issue: 41).

4 Danaharta is an asset management company that was established to buy up nonperforming loans from banking institutions so that they can refocus on their lending activities. Danamodal, on the other hand, is an institution meant to recapitalize banking institutions whose shareholders are unable to raise additional capital. The Corporate Debt Restructuring Committee's role is to provide a mechanism for banks and their debtors to work out feasible solutions to their debt problems.

5 In 1985, the public sector accounted for 31 percent of domestic demand (Bank Negara Malaysia, various years a, 1998 and 1999 issue: 31).

6 Under flexible exchange rates and free capital mobility across borders, it is theoretically possible that increased government spending will raise domestic interest rates and attract capital inflows. The consequent appreciation of the exchange rates will undermine exports and increase imports. The deterioration of net exports can nullify some of the impact of the fiscal impulse. See Mankiw (1997) for a simple exposition of these effects.

7 For example, since the sales tax is levied in the early stage of production, it fails to tax value added in later stages. This results in the effective tax rate depending upon the number of subsequent stages that the taxed commodity passes through. In addition, there is considerable incentive to push activities such as advertising and freight services beyond the point of impact of the tax (Narayanan 1991: 7–9).

8 This occurs because the tax is applied at the first stage of the production-distribution chain. As the taxed good passes through subsequent stages, a markup is applied to the purchase price that includes the tax. Consequently, the tax "pyramids" as it reaches the consumer, but the higher price paid by the consumer does not result in higher tax receipts to the government.

9 This refers to the multiple application of a tax to a given commodity as it goes through the production and distribution chain. Thus, the total tax attracted by a good is not determined by any objective criteria. Instead, it hinges on the number of stages it passes through. In Malaysia, a "ring system" and "refund system" attempt to minimize this cascading, but these are not entirely effective. See Narayanan (1991: 8) for more detail.

## References

Adam, C. and Cavendish, W. (1995) "Early privatizations," in K.S. Jomo (ed.) *Privatizing Malaysia*, Boulder, CO: Westview Press.

Ariff, M. (1999) "Fixing Malaysia's fixed exchange rate regime: some options," *Kajian Malaysia* [Journal of Malaysia Studies], 17(2): 1–20.

Asher, M.G. and Both, A. (1983) *Indirect Taxation in ASEAN*, Singapore: Singapore University Press.

Bank Negara Malaysia (various years a) *Annual Report*, various issues, Kuala Lumpur: Bank Negara Malaysia.

Bank Negara Mayalsia (various years b) *Quarterly Statistical Bulletin*, various issues, Kuala Lumpur: Bank Negara Malaysia.

Bank Negara Malaysia (2003) Statistics database, available on: http://www.bnm.gov.my.

Department of Information Services, Malaysia (various years) Budget speeches, Kuala Lumpur: Jabatan Perkhidmatan Penerangan Malaysia.

Jomo, K.S. (1995) "Introduction," in K.S. Jomo (ed.) *Privatizing Malaysia*, Boulder, CO: Westview Press.

Lee, Hock Lock (2001) *Financial Security in Old Age: Whither the Employees Provident Fund of Malaysia?*, Kualar Lumpur: Pelanduk Publications.

Malaysia (1971) *Second Malaysia Plan, 1971–1975*, Kuala Lumpur: Government Printer.

Malaysian Institute of Economic Research (MIER) (1987) "Overview of tax reform in Malaysia," paper prepared for the National Conference on Tax Reform, organized by the Malaysian Institute of Economic Research, Kuala Lumpur, December 7–9.

Mankiw, N.G. (1997) *Macroeconomics*, New York: Worth Publishers.

Narayanan, Suresh (1991) *The Value Added Tax in Malaysia: The Rationale, Design and Issues*, Kuala Lumpur: Institute of Strategic and International Studies.

Narayanan, Suresh (1996) "Fiscal reform in Malaysia: behind a successful experience," *Asian Survey* 36(9): 869–81.

Narayanan, Suresh *et al.* (1997) "The East Asian economic crisis: why was Malaysia vulnerable?" *Malaysian Journal of Economic Studies* 34(1 & 2): 93–112.

*New Straits Times* (various years) *New Straits Times*, various issues.

Rugayah, Mohammad (1995) "Public sector enterprises," in K.S. Jomo (ed.) *Privatizing Malaysia*, Boulder, CO: Westview Press.

*Star*, 8 January 2003.

Thong, Y.H. (1987) "Balance of payments issues and implications," in K.S. Jomo, K.H. Ling and S.K. Ahmad (eds) *Crisis and Response in the Malaysian Economy*, Kuala Lumpur: Malaysian Economic Association.

Treasury (2000) *Economic Report 2000/2001*, Kuala Lumpur: Percetakan Nasional Malaysia.

Umikalsum, M.N. (1991) Fiscal federalism in Malaysia, 1981–87, unpublished PhD thesis submitted to the Faculty of Economics and Administration, University of Malaya, Kuala Lumpur.

Yip, Y.H. (1987) "Regulation, deregulation or reregulation?" in K.S. Jomo, K.H. Ling and S.K. Ahmad (eds) *Crisis and Response in the Malaysian Economy*, Kuala Lumpur: Malaysian Economic Association.

Yong, P.K. (1987) "The industrial sector, deregulation and growth," in K.S. Jomo, K.H. Ling and S.K. Ahmad (eds) *Crisis and Response in the Malaysian Economy*, Kuala Lumpur: Malaysian Economic Association.

# 11 Mexico

*Sergio A. Luna and Rafael E. Gómez-Tagle M.*

## Introduction

What can governments do? What should they do? In the past thirty years, Mexico's response has touched on two extremes. While in 1982 the public balance had reached a deficit worth 14.8 percent of GDP, by 1992 it was showing a surplus of 1.5 percent of GDP. As a result, the description of Mexico's experience usually falls into the stereotype of a country that, having suffered the consequences of its excesses, is now an example of fiscal rectitude. However, to adopt such a simplistic view is equivalent to throwing away all of the lessons that were learnt during those years. We believe that in order to understand fiscal issues in Mexico, it is necessary to adopt a more comprehensive view. Therefore, this chapter is organized as follows. The next section offers a description of the structure of public finances in Mexico and its most relevant institutional features. Based on the former, the chapter develops an analytical framework which is then applied, in a subsequent section, to the review of fiscal issues in Mexico during the period 1970–2001. The final section offers our concluding remarks.

## The structure of fiscal accounts in Mexico

Mexico's fiscal accounts are highly centralized, particularly in terms of revenue. The 32 state and 2,433 municipal governments have the right to collect taxes on land, payroll, alcoholic beverages and public shows, among others. Nonetheless, revenue from these sources represents a marginal proportion of total budgets. For 2000, for example, our own estimates suggest that, on average, 70 percent of total funding at the municipal level comes from the federal government.[1]

Thus, a more detailed view of revenue at the level of the federal government is necessary (Figure 11.1). The federal public sector in Mexico is divided into three major categories: federal government, state-owned enterprises (SOEs) subject to direct budgetary control and SOEs under indirect budgetary control. The lion's share of income from SOEs comes from those subject to direct budgetary control, as this group includes the oil company PEMEX (Mexico's constitution grants ownership of oil resources to the state). Table 11.1 shows the contribution of both the federal government and the consolidated SOE sector to total federal revenue in much of the 1970–2001 period. This classification under-estimates the importance of oil-related

Consolidated budgetary revenue (T) = T.1. + T.2. + T.3.

T.1. Revenue federal government

T.1.1. Taxes

- T.1.1.1. Income tax
- T.1.1.2 Value-added tax
- T.1.1.3 Special taxes on products and services
  - Fuel
  - Other
- T.1.1.4 Outlays
- T.1.1.5 Foreign trade
- T.1.1.6 Other

T.1.2. Nontax sources

- T.1.2.1. Rights
  - Hydrocarbons
  - Other
- T.1.2.2. Products
- T.1.2.3. Rents

T.2. Revenue from SOEs direct budgetary control

T.2.1. Own income

- T.2.1.1. Current income
  - Sales of goods and services
  - Other (social security contributions and other sources)
- T.2.1.2. Capital income

T.2.2. Transfers from the federal government

- T.2.2.1 Current
- T.2.2.2. Capital

T.3. Revenue from SOEs indirect budgetary control

T.3.1. Own income

- T.3.1.1. Current income
  - Sales of goods and services
  - Other (social security contributions and other sources)
- T.3.1.2. Capital income

T.3.2. Transfers from the federal government

- T.3.2.1 Current
- T.3.2.2. Capital

*Figure 11.1* The structure of government revenue in Mexico.

Note

Consolidated budgetary revenue (T) = T.1. + T.2. + T.3.

revenue, as PEMEX contributes toward the federal government's finances via three mechanisms: (i) royalties on hydrocarbons; (ii) payments of VAT; and (iii) duties and royalties on profits from its exports. Therefore, and in spite of being classified as part of the federal government, items T.1.1.2., T.1.1.3. and T.1.2.1. in Figure 11.1 also reflect oil-related revenue. As a consequence, it is customary to offer an alternative view based on the distinction between oil and non-oil revenue sources (Figure 11.2).

Regarding revenue from the federal government, Figure 11.1 offers a breakdown of major sources divided into two groups: tax and nontax sources. The latter is, as noted earlier, mostly related to oil. Therefore, traditional sources of government

*Table 11.1* Revenue indicators for Mexico (as a % of GDP, average for the period)

| | *1977–80* | *1981–90* | *1991–99* |
|---|---|---|---|
| Consolidated budgetary revenue (T) | 22.2 | 27.5 | 22.4 |
| Federal government (T.1.) | 12.5 | 15.7 | 15.4 |
| Taxes (T.1.1.) | 10.1 | 10.2 | 10.6 |
| Income tax (T.1.1.1.) | 5.4 | 4.4 | 4.7 |
| VAT (T.1.1.2.) | 2.3 | 3.1 | 3.1 |
| SOEs direct + indirect budgetary control (T.2. + T.3.) | 9.7 | 11.8 | 7.0 |

income (i.e., taxes) have never gone beyond 16 percent of GDP (Table 11.1). The two major taxes in Mexico are the income tax and the value added tax, which together account for close to 8 percent of GDP on average for the period under analysis.

A similar institutional classification applies to government expenditure (Figure 11.3). Nevertheless, expenditure responsibilities are more decentralized.[2] Overall public expenditure in Mexico is divided into two broad categories: programmable and nonprogrammable. The former refers to conventional budgetary expenses made by the federal government and SOEs (both under direct and indirect budgetary control), while the latter has two major items: (i) interest payments on

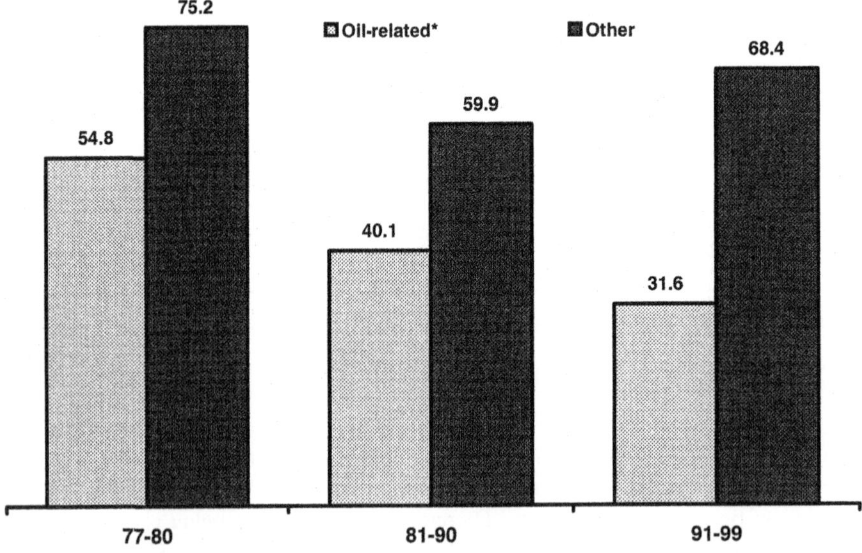


*Figure 11.2* Oil dependence of public finance (as a % of consolidated budgetary revenue).

Source: Ministry of Finance and Public Credit (2003).

Note

* Oil-related income has to do with the following revenue categories: T.2.1. (SOEs own income), T.1.1.3. (special taxes), and T.1.2.1.

Consolidated budgetary revenue (G) = FG + SOEG + SOXG

Total expenditure of federal government (FG) = G.1. + G.2.

G.1. Programmable expenditure

G.1.1 Current

G.1.1.1 Wages and salaries
G.1.1.2 Purchases
G.1.1.3 Other

G.1.2 Capital

G.1.2.1 Physical investment
G.1.2.2 Financial investment

G.1.3 Net transfers

G.1.3.1. Current
G.1.3.2 Capital

G.2. Nonprogrammable expenditure

G.2.1. Participations to states and municipalities

G.2.2 Interest payments on debt

G.2.2.1 Internal
G.2.2.2 External

Total expenditure of SOEs—direct budgetary control (SOED) = G.3. + G.4.

G.3. Programmable expenditure

G.3.1 Current

G.3.1.1 Wages and salaries
G.3.1.2 Purchases
G.3.1.3 Other

G.3.2 Capital

G.3.2.1 Physical investment
G.3.2.2 Financial investment

G.3.3 Net transfers

G.3.3.1. Current
G.3.3.2 Capital

G.4. Nonprogrammable expenditure

G.4.1. Participations to states and municipalities

G.4.2 Interest payments on debt

G.4.2.1 Internal
G.4.2.2 External

Total expenditures SOEs indirect budgetary control (SOXG) = G.5. + G.6

G.5. Programmable expenditure

G.5.1 Current

G.5.1.1 Wages and salaries
G.5.1.2 Purchases
G.5.1.3 Other

G.5.2 Capital

G.5.2.1 Physical investment
G.5.2.2 Financial investment

G.5.3 Net transfers

G.5.3.1. Current
G.5.3.2 Capital

G.6. Nonprogrammable expenditure

G.6.1. Participations to states and municipalities

G.6.2 Interest payments on debt

G.6.2.1 Internal
G.6.2.2 External

*Figure 11.3* The structure of government expenditure in Mexico.

debts, which appears on the expenditure bills of the federal government and the two institutional classifications of SOEs; and (ii) revenue-sharing with states and municipalities, which only appears in the expenditure bill of the federal government. This is the main channel through which resources collected on a federal basis are distributed among the lower levels of government.

Figure 11.4 summarizes this description. Along the vertical axis, the distinction is made among the three institutional components of the consolidated account. Thus, the sum of the balances of the federal government and the SOEs under direct budgetary control gives rise to the budgetary balance. When SOEs subject to indirect budgetary control are added, the result is the so-called economic balance, which represents the most aggregate measure of fiscal balances in Mexico. Along the horizontal axis, a second distinction is made in which the item of non-programmable expenditure common to the three institutional sectors (i.e., interest payments) is subtracted from the original balance, giving rise to the so-called primary balance. Thus, the consolidated budgetary account minus consolidated interest payments results in the concept shown in the last box on the right of Figure 11.4, namely, the primary economic balance.

At this point, it is convenient to offer a few more comments on current debt reporting.[3] Figures for external debt usually make a distinction between the federal

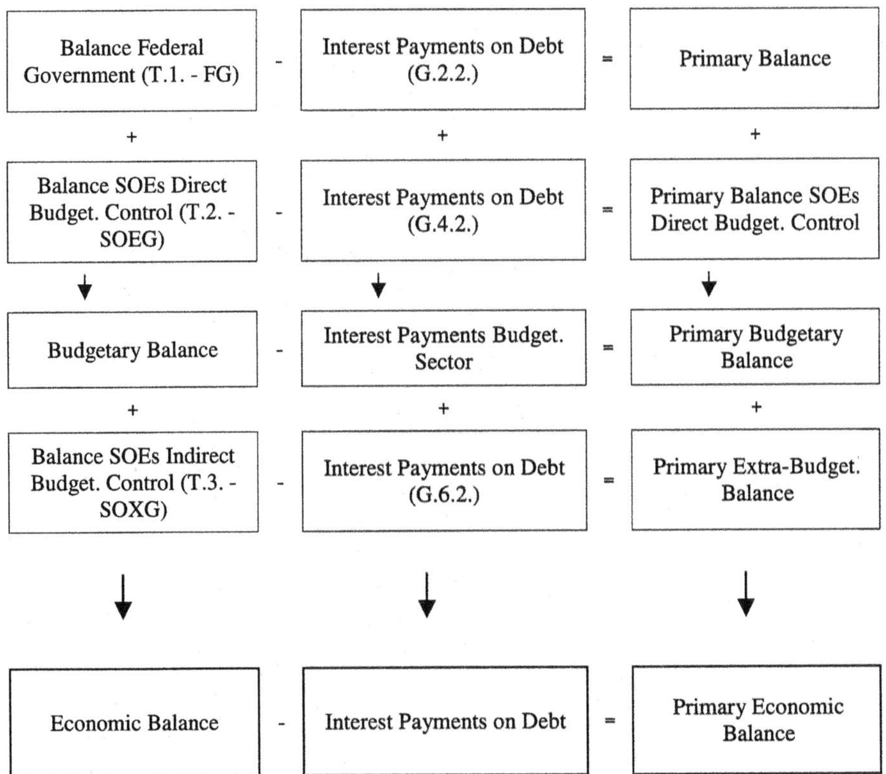


*Figure 11.4* Definitions of public balances employed in Mexico.

government, major SOEs (i.e., PEMEX, CFE) and development banks as well as a classifications based on maturity (short- vs. long-term instruments), debt holders and type of currency. Regarding internal debt, at the closing of 2001, 90 percent of the gross domestic debt was financed via securities, among which CETEs, with maturities ranging from 28 to 364 days, have long been the leading instrument in terms of determining benchmark rates. More recently, however, BONDES (with maturities from two to five years) constitute a larger proportion, as a more stable macroeconomic environment assists the effort to build a longer-term reference curve. At the end of 2001, CETES represented 25 percent of gross domestic debt, while BONDES accounted for 39 percent. Other instruments for the financing of internal debt include fixed rate bonds, Udibonos (an inflation-indexed bond) as well as issues from retirement savings systems.

Regarding size, Mexico's ratio of public debt to GDP (23.4 percent in 2001) was one of the lowest among the OECD countries. However, this figure does not consider the fiscal cost of IPAB, a program aimed at guaranteeing the solvency of the banking system during the 1995 crisis. These liabilities are not considered as official public debt because Congress has not granted that recognition. However, sensible accounting practices suggest they should be seen as part of outstanding financial commitments and this is precisely the principle followed by the Mexican government. In 2001, IPAB's net debt represented 11.75 percent of GDP.

There is another item to discuss: projects of financed investment, or PIDIREGAS, a scheme that went into operation right after the peso crisis of 1995. In order to carry on with some critical investment projects, the government commissioned their implementation and financing on the private sector with an explicit guarantee to purchase these projects. If the principle followed in the case of the IPAB is applied here as well, we should therefore treat these projects as liabilities that will soon materialize. This leads to additional debt worth 2.81 percent of GDP in 2001.

As in most countries, the difference between paid contributions to retirement systems and future claims, as well as its impact on public debt, remains a subject of debate. Santaella (2001) considers both liabilities from the scheme for private sector workers (IMSS) who are not yet included in the current transition to a pay-as-you-go system and those for the (unreformed) systems of retirement for public sector workers both at the federal and state levels. The assumptions behind these figures and the resulting ratio (135.9 percent of GDP in 1999) will only be meaningful in a comparison with similar exercises for other countries.

In the final analysis, what matters is the transparency with which things are managed. An example is the introduction, in 2001, of the concept of "public sector borrowing requirements" (PSBR), where the conventional measures of public finances discussed in this section are adjusted in order to take into account both nonrecurrent revenue and commitments related to the IPAB and PIDIREGAS, among others. Applying these criteria, the debt to GDP ratio for 2001 goes up to 40.8 percent, while the economic deficit (0.7 percent of GDP) translates into a PSBR deficit worth 3.3 percent of GDP. We believe the adoption of a more transparent approach represents a further step in a gradual process of fiscal consolidation in Mexico, a topic that we shall review. First, however, some analytical elements need to be discussed.

## Fiscal and social equilibrium: an analytical focus

Consider a country in which the goods and services that the government provides are not subject to externalities and that the consumption of each agent is proportional to his/her contribution in taxes. We also require that a single variable—say, income—is the sole determinant of taxes and consumption of government goods. Under these conditions, taxes are strictly identical to the marginal/average cost incurred in the production of goods made by the government. As if these restrictions were not enough, our time horizon is limited to a single generation. Hence, there are no financial markets and no demographic change.

Under these conditions, the work of the public administrator is limited to: (i) determining the quantity of goods demanded (N); (ii) collecting the required funds (T); and (iii) producing these goods (G). Nonetheless, the process is different from the one characterizing a private company under perfect competition. In fact, it can be said that the quantity to be produced, G, should be determined exogenously, given that there is a strict identity between the quantity to be consumed, N, and the quantity produced, G. We will refer to this peculiar structure as total market power (TMP). The problem can now be presented as follows:

- The combination of apparently competitive behavior (suggested by performance in terms of prices or taxes) and the TMP structure is inconsistent with profit maximization as a rule for government conduct;
- Thus the process through which the quantity is established—either G or N—is indeterminate; the government can efficiently produce zero or infinite goods; by severing the link connecting structure (TMP) with conduct (profit maximization, for example), the determination of quantities becomes independent of price.

Since Samuelson's (1955) breakthrough contribution to the theory of public finance, uncertainty about what the government optimizes is usually resolved via a "social welfare function" (SWF): agents are indifferent about who provides the required goods and thus the distinction between the government and the private sector disappears. In this respect, a SWF does not offer a solution to the question about what a government should do. Rather, it allows us to assume that this question has somehow been solved, perhaps by the ubiquitous "omniscient referee." In other words, the government's role is indeterminate unless "someone" makes a decision, and this has to be based on normative—not positive—judgments about the state of things.

In this sense, a SWF assumes some degree of government activity and as such, has a relationship with government expenditure, G. Assuming a unique correspondence between these two variables defines a "social balance" curve (Figure 11.5) which, in this first case, starts at the origin and has a slope of 45°. The way in which the resources needed are collected is expressed in the upper-right quadrant, which depicts the traditional relationship between tax revenue, T, and government expenditure, G. The resulting curve is none other than the "fiscal balance." This also starts at the origin and has a slope of 45°. It reflects the government efficiency

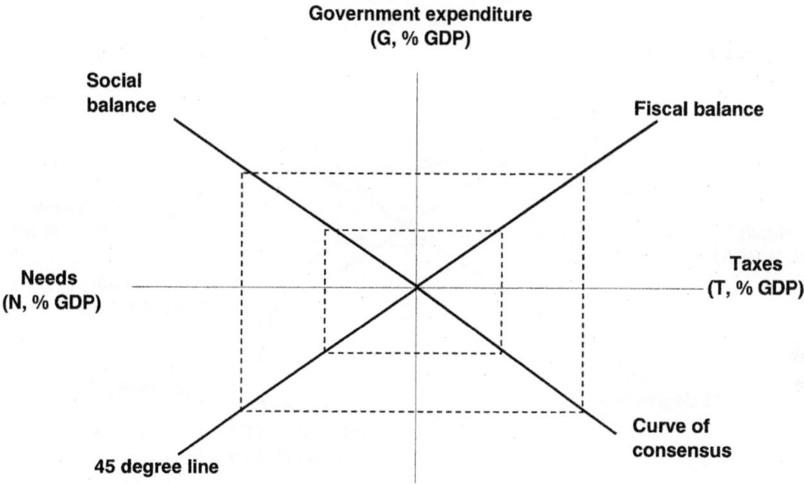


*Figure 11.5* Balance between fiscal and social needs in a stylized economy.

of perfect competition, as well as our assumption about a unitary time horizon. When we incorporate a third 45° line in the lower-left quadrant, we are ready to make a transformation between the social balance and fiscal balance curves, as illustrated in the lower-right quadrant. In such a simplified economy, the simultaneous fulfillment of social and fiscal needs is not only feasible, but is, in fact, the only possible result. We shall call this collection of points the "consensus curve."

Starting from this framework, we introduce a greater degree of realism by relaxing some assumptions:

- the time horizon is now intergenerational;
- the possibility of externalities is accepted (e.g., public goods, distinct criteria for determining taxes and allocating expenditure);
- the government can incur administrative deficiencies.

With financial markets and demographic change, the fiscal equilibrium curve is no longer the only option. Figure 11.6 illustrates a situation of growing deficits derived from the fact that agents will be more reluctant about paying taxes, the higher the fiscal charge is as a proportion of GDP. Why? Two things should be considered:

- There are externalities; this implies that government action means some kind of redistribution.
- In the extreme case where the state covers all of the agents' needs, it would have to spend more than 100 percent of GDP. The schedule for the social balance has an increasing gradient because at some point the government is less cost-effective than are the private parties in resolving their needs.

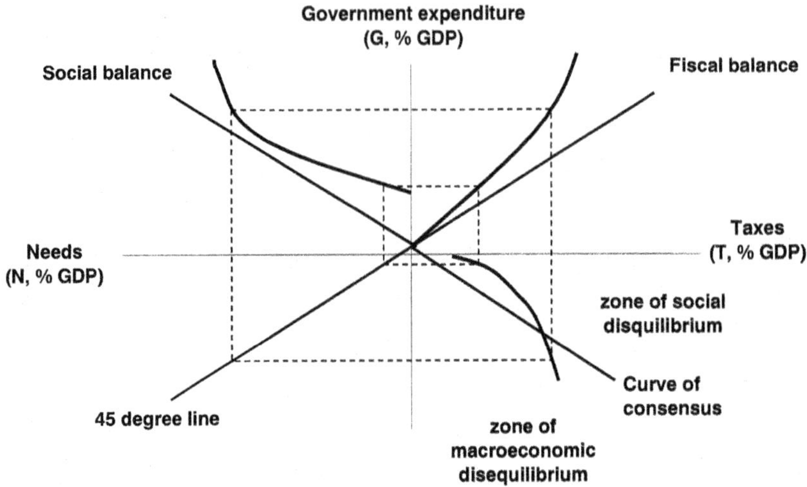


*Figure 11.6* Balance between fiscal and social needs in a less-stylized economy.

Finally, it should be noted that the curve of social balance in Figure 11.6 does not start at the origin; since the possibility of public deficits arises, the intercept reflects the financial cost of the indebtedness incurred. Thus, the natural consequence of the above is that we abandon the "curve of consensus" in the bottom-right quadrant. This also becomes a reference now in the face of a clear dilemma. Above that curve, we enjoy fiscal equilibrium at the cost of accepting a social welfare deficit. Below it, the fiscal balance takes second place and, in changing the emphasis to social needs, we run into a fiscal disequilibrium. Although this scheme does not capture all of the wealth of detail involved in the fiscal challenges, we believe it will be useful for describing Mexico's fiscal experience.

## Mexico's fiscal experience, 1970–2001

The application of the framework described in the previous section to actual Mexican data uses the concept of economic balance. Moreover, some simplifying assumptions are required. A social balance curve linking an unobserved SWF with government expenditure is necessarily a subjective element. In this respect, we have defined its intercept as the average proportion of interest payments during a specified period. Based on this data, an exponential trajectory is projected based on the arguments discussed in the previous section and we are maintaining the derivative of that function constant throughout all periods. Regarding the observations in the quadrant relating tax income and total government expenditure, these are the figures effectively registered. In the resulting graphs, we shall only use some points in this space to suggest the shape of the "curve of consensus." This procedure is applied to three periods in Mexico's fiscal accounts.

### *The state option, 1970–80*

Figure 11.7 illustrates the application of our framework to the 1970–80 period. The trajectory observed in the fiscal equilibrium quadrant is well defined; as the decade goes on, the magnitudes increase, and there is a growing deviation toward the fiscal deficit zone. This is due to the fact that the change in the ideological orientation on the role of the state in the economy led to a self-sustainable and explosive pace of spending that was not accompanied by a rise in tax-collection capacities.

The change in the pendulum in favor of greater participation by the state in the economy is a generalized phenomenon of the 1970s.[4] In the case of Mexico, its application was influenced by the view in which intervention by the state—as the only entity with sufficient resources and capacities to eliminate structural bottlenecks—is a precondition for development. Between 1970 and 1975, government spending rose from 20 to 30 percent of GDP. Nonetheless, these numbers say little about the nature of that spending and reveal even less about their own hidden dynamics.

The channeling of increased government spending has two alternatives: (i) "the market option" or monetary transfers which allow recipients to acquire goods and services produced by private companies; or (ii) "the state option" which consists of the direct production of these goods and services in SOEs. The second is ideologically closer to Mexico's tradition of those years. For reasons of space, it is enough to state that in 1980, 60.5 percent of total programmable public spending corresponded to decentralized entities and companies, whose number rose from 84 in 1970 to a record of 1,155 in 1982. For our purposes, the "state option" implies the following:

- The programmatic dispersion of government revenue sources. A large part of public revenue arises not from conventional sources (i.e., taxes), but from the sale of goods and services by SOEs.

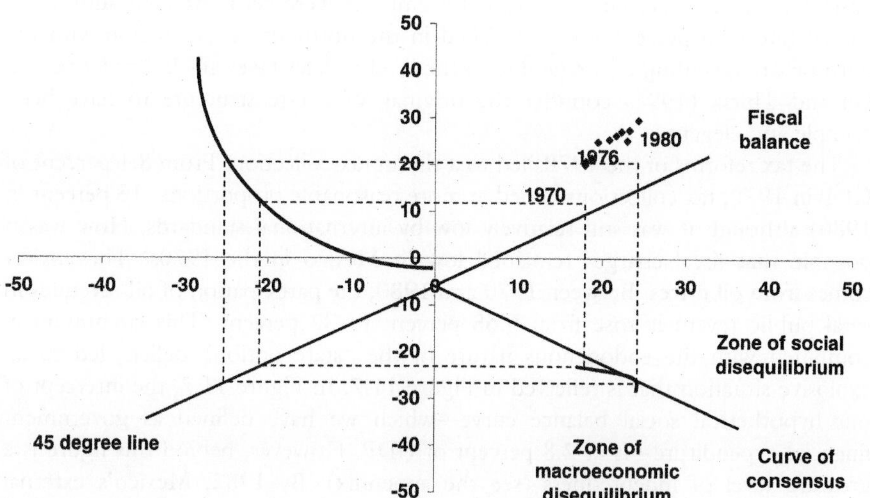


*Figure 11.7* Fiscal and social needs in Mexico, 1970–80 (as a % of GDP).

- The programmatic dispersion of sources of government expenditure. Based on the argument of social justice, many products made by SOEs were sold at prices below their production costs.

The former led to an absence of market discipline. A subsidy a SOE offers by selling below production costs has the following shortcomings:

1 Given that no access criterion is established, this implies a generalized subsidy, with a nil impact on income distribution.
2 It creates severe distortions, because it changes the allocation of resources by showing no relative scarcity.
3 It leads to lack of transparency and therefore serious administrative problems. Moreover, the accounting difficulties involved might foster irregular practices and corruption.
4 The inability to distinguish between good and bad performance among SOEs could lead to an explosive bias toward losses. No administrator will report earnings that cover the losses of other managers.

In sum, the adoption of the "state option" in Mexico offered sufficient incentives to create an explosive combination of revenue and expenditure dynamics: once it goes beyond a certain point, the deficit escapes all control.

In this respect, it is fair to say that the convenience of relying on conventional revenue sources did not go unnoticed. At the beginning of the 1970s, efforts were concentrated on the dual goals of modernization and simplification. Indirect taxes rose, for example, from 37 percent of total tax collection in 1970 to 55 percent in 1980. This reflects the introduction, in the latter year, of the value added tax (VAT), which, according to Urzúa (1994) substituted 25 federal and 300 local taxes. The basic VAT rate was set at 10 percent, but basic agricultural goods and a basic consumer basket either remained exempt or were zero-rated. In addition, a special rate of 6 percent was established in the northern border region with the purpose of preventing arbitrage due to the level of sales taxes at US border towns. Gil and Thirsk (1997) consider the original VAT rate structure to have been "simple and elegant."

The tax reforms of the 1970s led to a rise in tax collection. From 8.1 percent of GDP in 1970, tax collections ended at more reasonable proportions (15 percent in 1980) although it was still relatively low by international standards. How was it possible that fiscal charges remained low in Mexico in the 1970s? The answer comes from oil prices. Between 1970 and 1980, the participation of oil revenues in total public revenues rose from 0.65 percent to 32 percent. This circumstance, combined with the endogenous nature of the "state option" deficit, led to an explosive situation that is reflected in Figure 11.7. In Figure 11.7, the intercept of our hypothetical social balance curve—which we have defined as government financial expenditure—is at 2.8 percent of GDP. However, behind this figure is a growing level of indebtedness (see the appendix). By 1982, Mexico's external government debt had reached US$58.1 billion. As we shall see below, the consequences would not take long to appear.

### *Leviathan, 1981–90*

In 1981, the Mexican economy was characterized by: (i) very high and rising levels of foreign indebtedness, mostly featuring floating interest rates; (ii) dependence on oil, which in that year represented 70 percent of total export value and 31 percent of fiscal revenue; and (iii) a very deficient productive plant, due to the type of perverse incentives created by the "state option." Nonetheless, the opinion that prevailed was that the change required to sound the alarm bells would imply such a combination of international circumstances that its likelihood did not even merit consideration. Then, the unlikely happened.

According to Bulmer-Thomas (1994), the net barter terms of trade for the Latin American oil-producing countries fell 5 percent between 1980 and 1983. This does not include the substantial rise in international interest rates, which increased the severity of the shock. The results are well known: a tremendous crisis in the balance of payments that inaugurated the so-called lost decade in Mexico. The large number of studies this period has generated allows us to spend a very short time on this. Rather, we shall concentrate on describing the effects, as shown in Figure 11.8.

The rise in the financial cost of the public debt implies a substantial increase in the social balance curve intercept. In absolute terms, financial spending reached a historic high in 1983. Moreover, the virtual disappearance of external financing sources implied the "crowding out" of the private sector from the local funds market and a substantial increase in local interest rates; the banks' sole purpose was to finance public deficits.

The rise in interest rates had an impact on the principal debtor (the public sector) and strengthened the endogenous nature of expenditure growth, which also triggered an intense inflationary process. In a vicious circle, this gave rise to an even bigger rise in interest rates. Public revenues lost out in this mad dash due to the Oliveira-Tanzi effect on tax collection.[5]

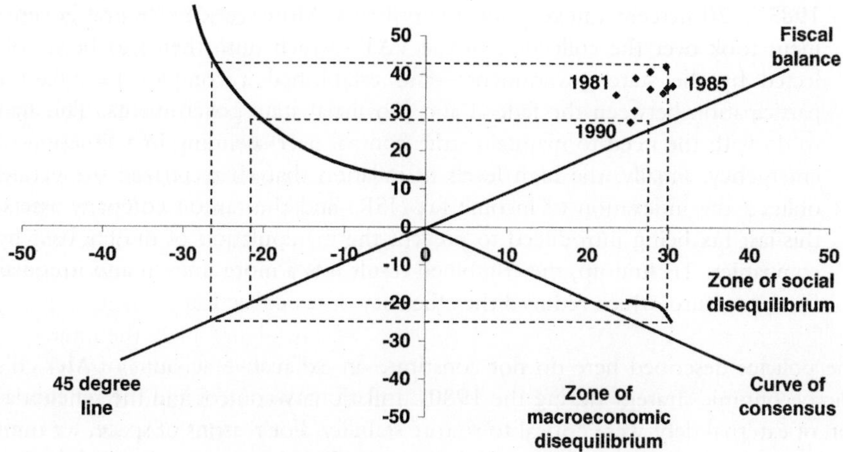


*Figure 11.8* Fiscal and social needs in Mexico, 1981–90 (as a % of GDP).

In sum, the substantial fiscal deficits registered in the upper-right quadrant of Figure 11.8 represent, like the Leviathan, a burden feeding from all that exists around it. Proof of this is the apparently surprising fact that in the lower-right quadrant, what we find is that the curve of consensus moves off and into the social deficit zone. Shouldn't it go in the opposite direction? The answer would be yes if the intercept of the social balance curve had remained constant. However, its displacement is more than proportional to that corresponding to the fiscal deficits, a fact that implies that what is available for social needs has been reduced. From this perspective and based on Mexico's experience of the 1980s, the rash justification of a fiscal deficit as a mechanism for promoting social well-being is most emphatically and sadly disqualified.

In order to prepare the ground for the discussion in the next subsection, we offer a brief description of the strategy implemented to combat the Leviathan:

1 *Privatization* is the distinctive feature of the swing in the world pendulum regarding the role of the state in the economy. In Mexico, the process reflects more pragmatic considerations: the need to increase state revenues and re-establish control over the spending process. Under these conditions, the number of SOEs fell from 872 in 1981 to 549 in 1990. Even today, exclusive public property persists in such sectors as oil and energy, due both to reasons of state revenue (surplus cash flows) and political considerations.
2 *Reducing programmable expenditure.* Given the endogenous nature of financial expenditure, efforts to re-establish equilibrium rest disproportionately on the other expenditure categories. One example is public investment, which registered an average annual change of −13.2 percent between 1981 and 1990. Its counterpart was a serious deterioration in infrastructure, both in the physical and in the human sense (health, education, attending to marginalized groups).
3 *Tax regulations.* The urgency to raise tax collections was expressed through changes in tax rates. To the general VAT tax rate of 15 percent was added, in 1983, a 20 percent category for luxury items. Moreover, the central government took over the collection of the VAT—which until then had been collected by the state governments—and established a complex formula for participation between the federal and provincial state governments. This had to do with the need to maintain strict control over spending in a situation of emergency. Finally, the high levels of inflation that characterized the period obliged the indexation of income tax (ISR) and the tax on company assets, this last tax being introduced to prevent the manipulation of the tax base by companies. To sum up, the combined result was a more uneven and irregular fiscal structure, which reduced the efficiency of tax collection.

The policies described here do not constitute an exhaustive account of Mexico's macroeconomic strategy during the 1980s. Inflationary control and the renegotiation of external debt were critical to restore stability. For reasons of space, we omit these matters from the discussion and move on directly to an analysis of the last period to be considered.[6]

### *The market option, 1991–2001*

The 1990s have often been characterized as a period of iron fiscal discipline, where deficits never exceeded 2.6 percent of GDP. As a result, the ratio of public debt to GDP in Mexico is today at one of the lowest levels among the OECD countries. Moreover, using the increasingly accepted criterion of long-term sustainability, and due to a timely reform in the pension system in the middle of the 1990s, the long-term fiscal situation also compares well by international standards.[7]

Meanwhile, it should be noted that the scale in Figure 11.9 is reduced relative to the one used for the two previous periods; in absolute terms, the fiscal magnitudes for the 1990s are lower. This reflects the dismantling of the "state option," expressed both by the low number of state-owned companies and by the privatization of services that were traditionally provided by the federal government.

These features—fiscal discipline and small government—appear to represent a new stereotype, particularly at the beginning of the decade when Mexico is frequently cited as an example of virtue based on learning from its past mistakes. This, in our opinion, is insufficient for characterizing what occurred throughout the last decade in terms of public finance in Mexico. We would begin by adding two limitations on the revenue side.

Tax collection reflects adaptations arising from distinct criteria, among which efficiency is not necessarily one of the main arguments. The example of the VAT is illustrative. In 1992, the general rate fell to 10 percent. When, in 1995, and as a result of the peso crisis, this rate returned to its original 15 percent, the enormous political cost incurred implies that even today, the VAT issue is a political taboo. Nonetheless, it has been demonstrated that the highest income brackets are the ones that capture the largest proportion of the benefits from special zero-rated or exempt tax regimes.[8]

Thus, Mexico's tax structure contains inconsistencies that are derived from the attempt to simultaneously fulfill the opposed aims of efficiency and income distribution. This has resulted in: (i) administrative complexity, which facilitates evasion;

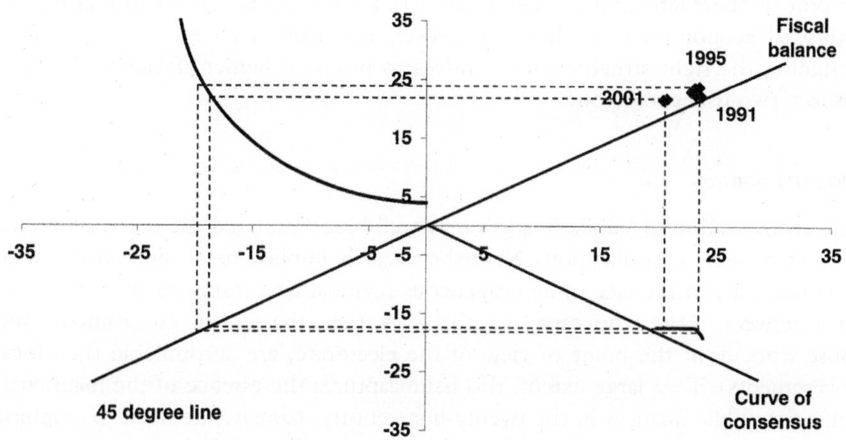


*Figure 11.9* Fiscal and social needs in Mexico, 1991–2001 (as a % of GDP).

(ii) an emphasis on direct rather than indirect taxes, which in an open economy again affects tax collection; and (iii) additional and discretionary methods of tax collection which introduce uncertainty into contributors' fiscal planning and can generate distortions. As a result, tax collection in Mexico is low by international standards and during the 1990s, it averaged 10.5 percent of GDP. Under these conditions, moreover, a large part of the effect of an increase in tax rates would be cancelled out by increased tax evasion. Silvani and Brondolo (1993) suggest that evasion represents between 30 and 37 percent of potential VAT and ISR collections.

The state of tax collection explains the dependence of Mexican public finance on nontax revenue. Between 1991 and 1999, this represented an average of 33 percent of total revenue. Oil revenue is by far the main component and the criteria used to manage PEMEX are strongly influenced by the needs of the federal government. This leads to two problems: (i) despite several administrative efforts, PEMEX does not enjoy managerial flexibility; and (ii) the federal government's dependence on this type of revenue severely limits the use of fiscal policy as an instrument of macroeconomic stabilization.

In sum, during the 1990s, fiscal policy in Mexico was marked by two strong restrictions—the condition of fiscal balance and limitations/exogeneity on the revenue side—that necessarily made spending the adjustment variable. In the mid-1990s, the restriction intensified due to the incorporation of the new commitments (i.e., reform of the pension system, the IPAB banking program and the PIDIREGAS scheme) implying an eventual increase in the intercept of the social balance curve in Figure 11.9. As a result, the public sector's capacity to attend to social needs in Mexico was severely limited, and this is reflected by the challenge to re-establish the curve of social consensus (lower-right quadrant) that still persists.

From this point of view, and given the restrictions on the balance and on tax revenue, the only alternative is to spend better. The size of the public sector is an example, given that the main problem in this area has to do with the quality, rather than the quantity, of personnel. In 1997, general government accounted for 11 percent of aggregate employment in Mexico, a lower proportion than that for the industrial economies as a whole.[9] However, the main challenge has to do with designing the right structure of incentives to promote higher efficiency.[10] In this respect, two issues stand out.

### *Decentralization*

The centralization of public finances may well have facilitated the macroeconomic process of fiscal consolidation. Nevertheless, this implied fiscal mechanisms with little flexibility in the face of heterogeneous regional circumstances, and a discrepancy between those who carry out the work (i.e., the federal government) and those who, from the point of view of the electorate, are accountable (i.e., local governments). To a large extent, this issue captures the essence of the main challenge for public finances in the twenty-first century, namely, the need to combine sound fiscal management with skill in the political process of decision-making.

In the 1990s, the emphasis of decentralization was on expenditure. Today, the federation is transferring resources to state and municipal governments in three ways (OECD 2000): (i) federal participation (about 3 percent of GDP), which are defined according to a pre-established percentage of state revenue, through the exercise of which it enjoys autonomy; (ii) federal contributions (about 4 percent of GDP), which from 1998, transferred to the local government level the administration of spending on basic education, health, infrastructure and the fight against poverty. These funds are specifically aimed at the stated programs, and only in the case of surpluses do the resources remain at the disposition of provincial state and municipal governments; and (iii) agreements to reallocate resources. The federal government can sign agreements with the state governments to transfer resources and responsibilities for specifically designated uses. In these cases, it is necessary for the applicant government to provide funds (locally collected taxes) equivalent to the amount provided by the federation.

Although decentralization is altogether advisable, we should be honest and admit that there is not a single "best practice" to follow. In countries such as Argentina and Canada, around 40 percent of total fiscal revenue is collected by local levels of government, while in Chile and the United Kingdom, this proportion is below 4 percent (Tijerina and Medellín 1998). A proper balance has to do with the capacity of subnational governments to collect taxes efficiently and to maintain an adequate degree of federal coordination.[11] Currently, 25 percent of all municipalities in Mexico receive 80.5 percent of total federal participations. Although extremely high, this concentration is even higher when total expenditure at the municipal level (i.e., federal plus locally collected funds) is considered (Figure 11.10). The former suggest a fact that cannot be stressed enough: municipalities in Mexico are better prepared at spending than at collecting taxes, a

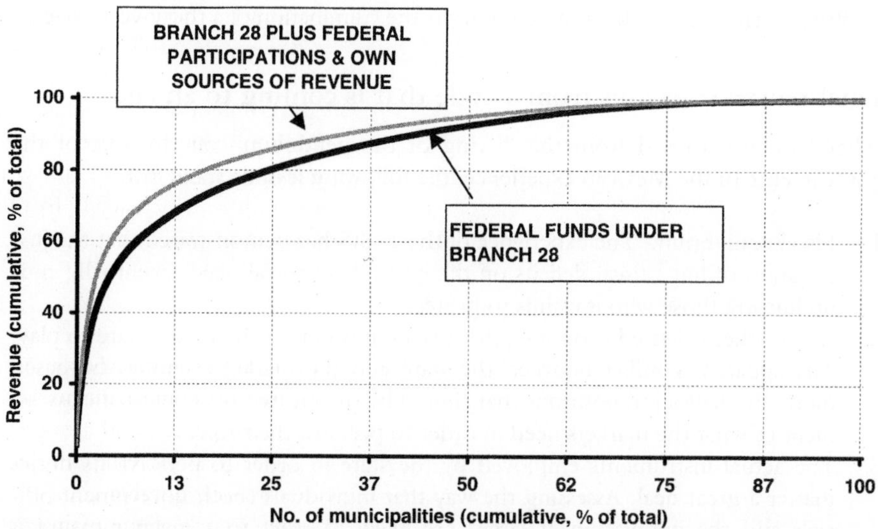


*Figure 11.10* Concentration of public revenue at the municipal level, 2000.

Source: Own estimates based on information from the National Institute of Statistics, Geography and Information (INEGI).

situation that, unless modified, can give rise to a severe inconsistency. Decentralization should be accompanied by coordination mechanisms among different levels of government in order to offer a swift and single response to unexpected macroeconomic shocks.

### *Social expenditure*

Mexico faces a serious challenge: the dividends of market reforms will fall below their full potential if they are not complemented by a strengthening in the basic capacities of the individual (health, food and education) to take advantage of the opportunities created. Subject to a strong budgetary constraint, the Mexican government has therefore been obliged to look for ways of increasing the social impact of fiscal expenditure. Although the process is underway and is certainly perfectible, it has been shown that when programs use adequate incentives, individuals respond. At its most aggregate dimension, a reallocation of the state's role is expressed by an increase in social spending (i.e., relative to health, education, social security and urban and rural development). In 2001, social expenditure represented 62.5 percent of programmable expenditure.

A similar transformation occurs in the design of programs aimed at combating extreme poverty. PROGRESA, introduced in 1997, is "designed to take into account the obvious complementarity between educational advance and progress in terms of nutrition and health" (OECD 2000: 103), in the sense that the support extended to 3.2 million families suffering from extreme poverty in 2001 is conditional on the fulfillment of certain commitments, such as sending children to school. In this respect, the main feature of Mexico's social policy is pragmatism; rather than being conceived as a substitute to the market, it seeks to recreate the basic conditions for its emergence. As such, perhaps it reflects the culmination of a thirty-year cycle.

## Final remarks: lessons from a cycle that is coming to an end

What have we learned from the "swing of the pendulum" on the role of the government? In the Mexican experience, the following lessons stand out:

1 Fiscal equilibrium. The experience of the 1980s has demonstrated that the justification of huge fiscal deficits on the grounds of social needs eventually ends up hurting those who it claims to protect.
2 In a market-oriented economy, there is an important role for the state to play. The apparent conflict between the state and the market seems to be based more on ideological positions that should be substituted by a pragmatic assessment of what the markets need in order to perform their role.
3 The actual instruments employed by the state in order to perform its duties matter a great deal. Assessing the way that individuals (both government officials and the population at large) are likely to react to a given measure is extremely important.
4 Tax policy should be guided by efficiency criteria, while issues of fairness and income distribution are better dealt with via expenditure policies.

5 Once the goals of expenditure policies have been clearly established, efficiency is also an important guideline. Three aspects seem to be particularly relevant:

   a The introduction of sound management practices that reward the maximization of available resources should be strongly encouraged.
   b Decentralization provides flexibility and accountability of public decisions. However, coordination and the promotion of a "level playing field" at the regional level should be part of a permanent dialogue among all levels of government.
   c Specific programs should make use of proper targeting and incentives in order to guarantee a high rate of social return.

In Mexico, the adoption of these principles has been a gradual process. In particular, fiscal reform aimed at increasing tax revenue is the only viable way to ensure higher spending in those areas in which current social conditions impede the generalized access to market opportunities, while at the same time guaranteeing the fiscal balance and reducing dependence on nontax sources. In other words, fiscal reform along these lines should be Mexico's main priority.

In this respect, the lessons accumulated during the past three decades imply that the nature, aims and instruments of the fiscal policy Mexico needs in the twenty-first century are clear from the technical point of view. The challenge, therefore, is of a political nature. In a democracy, support for this reform should be built from the bottom-up, and that requires providing the electorate—i.e., the taxpayer—with a comprehensive view of fiscal issues in which the need for fiscal balance is complemented by a proper understanding of the need for social balance. In sum, and as we have discussed, it implies that "someone" makes a decision and—rather than the "omniscient referee"—the only one who can make that decision is society as a whole.

## Acknowledgments

The opinions in this article are those of the authors and do not necessarily reflect the opinion of their respective organizations. The authors want to thank comments from participants in the PEO/Structure project on "Fiscal Policy Issues in the Pacific Region" and the contribution of Guillermina Rodriguez on the issue of decentralization.

## Notes

1 Details on expenditure by government levels can be found in Merino (2001).
2 On expenditure responsibilities by government levels, see Giugale and Webb (2000).
3 See Ministry of Finance and Public Credit (2003) at: www.shcp.gob.mx.
4 In 1971, Nixon declared "Now, I am a Keynesian" (Yergin and Stanislaw 1998: 60).
5 This refers to the deterioration in the real value of tax revenue due to inflation between the period in which the tax is imposed and its collection. For more on this, see Gil and Thirsk (1997).
6 For more on macroeconomic policy in the late 1980s, see Aspe (1993).
7 For more on the assessment of Mexico's long-term fiscal balance, see Sales and Videgaray (1999).

8 Tijerina and Guajardo (1998) calculate that if the VAT exemptions were eliminated, with 17.6 percent of additional tax collection, 50 percent of the poorest families would be compensated. In other words, for every peso benefit in exemptions, there is an opportunity cost of 4.7 pesos!

9 For example, in the US, the ratio is 15 percent, and in Canada and the European Union, it is 20 percent (OECD 2000).

10 For example, the OECD (2000) estimates that the present number of appointments (i.e., personnel who change with each administration) represents one-seventh of the total public workforce; this is certainly an excessive proportion.

11 For an analytical framework on decentralization, see Corbo (1995).

## References

Aspe, P. (1993) *Economic Transformation: The Mexican Way*, Cambridge, MA: MIT Press.

Bulmer-Thomas, V. (1994) *The Economic History of Latin America since Independence*, Cambridge: Cambridge University Press.

Corbo, Vito (1995) "Fiscal federalism and decentralization: a review of some efficiency and macroeconomic aspects," in M. Bruno and B. Pleskovic (eds) *Proceedings of the Annual World Bank Conference on Development Economics*, Washington, DC: World Bank.

Gil, F. and Thirsk, W. (1997) "Tax reform in Mexico," in W. Thirsk (ed.) *Tax Reform in Developing Countries*, Washington, DC: World Bank.

Giugale, M. and Webb, S. (2000) *Achievements and Challenges in Fiscal Decentralization, Lessons from Mexico*, Washington, DC: World Bank.

Merino, G. (2001) "Federalismo fiscal: diagnóstico y propuestas," *Una Agenda para las Finanzas Públicas de México*, Special Issue, *Gaceta de Economía* (Spring) ITAM: 145–84.

Ministry of Finance and Public Credit (2003) available on: www.shcp.gob.mx.

OECD (2000) *Economic Studies: México*, Paris: OECD.

Sales, C. and Videgaray, L. (1999) "The long-run sustainability of fiscal policy in Mexico: a generational accounting approach," *Economía Mexicana, Nueva Epoca* 8(2): 367–403.

Samuelson, P.A. (1955) "Diagrammatic exposition of a theory of public expenditure," *Review of Economics and Statistics* 37(Nov.): 350–6.

Santaella, J. (2001) "La viabilidad de la política fiscal 2000–2025," *Una Agenda para las Finanzas Públicas de México,* Special Issue, *Gaceta de Economía* (Spring) ITAM: 37–65.

Silvani and Brondolo (1993) "An analysis of VAT compliance," *General Trends in Taxation and the Tax Administration*, Panama City: Inter-American Center of Tax Administrations.

Tijerina, A. and Guajardo, J. (1998) *Propuesta de reforma en el impuesto al valor agregado*, research paper no. 2, Monterrey, Mexico: CADE.

Tijerina, A. and Medellín, A. (1998) *Fortalecimiento de los ingresos de los gobiernos estatales en México*, research paper no. 3, Monterrey, Mexico: CADE.

Urzúa, C. (1994) *An Appraisal of Recent Tax Reforms in México*, working paper IV–1994, Centro de Estudios Económicos, El Colegio de México.

Yergin, D. and Stanislaw, J. (1998) *The Commanding Heights*, New York: Simon & Schuster.

# 12 New Zealand

*Douglas Steel and Peter Gardiner*

## Introduction

This chapter discusses the development of fiscal policy in New Zealand in the past thirty years. There have been two distinct episodes in fiscal policy over this period: 1970–84 and 1984–present. For this reason, the discussion has been structured along chronological lines. The second section outlines the broad historical trends in fiscal policy prior to 1970, and then fiscal policy from 1970–84. The third section discusses events of 1984 and the fourth section covers the period from 1984 to the present. The final two sections discuss some fiscal policy legislation and issues that relate to fiscal policy in New Zealand today.

## Period one: 1970–84

### *Pre-1970*

The standard for fiscal policy in New Zealand between 1970 and 1984 was set in the prior two decades. During the 1950s and 1960s, the government's role in the economy continued to expand with ambitious infrastructure developments and interventionist policies. Major road, school, hospital and housing developments were to a large extent driven by demographic changes. The government also embarked on several projects aimed at broadening the economic base of the country including developments in forestry, energy and steel manufacturing.

The production and export of agricultural commodities, which earned around 85 percent of total foreign receipts, dominated the private sector. The main agricultural exports were wool, butter and lamb, and these commodities were exported through government-controlled boards. Almost all exports were sent to the United Kingdom. The New Zealand manufacturing sector had developed throughout the 1950s and 1960s, and was employing around 25 percent of the New Zealand labor force (Bassett 1998). Most manufacturing sectors were highly protected and regulated with import licensing and tariffs to limit competing imports. Additionally, government-owned financial institutions lent money to manufacturers at reduced interest rates. The government also subsidized some inputs to manufacturing, and the exchange rate was controlled to keep exports competitively priced.

Domestic prices and wages were constrained to ensure that inflation was kept under control. New Zealand had virtually no unemployment partly because of the large and expanding public sector. Taxes steadily rose over the 1960s to keep pace with government expenditure. Tax policy centered on income tax, to the point where the top marginal tax rate reached 77.5 percent in the 1950s. The New Zealand government's reliance on income tax as a source of tax revenue was high compared to other developed countries at this time (Bassett 1998).

Wages and prices steadily increased throughout the 1960s under the combined weight of government infrastructure investment that did not yield a high rate of return, and high cost structures created by a large government sector and protectionist policies. Under these conditions, it was not surprising that economic growth started to ease. Additionally, world demand began to drop, and the terms of trade took a turn for the worst when international wool prices collapsed in 1968. The New Zealand economy ended the 1960s in a somewhat delicate state.

### *1970–84*

The period between 1970 and 1984 was a difficult period for fiscal management in New Zealand. Severe changes in world demand, caused by the oil shocks of 1974 and 1979, reinforced the Keynesian "big government" position that had dominated fiscal policy in the decades prior to 1970. In response to increased oil prices and the subsequent deterioration in world demand, the government sought to strengthen its protectionist stance. New Zealand embarked on policies that emphasized export promotion (particularly in the agricultural sector), import substitution and self-sufficiency. New Zealand's policy response to the oil crisis was, in fact, similar to other developed nations at the time including Australia, the United States and Canada (Wells 1987). However, perhaps because of the country's higher dependency on its export sector, New Zealand's economic performance slipped against most other OECD countries.

Economic growth was the dominant focus of fiscal policy in the 1970s. This was to change in the early 1980s when persistent inflation and a burgeoning current account deficit became the major targets for government policy. However, there were inevitable problems in the 1970s with targeting growth since other macroeconomic variables like inflation are affected by growth. This often invoked a further policy response aimed at the emerging problem. The result was that fiscal policy in New Zealand had developed a short-term focus on growth, with additional policies used to target emerging problems.

One thing that did remain consistent until 1984 was a large and expanding public sector. Railways, communications and air travel were all operated by the state, and state-owned institutions played a dominant role in many other sectors of the economy including the financial, health and education sectors. In addition, the government tried to increase New Zealand's economic base with large-scale investments in the energy and exporting sectors. Substantial projects in such areas as gas exploration, oil refining, forestry, manufacturing, aluminum smelting and tourism were borne out of the government's desire to increase New Zealand's self-sufficiency and export base.

In the lead-up to the 1974 oil shock, inflation had crept up due to a strong surge in agricultural prices and increased government spending. The government, concerned about the effect inflation would have on real incomes, applied a general wage and price freeze for around twelve months. Immediately after the oil shock, the government instituted policies to mitigate the impact of rising oil prices on the economy. The road transport speed limit was reduced, weekend petrol sales were outlawed, and the price of petrol was increased to reduce consumption (Economic Summit Conference 1984). The oil shock caused a sharp decline in the terms of trade and the current account deficit grew.

Despite growing external demand problems, fiscal policy remained focused on growth to ease the current account deficit. The government tried to encourage growth with counter-cyclical spending initiatives such as export incentives and tax breaks, expansion of national employment schemes, and increased investment spending. These policies had the desired results: growth responded and unemployment was held to around 0.5 percent of the workforce until 1977 (Economic Summit Conference 1984). By 1977, growth was beginning to slow again, so fiscal spending was stepped up. The tax rate was lowered and substantial changes were made to the superannuation policy, lifting the total benefit payout. These measures achieved their objectives and growth picked up. However, the expanding economy renewed inflationary pressures and demand for imports, which caused a further deterioration in the current account balance. Unfortunately, government spending initiatives and declining tax revenue also pushed the government account into deficit. Figure 12.1 shows the fiscal balance as a percentage of GDP for the period 1972–2000. (It should be noted that there was a change in the accounting method used for the government accounts in the early 1990s such that the fiscal year ended in March up until 1989, and from then on, the fiscal year ended in June.)

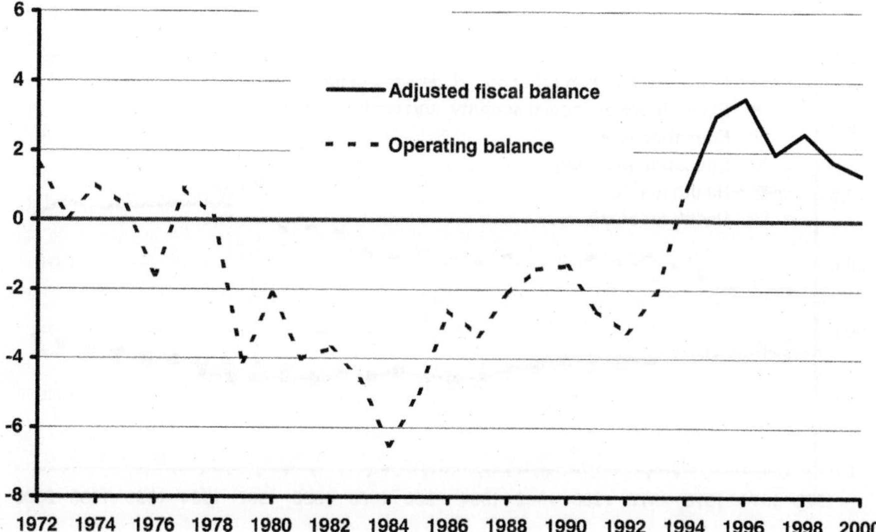


*Figure 12.1* Fiscal balance in New Zealand (as a % of GDP).

Source: New Zealand Treasury using budget data from the Minister of Finance (various years).

Throughout the 1970s, fiscal policy had been targeting growth, and it was hoped that this would encourage employment. The large government sector and several employment schemes also directly supported employment growth. However, the government provided a large and expanding welfare system for those on low incomes and those who could not work. In 1973, the government introduced a benefit for solo parents, and in 1975, the state-run pension scheme was updated. Furthermore, in 1977, the pension scheme was extended to include all New Zealanders 60 years and older. The government granted lower-income earners tax rebates and family assistance grants to help attain greater equality in income distribution. Between 1972 and 1984, government expenditure on welfare climbed from 23 to 30 percent of total expenditure. Over the same period, education expenditure fell from 20 percent of total expenditure to around 12 percent, while health expenditure fell from 17 percent to around 13 percent of government expenses. Figure 12.2 shows government expenditure on social security, health and education as a share of total expenditure over the period 1972–99. In real terms, government expenditure was expanding rapidly in order to keep pace with the growing and changing demographic profile of the New Zealand population.

A significant part of the economic strategy was to manipulate resource allocation through taxation. There was a wide range of tax increases and tax breaks, as well as subsidies, designed to promote exports. For example, a 10 percent sales tax was imposed on machinery purchases, although exporters and agriculturists were exempt. Additionally, the agricultural sector received substantial income support through various schemes.

Throughout the 1970s and early 1980s, trade policy maintained a commitment to encouraging export growth and discouraging import growth. These policies were implemented to meet several objectives. These included a broadening of New

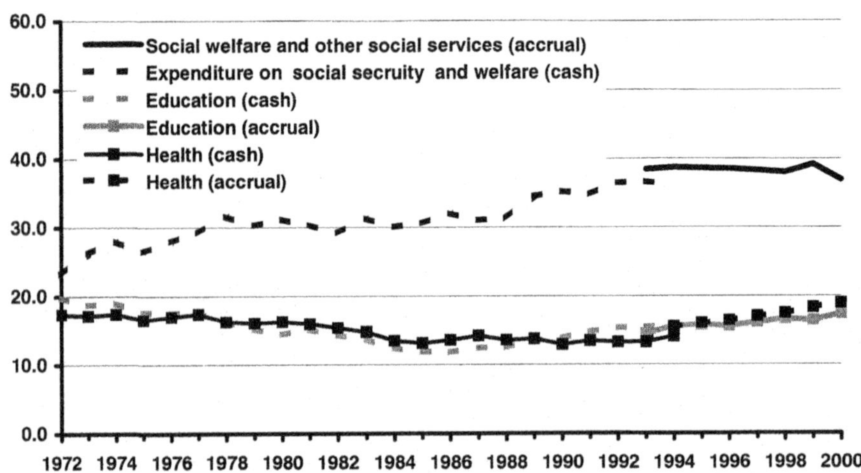


*Figure 12.2* Expenditure on welfare, health and education (as a % of total government expenditure).

Source: New Zealand Treasury using budget data from the Minister of Finance (various years).

Zealand's export base, protecting agricultural incomes and helping to control the current account deficit. Tax incentives and subsidies were given to manufacturers and exporters to encourage export diversification. For example, in the late 1970s, subsidies were granted for nontraditional agricultural exports. Farmers received government assistance to supplement incomes as declines in commodity prices were reducing incomes, especially after the 1974 and 1979 oil shocks. This supplementary income support included tax and interest rate concessions, minimum prices for products, and input subsidies for fertilizer and pest control. Imports were discouraged through import licensing and tariff controls, and the exchange rate was actively managed to maintain export competitiveness.

However, these policies had significant costs. Import controls and exchange rate devaluations contributed to input costs and inflation, which reduced the competitiveness of the export sector. In 1970, total assistance to the agricultural sector was \$NZ23 million. By 1980, this had risen to \$NZ341 million, and in 1984, total agricultural assistance had increased to over \$NZ1,000 million (Sandrey and Reynolds 1990). Although this trade policy had an impact on reducing the current account deficit, the impact was mitigated to some extent by the counter-cyclical spending initiatives of government. Figure 12.3 shows New Zealand's current account balance as a percentage of GDP from 1972 to 2000.

The government had trouble containing wage growth throughout the 1970s and early 1980s. The government relied mainly on influencing the first few wage settlements of the year, which then set a precedent for other wage negotiations. This allowed the government some control over the annual increase in wages, but little control over relative wage movements that were related to demand for skills (Wells 1987). In 1979, the government introduced the Remuneration Act, which gave it direct control over award wage rates. However, wages continued to climb, largely as a result of higher price inflation, which in fact was causing a decline in the real wage. The government tried to bring wage growth under control by

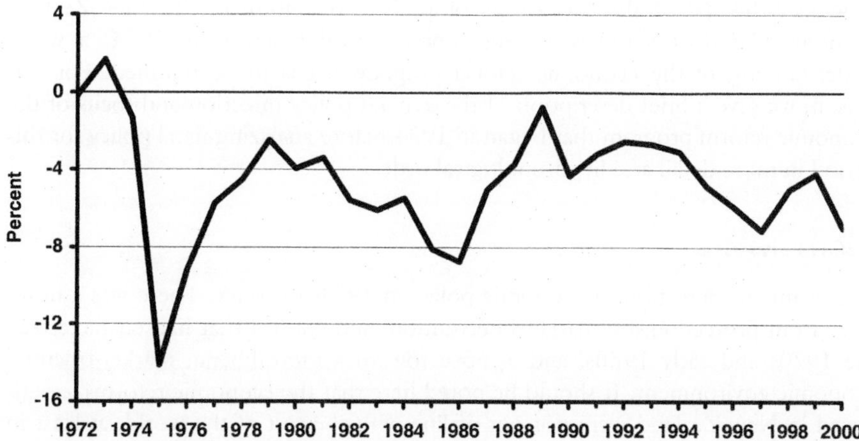


*Figure 12.3* Current account balance (as a % of GDP).

Source: Statistics New Zealand (2001).

entering into talks with unions and employers. However, these talks failed and wages continued to climb, as did inflation. In subsequent years, the government proposed a tax–wage trade-off, but this failed to get union approval, so a general wage and price freeze was imposed in mid-1982. By this time, government policy was now targeting inflation. Inflation had long been a problem, which fiscal policy had partly created by focusing on growth at the expense of other outcomes.

While the wage and price freezes were relatively effective, there were complementary factors that worked in the government's favor. These included a contraction in demand throughout 1982–83 and tax cuts that helped to soften the blow of the wage freeze (Economic Summit Conference 1984). The tax cuts contributed to a decline in the fiscal balance, which created an additional decline in the current account balance. The tax cuts also held consumption up, so that when the price and wage freezes were lifted in 1984, imports rose and the current account balance declined further. The mounting current account deficit and widespread speculation on the New Zealand currency intensified the pressure on the currency.

In the lead-up to the 1984 election, fiscal policy had evolved to the point where there was a large public sector and a substantial reliance on government intervention to allocate New Zealand's resource base. By 1984, government expenditure had grown to 38.3 percent of GDP, up from 24.9 percent of GDP in 1972. Significantly, government debt had reached high levels, unemployment and the current account deficit were growing, and a currency crisis provided the catalyst for a substantial deregulation of the New Zealand economy over the years to follow.

## A turning point: 1984

A pivotal year for the direction of economic policy in New Zealand was 1984. A growing fiscal deficit, ever-increasing public debt and an expanding current account deficit led many to believe that the economic structure of the economy could not be maintained. The economic crisis of the early 1980s, which came to a head in 1984, paved the way for a comprehensive reform of the New Zealand economy. To discuss the issues surrounding fiscal policy from 1984, a wider understanding of the economic reform program needs to be outlined. For this reason, we give a brief description of the general policy direction and focus of the economic reform program that began in 1984 before analyzing fiscal policy for this period in more detail and in chronological order.

### *Reform overview*

The change in direction of economic policy in 1984 was stark. There was a move away from protectionism, market intervention, and control that had characterized the 1970s and early 1980s, and a move toward a more liberal, market-oriented economic environment. It should be noted here that the economic reforms experienced in New Zealand were not out of line with the rest of the world, at least in terms of direction. However, the scope and depth of the reform program were perhaps larger than that experienced by most other countries.

The election of the Labour Party in July 1984 saw the beginning of an extensive program of economic reform that was to take place in New Zealand over the next one-and-a-half decades. As described earlier, in the 1970s and early 1980s, policy was focused on stabilization objectives. However, these objectives were not transparent. Stabilization efforts were made through intervention and demand management policies. The reforms that began in 1984 walked away from such stabilization efforts. There was greater focus on implementing stable policies rather than stabilization policies, and the emphasis had changed toward policies that were sustainable in the longer term. Evans *et al.* (1996) suggest that the key intellectual principles underlying the reforms in New Zealand can be characterized as the pursuit of coherent policies on a broad front, credibility and time consistency, a comparative institutional approach and efficient contracting arrangements.

To provide a better feel for the scope of the reforms that began in 1984, more detail is provided here. The following summary is based largely upon Evans *et al.* (1996). The timing of these reforms is discussed later when we discuss the evolution of fiscal policy over this period. The reforms (in no particular order) included the following:[1]

- *Financial market and monetary policy*: the removal of foreign exchange controls, the removal of interest rate controls, the floating of the New Zealand dollar, the move to fully funding fiscal deficits through bond issues, and the setting of specific targets for monetary policy.
- *Goods market*: the removal of price and rent freezes, the removal of agricultural subsidies and export assistance, the removal of import licensing and tariffs (although some low tariffs remained), and the introduction of light-handed regulation.
- *Labor market*: the lifting of the wage freeze and the introduction of a new employment law that replaced centralized bargaining structures with enterprise-based bargaining.
- *Public sector reform*: corporatization and privatization, changes to public sector employment conditions and contracting arrangements, a move to accrual accounting, tax reform, and specific targets for fiscal policy.
- *Tax reform*: broadening of the tax base, simplification of the system, and flattening of the tax scale. Generally there was a move to indirect taxation including the introduction of a goods and services tax (GST).

While this list is not complete, it provides a flavor of the scope of the changes over the last decade and a half.

## The second period: 1984–present

### *1984*

The main aim of fiscal policy following the 1984 general election was to restore fiscal balance. The fiscal deficit had ballooned to 6.5 percent of GDP in the lead-up to the election. Public debt had increased dramatically over the decade, reaching 31.5 percent of GDP in 1984 compared to 4.5 percent in 1974. Along with the aim of restoring fiscal balance came the decision to fully fund fiscal deficits with the issue of bonds. As a result, public debt continued to rise strongly from 1984. (The level and structure of debt are discussed later.) However, the funding of deficits through bonds allowed monetary policy to concentrate on reducing inflation.

The road to restoring fiscal balance was a long and winding one, and a fiscal surplus was not achieved until the 1994 fiscal year. Why did it take so long to achieve fiscal balance? To answer this question, we follow the paths of revenue and expenditure through time from 1985.

### *1985–88*

On the revenue side, there was strong growth from 1985 to 1988. Figure 12.4 shows government revenue as a percentage of GDP over the period 1972–2000. There were perhaps three main reasons for the strong growth from 1985 through to 1988. One reason was the economic growth that New Zealand experienced during this period, driven largely by robust export performance. Export volumes grew by an average of 5.2 percent per annum over this period. The second reason for the strong revenue growth was strong inflation. Following the removal of the wage and price freezes in 1984, consumer price inflation returned to double-digit rates in 1985 and remained there until the end of 1987. A third reason for the increase in government revenue was tax reform.

Wells (1996: 219) notes that the main objectives of tax reform since 1984 have been to broaden the tax base, simplify the system and flatten the rate scale. A major step to broadening the tax base was made in October 1986 with the introduction of a goods and services tax (GST). The GST replaced sales and indirect taxes, and there were no significant exemptions. The GST rate was initially set at 10 percent, although this was raised to 12.5 percent in 1989. Income taxes were restructured and reduced at the same time that the GST was introduced.

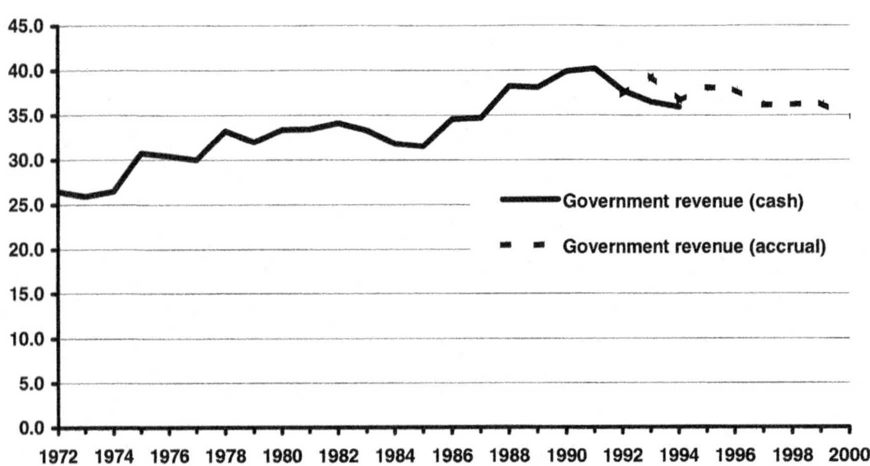


*Figure 12.4* Government revenue, 1972–2000 (as a % of GDP).

Source: New Zealand Treasury using budget data from the Minister of Finance (various years).

Expenditure growth lagged behind revenue growth in the financial years 1985 and 1986, bringing an improvement in the fiscal deficit in those years. There were significant reductions in expenditure on assistance to industry following the 1984 election. Partly offsetting this were rising finance costs from high debt levels and rising social welfare payments. Expenditure as a percentage of GDP fell in FY85 (as shown in Figure 12.5).

The corporatization and privatization of the public sector started in 1987, although the intention was signalled earlier in the 1984 budget. Trading departments were converted into state-owned enterprises (SOEs), and each SOE was to function as a business. Evans *et al.* (1996) note that SOEs did act commercially, typically reducing their workforces and pricing their services on a more commercial basis. The shedding of labor in state-owned enterprises helped push up the unemployment rate and associated fiscal costs. A major correction in world and New Zealand equity markets in 1987 and subsequent lackluster economic growth also helped to raise the unemployment rate.

Despite revenue growing faster than expenditure in 1984–88, the fiscal budget remained in deficit throughout (as illustrated in Figure 12.1). These persistent deficits and the decision in 1984 to fully fund these deficits through the issue of bonds resulted in an increase in the level of debt. As shown in Figure 12.6, net debt rose from 31.5 percent of GDP in 1984 to 46.4 percent in 1987. The higher debt levels helped push expenditure on debt servicing up from 5.2 percent of GDP in 1984 to 7.9 percent in 1988.

The sale of some SOEs occurred in 1988. Part of the revenue generated from these sales was used to retire debt, and as a result, net debt as a percentage of GDP fell to 41.5 percent in 1988. The proceeds from privatization went primarily to pay off debt that was denominated in foreign currency. The evolution of the denomination of New Zealand's public debt is shown in Figure 12.7. The repayment of foreign currency debt in 1988 is clear.

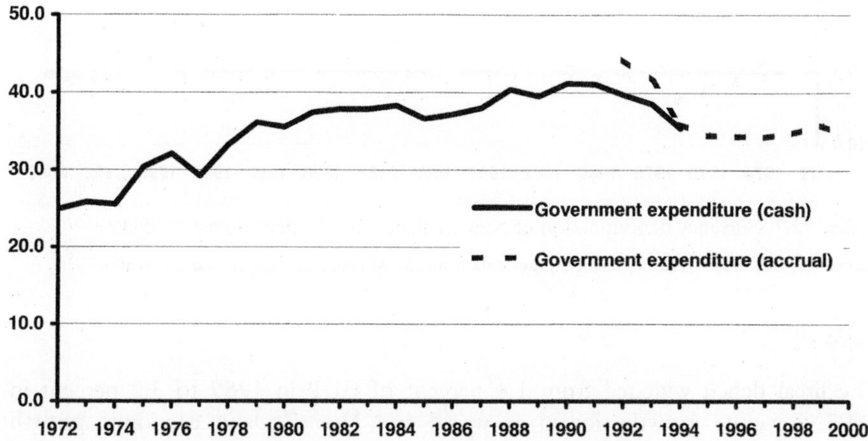


*Figure 12.5* Government expenditure, 1972–2000 (as a % of GDP).

Source: New Zealand Treasury using budget data from the Minister of Finance (various years).

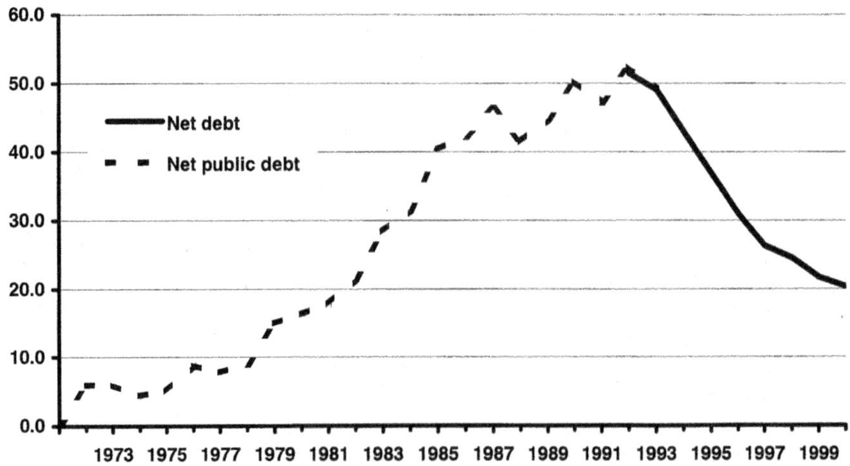


*Figure 12.6* Government net debt, 1972–2000 (as a % of GDP).

Source: New Zealand Treasury using budget data from the Minister of Finance (various years).

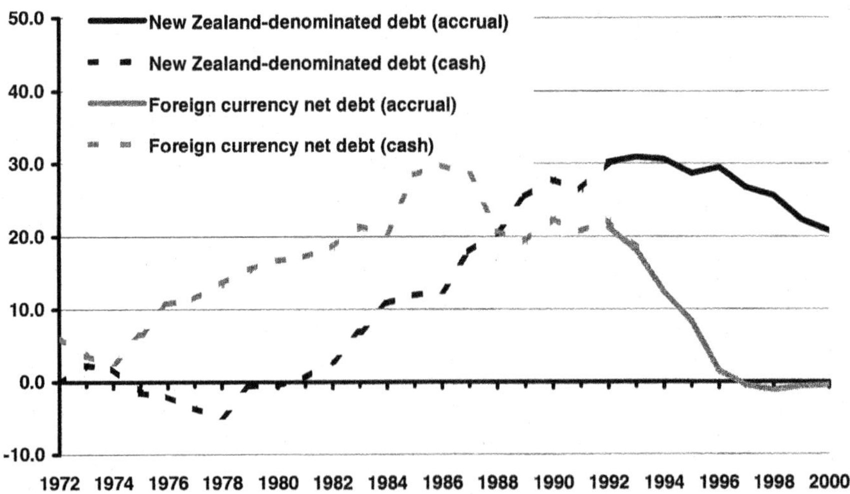


*Figure 12.7* Currency denomination of New Zealand's public debt (as a % of GDP).

Source: New Zealand Treasury using budget data from the Minister of Finance (various years).

### *1989–92*

The fiscal deficit widened from 1.4 percent of GDP in 1989 to 3.2 percent in 1992. Revenue growth slowed as world and New Zealand economic growth slowed in part as a fallout from the world equity market correction in 1987. However, revenue grew to 39.9 percent of GDP in 1990 as the corporate tax rate was lifted from 28 to 33 percent, and GST was lifted from 10 to 12.5 percent.

The effect of the world's economic slowdown on New Zealand government revenue postponed the targeted fiscal balance that policy had set out to achieve. However, the reforms continued. Two that are worth mentioning here because of their wider economic effects rather than their fiscal policy implications are the Reserve Bank of New Zealand Act (1989) and the Employment Contracts Act (1991).

The Reserve Bank of New Zealand Act (1989) essentially legislated the role of monetary policy. The act gave greater independence to the Reserve Bank and set price stability as the goal for monetary policy. The act followed the overall focus of policy since the change of economic direction in 1984 in that it made the objective of monetary policy explicit and increased the transparency of operations. The original monetary policy target was to get annual consumer price inflation (CPI) below 2 percent and once achieved, keep it within a band of 0–2 percent. However, this band was extended to 0–3 percent in 1996.

The Employment Contracts Act (1991) was another major piece of legislation. Again, this legislation had limited direct impact on the fiscal balance, but was a significant part of the deregulation of the New Zealand economy.

As mentioned previously, the labor shedding induced by corporatization and privatization through the latter years of the 1980s helped push up the unemployment rate. As a result, government expenditure on social security and welfare rose sharply, reaching 14.5 percent of GDP in 1990 as compared to 11.8 percent three years earlier. Figure 12.8 shows the level of government expenditure on social security and welfare from 1972 through to 2000.

On the expenditure side, there were significant changes between 1989 and 1992. These changes followed the National Party victory in the 1990 general election. The 1991 budget came to be known as "the mother of all budgets" and it included cuts to social welfare benefit rates and tighter eligibility criteria for receiving benefits. Superannuation rates were held constant so that the usual indexation

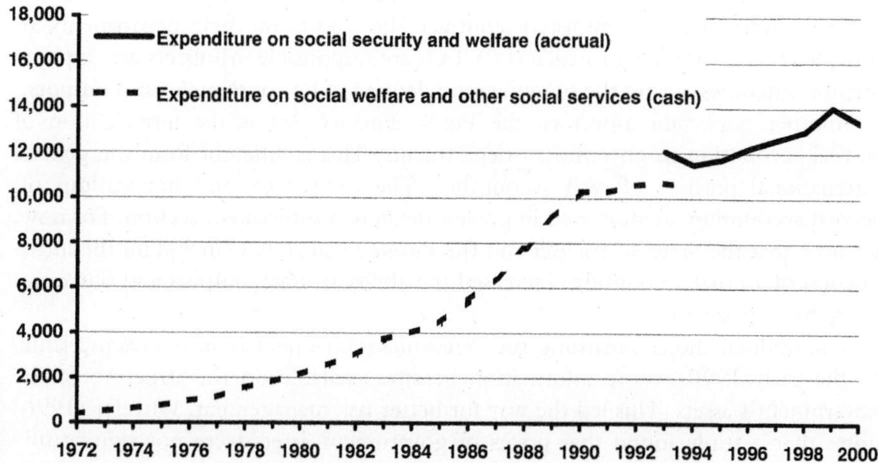


*Figure 12.8* Social security and welfare spending, 1972–2000 ($NZ million).

Source: New Zealand Treasury using budget data from the Minister of Finance (various years).

increase did not occur and the age of eligibility was gradually raised from 60 to 65. Looking forward to the present day, superannuation remains a large fiscal issue, perhaps the largest. (We discuss the superannuation issue later.)

It can be seen from Figure 12.8 that "the mother of all budgets" had a major impact on what had been ever-increasing social security and welfare expenditure. This impact is even more remarkable given that the unemployment rate increased from an average 7.1 percent in 1989 to an average 10.3 percent in 1992.

The larger fiscal deficit in 1992 compared to 1989 meant that net debt increased further over this period. Most of the increase was in New Zealand dollar-denominated debt, as shown in Figure 12.7. In line with the credibility and time-consistent principles of the economic reforms, attempts were made to make fiscal policy more transparent. It was thought that greater transparency would lead to more accountability, and more accountability would ultimately lead to better decision-making. This period saw much public sector reform through corporatization and privatization. The focus here was to improve efficiency in the public sector. Two key pieces of legislation with regard to corporatization were the State Sector Act (1988) and the Public Finance Act (1989).

The State Sector Act (1988) followed the State Owned Enterprises Act (1986) that decoupled ministers from the day-to-day management of SOEs. The new act changed the employment rules for government department heads. Prior to the act, it was unclear who was responsible for each government department and basically two views prevailed. The first was the traditional Westminster view that the minister is responsible for everything in his/her portfolio. The second, the so-called realist view, was that ministers could not be expected to take the rap for things they did not know about and did not authorize (Martin 1995). The State Sector Act establishes that CEOs of government departments are employed on fixed-term contracts under performance criteria that are agreed upon between the CEO and the minister, with the CEO being directly accountable to the minister.

The Public Finance Act (1989) gives the means to assess the performance of the CEOs. Under this act, ministers contract the CEOs of their departments to provide specific outputs for which the CEOs are responsible. Ministers are responsible for outcomes, where the outcomes are defined to be consequences of outputs.

Another important aspect to the Public Finance Act is the introduction of accrual accounting to government departments. This is different from the general international practice of cash accounting. The change to, and implications of, accrual accounting are discussed in greater detail in a subsequent section. For now, we note that the State Sector Act and the Public Finance Act (including the introduction of accrual accounting) increased the ability to track outputs and outcomes from the state sector.

The optimal choice regarding the denomination of debt is an interesting issue. In the early 1990s, more information became available on the structure of the government's assets. This led the way for better risk management. Wheeler (1996) notes that a study found that prices of government assets were not significantly sensitive to exchange rate movements, implying that holding foreign currency debt in the government's debt portfolio introduced significant variability to the government's net worth. This led to the objective of achieving zero net foreign currency debt. However, there has been debate on whether the policy of reducing foreign currency debt was optimal.

Fowlie and Wright (1997) show, using Bohn's (1990) generalized version of Barro's (1979) model of smoothing tax rates over time, that the strategy of retiring foreign currency-denominated debt may not have been optimal in the New Zealand case. Fowlie and Wright argue that higher domestic currency debt can undermine the credibility of monetary policy as surprise inflation can reduce the real value of the government's debt. This is particularly so when foreigners own a large fraction of the domestic-denominated debt.

### *1993–99*

After a decade of focusing fiscal policy on the fiscal balance, a fiscal surplus was finally achieved in the 1994 financial year. The fiscal balance turned around sharply in 1993 and 1994 as the economic fortunes of New Zealand lifted in line with the recovery in world economic growth. By 1996, the fiscal surplus was 3.6 percent of GDP. This strengthening of the fiscal accounts led to an income tax cut in 1996, and continued fiscal surpluses led to another income tax cut in 1998. Strong economic growth produced strong taxation revenue and reduced expenditure on social security and welfare. Revenue grew by 10.5 percent between 1992 and 1994, although it remained steady as a percentage of GDP at 36.6 percent in 1994.

Expenditure on health and education as a percentage of GDP rose in the second half of the 1990s. In 1994, expenditures on health and education were each at 5.6 percent of GDP. Expenditure in these areas rose to 6.6 percent and 5.9 percent of GDP in 1999, respectively. Expenditure on social welfare and other social services declined slightly as a percentage of GDP, from 13.9 percent in 1994 to 12.9 percent in 1999. The small decline mirrors a similar-sized decline in the unemployment rate over this period, which fell from an average 8.3 percent in 1994 to an average 7.3 percent in 1999.

The fiscal surpluses from 1994 on have been used to pay off debt. Privatization proceeds were also used to retire debt over this period. Figure 12.6 illustrates the dramatic fall in net debt over this period, and Figure 12.7 shows that the focus was on paying foreign currency-denominated debt first. In fact, by 1997 New Zealand had negative net foreign currency-denominated debt. New Zealand dollar-denominated debt has been decreasing since peaking at 30.9 percent of GDP in 1993.

Debt repayment has meant that financing costs have fallen. Total financing costs as a percentage of GDP peaked in 1988 at 7.9 percent, and have fallen steadily since to reach 2.3 percent in 2000 (Figure 12.9). This decline in financing costs has helped improve the fiscal balance while allowing spending on health and education to increase.

In 1994, the government moved to an accrual-based accounting framework. The move to accrual accounting completed a sequence of reforms aimed at improving the quality of government expenditure and constraining future governments by bringing greater transparency to government accounting. Some differences between the cash-based accounting framework and the accrual accounting system used in New Zealand are explained in more detail below.

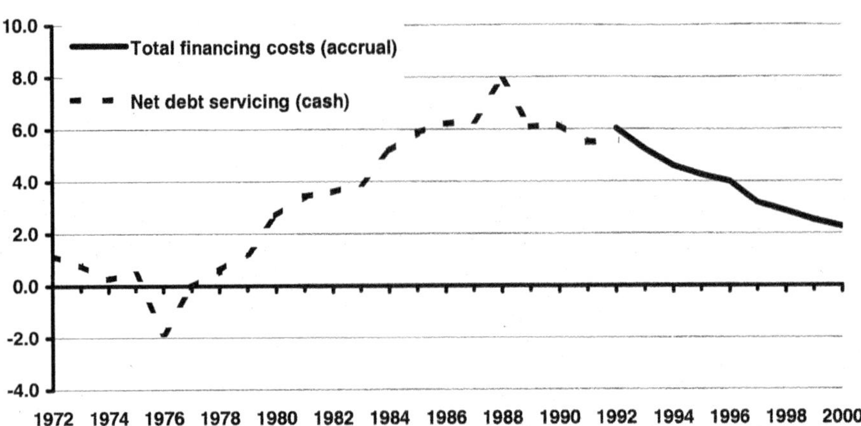


*Figure 12.9* Debt-financing costs, 1972–2000 (as a % of GDP).

Source: New Zealand Treasury using budget data from the Minister of Finance (various years).

The 1993–99 period saw the introduction of a unique piece of legislation with regard to fiscal policy. The Fiscal Responsibility Act (1994) reflected the general thinking from 1984 that fiscal policy should be aimed at the longer-term health of the economy. The Fiscal Responsibility Act, building on the State Sector Act (1988) and the Public Finance Act (1989), was aimed at making fiscal policy more transparent so that accountability was increased and uncertainty surrounding the longer-term future of fiscal management was reduced.

In a sense, the Fiscal Responsibility Act is the fiscal counterpart of the Reserve Bank of New Zealand Act which is the basis of monetary policy. Both acts focus on transparency of policy objectives with the aim of increasing accountability, thereby leading to better fiscal and monetary policy decisions and providing better economic outcomes. (The Fiscal Responsibility Act is discussed in greater detail below.) The success of the act is yet to be fully determined, as it is fundamentally a long-term policy prescription.

### *1999 to present*

The Labour Party won the November 1999 general election under mixed member proportional representation. It formed a coalition government with the Alliance Party, with parliamentary support from the Green Party. The coalition government moved away from the free-market economic philosophy that had been followed for the previous fifteen years. A freeze on tariff reductions, an increase in the top marginal tax rate, the introduction of a new employment law giving more power to unions, and the renationalization of accident insurance were four of many changes made by the new government. The impact of these and other changes on the fiscal situation are not yet clear.

## The Fiscal Responsibility Act (FRA)

The Fiscal Responsibility Act (FRA) was introduced in New Zealand in 1994, and its key purpose was to increase the transparency and accountability of fiscal policy. The act sets out principles for responsible fiscal management, aimed primarily at sound debt and risk management. It also put in place a system of disclosure statements whereby the government outlines short-, medium- and long-term fiscal policy strategies, and provides regular updates of fiscal performance and projections measured against strategic policy targets.

Like the Reserve Bank of New Zealand Act (RBA) of 1989, the FRA is more about policy processes than targets. The RBA provides a framework for conducting monetary policy whereby the government makes the policy goals explicit and policy is set in a transparent manner. Likewise, the FRA provides a framework for fiscal policy whereby fiscal goals are made explicit and policy is developed and conducted in a transparent manner. For example, the FRA's disclosure requirements include:

- a budget policy statement specifying broad strategic priorities for the upcoming budget, intentions for the next three years and long-term fiscal policy objectives;
- a fiscal strategy report that accompanies the budget and indicates whether the economic and fiscal update is in line with the government's short-term fiscal intentions as set out in the most recently published Budget Policy Statement. Where those intentions have changed, the government must state why and provide an amended version of them;
- the publication of a substantial array of fiscal information throughout the year.

In the past, the New Zealand government tended to lump all of these statements and reports into the annual budget policy statement. Because these reports were released on an annual basis, it was not unusual for a statement to include a number of major "surprises" in terms of both policy and fiscal performance. While it made the statements more interesting, markets generally do not like surprises. Hence, the disclosure regime attempts to drip-feed information to the public well in advance of comprehensive financial and policy statements.

Perhaps the most important aspect of the FRA is in terms of credibility. Like the RBA, the FRA formalizes the transparency of policy. While most of the changes to disclosure and policy processes may well have occurred without the compulsion of legislation, setting the framework out in a formal act adds a degree of credibility that any voluntarily observed guidelines would have lacked. Accrual accounting adds to the transparency of the government's accounts and helps give credibility to the FRA. By effectively taking the mystery out of policy setting, both the FRA and the RBA improve policy credibility and hence provide a more stable base for interaction with the wider community on policy issues.

The complete adoption of accrual accounting in 1994 was a major shift away from the standard international cash-based accounting system. The use of an accrual-based system provides a clear picture of the contractual and obligations of the government, hence giving a clearer picture of the overall fiscal position. Accrual accounting includes noncash items such as revaluations. For example, over 60 percent of the difference between the operating balance (under GAAP) and the adjusted financial balance shown in Figure 12.1 is due to a net foreign currency loss.

## Current and future fiscal policy issues

We now discuss perhaps the most important fiscal policy issue that is yet to be resolved in New Zealand, that is, superannuation. We all know the world is getting older as the baby boomers begin to enter their retirement years. The fiscal impacts of this demographic transition are probably the most important current fiscal issue for New Zealand and the rest of the world. The most obvious fiscal impact of an aging population is the increase in necessary expenditure through public pension provision and public health care. But what are governments doing to ensure that the funding of retirement expenses is met in an optimal way?

There has been a great deal of research into the fiscal impacts of the aging population. One report by Cook and Savage (1995) at the New Zealand Institute of Economic Research used a long-term model based on an accounting framework to examine the fiscal affordability of an aging population in New Zealand. The model projected future superannuation, education, health and social welfare benefits as a function of the demographic profile. Based on a range of demographic, economic and policy assumptions, these costs are forecast out to 2050. Other fiscal expenses, such as debt servicing and discretionary expenses, and revenues were forecast using assumptions about key economic variables. The model projects the main fiscal indicators: total government expenses, total government revenue, government operating balance, gross public debt, net public debt and net worth.

A central scenario using the likely future tracks of the key economic variables was investigated using the model. The fiscal forecasts generated by this scenario reveal that, if the assumptions underpinning the scenario actually eventuate, then the overall fiscal position would improve over time and the New Zealand superannuation scheme is affordable (Cook and Savage 1995: 5).

So what is the problem? Cook and Savage run a number of alternative scenarios and find that the model projections are sensitive to the underlying assumptions. The fiscal outcomes are particularly sensitive to assumptions about productivity and changes in the participation rate, both of which drive economic growth. Cook and Savage also find that the starting point from which New Zealand approaches the demographic pressures will be important in determining whether New Zealand returns to a period of accumulating debt. Any significant fiscal loosening could create a cycle of mounting debt and debt-servicing costs. This highlights the need to gain multiparty agreement on a sustainable superannuation policy. A credible and transparent superannuation policy with multiparty support would help to create certainty regarding the superannuation policy for New Zealanders. This would allow people to plan ahead for their retirement and would lead to a better outcome.

In October 2001, the Labour government passed as law the New Zealand Superannuation Bill, which established a fund to partially pre-fund future New

Zealand superannuation payments. The government will make annual capital contributions to the fund based on the expected future payments of superannuation and the expected annual return on investment of the fund's assets over a forty-year rolling horizon. To allow sufficient capital to accumulate, partial funding of superannuation payments from the fund will begin around 2020. The fund is expected to cover about 20 percent of total superannuation payments.

In the first three years of the fund's operation, the government plans to build toward making the full capital contributions to the superannuation fund. This transition period is to prevent undue pressure being placed on the government's fiscal position while structural surpluses are raised to the required levels. The government's contribution to the superannuation fund was $NZ600 million in the 2002 financial year. The 2002 budget has also earmarked $NZ1,200 million, $NZ1,800 million and $NZ2,100 million for the three following fiscal years.

Superannuation remains a contentious issue in New Zealand. The main opposition party has stated that it wishes to change the current funding arrangements.

## Acknowledgments

The assistance of Phil Briggs and Frances Gamble is gratefully acknowledged.

## Note

1 While the sequencing of economic reform is important, the aim here is to provide a broad understanding of the extensiveness of the reforms that have taken place.

## References

Barro, R.J. (1979) "On the determination of public debt," *Journal of Political Economy* 87(5): 940–71.

Bassett, M. (1998) *The State in New Zealand 1840–1984: Socialism Without Doctrines?*, Auckland: Auckland University Press.

Bohn, H. (1990) "Tax smoothing with financial instruments," *American Economic Review* 80(5): 1217–30.

Cook, D. and Savage, J. (1995) *The Fiscal Impacts of an Ageing Population*, New Zealand Institute of Economic Research Working Paper 95/33, Auckland: New Zealand Institute of Economic Research.

Economic Summit Conference (1984) *A Briefing on the New Zealand Economy*, Wellington: Government Printer.

Evans, L., Grimes, A., Wilkinson, B. and Teece, D. (1996) "Economic reform in New Zealand 1984–95: the pursuit of efficiency," *Journal of Economic Literature* 34(4):1856–902.

Fowlie, K. and Wright, J. (1997) "Optimal currency denomination of public debt in New Zealand," *New Zealand Economic Papers* 31(2): 137–51.

Martin, J. (1995) "Contracting and accountability," in Jonathon Boston (ed.) *The State Under Control*, Wellington: Bridget Williams Books Ltd.

Minister of Finance (various years) *Budget*, Wellington: Government Printer/PrintLink.

New Zealand Treasury (1995) *Fiscal Responsibility Act 1994: An Explanation*, Wellington: Government Printer/PrintLink, available on: www.treasury.govt.nz.

Sandrey, R. and Reynolds, R. (1990) *Farming Without Subsidies: New Zealand's Recent Experience*, Auckland: Ministry of Agriculture and Fisheries.

Statistics New Zealand (2001) INFOS (Information Network for Official Statistics) database. Auckland, available on: www.stats.govt.nz/domino/external/infos/ifwclient.nsf/htmldocs/infoshomepage?OpenDocument.

Stephens, B. (1987) "Social policy reforms: in retrospect and prospect," in A. Bollard and R. Buckle (eds) *Economic Liberalisation in New Zealand*, Sydney: Allen and Unwin, pp. 299–329.

Treasurer and Minister of Finance (2000) *Financial Statements of the Government of New Zealand for the Year Ended 30 June 2000*, Wellington: Government Printer/PrintLink, available on: www.treasury.govt.nz/financialstatements/year/jun00/statement.asp.

Wells, G. (1987) "The changing focus of fiscal policy," in A. Bollard and R. Buckle (eds) *Economic Liberalisation in New Zealand*, Sydney: Allen and Unwin, pp. 283–98.

Wells, G. (1996) "Fiscal policy," in B. Silverstone, A. Bollard and R. Lattimore (eds) *Contributions to Economic Analysis*, vol. 236, Amsterdam: Elsevier Science B.V.

Wheeler, G. (1996) *New Zealand's Experience with Autonomous Sovereign Debt Management*, available on: www.nzdmo.govt.nz.

# 13 Peru

*Eduardo Moreno and Jose L. Pereyra*

## Introduction

In the past decade, the Peruvian economy has faced deep changes that originated from fiscal and monetary policies, on the one hand, and natural disasters and external shocks, on the other. In examining fiscal behavior in Peru, the analysis takes into consideration three different periods: 1990–97, 1998 to the first half of 2000, and the second half of 2000 to the present.

In the first period, 1990–97, the Peruvian government launched an aggressive stabilization program aimed at liberalizing and deregulating the economy which faced hyperinflation, but it had almost no international reserves and was isolated from international financial markets. Under a successful stabilization process supported by sound monetary discipline, inflation was reduced from 7,650 percent to less than 7 percent, international reserves increased from US$510 million to more than US$10 billion and, due to strong fiscal policy, the fiscal imbalance went from 8.7 percent of GDP to an overall surplus of 0.2 percent of GDP in 1997, the first fiscal surplus in more than thirty-five years.

The second period, 1998 to the first half of the year 2000, is characterized by an economy facing external financial shocks and natural disasters, demand recession and a drop in tax collection. In addition to the effect of the recession on revenues, fiscal discipline was affected by an increase on both central government expenditure and tax benefits. All of these events provoked a performance that could create a serious fiscal imbalance and an unsustainable fiscal situation in the medium term.

Under such difficult circumstances, since the second half of 2000, the current government has begun an emergency fiscal program that is targeted toward reducing expenditures and restoring the active tax policy which focused on a gradual elimination of tax benefits and reduction in both tax evasion and tax elusion.

This chapter is intended to explain how these fiscal events happened, what their causes were and how Peruvian fiscal policy reacted. Even though it is difficult to provide a unique answer about how a government must behave under specific circumstances, lessons like these help to act prudently and with a long-term in sight.

## An overview of the Peruvian public sector

In this section we provide a brief description of the institutional arrangements underlying fiscal policy operations in Peru. The section begins with a description of the structure of the public sector, the relationship between the central government and other public entities, and their effects on fiscal policy. A section on the sources of financing of the fiscal deficit follows, including an analysis of how the public debt was generated and the function of the central government in indebtedness operations.

### *Structure of the public sector*

In terms of the structure of the Peruvian public sector,[1] the consolidated central government and local governments comprise general government in Peru (Table 13.1, Table 13.2 and Table 13.3). The consolidated central government is composed of the central government—this includes ministries, the Housing Fund, public entities and universities—and the rest of the central government which comprises the Social Security and Register Offices, and regulatory and charity institutions. Social security is administered by the health security institutions and the provisional institutions such as the National Pension Savings Fund, the National Pensions Office and the Consolidated Reserve Fund.

Peru's political structure is not organized as a federal republic; therefore, there is not a strong regional or state-level government in this country. Although regional governments were created in the late 1980s as a way to decentralize fiscal policy decisions, they were not allowed to raise taxes or issue debt; as a result, the national authorities basically set revenues and expenditures. In addition, regional authorities are appointed by the central government.

In the case of local governments, they are allowed by law to establish certain taxes, fees, and fines and to issue debt. They provide public goods at the local level and are allowed to set their budget in an autonomous way. However, in 2000, around 41 percent of local government's revenues came as a transfer from the central government, mainly as an earmarked tax of the Peruvian value added tax (VAT).

During the period 1990–99, an average of 82 percent of general government revenues were collected at the central government level, 10 percent of revenues corresponded to social security contributions, and the remainder came from local governments and other public entities (Table 13.4).

On the expenditure side, the structure of the general government budget is quite similar (Table 13.5). This shows that the fiscal policy-making process in Peru is a highly centralized process, where public resources are allocated by central government decisions. Therefore, central government developments explain most of the general government trends in Peru.

### *Budgetary practices*

The fiscal year begins on 1 January. The main fiscal instrument is the public sector budget, which is approved by the Congress. The budget covers much of the

*Table 13.1* Nonfinancial public sector operations, 1968–2000

| | Savings | | | Capital revenue | | | Capital expenditure | | | Overall balance | | |
|---|---|---|---|---|---|---|---|---|---|---|---|---|
| | Nominal[a] | Real[b] | % of GDP | Nominal[a] | Real[b] | % of GDP | Nominal[a] | Real[b] | % of GDP | Nominal[a] | Real[b] | % of GDP |
| 1968 | 5 | 1,453 | 2.6 | 2 | 515 | 0.9 | 10 | 3,079 | 5.5 | −4 | −1,112 | −2.0 |
| 1969 | 10 | 2,644 | 4.5 | 2 | 561 | 1.0 | 13 | 3,536 | 6.0 | −1 | −331 | −0.6 |
| 1970 | 11 | 2,754 | 4.4 | 2 | 402 | 0.6 | 14 | 3,678 | 5.9 | −2 | −522 | −0.8 |
| 1971 | 9 | 2,137 | 3.3 | 2 | 548 | 0.8 | 15 | 3,610 | 5.6 | −4 | −924 | −1.4 |
| 1972 | 7 | 1,587 | 2.4 | 2 | 357 | 0.5 | 17 | 3,860 | 5.8 | −9 | −1,915 | −2.9 |
| 1973 | 6 | 1,180 | 1.7 | 1 | 233 | 0.3 | 23 | 4,649 | 6.6 | −16 | −3,236 | −4.6 |
| 1974 | 12 | 1,979 | 2.6 | 2 | 363 | 0.5 | 44 | 7,603 | 9.9 | −31 | −5,261 | −6.9 |
| 1975 | 0 | 44 | 0.1 | 0 | 51 | 0.1 | 54 | 7,568 | 9.6 | −54 | −7,473 | −9.4 |
| 1976 | −9 | −945 | −1.2 | 2 | 170 | 0.2 | 70 | 7,563 | 9.4 | −77 | −8,338 | −10.3 |
| 1977 | −30 | −2,373 | −2.9 | 1 | 87 | 0.1 | 74 | 5,906 | 7.3 | −103 | −8,192 | −10.1 |
| 1978 | −13 | −639 | −0.8 | 6 | 308 | 0.4 | 96 | 4,817 | 5.9 | −103 | −5,147 | −6.3 |
| 1979 | 152 | 4,398 | 5.1 | 2 | 68 | 0.1 | 188 | 5,430 | 6.3 | −33 | −965 | −1.1 |
| 1980 | 149 | 2,648 | 2.9 | 34 | 604 | 0.7 | 418 | 7,428 | 8.2 | −235 | −4,176 | −4.6 |
| 1981 | 43 | 456 | 0.5 | 78 | 827 | 0.9 | 838 | 8,883 | 9.3 | −717 | −7,600 | −8.0 |
| 1982 | −18 | −114 | −0.1 | 214 | 1,361 | 1.4 | 1,511 | 9,607 | 10.2 | −1,315 | −8,361 | −8.8 |
| 1983 | −729 | −2,216 | −2.7 | 282 | 857 | 1.0 | 2,745 | 8,340 | 10.0 | −3,192 | −9,700 | −11.6 |
| 1984 | 366 | 541 | 0.6 | 578 | 854 | 1.0 | 5,616 | 8,299 | 9.5 | −4,672 | −6,904 | −7.9 |
| 1985 | 4,896 | 2,732 | 3.0 | 1,145 | 639 | 0.7 | 11,995 | 6,694 | 7.4 | −5,954 | −3,323 | −3.7 |
| 1986 | −4,355 | −1,399 | −1.4 | 1,245 | 400 | 0.4 | 19,969 | 6,416 | 6.5 | −23,079 | −7,415 | −7.5 |
| 1987 | −30,541 | −5,329 | −5.0 | 2,644 | 461 | 0.4 | 33,597 | 5,863 | 5.5 | −61,494 | −10,731 | −10.0 |
| 1988 | −267,513 | −7,043 | −7.2 | 9,038 | 238 | 0.2 | 175,474 | 4,620 | 4.7 | −433,949 | −11,425 | −11.7 |
| 1989 | −6,191,653 | −5,945 | −6.9 | 361,696 | 347 | 0.4 | 4,118,635 | 3,954 | 4.6 | −9,948,592 | −9,552 | −11.1 |
| 1990 | −300 | −4,517 | −5.5 | 5 | 77 | 0.1 | 180 | 2,717 | 3.3 | −475 | −7,157 | −8.7 |
| 1991 | 209 | 656 | 0.8 | 73 | 229 | 0.3 | 1,027 | 3,223 | 3.8 | −745 | −2,338 | −2.8 |
| 1992 | 311 | 577 | 0.7 | 147 | 273 | 0.3 | 2,214 | 4,107 | 4.9 | −1,755 | −3,257 | −3.9 |
| 1993 | 1,503 | 1,896 | 2.2 | 72 | 91 | 0.1 | 3,695 | 4,662 | 5.3 | −2,121 | −2,675 | −3.1 |
| 1994 | 2,913 | 2,913 | 3.0 | 135 | 135 | 0.1 | 5,804 | 5,804 | 5.9 | −2,756 | −2,756 | −2.8 |
| 1995 | 2,830 | 2,510 | 2.3 | 21 | 19 | 0.0 | 6,652 | 5,898 | 5.5 | −3,800 | −3,369 | −3.1 |
| 1996 | 5,338 | 4,282 | 3.9 | 173 | 139 | 0.1 | 6,905 | 5,539 | 5.0 | −1,394 | −1,118 | −1.0 |
| 1997 | 8,170 | 6,090 | 5.2 | 73 | 54 | 0.0 | 7,989 | 5,956 | 5.1 | 253 | 189 | 0.2 |
| 1998 | 6,590 | 4,596 | 4.0 | 242 | 169 | 0.1 | 8,160 | 5,691 | 4.9 | −1,329 | −927 | −0.8 |
| 1999 | 3,103 | 2,075 | 1.8 | 156 | 104 | 0.1 | 8,741 | 5,845 | 5.0 | −5,482 | −3,665 | −3.1 |
| 2000 | 1,558 | 1,004 | 0.8 | 208 | 134 | 0.1 | 7,708 | 4,966 | 4.1 | −5,942 | −3,829 | −3.2 |

| | External financing | | | Privatization | | | Domestic financing | | |
|---|---|---|---|---|---|---|---|---|---|
| | Nominal[a] | Real[b] | % of GDP | Nominal[a] | Real[b] | % of GDP | Nominal[a] | Real[b] | % of GDP |
| 1968 | 3 | 853 | 1.5 | 0 | 0 | 0.0 | 1 | 259 | 0.5 |
| 1969 | 5 | 1,313 | 2.2 | 0 | 0 | 0.0 | −4 | −982 | −1.7 |
| 1970 | 3 | 753 | 1.2 | 0 | 0 | 0.0 | −1 | −231 | −0.4 |
| 1971 | 1 | 183 | 0.3 | 0 | 0 | 0.0 | 3 | 741 | 1.1 |
| 1972 | 5 | 1,075 | 1.6 | 0 | 0 | 0.0 | 4 | 840 | 1.3 |
| 1973 | 11 | 2,242 | 3.2 | 0 | 0 | 0.0 | 5 | 994 | 1.4 |
| 1974 | 21 | 3,539 | 4.6 | 0 | 0 | 0.0 | 10 | 1,723 | 2.2 |
| 1975 | 27 | 3,824 | 4.8 | 0 | 0 | 0.0 | 26 | 3,649 | 4.6 |
| 1976 | 27 | 2,904 | 3.6 | 0 | 0 | 0.0 | 50 | 5,434 | 6.7 |
| 1977 | 50 | 3,993 | 4.9 | 0 | 0 | 0.0 | 53 | 4,199 | 5.2 |
| 1978 | 35 | 1,771 | 2.2 | 0 | 0 | 0.0 | 67 | 3,376 | 4.1 |
| 1979 | 81 | 2,340 | 2.7 | 0 | 0 | 0.0 | −48 | −1,375 | −1.6 |
| 1980 | 100 | 1,777 | 2.0 | 0 | 0 | 0.0 | 135 | 2,399 | 2.6 |
| 1981 | 180 | 1,908 | 2.0 | 0 | 0 | 0.0 | 537 | 5,692 | 6.0 |
| 1982 | 1,033 | 6,568 | 6.9 | 0 | 0 | 0.0 | 282 | 1,793 | 1.9 |
| 1983 | 1,814 | 5,513 | 6.6 | 0 | 0 | 0.0 | 1,378 | 4,187 | 5.0 |
| 1984 | 3,502 | 5,175 | 5.9 | 0 | 0 | 0.0 | 1,170 | 1,729 | 2.0 |
| 1985 | 9,168 | 5,117 | 5.7 | 0 | 0 | 0.0 | −3,214 | −1,794 | −2.0 |
| 1986 | 12,915 | 4,149 | 4.2 | 0 | 0 | 0.0 | 10,164 | 3,266 | 3.3 |
| 1987 | 21,787 | 3,802 | 3.5 | 0 | 0 | 0.0 | 39,706 | 6,929 | 6.5 |
| 1988 | 185,893 | 4,894 | 5.0 | 0 | 0 | 0.0 | 248,056 | 6,531 | 6.7 |
| 1989 | 5,061,799 | 4,860 | 5.6 | 0 | 0 | 0.0 | 4,886,794 | 4,692 | 5.4 |
| 1990 | 342 | 5,151 | 6.3 | 0 | 0 | 0.0 | 133 | 2,007 | 2.4 |
| 1991 | 1,106 | 3,473 | 4.1 | 1 | 4 | 0.0 | −363 | −1,139 | −1.4 |
| 1992 | 1,447 | 2,685 | 3.2 | 69 | 128 | 0.2 | 239 | 444 | 0.5 |
| 1993 | 2,107 | 2,658 | 3.0 | 300 | 378 | 0.4 | −286 | −361 | −0.4 |
| 1994 | 2,383 | 2,383 | 2.4 | 5,032 | 5,032 | 5.1 | −4,660 | −4,660 | −4.7 |
| 1995 | 3,048 | 2,702 | 2.5 | 2,151 | 1,907 | 1.8 | −1,398 | −1,240 | −1.2 |
| 1996 | 1,092 | 876 | 0.8 | 5,279 | 4,234 | 3.9 | −4,976 | −3,992 | −3.6 |
| 1997 | −591 | −440 | −0.4 | 1,492 | 1,112 | 0.9 | −1,155 | −861 | −0.7 |
| 1998 | 642 | 448 | 0.4 | 764 | 533 | 0.5 | −77 | −54 | 0.0 |
| 1999 | −111 | −74 | −0.1 | 1,318 | 882 | 0.8 | 4,274 | 2,858 | 2.4 |
| 2000 | 2,280 | 1,469 | 1.2 | 1,427 | 920 | 0.8 | 2,235 | 1,440 | 1.2 |

Notes

a 1968–89 in nuevos soles; 1990–2000 in millions of nuevos soles.

b In millions of 1994 nuevos soles.

*Table 13.2* General government operations in Peru, 1968–2000

| | *Current revenue* | | | *Current expenditure* | | | *Savings* | | | *Capital revenue* | | | *Capital expenditure* | | | *Overall balance* | | |
|---|---|---|---|---|---|---|---|---|---|---|---|---|---|---|---|---|---|---|
| | *Nominal*[a] | *Real*[b] | *% of GDP* | *Nominal*[a] | *Real*[b] | *% of GDP* | *Nominal*[a] | *Real*[b] | *% of GDP* | *Nominal*[a] | *Real*[b] | *% of GDP* | *Nominal*[a] | *Real*[b] | *% of GDP* | *Nominal*[a] | *Real*[b] | *% of GDP* |
| 1968 | 40 | 11,884 | 21.1 | 35 | 10,416 | 18.5 | 5 | 1,467 | 2.6 | 3 | 973 | 1.7 | 10 | 3,015 | 5.3 | −2 | −575 | −1.0 |
| 1969 | 44 | 12,113 | 20.7 | 36 | 9,913 | 16.9 | 8 | 2,200 | 3.8 | 3 | 763 | 1.3 | 10 | 2,794 | 4.8 | 1 | 169 | 0.3 |
| 1970 | 46 | 11,964 | 19.3 | 38 | 9,750 | 15.7 | 9 | 2,214 | 3.6 | 1 | 351 | 0.6 | 11 | 2,764 | 4.5 | −1 | −199 | −0.3 |
| 1971 | 49 | 11,863 | 18.4 | 43 | 10,455 | 16.2 | 6 | 1,408 | 2.2 | 1 | 293 | 0.5 | 14 | 3,278 | 5.1 | −7 | −1,577 | −2.4 |
| 1972 | 56 | 12,552 | 18.9 | 51 | 11,489 | 17.3 | 5 | 1,064 | 1.6 | 1 | 190 | 0.3 | 14 | 3,252 | 4.9 | −9 | −1,999 | −3.0 |
| 1973 | 65 | 12,908 | 18.4 | 63 | 12,393 | 17.7 | 3 | 514 | 0.7 | 0 | 59 | 0.1 | 16 | 3,176 | 4.5 | −13 | −2,603 | −3.7 |
| 1974 | 86 | 14,754 | 19.3 | 76 | 13,004 | 17.0 | 10 | 1,750 | 2.3 | 1 | 100 | 0.1 | 21 | 3,621 | 4.7 | −10 | −1,771 | −2.3 |
| 1975 | 111 | 15,391 | 19.4 | 107 | 14,840 | 18.7 | 4 | 551 | 0.7 | 0 | 18 | 0.0 | 29 | 4,009 | 5.1 | −25 | −3,439 | −4.3 |
| 1976 | 137 | 14,780 | 18.3 | 143 | 15,454 | 19.1 | −6 | −674 | −0.8 | 1 | 101 | 0.1 | 40 | 4,318 | 5.3 | −45 | −4,890 | −6.1 |
| 1977 | 190 | 15,096 | 18.6 | 220 | 17,481 | 21.5 | −30 | −2,385 | −2.9 | 0 | 35 | 0.0 | 45 | 3,572 | 4.4 | −74 | −5,921 | −7.3 |
| 1978 | 306 | 15,330 | 18.8 | 332 | 16,600 | 20.4 | −25 | −1,269 | −1.6 | 6 | 305 | 0.4 | 60 | 3,015 | 3.7 | −79 | −3,979 | −4.9 |
| 1979 | 634 | 18,305 | 21.3 | 516 | 14,891 | 17.3 | 118 | 3,414 | 4.0 | 2 | 68 | 0.1 | 136 | 3,920 | 4.6 | −15 | −438 | −0.5 |
| 1980 | 1,193 | 21,199 | 23.4 | 1,035 | 18,392 | 20.3 | 158 | 2,808 | 3.1 | 7 | 124 | 0.1 | 291 | 5,171 | 5.7 | −126 | −2,239 | −2.5 |
| 1981 | 1,828 | 19,376 | 20.4 | 1,779 | 18,857 | 19.8 | 49 | 519 | 0.5 | 19 | 201 | 0.2 | 500 | 5,300 | 5.6 | −432 | −4,579 | −4.8 |
| 1982 | 2,957 | 18,800 | 19.9 | 2,922 | 18,578 | 19.6 | 35 | 223 | 0.2 | 44 | 280 | 0.3 | 680 | 4,323 | 4.6 | −601 | −3,821 | −4.0 |
| 1983 | 4,546 | 13,812 | 16.6 | 5,892 | 17,903 | 21.5 | −1,346 | −4,091 | −4.9 | 37 | 112 | 0.1 | 1,167 | 3,546 | 4.2 | −2,476 | −7,524 | −9.0 |
| 1984 | 11,199 | 16,550 | 18.9 | 12,110 | 17,895 | 20.4 | −911 | −1,346 | −1.5 | 216 | 319 | 0.4 | 2,644 | 3,907 | 4.5 | −3,339 | −4,934 | −5.6 |
| 1985 | 33,030 | 18,433 | 20.4 | 32,636 | 18,213 | 20.2 | 394 | 220 | 0.2 | 498 | 278 | 0.3 | 5,894 | 3,289 | 3.6 | −5,002 | −2,792 | −3.1 |
| 1986 | 56,575 | 18,177 | 18.3 | 61,073 | 19,622 | 19.8 | −4,498 | −1,445 | −1.5 | 347 | 111 | 0.1 | 12,300 | 3,952 | 4.0 | −16,451 | −5,285 | −5.3 |
| 1987 | 89,821 | 15,674 | 14.6 | 122,210 | 21,326 | 19.9 | −32,389 | −5,652 | −5.3 | 493 | 86 | 0.1 | 20,952 | 3,656 | 3.4 | −52,848 | −9,222 | −8.6 |
| 1988 | 508,339 | 13,384 | 13.7 | 667,023 | 17,562 | 17.9 | −158,684 | −4,178 | −4.3 | 1,652 | 43 | 0.0 | 89,320 | 2,352 | 2.4 | −246,352 | −6,486 | −6.6 |
| 1989 | 9,680,469 | 9,294 | 10.8 | 15,578,249 | 14,957 | 17.3 | −5,897,780 | −5,663 | −6.6 | 35,696 | 34 | 0.0 | 2,809,507 | 2,697 | 3.1 | −8,671,591 | −8,326 | −9.6 |
| 1990 | 720 | 10,850 | 13.2 | 1,039 | 15,653 | 19.1 | −319 | −4,803 | −5.9 | 2 | 24 | 0.0 | 109 | 1,641 | 2.0 | −426 | −6,419 | −7.8 |
| 1991 | 4,115 | 12,915 | 15.4 | 3,974 | 12,473 | 14.9 | 141 | 442 | 0.5 | 33 | 103 | 0.1 | 750 | 2,355 | 2.8 | −577 | 1,419 | −2.2 |
| 1992 | 7,485 | 13,886 | 16.7 | 7,482 | 13,880 | 16.6 | 3 | 6 | 0.0 | 57 | 105 | 0.1 | 1,794 | 3,328 | 4.0 | −1,734 | 4,324 | −3.9 |
| 1993 | 11,474 | 14,474 | 16.6 | 10,811 | 13,638 | 15.6 | 663 | 836 | 1.0 | −28 | −35 | 0.0 | 3,011 | 3,799 | 4.3 | −2,377 | 5,425 | −3.4 |
| 1994 | 17,025 | 17,025 | 17.3 | 15,259 | 15,259 | 15.5 | 1,766 | 1,766 | 1.8 | 357 | 357 | 0.4 | 5,153 | 5,153 | 5.2 | −3,031 | 7,782 | −3.1 |
| 1995 | 21,470 | 19,036 | 17.8 | 19,353 | 17,160 | 16.0 | 2,117 | 1,877 | 1.8 | 329 | 292 | 0.3 | 6,046 | 5,361 | 5.0 | −3,601 | 9,646 | −3.0 |
| 1996 | 25,288 | 20,283 | 18.5 | 21,145 | 16,961 | 15.4 | 4,143 | 3,323 | 3.0 | 613 | 492 | 0.4 | 6,323 | 5,072 | 4.6 | −1,567 | 13,236 | −1.1 |
| 1997 | 29,712 | 22,150 | 18.9 | 23,368 | 17,421 | 14.9 | 6,344 | 4,729 | 4.0 | 224 | 167 | 0.1 | 7,272 | 5,421 | 4.6 | −704 | 15,399 | −0.4 |
| 1998 | 31,261 | 21,802 | 18.8 | 25,787 | 17,984 | 15.5 | 5,474 | 3,818 | 3.3 | 571 | 398 | 0.3 | 7,115 | 4,962 | 4.3 | −1,070 | 15,453 | −0.6 |
| 1999 | 30,653 | 20,497 | 17.5 | 29,125 | 19,475 | 16.7 | 1,528 | 1,022 | 0.9 | 577 | 386 | 0.3 | 7,560 | 5,055 | 4.3 | −5,455 | 14,700 | −3.1 |
| 2000 | 33,077 | 21,312 | 17.7 | 31,730 | 20,444 | 17.0 | 1,347 | 868 | 0.7 | 554 | 357 | 0.3 | 6,815 | 4,391 | 3.6 | −4,913 | 14,638 | −2.6 |

Notes

a 1968–89 in nuevos soles; 1990–2000 in millions of nuevos soles.

b In millions of 1994 nuevos soles.

*Table 13.3* Central government operations in Peru, 1968–2000

| | *Current revenue* | | | *Current expenditure* | | | *Savings* | | | *Capital revenue* | | | *Capital expenditure* | | | *Overall balance* | | |
|---|---|---|---|---|---|---|---|---|---|---|---|---|---|---|---|---|---|---|
| | *Nominal*[a] | *Real*[b] | *% of GDP* | *Nominal*[a] | *Real*[b] | *% of GDP* | *Nominal*[a] | *Real*[b] | *% of GDP* | *Nominal*[a] | *Real*[b] | *% of GDP* | *Nominal*[a] | *Real*[b] | *% of GDP* | *Nominal*[a] | *Real*[b] | *% of GDP* |
| 1968 | 30 | 9,065 | 16.1 | 27 | 8,168 | 14.5 | 3 | 897 | 1.6 | 0 | 0 | 0.0 | 6 | 1,827 | 3.2 | −3 | −930 | −1.6 |
| 1969 | 34 | 9,395 | 16.0 | 28 | 7,772 | 13.3 | 6 | 1,622 | 2.8 | 0 | 47 | 0.1 | 6 | 1,776 | 3.0 | 0 | −106 | −0.2 |
| 1970 | 39 | 10,019 | 16.2 | 32 | 8,342 | 13.5 | 6 | 1,677 | 2.7 | 0 | 45 | 0.1 | 10 | 2,573 | 4.1 | −3 | −850 | −1.4 |
| 1971 | 41 | 9,935 | 15.4 | 37 | 8,960 | 13.9 | 4 | 976 | 1.5 | 0 | 81 | 0.1 | 12 | 3,018 | 4.7 | −8 | −1,961 | −3.0 |
| 1972 | 45 | 10,159 | 15.3 | 42 | 9,511 | 14.3 | 3 | 648 | 1.0 | 0 | 95 | 0.1 | 14 | 3,176 | 4.8 | −11 | −2,433 | −3.7 |
| 1973 | 53 | 10,505 | 15.0 | 52 | 10,291 | 14.7 | 1 | 214 | 0.3 | 0 | 57 | 0.1 | 15 | 3,051 | 4.4 | −14 | −2,780 | −4.0 |
| 1974 | 68 | 11,682 | 15.2 | 62 | 10,717 | 14.0 | 6 | 965 | 1.3 | 0 | 84 | 0.1 | 20 | 3,468 | 4.5 | −14 | −2,418 | −3.2 |
| 1975 | 88 | 12,240 | 15.5 | 91 | 12,603 | 15.9 | −3 | −364 | −0.5 | 0 | 0 | 0.0 | 28 | 3,896 | 4.9 | −31 | −4,260 | −5.4 |
| 1976 | 111 | 11,961 | 14.8 | 123 | 13,262 | 16.4 | −12 | −1,301 | −1.6 | 1 | 78 | 0.1 | 37 | 4,010 | 5.0 | −48 | −5,234 | −6.5 |
| 1977 | 154 | 12,227 | 15.1 | 193 | 15,362 | 18.9 | −39 | −3,135 | −3.9 | 0 | 29 | 0.0 | 40 | 3,191 | 3.9 | −79 | −6,296 | −7.8 |
| 1978 | 263 | 13,150 | 16.2 | 291 | 14,568 | 17.9 | −28 | −1,418 | −1.7 | 1 | 52 | 0.1 | 58 | 2,886 | 3.5 | −85 | −4,252 | −5.2 |
| 1979 | 551 | 15,895 | 18.5 | 442 | 12,753 | 14.8 | 109 | 3,142 | 3.7 | 1 | 37 | 0.0 | 129 | 3,709 | 4.3 | −18 | −530 | −0.6 |
| 1980 | 1,017 | 18,072 | 20.0 | 898 | 15,957 | 17.6 | 119 | 2,115 | 2.3 | 2 | 36 | 0.0 | 263 | 4,673 | 5.2 | −142 | −2,523 | −2.8 |
| 1981 | 1,517 | 16,080 | 16.9 | 1,504 | 15,942 | 16.7 | 13 | 138 | 0.1 | 6 | 64 | 0.1 | 439 | 4,653 | 4.9 | −420 | −4,452 | −4.7 |
| 1982 | 2,476 | 15,742 | 16.6 | 2,456 | 15,615 | 16.5 | 20 | 127 | 0.1 | 18 | 114 | 0.1 | 595 | 3,783 | 4.0 | −557 | −3,541 | −3.7 |
| 1983 | 3,730 | 11,333 | 13.6 | 5,070 | 15,406 | 18.5 | −1,340 | −4,073 | −4.9 | 11 | 33 | 0.0 | 1,019 | 3,096 | 3.7 | −2,348 | −7,135 | −8.6 |
| 1984 | 9,473 | 13,999 | 15.9 | 10,501 | 15,518 | 17.7 | −1,028 | −1,519 | −1.7 | 173 | 256 | 0.3 | 2,360 | 3,488 | 4.0 | −3,215 | −4,751 | −5.4 |
| 1985 | 28,214 | 15,745 | 17.4 | 28,816 | 16,081 | 17.8 | −602 | −336 | −0.4 | 365 | 204 | 0.2 | 5,052 | 2,819 | 3.1 | −5,289 | −2,952 | −3.3 |
| 1986 | 45,680 | 14,676 | 14.8 | 52,752 | 16,948 | 17.1 | −7,072 | −2,272 | −2.3 | 251 | 81 | 0.1 | 10,968 | 3,524 | 3.5 | −17,789 | −5,715 | −5.8 |
| 1987 | 67,553 | 11,788 | 11.0 | 104,333 | 18,206 | 17.0 | −36,780 | −6,418 | −6.0 | 129 | 23 | 0.0 | 17,326 | 3,023 | 2.8 | −53,977 | −9,419 | −8.8 |
| 1988 | 411,163 | 10,826 | 11.1 | 567,993 | 14,955 | 15.3 | −156,830 | −4,129 | −4.2 | 1,044 | 27 | 0.0 | 68,623 | 1,807 | 1.8 | −224,409 | −5,908 | −6.0 |
| 1989 | 7,703,442 | 7,396 | 8.6 | 13,694,994 | 13,149 | 15.2 | −5,991,552 | −5,753 | −6.7 | 13,000 | 12 | 0.0 | 2,439,967 | 2,343 | 2.7 | −8,418,519 | −8,083 | −9.4 |
| 1990 | 623 | 9,381 | 11.4 | 959 | 14,451 | 17.6 | −337 | −5,070 | −6.2 | 0 | 4 | 0.0 | 96 | 1,447 | 1.8 | −432 | −6,513 | −7.9 |
| 1991 | 3,193 | 10,023 | 12.0 | 3,354 | 10,528 | 12.6 | −161 | −505 | −0.6 | 23 | 74 | 0.1 | 523 | 1,641 | 2.0 | −660 | −2,072 | −2.5 |
| 1992 | 6,059 | 11,241 | 13.5 | 6,399 | 11,872 | 14.2 | −341 | −632 | −0.8 | 28 | 51 | 0.1 | 1,438 | 2,667 | 3.2 | −1,750 | −3,248 | −3.9 |
| 1993 | 9,424 | 11,889 | 13.6 | 9,336 | 11,777 | 13.5 | 88 | 111 | 0.1 | −58 | −74 | −0.1 | 2,544 | 3,210 | 3.7 | −2,515 | −3,172 | −3.6 |
| 1994 | 14,386 | 14,386 | 14.6 | 13,489 | 13,489 | 13.7 | 898 | 898 | 0.9 | 324 | 324 | 0.3 | 4,341 | 4,341 | 4.4 | −3,120 | −3,120 | −3.2 |
| 1995 | 18,319 | 16,243 | 15.2 | 17,568 | 15,577 | 14.5 | 752 | 666 | 0.6 | 274 | 243 | 0.2 | 5,031 | 4,460 | 4.2 | −4,005 | −3,551 | −3.3 |
| 1996 | 21,522 | 17,263 | 15.7 | 18,969 | 15,215 | 13.9 | 2,553 | 2,048 | 1.9 | 578 | 463 | 0.4 | 5,048 | 4,049 | 3.7 | −1,918 | −1,538 | −1.4 |
| 1997 | 25,001 | 18,638 | 15.9 | 20,723 | 15,449 | 13.2 | 4,278 | 3,189 | 2.7 | 192 | 143 | 0.1 | 5,795 | 4,320 | 3.7 | −1,324 | −987 | −0.8 |
| 1998 | 26,174 | 18,254 | 15.7 | 22,876 | 15,954 | 13.7 | 3,298 | 2,300 | 2.0 | 533 | 372 | 0.3 | 5,623 | 3,921 | 3.4 | −1,792 | −1,250 | −1.1 |
| 1999 | 25,334 | 16,940 | 14.5 | 25,471 | 17,032 | 14.6 | −138 | −92 | −0.1 | 539 | 360 | 0.3 | 5,900 | 3,945 | 3.4 | −5,499 | −3,677 | −3.1 |
| 2000 | 27,515 | 17,728 | 14.7 | 27,831 | 17,932 | 14.9 | −316 | −204 | −0.2 | 530 | 342 | 0.3 | 5,232 | 3,371 | 2.8 | −5,019 | −3,234 | −2.7 |

Notes

a 1968–89 in nuevos soles; 1990–2000 in millions of nuevos soles.

b In millions of 1994 nuevos soles.

*Table 13.4* Central government current revenue, 1968–2000

| | *Income tax* | | | *Custom duties* | | | *Sales tax or VAT* | | | *Excise taxes* | | |
|---|---|---|---|---|---|---|---|---|---|---|---|---|
| | *Nominal*[a] | *Real*[b] | *% of GDP* | *Nominal*[a] | *Real*[b] | *% of GDP* | *Nominal*[a] | *Real*[b] | *% of GDP* | *Nominal*[a] | *Real*[b] | *% of GDP* |
| 1968 | 7 | 1,970 | 3.5 | 7 | 2,161 | 3.8 | 6 | 1,881 | 3.3 | 2 | 671 | 1.2 |
| 1969 | 8 | 2,301 | 3.9 | 8 | 2,178 | 3.7 | 7 | 1,820 | 3.1 | 3 | 895 | 1.5 |
| 1970 | 12 | 3,034 | 4.9 | 8 | 2,092 | 3.4 | 8 | 1,971 | 3.2 | 3 | 765 | 1.2 |
| 1971 | 9 | 2,209 | 3.4 | 9 | 2,154 | 3.3 | 9 | 2,150 | 3.3 | 4 | 895 | 1.4 |
| 1972 | 10 | 2,202 | 3.3 | 8 | 1,762 | 2.6 | 10 | 2,231 | 3.4 | 5 | 1,029 | 1.5 |
| 1973 | 15 | 2,925 | 4.2 | 9 | 1,800 | 2.6 | 12 | 2,433 | 3.5 | 5 | 954 | 1.4 |
| 1974 | 20 | 3,488 | 4.6 | 10 | 1,764 | 2.3 | 17 | 2,948 | 3.8 | 6 | 974 | 1.3 |
| 1975 | 24 | 3,360 | 4.2 | 18 | 2,529 | 3.2 | 24 | 3,285 | 4.1 | 7 | 960 | 1.2 |
| 1976 | 23 | 2,486 | 3.1 | 18 | 1,940 | 2.4 | 32 | 3,498 | 4.3 | 12 | 1,339 | 1.7 |
| 1977 | 30 | 2,417 | 3.0 | 20 | 1,564 | 1.9 | 44 | 3,539 | 4.4 | 20 | 1,591 | 2.0 |
| 1978 | 43 | 2,151 | 2.6 | 39 | 1,956 | 2.4 | 78 | 3,907 | 4.8 | 40 | 2,014 | 2.5 |
| 1979 | 118 | 3,394 | 3.9 | 68 | 1,966 | 2.3 | 162 | 4,671 | 5.4 | 60 | 1,738 | 2.0 |
| 1980 | 298 | 5,295 | 5.8 | 158 | 2,808 | 3.1 | 281 | 4,993 | 5.5 | 89 | 1,581 | 1.7 |
| 1981 | 303 | 3,212 | 3.4 | 321 | 3,403 | 3.6 | 461 | 4,886 | 5.1 | 148 | 1,569 | 1.6 |
| 1982 | 480 | 3,052 | 3.2 | 475 | 3,020 | 3.2 | 767 | 4,877 | 5.2 | 383 | 2,435 | 2.6 |
| 1983 | 649 | 1,972 | 2.4 | 714 | 2,169 | 2.6 | 1,125 | 3,418 | 4.1 | 771 | 2,343 | 2.8 |
| 1984 | 1,422 | 2,101 | 2.4 | 1,779 | 2,629 | 3.0 | 2,066 | 3,053 | 3.5 | 2,361 | 3,489 | 4.0 |
| 1985 | 3,459 | 1,930 | 2.1 | 5,592 | 3,121 | 3.5 | 5,129 | 2,862 | 3.2 | 10,416 | 5,813 | 6.4 |
| 1986 | 9,853 | 3,166 | 3.2 | 8,757 | 2,813 | 2.8 | 5,828 | 1,872 | 1.9 | 15,669 | 5,034 | 5.1 |
| 1987 | 13,126 | 2,291 | 2.1 | 14,069 | 2,455 | 2.3 | 9,231 | 1,611 | 1.5 | 25,984 | 4,534 | 4.2 |
| 1988 | 86,829 | 2,286 | 2.3 | 54,881 | 1,445 | 1.5 | 95,839 | 2,523 | 2.6 | 111,732 | 2,942 | 3.0 |
| 1989 | 1,255,000 | 1,205 | 1.4 | 1,266,000 | 1,216 | 1.4 | 2,225,000 | 2,136 | 2.5 | 1,935,000 | 1,858 | 2.1 |
| 1990 | 37 | 558 | 0.7 | 64 | 961 | 1.2 | 109 | 1,644 | 2.0 | 228 | 3,441 | 4.2 |
| 1991 | 250 | 783 | 0.9 | 336 | 1,053 | 1.3 | 765 | 2,401 | 2.9 | 1,196 | 3,754 | 4.5 |
| 1992 | 749 | 1,390 | 1.7 | 650 | 1,206 | 1.4 | 1,702 | 3,157 | 3.8 | 1,743 | 3,234 | 3.9 |
| 1993 | 1,406 | 1,774 | 2.0 | 1,228 | 1,549 | 1.8 | 3,534 | 4,459 | 5.1 | 1,611 | 2,033 | 2.3 |
| 1994 | 2,526 | 2,526 | 2.6 | 1,700 | 1,700 | 1.7 | 5,954 | 5,954 | 6.0 | 2,267 | 2,267 | 2.3 |
| 1995 | 3,462 | 3,070 | 2.9 | 2,144 | 1,901 | 1.8 | 7,646 | 6,779 | 6.3 | 2,486 | 2,204 | 2.1 |
| 1996 | 4,981 | 3,995 | 3.6 | 2,308 | 1,851 | 1.7 | 8,578 | 6,881 | 6.3 | 2,761 | 2,215 | 2.0 |
| 1997 | 5,710 | 4,257 | 3.6 | 2,471 | 1,842 | 1.6 | 10,344 | 7,712 | 6.6 | 3,365 | 2,509 | 2.1 |
| 1998 | 5,861 | 4,088 | 3.5 | 2,891 | 2,016 | 1.7 | 11,040 | 7,699 | 6.6 | 3,427 | 2,390 | 2.1 |
| 1999 | 5,072 | 3,391 | 2.9 | 2,848 | 1,905 | 1.6 | 11,029 | 7,375 | 6.3 | 3,446 | 2,304 | 2.0 |
| 2000 | 5,130 | 3,305 | 2.7 | 2,913 | 1,877 | 1.5 | 11,996 | 7,729 | 6.4 | 3,421 | 2,204 | 1.8 |

Notes
a 1968–89 in nuevos soles; 1990–2000 in millions of nuevos soles.
b In millions of 1994 nuevos soles.

central government operations, but some institutions—such as health security institutions, local governments and state-owned enterprises—are not included in the public sector budget. The annual budget sets the limits to nonfinancial expenditures and public debt service (both domestic and foreign). It also includes a detailed projection of current revenues (tax and nontax revenues) and domestic and foreign debt disbursements to finance the projected level of expenditure and public debt service.

The budgetary process starts in May with the definition of the macroeconomic assumptions for the following year, mainly the real growth rate, the rate of inflation, the exchange rate and the level of exports. The Ministry of Finance, the central bank, and the Tax Collection Agency jointly forecast the next-year revenue aggregate target; this variable is then used in the expenditure estimates that are made by each budget-spending department. Then, the budget proposal is passed to the Congress before 30 August and it must be approved by the Congress no later than 30 November; otherwise the executive branch will enact the budget by decree.

The Congress cannot increase expenditures further than that proposed by the executive branch and any provision for tax exemption or benefit requires a

| *Other taxes & tax refunds* | | | *Total tax revenue* | | | *Nontax revenue* | | | *Total current revenue* | | |
|---|---|---|---|---|---|---|---|---|---|---|---|
| *Nominal*[a] | *Real*[b] | *% of GDP* | *Nominal*[a] | *Real*[b] | *% of GDP* | *Nominal*[a] | *Real*[b] | *% of GDP* | *Nominal*[a] | *Real*[b] | *% of GDP* |
| 5 | 1,365 | 2.4 | 27 | 8,048 | 14.3 | 3 | 1,016 | 1.8 | 30 | 9,065 | 16.1 |
| 4 | 1,012 | 1.7 | 30 | 8,206 | 14.0 | 4 | 1,189 | 2.0 | 34 | 9,395 | 16.0 |
| 3 | 817 | 1.3 | 33 | 8,679 | 14.0 | 5 | 1,340 | 2.2 | 39 | 10,019 | 16.2 |
| 5 | 1,174 | 1.8 | 35 | 8,581 | 13.3 | 6 | 1,354 | 2.1 | 41 | 9,935 | 15.4 |
| 7 | 1,559 | 2.3 | 39 | 8,784 | 13.2 | 6 | 1,375 | 2.1 | 45 | 10,159 | 15.3 |
| 6 | 1,145 | 1.6 | 47 | 9,257 | 13.2 | 6 | 1,248 | 1.8 | 53 | 10,505 | 15.0 |
| 6 | 1,062 | 1.4 | 60 | 10,236 | 13.4 | 8 | 1,446 | 1.9 | 68 | 11,682 | 15.2 |
| 8 | 1,047 | 1.3 | 80 | 11,180 | 14.1 | 8 | 1,060 | 1.3 | 88 | 12,240 | 15.5 |
| 13 | 1,458 | 1.8 | 99 | 10,721 | 13.3 | 11 | 1,240 | 1.5 | 111 | 11,961 | 14.8 |
| 25 | 1,962 | 2.4 | 139 | 11,074 | 13.7 | 14 | 1,153 | 1.4 | 154 | 12,227 | 15.1 |
| 44 | 2,222 | 2.7 | 245 | 12,251 | 15.1 | 18 | 899 | 1.1 | 263 | 13,150 | 16.2 |
| 88 | 2,534 | 2.9 | 496 | 14,303 | 16.6 | 55 | 1,592 | 1.8 | 551 | 15,895 | 18.5 |
| 115 | 2,044 | 2.3 | 941 | 16,721 | 18.5 | 76 | 1,350 | 1.5 | 1,017 | 18,072 | 20.0 |
| 149 | 1,579 | 1.7 | 1,382 | 14,649 | 15.4 | 135 | 1,431 | 1.5 | 1,517 | 16,080 | 16.9 |
| 144 | 916 | 1.0 | 2,249 | 14,299 | 15.1 | 227 | 1,443 | 1.5 | 2,476 | 15,742 | 16.6 |
| 102 | 310 | 0.4 | 3,361 | 10,212 | 12.2 | 369 | 1,121 | 1.3 | 3,730 | 11,333 | 13.6 |
| 329 | 486 | 0.6 | 7,957 | 11,759 | 13.4 | 1,516 | 2,240 | 2.6 | 9,473 | 13,999 | 15.9 |
| 510 | 285 | 0.3 | 25,106 | 14,011 | 15.5 | 3,108 | 1,734 | 1.9 | 28,214 | 15,745 | 17.4 |
| 1,293 | 415 | 0.4 | 41,400 | 13,301 | 13.4 | 4,280 | 1,375 | 1.4 | 45,680 | 14,676 | 14.8 |
| 83 | 15 | 0.0 | 62,493 | 10,905 | 10.2 | 5,060 | 883 | 0.8 | 67,553 | 11,788 | 11.0 |
| 27,306 | 719 | 0.7 | 376,587 | 9,915 | 10.1 | 34,576 | 910 | 0.9 | 411,163 | 10,826 | 11.1 |
| 588,442 | 565 | 0.7 | 7,269,442 | 6,980 | 8.1 | 434,000 | 417 | 0.5 | 7,703,442 | 7,396 | 8.6 |
| 149 | 2,251 | 2.7 | 588 | 8,856 | 10.8 | 35 | 525 | 0.6 | 623 | 9,381 | 11.4 |
| 410 | 1,286 | 1.5 | 2,958 | 9,283 | 11.1 | 236 | 740 | 0.9 | 3,193 | 10,023 | 12.0 |
| 572 | 1,061 | 1.3 | 5,416 | 10,048 | 12.0 | 643 | 1,193 | 1.4 | 6,059 | 11,241 | 13.5 |
| 699 | 881 | 1.0 | 8,478 | 10,696 | 12.2 | 946 | 1,193 | 1.4 | 9,424 | 11,889 | 13.6 |
| 420 | 420 | 0.4 | 12,866 | 12,866 | 13.1 | 1,520 | 1,520 | 1.5 | 14,386 | 14,386 | 14.6 |
| 475 | 421 | 0.4 | 16,212 | 14,374 | 13.4 | 2,108 | 1,869 | 1.7 | 18,319 | 16,243 | 15.2 |
| 408 | 327 | 0.3 | 19,036 | 15,269 | 13.9 | 2,485 | 1,994 | 1.8 | 21,522 | 17,263 | 15.7 |
| 231 | 172 | 0.1 | 22,122 | 16,492 | 14.1 | 2,879 | 2,147 | 1.8 | 25,001 | 18,638 | 15.9 |
| −224 | −156 | −0.1 | 22,995 | 16,037 | 13.8 | 3,179 | 2,217 | 1.9 | 26,174 | 18,254 | 15.7 |
| −522 | −349 | −0.3 | 21,873 | 14,626 | 12.5 | 3,460 | 2,314 | 2.0 | 25,334 | 16,940 | 14.5 |
| −796 | −513 | −0.4 | 22,663 | 14,602 | 12.1 | 4,851 | 3,126 | 2.6 | 27,515 | 17,728 | 14.7 |

comment by the Ministry of Finance. In addition, supplementary budgets follow the same procedures as the budget itself; any requirement for increasing expenditure or transfer of funds requires approval from the Congress.

There are a group of laws enacted by the Congress that complement budget practices; these laws are: the Law of Financial Equilibrium which states the amount of deficit to be financed within the year according to the maximum level of spending and estimated revenues; the Law of Borrowing which fixes the maximum amount of borrowing from abroad and from domestic sources; and the Law of Budget Management which sets the fundamentals of the budget procedures followed by public sector entities.

Starting in fiscal year 2000, the Law of Fiscal Prudence and Transparency (enacted in December 1999) established quantitative limits to the nonfinancial public sector deficit (1 percent of GDP) and to the rate of growth of real public nonfinancial expenditure (2 percent per annum). It also forced the executive branch to make public three-year forecasts of the main macroeconomic indicators (i.e., GDP, inflation, exchange rate, imports and exports) and a complete set of fiscal variables (revenues, expenditures and fiscal balance). A declaration of the fiscal policy's medium-term goals and a list of measures to be undertaken in order

*Table 13.5* Central government expenditures, 1968–2000

| | *Components of current expenditure* | | | | | | | | | | | |
|---|---|---|---|---|---|---|---|---|---|---|---|---|
| | *Total expenditure* | | | *Total current expenditure* | | | *Wages and salaries* | | | *Goods and services* | | |
| | *Nominal*[a] | *Real*[b] | *% of GDP* | *Nominal*[a] | *Real*[b] | *% of GDP* | *Nominal*[a] | *Real*[b] | *% of GDP* | *Nominal*[a] | *Real*[b] | *% of GDP* |
| 1968 | 33 | 9,995 | 17.7 | 27 | 8,168 | 14.5 | 14 | 4,348 | 7.7 | 4 | 1,251 | 2.2 |
| 1969 | 34 | 9,548 | 16.3 | 28 | 7,772 | 13.3 | 15 | 4,240 | 7.2 | 4 | 1,098 | 1.9 |
| 1970 | 42 | 10,915 | 17.6 | 32 | 8,342 | 13.5 | 17 | 4,460 | 7.2 | 5 | 1,404 | 2.3 |
| 1971 | 49 | 11,977 | 18.5 | 37 | 8,960 | 13.9 | 20 | 4,830 | 7.5 | 6 | 1,477 | 2.3 |
| 1972 | 56 | 12,687 | 19.1 | 42 | 9,511 | 14.3 | 23 | 5,083 | 7.6 | 8 | 1,715 | 2.6 |
| 1973 | 67 | 13,342 | 19.0 | 52 | 10,291 | 14.7 | 26 | 5,168 | 7.4 | 10 | 1,929 | 2.8 |
| 1974 | 83 | 14,184 | 18.5 | 62 | 10,717 | 14.0 | 29 | 4,988 | 6.5 | 14 | 2,358 | 3.1 |
| 1975 | 118 | 16,499 | 20.8 | 91 | 12,603 | 15.9 | 39 | 5,404 | 6.8 | 22 | 3,008 | 3.8 |
| 1976 | 160 | 17,272 | 21.4 | 123 | 13,262 | 16.4 | 52 | 5,567 | 6.9 | 32 | 3,484 | 4.3 |
| 1977 | 233 | 18,553 | 22.9 | 193 | 15,362 | 18.9 | 70 | 5,593 | 6.9 | 65 | 5,166 | 6.4 |
| 1978 | 349 | 17,454 | 21.5 | 291 | 14,568 | 17.9 | 97 | 4,868 | 6.0 | 80 | 4,023 | 4.9 |
| 1979 | 571 | 16,462 | 19.1 | 442 | 12,753 | 14.8 | 148 | 4,265 | 5.0 | 89 | 2,578 | 3.0 |
| 1980 | 1,161 | 20,631 | 22.8 | 898 | 15,957 | 17.6 | 286 | 5,082 | 5.6 | 212 | 3,767 | 4.2 |
| 1981 | 1,943 | 20,595 | 21.6 | 1,504 | 15,942 | 16.7 | 551 | 5,840 | 6.1 | 296 | 3,138 | 3.3 |
| 1982 | 3,051 | 19,398 | 20.5 | 2,456 | 15,615 | 16.5 | 943 | 5,996 | 6.3 | 614 | 3,904 | 4.1 |
| 1983 | 6,089 | 18,502 | 22.2 | 5,070 | 15,406 | 18.5 | 1,776 | 5,396 | 6.5 | 1,023 | 3,108 | 3.7 |
| 1984 | 12,861 | 19,005 | 21.6 | 10,501 | 15,518 | 17.7 | 3,741 | 5,528 | 6.3 | 1,532 | 2,264 | 2.6 |
| 1985 | 33,868 | 18,900 | 20.9 | 28,816 | 16,081 | 17.8 | 9,256 | 5,165 | 5.7 | 5,481 | 3,059 | 3.4 |
| 1986 | 63,720 | 20,472 | 20.6 | 52,752 | 16,948 | 17.1 | 18,435 | 5,923 | 6.0 | 8,877 | 2,852 | 2.9 |
| 1987 | 121,659 | 21,230 | 19.8 | 104,333 | 18,206 | 17.0 | 38,498 | 6,718 | 6.3 | 14,440 | 2,520 | 2.4 |
| 1988 | 636,616 | 16,762 | 17.1 | 567,993 | 14,955 | 15.3 | 172,392 | 4,539 | 4.6 | 60,545 | 1,594 | 1.6 |
| 1989 | 16,134,961 | 15,492 | 17.9 | 13,694,994 | 13,149 | 15.2 | 4,294,279 | 4,123 | 4.8 | 1,378,961 | 1,324 | 1.5 |
| 1990 | 1,055 | 15,898 | 19.4 | 959 | 14,451 | 17.6 | 200 | 3,019 | 3.7 | 133 | 1,999 | 2.4 |
| 1991 | 3,877 | 12,168 | 14.5 | 3,354 | 10,528 | 12.6 | 911 | 2,859 | 3.4 | 552 | 1,733 | 2.1 |
| 1992 | 7,837 | 14,539 | 17.4 | 6,399 | 11,872 | 14.2 | 1,770 | 3,284 | 3.9 | 966 | 1,792 | 2.1 |
| 1993 | 11,880 | 14,987 | 17.2 | 9,336 | 11,777 | 13.5 | 2,659 | 3,355 | 3.8 | 1,413 | 1,783 | 2.0 |
| 1994 | 17,830 | 17,830 | 18.1 | 13,489 | 13,489 | 13.7 | 3,866 | 3,866 | 3.9 | 2,570 | 2,570 | 2.6 |
| 1995 | 22,598 | 20,037 | 18.7 | 17,568 | 15,577 | 14.5 | 5,098 | 4,520 | 4.2 | 3,928 | 3,483 | 3.3 |
| 1996 | 24,017 | 19,265 | 17.5 | 18,969 | 15,215 | 13.9 | 5,433 | 4,358 | 4.0 | 5,129 | 4,114 | 3.7 |
| 1997 | 26,518 | 19,769 | 16.9 | 20,723 | 15,449 | 13.2 | 6,397 | 4,769 | 4.1 | 5,319 | 3,965 | 3.4 |
| 1998 | 28,498 | 19,875 | 17.1 | 22,876 | 15,954 | 13.7 | 6,979 | 4,867 | 4.2 | 6,022 | 4,200 | 3.6 |
| 1999 | 31,371 | 20,977 | 18.0 | 25,471 | 17,032 | 14.6 | 7,774 | 5,198 | 4.4 | 6,210 | 4,153 | 3.6 |
| 2000 | 33,063 | 21,303 | 17.7 | 27,831 | 17,932 | 14.9 | 8,180 | 5,271 | 4.4 | 7,068 | 4,554 | 3.8 |

Notes
a 1968–89 in nuevos soles; 1990–2000 in millions of nuevos soles.
b In millions of 1994 nuevos soles.

to achieve them were also required by this law. This document is called the Multi-Annual Macroeconomic Framework and was intended to improve transparency and predictability in the process of fiscal policy-making, thereby reducing the level of uncertainty about public sector behavior.

## Fiscal developments

In this section, the evolution of the main fiscal developments during the period 1990–2000 is presented. Fluctuation in central government expenditures and revenues is explained in some detail in order to cast light on the fiscal policy measures that were undertaken, with special emphasis on the stabilization and reform process in the 1990s.

The evolution of Peruvian fiscal policy in the past decade has been characterized by three main stages: (1) stabilization and recovery; (2) external shocks and fiscal imbalance; and (3) adjustment policy. In the following sections, it can be seen how these periods developed and how it affected the economy.

*mponents of current expenditure*

| *nsfers* | | | *Interest* | | | *Total capital expenditure* | | | *Gross capital formation* | | | *Other* | | |
|---|---|---|---|---|---|---|---|---|---|---|---|---|---|---|
| *minal*[a] | *Real*[b] | *% of GDP* | *Nominal*[a] | *Real*[b] | *% o GDP* | *Nominal*[a] | *Real*[b] | *% o GDP* | *Nominal*[a] | *Real*[b] | *% of GDP* | *Nominal*[a] | *Real*[b] | *% of GDP* |
| 7 | 2,151 | 3.8 | 1 | 419 | 0.7 | 6 | 1,827 | 3.2 | 3 | 781 | 1.4 | 3 | 1,046 | 1.9 |
| 7 | 1,935 | 3.3 | 2 | 499 | 0.9 | 6 | 1,776 | 3.0 | 3 | 810 | 1.4 | 3 | 966 | 1.6 |
| 7 | 1,907 | 3.1 | 2 | 571 | 0.9 | 10 | 2,573 | 4.1 | 6 | 1,439 | 2.3 | 4 | 1,134 | 1.8 |
| 8 | 1,899 | 2.9 | 3 | 753 | 1.2 | 12 | 3,018 | 4.7 | 7 | 1,786 | 2.8 | 5 | 1,232 | 1.9 |
| 8 | 1,753 | 2.6 | 4 | 960 | 1.4 | 14 | 3,176 | 4.8 | 9 | 1,921 | 2.9 | 6 | 1,254 | 1.9 |
| 10 | 2,021 | 2.9 | 6 | 1,173 | 1.7 | 15 | 3,051 | 4.4 | 8 | 1,638 | 2.3 | 7 | 1,413 | 2.0 |
| 12 | 2,051 | 2.7 | 8 | 1,320 | 1.7 | 20 | 3,468 | 4.5 | 13 | 2,222 | 2.9 | 7 | 1,246 | 1.6 |
| 21 | 2,879 | 3.6 | 9 | 1,312 | 1.7 | 28 | 3,896 | 4.9 | 16 | 2,209 | 2.8 | 12 | 1,687 | 2.1 |
| 26 | 2,786 | 3.4 | 13 | 1,424 | 1.8 | 37 | 4,010 | 5.0 | 20 | 2,144 | 2.7 | 17 | 1,866 | 2.3 |
| 29 | 2,282 | 2.8 | 29 | 2,321 | 2.9 | 40 | 3,191 | 3.9 | 27 | 2,157 | 2.7 | 13 | 1,034 | 1.3 |
| 42 | 2,080 | 2.6 | 72 | 3,597 | 4.4 | 58 | 2,886 | 3.5 | 42 | 2,127 | 2.6 | 15 | 759 | 0.9 |
| 67 | 1,924 | 2.2 | 138 | 3,986 | 4.6 | 129 | 3,709 | 4.3 | 92 | 2,665 | 3.1 | 36 | 1,044 | 1.2 |
| 186 | 3,305 | 3.6 | 214 | 3,803 | 4.2 | 263 | 4,673 | 5.2 | 178 | 3,163 | 3.5 | 85 | 1,510 | 1.7 |
| 275 | 2,915 | 3.1 | 382 | 4,049 | 4.3 | 439 | 4,653 | 4.9 | 351 | 3,721 | 3.9 | 88 | 933 | 1.0 |
| 342 | 2,174 | 2.3 | 557 | 3,541 | 3.7 | 595 | 3,783 | 4.0 | 541 | 3,440 | 3.6 | 54 | 343 | 0.4 |
| 855 | 2,598 | 3.1 | 1,416 | 4,304 | 5.2 | 1,019 | 3,096 | 3.7 | 901 | 2,738 | 3.3 | 118 | 359 | 0.4 |
| ,973 | 2,916 | 3.3 | 3,255 | 4,810 | 5.5 | 2,360 | 3,488 | 4.0 | 2,075 | 3,066 | 3.5 | 285 | 421 | 0.5 |
| ,722 | 2,635 | 2.9 | 9,357 | 5,222 | 5.8 | 5,052 | 2,819 | 3.1 | 4,579 | 2,555 | 2.8 | 473 | 264 | 0.3 |
| ,320 | 3,958 | 4.0 | 13,120 | 4,215 | 4.2 | 10,968 | 3,524 | 3.5 | 8,335 | 2,678 | 2.7 | 2,633 | 846 | 0.9 |
| ,530 | 4,630 | 4.3 | 24,865 | 4,339 | 4.0 | 17,326 | 3,023 | 2.8 | 11,209 | 1,956 | 1.8 | 6,117 | 1,067 | 1.0 |
| ,716 | 3,547 | 3.6 | 200,340 | 5,275 | 5.4 | 68,623 | 1,807 | 1.8 | 46,219 | 1,217 | 1.2 | 22,404 | 590 | 0.6 |
| ,345 | 3,288 | 3.8 | 4,597,409 | 4,414 | 5.1 | 2,439,967 | 2,343 | 2.7 | 1,696,240 | 1,629 | 1.9 | 743,727 | 714 | 0.8 |
| 209 | 3,155 | 3.8 | 417 | 6,278 | 7.7 | 96 | 1,447 | 1.8 | 92 | 1,385 | 1.7 | 4 | 62 | 0.1 |
| 856 | 2,687 | 3.2 | 1,035 | 3,249 | 3.9 | 523 | 1,641 | 2.0 | 504 | 1,583 | 1.9 | 18 | 57 | 0.1 |
| ,665 | 3,089 | 3.7 | 1,998 | 3,707 | 4.4 | 1,438 | 2,667 | 3.2 | 1,115 | 2,069 | 2.5 | 322 | 598 | 0.7 |
| ,375 | 2,996 | 3.4 | 2,888 | 3,643 | 4.2 | 2,544 | 3,210 | 3.7 | 2,150 | 2,712 | 3.1 | 394 | 497 | 0.6 |
| 493 | 3,493 | 3.5 | 3,560 | 3,560 | 3.6 | 4,341 | 4,341 | 4.4 | 3,342 | 3,342 | 3.4 | 999 | 999 | 1.0 |
| 518 | 4,006 | 3.7 | 4,023 | 3,567 | 3.3 | 5,031 | 4,460 | 4.2 | 3,955 | 3,507 | 3.3 | 1,075 | 954 | 0.9 |
| ,118 | 4,105 | 3.7 | 3,289 | 2,638 | 2.4 | 5,048 | 4,049 | 3.7 | 3,921 | 3,145 | 2.9 | 1,128 | 904 | 0.8 |
| 217 | 4,635 | 4.0 | 2,789 | 2,079 | 1.8 | 5,795 | 4,320 | 3.7 | 4,448 | 3,316 | 2.8 | 1,347 | 1,004 | 0.9 |
| 756 | 4,712 | 4.1 | 3,119 | 2,175 | 1.9 | 5,623 | 3,921 | 3.4 | 4,964 | 3,462 | 3.0 | 659 | 459 | 0.4 |
| 813 | 5,224 | 4.5 | 3,674 | 2,457 | 2.1 | 5,900 | 3,945 | 3.4 | 5,652 | 3,780 | 3.2 | 248 | 166 | 0.1 |
| 508 | 5,482 | 4.6 | 4,074 | 2,625 | 2.2 | 5,232 | 3,371 | 2.8 | 4,749 | 3,060 | 2.5 | 483 | 312 | 0.3 |

### *1990–97: Stabilization and recovery*

In 1990, the government launched a stabilization program that was intended to liberalize and modernize the economy, and thereby re-establish fiscal and monetary equilibrium and also open up the economy to competition and foreign investment. Due to strong monetary discipline maintained by the central bank, inflation was reduced from 7,650 percent in 1990 to 6.5 in 1997, as Peru went from an entangled economy to a private-oriented economy led by market forces. Most major state-owned enterprises had been privatized in the past eight years, regulatory regimes were abolished, and price controls, direct subsidies and restrictions on foreign investment were eliminated.

During the first two years, the stabilization program had as its objective the elimination of the hyperinflationary process, so as to generate public savings and to reverse the country's isolation from the international financial community. This program was constituted by a set of fiscal reforms and commercial and financial liberalization, whereby interest rates were determined by the market, the monopoly of the public sector and of most subsidies was eliminated, and the economy was opened up to foreign goods and services. This adjustment process occurred simultaneously during a period of external credits suspension and a deterioration in the terms of trade.

The stabilization policy was based on discretionary management of the monetary base and a floating exchange rate policy with intervention by the central bank to avoid abrupt fluctuations. The program imposed austerity in fiscal policy, limiting government expenditure to the availability of tax resources and external sources of financing.

In 1990–92, the main objective of economic policy was to consolidate the stabilization process and to define an adequate framework for growth in the medium term through the accomplishment of a series of structural reforms. This stage also emphasized the beginning of the privatizations linked to the public service sector, the Central Bank Autonomy Law.

The new direction of economic policy also encouraged negotiations to end the isolation of Peru to external financing. The process started with the multilateral institutions agreements in 1991 followed by the Paris Club and finally with the commercial banks in the context of the Brady Plan.

The debt-restructuring agreement under the Brady Plan was signed in 1997. As a result of this agreement, Peru issued bonds with a nominal value of US$4,873 million in exchange for debt. The debt reduction has had a positive impact on the country's external credit rating, with medium- and long-term external public debt declining from 41 to 29 percent of GDP between 1996 and 1997.

### *Central government revenue trends*

Tax revenue increased from 10.8 percent of GDP in 1990 to 14.1 percent in 1997. Tax reform implemented during this period was devoted to generating greater resources for the treasury and to simplifying administrative tax procedures and reducing tax evasion. During the first two years, the main characteristics of the tax policy were simplification of tax legislation and modification of the base and tax rates on taxes of a permanent character (emphasizing the increase of the excise tax rate on fuels). In addition, in order to increase fiscal resources and reduce the fiscal gap more quickly, a set of temporary and extraordinary taxes was introduced. These measures improved the tax structure, even though it preserved a relative tax dispersion that impeded consolidation of the tax system based only on permanent taxes.

The main effort of tax reform took place in late 1992. After the reform, the tax system was composed mainly of four taxes: income tax, value added tax, excise tax and import tax. Efforts to improve the tax system later continued, with the reduction in exemptions and abolishment of taxes.

### *Central government expenditure trends*

Total expenditure as a percentage of GDP dropped substantially from 19.4 percent in 1990 to 16.9 percent in 1997. This remarkable effort in reducing expenses was due to strong fiscal discipline, reallocation of resources and rationalization of all expenses. In order to control expenditures, the new Cash Management Committee strictly enforced the policy of limiting expenditures to available resources.

The stabilization program reduced public expenses with the elimination of most subsidies on controlled prices, the reduction and elimination of budgetary subsidies to nonprofitable companies, and cuts on certain public nonproductive investments. To increase efficiency and effectively reduce expenditure pressures, a process of reforms on public administration was implemented. The main policies of this reform were:

- Rationalization of public servants. The government undertook a process of evaluation of public servants to match real needs and to increase the quality of human resources. As a result, the number of public employees dropped from 714,000 in 1990 to 645,000 in 1992.
- Reduction in the number of public entities. The government reduced and merged some ministries and public institutions.
- Privatization of public enterprises.

On the other hand, in contrast to previous policies, social expenditure was supported; expenditures on poverty relief programs and in education, social and economic infrastructure were increased. To improve readiness in applying social policies, the government created specialized institutions such as FONCODES (Compensation and Social Development Fund) and INFES (National Education and Social Infrastructure Institute). To this end, there was a notable increase in social expenditure to mix growth with equity. The greater expenditure was financed almost exclusively by the tax reform and the privatization processes.

Debt service represented a considerable share of expenditures during this period, especially in the first years. This came as a result of the policies of the previous government to reduce debt payments to a minimum, which produced an increase in the arrears of the external public debt.

### *1998–2000: External shocks and fiscal imbalance*

During this period, the Peruvian economy faced four shocks that influenced productive sectors and aggregate demand; three of the shocks came from a foreign crisis and the other from natural phenomena. The first shock was the Asian crisis, which affected prices of commodities in mining (the price of copper reached a fifty-year low) and other export sectors.

Right after the Asian crisis had begun, the country was hit by the El Niño phenomena. This raised the temperature in the ocean by 10 degrees Celsius, creating fish migration, and causing torrential rains and floods that destroyed a large part of the country's agriculture and roads. The loss in infrastructure, export sales and agricultural products has been calculated to be US$1.6 billion, and is reflected in the current account deficit of 5.9 percent of GDP in 1998. The effects of the Russian crisis motivated a stock market drop of 21 percent and local banks began to have trouble finding international loans.

The Brazilian crisis also affected the flow of external resources, as international markets feared that the contagion would spread throughout the region. As a result, credit to the productive sectors was seriously affected. All of these supply-side factors affected aggregate demand; after an expansion of 6.7 percent in 1997, aggregate demand showed successive contractions of 0.9 and 2.6 percent in 1998 and 1999, respectively.

The overall balance of the nonfinancial public sector plunged from a surplus of 0.2 percent of GDP in 1997 to a deficit of 3 percent in 2000. Most of the increase in the fiscal deficit comes from the reduction in central government tax revenue, due to the contraction in aggregate demand but also to a moderate expansion in public expenses. Both factors contributed toward the anti-cyclical response of fiscal policy.

A considerable share of the expenditure increase was applied to finance emergency, rehabilitation and reconstruction programs, intended to restore the damage caused by El Niño. Payroll expenditures also increased, as wage and salary increases were granted to all central government active workers and pensioners in August 1997 and April 1999. Goods and services expenditure rose from 3.4 to 3.7 percent of GDP due mainly to government aid to the population affected by El Niño. The low dynamism of domestic demand offset the application of significant expenditure cuts in central government expenditure.

Regarding tax policy, the government applied a new set of tax exemptions and benefits. Even though their effect was not considerable, they implied a backward step in the tax reform process. The main benefits were:

- investment promotion in the Amazon (through VAT, income and excise tax benefits);
- VAT exemptions of social real property sales;
- tax rate reduction on rice sales;
- the Agricultural Promotion Law (income tax reduction).

### *Current adjustment policy*

The central aim of the current fiscal policy is to eliminate the fiscal gap in the short run so as to avoid an unsustainable position in the medium term. Fiscal policy advocates drastic constraint in government expenditure and expansion in tax collection. Reflecting this, from July 2000, the government has adopted extraordinary measures of financial and economic character that are directed at rationalizing government expenditure, improving tax collection and making possible the availability of fiscal resources.

The main fiscal austerity measures included:

- reduction in the upper limits of National Treasury expenditures in the third and fourth quarters below the targets set in the Budget Law;
- fiscal discipline policies referred to in the budget implementation for wages and salaries, goods and services, and contracting and administration of public institutions of their own resources;

- reduction in the Budget Law of 2001, nonfinancial expenditures to 5 percent (US$360 million);
- a stand-by agreement with the IMF. The government is committed to reducing the fiscal deficit from 3.0 percent of GDP in 2000 to 1.5 percent in 2001, in line with the limits set in the Law of Fiscal Prudence and Transparency.

As a result, nonfinancial expenditure of the central government fell 6.7 and 9.0 percent in real terms during the third and fourth quarters, respectively. Nonfinancial expenditure in these two quarters was also lower than that registered in the second quarter, even though the second quarter expenses included traditional wage bonuses for the National Holiday (July) and Christmas. For 2001, nonfinancial expenditure of the central government is expected to be reduced 6 percent in real terms with respect to 2000.

On the revenue side, Congress passed laws proposed by the executive branch limiting the scope of tax stability agreements and reducing long-lasting benefits for the mining and energy sectors with the elimination of tax incentives that originated at the beginning of the 1990s. At that time, incentives were introduced to promote large investments in the economy; clearly the context for such incentives is very different today.

Modifications to income tax were introduced and were directed to reduce evasion. The main charges are referred to regulations of transactions (including transfer pricing) operations with foreign fiscal paradises, limits on carry-over losses, and depreciation and reduction of exemptions.

At the beginning of 2001, the Congress approved the executive branch's initiative to stop new exemptions or tax benefits. The Congress later permitted the executive branch to regulate in tax matters and to reduce the number of tax benefits and exemptions.

On the public debt side, the government will issue sovereign bonds up to US$500 million, with the aim of promoting the Peruvian capital market and at the same time, obtaining resources and allowing for more efficient administration of the public debt.

## Fiscal policy dynamics

This section looks at the accomplishments of the 1990s' tax reform, the successful privatization process and the new legal framework that supported these efforts including the Law of Prudence and Fiscal Transparency which set out the fiscal rules, transparency procedures and the benefits from the stabilization fund.

### *Reforms*

An overview of fiscal policy in Peru focuses on four main reforms that occurred in the 1990s:

- The tax reform launched at the beginning of the decade that was devoted to establishing a simple, neutral and fair tax system. This transformed a chaotic tax situation into a modern tax administration.

- The privatization process which aimed to attain a suitable economic environment in terms of an open and competitive economy.
- Reform of the pension system.
- The new fiscal law that was enacted to support prudent and responsible fiscal behavior in order to stabilize the fiscal achievements that had been gained from the beginning of the 1990s and also to establish basic macroeconomic conditions for the long term.

### *Tax reform*

The tax reform was successful in terms of providing higher tax collections in a more efficient manner. At the beginning of the 1990s, the Peruvian tax system was characterized by approximately 200 taxes including special contributions and earmarked taxes. Multiple benefits and tax exemptions were granted to almost all geographical zones of the country, to economic sectors that were considered to be the most important, and to industrial companies, depending on the volume on their investment (micro, small and medium-sized companies). This situation generated an inefficient tax system that was difficult to manage and supervise, and also resulted in a deterioration in tax revenue.

In 1990, almost 40 percent of tax collections came from the excise tax, especially on gasoline, and 22 percent came from earmarked taxes and extraordinary contributions. Revenue from the income tax was only 6 percent of the total tax collection and the value added tax (IGV) represented 18 percent. The Peruvian economic scenario was basically that of an economy that was protected and extremely regulated by the state, with state-owned enterprises playing a significant role in economic activity and in the overall deficit expansion. Price controls, direct subsidies and restrictions on foreign investment also characterized the economy.

Between 1990 and 1992, a successful tax reform was carried out. The reforms aimed to eliminate most exonerations, earmarked taxes and other benefits in order to build a modern tax system that was simple and easy to manage. This fiscal change is reflected in the considerable increase in the tax burden and the first economic surplus in thirty-five years.

The new tax structure reflects three basic principles: (i) neutrality;[2] (ii) simplicity; and (iii) equity. Since 1993, the Peruvian tax scheme has become one of the simplest in the region, represented by only four taxes: income tax, value added tax (IGV), excise tax and import taxes. The value added tax contributes to 44 percent of the tax collection, 19 percent comes from the income tax and only 13 percent comes from the excise tax.

The structure of these taxes was also modified as follows:

- Income tax. The personal income tax structure was simplified from nine tax brackets in 1990 to five in 1992, and finally to two tax brackets in 1994. The marginal tax rate was also reduced from 45 percent in 1990 to 37 percent in 1992, and to 30 in 1994.[3]

- Selective tax. There was a reduction in the number of goods subject to selective taxes (for example, electronic appliances, perfumes and jewelry).
- For the VAT, there was a reduction in the number of exemptions and tax earmarks.
- Import taxes. The reform resulted in a reduction in the number of rates, from 56 in the first semester of 1990 to three since September 1990, and finally to two in 1991. The average tax rate was reduced from 66 percent in 1990 to 17 percent in 1991 and to 13 percent in 1997.[4]

There was also reform in tax administration, and the once corrupt and inefficient tax authority was completely revamped, giving birth to a new institution, the National Tax Superintendence (SUNAT), and reorganization and modernization of customs (ADUANAS).

However, in recent years due to political factors, the essence of these principles has been surpassed by a number of tax benefits that are given to sectors and regions in order to reactivate the economy.

### *Privatization*

Since the 1960s, the state has extended its participation in production activities, providing support to strategic sectors that cannot be in private hands because of national security. Reflecting this viewpoint, participation of state-owned companies as a percentage of GDP increased from 1.5 percent in 1968 to 15 percent in 1988 (currently this ratio is about 5 percent of GDP). However, as part of the economic reforms, privatization was viewed as important in releasing the state from its activity as a producer of private goods and services and at the same time, reinforcing its role as supplier of basic services in health, education, justice, safety and basic infrastructure.

The effects of the privatization process are multiple, at both the macroeconomic and microeconomic levels. Privatization has contributed to greater economic stability and has permitted an increase in the productive capacity of the country. At the same time, this process has contributed toward improvement in the fiscal accounts, allowing the government to provide more and better services. Finally, the change has had a favorable impact on employment in the medium term.

Since 1991, privatization receipts have totaled US$8,335 million due to successful sales in almost all sectors. For example, in 1994, the majority of shareholder stock in the National Telecommunications Company was sold to Telefonica of Spain for US$1,392 million and involved committing investments of more than US$610 million. Two years later, the remaining state participation was sold for US$1,240 million. These changes produced an impressive improvement in the quality of services, and expansion of the network and the number of phones installed. For example, the number of lines doubled between 1994 and 1997, the number of months waiting for a line was reduced from thirty-three months to less than two months, and the number of TV cable customers increased from 6,000 to 252,000.

This boom in privatization has also encompassed key sectors such as electricity, mining, financial services and many others. The benefits from the more than 220 privatization and concession processes are remarkable. Some of these are described below:

- Losses and pressures on the fiscal deficit from state-owned companies no longer hamper the state. Under the new administration, these companies are now productive and successful. As a result, the state has more resources available to be directed toward addressing poverty and for programs in social policy, education, health, public safety and justice.
- There has been an impressive improvement in the quality and coverage of public services at competitive rates that, in some cases have dropped, thanks to efficient administrative procedures, modern technology and infrastructure improvements.
- Middle- and long-term productive employment has been generated. In recent years, the country's productive capacity is better as a consequence of private investment in sectors such as telecommunications, mining and electricity. As a result, companies are stronger and more competitive, and now have greater access to more reliable external market knowledge, as well as to the capital needed to continue their growth.
- Privatization also transformed privatized companies' workers and a great number of Peruvians into stockholders. The preferential right of workers to purchase up to 10 percent of the shares was guaranteed by legislation, while ordinary citizens can purchase shares through the Citizen Participation System. Up to 1998, approximately 16,000 workers exercised their right to purchase shares amounting to US$236 million. Additionally, under the Citizen Participation System, 410,000 Peruvians became owners of solid, profitable shares in companies such as Telefonica S.A., Luz del Sur and Banco Continental.

### *Pension system reform*

One of the impressive reforms introduced was the reform of the pension system—from a distribution system managed by a public entity (Instituto Peruano de Seguridad Social or IPSS) to one based on individual capitalization managed by private companies (Administradoras de Fondos de Pensiones or AFPs)—in December 1992. The AFPs started their operations in the second semester of 1993. Under the new system, each person accumulates his/her own pension funds in a similar way as is done in a savings account. The AFPs invest the funds in a financial instruments portfolio, subject to guarantee and public regulation as well as monitoring and supervision by the Superintendence who looks after the safety of the provisional funds and its technical management.

In short, the pension reform presented benefits in terms of capital accumulation and transparency of the new system. However, the pension reform has a fiscal cost. Specifically, this cost is composed of (i) recognition bonds that have been issued or will be issued to workers who have switched from the public to the private system; and (ii) the additional unfounded liabilities accrued under the public system for both current and future workers. In the case of Peru, these costs are relatively low compared to international standards. The cost is expected to reach a peak of 1.0 percent of GDP by 2020. The low cost is due to the low coverage of the public pension system.

### *The Law of Fiscal Prudence and Transparency*

The Law of Fiscal Prudence and Transparency—enacted on 27 December 1999—is aimed at contributing to economic stability and economic growth through a sound fiscal framework for the medium term. The law restricts the fiscal deficit of the consolidated public sector, limits the growth of nonfinancial expenditures of the general government and establishes a stabilization fund for current income fluctuations associated with the business cycle. In election years, the law imposes additional restrictions on both the consolidated public sector deficit and general government nonfinancial expenditures.

In order to give transparency and reliability to fiscal management, the law establishes the publication of a three-year macroeconomic framework containing the fundamental principles of fiscal policy, as well as macroeconomic forecasts for variables such as income and fiscal expenditures, investment and public indebtedness. It also describes the way in which the macroeconomic framework is to be approved and published, so that the government's fiscal policy intentions will be clearly understood by economic agents.

The quantitative rules specified in the law include the following:

- The consolidated public sector deficit will be no greater than 2 percent of GDP in 2000, 1.5 percent in 2001 and 1 percent thereafter.
- General government expenditure will grow by no more than 2 percent in real terms.
- Total public sector debt—adjusted by exchange rate variations, issues of new provisional bonds, variations in public sector deposits and debt assumed by the public sector—will increase by no more than the deficit.
- In election years, general government nonfinancial expenditure between January and July will be no greater than 60 percent of the total foreseen in the annual budget. The public sector deficit for the first semester will be no greater than 50 percent of the deficit anticipated for the year.

The law also stipulates the following exception rules: (i) in cases of national emergency or international crises, the executive branch can request Congress to suspend any of the quantitative rules for one year; and (ii) if there is evidence that GDP is decreasing or could decrease in real terms in the following period, the fiscal deficit as a percentage of GDP can be allowed to exceed the 1 percent rule, but in no case will be greater than 2 percent.

The following are the resources of the Fiscal Stabilization Fund:

- current revenues from ordinary sources exceeding the average of the last three years by 0.3 percent of GDP;
- 75 percent of privatization revenues;
- 50 percent of net revenue from concessions;

- accumulated savings will be no greater than 3 percent of GDP and the excess will be destined to the consolidated provisional reserve fund or to the reduction of public debt;
- use of fund resources will be contingent on an expected decrease in ordinary revenues of more than 0.3 percent of GDP relative to the average of the last three years, adjusted by significant changes in tax policy.

Transparency procedures identified in the law include the following:

- The Multi-Annual Macroeconomic Framework includes the Statement of Fiscal Policy Principles, which contains the economic policy guidelines and long-run fiscal objectives. Additionally, the framework presents the three-year targets for fiscal policy, as well as macroeconomic forecasts, fiscal revenues and expenditures, investment and public indebtedness. The central bank will issue a technical report, which will include an analysis of the compatibility of the framework with the forecasts for the balance of payments and international reserves and with the monetary policy.
- The law establishes the way in which the framework will be approved and published, as well as the format of performance reports, the Responsibility Fulfillment Statement and the Interpretation and Prohibition Procedures, which are designed to convey to the public the intentions of the government concerning fiscal matters.

## Conclusion: policy issues and future prospects

In the future, fiscal policy will be devoted to restoring financial balance without affecting economic reactivation or taking away resources that are required by the private sector. In accordance with this principle, the goal of tax policy is to expand the tax base and reduce tax rates in the future. Thus, most of the policy actions will depend not only on adequate measures, but also on the efficient administrative capacity in tax collection that is consistent with long-term objectives.

The government will continue with a constant real growth of nonfinancial public expenditure following the expenditure rule stipulated by the Law of Fiscal Prudence and Transparency. The expenditure side of fiscal policy will be accomplished by an objective administration directing expenditure toward potential allocations such as social expenditure, education and health, and toward improving the quality and effectiveness of the services provided by the state.

### *The domestic debt market*

In developing debt policy, it is prudent to embrace a gradual policy so that the market can support the financing needs of the public sector. In the medium term, a more active management of debt policy is foreseeable. This policy would be geared toward the following measures:

- Development of the domestic capital market. Arising as a domestic capital market agent, government issue of titles makes possible the generation of a yield curve, which serves as a benchmark for domestic operations and reduces the need for external debt-reducing adverse effects of external shocks.
- Creation of an institutional framework that provides the mechanisms for the development of these operations. This step is fundamental, since the Treasury does not have a reputation as an issuer of titles in the capital market.
- Generation of resources for service of the external debt. Although fiscal adjustment and privatization constitute important mechanisms for generation of resources, servicing of the external debt will require additional sources that are not subject to currency risk in the medium term.
- Management of short-term debt. What would be convenient is the introduction of the Treasury's short-term liabilities (i.e., treasury drafts) to improve management of the Treasury's liquidity, taking into account the short-term fluctuations or seasonality of public finances.

It is very important to guarantee the domestic financing framework as an additional source of resources to avoid adverse effects from external or nature shocks, as has happened in the past. It is also highly recommended that this domestic framework be maintained in a transparent and reliable way. Prudent treasury management will contribute toward providing the necessary financial support to fiscal policy in the long term.

Although the tax structure was satisfactory for most of the 1990s, it is necessary to pursue strong fiscal discipline especially in the rationalization of tax exemptions, improvement in the mechanisms for tax collection, and reduction in tax avoidance and in all practices against neutrality and equity of the current tax system.

There is also the need to continue the reform of import taxes. The current 13 percent average rate is one of the highest in the region, generating a loss of competitiveness for local producers. To assure neutrality of fiscal policy,[5] the reform should also reduce tariff dispersion, which currently ranges from 4 to 30 percent due to the surtax on agricultural goods. Fiscal policy should aim at a single rate of 5 or 6 percent over the medium term.

Recently, due to the political environment, there has been a slowdown in the privatization process. However, there is still interest from investors in other privatization projects and concessions in ports and airports, mining, telecommunications and the electricity distribution sectors. The Peruvian state still owns enterprises in the oil, electricity generation, transportation and public utilities sectors. Sale of these enterprises could generate US$3,000 million in revenue to the government and investment of US$5,000 million. In the electricity generation sector, for example, there is a group of firms that includes Mantaro, Egasa, Electro Andes, Egesur, San Gaban and Egemsa. There are also two electricity transmission firms (Etecen and Etesur) and a set of distribution firms such as Electro Suroeste, Sureste, Sur, Puno, Ucayali and Oriente. Privatization of these enterprises could result in revenue of US$2,400 million.

In the mining and petroleum production sectors, a group of oil refineries (such as Talara, Conchan and Iquitos) could be sold. In addition, the pipeline that is run by Petroperu could be given in concession to the private sector. Moreover, there remain some units of Centromin and Mineroperu to be sold (like Imex, Bayovar, among others). These assets could generate upward of US$300 million in privatization receipts.

In the services sector, ports managed by Enapu and airfields by Corpac will be transferred to the private sector. These transactions could generate up to US$100 million. In addition to these operations, the selling of state-owned buildings and proceeds from previous privatizations could generate as much as US$200 million in additional revenue. Cash revenue from the privatization of Sedapal and other water supply enterprises are not expected. These firms, and the road system, could be given in concession to the private sector.

It is necessary to grant a high priority to infrastructure concessions, in order to increase efficiency and reduce public expenditures. Public savings could be oriented to respond to social needs.

## Notes

1 The institutional coverage of public finance statistics produced by the Central Bank of Peru (Banco Central de Reserva del Perú, 1999) follows international standards and includes both in-budget and off-budget operations of the central government, the social security system, regional and local governments, state-owned enterprises and other public entities (such as universities, regulatory agencies, and decentralized institutions). It also includes all public funds such as the Consolidated Pension Fund and National Savings Fund.

2 Neutrality in the sense of applying a uniform effective rate to all economic activities and allowing the market to conduct the investment according to the profitability rate of each sector; and without distortions that could cause exemptions, reduced taxes for selective geographical zones or productive sectors.

3 In December 1999, the government further reduced the marginal tax rate from 30 to 20 percent.

4 In 1997, an ad valorem surtax was introduced for some agricultural goods. However, the average rate remains at 13 percent.

5 It is important to note that there is a practical impossibility in distinguishing between final and intermediate goods, as some goods may be an input for some goods and a final good for others. Thus multiple rates can ultimately hurt local production and generate artificial profitability.

## References

Banco Central de Reserva del Perú (1999). *Memorias 1990–2000*, Lima: Banco Central de Reserva del Perú.

von Hagen, J. (1999) *Strengthening Fiscal Institutions*, Bonn: Centre for European Integration Studies.

# 14 The Philippines

*Cayetano W. Paderanga, Jr*

## Introduction

The Philippines has had a volatile economic record for the past two decades. During that period, it has experienced one deep and two relatively minor recessions. The deep recession was the result of a crisis that started with a political event (the assassination of Senator Benigno Aquino) and culminated with the downfall of President Ferdinand Marcos in 1985. The minor crises happened in 1990, in the aftermath of the most serious coup attempt against President Corazon Aquino, and in 1997, as part of the Asian currency crisis. Table 14.1 lists the related balance-of-payments crisis that accompanied these economic downturns.

A major cause and effect of this overall volatility is the deterioration in the fiscal position of the government. The continued structural deficit introduces an underlying instability into the system that reduces the economy's ability to absorb external and random internal shocks. Otherwise minor perturbations become large fluctuations because of the underlying imbalances. At the same time, economic volatility introduces uncertainty into the tax base, reduces stability and predictability in the taxpayers' ability to pay, and may unduly complicate the collection process. This underlying interaction argues for structural changes designed to reduce volatility and create a stable fiscal balance.

## Taxes and public sector resource mobilization in the Philippines

### *National and local government revenues and expenditures*

In the past fifteen years since the Aquino administration supplanted the Marcos regime, the Philippine government has implemented various changes in its revenue and expenditure patterns. Soon after the takeover of the Marcos regime, the government initiated a series of attempts to overhaul the tax system by restructuring the types and rates of taxes to be imposed. Those taxes that pertained to the national government are discussed in this chapter.

As far as comparative national and local government budget activities are concerned, the most significant event is the passage of the Local Government Code (LGC) in 1991. The code increased the local governments' share of internal

*Table 14.1* Episodes of balance-of-payments crisis in the Philippines

| *Date* | *Immediate precipitant* | *Underlying precipitant* | *Average GDP growth rate: past 4–5 years* |
|---|---|---|---|
| Nov.–Dec. 1949 | 1949 presidential election | Rising trade deficit, rapid fall of reserves from $420 to $260 million | 18.0 |
| Nov.–Dec. 1957 | 1957 presidential election | Trade deficit pressure inherent in import substitution; reserves fell from $160 to $71 million | 7.0 |
| Nov.–Dec. 1969 | 1969 presidential election | Trade deficit explosion; rising debt service | 5.4 |
| 1980–83 | Oil shock, rise in world interest rate, political turmoil | Trade deficit pressure; rapid rise in debt service | 6.4 |
| 1990 | Gulf War, natural calamities | Trade deficit pressure; debt service explosion | 4.5 |
| 1997–99 | Natural calamities; oil price rebound; presidential election | Trade deficit pressure; still considerable debt service | 5.0 |

Source: Fabella (1994: 144), except data for 1997–99.

revenue taxes and increased the power of the provinces, municipalities and villages (*barangays*) to impose fees and some taxes. The increased internal revenue allocation is especially mentioned as the reason for the increase in local government resources in the past decade.

Table 14.2 shows the revenues of national and local government in the period 1975–2000. The increase in local government resources as a percentage of gross domestic product (GDP) is shown in Figure 14.1. While the national government's share of GDP decreased slightly in the last decade, local government's share has shown a secular increase. Figure 14.2 shows how the proportions of national and local government to total public expenditures have changed.

According to the income and expenditure patterns of local governments in 1980–99, the increase in the share of tax revenue relative to operating and miscellaneous revenue and capital revenue is very palpable. Starting in 1991, the share of tax revenue jumped from 69 to 84 percent and continued to increase to 87 percent as of 1999. What should not go unnoticed, however, is the increase in the share of public services on the expenditure side. This increased from only about 40 percent at the start of the 1980s to 50 percent in 1999. However, the increase started much earlier in 1986, when the Aquino administration took over. Still, the share of capital outlays and maintenance and operating expenses indicate that increased resources have not gone toward an increased proportion for direct program expenses and capital investments. This trend must be reversed in the long run as much as possible.

### *National government revenue patterns*

The Philippine tax effort—which is dominated by developments in national government revenue—has generally been disappointing, especially in comparison to the impressive levels in the ASEAN region (see Table 14.3). The improvement in the tax effort in the late 1990s remains insufficient to cover the financial operations of the government. From 1975, the tax effort peaked at 17 percent in 1997, but it started to deteriorate in the following year and slid further in the subsequent three years. In 2000, the tax effort stood at 13.6 percent as the growth of tax earnings decelerated since 1997 and hit its lowest growth rate of 1.1 percent in 1998.

The lowest tax ratio of 9.6 percent was registered during the crisis period of 1984. Thereafter, the tax effort has improved with the implementation of various measures to increase tax earnings. Specifically, the 1986 Tax Reform Program led to improved mobilization of resources to finance public sector projects.

In the 1990s, a number of changes in the revenue structure (which moved towards direct taxation) turned out to be more beneficial as a greater tax burden was redirected toward household groups that had a greater ability to pay. From 1986, the share of direct taxes to GDP has been rising faster than in the case of indirect taxes. The share of direct taxes to total national income increased from 3.2 percent in 1986 to 6.9 percent in 1998, while the share of indirect taxes inched up slightly from 4.4 percent to 4.8 percent in the same period. Part of the increase in indirect taxes came from the introduction of the value added tax (VAT) that was supposed to serve as a substitute for transfer taxes. However, the disappointing

*Table 14.2* National and local government revenue, 1975–2000 (million pesos, unless otherwise noted)

| | *1975* | *1976* | *1977* | *1978* | *1979* | *1980* | *1981* | *1982* | *1983* | *1984* |
|---|---|---|---|---|---|---|---|---|---|---|
| A. National government (NG) revenue | 16,856 | 18,089 | 19,959 | 24,073 | 29,470 | 34,731 | 35,933 | 38,205 | 45,632 | 56,861 |
| Tax revenue | 13,753 | 15,327 | 16,955 | 20,441 | 25,956 | 30,533 | 31,423 | 33,779 | 39,524 | 50,118 |
| B. Local government (LG) revenue | 2,344 | 1,813 | 2,625 | 2,847 | 3,687 | 4,573 | 5,102 | 5,929 | 6,700 | 7,349 |
| Tax revenue | 1,454 | 1,164 | 1,897 | 2,012 | 2,682 | 3,281 | 3,805 | 4,501 | 5,040 | 5,454 |
| C. Total (A + B) | 19,200 | 19,902 | 22,584 | 26,920 | 33,157 | 39,304 | 41,035 | 44,134 | 52,332 | 64,210 |
| D. As a share of total government revenue (%) | | | | | | | | | | |
| NG revenue | 87.79 | 90.89 | 88.38 | 89.42 | 88.88 | 88.36 | 87.57 | 86.57 | 87.20 | 88.56 |
| LG revenue | 12.21 | 9.11 | 11.62 | 10.58 | 11.12 | 11.64 | 12.43 | 13.43 | 12.80 | 11.44 |
| E. Ratio of tax revenue to GDP (%) | | | | | | | | | | |
| NG tax revenue | 12.74 | 12.05 | 11.66 | 12.22 | 12.79 | 12.53 | 11.16 | 10.65 | 10.71 | 9.56 |
| LG tax revenue | 1.35 | 0.92 | 1.30 | 1.20 | 1.32 | 1.35 | 1.35 | 1.42 | 1.37 | 1.04 |
| Combined NG & LG tax revenues | 17.79 | 15.64 | 15.53 | 16.10 | 16.34 | 16.12 | 14.57 | 13.91 | 14.18 | 12.24 |
| Nominal GDP | 107,950 | 127,211 | 145,451 | 167,249 | 202,900 | 243,749 | 281,596 | 317,177 | 369,077 | 524,481 |

| | *1985* | *1986* | *1987* | *1988* | *1989* | *1990* | *1991* | *1992* | *1993* | *1994* |
|---|---|---|---|---|---|---|---|---|---|---|
| A. National government (NG) revenue | 68,961 | 79,245 | 103,214 | 112,861 | 152,410 | 180,902 | 220,787 | 242,715 | 260,405 | 336,160 |
| Tax revenue | 61,253 | 65,491 | 85,923 | 90,352 | 122,462 | 151,698 | 182,275 | 208,706 | 230,170 | 271,305 |
| B. Local government (LG) revenue | 8,510 | 8,661 | 8,923 | 13,359 | 15,281 | 19,062 | 23,900 | 27,434 | 44,210 | 59,830 |
| Tax revenue | 6,199 | 6,537 | 6,777 | 8,053 | 9,654 | 13,005 | 16,484 | 23,086 | 38,166 | 51,401 |
| C. Total (A + B) | 77,471 | 87,906 | 112,137 | 126,220 | 167,691 | 199,964 | 244,687 | 270,149 | 304,615 | 395,990 |

| | | | | | | | | | | |
|---|---|---|---|---|---|---|---|---|---|---|
| D. As a share of total government revenue (%) | | | | | | | | | | |
| NG revenue | 89.01 | 90.15 | 92.04 | 89.42 | 90.89 | 90.47 | 90.23 | 89.85 | 85.49 | 84.89 |
| LG revenue | 10.99 | 9.85 | 7.96 | 10.58 | 9.11 | 9.53 | 9.77 | 10.15 | 14.51 | 15.11 |
| E. Ratio of tax revenue to GDP (%) | | | | | | | | | | |
| NG tax revenue | 10.71 | 10.76 | 12.58 | 11.31 | 13.23 | 14.08 | 14.61 | 15.44 | 15.61 | 16.03 |
| LG tax revenue | 1.08 | 1.07 | 0.99 | 1.01 | 1.04 | 1.21 | 1.32 | 1.71 | 2.59 | 3.04 |
| Combined NG & LG tax revenues | 13.55 | 14.44 | 16.42 | 15.79 | 18.12 | 18.56 | 19.61 | 19.99 | 20.66 | 23.39 |
| Nominal GDP | 571,883 | 608,887 | 682,764 | 799,182 | 925,444 | 1,077,237 | 1,248,011 | 1,351,559 | 1,474,457 | 1,692,932 |

| | *1995* | *1996* | *1997* | *1998* | *1999* | *2000* |
|---|---|---|---|---|---|---|
| A. National government (NG) revenue | 361,220 | 410,449 | 471,843 | 462,515 | 478,502 | 505,725 |
| Tax revenue | 310,517 | 367,894 | 412,165 | 416,585 | 431,688 | 451,941 |
| B. Local government (LG) revenue | 67,840 | 76,109 | 93,666 | 100,226 | 120,349 | |
| Tax revenue | 58,938 | 65,047 | 80,772 | 87,391 | 104,836 | 146,484 |
| C. Total (A + B) | 429,060 | 486,558 | 565,509 | 562,741 | 598,851 | 505,725 |
| D. As a share of total government revenue (%) | | | | | | |
| NG revenue | 84.19 | 84.36 | 83.44 | 82.19 | 79.90 | na |
| LG revenue | 15.81 | 15.64 | 16.56 | 17.81 | 20.10 | na |
| E. Ratio of tax revenue to GDP (%) | | | | | | |
| NG tax revenue | 16.29 | 16.94 | 16.98 | 15.55 | 14.41 | 13.60 |
| LG tax revenue | 3.09 | 2.99 | 3.33 | 3.26 | 3.50 | 4.41 |
| Combined NG & LG tax revenues | 22.51 | 22.40 | 23.30 | 21.01 | 19.99 | 15.22 |
| Nominal GDP | 1,906,328 | 2,171,922 | 2,426,743 | 2,678,187 | 2,996,371 | 3,322,626 |

Sources: Bureau of Treasury; Commission on Audit for National and Local Governments.

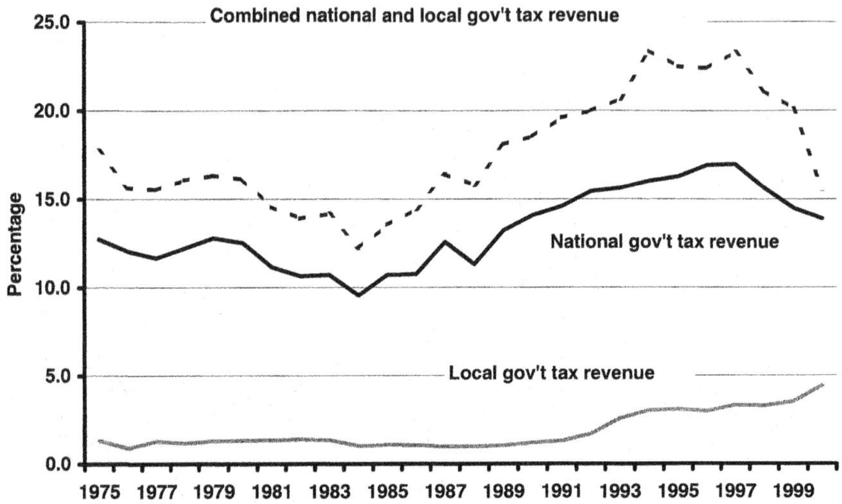


*Figure 14.1* National and local government tax revenue in the Philippines, 1975–2000 (as a % of nominal GDP).

Sources: Bureau of Treasury; Commission on Audit for National and Local Governments.

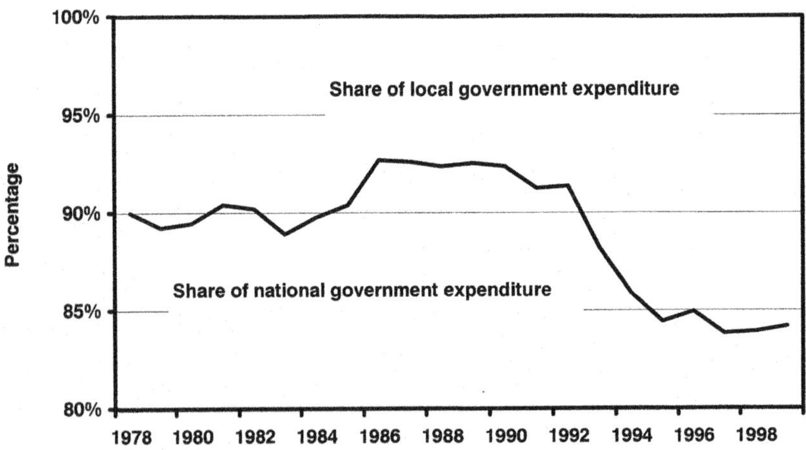


*Figure 14.2* National and local government expenditure pattern in the Philippines, 1978–99 (as a % of total expenditures).

*Table 14.3* Revenue generation and structure in selected Asian countries, 1990–96 average (as a % of GDP)

| | *The Philippines* | *Indonesia* | *Korea* | *Malaysia* | *Thailand* |
|---|---|---|---|---|---|
| Tax revenue | 15.6 | 15.8 | 16.6 | 20.4 | 16.7 |
| Taxes on income, profits and capital gains | 2.3 | 9.3 | 5.9 | 9.2 | 5.2 |
| Of which: corporate income tax | 2.1 | 4.9 | 2.4 | 6.8 | 3.0 |
| Domestic taxes on goods and services | 4.8 | 5.0 | 6.3 | 6.0 | 7.5 |
| Taxes on international trade and transactions | 4.8 | 0.9 | 1.4 | 3.9 | 3.3 |
| Nontax revenue | 2.7 | 1.9 | 2.6 | 6.8 | 2.0 |
| Total revenue | 18.3 | 17.7 | 19.2 | 27.2 | 18.6 |

Source: International Monetary Fund (2000).

yield in the VAT and the continuing inadequacy of revenues to meet expenditure needs have caused the government to delay the second step, i.e., it has not yet fulfilled its commitment to remove all transfer taxes. This has increased the yield from indirect taxes, but has also increased the burden on those sectors already paying taxes.

Starting in 1984, the tax effort improved as a result of the 1986 tax reform program. However, beginning in 1994, the tax revenue effort began to deteriorate and reverted back to a low of 13.6 percent in 2000 from a high of 19.4 percent in 1994. There are several possible reasons for this: (i) many tax measures passed by Congress—such as the adoption of a simplified income tax system for nonfixed income tax filers—eroded the tax base; (ii) the tax collection machinery failed to make the necessary administrative adjustments to keep up with the recent tax laws (e.g., inadequate preparation for the implementation of VAT); (iii) an intensification of governance problems in the tax area; and (iv) tariff reductions due to trade liberalization.

Dependence on the strength of tax collection from property and net income and profits has increased. As countries expand their markets through open trade, the last point related to tariff liberalization will have added significance in the future. As the Philippines gradually dismantles its tariff walls and the yield from trade taxes declines as the AFTA and the GATT Uruguay Round trade accord become operative, then dependence on trade taxes will have to be reduced. As a result, the government will have to tap internal indirect and direct taxes to fund the budget. The experience of most countries suggests that domestic indirect taxes progressively replace foreign trade taxes, and direct taxes show greater predominance soon thereafter. For the Philippines, internal indirect taxes as a percentage of GDP have been fairly constant. Therefore, unless collections from direct taxes are aggressively improved, the government's revenue collections will not be able to catch up with the size of its spending.

Meanwhile, nontax revenues in the Philippines became more significant during 1995–99 mainly due to the proceeds from sale of sequestered assets and the privatization of some state-operated enterprises. Sales of government assets turned in large, one-time inflows to the national treasury. A recent law requiring government corporations to remit 50 percent of their net income as dividends to the national government has also brought forward additional nontax revenue for the Bureau of Treasury.

However, these temporary revenue sources distort the long-run fiscal picture of the government. Proceeds from privatization are nonrecurring and reflect a corresponding loss of government assets. With lower net worth, the government is in a weaker position to service fiscal deficits in the future. At the same time, the higher dividends going to the national treasury have neutral effects. While it improves the financial picture of the national government, it weakens those of affected corporations. Hence, problems arise when these nonrecurring and higher dividends from corporations are treated as a permanent and real revenue gain, and the proceeds are used for recurring expenditures. The national government would then be faced with larger deficits in the future as privatization proceeds dry up and financial conditions of state corporations deteriorate, while the national government budget rises beyond its limits. This could also be cited as one of the causes of the deterioration in the revenue effort seen in recent years.

### *National government expenditure patterns*

Closer examination of the national government's fiscal expenditure suggests that, as a percentage of GDP, it has been tracking the country's growth path. In the crisis period of 1984, the lowest share of 12.8 percent was recorded. After achieving the highest expenditure to GDP ratio of 20.2 percent in 1990, government spending went on a downtrend in subsequent years but is back on track at 19.3 percent in 2000.

Of total government spending, the share of capital expenditures is continuously being reduced. After receiving the largest share for more than a quarter of the early 1980s, the proportion of capital spending was cut to a single-digit rate in the late 1990s. The low budgetary share of capital spending suggests that there is serious underspending in physical infrastructure. Studies have shown that the failure of the government to implement projects is caused not only by lower budgetary appropriation, but also by bureaucratic delays and low absorptive capability of the government infrastructure machinery. Note that this seriously undermines the appropriate role of government in sustaining growth by providing physical and social infrastructure, especially in human capital.

Meanwhile, the amount of spending that has been directed toward the servicing of liabilities of the public sector has continued to escalate. Interest payments have continuously accounted for a significant share of total expenditures. From a single-digit average of 3.0 percent and 6.8 percent in 1975–79 and 1980–83, respectively, interest payments surged to an average of 29.1 percent in 1990–94 and 18.7 percent in 1995–99. The largest share of 33.7 percent was posted in 1988. The unprecedented large government deficits and borrowing in the last two-and-a-half years can be expected to place upward pressure on interest payments in the near future.

### *National government deficit financing*

The national government's fiscal position has mostly been in deficit since 1975, with the exception of surpluses recorded in 1994 to 1997. Review of the Philippine fiscal balance suggests that the large budget deficits can be traced to the large revenue shortfall arising from the rapid implementation of large public investment projects. After successfully turning up surpluses in 1994 to 1997, the total deficit soared to P50 billion in 1998, P111.7 billion in 1999 and P136.1 billion in 2000 (Table 14.4).

In recent years, the large fiscal deficits have been financed by foreign borrowing to a significant extent. Historically, foreign borrowing was high in 1978–83, but it started to decline in the mid-1980s as foreign loans became scarce. During the crisis years of 1983–84, the ratio of net external financing to the fiscal deficit rose again. Then in 1984–91, the government tapped domestic financing to manage its deficits. Subsequently, in the late 1990s, after posting surpluses for four consecutive years, external finance became increasingly important once again. In 1999 alone, total borrowings from foreign sources was 45.6 percent (Table 14.5).

The long-run consequences of large external borrowings can be analyzed by looking at the primary surplus—that is, total revenues less nondebt expenditures. Without large interest payments, the fiscal position of the national government would be more manageable. From only P20.1 billion in 1987, the national government was able to build up a primary surplus amounting to P49.8 billion in 1998. The highest level of primary surplus was reached in 1994 at P95.4 billion.

## Fiscal policy for sustainable growth

The sustainability of economic growth can be assessed in two ways: (i) analyses of the attainment of fiscal balance on a sustainable basis; and (ii) an examination of how the mix of government spending and taxation influence economic growth. During periods of stabilization, the government's immediate aim should be to close the fiscal gap in the short run. Nonetheless, in a process of recovery, which the Philippines is undergoing at this time, a higher growth path should be achieved by attaining fiscal balance but not at the expense of investments in infrastructure and human capital.

## Sustainability of the fiscal balance

### *The savings–investment gap*

One of the reasons for the failure of the Philippine economy to grow on a sustainable basis is its inability to accumulate savings to finance its public investments. Although gross domestic saving rates have improved in recent years, negative rates were attained for the period 1990–97. The slow accumulation of savings by the

*Table 14.4* National government account balances (million pesos)

| *Items* | *1980* | *1982* | *1984* | *1986* | *1988* | *1990* | *1992* | *1994* | *1996* | *1998* | *2000* |
|---|---|---|---|---|---|---|---|---|---|---|---|
| 1. Total revenues | 34,731 | 38,205 | 56,861 | 79,245 | 112,861 | 180,902 | 242,715 | 336,160 | 410,449 | 462,515 | 505,725 |
| a. Total taxes | 30,533 | 33,779 | 50,118 | 65,491 | 90,352 | 151,698 | 208,706 | 271,305 | 367,894 | 416,585 | 451,941 |
| Direct taxes | 8,957 | 8,668 | 12,410 | 19,353 | 27,793 | 49,645 | 70,371 | 92,269 | 136,921 | 184,383 | na |
| Taxes on net income and profits | 8,761 | 8,406 | 12,139 | 19,148 | 27,409 | 49,366 | 70,123 | 91,886 | 136,356 | 183,914 | na |
| Taxes on property | 196 | 262 | 271 | 205 | 384 | 279 | 248 | 383 | 565 | 469 | na |
| Indirect taxes | 9,332 | 12,243 | 18,793 | 26,659 | 33,207 | 50,745 | 57,285 | 76,025 | 107,689 | 128,716 | na |
| Tax on international trade | 9,904 | 12,253 | 17,756 | 17,851 | 25,580 | 46,570 | 73,577 | 82,318 | 104,850 | 76,371 | na |
| Other taxes | 640 | 736 | 1,159 | 1,628 | 3,772 | 4,738 | 7,473 | 20,693 | 18,434 | 27,116 | na |
| b. Nontax revenues | 4,198 | 4,406 | 6,743 | 13,756 | 22,509 | 28,423 | 34,008 | 64,856 | 42,555 | 45,930 | 53,784 |
| 2. Total expenditures | 38,118 | 52,610 | 66,926 | 110,497 | 136,067 | 218,096 | 258,680 | 319,874 | 404,193 | 512,496 | 641,835 |
| a. Current operating expenditures | 24,516 | 31,746 | 42,873 | 71,330 | 113,595 | 161,840 | 219,505 | 277,274 | 353,062 | 467,920 | 579,978 |
| Of which: | | | | | | | | | | | |
| Interest payments | 2,296 | 3,560 | 10,409 | 20,953 | 45,866 | 71,113 | 79,539 | 79,123 | 76,522 | 99,792 | 140,894 |
| Domestic | 1,098 | 2,312 | 6,141 | 15,156 | 32,183 | 53,727 | 63,112 | 59,806 | 59,002 | 73,525 | 93,575 |
| Foreign | 1,198 | 1,248 | 4,268 | 5,797 | 13,682 | 17,386 | 16,427 | 19,317 | 17,520 | 26,267 | 47,319 |
| Personal services | 9,331 | 10,647 | 16,854 | 24,991 | 40,795 | 64,289 | 74,337 | 92,678 | 123,226 | 172,889 | 180,999 |
| b. Capital outlays | 8,405 | 9,278 | 9,786 | 11,683 | 15,233 | 38,236 | 46,125 | 33,606 | 47,955 | 43,478 | 58,687 |
| c. Net lending and equity | 5,197 | 11,586 | 14,267 | 27,484 | 7,239 | 2,769 | −6,950 | 8,994 | 3,176 | 1,098 | 3,170 |
| 3. Total surplus/(deficit): (1) − (2) | −3,387 | −14,405 | −10,065 | −31,252 | −23,206 | −37,194 | −15,966 | 16,286 | 6,256 | −49,981 | −136,110 |
| 4. Expenditures excl. interest payments | 35,822 | 49,050 | 56,517 | 89,544 | 90,201 | 146,983 | 179,141 | 240,751 | 327,671 | 412,704 | 500,941 |
| 5. Primary surplus/(deficit): (1) − (4) | −1,091 | −10,845 | 344 | −10,299 | 22,660 | 33,919 | 63,574 | 95,409 | 82,778 | 49,811 | 4,784 |

Source: Bureau of Treasury.

*Table 14.5* Distribution of national government financing, 1975–2000

| *Items* | *1975* | *1976* | *1977* | *1978* | *1979* | *1980* | *1981* | *1982* | *1983* | *1984* | *1985* | *1986* | *1987* |
|---|---|---|---|---|---|---|---|---|---|---|---|---|---|
| Total financing (million pesos) | 1,374 | 1,445 | 2,402 | 4,071 | 3,847 | 3,496 | 14,820 | 11,199 | 12,028 | 18,004 | 12,531 | 32,029 | 41,118 |
| Total financing: (a) + (b) | 100.00 | 100.00 | 100.00 | 100.00 | 100.00 | 100.00 | 100.00 | 100.00 | 100.00 | 100.00 | 100.00 | 100.00 | 100.00 |
| a. Net foreign borrowing | 17.61 | 3.53 | 10.41 | 45.49 | 82.79 | 68.76 | 40.43 | 41.05 | 45.20 | 11.13 | −2.71 | 11.18 | 16.49 |
| Gross borrowing | 24.45 | 12.18 | 32.89 | 55.64 | 95.68 | 87.39 | 45.37 | 48.11 | 63.88 | 28.15 | 29.56 | 30.50 | 37.50 |
| Less: payments | 6.84 | 8.65 | 22.48 | 10.14 | 12.89 | 18.62 | 4.94 | 7.06 | 18.68 | 17.02 | 32.27 | 19.32 | 21.01 |
| b. Net domestic borrowing | 82.39 | 96.47 | 89.59 | 54.51 | 17.21 | 31.24 | 59.57 | 58.95 | 54.80 | 88.87 | 102.71 | 88.82 | 83.51 |
| Gross borrowing | 103.86 | 116.75 | 342.80 | 241.69 | 252.12 | 144.94 | 83.69 | 94.12 | 67.31 | 95.21 | 125.91 | 110.72 | 142.56 |
| Less: payments | 21.47 | 20.28 | 253.21 | 187.18 | 234.91 | 113.70 | 24.12 | 35.17 | 12.51 | 6.34 | 23.20 | 21.89 | 59.05 |

| *Items* | *1988* | *1989* | *1990* | *1991* | *1992* | *1993* | *1994* | *1995* | *1996* | *1997* | *1998* | *1999* | *2000* |
|---|---|---|---|---|---|---|---|---|---|---|---|---|---|
| Total financing (million pesos) | 39,329 | 28,660 | 19,270 | 41,248 | 152,637 | −15,653 | −21,937 | 10,969 | 43,319 | −27,113 | 88,896 | 181,698 | 198,271 |
| Total financing: (a) + (b) | 100.00 | 100.00 | 100.00 | 100.00 | 100.00 | 100.00 | 100.00 | 100.00 | 100.00 | 100.00 | 100.00 | 100.00 | 100.00 |
| a. Net foreign borrowing | 10.79 | 28.65 | 21.42 | 16.68 | 9.43 | −82.49 | 52.77 | −121.67 | −13.86 | 25.15 | 13.89 | 45.57 | 39.72 |
| Gross borrowing | 43.96 | 69.62 | 126.65 | 55.97 | 22.37 | −244.19 | −55.99 | 153.46 | 50.68 | −84.81 | 54.34 | 66.24 | 60.66 |
| Less: payments | 33.18 | 40.97 | 105.24 | 39.29 | 12.94 | −161.70 | −108.77 | 275.13 | 64.54 | −109.96 | 40.45 | 20.67 | 20.94 |
| b. Net domestic borrowing | 89.21 | 71.35 | 78.58 | 83.32 | 90.57 | 182.49 | 47.23 | 221.67 | 113.86 | 74.85 | 86.11 | 54.43 | 60.28 |
| Gross borrowing | 120.37 | 129.83 | 156.19 | 156.91 | 97.06 | 108.54 | −21.07 | 534.72 | 144.47 | 8.96 | 118.47 | 88.31 | 83.16 |
| Less: payments | 31.15 | 58.48 | 77.60 | 73.59 | 6.48 | −73.95 | −68.30 | 313.05 | 30.61 | −65.89 | 32.35 | 33.88 | 22.88 |

Source: Bureau of Treasury.

public sector has been offsetting the high saving levels achieved by the private sector. Private savings as a percentage of GNP improved significantly to 4.5 percent in 1998–99 from −9.2 percent in 1996–97. On the other hand, public savings dragged overall savings as it slipped from 4.4 percent in 1996–97 to an average of 1.1 percent in 1998–99.

Given the slow pace of savings accumulation, the savings–investment gap has been negative for seventeen consecutive years (1980–97). Essentially this can be traced to the low savings rate since investments have not attained very high levels. From P100 million in 1986, total investments slowly inched up to around P600 million in 1999. The investment crunch is largely due to poor private sector investments, which were also negative during 1986–99.

Gross capital formation can be financed either by gross domestic savings or by a current account deficit. With a growing trade gap, there is greater pressure for the private sector to generate private savings and for the government to exhibit a large primary surplus. If the economy has more exports than imports, there is less pressure on the fiscal sector to skimp on essential public infrastructure and investment in human capital in order to show a surplus.

Meanwhile, the trade balance also shows that for the period 1980–97, the same years when the savings–investment gap turned negative, outflows exceeded inflows. It was only in the years 1998 and 1999 that positive trade gaps were observed. Hence, the increase in private savings can be explained by the improvement in the trade positions of the country.

### *Tax buoyancy*

Tax buoyancy, which measures the point elasticity of taxes with respect to changes in GDP, stagnated to 0.3 and 0.4 in 1999 and 2000, respectively. This implies that increases in economic activity lead to much lower percentage increases in tax revenue, contrary to what the literature suggests. One possible explanation is the poor revenue collection mechanism, which allows huge leaks in tax revenue (Table 14.6).

Meanwhile, the rise in tax effort has been slow despite the many tax laws and new administrative measures passed by the authorities. There is a growing consensus among policy-makers and tax researchers that losses due to tax evasion of personal income taxes are extremely large. In 1999, tax buoyancy for taxes on net income and profits was depressed to 0.01 from a range of 1.5–1.7 in earlier years beginning in 1994. There is a pressing need to address the administrative problems that allow tax evasion.

### *The debt ratio*

One of the major threats to the long-term fiscal position of the national government is its large stock of outstanding debt and the costs of servicing that debt in the long term. During the Aquino administration, the government's decision to assume the servicing and liabilities of the Philippine National Bank, the Development Bank of the Philippines and other public institutions largely contributed to

*Table 14.6* National government tax buoyancy (elasticity), 1976–2000

| | *1976* | *1977* | *1978* | *1979* | *1980* | *1981* | *1982* | *1983* | *1984* | *1985* | *1986* | *1987* | *1988* |
|---|---|---|---|---|---|---|---|---|---|---|---|---|---|
| Total revenues | 0.4 | 0.7 | 1.4 | 1.1 | 0.9 | 0.2 | 0.5 | 1.2 | 0.6 | 2.4 | 2.3 | 2.5 | 0.5 |
| a. Total taxes | 0.6 | 0.7 | 1.4 | 1.3 | 0.9 | 0.2 | 0.6 | 1.0 | 0.6 | 2.5 | 1.1 | 2.6 | 0.3 |
| Direct taxes | 2.0 | 0.7 | 1.2 | 1.1 | 1.4 | 0.7 | −1.0 | 0.5 | 0.8 | 5.7 | 0.4 | 1.1 | 1.5 |
| Taxes on net income and profits | 1.8 | 0.9 | 0.6 | 1.6 | 1.4 | 0.7 | −1.1 | 0.5 | 0.8 | 5.9 | 0.4 | 1.1 | 1.5 |
| Taxes on property | 24.0 | −3.1 | 34.6 | −2.9 | −0.1 | 0.7 | 1.6 | 0.9 | −0.2 | −4.0 | 2.9 | 1.4 | 3.6 |
| Indirect taxes | 4.0 | 0.0 | 0.3 | 1.6 | 0.3 | 0.4 | 1.9 | 0.4 | 1.0 | 2.3 | 2.7 | 2.9 | −0.4 |
| Tax on international | −1.5 | −0.1 | 4.0 | 0.9 | 0.3 | −0.1 | 2.0 | 2.1 | 0.2 | 0.4 | −0.5 | 3.9 | −0.2 |
| Other taxes | 2.0 | 20.5 | −3.7 | −0.1 | 1.2 | −1.3 | 3.4 | 1.1 | 0.8 | 1.4 | 3.8 | 0.5 | 7.0 |
| b. Nontax revenue | −0.5 | 0.6 | 1.4 | −0.2 | 1.0 | 0.5 | −0.2 | 1.9 | 0.4 | 1.6 | 12.1 | 2.1 | 1.8 |

| | *1989* | *1990* | *1991* | *1992* | *1993* | *1994* | *1995* | *1996* | *1997* | *1998* | *1999* | *2000* |
|---|---|---|---|---|---|---|---|---|---|---|---|---|
| Total revenues | 2.2 | 1.1 | 1.4 | 1.2 | 0.8 | 2.0 | 0.6 | 1.0 | 1.3 | −0.2 | 0.3 | 0.5 |
| a. Total taxes | 2.2 | 1.5 | 1.3 | 1.7 | 1.1 | 1.2 | 1.1 | 1.3 | 1.0 | 0.1 | 0.3 | 0.4 |
| Direct taxes | 2.4 | 1.8 | 1.5 | 1.8 | 0.7 | 1.6 | 1.7 | 1.6 | 1.8 | 1.1 | 0.0 | −9.2 |
| Taxes on net income and profits | 2.4 | 1.9 | 1.5 | 1.8 | 0.7 | 1.5 | 1.7 | 1.6 | 1.7 | 1.2 | 0.0 | na |
| Taxes on property | 4.5 | −3.5 | −2.0 | 3.8 | −1.1 | 4.8 | 0.7 | 2.5 | 4.8 | −4.5 | 1.9 | na |
| Indirect taxes | 1.7 | 1.3 | 0.1 | 1.4 | 1.7 | 1.0 | 0.9 | 1.9 | 1.8 | −0.1 | 0.7 | −9.2 |
| Tax on international | 3.3 | 1.2 | 2.5 | 1.6 | 1.4 | 0.0 | 1.5 | 0.5 | −0.8 | −1.9 | 1.1 | −9.2 |
| Other taxes | −0.9 | 2.8 | 0.2 | 6.3 | −1.4 | 14.7 | −1.7 | 1.0 | 1.3 | 2.7 | −1.7 | −9.2 |
| b. Nontax revenue | 2.1 | −0.3 | 2.2 | −1.4 | −1.2 | 7.7 | −1.7 | −1.2 | 3.4 | −2.2 | 0.2 | 1.4 |

Source: Bureau of Treasury.

*Table 14.7* Public sector[a] debt, 1965–2000

| *Year* | *Level (billion pesos)* | | | *Growth rate (%)* | | | *As a % of total* | | *As a % of GNP* | |
|---|---|---|---|---|---|---|---|---|---|---|
| | *Internal debt* | *External debt* | *Total debt* | *Internal debt* | *External debt* | *Total debt* | *Internal debt* | *External debt* | *Internal debt* | *External debt* |
| 1965 | 1.9 | 1.0 | 2.9 | — | — | — | 66.9 | 33.1 | 8.6 | 4.3 |
| 1966 | 2.1 | 1.1 | 3.1 | 5.9 | 10.3 | 7.3 | 66.0 | 34.0 | 8.3 | 4.3 |
| 1967 | 2.5 | 1.6 | 4.0 | 21.2 | 47.3 | 30.1 | 61.5 | 38.5 | 9.4 | 5.9 |
| 1968 | 2.7 | 1.7 | 4.3 | 6.8 | 6.2 | 6.6 | 61.7 | 38.3 | 9.0 | 5.6 |
| 1969 | 3.5 | 2.2 | 5.7 | 33.0 | 30.3 | 31.9 | 62.1 | 37.9 | 10.8 | 6.6 |
| 1970 | 4.0 | 4.2 | 8.2 | 13.6 | 93.2 | 43.8 | 49.1 | 50.9 | 10.4 | 10.7 |
| 1971 | 4.3 | 5.2 | 9.5 | 6.6 | 25.4 | 16.2 | 45.1 | 54.9 | 9.1 | 11.1 |
| 1972 | 5.6 | 6.6 | 12.2 | 30.8 | 26.6 | 28.5 | 45.9 | 54.1 | 10.6 | 12.5 |
| 1973 | 7.3 | 7.6 | 14.9 | 30.1 | 15.4 | 22.1 | 48.9 | 51.1 | 10.7 | 11.2 |
| 1974 | 9.9 | 9.4 | 19.3 | 35.4 | 23.2 | 29.2 | 51.3 | 48.7 | 10.5 | 10.0 |
| 1975 | 11.0 | 14.0 | 25.0 | 11.3 | 49.0 | 29.7 | 44.0 | 56.0 | 10.2 | 13.0 |
| 1976 | 13.2 | 14.3 | 27.4 | 19.9 | 1.9 | 9.8 | 48.0 | 52.0 | 10.5 | 11.3 |
| 1977 | 15.3 | 13.8 | 29.0 | 15.8 | −3.4 | 5.8 | 52.6 | 47.4 | 10.6 | 9.5 |
| 1978 | 17.8 | 22.0 | 39.9 | 16.9 | 59.9 | 37.3 | 44.7 | 55.3 | 10.7 | 13.3 |
| 1979 | 19.1 | 17.1 | 36.1 | 7.0 | −22.6 | −9.3 | 52.8 | 47.2 | 9.4 | 8.4 |
| 1980 | 42.1 | 34.9 | 77.0 | 120.6 | 104.5 | 113.0 | 54.7 | 45.3 | 17.4 | 14.4 |
| 1981 | 59.0 | 46.1 | 105.1 | 40.1 | 32.0 | 36.4 | 56.2 | 43.8 | 21.1 | 16.5 |
| 1982 | 73.7 | 61.5 | 135.3 | 25.0 | 33.5 | 28.7 | 54.5 | 45.5 | 23.7 | 19.8 |
| 1983 | 107.6 | 138.6 | 246.2 | 45.9 | 125.4 | 82.0 | 43.7 | 56.3 | 29.8 | 38.4 |
| 1984 | 127.4 | 232.6 | 360.0 | 18.5 | 67.8 | 46.2 | 35.4 | 64.6 | 25.3 | 46.2 |
| 1985 | 297.7 | 325.6 | 623.3 | 133.6 | 40.0 | 73.1 | 47.8 | 52.2 | 54.0 | 59.0 |
| 1986 | 408.0 | 407.1 | 815.1 | 37.0 | 25.0 | 30.8 | 50.1 | 49.9 | 69.3 | 69.2 |
| 1987 | 418.5 | 432.1 | 850.6 | 2.6 | 6.1 | 4.4 | 49.2 | 50.8 | 62.9 | 64.9 |
| 1988 | 461.8 | 399.8 | 861.6 | 10.3 | −7.5 | 1.3 | 53.6 | 46.4 | 59.0 | 51.1 |
| 1989 | 555.3 | 402.0 | 957.2 | 20.2 | 0.6 | 11.1 | 58.0 | 42.0 | 61.3 | 44.4 |
| 1990 | 623.2 | 552.3 | 1,175.4 | 12.2 | 37.4 | 22.8 | 53.0 | 47.0 | 58.2 | 51.5 |
| 1991 | 848.0 | 599.5 | 1,447.5 | 36.1 | 8.6 | 23.1 | 58.6 | 41.4 | 67.6 | 47.8 |
| 1992 | 818.3 | 1,003.8 | 1,822.1 | −3.5 | 67.4 | 25.9 | 44.9 | 55.1 | 59.5 | 73.0 |
| 1993 | 1,260.7 | 652.1 | 1,912.8 | 54.1 | −35.0 | 5.0 | 65.9 | 34.1 | 84.0 | 43.5 |
| 1994 | 1,289.2 | 660.2 | 1,949.4 | 2.3 | 1.2 | 1.9 | 66.1 | 33.9 | 74.2 | 38.0 |
| 1995 | 1,453.6 | 713.5 | 2,167.1 | 12.8 | 8.1 | 11.2 | 67.1 | 32.9 | 74.2 | 36.4 |
| 1996 | 1,502.6 | 734.6 | 2,237.2 | 3.4 | 3.0 | 3.2 | 67.2 | 32.8 | 66.4 | 32.5 |
| 1997 | 1,586.9 | 1,082.4 | 2,669.3 | 5.6 | 47.3 | 19.3 | 59.5 | 40.5 | 62.8 | 42.8 |
| 1998 | 1,721.2 | 1,230.3 | 2,951.5 | 8.5 | 13.7 | 10.6 | 58.3 | 41.7 | 61.1 | 43.7 |
| 1999 | 2,196.6 | 1,469.7 | 3,666.3 | 27.6 | 19.5 | 24.2 | 59.9 | 40.1 | 69.6 | 46.6 |
| 2000[b] | 2,116.8 | 1,626.3 | 3,743.1 | na | na | na | 56.6 | 43.4 | 60.4 | 46.4 |

Source: Department of Finance.

Notes

a The public sector includes the national government, 14 monitored government-owned and -controlled corporations (GOCCs), Central Bank/Central Bank-Board of Liquidators/Bangko Sentral ng Pilipinas (CB/CB-BOL/BSP) and government financial institutions (GFIs).

b Refers to March 2000.

the rising national government debt. Similarly, the budgetary assistance provided by the national government for the restructuring of the central bank further depressed the country's fiscal position (Table 14.7).

The debt service ratio (i.e., the ratio of total public sector debt to nominal GDP) has been on an upsurge. Figure 14.3 shows that from an average of 0.2 in the 1970s, the debt service ratio went up to over 1 in the 1990s. In terms of levels, total public sector debt has escalated to P3.7 trillion in 1999 from merely P957.2 billion in 1989, which was already twelve times more than its 1980 level of P77.0 billion. Of the total public sector debt, the debt structure has changed to an almost

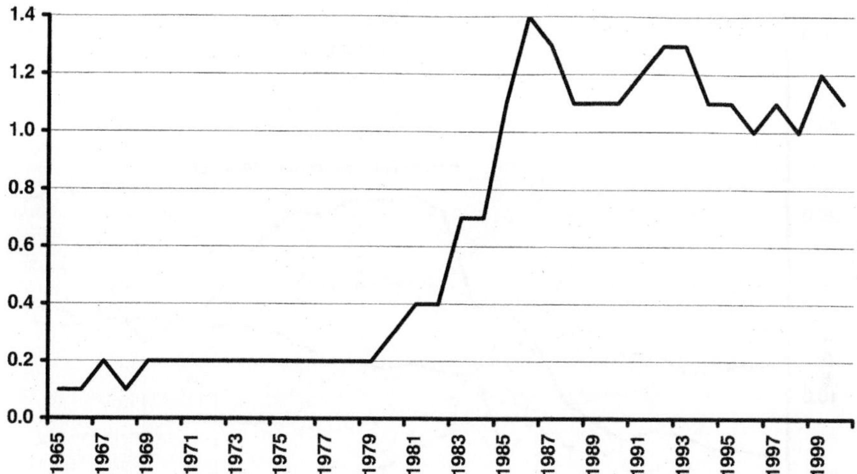


*Figure 14.3* Ratio of total public sector debt to nominal gross domestic product, 1965–2000.

Source: Department of Finance.

equal sharing between internal and external sources in the late 1990s. This is contrary to its structure in the 1980s, when a larger proportion of debt was taken from external sources.

### *Impact of government spending and debt on economic growth*

The rapid expansion of government expenditure in 1986–93 does not indicate an inordinate growth in the size of the government, but rather is attributable to a large debt service that accounted for approximately one-third of the government budget during that period. Total government expenditures (net of debt service) actually contracted between 1975 and 1993. The period 1986–93 marked the obvious rise in debt service. Consequently, this debt burden hampered the government's capacity to provide services to the people and to build the necessary infrastructure to push the economy into a higher growth orbit.

### *Budgetary priorities*

Looking at the allocation of national government expenditures across sectors, Figure 14.4 clearly shows that the social service sector continues to capture the largest share of aggregate government expenditures. Expenditure in this sector grew substantially in both nominal and real terms in 1986–2000 due to developments in the macroeconomic environment following the economic turnaround in 1987. As of 1999, allocation for social services stood at 33.23 percent after being cut to 21.97 percent in 1990. Despite this improvement, the Philippine social allocation ratio continues to be below the United Nations Development Programme norm of 40 percent. Among the social service sectors, education was the largest

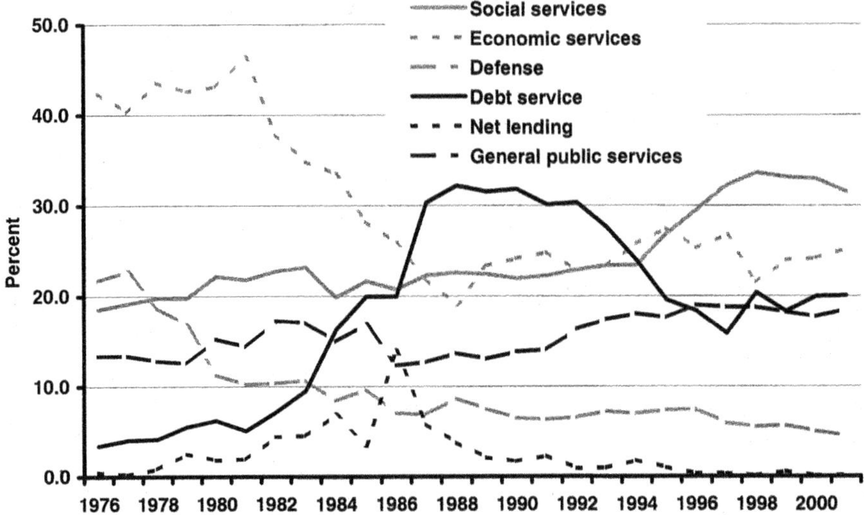


*Figure 14.4* Sectoral distribution of national government expenditures, 1976–2000.

Source: Department of Budget and Management.

recipient, taking up approximately 15 percent of the total budget or 60 percent of total social service sector expenditures (Table 14.8).

At the same time, government spending for economic services is continuously being cut, and it declined to its lowest share of 21.5 percent in 1998 from a peak of 46.48 percent in 1981. Allocation for infrastructure (i.e., power and energy, water resources development, and transportation and communication) has been squeezed to a low of 9.53 percent in 1998 from more than 29 percent in 1980. This infrastructure deficiency, due partly to the low levels of government spending on infrastructure and institutional weaknesses, emerged as one of the major bottlenecks in the economy.

The World Bank (1992) gave four primary explanations for the current crisis in economic infrastructure:

1 A failure by government to develop a strategic vision for its economic infrastructure and to take the necessary decisions to realize such a program.
2 Irregular, and in some cases declining, levels of maintenance and rehabilitation expenditure have reduced the country's ability to extract economic services from existing infrastructure assets.
3 Regulatory failures (including pricing) have constrained the supply of services by the private sector and government corporations, and have caused demand to swell beyond the capacity of these service providers. This, in turn, has resulted in rationing, outages, accelerated deterioration of assets and financial and macroeconomic instability.
4 Infrastructure investments have been inefficiently distributed across regions.

*Table 14.8* Sectoral allocation of national government expenditures, 1980–2000 (% of total expenditures)

| | *1980* | *1982* | *1984* | *1986* | *1988* | *1990* | *1992* | *1994* | *1996* | *1998* | *2000*[a] |
|---|---|---|---|---|---|---|---|---|---|---|---|
| Economic services | 43.17 | 37.92 | 33.55 | 25.89 | 19.05 | 24.17 | 22.89 | 25.76 | 25.33 | 21.51 | 24.20 |
| Agricultural, agrarian reform and natural resources | 6.01 | 7.03 | 7.15 | 6.41 | 6.22 | 6.92 | 6.52 | 5.62 | 6.34 | 8.32 | 5.68 |
| Trade and industry | 1.19 | 5.01 | 2.55 | 1.48 | 0.88 | 1.08 | 1.17 | 0.90 | 1.72 | 1.01 | 0.54 |
| Tourism | 0.54 | 0.39 | 0.29 | 0.22 | 0.13 | 0.16 | 0.11 | 0.14 | 0.21 | 0.20 | 0.15 |
| Power and energy | 8.88 | 6.45 | 2.19 | 1.84 | 1.46 | 0.54 | 0.81 | 2.04 | 0.94 | 0.33 | 0.63 |
| Water resource dev't and flood control | 2.60 | 1.79 | 0.19 | 2.11 | 1.15 | 1.08 | 1.13 | 1.31 | 1.06 | 1.33 | 1.01 |
| Communications, roads and other transportation | 21.09 | 19.05 | 16.51 | 11.27 | 8.13 | 10.49 | 11.87 | 8.22 | 10.99 | 9.85 | 9.41 |
| Other economic services | 2.31 | 6.76 | 6.06 | 4.91 | 3.93 | 3.11 | 1.69 | 0.46 | 1.38 | 0.70 | 0.82 |
| Subsidy to local gov't units | 0.00 | 0.00 | 0.00 | 0.00 | 0.00 | 0.00 | 1.56 | 4.70 | 4.90 | 5.06 | 5.75 |
| Social services | 22.19 | 22.77 | 19.87 | 20.76 | 22.62 | 21.97 | 22.94 | 23.41 | 29.52 | 33.68 | 32.99 |
| Education, culture and manpower dev't | 12.18 | 12.86 | 12.79 | 14.66 | 13.97 | 15.77 | 13.48 | 14.08 | 16.57 | 19.31 | 19.06 |
| Health | 3.74 | 4.03 | 5.13 | 4.47 | 3.49 | 3.76 | 3.69 | 2.52 | 2.25 | 2.88 | 2.58 |
| Social security and labor welfare | 1.47 | 1.23 | 0.89 | 0.80 | 0.67 | 0.86 | 1.49 | 1.18 | 1.86 | 4.12 | 4.28 |
| Land distribution (CARP) | 0.00 | 0.00 | 0.00 | 0.00 | 0.21 | 0.19 | 1.63 | 0.00 | 0.00 | 0.00 | 0.38 |
| Housing and community dev't | 2.32 | 2.65 | 3.50 | 0.92 | 0.36 | 0.23 | 0.47 | 0.60 | 0.88 | 0.50 | 0.71 |
| Other Social Services | 0.09 | 1.03 | 0.90 | 0.81 | 3.60 | 1.63 | 0.80 | 0.12 | 0.13 | 0.16 | 0.14 |
| Subsidy to local gov't units | 0.00 | 0.00 | 0.00 | 0.00 | 0.00 | 0.00 | 0.71 | 4.87 | 5.18 | 5.35 | 6.07 |
| Defense | 11.29 | 10.40 | 8.42 | 7.04 | 8.67 | 6.51 | 6.60 | 7.00 | 7.44 | 5.55 | 5.04 |
| Domestic security | 12.90 | 10.25 | 10.68 | 9.72 | 6.94 | 7.52 | 6.34 | 7.22 | 7.39 | 5.94 | 5.68 |
| Peace and order | 3.99 | 0.00 | 0.00 | 0.00 | 0.00 | 0.00 | 0.00 | 0.00 | 0.00 | 0.00 | 0.00 |
| General public services | 15.27 | 17.32 | 14.99 | 12.32 | 13.67 | 13.84 | 16.34 | 18.08 | 19.04 | 18.79 | 17.73 |
| General administration | 7.13 | 5.78 | 6.68 | 7.06 | 5.04 | 5.15 | 6.56 | 6.54 | 6.89 | 7.39 | 6.37 |
| Public order and safety | 1.11 | 5.10 | 5.85 | 5.58 | 4.75 | 5.49 | 5.68 | 5.68 | 6.13 | 6.81 | 7.03 |
| Other general public services | 4.35 | 3.52 | 4.56 | 4.27 | 2.91 | 2.41 | 0.17 | 1.51 | 0.68 | 0.58 | 0.25 |
| Subsidy to local gov't units | 0.00 | 0.00 | 0.00 | 0.00 | 0.00 | 0.00 | 1.68 | 3.71 | 3.93 | 4.05 | 4.60 |
| Net lending | 1.83 | 4.45 | 6.91 | 14.01 | 3.80 | 1.69 | 0.86 | 1.78 | 0.28 | 0.09 | 0.06 |
| Debt service | 6.24 | 7.15 | 16.25 | 19.99 | 32.19 | 31.82 | 30.37 | 23.96 | 18.39 | 20.39 | 19.98 |
| Total | 100.00 | 100.00 | 100.00 | 100.00 | 100.00 | 100.00 | 100.00 | 100.00 | 100.00 | 100.00 | 100.00 |

Source: Department of Budget and Management.

Meanwhile, the allocation for agriculture does not seem sufficient to support the sector's growth. From 6.9 percent and 7.3 percent in 1989 and 1990, respectively, the government budget for agriculture was trimmed down to 4.7 percent in 1998 and 5.7 percent in 1999.

In contrast, the large share of general public services has been fairly stable at a little more than 18 percent of the total. While a significant amount of government resources could be saved yearly by reducing outlays on general public administration, interviews with officials in both the executive and legislative branches indicate no support for pursuing reforms in this direction.

If these trends of rising allocation for general public services and decreasing budget for economic services continue to prevail, it would result in a weaker contribution of the government to sustainable growth. It would mean that the national government would be spending more in areas that are less important (for example, general public services) and less in areas that are crucial for sustaining economic growth (i.e., economic and social services).

## Debt management

Among the immediate problems faced by Philippine economic managers is the large debt overhang, and this problem remains unaddressed; hence, debt management will be a crucial issue in the coming years. The question pertaining to the sustainability of public debt can be examined by comparing sustainable debt payments, which is expressed in terms of interest rates, with the actual "sustained expected interest rate." Long-run solvency requires that the permanent primary surplus be equal to the following:[1]

$$ps^* = (r - n)d_t - (phat + n)\, m^* \qquad (14.1)$$

where: $ps^*$ = primary surplus
$r$ = long-term real interest rate
$d_t$ = debt/nominal GDP
$n$ = long-run real growth rate
$phat$ = "equilibrium" rate of inflation
$m^*$ = inverse of base money velocity.

Equation (14.1) can then be rearranged to estimate the interest rate, $r^*$, that is needed for long-term sustainability. This would reflect the combination of the primary surplus, the long-run GDP growth rate, the inflation rate and the interest rate needed for debt to be sustainable, assuming that the base money velocity is fairly constant. Hence:

$$r^* = n + [ps + (phat + n)m^*] \,/\, d_t. \qquad (14.2)$$

The resulting $r^*$ is then compared with the actual interest rate (91-day Treasury bill rate). If the sustainable interest rate $r^*$ is greater than the actual interest rate r, then the debt level is sustainable assuming that magnitudes persist over the long run. Therefore, any policy that increases r* enhances long-run solvency or debt sustainability.

Figures 14.5a to 14.5c show the Philippines' struggle to manage the debt problem for the period 1975–99. Figure 14.5a uses actual data for GDP growth and inflation rates, Figure 14.5b uses average GDP growth and inflation rates for

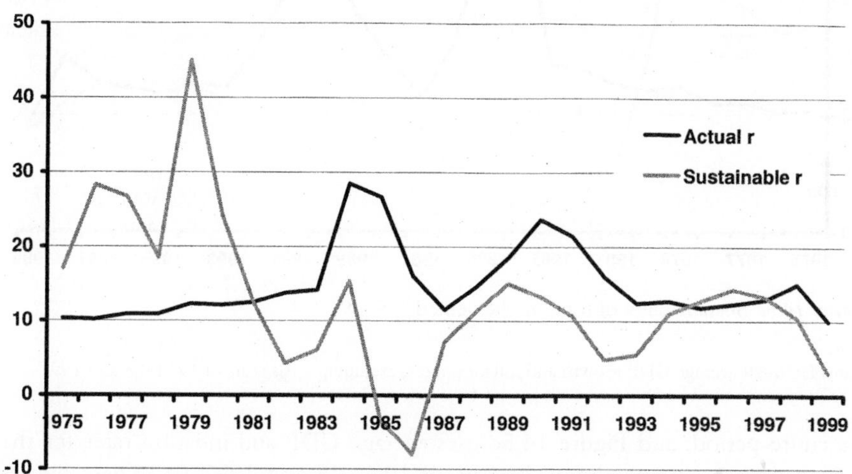


*Figure 14.5a* Sustainability of total public debt, 1975–99.

Note
Using actual GDP growth and inflation rates.

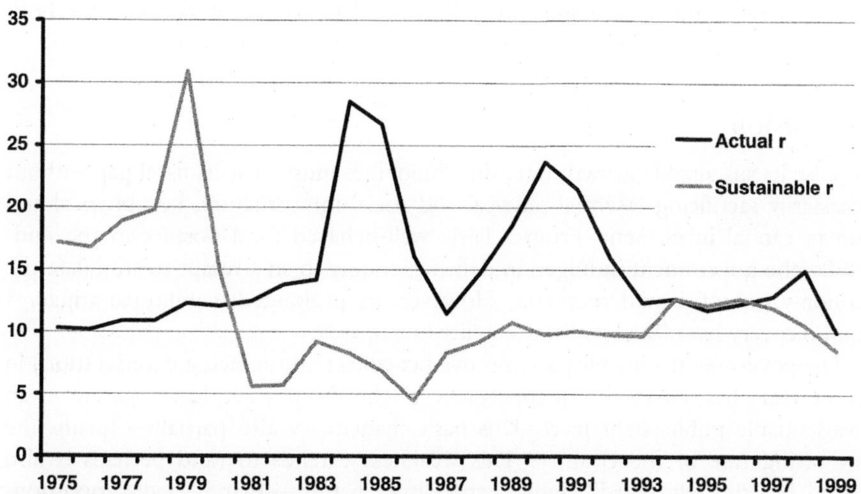


*Figure 14.5b* Sustainability of total public debt, 1975–99.

Note
Using 1975–99 average GDP growth and inflation rates.

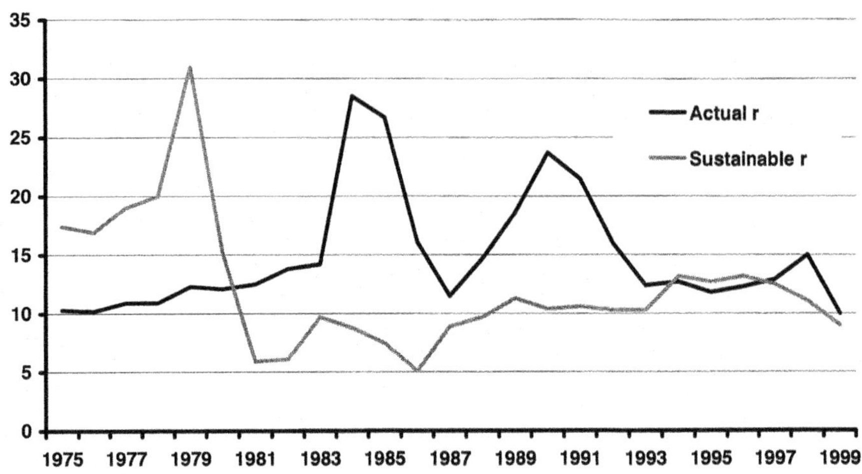


*Figure 14.5c* Sustainability of total public debt, 1975–99.

Note
Using 1975–99 average GDP growth and inflation rates, excluding crisis years of 1984–85 and 1997–98.

the entire period, and Figure 14.5c uses average GDP and inflation rates for the same period, excluding the crisis years of 1984–85 and 1997–98. These figures show how macroeconomic imbalances have deteriorated the country's ability to sustain its debt problems. Figure 14.5a shows how the country's fiscal position has been fluctuating from sustainable to unsustainable levels. However, Figures 14.5b and 14.5c show a clearer picture of the country's long-run insolvency. Similar assessments were made for internal and external debt. Although more fluctuations were observed, the unsustainability of public debt in recent periods, for both internal and external debt, are consistently highlighted for all observations.

## Conclusion

To raise its sustainable growth rate, the Philippines must close its fiscal gap without necessarily sacrificing essential physical and social infrastructure, i.e., physical and human capital investment. From a fairly well-behaved fiscal posture in the mid-1990s, the government indulged in deficit spending in an attempt to stimulate the economy out of a mild recession. However, its prolonged inability to trigger a rapid recovery has placed its fiscal stability in jeopardy.

The government's inability to improve tax collection (in fact, a deterioration) in recent years has led to the disappearance of the primary surplus, resulting in an unsustainable public debt level. This basic inadequacy also partially explains the low saving rate of the country. This weakness extends to (and perhaps is also caused by) the "distorted" public expenditure pattern—that is, a disproportionately large share of expenditure going to personnel services (70 percent) and much less to maintenance and operating expenses (20 percent) and capital expenditure (10 percent).

On the revenue side, the inability to collect direct taxes has resulted in an overdependence on indirect taxes (which is also declining, especially in some specific taxes). In order to increase its tax effort, the government has concentrated its efforts toward finding other taxes that can be imposed on the sectors already paying taxes, courting the possibility of getting on the backward-bending section of the Laffer curve.

The structural reforms in the fiscal area are quite obvious but are very difficult to implement and requires political will that, up to now, has been difficult to summon. The government must improve its tax administration, collecting a few core taxes that are easy to understand and accept, and abolishing many complicated taxes. It must also undertake reform on the expenditure side, reducing personnel services drastically and at the same time, perhaps, reducing red tape and bureaucratic lethargy. Agencies may have to be closed and the government taken out of some activities where its functions are unclear. Both thrusts will require tremendous effort and commitment, but only then can the fiscal area be conducive to sustainable rapid growth.

## Note

1 The following analyses follows Montiel (1993).

## References

Diokno, Benjamin E. (1994) "Taxes and public sector resource mobilization in the Philippines," in R.V. Fabella and H. Sakai (eds) *Resource Mobilization and Resource Use in the Philippines*, Tokyo: Institute of Developing Economies, pp. 147–65.

Diokno, Benjamin E. (1995) "Fiscal policy for sustainable growth," in R.V. Fabella and H. Sakai (eds) *Towards Sustained Growth*, Tokyo: Institute of Developing Economies, pp. 33–56.

Fabella, Raul V. (1994) "Investment and the allocation of resources under macroeconomic instability," in R.V. Fabella and H. Sakai (eds) *Resource Mobilization and Resource Use in the Philippines*, Tokyo: Institute of Developing Economies, pp. 127–46.

International Monetary Fund (2000) *International Financial Statistics*, Washington, DC: International Monetary Fund.

Manasan, Rosario G. *et al.* (1996) *Financing Social Programs in the Philippines: Public Policy and Budget Restructuring*, Manila: Philippine Institute for Development Studies.

Montiel, Peter J. (1993) *Fiscal Aspects of Developing Country Debt Problems and Debt and Debt-Service Reduction Operations: A Conceptual Approach*, World Bank Policy Research Working Paper No. WPS 1073 (January), Washington, DC: World Bank.

Paderanga, Cayetano Jr. (1995) "Debt management in the Philippines," in R.V. Fabella and H. Sakai (eds) *Towards Sustained Growth*, Tokyo: Institute of Developing Economies, pp. 57–108.

World Bank (1992) *The Philippines: An Opening for Sustained Growth*, World Bank Report No. 11061-PH, Country Department I, East Asia and Pacific Region, Washington, DC: World Bank.

# 15 Singapore

*Tan Khee Giap and Soon Lee Ying*

## Introduction

Singapore has been recording budget surpluses almost every year for more than three decades. The budget surpluses are the outcome of the government's prudent fiscal policy that has become a cornerstone of the macroeconomic stability underpinning Singapore's impressive economic growth. While economists have long advocated sound fiscal policies to sustain long-term growth, few countries have displayed the commitment to long-term goals that has come to characterize Singapore's formulation of budgetary policies. The country's experience is interesting amidst growing awareness of the role that public sector savings can play in the wealth accumulation of a nation, and the circumstances under which this is justified (Hemming and Daniel 1995; Chalk and Hemming 1998).

The aim of this study is to obtain an understanding of the nature of Singapore's budget surplus so that it may provide some insight into the government's conservative fiscal policy stance. In the process, the study also provides an update of the government's fiscal response during the Asian financial crisis. The chapter also presents some budgetary projections that throw light on the size of the future budget surplus.

The chapter is divided into seven sections. The first section provides an overview of the public sector in Singapore. This is followed by an examination of the size of the budget balance and the sources of the surplus. While the budget surplus is one aspect of sound fiscal policy, expenditure and tax policies are also integral components. An important aspect of sound fiscal management concerns how the government allocates its expenditure and how taxes are structured. Some crucial guiding principles and rules pertaining to fiscal management reform undertaken in the 1990s are examined in the subsequent section. The fifth section examines how the surpluses have been spent; this is followed by a discussion of future fiscal projections that take into account the aging population and economic restructuring as Singapore enters the new millennium. The chapter concludes with summary remarks and policy implications.

## The size of the government and the public sector in Singapore

It is useful to begin with some idea of the size of the public sector in the Singapore economy from an international perspective. A simple exercise that compares the relative size of government is to fit a trend line of the share of government expenditure against per capita income over a cross-section of countries. This is shown in Figure 15.1 where trend lines were fitted for two years, 1980 and 1998, for two measures of the size of government—the percentage of total government expenditure to GDP and the percentage of tax revenue to GDP—for a sample of Asian and Western industrialized countries. As can be seen from Figure 15.1, the size of the government in Singapore, as measured by government expenditure as a percentage of GDP, was slightly below that predicted for a country at Singapore's level of per capita income in 1980. By 1998, public expenditure had fallen to a level that was significantly lower than that predicted on the basis of per capita income. The same trend is noted in the share of tax revenue to GDP. As will be seen in the next section, the reduced size of the public sector is the outcome of a deliberate policy to reduce the size of government over time.

However, it is well known that the influence of the Singapore government in economic activity extends beyond the central government's finances. A significant part of the government's functions is, in fact, channeled through statutory boards (SBs); these are semi-autonomous agencies that were established in the 1960s to handle specific concerns, initially in the areas of housing and economic development, and subsequently in almost every important economic and social field.[1] In addition, there are government-linked companies (GLCs); these are incorporated entities that are either wholly or partly government-owned, and are found in a wide range of basically private sector activities, including manufacturing, shipbuilding and ship repair, trading, financial services, construction and property development, tourism and leisure. The share of these two sectors is large,[2] although they have been declining as a result of privatization and as the government has divested its share in GLCs, in line with its objective to give the private sector a greater role in the economy.

While it is desirable to examine the fiscal balance for the broadest measure of the public sector, consolidated budgetary accounts of the public sector are not available.[3] Transactions of SBs that are reflected in the central government budget consist only of net loans and grants given to SBs and dividends and taxes received from them. The SBs have been running overall surpluses between 1987 and 1997 (Table 15.1). Since 1987, the SBs have been required to transfer 20 percent of their annual operating surplus to the government. GLCs are required to remain viable without budgetary support.

Finally, official published public finance statistics do not provide a consistent time series; hence, this chapter for the most part relies on various issues of the IMF's *Government Finance Statistics.* However, data from this source are available only from 1972 and the most recent data available are for 1997.

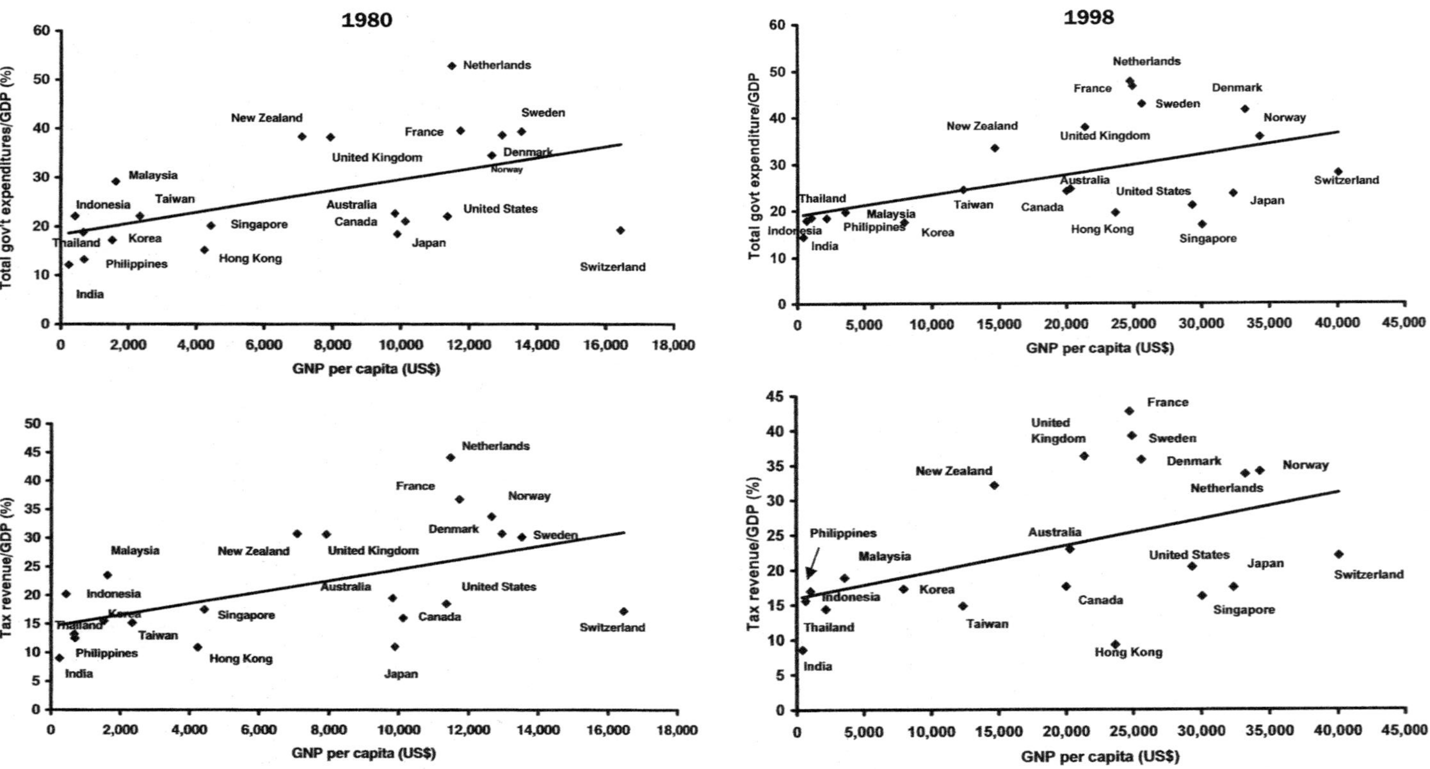


*Figure 15.1* Size of government, international comparisons, 1980 and 1998.

*Table 15.1* Budget balance of statutory boards in Singapore, 1966–98 (S$ million)

| | *Current surplus/deficit* | *Overall surplus/deficit* |
|---|---|---|
| 1966 | 39 | −127 |
| 1967 | 54 | −220 |
| 1968 | 78 | −291 |
| 1969 | 74 | −104 |
| 1970 | 112 | −110 |
| 1971 | 140 | −207 |
| 1972 | 234 | −347 |
| 1973 | 305 | −232 |
| 1974 | 246 | −713 |
| 1975 | 272 | −1,067 |
| 1976 | 725 | −882 |
| 1977 | 835 | −903 |
| 1978 | 1,213 | −306 |
| 1979 | 1,276 | −250 |
| 1980 | 1,822 | −277 |
| 1981 | 2,202 | −780 |
| 1982 | 2,651 | −2,060 |
| 1983 | 2,730 | −2,839 |
| 1984 | 5,623 | 354 |
| 1985 | 3,320 | −910 |
| 1986 | 3,349 | −174 |
| 1987 | 3,242 | 425 |
| 1988 | na | 1,079.2 |
| 1989 | na | 2,170 |
| 1990 | na | 2,369.9 |
| 1991 | na | 2,847.7 |
| 1992 | na | 1,673.1 |
| 1993 | na | 2,192 |
| 1994 | na | 2,368.8 |
| 1995 | na | 2,156 |
| 1996 | na | 1,786.7 |
| 1997 | na | 1,459.3 |
| 1998* | na | −23.2 |

Source: Ministry of Finance (various years).

Notes
na = Not available.
* Estimate.

## Fiscal balance

The fiscal stance underpinning the formulation of the government's budgetary policies over the past decade can be seen in the following statement:

> Government long-term budget policy is three-fold: (1) there must be an overall balanced budget. Over a five-year planning period, recurrent and development expenditure outlays should not exceed total revenue collection; (2) the share of national resources taken up by the public sector must be gradually reduced; (3) the effectiveness and efficiency of public services should be

> enhanced. As far as possible, programs should be self-financing and subsidies kept to a minimum. In general, public services should be provided at least cost to the taxpayer.
>
> (Ministry of Finance 1988)

In the light of this statement, Figure 15.2 presents Singapore's budget surplus for two different measures of the budget balance, the overall balance and the current balance. The current balance is the balance on current transactions (i.e., current revenue less current expenditure). Current revenue consists of tax revenue and nontax revenue, the latter consisting largely of investment income, charges and fees. On the expenditure side, current expenditures refer to operational expenditures, inclusive of debt servicing. As Figure 15.2 shows, the current balance has been recording surpluses in excess of 10 percent of GDP since 1987. At these levels, government savings have been well in excess of development expenditure needs, which between 1988 and 1997 averaged 5 percent of GDP. It was only briefly in the mid-1980s, when the economy was hit by a severe recession as a result of which development expenditure rose to 12 percent of GDP (in 1986 and 1987), that the current balance fell short of development expenditure.

The overall budget balance is the balance of total revenue less total expenditure plus net lending (i.e., gross lending less repayments) (Table 15.2). Taking the current balance, development expenditure and net lending are added to the expenditure side, and on the revenue side, it includes capital revenue. Gross lending goes mainly to statutory boards to finance development expenditure, most of which consists of loans to the Housing and Development Board for construction of public housing.

Between 1972 and 1986, the government ran modest overall budget surpluses, except in 1973 and 1976 when small deficits (of less than 1 percent of GDP) were

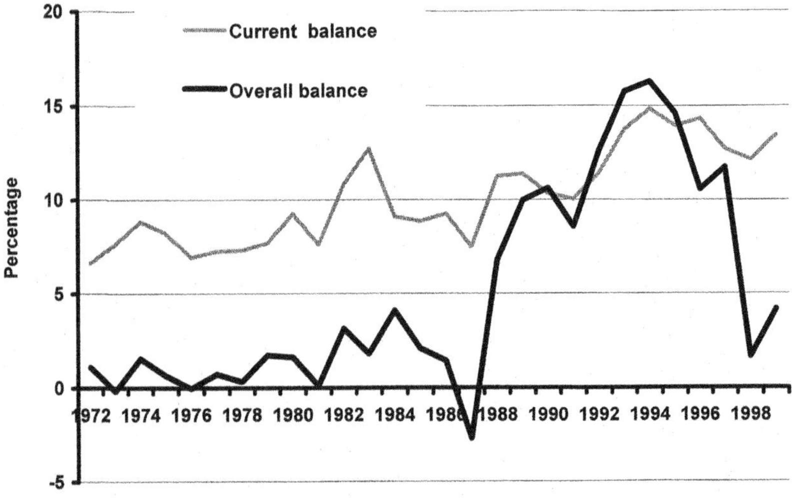


*Figure 15.2* Singapore's budget balances, 1972–99 (as a % of GDP).

*Table 15.2* Fiscal aggregates, 1972–99 (as a % of GDP)

| | *Current balance* | *Overall balance* | *Total revenue* | *Current revenue* | *Tax revenue* | *Nontax current revenue* | *Capital revenue* | *Current expenditure* | *Debt service* | *Current expenditure less debt service* | *Development expenditure* | *Net lending* |
|---|---|---|---|---|---|---|---|---|---|---|---|---|
| 1972 | 6.66 | 1.11 | 22.21 | 21.46 | 14.73 | 6.74 | 0.52 | 14.81 | 1.75 | 13.05 | 1.62 | 4.17 |
| 1973 | 7.66 | −0.18 | 22.27 | 20.68 | 14.98 | 5.69 | 1.52 | 13.02 | 1.46 | 11.56 | 1.62 | 6.89 |
| 1974 | 8.84 | 1.56 | 21.64 | 20.52 | 15.33 | 5.19 | 1.13 | 11.67 | 1.41 | 10.26 | 1.93 | 4.89 |
| 1975 | 8.24 | 0.65 | 24.98 | 23.16 | 16.92 | 6.23 | 1.82 | 14.91 | 1.62 | 13.29 | 2.54 | 6.46 |
| 1976 | 6.95 | −0.03 | 23.67 | 22.61 | 16.38 | 6.23 | 1.06 | 15.66 | 2.14 | 13.53 | 3.99 | 3.91 |
| 1977 | 7.28 | 0.72 | 24.63 | 24.03 | 17.05 | 6.98 | 0.60 | 16.74 | 2.69 | 14.05 | 3.82 | 3.34 |
| 1978 | 7.34 | 0.31 | 23.53 | 23.24 | 16.39 | 6.85 | 0.29 | 15.90 | 2.99 | 12.91 | 3.89 | 3.42 |
| 1979 | 7.71 | 1.72 | 24.95 | 23.52 | 16.53 | 6.99 | 1.43 | 15.81 | 3.10 | 12.71 | 4.07 | 3.35 |
| 1980 | 9.27 | 1.63 | 26.11 | 25.09 | 17.52 | 7.56 | 1.02 | 15.82 | 2.95 | 12.87 | 4.45 | 4.20 |
| 1981 | 7.63 | 0.11 | 29.20 | 26.13 | 18.50 | 7.63 | 3.06 | 18.50 | 2.62 | 15.88 | 4.96 | 5.62 |
| 1982 | 10.82 | 3.16 | 30.87 | 27.71 | 19.68 | 8.04 | 3.16 | 16.89 | 2.88 | 14.01 | 4.62 | 6.20 |
| 1983 | 12.71 | 1.80 | 31.90 | 29.77 | 19.44 | 10.33 | 2.13 | 17.06 | 4.38 | 12.68 | 5.46 | 7.58 |
| 1984 | 9.11 | 4.10 | 29.21 | 28.59 | 18.41 | 10.19 | 0.61 | 19.48 | 4.73 | 14.75 | 6.67 | −1.05 |
| 1985 | 8.87 | 2.10 | 37.93 | 27.66 | 16.44 | 11.22 | 10.27 | 18.80 | 3.08 | 15.72 | 8.39 | 8.65 |
| 1986 | 9.26 | 1.44 | 38.42 | 26.72 | 13.37 | 13.35 | 11.70 | 17.46 | 3.05 | 14.40 | 11.90 | 7.63 |
| 1987 | 7.50 | −2.71 | 32.12 | 30.13 | 13.86 | 16.27 | 2.00 | 22.62 | 8.83 | 13.79 | 12.91 | −0.70 |
| 1988 | 11.25 | 6.82 | 28.31 | 27.13 | 14.72 | 12.41 | 1.18 | 15.87 | 2.78 | 13.09 | 7.12 | −1.50 |
| 1989 | 11.39 | 9.99 | 29.29 | 26.65 | 16.32 | 10.34 | 2.64 | 15.27 | 2.70 | 12.57 | 6.98 | −2.95 |
| 1990 | 10.35 | 10.62 | 31.96 | 26.40 | 15.15 | 11.25 | 5.56 | 16.05 | 2.99 | 13.07 | 4.96 | 0.33 |
| 1991 | 10.03 | 8.57 | 30.86 | 26.46 | 15.84 | 10.62 | 4.40 | 16.43 | 3.49 | 12.93 | 4.78 | 1.08 |
| 1992 | 11.42 | 12.61 | 33.01 | 26.56 | 16.96 | 9.60 | 6.45 | 15.14 | 2.46 | 12.69 | 4.53 | 0.73 |
| 1993 | 13.75 | 15.76 | 36.15 | 27.16 | 17.17 | 9.99 | 9.00 | 13.41 | 1.33 | 12.09 | 4.19 | 2.79 |
| 1994 | 14.84 | 16.28 | 35.66 | 26.38 | 17.56 | 8.82 | 9.28 | 11.54 | 1.07 | 10.47 | 2.60 | 5.24 |
| 1995 | 13.95 | 14.61 | 36.22 | 26.47 | 16.56 | 9.91 | 9.75 | 12.53 | 1.03 | 11.49 | 3.70 | 5.38 |
| 1996 | 14.34 | 10.56 | 38.50 | 29.39 | 16.74 | 12.65 | 9.11 | 15.05 | 0.86 | 14.19 | 6.22 | 6.67 |
| 1997 | 12.71 | 11.73 | 38.11 | 24.48 | 16.11 | 8.36 | 13.64 | 11.77 | 0.70 | 11.07 | 5.05 | 9.56 |
| 1998 | 12.14 | 1.66 | 29.86 | 23.62 | 15.56 | 0.84 | 6.24 | 11.48 | 0.71 | 10.76 | 8.87 | 7.85 |
| 1999 | 13.46 | 4.17 | 29.40 | 24.79 | 14.91 | 9.88 | 4.61 | 11.33 | 0.58 | 10.75 | 7.40 | 6.50 |

Sources: IMF (various years); Department of Statistics (various years).

recorded. The only other time that the overall budget went into a deficit was in 1987, when the deficit reached 3 percent of GDP, but this was the result of unusually large charges for debt servicing.[4] Singapore has a large domestic public debt, which in 1997 stood at $102,371.9 million or 72 percent of nominal GDP. A good part of this debt is the result of the requirement that CPF balances be invested in government bonds (or in advance deposits with the Monetary Authority of Singapore or MAS, to be converted to bonds in due course).

Since 1987, the overall surplus has been rising sharply, reaching a peak of 16 percent of GDP in 1995. Between 1992 and 1994, the overall surplus exceeded the current surplus as development expenditure fell sharply; debt servicing was low, while at the same time, capital revenue increased. Hence, although the government had targeted a structural balance in the overall budget in the medium term, it has been running unusually large surpluses averaging 11 percent of GDP in 1988–97.

However, the financial crisis of 1997 led to a steep fall in the overall budget balance in 1998 as development expenditure and net lending rose sharply, and as revenue fell with the stall in economic activity. In 1998, a modest overall budget surplus of 1.6 percent of GDP was recorded; the overall budget surplus rose to 4 percent of GDP in 1999 due to a strong economic recovery.[5]

A breakdown of the major components of expenditures (Figure 15.3) and revenues (Figure 15.4 and Figure 15.5) provides some insight into the large budget surpluses that characterized the 1990s. On the expenditure side, after increases in development expenditure to 12 percent of GDP in 1985–86, which was mainly due to counter-cyclical measures undertaken in response to the recession, development expenditure was cut back sharply after 1987, reaching as low as 2.6 percent of GDP in 1994. This was possible because most of the capital expenditure on infrastructure and housing had been completed.[6] Development expenditure rose to average 5.6 percent of GDP in 1996–97 as the government embarked on a program to upgrade old housing estates. Other priority areas of development expenditure during this period included health care (expanding and upgrading of hospitals and other health care facilities) and transport (the expansion of the existing Mass Rapid Transit or MRT system and the construction of the light rail transit system). In response to the slowdown in 1998, development expenditure increased to 9 percent in 1998. The increase went mainly to the education sector for the construction of schools to cater to single-session secondary schools, and to finance the expansion of IT infrastructure in schools and tertiary institutions. Development spending in transport fell because the LTA issued bonds to partially fund land transport projects in 1999. Net lending rose after 1993, after a period (1987–90) when repayments exceeded gross lending, as the government increased lending to statutory boards for housing and transport projects.

Throughout the period under study, current expenditure remained largely constant (Figure 15.3). Reflecting the government's goal to curb growth of operating expenses, current expenditure (excluding debt servicing) which had averaged about 13.5 percent of GDP in 1972–86, fell to 12.4 percent in 1987–97. The fall in operating expenditure was possible due to a number of factors: (i) the government's strong commitment to keep the administration lean, relying on increases in

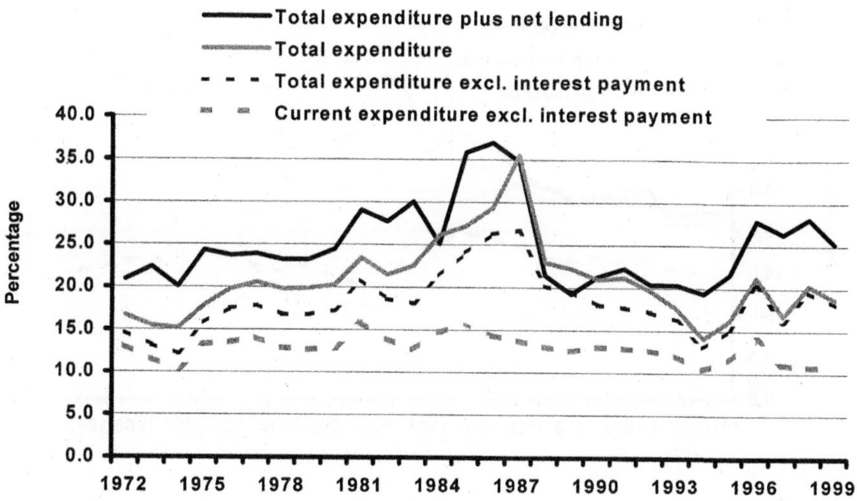


*Figure 15.3* Government expenditure, 1972–99 (as a % of GDP).

productivity through computerization and information technology to improve delivery of services; (ii) the government's aversion to subsidies and emphasis on aggressive cost recovery. Examples of this is the upgrading of public housing where the cost is partly borne by owners and the revamp of the health care benefits in the public sector in 1994 that mandated greater cost-sharing by employees; and (iii) the fact that public sector annual pay adjustments follow the annual recommendations of the National Wages Council,[7] which has effectively pegged the growth of public sector wages to that of the performance of the economy; it is particularly significant that in both the 1985 recession and the slowdown in 1998 that the wage bill fell because of wage restraint announced by the NWC as well as mandatory CPF cuts.

On the revenue side, total revenue has been trending upward strongly, averaging 25 percent of GDP in the 1970s to 35 percent in the 1990s (Figure 15.4), but the increase has been exclusively due to the increasing share of nontax revenue. Although tax revenue trended upward until 1982, when it reached almost 20 percent of GDP (Figure 15.5) and then fell sharply in the mid-1980s, it has remained relatively stable through the 1990s averaging about 16 percent of GDP. The flattening of tax revenue is due to generally lower tax rates that have not been entirely offset by a broader tax base since the switch to a broad consumption-based value added tax in 1994.

In contrast, current nontax revenue (consisting mainly of investment income, fees and charges) rose from an average of 5 percent of GDP in the 1970s to 11 percent of GDP since 1983 (Figure 15.6). At its peak in 1987, nontax current revenue contributed to more than half of current revenue and through the 1990s, its contribution averaged 38 percent. The main source comes from investment income, which contributed about two-thirds of current nontax revenue in 1990–97, or an average of 3 percent of GDP over this period. Investment income

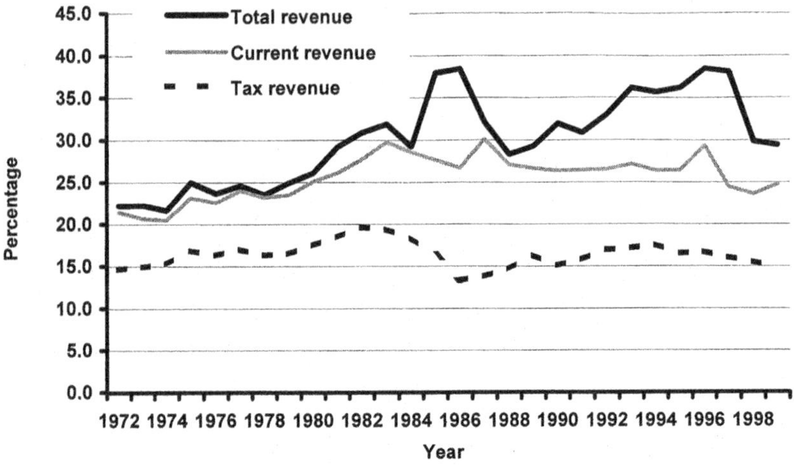


*Figure 15.4* Government revenue, 1972–99 (as a % of GDP).

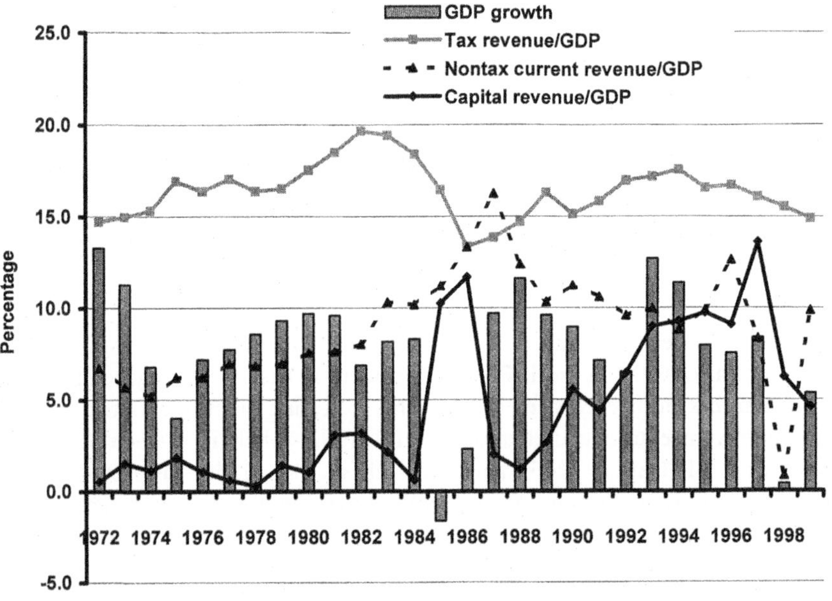


*Figure 15.5* Composition of revenue and GDP growth.

is generated mainly from investments of the government's budget surpluses and CPF funds managed by the GIC (Government Investment Corporation) and from foreign reserves managed by the MAS. The high proportion of revenue from fees and charges is due to widespread use of user charges (this includes the regulation of ownership of motor vehicles and development charges).

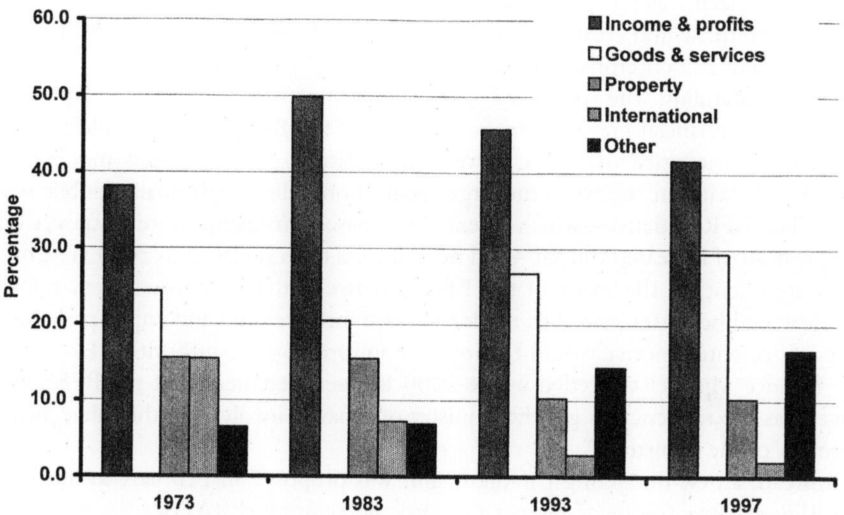


*Figure 15.6* Composition of tax revenue.

The other source of nontax revenue is capital revenue, which has also been rising sharply, from 1 percent of GDP in 1988 to 13 percent in 1997. Revenue from this source consists mainly of land sales, predominantly long leases rather than outright sales. The official policy on land sales is an orderly release to ensure that supply meets demand. Hence, land sales for private housing in the mid-1990s were accelerated when speculative demand drove housing prices to unprecedented levels.

In short, the build-up of large budget surpluses between 1988 and 1997 has primarily been a result of the sharp increase in nontax revenue, of which capital revenue from land sales has been a significant contributor. At the same time, deliberate policies to control operating expenditure bore fruit. The priority given to controlling operating expenditure was, in fact, instituted in anticipation of the fall in tax revenue as the government moved toward a lower tax regime. In the next section, we turn to an examination of Singapore's tax and expenditure policies.

## Recent guiding principles on tax and expenditure policies reform

In 1994, the Ministry of Finance launched an initiative coined as Budgeting for Results (BFR) with the intention of improving financial management in the public sector. Following the principle of BFR, fourteen organizations were commissioned as Autonomous Agencies (AAs) in April 1995. In 1996, another 102 ministry headquarters, departments and government-funded statutory boards (SBs) were being managed as AAs. This move was intended to enable the entire civil service and all SBs with "greater autonomy and flexibility to respond quickly to changes, along with incentives for efficient and superior performance and the wherewithal to nurture enterprise and creativity" with the ultimate "objective of creating a leaner, more efficient and enterprising public service."

Notwithstanding the proposed good intentions, some quarters expressed concern that financial management reforms under the BFR initiative could lead to increases in the price of public services or create a profit-oriented mindset in government without regard to the larger goal of providing high-quality public services. The BFR initiative—which essentially is based on giving more resources on the promise of increased output—had nevertheless been replaced in 2000. The original argument on the merit of the BFR initiative is that a more efficient public sector would be better placed to moderate price increases and any unjust price hike or profit-oriented motive would be closely monitored by the authorities. However, the Finance Minister conceded in the 2000 Budget Statement that the BFR initiative "has the tendency to get the Ministry of Finance involved in the micro management of the ministries."

Instead, a new budgeting paradigm shift was proposed in February 2000 from the BFR initiative to one of Budget Resource Accounting (BRA) by

> encouraging ministries to get the most out of their allotted resources. Within that budgetary framework, ministries are assured of a built-in increase for their base budget that is dependent on the GDP growth rate. Any increase in budgetary provision beyond that would have to be justified on the basis of the priority of their programs against others.
>
> (Ministry of Finance 2000)

This BRA principle is a fine-tuning over the previous BFR initiative since ministries are now being encouraged to not just look at the output generated by their programs, but also to examine the intended desired outcomes. It was further proposed that over 2001 and 2002, further concepts pertaining to BRA be introduced so as to ensure that ministries look at the total cost of providing services rather than just the cash cost alone. Among the major implications under the new BRA principle is that the GDP growth rate forecast that is traditionally provided by the Ministry of Trade and Industry becomes one of the crucial integrals in the budgeting process. Inability to provide reasonably accurate economic growth forecasts could not only deny or overprovide resources to various ministries, but could also distort projected revenues and hence overall budgetary balances (we shall discuss this further in the section on future fiscal projections).

### *Tax policies*

The government's formulation of tax policies reflects its long-term goal to provide an environment that is conducive to investment and work effort, while at the same time meeting equity goals. There is no capital gains tax. In the 1970s, the formulation of tax policies concentrated on the liberal use of tax incentives to attract foreign direct investment. Income tax rates were necessarily high to generate revenue since raising revenue through indirect taxes was limited given Singapore's free-port status. Since the mid-1980s, under pressure to stay internationally competitive, corporate tax rates have been gradually lowered from 55 percent in the early 1980s to the current level of 26 percent. Personal income tax rates have also been reduced accordingly with the tax rate for the highest income bracket currently at 28 percent. The effective tax rate is significantly lower as tax preferences are granted to encourage the achievement of socially desired goals (such as encouraging parental care, encouraging higher female labor force participation and fostering a higher birth rate).

Income tax rates were also reduced because of the introduction of a value added tax, or the Goods and Services (GST) tax as it is called, in 1994. The GST implemented in Singapore is a consumption-type value added tax. Under the GST, only exports and narrowly specified international services are zero rated, while businesses with turnover of less than S$1 million are exempt.[8] At the time of implementation, the government announced that the rate would be fixed at 3 percent for five years and would be reviewed with the aim to gradually raise it. However, the GST has remained at 3 percent since implementation. Various rebates were granted through personal income tax to offset some of the regressivity of the GST in the initial years of implementation.

The GST was also deemed necessary in response to demographic changes in the population, namely, the rapid aging of the country's population. A shift to a broad consumption-based tax will offset part of the fall in the tax base as the country's labor force ages.

The structure of tax revenue has remained largely unchanged since 1972. As shown in Figure 15.5, between 40 to 50 percent of tax revenue comes from personal and corporate income taxes. Indirect taxes on goods and services make up another one-fifth to one-quarter of tax revenue. Until 1993, such taxes were concentrated in a narrow range of goods and services, mainly motor vehicles, petroleum products, tobacco and betting. Since 1994, with the introduction of the GST, taxes on goods and services have contributed to almost 30 percent of tax revenue, an increase from 26 percent in 1993.

The increase in "Other" in the proportion of tax revenue reflects the growing presence of foreign workers in the economy. The government levies charges of between $350 (for semi-skilled) to $500 (for unskilled) per foreign worker to regulate employment of foreign workers in the economy. Figures are not available separately for revenue from foreign worker levies but Asher (1996) estimated that in 1994–95, revenue from foreign worker levies generated 7.5 percent of total tax revenue, equivalent to 1.3 percent of GDP which is higher than the 1.1 percent from GST.

### *Expenditure policy*

On the expenditure side, policies have been targeted at investment in social goods that reap long-term benefits and in providing infrastructure. Figure 15.7 provides the breakdown of total expenditure as a percentage of GDP for the period 1972–97 by functions of government. Expenditure on security represents the single largest item in the budget, averaging between 5 to 6 percent of GDP, while

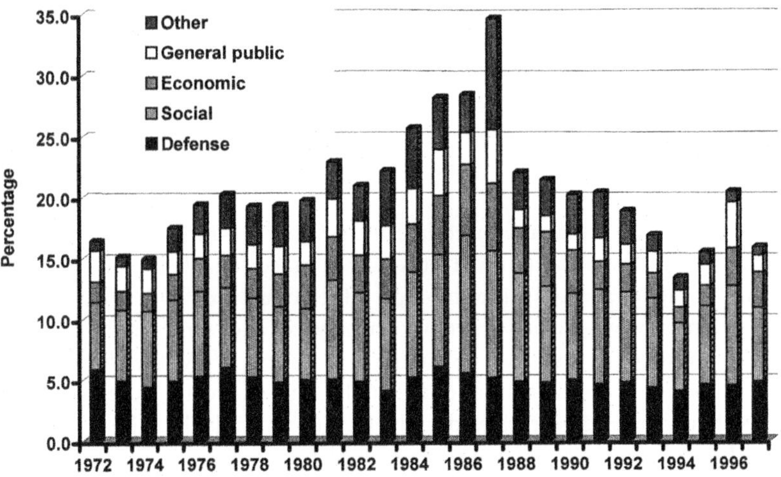


*Figure 15.7* Functional allocation of expenditures (as a % of GDP).

social expenditure—which covers education, health, housing and social security—has consistently been the largest functional area of public expenditure. Expenditures in these social services averaged between 5–7 percent of GDP through the 1970s. These were noticeably higher in the 1980s, and were highest during 1986–87, constituting more than 10 percent of GDP due to the acceleration of public housing construction (Figure 15.8). It can also be seen from Figure 15.8 that education has been consistently the most important item of social expenditure throughout the period, a reflection of the priority that education plays in the government's overall development strategy.

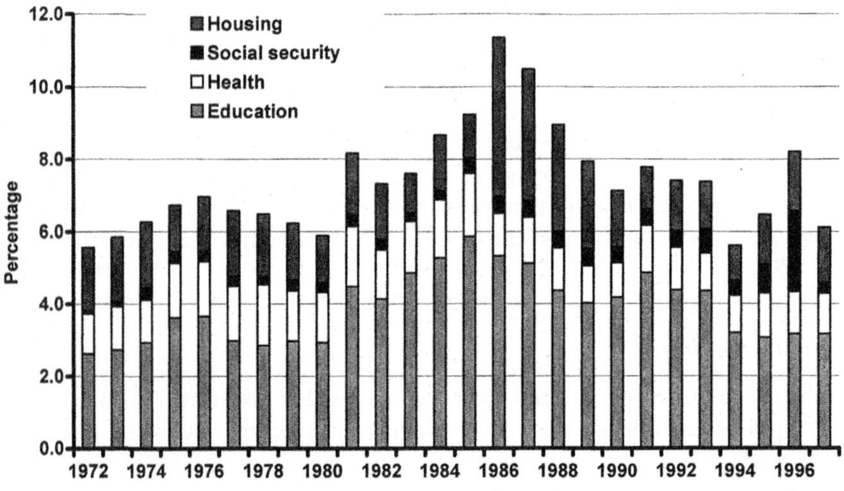


*Figure 15.8* Allocation of social expenditures (as a % of GDP).

Allocations to economic services vary between years, with the highest allocation in 1986–87 when it constituted more than 5 percent of GDP. Generally, the 1980s saw the largest allocations in this category and most of it is attributed to expenditure on transport. The share of general public services in the1990s was less than 2 percent in most years, significantly lower than that of earlier years.

The "Other" category consists largely of interest on internal public debt. This refers to interest paid to government securities. In spite of a persistent budget surplus, Singapore has a large internal public debt. This is because of the statutory requirement that the CPF and other financial institutions must invest a certain proportion of their deposits in government securities.

## How the surplus is spent

Although fiscal policy has a limited role as a tool for discretionary demand management in Singapore because of the openness of the economy,[9] the government increased development spending aggressively during the 1985–86 recession. In the 1998 slowdown, although development expenditure had increased, the primary response to the financial crisis caused by the collapse of regional currencies was a set of aggressive cost-reduction measures aimed at providing relief to private business measures including: a 10 percentage point reduction in employer contribution to the CPF; rebates or suspension of user charges for a wide range of services provided by the public sector such as utilities and rental; property tax rebates; foreign worker levy cuts; and a 10 percent corporate tax cut for year of assessment 1999.

The surpluses have been used as a tool for income redistribution through the government subsidy for public housing, i.e., the government has emphasized that the pace of upgrading of public housing would depend on the size of budget surpluses. Rather than instituting permanent tax preferences to lower-income groups, the government grants rebates through the income tax on an *ad hoc* basis to provide relief to lower-income groups, depending on the size of the budget surplus.

Since 1992–93, part of the surplus has been allocated to two funds to help finance future growth of social expenditures: the Edu-save Endowment Fund and Medi-save Endowment Fund (Table15.3).[10] Most of the surplus has been channeled to asset accumulation, mainly through overseas portfolio investment for which figures are not available, and into foreign reserves. A product of the budget

*Table 15.3* Uses of the budget surplus, 1992–97 (S$ million)

| | *Edu-save* | *Medi-save* | *CPF top-up* |
|---|---|---|---|
| 1992 | 1,000 | — | — |
| 1993 | 1,000 | 200 | 242.5 |
| 1994 | 1,000 | 100 | — |
| 1995 | 1,000 | 100 | 798.4 |
| 1996 | 500 | 100 | 460.9 |
| 1997 | 500 | 100 | 781.0 |

Sources: Ministry of Finance (various years).

surplus (and also the CPF savings) is its effect on the monetary base. The budget surplus contracts the monetary base and the Monetary Authority of Singapore buys foreign exchange to offset the reduction in money supply. The result is the translation of the budget surplus into foreign exchange reserves.

As the budget surplus builds up, the government has taken precautionary measures to protect reserves. In 1991, the Elected Presidency Law was passed which gives the president the right to veto the annual budgets of the government, statutory boards and key government companies. The president also has the power to scrutinize and, if necessary, veto any large item expenditure by a statutory board or government company. The EPL requires the concurrence of the president before the reserves can be used by the government of the day.

At the time of preparation of this chapter, a bill to amend the constitution had been introduced that mandates that at least half of the investment income earned from past reserves (the exact amount to be decided by the Minister of Finance each year) will be locked away as past reserves, instead of being treated as current reserves which can be spent by the government of the day. The amendment will also redefine net investment income to include interest earned from loans by government to the statutory boards. These measures will act as additional safeguards to reserves.

## Future fiscal projections

It is well understood that fiscal projections are not just quantitative assignments *per se* and, in retrospect, it is known to be a highly precarious task. With regard to general fiscal guidelines, the government has consistently argued over the decades on a balanced budget by "containing all development and operating expenditures at a level that can be financed by operating revenues" and "surpluses would be accumulated in good years as buffer against periods of economic downturns." Furthermore, "our financial reserves are therefore of crucial importance, not only to see us through times of crisis but also securing investor confidence in the future." Such fiscal policy guidelines clearly imply generational impacts and intertemporal implications, which are derived from the philosophy of "preparing for crises during period of stability" as a long-term strategy of nationhood survival consistently argued by the ruling government.

In fact, such philosophy of "generational-surplus-budgeting" was further institutionalized when a Constitutional Amendment Bill was moved and approved by the Parliament in January 2001 to require the government to protect at least 50 percent of the net investment income (NII) earned from past reserves. The composition of operating revenue has since been changed to include a new item called "NII contribution" defined as the subset or portion of NII that is available for the government of the day to spend. The government has also reclassified expenditures on land reclamation projects that were previously funded as development expenditure using current revenues, which could now become a disincentive for future governments to take on such projects, as benefits would only accrue in the long term. Under the new arrangement, since fiscal year 2001, land reclamation would be viewed as a long-term investment whose expenditures will be funded from capital receipts from land sales.

On the expenditure side, although its impact can be simulated and quantified, qualitative observations on Singapore's future fiscal positions can be viewed from Singapore's aging population and ongoing economic restructuring. The former is related to the burden of health care and old folks' home expenditures and the latter is linked to human resource investment and foreign talent recruitment drive as the republic gravitates toward an information technology-driven, knowledge-based economy (ITKBE). Under the ITKBE, government development expenditures on workers' retraining schemes and education-based hard and soft infrastructure are bound to rise. Confronted with the potential burden of state expenditures on health care and old folks' welfare maintenance resulting from the rapid aging population, the government has and is attempting to further privatize such responsibilities to the ultimately more efficient private sector. As the new residential population target has been raised to 5.5 million by 2015, successful recruitment of foreign talent to Singapore may marginally mitigate the aging population profile and its associated burdens.

On the revenue side, the burden of personal income tax revenue as a ratio of GDP has been capped at 8 percent since the 1980s. In the new millennium, we are likely to see further lowering of the personal income tax revenue to GDP ratio as was evident in the 2001 budget statement where further lowering of income tax across all income bands, with the top band being reduced by 2 percent from the current 28 percent, was proposed in 2001. Regular introduction of income tax rebates imply a lower percentage of tax-paying employees amounting to about 35 percent of the workforce with the bulk of the income tax being paid by the top few income brackets. Such policies are in line with the principle of moving the tax incidence from indirect income tax to direct goods and services taxes, and thus to further stimulate work incentive and encourage saving by leaving more earnings in the hands of employees and taxing directly on consumption instead which presently stands at 3 percent.

With regard to the corporate income tax, which currently stands at 24.5 percent, Singapore is already amongst the lowest in the world, just slightly higher than Ireland (24 percent) and Hong Kong (16 percent). Given the unique features of the Singapore economy as reflected in a highly restricted transportation land use, limited land space, higher population density resulting from increasing participation of skilled and unskilled foreign labor, future or longer-term sources of tax revenue are likely to increasingly come from transportation taxes, land sales proceeds, consumption tax or GST and foreign worker levies. As far as the potential of the future corporate income tax and personal income tax revenues are concerned, inevitably these will be increasingly dependent upon Singapore's largely external demand-driven economy over which the government would have little control as the republic plugs itself completely into the globalization of trade and services.

## Conclusion

An important factor in Singapore's economic success over the last three decades is the government's fiscal policy. Budgetary policies have been prudent, administered by an efficient public sector exercising strong fiscal responsibility, underpinned by the philosophy that the government should live within its means. The result has been a build-up of large public sector savings that has translated into an accumulation of strong foreign reserves, an important factor that has underpinned long-term investor confidence in the Singapore economy.

Government spending has focused on providing goods and services that enhance the productive capacity of the economy especially in the areas of education, housing, health and physical infrastructure, and in the area of taxation policy on creating an environment that is conducive to investment and work effort and responsive to the competitive environment engendered by globalization.

It cannot be over-emphasized that Singapore's ability to exercise strong fiscal discipline is also due to a number of unique factors. First, it is a small city-state with an educated labor force; with that comes fiscal advantages such as a large tax base (relative to the size of the population) and high tax compliance since enforcement is relatively easy. A small country also facilitates cohesiveness in decision-making and in soliciting support for policies that would have been otherwise unpopular.

In countries experiencing large budget surpluses, the tendency is either to spend it, lower taxes, or to reduce existing public debt. Generally if a government running a surplus can increase intertemporal social welfare by lowering taxes or increasing expenditure, then some or all of the surpluses should be spent. Ultimately whether budget surpluses should be reduced or accumulated as reserves for the benefit of future generations depends on intergenerational equity concerns. Owing to the size of the country, the lack of natural resources and the country's rapidly aging population that is expected to erode the tax base, the Singapore government's fiscal policy clearly favors protecting the reserves for future generations.

## Notes

1 Statutory boards enjoy a greater degree of autonomy and flexibility in their day-to-day operations and finances than the central government does. Currently the major statutory boards are the Housing Development Board, the Economic Development Board, Jurong Town Corporation, the Central Provident Fund (CPF), the Public Utilities Board, the Monetary Authority of Singapore, the Port of Singapore Authority, the Urban Redevelopment Authority, and Changi Airport Authority of Singapore.

2 According to an IMF study (Carling 1995: 20, fn 2) which cited a Department of Statistics estimate, the share of the central government in terms of value added is 5.3 percent but this share is 10.4 percent and 7.2 percent for statutory boards and GLCs, respectively. In 1987, there were an estimated 500 GLCs.

3 A comprehensive study of the inconsistencies in official budgetary data can be found in Asher (1989). The government accounts are organized around ten funds, of which the Consolidated Fund, the Development Fund, the Sinking Fund and the Skills Development Fund are the most important. Budgetary data presented in government publications include only transactions of the Consolidated and Development Funds. Interfund transfers such as transfers to the Sinking Fund (a fund set up for the redemption of loans) are treated as expenditures, as are transfers to various endowment funds such as Edu-save and Medi-save. Hence, Asher points out that the official data tend to over-state expenditure (because intra-government expenses are recorded as expenditures and transfers to endowment funds are also considered expenditures), while revenue tends to be understated.

4 The increase in debt servicing in 1987 was due both to a one-off payment of back-dated interest payable on CPF advance deposits that were converted to registered stocks in 1987 and interest payable on new borrowings. Excluding debt servicing, the budget would have registered a surplus, since debt servicing in that year accounted for 8 percent of GDP (see Table 15.2).

5 Data for 1998–99 are taken from Singapore official statistics and are not strictly comparable to the IMF data (see Table 15.2).

6 By the early 1990s, home ownership had reached 90 percent of the population, of which 87 percent lived in public housing.

7 The NWC is a tripartite council—involving representatives from unions, employer organizations and the government and chaired by an academic—that engages in annual recommendations of wage increases for the economy as a whole. Its recommendations have traditionally been adopted by the public sector in its annual adjustment of salaries and annual bonuses.

8 Zero rating means that the enterprise need not pay tax on sales but can claim tax paid on purchases, while exemption means that an enterprise need not pay tax on sales but also cannot claim tax paid on purchases. Allocation to these funds is not classified as expenditures but as allocations of the surplus. Such allocations totaled S$1.5 billion (2 percent of GDP) in 1992–93 (see Carling 1995: 23).

9 Singapore is a highly open economy and any stimulation of aggregate demand using fiscal policy would primarily lean to an increase in imports given the high import content of domestic expenditure. Second, fiscal policy in a flexible exchange rate regime would be ineffective in the tradition of the Fleming–Mundell model, i.e., any attempt to stimulate aggregate demand by running a budget deficit will lead to the incipient rise in the domestic interest rate and an appreciation in the domestic currency which will, in turn, reduce next exports and output.

10 These are capital funds, the annual interest earnings of which will finance transfers to households for certain education and medical expenses.

## References

Asher, Mukul (1996) "Singapore's fiscal policies in international perspective," in Mukul Asher and Amina Tyabji (eds) *Fiscal System of Singapore: Trends, Issues and Directions*, Singapore: National University of Singapore, Center for Advanced Studies.

Asher, Mukul (1989) *Fiscal System and Practices in Singapore*, Singapore: Institute of Southeast Asian Studies.

Carling, Robert G. (1995) "Fiscal and monetary policies," in Kenneth Bercuson (ed.) *Singapore: A Case Study in Rapid Development*, Washington, DC: International Monetary Fund.

Chalk, N. and Hemming, R. (1998) *What Should be Done with a Fiscal Surplus?*, IMF discussion paper, Fiscal Affairs Department, Washington, DC: International Monetary Fund.

Department of Statistics (various years) *Yearbook of Statistics, Singapore*, Singapore: Department of Statistics.

Hemming, R. and Daniel, J. (1995) *When is a Fiscal Surplus Appropriate?*, IMF paper on policy analysis and assessment, Washington, DC: International Monetary Fund.

International Monetary Fund (various years) *Government Finance Statistics Yearbook*, various issues, Washington, DC: International Monetary Fund.

Ministry of Finance (1988) *FY1988 Budget*, Singapore: Ministry of Finance.

Ministry of Finance (2000) *FY2002 Budget*, Singapore: Ministry of Finance.

Ministry of Finance (various years) *Economic Survey of Singapore*, various issues, Singapore: Ministry of Finance.

# 16 Chinese Taipei

*Cheng-Mount Cheng*

## Introduction

Chinese Taipei is known as a member of the four Asian dragons. Its successful economic development can be partly attributed to the government's successful implementation of fiscal policy, the main objective of which is to maintain economic momentum in good times and to stimulate the economy when things are not going well. Under guidelines issued to financial administrations, it is clearly specified that the agency should allocate financial resources efficiently to support major construction programs and coordinate fiscal policies to support economic development. Other objectives for financial administration include strict enforcement of budgeting and operation of government bonds to establish a sound financial status, and improvement in the tax structure so as to promote economic development. Clearly, fiscal policy in Chinese Taipei has many facets. Improper fiscal policy may have an opposite effect on the goal that it originally intended to achieve. Therefore, how to practice fiscal policy wisely is an important issue for the government in Chinese Taipei.

In the following, we give a brief description of the fiscal system in Chinese Taipei and the government's fiscal performance since 1970. Subsequently, we discuss the current situation and challenges the government now faces.

## Overview of the fiscal system

In recent years, there has been a dramatic change in the government's fiscal balance. Prior to 1989, the general government basically maintained a balanced budget. At the same time, economic growth was sustained at a rapid pace. However, beginning in 1989, the central government's fiscal deficit expanded significantly. This is particularly true in fiscal year 1992 when outstanding debts of the central government increased to a historical record. To prevent the fiscal situation from worsening, the central government had to cut back on consumption expenditures and engaged in reforms. In 1995, the Legislative Yuan passed the Public Debt Law which stipulated that the outstanding debt of the general government must not exceed 48.0 percent of the average GNP in the previous three years, and the outstanding debt of the central government must not exceed 28.8 percent. At the same time, the fiscal deficit of the general government must not exceed 15 percent of the expenditure budget in the current fiscal year. After the reform had taken effect, in FY1998 and FY1999, the central government had improved its fiscal condition. In the next section, we will first introduce the government and tax structure and then the budget process in Chinese Taipei.

### *The government and tax structure*

In Chinese Taipei, there are four layers of government. At the top is the central government, with the Executive Yuan as the main executive branch. At the next level is the provincial and municipal governments that are supervised directly under the central government. The third layer of government is the counties and cities that are under the provincial government, and at the bottom are the township offices that are under the county government.

Of these four levels of government, the central government clearly is the greatest in terms of revenue and expenditure (Table 16.1). For instance, in FY1976, the central government's revenue and expenditure reached NT$96.2 billion and NT$87.0 billion, respectively, representing 53.3 and 52.3 percent of revenue and expenditure for all governments. On the other hand, combined revenue and expenditure of Taipei municipal and Taiwan provincial governments amounted to NT$51.1 billion and NT$48.7 billion respectively, or 28.3 and 29.3 percent of revenue and expenditure for all governments. Revenue and expenditure for local governments, which includes county and city government and township offices, only reached NT$33.2 billion and NT$30.6 billion, making up 18.4 and 18.3 percent of revenue and expenditure for all governments.

As another indication of the relative size of the central government, consider Kaohsiung City which in 1979 became Kaohsiung Municipality. Even with this change, the central government comprised a 55.6 and 54.3 percent share of revenue and expenditure for all governments, while the share of Taipei, Kaohsiung and Taiwan provincial governments combined reached 28.4 and 29.0 percent, and local governments had 16.1 and 16.6 percent.

In 1999, the Taiwan provincial government was streamlined. As a result, the share of the central government in terms of revenue and expenditure to all governments jumped to 65.3 and 66.5 percent in FY2000. Meanwhile, the share of revenue and expenditure of the Taipei and Kaohsiung governments remained at 10.8 and 10.3 percent, respectively, while local government's shares increased to 23.8 and 23.2 percent, respectively.

In general, revenue of all levels of government comes from two sources—current and capital accounts. Current account revenue includes tax revenue and nontax revenue. The former consists of revenue from income tax, property tax, tax on goods and services, tariffs and other taxes, while the latter is made up of income from government property, income from public enterprises, administrative fees, fines and other nontax revenue. Capital account revenue is generated from government financing, that is, from issuing public bonds or loans.

Expenditures can also be separated into current account and capital account components. Current account expenditure includes the government's expenditure on goods and services, wages and salaries, interest payments, and subsidies

*Table 16.1* Revenues and expenditures of all levels of government in Chinese Taipei, 1970–2000 (NT$ million)

| Fiscal year | Central gov't | | Taipei municipal gov't | | Kaohsiung municipal gov't | | Taiwan provincial gov't | | County and city gov't | | Township office | |
|---|---|---|---|---|---|---|---|---|---|---|---|---|
| | *Revenue* | *Expenditure* | *Revenue* | *Expenditure* | *Revenue* | *Expenditure* | *Revenue* | *Expenditure* | *Revenue* | *Expenditure* | *Revenue* | *Expenditure* |
| 1970 | 32,382 | 30,667 | 3,360 | 3,554 | — | — | 13,386 | 13,266 | 7,965 | 7,695 | 2,214 | 2,060 |
| 1971 | 36,141 | 34,948 | 3,920 | 3,901 | — | — | 13,579 | 13,553 | 9,348 | 8,955 | 2,366 | 2,243 |
| 1972 | 41,749 | 39,828 | 4,604 | 4,604 | — | — | 15,168 | 15,062 | 9,481 | 9,251 | 2,549 | 2,358 |
| 1973 | 56,967 | 48,229 | 5,571 | 5,060 | — | — | 19,039 | 18,511 | 11,069 | 10,180 | 3,004 | 2,596 |
| 1974 | 72,158 | 53,121 | 7,242 | 5,834 | — | — | 22,769 | 20,833 | 14,943 | 13,969 | 4,039 | 3,526 |
| 1975 | 81,808 | 74,830 | 9,263 | 8,784 | — | — | 32,679 | 32,363 | 21,199 | 21,059 | 5,561 | 5,068 |
| 1976 | 96,186 | 86,976 | 13,010 | 11,327 | — | — | 38,127 | 37,323 | 26,347 | 24,498 | 6,855 | 6,060 |
| 1977 | 113,021 | 107,289 | 15,987 | 15,987 | — | — | 40,720 | 39,942 | 30,141 | 29,635 | 8,310 | 7,675 |
| 1978 | 138,485 | 130,077 | 18,771 | 18,771 | — | — | 49,566 | 47,916 | 34,865 | 34,565 | 8,804 | 8,223 |
| 1979 | 176,922 | 153,046 | 22,269 | 21,420 | — | — | 59,801 | 55,853 | 43,767 | 41,723 | 11,469 | 10,730 |
| 1980 | 218,669 | 201,793 | 28,584 | 28,011 | 8,684 | 8,359 | 74,221 | 71,847 | 49,511 | 48,515 | 13,866 | 13,110 |
| 1981 | 272,381 | 272,381 | 34,690 | 34,690 | 10,949 | 10,949 | 105,692 | 105,692 | 63,786 | 62,946 | 16,982 | 16,334 |
| 1982 | 310,445 | 310,445 | 40,821 | 39,895 | 12,875 | 14,228 | 112,924 | 112,924 | 73,103 | 72,955 | 19,707 | 18,394 |
| 1983 | 319,518 | 319,518 | 43,448 | 40,880 | 13,824 | 13,824 | 110,556 | 110,556 | 76,890 | 76,298 | 20,232 | 19,213 |
| 1984 | 316,192 | 316,192 | 46,617 | 41,920 | 13,966 | 13,537 | 129,048 | 128,927 | 81,302 | 79,622 | 21,658 | 21,063 |
| 1985 | 361,987 | 353,871 | 50,750 | 49,047 | 16,359 | 15,843 | 123,288 | 123,288 | 87,932 | 87,856 | 24,346 | 23,813 |
| 1986 | 405,721 | 405,721 | 53,357 | 53,357 | 17,431 | 17,431 | 140,126 | 140,126 | 93,897 | 93,493 | 25,394 | 24,845 |
| 1987 | 451,036 | 418,962 | 59,173 | 57,244 | 19,764 | 18,123 | 143,244 | 143,244 | 108,167 | 100,829 | 29,687 | 27,932 |
| 1988 | 539,753 | 470,255 | 69,340 | 62,265 | 23,206 | 22,287 | 131,404 | 129,854 | 130,826 | 120,570 | 36,261 | 35,383 |
| 1989 | 613,376 | 549,200 | 73,823 | 73,823 | 25,424 | 24,598 | 186,849 | 186,849 | 161,612 | 158,739 | 45,524 | 44,286 |
| 1990 | 707,906 | 673,201 | 82,778 | 75,570 | 31,797 | 31,797 | 214,669 | 214,669 | 169,695 | 173,830 | 51,794 | 50,553 |
| 1991 | 804,558 | 804,558 | 129,013 | 129,013 | 34,986 | 34,986 | 216,993 | 216,993 | 197,738 | 199,318 | 53,108 | 51,379 |
| 1992 | 945,225 | 945,225 | 125,333 | 122,140 | 44,947 | 38,663 | 279,941 | 279,941 | 273,853 | 232,380 | 87,697 | 83,567 |
| 1993 | 1,031,131 | 1,031,131 | 123,099 | 120,100 | 47,885 | 47,885 | 292,484 | 292,484 | 308,246 | 294,328 | 93,268 | 89,343 |
| 1994 | 1,024,255 | 1,024,255 | 126,963 | 126,963 | 48,889 | 48,889 | 360,400 | 360,400 | 318,645 | 314,104 | 112,511 | 107,657 |
| 1995 | 1,012,521 | 996,698 | 123,990 | 123,990 | 52,256 | 52,256 | 338,604 | 338,604 | 350,198 | 348,992 | 114,140 | 108,373 |
| 1996 | 1,092,526 | 1,085,077 | 142,543 | 142,543 | 52,973 | 52,973 | 385,876 | 385,876 | 377,395 | 376,689 | 128,585 | 123,297 |
| 1997 | 1,151,762 | 1,151,762 | 156,035 | 146,604 | 57,901 | 57,901 | 406,341 | 406,341 | 413,357 | 413,590 | 132,321 | 126,905 |
| 1998 | 1,301,428 | 1,187,011 | 176,505 | 176,060 | 59,926 | 59,926 | 399,388 | 399,388 | 392,217 | 407,136 | 127,711 | 123,598 |
| 1999 | 1,285,207 | 1,281,996 | 162,270 | 162,270 | 64,228 | 64,228 | 344,537 | 344,540 | 394,972 | 414,905 | 139,262 | 135,044 |
| 2000[a] | 1,985,645 | 2,234,769 | 241,274 | 254,276 | 88,331 | 92,217 | — | — | 559,764 | 605,359 | 165,523 | 174,499 |

Source: Directorate-General of Budget, Accounting, and Statistics (DGBAS), Executive Yuan (1999).

Note
a Figures refer to the amount of budgets.

and transfer payments to other levels of government. Capital account expenditure, on the other hand, includes government's acquisition of capital assets, land, fixed capital assets and intangible assets, capital transfers and public debt repayment.

It is obvious that the central government plays a dominant role in the fiscal system. In terms of revenue distribution, the central government collects the income tax, customs duties, commodity tax, security transaction tax, future transaction tax, mining lot tax, distribution tax,[1] and so on. The central government also receives revenue from monopolies, public enterprises' surpluses, fines and indemnities, fees, property revenues, trust revenue, revenue from issuing bonds and loans, and miscellaneous revenue. Tax revenue for the municipal and the provincial governments includes the business tax, stamp tax, license tax, distribution tax and harbor construction dues.[2] Tax revenue for county and city governments includes the land tax,[3] house tax, slaughter tax, amusement tax, deeds tax, education surtax and distribution tax.

Total tax revenues contain tax revenue and monopoly revenue (Table 16.2). In FY1970, the national tax, provincial and municipal tax, and municipal and city tax registered NT$20.0 billion, NT$6.8 billion, and NT$3.8 billion, respectively, while monopoly revenue amounted to NT$6.0 billion. This represents shares of 54.5, 18.7, 10.4 and 16.4 percent, respectively. It is noteworthy that the share of monopoly revenue to total tax revenues has been declining over time. In FY2000, because of the streamlining of the Taiwan provincial government, the share of the national tax jumped to 77.8 percent, while the share of the municipal and city tax rose to 17.9 percent. On the other hand, the share of monopoly revenue declined to only 4.3 percent.

Because of the asymmetry in the collection and distribution of tax revenue among the different levels of government, and to increase the fiscal independence of local governments, the central government in 1999 revised the Fiscal Distribution Act, which can be summarized as follows:

- The fiscal system includes the central government, the municipal governments, county and city governments, and townships; the provincial government has been streamlined.
- The tax structure includes the national tax, municipal tax, and county and city tax; the business tax will be classified under the national tax.
- The central government will distribute 10 percent of the income tax and commodity tax to local governments.
- Adding tax for tobacco and alcohols, 20 percent of the tax revenue will be distributed to local governments according to their demographic ratios.
- Revenue from the stamp tax and license tax on motor vehicles will be distributed to local governments.
- The system of the distribution tax should be formalized and put into a formula to prevent arbitrary changes.

*Table 16.2* Total tax revenue, 1970–2000 (NT$ million)

| *Fiscal year* | *National tax* | *Provincial and municipal tax* | *Municipal and city tax* | *Monopoly revenue* | *Total* |
|---|---|---|---|---|---|
| 1970 | 19,998 | 6,840 | 3,819 | 6,007 | 36,664 |
| 1971 | 22,366 | 7,695 | 4,187 | 6,438 | 40,685 |
| 1972 | 27,466 | 9,026 | 4,542 | 6,942 | 47,976 |
| 1973 | 36,253 | 11,480 | 5,361 | 7,634 | 60,727 |
| 1974 | 56,605 | 17,567 | 6,743 | 7,939 | 88,854 |
| 1975 | 57,964 | 19,433 | 6,992 | 13,115 | 97,504 |
| 1976 | 70,151 | 27,080 | 9,752 | 14,784 | 121,767 |
| 1977 | 80,146 | 31,004 | 11,548 | 16,608 | 139,305 |
| 1978 | 98,617 | 37,580 | 12,852 | 19,145 | 168,194 |
| 1979 | 131,750 | 51,903 | 15,692 | 21,176 | 220,521 |
| 1980 | 155,462 | 63,537 | 18,187 | 24,162 | 261,349 |
| 1981 | 180,106 | 81,176 | 19,805 | 33,963 | 315,049 |
| 1982 | 172,531 | 62,170 | 65,795 | 37,594 | 338,090 |
| 1983 | 171,793 | 63,880 | 66,805 | 39,900 | 342,379 |
| 1984 | 194,064 | 73,948 | 75,200 | 40,152 | 383,364 |
| 1985 | 200,768 | 76,880 | 75,460 | 41,738 | 394,846 |
| 1986 | 195,791 | 82,832 | 78,353 | 44,824 | 401,800 |
| 1987 | 226,311 | 90,687 | 98,320 | 46,137 | 461,455 |
| 1988 | 286,232 | 100,900 | 124,505 | 46,409 | 558,046 |
| 1989 | 361,427 | 109,012 | 159,313 | 47,666 | 677,418 |
| 1990 | 505,926 | 145,367 | 143,519 | 52,921 | 847,733 |
| 1991 | 442,353 | 145,114 | 161,041 | 60,113 | 808,621 |
| 1992 | 473,256 | 173,385 | 262,469 | 58,513 | 967,624 |
| 1993 | 515,165 | 198,925 | 269,297 | 62,109 | 1,045,496 |
| 1994 | 571,481 | 229,363 | 261,934 | 64,703 | 1,127,481 |
| 1995 | 662,201 | 251,431 | 257,223 | 61,408 | 1,232,264 |
| 1996 | 661,414 | 260,122 | 220,302 | 55,959 | 1,197,797 |
| 1997 | 706,200 | 269,275 | 237,798 | 58,179 | 1,271,453 |
| 1998 | 808,298 | 293,087 | 238,220 | 57,448 | 1,397,052 |
| 1999 | 788,392 | 302,397 | 208,951 | 55,322 | 1,355,062 |
| 2000[a] | 1,563,418 | — | 358,879 | 86,313 | 2,008,610 |

Source: Directorate-General of Budget, Accounting and Statistics, Executive Yuan (1999).

Note
a Figures refer to the amount of budgets. The surtax and temporary tax are included.

### *The budget process*

In Chinese Taipei, each layer of government must draw up a program and raise the required funds before it launches a construction project or before it starts to provide services. In this way, it can smoothly carry out administration of the programs and provide the maximal allocation of national resources. The general budget for the central government and the budget for subordinate government agencies are prepared in five stages as follows:

1 From June to August of a year, the Executive Yuan shall draw up annual programs, plan the budget, and set receipt and expenditure policies for the next

fiscal year. Major tasks include setting of administration guidelines, the general summary of administration programs, the budgeting guidelines for central and local governments, and the rules for preparation and review of both the general budget for the central government and the budget for subordinate government agencies.

2 From September to October of a year, the Executive Yuan shall set the scale of the general budget for the central government and approve the expenditure budget lines for each government agency. Each operating agency shall prepare operation programs during the period. Major tasks include preparation of administration programs by each government agency, setting of expenditure budget lines for each central government agency and granting of budget lines for provincial and municipal governments, and preparation of operation programs and budgets for all subordinate agencies.

3 From November of a year to January of the following year, each government agency shall prepare its annual expenditure estimates and the Executive Yuan shall approve such estimates. Major tasks during the period include preparation of annual expenditure estimates by each government agency, rescreening of such estimates, screening of annual expenditure estimates for subordinate agencies, submission of annual operation programs, and calling of meetings of the Budget Review Committee.

4 From February to March of the next year, the Executive Yuan shall compile and prepare the general budget proposal, the budgets for subordinate agencies, and the consolidated budget tables. According to provisions of the Budget Law, all government agencies shall submit their agency budget proposals via their superior to the Executive Yuan prior to a deadline. The Directorate-General of Budget, Accounting and Statistics (DGBAS) of the Executive Yuan shall combine these agency budget proposals and compile them into the central government budget proposal. Following the passage of the cabinet meeting, the Executive Yuan shall submit the central government budget proposal to the Legislative Yuan prior to a deadline for legislation.

5 From April to May of the next year, the Legislative Yuan shall review the central government budget proposal. The Legislative Yuan shall invite the Premier, the DGBAS Director-General and the Finance Minister to report on the administrative programs and the process of preparing the annual revenue and annual expenditure budget. Different parts of the proposal are reviewed first by relevant committees and subsequently by the whole committees of the Legislative Yuan during the first reading. Then the proposal is submitted to the floor of the Legislative Yuan for the second and third readings. After passage by the Legislative Yuan, the President shall promulgate central government budget.

## *Overall fiscal position*

The fiscal year begins on 1 July of the same year and ends on 30 June in the following year. In the 1970s and 1980s, the government (in the remainder of the chapter, "government" is used to represent all levels of government unless specified otherwise) generally maintained a balanced budget. However, in FY1989, faced with a slowdown in domestic economic growth from double figures to about 6 percent, and given the fact that the outlook for the global economy was not bright, the central government decided to increase public spending to stimulate domestic consumption and investment. As a result, the government's budget deficit jumped to NT$318.0 billion and since then, the budget has been in the red (Table 16.3). The ratio of the budget deficit to GNP also jumped to 8.4 percent in FY1989, but declined gradually to 2.6 percent by FY1999. This trend suggests that the government in general did attempt to amend its over-spending of FY1989 and abide by fiscal discipline.

Separating the budget balance into the current account and capital account, we can see that the government has a surplus in the former but a deficit in the latter. With respect to government revenues, the current account contributed to 98.3 percent of revenues, while the capital account contributed only 1.7 percent in FY1971. However, the proportion of the current account gradually declined to 93.0 percent in FY1999, while that of the capital account rose to 7.0 percent. This reflects the fact that government financing has become more important for the budget.

The sources of government revenue were mainly from taxes, monopoly revenue, surplus of public enterprises and public utilities, proceeds from issues of public bonds, receipts from loans for economic construction and others (Table 16.4). Tax revenue is the largest source. The ratio of tax revenue to total government revenues reached as high as 69.4 percent in FY1979 and as low as 52.0 percent in FY1991. Overall, the ratio has been declining, and the government has had to rely more heavily on other sources. Monopoly revenue used to be another main source of government revenue, but because of the opening of markets and greater competition, monopoly revenue does not contribute as much as it did in the past. For example, the ratio of monopoly revenue to total government revenue declined from 11.7 percent in FY1970 to 2.4 percent in FY1999. On the other hand, surplus of public enterprises and public utilities has become a reliable source of government revenue. As a ratio of total government revenue, the surplus of public enterprises and utilities has been about 8 percent in recent years and even reached as high as 15.6 and 14.1 percent in FY1998 and FY1999, respectively. The ratio of proceeds from issues of public bonds and receipts from loans for economic construction has varied, complementing the other sources of government revenue.

With respect to government expenditure, current account expenditures amounted to 73.0 percent of total government expenditures while the capital account took up the rest of the share in FY1970. In FY1989, the share of the current account had declined to 46.6 percent, while the share of the capital account rose to 53.4 percent. Since then, the share of the current account has gradually climbed back to around 70 percent.

General administration, national defense, education, science and culture, economic development, social security and obligation were the main items of government expenditure (Table 16.5). Spending on national defense used to be the largest expenditure of the government, with its share of total government expenditures reaching as high as 35.9 percent in FY1970. However, this ratio has declined steadily, and by FY1999, it had dropped to 12.9 percent.

*Table 16.3* Comparison of net revenue and expenditure[a] of general government by current and capital accounts, 1970–2000 (NT$ million)

| *Fiscal year* | *Net revenues* | | | *Net expenditures* | | | *Surplus or deficit* | | |
|---|---|---|---|---|---|---|---|---|---|
| | *Total* | *Current* | *Capital* | *Total* | *Current* | *Capital* | *Total* | *Current* | *Capital* |
| 1970 | 48,287 | 46,586 | 1,701 | 49,153 | 35,901 | 13,252 | −866 | 10,685 | −11,551 |
| 1971 | 52,843 | 51,960 | 883 | 54,829 | 39,732 | 15,097 | −1,986 | 12,228 | −14,214 |
| 1972 | 63,377 | 62,409 | 968 | 63,668 | 47,528 | 16,140 | −291 | 14,881 | −15,172 |
| 1973 | 82,281 | 80,181 | 2,100 | 79,856 | 56,476 | 23,380 | 2,425 | 23,705 | −21,280 |
| 1974 | 110,054 | 107,550 | 2,504 | 89,934 | 62,781 | 27,153 | 20,120 | 44,769 | −24,649 |
| 1975 | 126,311 | 123,238 | 3,073 | 126,436 | 82,915 | 43,521 | −125 | 40,323 | −40,448 |
| 1976 | 156,124 | 152,063 | 4,061 | 149,594 | 95,699 | 50,895 | 9,530 | 56,365 | −46,835 |
| 1977 | 180,225 | 176,113 | 4,112 | 187,660 | 111,953 | 75,708 | −7,435 | 64,160 | −71,596 |
| 1978 | 216,168 | 209,638 | 6,530 | 221,479 | 131,857 | 89,622 | −5,311 | 77,780 | −83,092 |
| 1979 | 276,559 | 268,724 | 7,836 | 246,888 | 154,307 | 92,581 | 29,671 | 114,416 | −84,745 |
| 1980 | 340,715 | 327,649 | 13,066 | 340,363 | 213,738 | 126,625 | 352 | 113,911 | −113,559 |
| 1981 | 411,712 | 390,881 | 20,831 | 425,731 | 264,906 | 160,825 | −14,020 | 125,975 | −139,994 |
| 1982 | 454,461 | 435,156 | 19,305 | 487,253 | 302,278 | 184,975 | −32,792 | 132,878 | −165,670 |
| 1983 | 461,117 | 448,294 | 12,823 | 489,894 | 334,612 | 155,282 | −28,778 | 113,681 | −142,459 |
| 1984 | 515,911 | 503,021 | 12,890 | 506,224 | 342,524 | 163,699 | 9,690 | 160,496 | −150,809 |
| 1985 | 542,602 | 531,075 | 11,527 | 546,338 | 382,713 | 163,625 | −3,735 | 148,362 | −152,098 |
| 1986 | 584,838 | 566,944 | 17,895 | 616,718 | 434,112 | 182,606 | −31,880 | 132,831 | −164,711 |
| 1987 | 650,203 | 629,488 | 20,715 | 641,911 | 443,239 | 198,672 | 8,292 | 186,249 | −177,957 |
| 1988 | 765,439 | 737,872 | 27,567 | 726,468 | 485,901 | 240,567 | 38,971 | 251,971 | −213,001 |
| 1989 | 921,575 | 890,664 | 30,911 | 1,207,351 | 577,967 | 629,384 | −285,775 | 312,697 | −598,473 |
| 1990 | 1,092,401 | 1,053,410 | 38,991 | 1,097,518 | 702,812 | 394,706 | −5,116 | 350,599 | −355,715 |
| 1991 | 1,049,931 | 997,536 | 52,395 | 1,275,613 | 823,188 | 452,425 | −225,682 | 174,348 | −400,030 |
| 1992 | 1,257,568 | 1,218,653 | 38,915 | 1,561,930 | 919,058 | 642,872 | −304,362 | 299,595 | −603,957 |
| 1993 | 1,416,334 | 1,352,986 | 63,348 | 1,756,306 | 1,025,405 | 730,902 | −339,972 | 327,581 | −667,553 |
| 1994 | 1,502,754 | 1,441,922 | 60,832 | 1,826,367 | 1,163,298 | 663,069 | −323,613 | 278,624 | −602,237 |
| 1995 | 1,559,429 | 1,522,624 | 36,805 | 1,910,066 | 1,328,425 | 581,641 | −350,637 | 194,199 | −544,836 |
| 1996 | 1,604,184 | 1,550,943 | 53,241 | 1,843,786 | 1,383,725 | 460,061 | −239,602 | 167,218 | −406,820 |
| 1997 | 1,704,759 | 1,629,420 | 75,338 | 1,878,764 | 1,463,449 | 415,315 | −174,005 | 165,972 | −339,976 |
| 1998 | 2,053,458 | 1,960,620 | 92,838 | 1,992,593 | 1,545,052 | 447,542 | 60,865 | 415,568 | −354,704 |
| 1999 | 2,004,394 | 1,867,081 | 137,313 | 2,050,004 | 1,554,405 | 495,598 | −45,609 | 312,676 | −358,286 |
| 2000[b] | 2,747,926 | 2,643,889 | 104,036 | 3,068,509 | 2,581,837 | 486,672 | −320,583 | 62,052 | −382,636 |

Source: Directorate-General of Budget, Accounting and Statistics, Executive Yuan (1999).

Notes

a Revenue does not include the proceeds from issues of public debt, receipts from loans for economic construction. Expenditures do not include principle repayments.

b The figures refer to annual budget appropriation; figures of the annexed budget are not included.

*Table 16.4* Revenues of general government by source, 1970–2000 (NT$ million)

| *Fiscal year* | *Tax revenue* | *Monopoly revenue* | *Surplus of public enterprise and utilities* | *Proceeds from issue of public bonds* | *Receipts from loans for economic construction* | *Other* | *Total* |
|---|---|---|---|---|---|---|---|
| 1970 | 30,657 | 6,007 | 4,938 | 2,500 | 428 | 6,685 | 51,215 |
| 1971 | 34,248 | 6,438 | 6,034 | 2,800 | 466 | 6,124 | 56,110 |
| 1972 | 41,034 | 4,942 | 7,686 | 1,900 | 701 | 7,715 | 63,978 |
| 1973 | 53,093 | 7,634 | 12,662 | 2,901 | 1,225 | 8,862 | 86,377 |
| 1974 | 80,915 | 7,939 | 9,906 | 900 | 744 | 11,295 | 111,699 |
| 1975 | 84,389 | 13,115 | 14,227 | 400 | 1,009 | 14,580 | 127,720 |
| 1976 | 106,983 | 14,748 | 16,570 | 4,600 | 1,913 | 17,786 | 162,600 |
| 1977 | 122,657 | 16,608 | 18,536 | 3,106 | 1,524 | 22,384 | 184,815 |
| 1978 | 149,048 | 19,145 | 21,732 | 6,510 | 5,862 | 26,242 | 228,539 |
| 1979 | 199,345 | 21,176 | 22,764 | 5,600 | 2,894 | 33,274 | 285,053 |
| 1980 | 237,187 | 24,162 | 33,106 | — | 4,612 | 46,260 | 345,327 |
| 1981 | 281,087 | 33,962 | 41,107 | 4,000 | 3,717 | 55,556 | 419,429 |
| 1982 | 300,496 | 37,594 | 55,628 | 13,382 | 6,806 | 60,742 | 474,648 |
| 1983 | 302,478 | 39,901 | 60,486 | 22,300 | 7,778 | 58,252 | 491,195 |
| 1984 | 343,212 | 40,152 | 63,022 | 9,779 | 5,982 | 69,527 | 531,674 |
| 1985 | 253,109 | 41,738 | 76,779 | 24,088 | 7,102 | 70,977 | 473,793 |
| 1986 | 356,975 | 44,824 | 99,646 | 28,800 | 7,441 | 83,392 | 621,078 |
| 1987 | 415,318 | 46,137 | 102,626 | 48,339 | 8,457 | 86,122 | 706,999 |
| 1988 | 511,637 | 46,409 | 111,727 | 76,540 | 9,504 | 95,667 | 851,484 |
| 1989 | 629,753 | 47,666 | 128,210 | 117,397 | 313,138 | 115,947 | 1,352,111 |
| 1990 | 794,812 | 52,921 | 121,418 | 15,831 | 72,855 | 123,250 | 1,181,087 |
| 1991 | 748,508 | 60,113 | 94,835 | 145,003 | 136,605 | 146,475 | 1,331,539 |
| 1992 | 909,110 | 58,514 | 141,045 | 312,903 | 89,133 | 148,900 | 1,659,605 |
| 1993 | 983,387 | 62,109 | 166,471 | 340,886 | 99,609 | 204,367 | 1,856,829 |
| 1994 | 1,062,778 | 64,703 | 184,914 | 108,327 | 231,135 | 190,359 | 1,842,216 |
| 1995 | 1,170,856 | 61,408 | 141,956 | 75,104 | 389,432 | 185,209 | 2,023,965 |
| 1996 | 1,141,838 | 55,959 | 181,094 | 115,769 | 249,676 | 225,294 | 1,969,630 |
| 1997 | 1,213,274 | 58,179 | 180,797 | 136,265 | 199,991 | 252,509 | 2,041,015 |
| 1998 | 1,339,605 | 57,448 | 361,574 | 59,904 | 176,262 | 294,831 | 2,289,624 |
| 1999 | 1,299,740 | 55,322 | 324,851 | 77,558 | 112,444 | 324,482 | 2,194,397 |
| 2000[a] | 1,922,297 | 86,313 | 408,219 | 394,000 | 64,558 | 331,097 | 3,206,484 |

Source: Directorate-General of Budget, Accounting and Statistics, Executive Yuan (1999).

Note

a The figures are those of annual budget appropriation and figures of annexed budget are not included.

Expenditure on economic development is another important component of government spending. In fact, in FY1975, spending on economic development surpassed expenditure on national defense to become the government's largest expenditure item. In FY1996, social security took the lead. From this we can see that the government's policy priority has switched from national defense to economic development and now to social security.

*Table 16.5* Expenditures of general government by use, 1970–2000 (NT$ million)

| *Fiscal year* | *Total* | *General administration* | *National defense* | *Education, science and culture* | *Economic development* | *Social security and pension* | *Obligations* | *Miscellaneous* |
|---|---|---|---|---|---|---|---|---|
| 1970 | 47,127 | 6,249 | 17,629 | 7,992 | 8,795 | 4,712 | 756 | 994 |
| 1971 | 51,943 | 6,913 | 19,259 | 9,636 | 8,512 | 5,683 | 946 | 994 |
| 1972 | 60,930 | 8,264 | 19,305 | 11,046 | 11,659 | 8,102 | 990 | 1,564 |
| 1973 | 76,872 | 8,279 | 24,795 | 13,512 | 18,207 | 8,663 | 1,062 | 2,354 |
| 1974 | 87,042 | 12,248 | 24,617 | 14,994 | 22,698 | 9,719 | 996 | 1,770 |
| 1975 | 123,557 | 19,377 | 30,231 | 20,741 | 37,486 | 12,657 | 957 | 2,108 |
| 1976 | 146,593 | 17,859 | 37,013 | 23,783 | 47,603 | 16,940 | 763 | 2,632 |
| 1977 | 187,659 | 22,493 | 47,005 | 28,277 | 66,693 | 20,428 | 593 | 2,170 |
| 1978 | 221,499 | 21,740 | 62,466 | 38,990 | 71,280 | 24,489 | 368 | 2,166 |
| 1979 | 246,888 | 24,936 | 70,464 | 41,228 | 77,567 | 29,118 | 339 | 3,236 |
| 1980 | 340,364 | 32,031 | 103,141 | 52,846 | 108,860 | 38,224 | 1,827 | 3,435 |
| 1981 | 425,579 | 42,219 | 104,623 | 75,409 | 145,365 | 51,143 | 1,756 | 5,064 |
| 1982 | 486,980 | 50,137 | 119,641 | 87,422 | 147,480 | 71,542 | 2,391 | 8,367 |
| 1983 | 489,607 | 54,480 | 134,155 | 96,267 | 121,184 | 75,501 | 4,197 | 3,823 |
| 1984 | 506,247 | 53,648 | 123,418 | 98,564 | 138,613 | 81,714 | 5,657 | 4,633 |
| 1985 | 545,995 | 61,968 | 135,243 | 111,522 | 138,021 | 88,400 | 6,032 | 4,809 |
| 1986 | 617,180 | 70,077 | 153,588 | 129,018 | 154,534 | 98,728 | 6,394 | 4,841 |
| 1987 | 641,318 | 72,074 | 148,798 | 133,700 | 171,364 | 102,482 | 6,989 | 5,911 |
| 1988 | 725,601 | 80,222 | 160,375 | 147,183 | 192,406 | 131,427 | 8,000 | 5,988 |
| 1989 | 1,205,343 | 97,299 | 187,908 | 205,000 | 541,385 | 151,567 | 10,701 | 11,483 |
| 1990 | 1,093,585 | 125,786 | 210,974 | 227,271 | 302,281 | 199,769 | 16,755 | 10,749 |
| 1991 | 1,270,652 | 153,278 | 227,099 | 288,077 | 322,087 | 234,221 | 33,398 | 12,492 |
| 1992 | 1,555,732 | 198,348 | 239,398 | 324,834 | 461,821 | 286,858 | 33,936 | 10,537 |
| 1993 | 1,747,645 | 208,961 | 253,511 | 350,351 | 545,641 | 311,347 | 63,892 | 13,942 |
| 1994 | 1,826,366 | 216,069 | 321,821 | 382,197 | 468,080 | 351,303 | 75,179 | 11,717 |
| 1995 | 1,515,066 | 222,403 | 269,960 | 357,487 | 438,152 | 415,196 | 194,890 | 11,978 |
| 1996 | 1,843,786 | 243,973 | 284,926 | 374,401 | 329,135 | 495,155 | 106,061 | 10,135 |
| 1997 | 1,878,763 | 244,757 | 291,920 | 375,822 | 295,035 | 543,320 | 115,630 | 12,279 |
| 1998 | 1,992,594 | 257,265 | 312,286 | 411,513 | 335,012 | 545,291 | 115,896 | 15,331 |
| 1999 | 2,050,004 | 279,113 | 286,572 | 429,127 | 351,102 | 551,344 | 140,910 | 11,836 |
| 2000[a] | 3,068,510 | 493,270 | 353,770 | 637,038 | 399,652 | 848,495 | 282,015 | 54,270 |

Source: Directorate-General of Budget, Accounting and Statistics, Executive Yuan (1999).

Note

a The figures are those of annual budget appropriation and figures of annexed budget are not included.

### *Fiscal deficit dynamics*

How does the government finance its budget? In FY1976, net borrowing of the government amounted to NT$6.6 billion, with NT$4.6 billion of the proceeds coming from the issue of public bonds, NT$1.9 billion of receipts coming from loans for economic construction, NT$3.5 billion was from a surplus in the previous fiscal year, and NT$3.1 billion of spending came from principle repayment (Table 16.6). With the exception of FY1980, proceeds from issue of public bonds have been a major source of financing for the government, representing as high as 184.3 percent and as low as 19.8 percent of net borrowing. Loans for economic construction are another source of financing, and its importance has been growing in recent years. On the other hand, surpluses from previous fiscal years have

*Table 16.6* Financing of general government, 1976–2000 (NT$ million)

| *Fiscal year* | *Net borrowing* | *Proceeds from issue of public bonds* | *Receipts from loans for economic construction* | *Surplus of previous fiscal year* | *Principle repayment* |
|---|---|---|---|---|---|
| 1976 | 6,579 | 4,600 | 1,913 | 3,466 | 3,401 |
| 1977 | 8,771 | 3,106 | 1,524 | 8,973 | 4,832 |
| 1978 | 12,056 | 6,510 | 5,862 | 5,104 | 5,420 |
| 1979 | 3,038 | 5,600 | 2,894 | 2,367 | 7,823 |
| 1980 | 23,174 | — | 4,612 | 23,595 | 5,034 |
| 1981 | 18,506 | 4,000 | 3,717 | 18,278 | 7,489 |
| 1982 | 29,818 | 13,382 | 6,806 | 16,118 | 6,488 |
| 1983 | 31,774 | 22,300 | 7,778 | 9,961 | 8,264 |
| 1984 | 5,418 | 9,779 | 5,982 | 2,483 | 12,825 |
| 1985 | 16,046 | 24,088 | 7,102 | 2,246 | 17,391 |
| 1986 | 35,423 | 28,800 | 7,441 | 15,125 | 15,943 |
| 1987 | 37,416 | 48,339 | 8,457 | 844 | 20,224 |
| 1988 | 61,730 | 76,540 | 9,504 | 1,147 | 25,461 |
| 1989 | 428,755 | 117,397 | 313,138 | 30,422 | 32,203 |
| 1990 | 41,510 | 15,831 | 72,855 | 22,053 | 69,229 |
| 1991 | 247,743 | 145,003 | 136,605 | 107,147 | 141,012 |
| 1992 | 319,047 | 312,903 | 89,133 | 51,197 | 134,186 |
| 1993 | 375,047 | 340,886 | 99,609 | 37,540 | 102,988 |
| 1994 | 334,367 | 108,327 | 231,135 | 82,280 | 87,375 |
| 1995 | 378,445 | 75,104 | 389,432 | 78,771 | 164,863 |
| 1996 | 257,682 | 115,769 | 249,676 | 54,348 | 162,111 |
| 1997 | 181,318 | 136,265 | 199,991 | 33,049 | 187,988 |
| 1998 | 59,827 | 59,904 | 176,262 | 35,726 | 212,065 |
| 1999 | 45,900 | 77,558 | 112,444 | 23,739 | 167,842 |
| 2000[a] | 320,654 | 394,000 | 64,558 | 93,625 | 231,529 |

Source: Directorate-General of Budget, Accounting and Statistics, Executive Yuan (1999).

Note
a The figures are those of annual budget appropriation and figures of the annexed budget are not included.

become relatively trivial. With the increase in net borrowing, the burden of principle repayment has also been rising sharply.

Only the central government and the provincial and municipal governments have the right to issue public bonds. In FY1976, the central government consolidated the issuing of public bonds. In FY1992, the central government classified the issuing into two categories. In the first category, public bonds and loans are issued to support construction funds that are not self-redeemable in nature while in the second category, bonds are used for construction funds that are self-redeemable.

With regard to the outstanding debt of the central government, in FY1985, the ratio of outstanding debt to central government expenditure was only 12.3 percent (Table 16.7). By FY1999, however, this ratio had risen to 94.3 percent; at the same time, the ratio of outstanding debt to GNP also increased from 1.8 percent in FY1985 to 14.7 percent in FY1999.

*Table 16.7* Outstanding debt of central government to expenditures and gross national product[a], 1985–99 (NT$ million)

| *Fiscal year* | *Outstanding debt* | | | | *Total expenditure* | *Gross national product* | *% of outstanding debt to expenditures* | *% of outstanding debt to GNP* |
|---|---|---|---|---|---|---|---|---|
| | *Total* | *First category public bonds and loans* | | *Second category public bonds* | | | | |
| | | *Public bonds* | *Loans* | | | | | |
| 1985 | 43,628 | 41,620 | 2,008 | — | 353,871 | 2,449,539 | 12.3 | 1.8 |
| 1986 | 60,067 | 58,375 | 1,692 | — | 105,721 | 2,680,483 | 56.8 | 2.2 |
| 1987 | 89,621 | 86,750 | 2,871 | — | 422,977 | 3,134,828 | 21.2 | 2.9 |
| 1988 | 139,489 | 129,625 | 3,864 | 6,000 | 483,886 | 3,442,690 | 28.8 | 4.1 |
| 1989 | 191,018 | 158,000 | 8,018 | 25,000 | 562,240 | 3,801,819 | 34.0 | 5.0 |
| 1990 | 201,165 | 122,375 | 33,790 | 45,000 | 726,014 | 4,227,304 | 27.7 | 4.8 |
| 1991 | 266,879 | 176,750 | 40,129 | 50,000 | 875,813 | 4,635,911 | 30.5 | 5.8 |
| 1992 | 568,518 | 409,970 | 48,937 | 109,611 | 1,099,219 | 5,199,918 | 51.7 | 10.9 |
| 1993 | 800,849 | 578,250 | 95,553 | 127,046 | 1,179,194 | 5,743,534 | 67.9 | 13.9 |
| 1994 | 917,232 | 641,506 | 135,226 | 140,500 | 1,098,333 | 6,282,384 | 83.5 | 14.6 |
| 1995 | 1,110,796 | 811,699 | 159,242 | 139,855 | 1,166,440 | 6,823,543 | 95.2 | 16.3 |
| 1996 | 1,233,815 | 901,143 | 198,601 | 134,071 | 1,204,279 | 7,431,749 | 102.5 | 16.6 |
| 1997 | 1,397,086 | 1,017,427 | 240,912 | 138,747 | 1,385,094 | 8,057,155 | 100.9 | 17.3 |
| 1998 | 1,396,633 | 972,427 | 291,709 | 132,497 | 1,260,039 | 8,732,893 | 110.8 | 16.0 |
| 1999 | 1,348,552 | 919,327 | 296,728 | 132,497 | 1,430,688 | 9,195,795 | 94.3 | 14.7 |

Source: Directorate-General of Budget, Accounting and Statistics, Executive Yuan (1999).

Note

a First category public bonds and loans are not self-redeemable, while second category public bonds are self-redeemable.

*Table 16.8* Outstanding public bonds and foreign debt of central government, 1976–99[a] (NT$ million)

| *Fiscal year* | *Total* | *Public bonds* | *Foreign debt* | |
|---|---|---|---|---|
| | | | *Direct foreign debt* | *Guaranteed obligations* |
| 1976 | 74,287.4 | 8,607.7 | 13,368.9 | 52,310.8 |
| 1977 | 91,552.9 | 8,573.3 | 13,695.6 | 69,283.9 |
| 1978 | 111,471.4 | 12,670.8 | 14,142.1 | 84,658.4 |
| 1979 | 111,105.0 | 13,310.4 | 13,132.1 | 84,662.5 |
| 1980 | 135,024.9 | 10,910.4 | 12,211.6 | 111,902.9 |
| 1981 | 167,241.4 | 10,600.0 | 11,565.7 | 145,075.7 |
| 1982 | 218,340.4 | 19,480.0 | 11,442.8 | 187,417.6 |
| 1983 | 250,456.1 | 36,860.0 | 10,457.9 | 203,138.2 |
| 1984 | 229,169.3 | 34,490.0 | 10,528.5 | 184,150.9 |
| 1985 | 212,316.3 | 41,620.0 | 9,182.3 | 161,514.0 |
| 1986 | 180,477.6 | 58,375.0 | 7,807.7 | 114,294.9 |
| 1987 | 150,990.6 | 86,750.0 | 5,579.1 | 58,661.5 |
| 1988 | 163,173.1 | 135,625.0 | 4,564.2 | 22,983.9 |
| 1989 | 199,384.7 | 183,000.0 | 3,765.0 | 12,619.7 |
| 1990 | 160,770.8 | 147,375.0 | 3,295.2 | 10,100.6 |
| 1991 | 213,381.5 | 202,250.0 | 3,859.0 | 7,272.6 |
| 1992 | 376,128.9 | 367,875.0 | 3,012.4 | 5,241.5 |
| 1993 | 557,953.2 | 550,500.0 | 3,047.0 | 4,406.2 |
| 1994 | 642,279.5 | 636,000.0 | 2,575.3 | 3,704.2 |
| 1995 | 730,329.9 | 724,750.0 | 2,061.2 | 3,518.7 |
| 1996 | 788,922.2 | 785,000.0 | 1,781.5 | 2,140.7 |
| 1997 | 941,730.8 | 939,250.0 | 1,431.2 | 1,049.7 |
| 1998 | 989,879.8 | 988,000.0 | 1,390.0 | 489.9 |
| 1999 | 965,957.7 | 964,900.0 | 1,057.7 | — |

Source: Directorate-General of Budget, Accounting and Statistics, Executive Yuan (1999).

Note

a 1949 Patriotic Bonds are included in domestic debt (before FY1970). The figures are based on transaction occurrence.

Besides financing domestically, the central government also borrows from overseas. In the early 1980s, the central government had a great deal of external public debt (Table 16.8). In FY1981, for example, the central government owed NT$10.6 billion in public bonds, NT$11.6 billion in direct foreign debt and NT$145.1 billion in guaranteed obligation. Nonetheless, with the large surplus from exports of goods and services, the public debt service ratio—which is equal to the external public debt divided by the foreign exchange income from exports—was only slightly above 4 percent (Table 16.9). In the 1990s, the central government relied less on external debt and external public debt was reduced to only US$17.6 million. As a result, the public debt service ratio dropped to a negligible 0.01 percent in 1999.

In summary, government expenditure has been growing faster than revenue in recent years, and this has resulted in an increasing budget deficit. The government has mainly relied on issuance of bonds and loans to finance the deficit. With

*Table 16.9* Public debt service ratio, 1976–99

| *Calendar year* | *External public debt*[a] *(US$ million)* *(1)* | *Foreign exchange income from goods and services* *(US$ million)* *(2)* | *Public debt service ratio* *(%)* *= (1)/(2)* |
|---|---|---|---|
| 1976 | 312.5 | 8,967 | 3.49 |
| 1977 | 470.7 | 10,869 | 4.33 |
| 1978 | 631.2 | 14,426 | 4.38 |
| 1979 | 720.9 | 18,414 | 3.91 |
| 1980 | 980.7 | 22,627 | 4.33 |
| 1981 | 1,063.3 | 26,080 | 4.08 |
| 1982 | 1,263.0 | 25,691 | 4.92 |
| 1983 | 1,284.3 | 28,832 | 4.45 |
| 1984 | 1,698.6 | 34,735 | 4.89 |
| 1985 | 1,416.9 | 35,424 | 4.00 |
| 1986 | 2,113.8 | 46,296 | 4.57 |
| 1987 | 1,956.1 | 61,477 | 3.18 |
| 1988 | 438.1 | 71,565 | 0.61 |
| 1989 | 541.7 | 73,959 | 0.73 |
| 1990 | 398.8 | 74,896 | 0.53 |
| 1991 | 269.7 | 85,030 | 0.32 |
| 1992 | 323.2 | 92,385 | 0.35 |
| 1993 | 99.9 | 98,836 | 0.10 |
| 1994 | 89.3 | 106,665 | 0.08 |
| 1995 | 90.9 | 127,048 | 0.07 |
| 1996 | 48.3 | 132,666 | 0.04 |
| 1997 | 47.5 | 139,756 | 0.03 |
| 1998 | 31.2 | 127,740 | 0.02 |
| 1999 | 17.6 | 133,909 | 0.01 |

Source: Directorate-General of Budget, Accounting and Statistics, Executive Yuan (1999).

Note

a External public debt represents direct debt of the central government (repayment and interest), central government guaranteed obligations and debt guaranteed by public financial institutions. Debt guaranteed by public financial institutions are not included since 1996.

respect to foreign debt, the government has been decreasing direct foreign debt and guaranteed obligations. Taken all together, the continued capital account deficit has led to a gradual deterioration in the government's fiscal health.

## Fiscal consolidation issues

Currently the government faces four challenges in the area of fiscal policy. These challenges are: (i) continued increase in the fiscal deficit; (ii) asymmetry in the distribution of revenues between central and local governments; (iii) poor structure in the government's revenue; and (iv) debt management.

### *Continued increase in the fiscal deficit*

As the previous discussion shows, the government's fiscal deficit grew due to several factors. One of these factors is the growth in government expenditure exceeding growth in revenue. From FY1970 to FY2000, the average growth rate of government net expenditure was 15.8 percent compared to 14.5 percent in growth of net revenue. From FY1989 to FY2000, the contrast is even more obvious with net expenditure growing at an average rate of 14.9 percent, while net revenue expanded at only 11.8 percent. This indicates that the government has had to resort to more financing to cover up the gaping fiscal deficit, but the financing itself has caused the deficit to grow.

The main reason behind the increase in government expenditure is rising government personnel fees and rapid increases in social welfare spending. With four layers of government, there is an overlapping of business among all levels of government and thus many redundant public employees. The share of government personnel fees to net expenditure is about 35 percent in Chinese Taipei; this ratio is relatively high compared to 30 percent in the US and European countries and 25 percent in Japan, Korea and Singapore.

With regard to the increase in spending on social welfare, the ratio of social security and pension spending to government expenditure reached 26.9 percent in FY1996. In FY2000, the ratio was even higher at 27.7 percent. From FY1989 to FY2000, the growth rate of social security and pension spending averaged 17.6 spending.

A second factor is the shrinking of the tax revenue base. Tax revenue is the most important source of government revenue. However, in recent years, growth of tax revenue has slowed, and because the growth of tax revenue did not match that of GNP, the ratio of the former to the latter has declined over time (Table 16.10). This is a cause for some concern for the government. In addition, in 2000, the central government consolidated the business and personal income tax, resulting in an estimated NT$30 billion tax loss. The government also lowered the business tax for financial institutions from 5 percent to 2 percent in 1999, and this will further bring down tax revenue by NT$76 billion. The temporary suspension of the land tax because of the earthquake in 1999 will further cut tax revenue by NT$31.6 billion.

### *Asymmetry in the distribution of revenues between central and local governments*

The distribution of the tax revenue cannot satisfy the needs of local governments. Most of the taxes are collected by the central government and local governments always complain that they do not have a large enough share of the tax revenue to cover its basic needs. Among the subordinate governments, the Taipei municipality has the highest revenue ratio (i.e., revenue divided by expenditure) at 88.4 percent, followed by Kaohsiung municipality at 78.7 percent. Revenue ratios among county governments are only around 45 percent with some degree of variance. In a way, the centralization of tax revenue could make the use of taxes more

*Table 16.10* Comparison between tax revenues, gross national product and population, 1975–99

| *Fiscal year* | *Tax revenues* | | *Gross national product (current prices)* | | *Population (end of year)* | *Tax revenue/ GNP* | *Tax revenue/ population* |
|---|---|---|---|---|---|---|---|
| | *Amount (NT$ million)* | *Growth rate (%)* | *Amount (NT$ million)* | *Growth rate (%)* | *(1,000 persons)* | *(%)* | *(NT$)* |
| 1975 | 97,504 | 9.7 | 554,142 | 11.0 | 15,852 | 17.6 | 6,151 |
| 1976 | 121,767 | 24.9 | 642,537 | 16.0 | 16,150 | 19.0 | 7,540 |
| 1977 | 139,305 | 14.4 | 759,540 | 18.2 | 16,508 | 18.3 | 8,439 |
| 1978 | 168,194 | 20.7 | 896,098 | 18.0 | 16,813 | 18.8 | 10,004 |
| 1979 | 220,521 | 31.1 | 1,093,349 | 22.0 | 17,136 | 20.2 | 12,869 |
| 1980 | 261,349 | 18.5 | 1,334,257 | 22.0 | 17,479 | 19.6 | 14,952 |
| 1981 | 315,049 | 20.5 | 1,634,120 | 22.5 | 17,805 | 19.3 | 17,694 |
| 1982 | 338,090 | 7.3 | 1,838,429 | 12.5 | 18,136 | 18.4 | 18,642 |
| 1983 | 342,379 | 1.3 | 1,986,885 | 8.1 | 18,458 | 17.2 | 18,549 |
| 1984 | 383,364 | 12.0 | 2,244,953 | 13.0 | 18,733 | 17.1 | 20,465 |
| 1985 | 394,846 | 3.0 | 2,449,539 | 9.1 | 19,013 | 16.1 | 20,767 |
| 1986 | 401,800 | 1.8 | 2,680,483 | 9.4 | 19,258 | 15.0 | 20,864 |
| 1987 | 461,455 | 14.8 | 3,134,828 | 17.0 | 19,455 | 14.7 | 23,719 |
| 1988 | 558,046 | 20.9 | 3,442,690 | 9.8 | 19,673 | 16.2 | 28,366 |
| 1989 | 677,418 | 21.4 | 3,801,819 | 10.4 | 19,904 | 17.8 | 34,034 |
| 1990 | 847,733 | 25.1 | 4,227,304 | 11.2 | 20,107 | 20.1 | 42,161 |
| 1991 | 808,621 | −4.6 | 4,635,911 | 9.7 | 20,353 | 17.4 | 39,730 |
| 1992 | 967,624 | 19.7 | 5,199,918 | 12.2 | 20,557 | 18.6 | 47,070 |
| 1993 | 1,045,496 | 8.0 | 5,743,534 | 10.5 | 20,803 | 18.2 | 50,257 |
| 1994 | 1,127,481 | 7.8 | 6,282,384 | 9.4 | 20,995 | 17.9 | 53,702 |
| 1995 | 1,232,264 | 9.3 | 6,823,543 | 8.6 | 21,178 | 18.1 | 58,186 |
| 1996 | 1,197,797 | −2.8 | 7,431,749 | 8.9 | 21,357 | 16.1 | 56,085 |
| 1997 | 1,271,453 | 6.1 | 8,057,155 | 8.4 | 21,525 | 15.8 | 59,069 |
| 1998 | 1,397,052 | 9.9 | 8,732,893 | 8.4 | 21,743 | 16.0 | 64,253 |
| 1999 | 1,355,062 | −3.0 | 9,195,795 | 5.3 | 21,929 | 14.7 | 61,793 |

Source: Directorate-General of Budget, Accounting and Statistics, Executive Yuan (1999).

efficient and could prevent corruption or misuse of taxes at the local government level. However, if local governments do not have enough control over the taxes that belong to them, then they will try to levy different kinds of tax on private business firms. This will make the operation of businesses more difficult because business people then have to figure out each individual tax system in the different areas. As mentioned earlier, the central government revised the Fiscal Distribution Act in 1999, but distribution of tax revenues toward a fair allocation remains under study.

### *The poor structure of government revenue*

In the central government's budget, revenues from one-time selling of public enterprise stocks and from unstable tax sources (like the security tax) weigh too heavily in the pool of government revenue. If the domestic stock market were to turn bearish, this could have a serious impact on government revenue. Another issue relates to the efficient use of public property. The government owns a significant amount of land and other property; yet the profits from public property are less than 1 percent of government revenue. How to extract more profit from public property is a crucial question and the answer will require improved management of land properties.

### *Debt management*

From FY1989 to FY2000, over-borrowing became a serious problem for the Chinese Taipei government. The ratio of central government outstanding debt to expenditure is 14.4 percent, which is close to the 15 percent limit that is stipulated by law. This will limit the capability of the central government to issue new bonds. With increased borrowings, the government needs to be more dexterous in its debt management. For instance, the timing of issuing bonds is acclimatized with the needs of the treasury and its lacks consideration for pro-activity and market orientation. Because of the poor market efficiency for public bonds, the interest rates on public bonds cannot be used to generate a yield curve for the bond markets. Moreover, there is no self-redemption plan in advance for the maturity of public bonds and loans; rather it will depend on the government's fiscal condition at the time the bonds and loans are due. In the end, the government may have to increase the budget or add a special budget for the redemption of public bonds and loans, but this creates an unstable shock for the purposes of fiscal policy itself.

## Conclusion

As Chinese Taipei matures as a democracy, fiscal policy will require the coordination of both economic and political wisdom. For instance, during the past election campaign, candidates often used increases in social welfare spending as their propaganda. But once elected, to carry out these promises would lead to a deterioration of the government's fiscal health. Hence, how to educate people and public employees about the importance of fiscal prudence remains the holy tasks of economists.

## Notes

1 All levels of government, according to the law, collect the distribution tax and each level receives a certain proportion of the tax. The distribution tax includes: estate and gift tax of the central government; business tax and stamp tax of the municipal government; business tax, stamp tax, land value increment tax, slaughter tax, land value tax, house tax, and deeds tax of the county and city governments.
2 Beginning from FY1991, harbor construction dues are classified under nontax revenue.
3 The land tax contains the agricultural land tax, the land value tax and the land value increment tax.

## References

Directorate-General of Budget, Accounting, and Statistics (DGBAS), Executive Yuan (1999) *Yearbook of Financial Statistics of the ROC, 1999*, Taipei: DGBAS.

Directorate-General of Budget, Accounting, and Statistics (DGBAS), Executive Yuan (2003) available on: http://www.dgbas.gov.tw/.

Ministry of Finance (2003) available on: http://www.mof.gov.tw/.

# 17 The United States

*Robert Dekle and Jeffrey B. Nugent*

## Introduction

A decade ago, the United States was widely criticized for its persistent failure to get its fiscal house in order, causing interest rates in the US to rise in order to attract the capital from abroad to cover its twin deficits. This failure was seen not only as a cause of the third world debt crises of the 1980s, but was also viewed as severely distorting the normal pattern for an advanced industrial country of net capital outflows and crowding out private investment and R&D expenditures, thereby contributing to the rather alarming secular decline in the rates of total factor productivity growth and real income growth. Subsequently, during the 1990s, however, the US managed to eliminate its fiscal deficits and seemed poised to generate fiscal surpluses for the first decade of the new millenium.

The aims of this chapter are to take stock of the changing fiscal position of the United States and to identify both the determinants and effects of these changes. How the US adjusts to its situation of projected fiscal surpluses over the next decade will have important long-term consequences not only for the US itself, but also, because of this country's size and influence, for the rest of the world.

This chapter is organized as follows. The next section is devoted to the evolution of government budgets over recent decades, especially since 1970. This is followed by some explanations for these patterns and an analysis of their effects. The chapter then proceeds to look ahead and the final section provides some conclusions.

## The evolution of fiscal balances of both federal and state and local governments

As is well known, the overall government fiscal position in the United States depends on decisions at two quite distinct levels of government, the federal government and a multiplicity of state and local governments.

### *The overall budget*

We begin, however, in Table 17.1 with the evolution of both types of expenditures as well as those of gross domestic product (GDP) and gross private domestic investment, all of which are expressed in constant 1996 prices. Over the 1960–99 period, total government expenditures more than tripled in real terms while GDP almost quadrupled. The somewhat slower growth of government expenditures was the result of accelerated (almost fivefold) growth of state and local expenditures and decelerating federal government expenditures which rose by only 85 percent over this forty-year period. Federal government expenditures rose sharply during the 1960s much of which was due to the Vietnam War build-up. Federal government expenditures then moderated somewhat in the 1970s while defense expenditures were being reduced in real terms before rising again in the early 1980s and then falling sharply in real terms from 1987 to 1999.

Table 17.2 shows the decline in government expenditures relative to GDP. The share of government expenditures in GDP fell from a peak of 23.41 percent in 1967 to about 17.5 percent in 1998–99. The bulk of this decline occurred between 1987 and 1998, and is largely attributable to the reduction in defense expenditures from 7.4 percent of GDP in 1987 to 3.9 percent in 1999. Notice that federal nondefense expenditures remained relatively constant in proportion to GDP at about 2.3 percent. State and local government expenditures, however, rose from 9 percent of GDP in 1960 to 12.8 percent in 1975. Yet, they, too, declined modestly relative to GDP between 1975 and 1998–99.

Table 17.3 shows the same pattern of expenditures in relation to GDP, but in greater detail. In particular, while consumption expenditures have always dominated investment expenditures at both levels of government, and much of the reduction occurred in defense, a significant portion of the decline in government spending in relation to GDP occurred in investment expenditures (from 5.42 percent of GDP in 1960 to 3.20 percent in 1999).

### *The scope and evolution of the federal budget*

The federal government budget consists of four main types of funds: general, special, trust and revolving. General funds are those from corporate and individual income taxes that go into a general multipurpose account, with no direct link between expenditures and revenues. Trust funds are designated by law to be used only for specific purposes. The advantage of trust funds is that they are somewhat less vulnerable to being raided so as to support other unrelated services. Since special funds, such as the Land and Water Conservation Fund and the National Wildlife Refuge Fund, are based on user fees and other earmarked revenues, they are quite similar to trust funds, though somewhat less well protected from diversion than trust funds. Revolving funds are those which arise from incomes and outlays of agencies and which appear in the budget only on a net basis, i.e., as the difference between receipts and outlays. Among these are government-owned enterprises such as the US Postal Service.

The expenditure side of the government budget includes both expenditures for wages and salaries of government employees that constitute government expenditures in the national accounts and transfer payments.

Certain government-sponsored (but not government-owned enterprises) such as the Government National Mortgage Association (Fannie Mae) and the Federal

*Table 17.1* Gross domestic product, gross private domestic investment and government expenditures in the US, 1960–99 (billion of 1996 dollars)

| *Year* | *GDP* | *GDP deflator* | *Gross private domestic investment* | *Government expenditures* | | | | |
|---|---|---|---|---|---|---|---|---|
| | | | | *Total* | *Federal* | | | *State and local* |
| | | | | | *Total* | *Nat'l defense* | *Non-defense* | |
| 1960 | 2,357.2 | 0.224 | 352.6 | 508.6 | 294.5 | 246.7 | 47.8 | 214.1 |
| 1961 | 2,412.1 | 0.226 | 345.7 | 537.1 | 307.2 | 256.8 | 49.9 | 229.9 |
| 1962 | 2,557.6 | 0.229 | 384.2 | 576.5 | 335.3 | 273.9 | 61.5 | 241.2 |
| 1963 | 2,668.2 | 0.232 | 404.5 | 597.3 | 338.5 | 270.4 | 68.1 | 258.3 |
| 1964 | 2,822.7 | 0.235 | 433.8 | 616.5 | 339.0 | 262.6 | 76.5 | 277.4 |
| 1965 | 3,002.8 | 0.240 | 492.9 | 640.9 | 342.4 | 260.2 | 82.1 | 298.6 |
| 1966 | 3,199.5 | 0.247 | 532.2 | 706.5 | 382.7 | 299.2 | 83.9 | 323.9 |
| 1967 | 3,279.5 | 0.254 | 505.6 | 767.9 | 419.9 | 337.3 | 82.6 | 348.4 |
| 1968 | 3,435.6 | 0.266 | 532.2 | 802.1 | 429.7 | 347.5 | 82.2 | 372.4 |
| 1969 | 3,543.2 | 0.278 | 562.4 | 807.7 | 417.5 | 333.0 | 84.5 | 390.2 |
| 1970 | 3,549.4 | 0.293 | 520.3 | 809.4 | 397.4 | 310.3 | 87.1 | 412.1 |
| 1971 | 3,660.2 | 0.308 | 577.9 | 814.0 | 381.4 | 288.6 | 92.8 | 433.0 |
| 1972 | 3,854.2 | 0.322 | 645.1 | 839.3 | 390.3 | 290.5 | 100.1 | 448.7 |
| 1973 | 4,073.1 | 0.340 | 718.8 | 846.4 | 375.7 | 276.0 | 99.7 | 470.7 |
| 1974 | 4,061.7 | 0.370 | 674.9 | 872.4 | 374.0 | 269.8 | 104.2 | 498.4 |
| 1975 | 4,050.3 | 0.404 | 570.2 | 894.4 | 376.7 | 267.3 | 109.5 | 517.7 |
| 1976 | 4,262.6 | 0.428 | 682.4 | 898.6 | 375.3 | 264.6 | 110.8 | 523.3 |
| 1977 | 4,455.7 | 0.456 | 792.5 | 910.9 | 386.0 | 268.9 | 117.3 | 524.9 |
| 1978 | 4,709.9 | 0.487 | 894.4 | 934.6 | 393.7 | 270.8 | 122.7 | 541.2 |
| 1979 | 4,870.1 | 0.527 | 931.0 | 955.5 | 401.5 | 278.4 | 123.3 | 553.7 |
| 1980 | 4,872.3 | 0.574 | 832.9 | 992.9 | 427.5 | 295.6 | 131.8 | 565.4 |
| 1981 | 4,993.9 | 0.627 | 910.3 | 1,007.0 | 449.4 | 315.5 | 134.0 | 557.6 |
| 1982 | 4,900.3 | 0.665 | 776.0 | 1,029.0 | 470.3 | 343.3 | 127.0 | 558.7 |

| | | | | | | | | |
|---|---|---|---|---|---|---|---|---|
| 1983 | 5,105.6 | 0.692 | 814.9 | 1,062.9 | 497.4 | 364.7 | 132.9 | 565.5 |
| 1984 | 5,477.4 | 0.717 | 1,024.4 | 1,115.3 | 524.2 | 394.9 | 129.3 | 591.1 |
| 1985 | 5,689.8 | 0.740 | 994.4 | 1,186.2 | 558.3 | 421.9 | 136.4 | 627.9 |
| 1986 | 5,885.7 | 0.757 | 987.6 | 1,245.5 | 579.9 | 439.1 | 140.8 | 665.6 |
| 1987 | 6,092.6 | 0.778 | 1,004.0 | 1,282.0 | 591.5 | 451.2 | 140.4 | 690.5 |
| 1988 | 6,349.1 | 0.805 | 1,020.5 | 1,288.8 | 575.0 | 442.3 | 132.7 | 713.8 |
| 1989 | 6,568.7 | 0.836 | 1,044.6 | 1,316.6 | 577.5 | 434.6 | 142.8 | 739.2 |
| 1990 | 6,683.5 | 0.868 | 992.4 | 1,360.6 | 585.5 | 431.8 | 153.9 | 775.1 |
| 1991 | 6,669.2 | 0.898 | 891.5 | 1,376.5 | 587.6 | 428.4 | 159.2 | 788.9 |
| 1992 | 6,891.1 | 0.917 | 945.1 | 1,385.5 | 582.9 | 412.8 | 170.1 | 802.6 |
| 1993 | 7,054.1 | 0.942 | 1,014.3 | 1,373.2 | 560.0 | 387.5 | 172.5 | 813.2 |
| 1994 | 7,337.8 | 0.961 | 1,141.2 | 1,381.3 | 542.0 | 369.4 | 172.6 | 839.2 |
| 1995 | 7,537.1 | 0.982 | 1,164.9 | 1,397.3 | 531.1 | 357.1 | 174.1 | 866.2 |
| 1996 | 7,813.2 | 1.000 | 1,242.7 | 1,421.9 | 531.6 | 357.0 | 174.6 | 890.4 |
| 1997 | 8,165.1 | 1.017 | 1,361.1 | 1,456.8 | 529.0 | 346.7 | 182.3 | 927.8 |
| 1998 | 8,516.3 | 1.029 | 1,488.6 | 1,487.2 | 523.7 | 338.9 | 184.8 | 963.4 |
| 1999 | 8,861.0 | 1.044 | 1,553.7 | 1,560.5 | 546.9 | 349.4 | 197.5 | 1,013.6 |

Source: US GPO (2000: Table B1).

*Table 17.2* Gross private domestic investment, current account balances and government, 1960–99 (as a % of GDP)

| *Year* | *Nominal GDP (US$ b)* | *Gross domestic investment* | *Current account balance* | *Government consumption expenditures and gross investment* | | | | |
|---|---|---|---|---|---|---|---|---|
| | | | | | *Federal* | | | *State and local* |
| | | | | *Total* | *Total* | *Nat'l defense* | *Non-defense* | |
| 1960 | 527.4 | 14.96 | 0.53 | 21.58 | 12.50 | 10.47 | 2.03 | 9.08 |
| 1961 | 545.7 | 14.33 | 0.70 | 22.26 | 12.74 | 10.65 | 2.07 | 9.53 |
| 1962 | 586.5 | 15.02 | 0.58 | 22.54 | 13.11 | 10.71 | 2.40 | 9.43 |
| 1963 | 618.7 | 15.16 | 0.71 | 22.39 | 12.69 | 10.13 | 2.55 | 9.68 |
| 1964 | 664.4 | 15.37 | 1.03 | 21.84 | 12.01 | 9.30 | 2.71 | 9.83 |
| 1965 | 720.1 | 16.41 | 0.75 | 21.34 | 11.40 | 8.67 | 2.74 | 9.94 |
| 1966 | 789.3 | 16.63 | 0.38 | 22.08 | 11.96 | 9.35 | 2.62 | 10.12 |
| 1967 | 834.1 | 15.42 | 0.31 | 23.41 | 12.80 | 10.29 | 2.52 | 10.62 |
| 1968 | 911.5 | 15.49 | 0.07 | 23.35 | 12.51 | 10.12 | 2.39 | 10.84 |
| 1969 | 985.3 | 15.87 | 0.04 | 22.80 | 11.78 | 9.40 | 2.39 | 11.01 |
| 1970 | 1,039.7 | 14.66 | 0.22 | 22.80 | 11.20 | 8.74 | 2.45 | 11.61 |
| 1971 | 1,128.6 | 15.79 | −0.13 | 22.24 | 10.42 | 7.89 | 2.53 | 11.83 |
| 1972 | 1,240.4 | 16.74 | −0.47 | 21.78 | 10.13 | 7.54 | 2.60 | 11.64 |
| 1973 | 1,385.5 | 17.65 | 0.52 | 20.78 | 9.22 | 6.78 | 2.45 | 11.56 |
| 1974 | 1,501.0 | 16.62 | 0.13 | 21.48 | 9.21 | 6.64 | 2.56 | 12.27 |
| 1975 | 1,635.2 | 14.08 | 1.11 | 22.08 | 9.30 | 6.60 | 2.70 | 12.78 |
| 1976 | 1,823.9 | 16.01 | 0.24 | 21.08 | 8.81 | 6.21 | 2.60 | 12.28 |
| 1977 | 2,031.4 | 17.79 | −0.71 | 20.44 | 8.66 | 6.04 | 2.63 | 11.78 |
| 1978 | 2,295.9 | 18.99 | −0.66 | 19.84 | 8.36 | 5.75 | 2.60 | 11.49 |
| 1979 | 2,566.4 | 19.12 | −0.01 | 19.62 | 8.25 | 5.72 | 2.53 | 11.37 |
| 1980 | 2,795.6 | 17.09 | 0.08 | 20.38 | 8.77 | 6.07 | 2.70 | 11.60 |
| 1981 | 3,131.3 | 18.23 | 0.16 | 20.16 | 9.00 | 6.32 | 2.68 | 11.16 |
| 1982 | 3,259.2 | 15.84 | −0.19 | 21.00 | 9.60 | 7.00 | 2.59 | 11.40 |

| | | | | | | | | |
|---|---|---|---|---|---|---|---|---|
| 1983 | 3,534.9 | 15.96 | −1.11 | 20.82 | 9.74 | 7.14 | 2.60 | 11.08 |
| 1984 | 3,932.7 | 18.70 | −2.41 | 20.36 | 9.57 | 7.21 | 2.36 | 10.79 |
| 1985 | 4,213.0 | 17.48 | −2.83 | 20.85 | 9.81 | 7.42 | 2.40 | 11.03 |
| 1986 | 4,452.9 | 16.78 | −3.35 | 21.16 | 9.85 | 7.46 | 2.39 | 11.31 |
| 1987 | 4,742.5 | 16.48 | −3.43 | 21.04 | 9.71 | 7.41 | 2.30 | 11.33 |
| 1988 | 5,108.3 | 16.07 | −2.41 | 20.30 | 9.06 | 6.97 | 2.09 | 11.24 |
| 1989 | 5,489.1 | 15.90 | −1.80 | 20.04 | 8.79 | 6.62 | 2.17 | 11.25 |
| 1990 | 5,803.2 | 14.85 | −1.37 | 20.36 | 8.76 | 6.46 | 2.30 | 11.60 |
| 1991 | 5,986.2 | 13.37 | 0.07 | 20.64 | 8.81 | 6.42 | 2.39 | 11.83 |
| 1992 | 6,318.9 | 13.71 | −0.80 | 20.11 | 8.46 | 5.99 | 2.47 | 11.65 |
| 1993 | 6,642.3 | 14.38 | −1.28 | 19.47 | 7.94 | 5.49 | 2.44 | 11.53 |
| 1994 | 7,054.3 | 15.55 | −1.72 | 18.82 | 7.39 | 5.03 | 2.35 | 11.44 |
| 1995 | 7,400.5 | 15.46 | −1.53 | 18.54 | 7.05 | 4.74 | 2.31 | 11.49 |
| 1996 | 7,813.2 | 15.91 | −1.65 | 18.20 | 6.80 | 4.57 | 2.23 | 11.40 |
| 1997 | 8,300.8 | 16.67 | −1.73 | 17.84 | 6.48 | 4.25 | 2.23 | 11.36 |
| 1998 | 8,759.9 | 17.48 | −2.52 | 17.46 | 6.15 | 3.98 | 2.17 | 11.31 |
| 1999 | 9,248.4 | 17.53 | −2.59 | 17.61 | 6.17 | 3.94 | 2.23 | 11.44 |

Source: US GPO (2000).

*Table 17.3* GDP and government expenditures by type, 1960–99 (as a % of GDP, based on data in current prices)

| *Year* | *GDP* | *Government consumption expenditure and gross investment* | | | | | | | | | | |
|---|---|---|---|---|---|---|---|---|---|---|---|---|
| | | *Total* | *Federal* | | | | | | | *State and local* | | |
| | | | *Total* | *National defense* | | | *Nondefense* | | | *Total* | *Con. exp.* | *Gross inv.* |
| | | | | *Total* | *Con. exp.* | *Gross inv.* | *Total* | *Con. exp.* | *Gross inv.* | | | |
| 1960 | 527.4 | 21.60 | 12.50 | 10.50 | 8.12 | 2.33 | 2.03 | 1.65 | 0.37 | 9.08 | 6.45 | 2.64 |
| 1970 | 1,039.7 | 22.80 | 11.20 | 8.74 | 7.57 | 1.17 | 2.45 | 2.09 | 0.36 | 11.60 | 8.85 | 2.77 |
| 1971 | 1,128.6 | 22.20 | 10.40 | 7.89 | 7.03 | 0.85 | 2.53 | 2.16 | 0.37 | 11.80 | 9.16 | 2.67 |
| 1972 | 1,240.4 | 21.80 | 10.10 | 7.54 | 6.63 | 0.90 | 2.60 | 2.23 | 0.36 | 11.60 | 9.17 | 2.47 |
| 1973 | 1,385.5 | 20.80 | 9.22 | 6.78 | 5.96 | 0.81 | 2.45 | 2.09 | 0.35 | 11.60 | 9.16 | 2.40 |
| 1974 | 1,501.0 | 21.50 | 9.21 | 6.64 | 5.83 | 0.81 | 2.56 | 2.19 | 0.37 | 12.30 | 9.63 | 2.64 |
| 1975 | 1,635.2 | 22.10 | 9.30 | 6.60 | 5.71 | 0.88 | 2.70 | 2.31 | 0.39 | 12.80 | 10.10 | 2.67 |
| 1976 | 1,823.9 | 21.10 | 8.81 | 6.21 | 5.37 | 0.83 | 2.60 | 2.20 | 0.40 | 12.30 | 9.87 | 2.40 |
| 1977 | 2,031.4 | 20.40 | 8.66 | 6.04 | 5.21 | 0.82 | 2.63 | 2.24 | 0.39 | 11.80 | 9.67 | 2.11 |
| 1978 | 2,295.9 | 19.80 | 8.36 | 5.75 | 4.97 | 0.77 | 2.60 | 2.18 | 0.42 | 11.50 | 9.33 | 2.15 |
| 1979 | 2,566.4 | 19.60 | 8.25 | 5.72 | 4.88 | 0.83 | 2.53 | 2.13 | 0.40 | 11.40 | 9.16 | 2.21 |
| 1980 | 2,795.6 | 20.40 | 8.77 | 6.07 | 5.20 | 0.86 | 2.70 | 2.28 | 0.42 | 11.60 | 9.32 | 2.29 |
| 1981 | 3,131.3 | 20.20 | 9.00 | 6.32 | 5.39 | 0.92 | 2.68 | 2.27 | 0.41 | 11.20 | 9.09 | 2.07 |
| 1982 | 3,259.2 | 21.00 | 9.60 | 7.00 | 5.94 | 1.07 | 2.59 | 2.20 | 0.39 | 11.40 | 9.41 | 1.99 |
| 1983 | 3,534.9 | 20.80 | 9.74 | 7.14 | 5.96 | 1.19 | 2.60 | 2.19 | 0.41 | 11.10 | 9.20 | 1.88 |
| 1984 | 3,932.7 | 20.40 | 9.57 | 7.21 | 5.97 | 1.24 | 2.36 | 1.96 | 0.39 | 10.80 | 8.89 | 1.90 |
| 1985 | 4,213.0 | 20.80 | 9.81 | 7.42 | 6.05 | 1.36 | 2.40 | 2.00 | 0.40 | 11.00 | 9.03 | 2.00 |
| 1986 | 4,452.9 | 21.20 | 9.85 | 7.46 | 6.05 | 1.41 | 2.39 | 2.00 | 0.39 | 11.30 | 9.23 | 2.08 |
| 1987 | 4,742.5 | 21.00 | 9.71 | 7.41 | 6.01 | 1.40 | 2.30 | 1.90 | 0.40 | 11.30 | 9.26 | 2.07 |
| 1988 | 5,108.3 | 20.30 | 9.06 | 6.97 | 5.77 | 1.20 | 2.09 | 1.73 | 0.36 | 11.20 | 9.16 | 2.08 |
| 1989 | 5,489.1 | 20.00 | 8.79 | 6.62 | 5.47 | 1.14 | 2.17 | 1.81 | 0.37 | 11.30 | 9.16 | 2.09 |
| 1990 | 5,803.2 | 20.40 | 8.76 | 6.46 | 5.32 | 1.14 | 2.30 | 1.91 | 0.38 | 11.60 | 9.41 | 2.19 |
| 1991 | 5,986.2 | 20.60 | 8.81 | 6.42 | 5.36 | 1.06 | 2.39 | 1.97 | 0.41 | 11.80 | 9.62 | 2.21 |
| 1992 | 6,318.9 | 20.10 | 8.46 | 5.99 | 5.02 | 0.97 | 2.47 | 2.04 | 0.43 | 11.60 | 9.52 | 2.13 |
| 1993 | 6,642.3 | 19.50 | 7.94 | 5.49 | 4.66 | 0.84 | 2.44 | 2.01 | 0.43 | 11.50 | 9.48 | 2.05 |
| 1994 | 7,054.3 | 18.80 | 7.39 | 5.03 | 4.27 | 0.76 | 2.35 | 1.96 | 0.38 | 11.40 | 9.39 | 2.04 |
| 1995 | 7,400.5 | 18.50 | 7.05 | 4.74 | 4.02 | 0.71 | 2.31 | 1.92 | 0.39 | 11.50 | 9.39 | 2.11 |
| 1996 | 7,813.2 | 18.20 | 6.80 | 4.57 | 3.87 | 0.69 | 2.23 | 1.83 | 0.40 | 11.40 | 9.30 | 2.10 |
| 1997 | 8,300.8 | 17.80 | 6.48 | 4.25 | 3.67 | 0.57 | 2.23 | 1.84 | 0.39 | 11.40 | 9.23 | 2.14 |
| 1998 | 8,759.9 | 17.50 | 6.15 | 3.98 | 3.42 | 0.55 | 2.17 | 1.75 | 0.41 | 11.30 | 9.22 | 2.09 |
| 1999 | 9,248.4 | 17.60 | 6.17 | 3.94 | 3.36 | 0.58 | 2.23 | 1.77 | 0.45 | 11.40 | 9.27 | 2.17 |

Source: US GPO (2000).

Home Loan Mortgage Company (Freddie Mac), however, are excluded from the budget altogether. Although these corporations are sponsored by government and serve certain public purposes (for which certain subsidies may be provided), they are operated as private enterprises and treated as such by excluding them from the budget.[1]

Prior to 1968, the trust funds were not included in the federal budget. Since that time, they are in the budget but are reported in a separate "off-budget" category. Since they are of growing importance in the federal budget, their inclusion allows the government budget to more fully convey the relation between revenues and outlays of the government as a whole. Table 17.4 provides a breakdown

*Table 17.4* Federal government receipts and outlays by budget type, 1960–2000 (fiscal years, US$ billion)

| *Year* | *Total* | | *On-budget* | | *Off-budget* | |
|---|---|---|---|---|---|---|
| | *Receipts* | *Outlays* | *Receipts* | *Outlays* | *Receipts* | *Outlays* |
| 1960 | 92.5 | 92.2 | 81.9 | 81.3 | 10.6 | 10.9 |
| 1961 | 94.4 | 97.7 | 82.3 | 86.0 | 12.1 | 11.7 |
| 1962 | 99.7 | 106.8 | 87.4 | 93.3 | 12.3 | 13.5 |
| 1963 | 106.6 | 111.3 | 92.4 | 96.4 | 14.2 | 15.0 |
| 1964 | 112.6 | 118.5 | 96.2 | 102.8 | 16.4 | 15.7 |
| 1965 | 116.8 | 118.2 | 100.1 | 101.7 | 16.7 | 16.5 |
| 1966 | 130.8 | 134.5 | 111.7 | 114.8 | 19.1 | 19.7 |
| 1967 | 148.8 | 157.5 | 124.4 | 137.0 | 24.4 | 20.4 |
| 1968 | 153.0 | 178.1 | 128.1 | 155.8 | 24.9 | 22.3 |
| 1969 | 186.9 | 183.6 | 157.9 | 158.4 | 29.0 | 25.2 |
| 1970 | 192.8 | 195.6 | 159.3 | 168.0 | 33.5 | 27.6 |
| 1971 | 187.1 | 210.2 | 151.3 | 177.3 | 35.8 | 32.8 |
| 1972 | 207.3 | 230.7 | 167.4 | 193.8 | 39.9 | 36.9 |
| 1973 | 230.8 | 245.7 | 184.7 | 200.1 | 46.1 | 45.6 |
| 1974 | 263.2 | 269.4 | 209.3 | 217.3 | 53.9 | 52.1 |
| 1975 | 279.1 | 332.3 | 216.6 | 271.9 | 62.5 | 60.4 |
| 1976 | 298.1 | 371.8 | 231.7 | 302.2 | 66.4 | 69.6 |
| 1977 | 355.6 | 409.2 | 278.7 | 328.5 | 76.8 | 80.7 |
| 1978 | 399.6 | 458.7 | 314.2 | 369.1 | 85.4 | 89.7 |
| 1979 | 463.3 | 504.0 | 365.3 | 404.1 | 98.0 | 100.0 |
| 1980 | 517.1 | 590.9 | 403.9 | 476.6 | 113.2 | 114.3 |
| 1981 | 599.3 | 678.2 | 469.1 | 543.1 | 130.2 | 135.2 |
| 1982 | 617.8 | 745.8 | 474.3 | 594.4 | 143.5 | 151.4 |
| 1983 | 600.6 | 808.4 | 453.2 | 661.3 | 147.3 | 147.1 |
| 1984 | 666.5 | 851.9 | 500.4 | 686.1 | 166.1 | 165.8 |
| 1985 | 734.1 | 946.4 | 547.9 | 769.6 | 186.2 | 176.8 |
| 1986 | 769.2 | 990.5 | 569.0 | 807.0 | 200.2 | 183.5 |
| 1987 | 854.4 | 1,004.1 | 641.0 | 810.3 | 213.4 | 193.8 |
| 1988 | 909.3 | 1,064.5 | 667.8 | 861.8 | 241.5 | 202.7 |
| 1989 | 991.2 | 1,143.7 | 727.5 | 932.8 | 263.7 | 210.9 |
| 1990 | 1,032.0 | 1,253.2 | 750.3 | 1028.1 | 281.7 | 225.1 |
| 1991 | 1,055.0 | 1,324.4 | 761.2 | 1082.7 | 293.9 | 241.7 |
| 1992 | 1,091.3 | 1,381.7 | 788.9 | 1129.3 | 302.4 | 252.3 |
| 1993 | 1,154.4 | 1,409.5 | 842.5 | 1142.9 | 311.9 | 266.6 |
| 1994 | 1,258.6 | 1,461.9 | 923.6 | 1182.5 | 335.0 | 279.4 |
| 1995 | 1,351.8 | 1,515.8 | 1,000.8 | 1227.2 | 351.1 | 288.7 |
| 1996 | 1,453.1 | 1,560.6 | 1,085.6 | 1259.7 | 367.5 | 300.9 |
| 1997 | 1,579.3 | 1,601.3 | 1,187.3 | 1290.7 | 392.0 | 310.6 |
| 1998 | 1,721.8 | 1,652.6 | 1,306.0 | 1336.0 | 415.8 | 316.6 |
| 1999 | 1,827.5 | 1,703.0 | 1,383.0 | 1382.3 | 444.5 | 320.8 |
| 2000 | 1,956.3 | 1,789.6 | 1,479.5 | 1460.6 | 476.8 | 328.9 |

Source: US GPO (2000: Table B-76).

of the unified federal budget into "on-budget" and "off-budget" categories. These two sides of the unified budget have frequently been at odds with one another, serving to moderate the overall budget deficits. The "off-budget" has been in surplus for thirty of the forty years between 1960 and 2000 and for every year beginning in 1983. By contrast, the "on-budget" has been in surplus in only a few of the forty years, two of which have occurred only in 1999 and 2000. Both components of the budget were reasonably well balanced until 1967 at which time the "on-budget" deficit started to grow quite rapidly to well over $100 billion in 1982, over $200 billion in 1983, $238 billion in 1986 and over $300 billion between 1991 and 1993. After 1993, however, this deficit was reduced sharply and turned into a surplus by 1999. The "off-budget" began running deficits in 1976, with the deficits gradually increasing until 1983. The social security trust fund was a major factor behind the worsening situation of the "off-government budget." Since social security in the US is a pay-as-you-go system, much of this worsening situation was due to gradually expanding benefits, stagnant social security taxes and an aging population. In 1983, social security taxes were raised, allowing the system to remain viable for another decade or two, and turning the "off-budget" into a surplus in 1983 with substantial surpluses beginning in 1988.

Table 17.5 disaggregates both the total receipts and outlays of the federal government into a number of categories. On the receipts side, the share of individual income taxes rose gradually from about 44 percent in the early 1960s to a little over 48 percent in the early 1980s. The tax cuts of the early Reagan years reduced the share of such taxes in federal revenues back down to about 44 percent, though through some tightening of loopholes, other measures, and rapid income growth, it increased to 48 percent by 1998. By contrast, the share of corporation income taxes declined steadily from 23.2 percent in 1960 to 12.5 percent in 1980 before falling sharply to a little over 6 percent by 1983 as a result of the Reagan tax cuts. Subsequent adjustments to tax rates and increased exemptions had the effect of raising the share back to around 10 percent from 1993 to 1999. The aforementioned adjustments in social security taxes in the early 1980s had the effect of increasing their share from about 30 percent to 37 percent by the early 1990s. The relative importance of "other" (mostly indirect) taxes declined in relative importance from almost 17 percent in 1960 to about 8 percent beginning in 1996.

On the expenditures side, there were dramatic reductions in the shares of both national defense and international affairs (such as foreign aid) in total expenditures. These were offset by sharply rising shares of expenditures on health, medicare, income security, social security and net interest, mostly in the form of transfer payments (Table 17.6). Much of these increases, especially in health and medicare, was due to rising costs.

On the revenue side, there have been growing numbers of exemptions and exclusions, e.g., for the contributions and earnings of employer pension programs, employer medical insurance and care programs, and interest payments on owner-occupied housing. These accounted for over $230 billion in revenue losses in the 2001 budget.

receipts and outlays by type, 1960–2000 (as a % of total)

| Year | Receipts | | | | | Outlays (on-budget and off-budget) | | | | | | | | |
|---|---|---|---|---|---|---|---|---|---|---|---|---|---|---|
| | Total | Individual income tax | Corporation income tax | Social insurance and retirement | Other | Total | National defence | Int'l affairs | Health | Medicare | Income security | Social security | Net interest | Other |
| 1960 | 92.5 | 44.0 | 23.2 | 15.9 | 16.9 | 92.2 | 52.2 | 3.3 | 0.9 | na | 8.0 | 12.6 | 7.5 | 15.6 |
| 1961 | 94.4 | 43.8 | 22.3 | 17.4 | 16.6 | 97.7 | 50.8 | 3.3 | 0.9 | na | 9.9 | 12.8 | 6.9 | 15.6 |
| 1962 | 99.7 | 45.7 | 20.6 | 17.1 | 16.6 | 106.8 | 49.0 | 5.2 | 1.1 | na | 8.6 | 13.5 | 6.5 | 16.1 |
| 1963 | 106.6 | 44.7 | 20.3 | 18.6 | 16.5 | 111.3 | 48.0 | 4.8 | 1.4 | na | 8.4 | 14.2 | 6.9 | 16.4 |
| 1964 | 112.6 | 43.3 | 20.9 | 19.5 | 16.4 | 118.5 | 46.2 | 4.1 | 1.5 | na | 8.2 | 14.0 | 6.9 | 19.1 |
| 1965 | 116.8 | 41.8 | 21.8 | 19.0 | 17.4 | 118.2 | 42.8 | 4.5 | 1.5 | na | 8.0 | 14.8 | 7.3 | 21.2 |
| 1966 | 130.8 | 42.4 | 23.0 | 19.5 | 15.1 | 134.5 | 43.2 | 4.2 | 1.9 | 0.1 | 7.2 | 15.4 | 7.0 | 21.2 |
| 1967 | 148.8 | 41.3 | 22.9 | 21.9 | 13.9 | 157.5 | 45.3 | 3.6 | 2.2 | 1.7 | 6.5 | 13.8 | 6.5 | 20.4 |
| 1968 | 153.0 | 44.9 | 18.8 | 22.2 | 14.2 | 178.1 | 46.0 | 3.0 | 2.5 | 2.6 | 6.6 | 13.4 | 6.2 | 19.7 |
| 1969 | 186.9 | 46.7 | 19.6 | 20.9 | 12.8 | 183.6 | 44.9 | 2.5 | 2.8 | 3.1 | 7.1 | 14.9 | 6.9 | 17.8 |
| 1970 | 192.8 | 46.9 | 17.0 | 23.0 | 13.1 | 195.6 | 41.8 | 2.2 | 3.0 | 3.2 | 8.0 | 15.5 | 7.4 | 19.0 |
| 1971 | 187.1 | 46.1 | 14.3 | 25.3 | 14.3 | 210.2 | 37.5 | 2.0 | 3.2 | 3.1 | 10.9 | 17.1 | 7.0 | 19.0 |
| 1972 | 207.3 | 45.7 | 15.5 | 25.4 | 13.4 | 230.7 | 34.3 | 2.1 | 3.8 | 3.3 | 12.0 | 17.4 | 6.7 | 20.5 |
| 1973 | 230.8 | 44.7 | 15.7 | 27.3 | 12.3 | 245.7 | 31.2 | 1.7 | 3.8 | 3.3 | 11.5 | 20.0 | 7.0 | 21.5 |
| 1974 | 263.2 | 45.2 | 14.7 | 28.5 | 11.6 | 269.4 | 29.4 | 2.1 | 4.0 | 3.6 | 12.5 | 20.8 | 7.9 | 19.6 |
| 1975 | 279.1 | 43.9 | 14.6 | 30.3 | 11.3 | 332.3 | 26.0 | 2.1 | 3.9 | 3.9 | 15.1 | 19.5 | 7.0 | 22.5 |
| 1976 | 298.1 | 44.2 | 13.9 | 30.5 | 11.5 | 371.8 | 24.1 | 1.7 | 4.2 | 4.3 | 16.4 | 19.9 | 7.2 | 22.2 |
| 1977 | 355.6 | 44.3 | 15.4 | 30.0 | 10.3 | 409.2 | 23.8 | 1.6 | 4.2 | 4.7 | 14.9 | 20.8 | 7.3 | 22.7 |
| 1978 | 399.6 | 45.3 | 15.0 | 30.3 | 9.4 | 458.7 | 22.8 | 1.6 | 4.0 | 5.0 | 13.4 | 20.5 | 7.7 | 25.0 |
| 1979 | 463.3 | 47.0 | 14.2 | 30.0 | 8.8 | 504.0 | 23.1 | 1.5 | 4.1 | 5.3 | 13.2 | 20.7 | 8.5 | 23.9 |
| 1980 | 517.1 | 47.2 | 12.5 | 30.5 | 9.8 | 590.9 | 22.7 | 2.2 | 3.9 | 5.4 | 14.7 | 20.1 | 8.9 | 22.2 |
| 1981 | 599.3 | 47.7 | 10.2 | 30.5 | 11.6 | 678.2 | 23.2 | 1.9 | 4.0 | 5.8 | 14.7 | 20.6 | 10.1 | 19.7 |
| 1982 | 617.8 | 48.2 | 8.0 | 32.6 | 11.2 | 745.8 | 24.9 | 1.7 | 3.7 | 6.3 | 14.4 | 20.9 | 11.4 | 16.8 |
| 1983 | 600.6 | 48.1 | 6.2 | 34.8 | 10.9 | 808.4 | 26.0 | 1.5 | 3.5 | 6.5 | 15.2 | 21.1 | 11.1 | 15.1 |
| 1984 | 666.5 | 44.8 | 8.5 | 35.9 | 10.8 | 851.9 | 26.7 | 1.9 | 3.6 | 6.8 | 13.2 | 20.9 | 13.0 | 13.9 |
| 1985 | 734.1 | 45.6 | 8.4 | 36.1 | 10.0 | 946.4 | 26.7 | 1.7 | 3.5 | 7.0 | 13.6 | 19.9 | 13.7 | 13.9 |
| 1986 | 769.2 | 45.4 | 8.2 | 36.9 | 9.5 | 990.5 | 27.6 | 1.4 | 3.6 | 7.1 | 12.1 | 20.1 | 13.7 | 14.4 |
| 1987 | 854.4 | 46.0 | 9.8 | 35.5 | 8.7 | 1,004.1 | 28.1 | 1.2 | 4.0 | 7.5 | 12.3 | 20.7 | 13.8 | 12.6 |
| 1988 | 909.3 | 44.1 | 10.4 | 36.8 | 8.7 | 1,064.5 | 27.3 | 1.0 | 4.2 | 7.4 | 12.2 | 20.6 | 14.3 | 13.1 |
| 1989 | 991.2 | 45.0 | 10.4 | 36.3 | 8.4 | 1,143.7 | 26.6 | 0.8 | 4.2 | 7.4 | 11.9 | 20.3 | 14.8 | 14.0 |
| 1990 | 1,032.0 | 45.2 | 9.1 | 36.8 | 8.9 | 1,253.2 | 23.9 | 1.1 | 4.6 | 7.8 | 11.7 | 19.8 | 14.7 | 16.3 |
| 1991 | 1,055.0 | 44.3 | 9.3 | 37.5 | 8.8 | 1,324.4 | 20.6 | 1.2 | 5.4 | 7.9 | 12.9 | 20.3 | 14.7 | 17.1 |
| 1992 | 1,091.3 | 43.6 | 9.2 | 37.9 | 9.3 | 1,381.7 | 21.6 | 1.2 | 6.5 | 8.6 | 14.3 | 20.8 | 14.4 | 12.6 |
| 1993 | 1,154.4 | 44.2 | 10.2 | 37.1 | 8.6 | 1,409.5 | 20.7 | 1.2 | 7.1 | 9.3 | 14.7 | 21.6 | 14.1 | 11.4 |
| 1994 | 1,258.6 | 43.2 | 11.2 | 36.7 | 9.0 | 1,461.9 | 19.3 | 1.2 | 7.3 | 9.9 | 14.7 | 21.9 | 13.9 | 12.0 |
| 1995 | 1,351.8 | 43.7 | 11.6 | 35.8 | 8.9 | 1,515.8 | 18.0 | 1.1 | 7.6 | 10.6 | 14.6 | 22.2 | 15.3 | 10.8 |
| 1996 | 1,453.1 | 45.2 | 11.8 | 35.1 | 7.9 | 1,560.6 | 17.0 | 0.9 | 7.7 | 11.2 | 14.5 | 22.4 | 15.5 | 11.0 |
| 1997 | 1,579.3 | 46.7 | 11.5 | 34.2 | 7.6 | 1,601.3 | 16.9 | 1.0 | 7.7 | 11.9 | 14.4 | 22.8 | 15.2 | 10.1 |
| 1998 | 1,721.8 | 48.1 | 11.0 | 33.2 | 7.7 | 1,652.6 | 16.3 | 0.8 | 8.0 | 11.7 | 14.1 | 23.0 | 14.6 | 11.7 |
| 1999 | 1,827.5 | 48.1 | 10.1 | 33.5 | 8.3 | 1,703.0 | 16.1 | 0.9 | 8.3 | 11.2 | 14.0 | 22.9 | 13.5 | 13.2 |
| 2000 | 1,956.3 | 48.6 | 9.8 | 33.2 | 8.3 | 1,789.6 | 16.2 | 1.0 | 8.6 | 11.3 | 14.0 | 22.7 | 12.3 | 13.8 |

Source: US GPO (2000).

Note
na = Not available.

*Table 17.6* Federal payments to individuals by selected programs, 1960–2000[a]

| *Program* | *1960* | *1970* | *1980* | *1990* | *2000* |
|---|---|---|---|---|---|
| Total payments | | | | | |
| US$ billion | 24.2 | 64.8 | 278.5 | 584.1 | 1,055.7 |
| US$ billion (constant 1996$) | 109.0 | 232.9 | 510.3 | 683.8 | 980.1 |
| As a % of total federal outlays | 26.2 | 33.1 | 47.1 | 46.6 | 59.0 |
| As a % of GDP | 4.6 | 6.4 | 10.2 | 10.2 | 11.0 |
| Outlays for selected programs (US$ billion) | 11.4 | 29.7 | 117.1 | 246.4 | 403.2 |
| Social security (OASDI) | | | | | |
| Medicare (HI) | 0.0 | 4.8 | 23.8 | 65.9 | 132.4 |
| Medicaid | 0.0 | 2.7 | 14.0 | 41.1 | 116.1 |
| Food stamps | 0.0 | 0.6 | 9.1 | 15.9 | 19.7 |
| Family support (AFDC/TANF)[b] | 2.1 | 4.1 | 6.9 | 12.3 | 18.1 |
| Civil service retirement | 0.9 | 2.8 | 14.7 | 31.0 | 45.4 |
| Veteran's assistance[c] | 4.7 | 8.1 | 19.9 | 27.3 | 44.5 |
| Military retirement | 0.7 | 2.9 | 11.9 | 21.6 | 32.9 |
| Supplementary Security Income (SSI) | 0.0 | 0.0 | 5.7 | 11.5 | 30.0 |
| Recipients (millions) | | | | | |
| Social security (OASDI) | 14.8 | 26.2 | 35.6 | 39.8 | 44.8 |
| Medicare (HI) | 0.0 | 20.4 | 25.1 | 30.5 | 39.3 |
| Medicaid | 0.0 | 14.5 | 21.6 | 25.3 | 33.4 |
| Food stamps | 0.0 | 4.3 | 21.1 | 20.0 | 18.1 |
| Family support (AFDC/TANF) | 3.0 | 8.5 | 10.8 | 11.7 | 7.3[d] |

Source: Schick (2000: 118).

Notes

a Estimated.

b AFDC was replaced by Temporary Assistance for Needy Families (TANF) in 1997.

c Includes service and nonservice connected compensation; grants to states; hospital and medical care; and education, insurance, and burial benefits.

d Actual figures from 1999.

### *State and local government budgets*

Not surprisingly, there is considerable variation in state and local budgets from one state and locality to another. Some states have income taxes, while others do not; some have high sales taxes and others do not. Some have constitutional provisions prohibiting deficits while others do not. Generally speaking, however, as shown in Table 17.7, individual income taxes have been of growing importance in state and local government revenues, compensating for declining shares of property taxes and sales taxes. On the expenditure side, welfare and "other" expenditures[2] have been rising in importance while those on education and highways have been of declining importance.

… (as a % of total)

| Fiscal year[a] | Government revenue by source[b] | | | | | | | Government expenditure by function[c] | | | | |
|---|---|---|---|---|---|---|---|---|---|---|---|---|
| | Total (US$ billion) | Property taxes | Sales and gross receipts taxes | Individual income taxes | Corporate net income taxes | Transfers from federal gov't | Other[d] | Total | Education | Highways | Public welfare | Other[d] |
| 1970–71 | 144.9 | 26.12 | 22.93 | 8.21 | 2.36 | 18.04 | 22.34 | 150.7 | 39.43 | 12.01 | 12.10 | 36.46 |
| 1971–72 | 167.5 | 25.59 | 22.39 | 9.09 | 2.64 | 18.71 | 21.58 | 168.5 | 39.05 | 11.29 | 12.53 | 37.14 |
| 1972–73 | 190.2 | 24.09 | 22.10 | 9.46 | 2.85 | 20.64 | 21.14 | 181.4 | 38.44 | 10.26 | 13.00 | 38.29 |
| 1973–74 | 207.7 | 22.97 | 22.20 | 9.39 | 2.90 | 20.14 | 22.41 | 199.0 | 38.11 | 10.03 | 12.61 | 39.25 |
| 1974–75 | 228.2 | 22.57 | 21.83 | 9.40 | 2.91 | 20.61 | 22.67 | 230.7 | 38.08 | 9.76 | 12.20 | 39.95 |
| 1975–76 | 256.2 | 22.25 | 21.29 | 9.59 | 2.84 | 21.70 | 22.32 | 256.7 | 37.87 | 9.31 | 12.70 | 40.12 |
| 1976–77 | 285.2 | 21.93 | 21.27 | 10.26 | 3.22 | 21.90 | 21.44 | 274.2 | 37.48 | 8.41 | 13.09 | 41.02 |
| 1977–78 | 316.0 | 21.02 | 21.39 | 10.50 | 3.40 | 22.03 | 21.66 | 297.0 | 37.29 | 8.29 | 13.18 | 41.24 |
| 1978–79 | 343.2 | 18.92 | 21.63 | 10.76 | 3.53 | 21.90 | 23.26 | 327.5 | 36.47 | 8.68 | 12.79 | 42.05 |
| 1979–80 | 382.3 | 17.92 | 20.91 | 11.01 | 3.48 | 21.72 | 24.97 | 369.1 | 36.09 | 9.03 | 12.81 | 42.07 |
| 1980–81 | 423.4 | 17.71 | 20.30 | 10.96 | 3.34 | 21.33 | 26.36 | 407.4 | 35.78 | 8.49 | 13.28 | 42.45 |
| 1981–82 | 457.7 | 17.93 | 20.46 | 11.09 | 3.28 | 19.07 | 28.17 | 436.7 | 35.33 | 7.90 | 13.28 | 43.49 |
| 1982–83 | 486.8 | 18.31 | 20.60 | 11.33 | 2.93 | 18.49 | 28.35 | 466.5 | 35.13 | 7.86 | 13.06 | 43.96 |
| 1983–84 | 542.7 | 17.77 | 21.02 | 11.89 | 3.16 | 17.86 | 28.30 | 505.0 | 34.87 | 7.81 | 13.15 | 44.17 |
| 1984–85 | 598.1 | 17.35 | 21.13 | 11.76 | 3.20 | 17.75 | 28.81 | 553.9 | 34.79 | 8.12 | 12.90 | 44.19 |
| 1985–86 | 641.5 | 17.41 | 21.05 | 11.59 | 3.12 | 17.62 | 29.20 | 605.6 | 34.81 | 8.15 | 12.53 | 44.51 |
| 1986–87 | 686.9 | 17.65 | 20.98 | 12.22 | 3.26 | 16.72 | 29.17 | 657.1 | 34.49 | 7.97 | 12.58 | 44.97 |
| 1987–88 | 726.8 | 18.19 | 21.53 | 12.16 | 3.26 | 16.18 | 28.69 | 704.9 | 34.43 | 7.89 | 12.64 | 45.04 |
| 1988–89 | 786.1 | 18.11 | 21.16 | 12.44 | 3.30 | 16.01 | 28.98 | 762.4 | 34.62 | 7.62 | 12.84 | 44.92 |
| 1989–90 | 849.5 | 18.32 | 20.94 | 12.44 | 2.77 | 16.10 | 29.43 | 834.8 | 34.52 | 7.31 | 13.24 | 44.93 |
| 1990–91 | 902.2 | 18.62 | 20.57 | 12.12 | 2.47 | 17.07 | 29.15 | 908.1 | 34.06 | 7.15 | 14.36 | 44.43 |
| 1991–92 | 979.1 | 18.42 | 20.19 | 11.81 | 2.44 | 18.30 | 28.84 | 981.2 | 34.92 | 6.86 | 16.18 | 43.88 |
| 1992–93 | 1,041.6 | 18.22 | 20.13 | 11.83 | 2.54 | 19.07 | 28.22 | 1,033.2 | 33.13 | 6.62 | 16.52 | 43.73 |
| 1993–94 | 1,100.4 | 17.92 | 20.32 | 11.71 | 2.57 | 19.58 | 27.91 | 1,077.7 | 32.78 | 6.69 | 17.02 | 43.51 |
| 1994–95 | 1,169.5 | 17.40 | 20.29 | 11.79 | 2.69 | 19.56 | 28.28 | 1,149.9 | 32.90 | 6.71 | 17.11 | 43.29 |
| 1995–96 | 1,222.8 | 17.13 | 20.36 | 12.01 | 2.62 | 19.21 | 28.68 | 1,193.3 | 33.43 | 6.63 | 16.54 | 43.41 |

Source: US GPO (2000: Table B-84).

Notes

a Fiscal years are not the same for all state and local governments.

b Excludes revenues for expenditures of publicly owned utilities, liquor stores, and of insurance-trust activities. Intergovernmental receipts and payments between state and local governments are also excluded.

c Includes other taxes and charges and miscellaneous revenues.

d Includes expenditures for libraries, hospitals, health, employment security administration, veteran services, air transportation, water transport and terminals, parking facilities, and transit subsidies, police protection, correction, protective inspection and regulation, sewerage, natural resources, parks and recreation, housing and community development, solid waste management, financial administration, judicial and legal, general public buildings, other government administration, interest on general debt, and general expenditures, n.e.c.

## Explaining the changes

### *Explanations of changes in revenues and expenditures*

In this section, we turn to the explanation for the trends in revenue and expenditure patterns, in general, and the elimination of the federal budget deficit, in particular. Table 17.8 identifies the most important elements of tax legislation since 1980 and the estimated revenue impact of each.

For the 1980s, the single most important measure was the Economic Recovery Act of 1981 initiated at the urging of President Reagan. This act reduced both corporate and individual income tax rates and flattened them considerably. Since the tax reduction did not result in an increase in revenues as some had predicted

*Table 17.8* Major tax legislation, 1980–97

| *Year* | *Legislation* | *Estimated revenue impact*[a] |
|---|---|---|
| 1980 | *Omnibus Budget Reconciliation Act*: First use of the reconciliation process | +4 |
| 1981 | *Economic Recovery Tax Act*: Enacted six month after Ronald Reagan became president; indexed major features of the individual income tax | –749 |
| 1982 | *Tax Equity and Fiscal Responsibility Act*: Initiated by The Senate; repealed some of the tax breaks enacted the previous year | +98 |
| 1983 | *Social Security Amendments*: Increased revenue for Social Security system, which was on the brink of insolvency | +165 |
| 1984 | *Deficit Reduction Act*: Revenue gains and spending cuts were packaged together in a reconciliation bill | +51 |
| 1986 | *Tax Reform Act*: Designed to be revenue-neutral; lowered rate on highest individual income tax bracket from 50 to 28 percent; revenue loss offset by eliminating many tax expenditures | +11 |
| 1987 | *Budget Reconciliation Act*: Canceled Gramm-Rudman-Hollings sequestration of $23 billion | +23 |
| 1989 | *Omnibus Budget Reconciliation Act*: Included approximately $10 billion in spending cuts | +6 |
| 1990 | *Omnibus Budget Reconciliation Act*: Contained the Budget Enforcement Act, which introduced new controls on revenue and spending legislation | +137 |
| 1993 | *Omnibus Budget Reconciliation Act*: Raised highest individual tax rate to 39.6 percent | +240 |
| 1997 | *Taxpayer Relief Act*: Part of the balanced budget agreement between the president and Congress; expanded several major tax expenditures; estimated revenue loss much higher after first five years | –95 |

Source: Schick (2000: Table 7.1).

Note

a Revenue impact estimated at time of enactment; actual revenue impact usually diverges from these estimates.

(i.e., the Laffer curve) and was accompanied by substantial increases in military spending, it was soon realized that the tax cuts had gone too far and that attention had to be given to deficit reduction. As a result, there followed: (i) the Tax Equity and Fiscal Responsibility Act of 1982, aimed at reversing some of the tax reductions believed to be excessive in the previous years; (ii) the Social Security Amendments of 1983 which raised social security revenues; and (iii) the Deficit Reduction Act of 1984 which made another modest effort to control expenditures and increase revenues.

Then came the Balanced Budget and Emergency Deficit Control Act of 1985 (Gramm-Hollings-Rudman) which set ceilings on projected future deficits and proposed to enforce these ceilings by withholding appropriations once these ceilings were exceeded. This act received a great deal of attention and yet, as will be explained, was much less effective than had been hoped. As is pointed out in Table 17.8, more substantial revenue gains came from the Omnibus Budget Reconciliation Acts of 1989, 1990 and 1993. Although serious consideration was given to a statutory balanced budget amendment to the constitution as early as 1985, the proposal was eventually rejected.

In addition to these major tax bills, over time, several important procedural changes were also implemented. The congressional reforms of the 1970s reduced the power of the House Ways and Means Committee, the committee charged with initiating legislation in Congress. Prior to that, its monopoly on the drafting of tax and expenditure proposals and the small size of the committee allowed its committee chair to wield enormous power. In the reforms, some of its responsibilities became shared with other committees and the committee was substantially increased in size. The committee also went through rule changes from time to time affecting the ability of committee members to make amendments.

Another institutional reform was to increase the informational base available to legislators and other decision-makers by imposing requirements for increasingly detailed and clearly identified rules for analyzing the budgetary impacts of proposed new spending and revenue programs. The responsibilities for such assessments were given to the Office of Management and Budget (OMB) within the executive branch, and the Congressional Budget Office (CBO) within the legislative branch. With more and better information, legislators are less able to mislead other legislators into voting for programs by misrepresenting their benefits relative to costs.

It is clear from Table 17.8 that there were at least as many serious legislative efforts to reduce the budget deficit in the 1980s as in the 1990s. Yet, progress in reducing the deficits was largely confined to the 1990s. Why? One factor was the sharp reversal in military spending, rising rapidly in the early 1980s and then sharply declining from the late 1980s until 2000 subsequent to the disintegration of the Soviet bloc and the perceived reduction in its military threat.

Since actual deficits are greatly affected by economic conditions, improved economic conditions were another important factor contributing to deficit reduction. Both average unemployment and inflation rates were reduced in the 1990s and nominal interest rates declined by even more, suggesting that real interest rates were also reduced. All of these economic conditions, therefore, were favorable to deficit reduction. Yet, since the rate of growth in real GDP and employment was slightly higher in 1983–90 than during 1992–99, it is clear that there must have been more to deficit reduction than changed economic conditions.

Indeed, a comparison of the institutional rules and procedures of the Gramm-Hollings-Rudman Act of 1985 with those of the Budget Enforcement Act (BEA) of 1990 shows that changes in institutional rules also contributed to the greater success in deficit reduction in the 1990s. Gramm-Hollings-Rudman prescribed a predetermined deficit ceiling regardless of economic conditions. Achievement of the target was to be enforced by withdrawal (sequestration) of agency funding if the target could not be achieved. Yet, the increasing size of the projected deficits undermined the feasibility of using such rules and led to the use of accounting tricks to avoid the restrictions.

To remedy this, the BEA introduced three major rule changes: (i) it more realistically allowed the size of the deficit ceiling to be adjusted to economic conditions; (ii) it distinguished between two types of spending: "discretionary" spending (which is appropriated annually) and "direct" (legislated or mandatory) expenditures, the latter (like Social Security and Medicare) being nondiscretionary and dictated by rules set out in the laws; and (iii) spending caps were imposed on discretionary programs and PAYGO rules on mandated expenditures. By PAYGO was meant that any increases in mandated spending would have to be offset by revenue enhancement to cover the cost. Given the unpopularity of tax increases, this in effect strongly discouraged proposals to increase entitlements. Each of these new rules contributed to the BEA's success.

The original BEA of 1990 was achieved at great political cost to President Bush in that he had to sacrifice his promise of "no new taxes" and partly go along with the preferences of the opposition Democratic Congress. In 1993, it was President Clinton's turn to pay a cost, having to give up his campaign promise of health care reform and again to raise some taxes, in order to pass the Omnibus Budget Reconciliation Act of that year. Spending caps and PAYGO rules that were originally imposed for only a five-year period were extended, first through 1998, and subsequently through fiscal year 2002. The discretionary (annually appropriated) spending includes military spending and the operating costs of most government agencies. The caps on these expenditures meant that the reductions in military spending could not be used to offset increases in direct spending. In some years, moreover, there were even separate caps on military and other spending within the general category of discretionary spending, making it impossible to use the military spending reductions for financing increases in other discretionary spending. With PAYGO rules in place, with minor exceptions, legislated mandatory spending was kept relatively constant in relation to GDP. On the revenue side, not only were the income tax rates for high-income earners raised, but various tax exemptions were also phased out, accounting for the significant rise in federal receipts from both individual and corporate income taxes between 1991 and 1998 (Table 17.5).

### *The impact of the business cycle on the budget, spending and revenues*

The budget is significantly influenced by the business cycle. When the economy is booming, spending on unemployment and welfare declines, and tax revenues surge. On the other hand, when the economy is declining, unemployment and welfare claims increase, and tax revenues sag. To obtain estimates of the budget surplus at full employment, we first divide the budget surplus by GDP to reduce nonstationarity, and then regress the ratio:

$$\text{Budget surplus/GDP} = a + b^* \text{ OUTGAP} + e1$$

where the output gap, OUTGAP, is equal to,

$$\text{OUTGAP} = (\text{POTGDP} - \text{GDP})/\text{POTGDP}$$

and POTGDP is potential GDP. Potential GDP is simply extrapolated using the trend growth in output, about 3.2 percent per year between 1960 and 2000.

The full employment budget surplus to GDP ratio is the ratio that arises when output is at its full-employment level. Thus, it is equal to the coefficient estimate a. The coefficient b reflects the sensitivity of the budget surplus to GDP ratio to the output gap, and should be negative; that is, as actual output falls short of potential output, the output gap increases, and the budget surplus to GDP ratio should fall. If actual output surpasses potential output, the output gap falls, and the budget surplus to GDP ratio should increase.

The above budget surplus–GDP equation was estimated using annual data between 1960 and 2000. The estimation resulted in an estimate of −0.013 for coefficient a, and an estimate of −0.51 for coefficient b. Thus, the budget deficit to GDP ratio was about 1.3 percent. Hence from 1960, a structural budget deficit of 1.3 percent was built into the economy, implying that even when the economy was at full employment, the government would run a budget deficit. As hypothesized, a rise in the output gap of 1 percent was estimated to reduce the budget surplus to GDP ratio.

As mentioned above, especially in the late 1980s and early 1990s, there were tax hikes, and in the early 1990s, reductions in certain types of expenditures as a result of welfare reform and the end of the Cold War. Since 1975, the actual budget surplus has been lower than the full-employment surplus, suggesting that the government has been more expansionary. The gap between the two surplus measures was especially large in the mid-1980s, reflecting the Reagan tax cuts and military expansion programs. Yet, the reforms of the 1990s had an impact in raising the actual surpluses; only between 1995 and 1999 did the actual budget surplus to GDP ratio exceed the full-employment budget surplus to GDP ratio. Hence, the high budget surpluses of the late 1990s are not solely due to a booming economy but also to the tax and expenditure reforms of 1986–2000.

## The relation of changing fiscal balances to debt holdings, investment, productivity, growth and current and capital account balances

### *Description*

The aim of this section is to examine the possible effects of US fiscal trends on debt, investment, productivity, growth and capital account balances. We begin with its effects on debt accumulation. Consistent with the relatively persistent but relatively steady deficits in the unified budget revealed in Table 17.4 for the years prior to 1980, the ratios of debt to GDP fell from 35.5 percent in 1970 to 32.5 percent in 1975 and then remained constant until 1980. However, with the rapid increases in these deficits beginning in the early 1980s, and lasting until the early 1990s, these debt to GDP ratios increased to 43.2 percent in 1985, 63.1 percent in 1990 and 70.5 percent in 1995 before declining to 61.0 percent in 1999. The growth of debt has been equally rapid for marketable and nonmarketable forms of debt. Over the 1970–99 period, the average maturity of the outstanding debt has increased fairly significantly, though not since 1990.

The distribution of ownership of this debt changed over the period. The portion held by the Federal Reserve rose from 30 percent in 1988 to almost 44 percent in 1999. At the same time, the portion held by foreigners increased fairly sharply to 23 percent in 1999. The increasing shares of these debt holders have come at the expense of state and local governments and others (the domestic private sector) which moved away from government securities in search of higher returns elsewhere.

While indirect taxes are generally regressive, income taxes have been the major source of progressivity in US taxes. The progressivity of US income taxes was reduced significantly, however, in the Reagan tax reforms of the early 1980s. Table 17.9 provides some data relevant to the progressivity of individual income taxes in the United States between 1989 and 1996. By comparing the 1989 and 1996 entries in the share of adjusted gross income, one can see that income inequality has increased in the US between these years. Yet, in the last two sets of columns, it can be seen that those in the higher-income groups pay larger percentages of the total income taxes collected and pay higher percentages of their income in the form of taxes. These changes are largely the result of the 1990 and 1993 Omnibus Budget Reconciliation Acts discussed earlier.

What about possible effects of the fiscal budget deficits on the international current accounts? With the exception of 1971 and 1972, the current account remained in surplus until 1977. After this, it remained negative in all years except the recession years of 1980, 1981 and 1991. The largest current account deficits of 1982–86 slightly followed the years with large fiscal deficits, 1983–86. After 1993, however, the current account deficits increased with accelerating economic growth, despite the decline and eventual elimination of the fiscal deficits.

*Table 17.9* Shares of adjusted gross income and individual income taxes, by income class, 1989, 1992 and 1996

| *Income class*[a] *(US$)* | *Share of adjusted gross income*[b] *(%)* | | | *Share of individual income taxes*[a] *(%)* | | | *Income taxes as a percentage of adjusted gross income*[a] | | |
|---|---|---|---|---|---|---|---|---|---|
| | *1989* | *1992* | *1996* | *1989* | *1992* | *1996* | *1989* | *1992* | *1996* |
| 0– 10,000 | 3 | 3 | 3 | 0 | 0 | −1 | −0.2 | −1.5 | −5.8 |
| 10,000–20,000 | 8 | 9 | 8 | 2 | 2 | 1 | 3.4 | 2.8 | 1.1 |
| 20,000–30,000 | 10 | 10 | 10 | 6 | 6 | 5 | 7.6 | 7.8 | 7.6 |
| 30,000–50,000 | 20 | 21 | 19 | 16 | 16 | 14 | 10.3 | 10.2 | 10.3 |
| 50,000–75,000 | 21 | 21 | 19 | 19 | 19 | 17 | 12.0 | 11.7 | 12.1 |
| 75,000–100,000 | 11 | 11 | 11 | 13 | 12 | 12 | 14.6 | 14.3 | 14.7 |
| 100,000–200,000 | 13 | 12 | 13 | 17 | 17 | 17 | 17.9 | 17.4 | 18.2 |
| 200,000–500,000 | 7 | 7 | 8 | 11 | 12 | 14 | 22.7 | 23.2 | 25.3 |
| 500,000–1,000,000 | 3 | 3 | 3 | 5 | 6 | 7 | 24.1 | 25.8 | 30.1 |
| 1,000,000 or more | 5 | 5 | 7 | 10 | 11 | 15 | 24.4 | 26.8 | 31.7 |

Source: Schick (2000: Table 7.8).

Notes

a Adjusted gross income in constant 1996 dollars.

b Includes refunds of the earned income tax credit.

### *Government investment and economic growth*

Recently, an enormous amount of literature has attempted to estimate the impact of public capital on productivity growth.[3] Specifically, the idea that is being advanced is that an expansion of public investment spending should have a larger stimulative impact on private output than equal-sized increases in public consumption expenditure. This would be so if public investment would induce an increase in the rate of return to private capital and, thereby, stimulate private investment expenditure. Aschauer (1989) produced results consistent with this view, suggesting that any slowdown in infrastructure growth—such as that which occurred in the 1970s and again more recently—would slow the rate of growth of future potential output and productivity.

Gramlich, however, cites at least two econometric problems with this literature. First is the issue of common trends: the overall trend of public capital per capita closely mirrors the overall trend of national output per capita. Second is the issue of causality: does the leveling off of infrastructure capital reduce the growth of output, or does the reduced growth of output reduce the demand for infrastructure capital?

### *Trends in income inequality*

Many observers believe that inequality in the US has become worse over the last several decades. In 1980, the top-fifth's share of total family income claimed about 40 percent. The large middle three-fifths of families received close to 54 percent of total income. The poorest fifth got what remained. Then in the early 1980s, the gap began to widen, and this gap widened further in the 1990s. The top-fifth's share began rising, reaching almost half of all income by the end of the century, while the share going to the middle three-fifth dropped to 49 percent, and the share going to the bottom fifth also declined. During the 1990s, the incomes of people at or near the top grew twice as fast as those of people in the middle. Despite the decade's boom, median income barely increased.

Although the distribution of after-tax income is not readily available, compared to the late 1970s and early 1980s, taxes have become less progressive, although as mentioned, the progressivity of the tax was increased somewhat in the 1990 and 1993 Omnibus Budget Reconciliation Acts. Still the well-off have the largest effective tax rates (Table 17.10), and pay most of the taxes collected by the government. In fact, the well-off have increased their share of total taxes paid. While in 1989, those making over $100,000 (in 1996 dollars) paid about 43 percent of all taxes, in 1996, those making over $100,000 (in 1996 dollars) paid about 53 percent of all taxes. This was because although the progressivity of taxes was reduced, the incomes of the well-off were growing faster than the incomes of the less well-off.

*Table 17.10* Effective tax rate for all individuals and families, by cash income

| *Cash income ($)* | *Individuals and families (million)* | *People (million)* | *Average pretax income ($)* | *Effective tax rates (%)* | | | | |
|---|---|---|---|---|---|---|---|---|
| | | | | *Total* | *Individual income tax* | *Social insurance tax* | *Corporate income tax* | *Excise tax* |
| 0–10,000 | 16.3 | 27.9 | 6,030 | 7.6 | −3.2 | 6.3 | 0.6 | 3.9 |
| 10,000–20,000 | 19.3 | 37.5 | 14,900 | 11.6 | −0.3 | 8.3 | 1.3 | 2.3 |
| 20,000–30,000 | 16.0 | 34.3 | 24,800 | 17.0 | 4.0 | 9.6 | 1.6 | 1.7 |
| 30,000–40,000 | 13.7 | 32.7 | 34,700 | 20.0 | 6.6 | 10.3 | 1.6 | 1.4 |
| 40,000–50,000 | 10.8 | 28.7 | 44,700 | 22.1 | 8.1 | 11.1 | 1.5 | 1.3 |
| 50,000–75,000 | 16.3 | 47.9 | 61,200 | 23.9 | 9.7 | 11.5 | 1.6 | 1.1 |
| 75,000–100,000 | 7.6 | 23.1 | 86,000 | 25.9 | 11.9 | 11.2 | 1.9 | 0.9 |
| 100,000–200,000 | 6.0 | 18.4 | 132,000 | 27.8 | 14.5 | 9.1 | 3.6 | 0.6 |
| 200,000 or more | 1.8 | 5.1 | 491,000 | 35.3 | 22.5 | 3.5 | 8.9 | 0.3 |
| All incomes | 109.6 | 258.8 | 45,700 | 24.7 | 11.3 | 9.2 | 3.2 | 1.1 |

Source: Schick (2000: Table 7.9).

## Prospects for the future: the surplus, how long it will last and what to do with it?

The major substantive issue of the presidential election of 1990 was what to do with the projected fiscal surplus over the next ten years. As a result of the indecisive election, it remains an issue, with the growing recession strengthening the case for tax reductions. As a result, substantial cuts in taxes seem likely.

One of the lessons to be learned from past experience is that budgetary projections are subject to considerable error. Indeed, even the professionals of the CBO and the OMB have frequently disagreed not only on the magnitude of the budgetary effect of any individual proposal, but even on the direction of the effect. First, small errors in the projections of basic macroeconomic variables, especially when accumulated over a number of years, can make a big difference. Table 17.11, for example, shows the sensitivity of receipts, outlays and the projected surplus to overestimation of economic conditions. The first section in Table 17.11 shows the year-by-year effects through 2005 of the real rate of growth in the year 2000 being 1 percent less than that projected. The second section shows the corresponding effects arising from a 1 percent lower growth rate in each year between 2000 and 2005. The third section does the same for a rate of inflation 1 percent higher than

*Table 17.11* Budget sensitivity to variances from economic projections, FY2000–5[a] (US$ billion)

| | *2000* | *2001* | *2002* | *2003* | *2004* | *2005* |
|---|---|---|---|---|---|---|
| Real growth: 1 percentage point less than projected in 2000; growth at projected in later years[b] | | | | | | |
| Receipts | −9 | −18 | −22 | −22 | −23 | −24 |
| Outlays | 2 | 7 | 8 | 9 | 11 | 14 |
| Surplus decrease | −11 | −25 | −29 | −32 | −35 | −38 |
| Real growth: 1 percentage point less than projected each year; 2000–5 | | | | | | |
| Receipts | −9 | −27 | −50 | −73 | −99 | −126 |
| Outlays | 0 | 1 | 3 | 7 | 12 | 19 |
| Surplus decrease | −9 | −28 | −53 | −80 | −111 | −146 |
| Inflation: 1 percentage point more than projected each year, 2000–5 | | | | | | |
| Receipts | 9 | 27 | 47 | 66 | 88 | 112 |
| Outlays | 1 | 6 | 12 | 20 | 28 | 36 |
| Surplus increase | 7 | 21 | 34 | 46 | 60 | 76 |
| Interest rates: 1 percentage point more than projected each year, 2000–5 | | | | | | |
| Surplus | 1 | 4 | 4 | 5 | 5 | 6 |
| Outlays | 5 | 12 | 15 | 17 | 17 | 17 |
| Surplus decrease | −3 | −9 | −11 | −12 | −12 | −11 |

Source: Schick (2000: Table 1.6).

Notes

a Numbers may not add to totals due to rounding.

b Assumes half a percentage point rise in the unemployment rate.

that anticipated in the projection. The final section in the table does the same for an interest rate that is 1 percent higher than supposed in the budget projection.

From the results, it can be seen that any single projection error could result in a substantial reduction in the projected budget surplus. For example, the reduction in the real rate of economic growth in the first year alone would reduce the accumulated budget surplus over the period 2000–5 by $140 billion. A sustained shortfall of one percent per annum in the economic growth rate would reduce the surplus by $427 billion. As a result, the first issue to resolve is whether or not significant budgetary surpluses will emerge.

In fact, both the OMB and the CBO are presently projecting surpluses over the next ten years. Each of these agencies makes numerous rather-strong assumptions in arriving at their "baseline" projections. For example, the CBO's projections are based on a set of predetermined rules, e.g., that revenues as well as expenditures continue according to current laws and current policy. While for mandatory spending the requirements of law are fairly clear, this is not so for discretionary spending, which is subject to annual appropriations. Since, as the CBO itself notes, "No consensus exists about how best to project the continuation of current policy for discretionary programs" (CBO 2000b: 79), what the CBO has done in practice is to choose three alternative baseline scenarios: "capped,"[4] "freeze,"[5] and "inflated."[6] The projected surpluses emerging from the three alternative scenarios are given in Table 17.12 for the total "unified" budget as well as for the "on-budget" (discretionary) and "off-budget" (mandatory) components, separately. While there is very little difference in the "off-budget" or mandatory part of the budget between scenarios, there are extremely sizable differences between scenarios in the "on-budget" part.

Auerbach and Gale (2000) provide a critique of the CBO baseline projections of both discretionary "on-budget" and direct "off-budget" components of the budget. They argue that all scenarios are unrealistically optimistic in that required reductions in discretionary spending in nominal terms would be unrealistically large, especially considering that the ratio of such spending to GDP is already at an historical low. The fact that such cuts would have to be made in an environment of unprecedented surpluses makes these projections even more implausible. Auerbach and Gale feel that budget cutters will be doing well to keep the discretionary spending relative to GDP constant. As shown in the first column of Table 17.13, this modification alone would reduce the accumulated surplus over the years 2001–10 by somewhere between $800 billion and $2 trillion!

Auerbach and Gale also criticize the CBO's assumptions with respect to tax policy changes, in particular by assuming unrealistically large increases in both the

*Table 17.12* CBO baseline budget surplus projections, 2001–10 (US$ billion)

| *Baseline* | *On-budget* | *Off-budget* | *Total* |
|---|---|---|---|
| Capped | 3,387 | 2,388 | 5,774 |
| Freeze | 3,349 | 2,395 | 5,744 |
| Inflated | 2,173 | 2,388 | 4,561 |

Source: Auerbach and Gale (2000).

*Table 17.13* On-budget surpluses, 2001–10, under alternative views of current policy (US$ billion)

| | | | | |
|---|---|---|---|---|
| Include tax adjustment | No | Yes | No | Yes |
| Remove retirement trust funds from on-budget totals | No | No | Yes | Yes |
| Discretionary spending path | | | | |
| Capped baseline | 3,387 | 3,233 | 2,585 | 2,431 |
| Freeze baseline | 3,349 | 3,195 | 2,547 | 2,393 |
| Inflated baseline | 2,173 | 2,019 | 1,371 | 1,217 |
| Constant DS/GDP | 1,309 | 1,155 | 507 | 353 |

Source: Auerbach and Gale (2000).

number of taxpayers who would pay the "alternative minimum tax" and the number of tax exemptions that would be allowed to expire. As shown in the second column of Table 17.13, avoiding these assumptions would reduce the size of the "on-budget" surplus by more than $150 billion. Finally, in the third column of the table, one can see the implications of not allowing the projected surpluses in the Medicare (Part A) Trust Fund and civilian pension funds to be transferred to discretionary spending and counted as surpluses in this component of the budget. As shown in the last column, when all three of these presumably more realistic adjustments are made to the baseline projections of the CBO, the projected surplus for the entire decade would fall to a "mere" $353 billion, an amount equal to the annual deficit of a single year typical of the years between 1985 and 1993.

In contrast to such words of caution, the US debate assumes unquestioningly that, without large tax cuts, there will be a massive surplus. The debate concerns what adjustment(s) should be made to the baseline surplus. In our opinion, tax cuts and spending increases seem more likely than reducing the public debt. Whatever the actual mix chosen, the mix will have major consequences for not only the first decade of the millennium, but most likely for the subsequent one as well.

## Conclusion: lessons of the US experience

Some of the lessons of the successful US experience in turning from persistent fiscal deficits to fiscal surpluses, such as sharp declines in military expenditures, will be difficult to apply to other countries. The more transferable lessons would seem to be those concerning the institutional reforms that were made in the 1980s and 1990s. One of these was welfare reform, i.e., in providing stronger incentives for being employed. A second was providing more and better professional assessments of the budgetary implications of various proposals. Another is the imposition of constraints that are both sufficiently flexible, so as to be politically and administratively feasible, such as the spending caps on discretionary expenditures and PAYGO rules on law-mandated programs that were adopted in 1990 and 1993.

At present, however, with the prospect of looming surpluses over the next decade, even the present constraints will be severely tested. Indeed, large-scale tax reductions seem likely and with any increase in international tensions, expenditures could also rise substantially. If as a result, these constraints cannot be sustained, there is the danger that the US could soon again be running severe fiscal deficits. The long time it took for the US to rectify the large fiscal deficits of the early 1980s would seem to underscore the importance of not getting into that situation again.

A consequence of the institutional changes that have taken place over time has been that discretionary fiscal policy is less useful as a stabilization tool. There is a certain amount of automatic, built-in stabilization embedded in the budget process, but discretionary stabilization policy is increasingly limited to monetary policy. While this frees fiscal policy to pursue other goals, the only way that the stabilizing effect of the fiscal system can be retained is by strengthening the automatic stabilizers, such as making the time-phasing of replacement of public capital more strongly counter-cyclical.

## Notes

1 Credits to these organizations, however, do appear in an appendix to the budget.
2 These include expenditures on health, libraries, sewerage, waste management, police, recreation, housing, interest on debt and transportation subsidies.
3 See Gramlich (1994) for a review of this topic.
4 The "capped" baseline assumes that Congress complies with the statutory budget caps on discretionary spending through 2002 after which they grow at the rate of inflation.
5 The "freeze" baseline holds discretionary spending at the nominal level enacted for 2000 and 2001.
6 The "inflated" baseline allows discretionary spending to grow at the rate of inflation.

## References


Aschauer, David A. (1989) "Is public expenditure productive?" *Journal of Monetary Economics* 23: 177–200.

Auerbach, Alan J. and Gale, William G. (2000) "Perspectives on the budget surplus," University of California Working Paper, Berkeley, CA: University of California Press.

Congressional Budget Office (2000a) *The Budget and Economic Outlook: Fiscal Years 2001–2010*, Washington, DC: US Government Printing Office (US GPO).

Congressional Budget Office (2000b) *An Analysis of the President's Budgetary Proposals for the Fiscal Year 2001*, Washington, DC: US Government Printing Office (US GPO).

Crain, W. Mark, Tollison, Robert, Goff, Brian and Carson, Diek (1985) "Legislator specialization and the size of government," *Public Choice* 46: 311–14.

Gramlich, Edward M. (1994) "Infrastructure investment: a review essay," *Journal of Economic Literature* 32(3): 1176–96.

Schick, Allen (2000) *The Federal Budget: Politics, Policy and Process*, Washington, DC: Brookings Institution Press.

Strauch, Rolf (1998) "Information and public spending: an empirical study of budget processes in the US states," in R.R. Strauch and J. van Hagen (eds) *Institutions, Politics and Fiscal Policy*, Kluwer: Boston.

United States Government Printing Office (US GPO) (2000) *Economic Report of the President 2000*, Washington, DC: US GPO.

# 18 Vietnam

*Kim Chung Tran and Viet Lan Nguyen*

## Introduction

Vietnam is in the Southeast Asian region with a total area of 332,000 square kilometers. As of April 1999, the population stood at 76.3 million (General Statistic Office 1999). Growth in the population declined to 2.3 percent per year in the early 1990s to about 1.8 percent in the late 1990s. GDP per capita was US$240 in 1995 (World Bank 1998) or US$1,236 in terms of PPP (United Nations Development Program 1998).

In moving from a centrally planned economic regime, Vietnam has imposed reforms since 1986 and it has accelerated the transition process to a market economy since 1989. After fifteen years, the fiscal system has changed such that it now has almost all of the characteristics of a market fiscal system. This chapter is composed of five parts, following the introduction, it discusses fiscal reform in Vietnam since 1986 in terms of two aspects. First, reorganization of the fiscal system and policies reform are considered, and second, an overview of fiscal development is presented. This is followed by an assessment of fiscal reform in terms of macroeconomic indicators as well as indicators of poverty reduction. Subsequently, the chapter considers future prospects and challenges for the country, and provides some suggestions for further fiscal reform.

## Fiscal reform in Vietnam

### *Fiscal management reform in Vietnam*

#### *The reorganization the fiscal system*

Before 1990, the organization of the institutions involved in fiscal policy followed a centrally planned regime. The State Planning Committee decided how and who could receive the financial resources from the state. The Ministry of Finance took responsibility for collecting taxes and making payments according to the plan given by the State Planning Committee. The State Bank of Vietnam played the role of treasurer.

After 1990, in terms of budget collection, there have been three important administrative reforms related to fiscal organization. First, the General Tax Department and General Custom Office which were under the Ministry of Finance were reorganized and moved from the central government to the local government (Thin 1999). Second, the state Treasury was reorganized and is now separate from the general financial system. The Treasury has two levels: national and provincial. The Treasury takes care of all payments from the government budget as well as at the provincial level. Third, the National Budget Audit Department was set up to audit the finances and payments of the budget. Although this organization is a department of the government, its operation is separate from the government. In terms of spending moneys from the budget, the Ministry of Finance takes care of current expenditures and the Ministry of Planning and Investment takes the role of payments for investment.

### *Policies reform*

From 1975 to 1985, the fiscal system was based on a centrally planned regime. Fiscal revenues came from several main sources: (i) transfers from SOEs to the government; (ii) taxes on industrial and commercial activities of the private sector; (iii) taxes on agriculture; and (iv) revenue from external activities, mainly aid from the former Soviet Union and eastern European economies. Fiscal expenditures were devoted to certain major activities including (i) expenditure for accumulation; (ii) expenditures for government activities; (iii) subsidies for supply of consumption goods; and (iv) subsidies to SOEs.

During the period 1986–89, there were several mistakes made in policy reform. First, the government used the price of rice as the norm for determining other prices. Because the price of rice was determined to be lower than it was, fiscal revenue was very low. Second, there was a sharp reduction in purchasing power and tax mobilization has also been very low. As a result, a vicious cycle appeared.

Nevertheless, stabilization policies began to be imposed in early 1989 and were achieved in late 1989. Simultaneous with banking and monetary policies, tight financial fiscal policies were also implemented. This included reduction of almost all subsidies and resources to state-owned enterprises through prices as well as through credit. In addition, budget losses were compensated for not by issuing money but by loans (domestic and foreign). As a result, the budget situation was not too severe.

During 1990–97, the National Assembly passed many laws and ordinances related to taxes. Currently, nine taxes have been approved (Table 18.1). The Law on the State Budget (Socialist Republic of Vietnam 1997), one of the most important laws in the transition of the economy, was approved. However, compared to other transition economies, such as Poland, Vietnam took a long time to issue the tax codes and laws related to the budget. For example, Poland took about two to three years to do what Vietnam has taken almost ten years to complete (that is, changing the laws related to organizing of the budget system). It therefore can been said that Vietnam has followed a gradual approach in the transition process.

During this period, the decentralization process has been strongly emphasized (World Bank 1996). Changes in the tax and transfer system between the central

*Table 18.1* Tax code system in Vietnam

| *Name* | *Number* | *Date of approval* | *Date of implementation* | *Date of renewal* | *Date of implementation* |
|---|---|---|---|---|---|
| Turnover tax | 57-L/CTN | 10/5/1997 | 1/1/1997 | | |
| Agriculture tax | 23-L/CTN | 10/7/1993 | 1/1/1994 | | |
| Special excise tax | 05/1998/QH10 | 28/10/1995 | 1/1/1996 | 20/5/1998 | 1/1/1999 |
| Import-export duties | 64-LTC/HDNN | 4/1/1992 | 1/3/1992 | 20/5/1998 | 1/1/1999 |
| Land and housing tax | 69-LCT/HDNN8 | 31/7/1992 | 1/10/1992 | | |
| Land alienation tax | 35-L/CTN | 22/6/1994 | 1/7/94 | 21/12/1998 | 1/1/2000 |
| Income tax of high income earners | 33-L/CTN | 19/5/1994 | 1/6/1998 | | |
| Value added tax (VAT) | 57-L/CTN | 10/5/1997 | 1/1/1999 | | |
| Tax on overuse the agriculture land | 31-L/CTN | 15/3/1994 | 1/1/1994 | | |

Source: Vietnam Law Data.

and local governments permits greater local flexibility while ensuring that central priorities are protected. Furthermore, expenditure is directed toward human development. Subsidies to SOEs are strictly controlled (Overseas Economic Cooperation Fund 1996). Expenditures for social services have increased slightly, and the deficit has been covered by borrowing rather than printing money.

Since 1998, the Vietnam economy has undertaken even deeper reforms. First, the turnover tax and the profit tax have been replaced by a VAT tax and a company turnover tax. In addition, two new taxes have been implemented from 1 January 1999. These changes have created a new regime for the Vietnamese tax system, and in particular, the market mechanism has been applied on the tax system. The changes have also encouraged both taxpayers and tax collectors and strengthened the tax collection process. Second, the reforms have improved transparency. Together with the new phase of tax system reform, one very important decision of the government in this period was the declaration of formal publication of government fiscal information since 1998. In particular, the Ministry of Finance issued a circular letter to direct the conduct of government institutions implementing the transparency process. This process is a further step to reform in terms of improving transparency (World Bank and the International Monetary Fund 2000). Moreover, the Budget Law was renewed in November 2002. The most important point of the renewed Budget Law is the move toward more decentralization to local government and encouragement of the role of local people council committees on deciding the decentralized budget (Ba 2002).

## *Review of Vietnam's fiscal policy and system*

### *Before 1990*

Table 18.2 shows that prior to 1985, the budget deficit was higher than 10 percent of GDP. Although mobilization of revenues was high (30.8 and 25.8 percent of GDP in 1976–80 and 1980–85, respectively), total expenditure in these two periods was also high. It can be seen that current fiscal expenditures in these two periods was a major component of total expenditures. Moreover, the balance between domestic revenue and current expenditure in these two periods was −4.3 and −1.0, respectively, which means that domestic revenue was not sufficient to cover current expenditures. As a result, the government needed foreign resources to operate current activities of the government, and the accumulation resource had to be smaller than the amount borrowed.

In the period 1986–90, revenue as a percentage of GDP was 14.5 percent and the fiscal deficit was −6.5 percent. While revenue declined relative to previous periods, at the same time, the deficit was also reduced. This can be explained by the fact that in 1985, Vietnam began its transition process, and it was only then that finances from the private sector began to be taken into account. That is, GDP in this period was a bit different from what it was before 1985. Nevertheless, the balance between domestic revenue and current expenditure was −0.3, and it can be said that in this period, the government has been moving toward balancing current expenditures.

*Table 18.2* The fiscal budget in Vietnam before 1990 (as a % of GDP)

| | *Average 1976–80* | *Average 1981–85* | *Average 1986–90* |
|---|---|---|---|
| 1. Total revenue | 30.8 | 25.8 | 14.5 |
| Domestic revenue | 25.4 | 25.4 | 14.1 |
| Of which: taxes and fees | 20.6 | 23.6 | 13.4 |
| 2. Total expenditure | 42.2 | 39.1 | 21.0 |
| For accumulation | 17.3 | 14.5 | 7.3 |
| Of which: investment | 14.6 | 11.7 | 5.2 |
| Interest payment | 1.1 | 0.7 | 0.8 |
| Current expenditure | 23.8 | 23.9 | 13.0 |
| Balance between domestic revenue and current expenditure | −4.3 | −1.0 | −0.3 |
| 3. Budget deficit | −11.3 | −13.4 | -6.5 |

Source: CIEM (1997).

*From 1990 onwards*

Figure 18.1 shows that budget revenue as a percentage of GDP in 1991–99 has gone up and down. It was 13.5 percent of GDP in 1991, increased to 1996, and then decreased to 18.4 percent in 1998 and went even lower in 1999. Meanwhile, domestic revenue followed the same trend as total revenue, while the situation with total expenditure is almost the same as with expenditure. However, in 1993, total expenditures peaked a bit higher than the trend (at more than 25 percent of GDP). The balance between domestic revenue and current expenditure in this

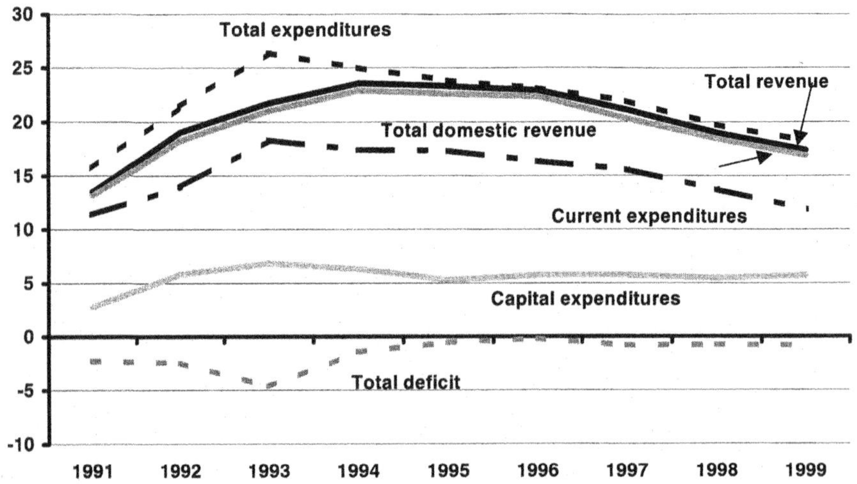


*Figure 18.1* An overview of the fiscal budget in Vietnam from 1990 onward (as a % of GDP).

Source: Adapted from various issues of GSO.

period is positive at about 5 percent of GDP. Two comments are made here. First, the government has savings and, second, fiscal management has made significant progress. As shown in Figure 18.1, the total budget deficit was under control. Moreover, the government was able to finance the deficit from domestic resources up to 1995 and reduced the deficit from 1995 onward.

Table 18.3 presents data on tax revenue as a percentage of GDP. The trend in the land and housing tax reflects the economic situation. As a percentage of GDP, the land and housing tax followed a rising trend, reaching 0.14 percent of GDP in 1996. In contrast, the agricultural tax followed a declining trend. The main reason for this is the booming market for land use transfers and the coming of foreign direct investment; as a result, the market on land use rights has been very active. However, with the decrease in activities in the land use rights market as well as the financial crisis of 1997, taxes from this source have declined to 0.08 percent of GDP in 1999. This is also the result of a reduction in the tax rate under the amendment of the law on land in 2000.

The most significant point is the rising trend of tax from joint venture enterprises. This source of tax revenue continuously increased from 0.28 percent of GDP in 1993 (the first time these enterprises had to pay a tax according to the law on foreign investment) to 1.23 percent in 1998 and 1.11 percent in 1999. This suggests that the joint venture sector in the economy has played an important role in tax revenue as well as the tax system. Taxes from import-export duties also played an important role in the tax system. They contributed about 4–5 percent of GDP and are the one of the highest contributors to the tax system. The trend of import-export duties follows the trend of total tax revenue, but it peaked at 5.8 percent in 1995, one year ahead of the peak in total tax revenue (19.6 percent in 1996). Subsequently, the contribution of import-export duties declined and in 1999, it was 4.13 percent of GDP.

Taxes from SOEs, in general, contributed about 6.8–9.6 percent of GDP over the period. The trend was generally upward until 1996 and since then, the ratio of taxes from SOEs has declined to 6.8 percent in 1999. The trend in taxes from SOEs was also affected by the financial crisis. In particular, the turnover tax was stable during 1990–98, and it decreased in 1999. Moreover, the profit tax was rather stable and contributed a share of about 2–3 percent of GDP. At the same time, the contribution from capital use charges remained stable at a rate of about 0.3–0.6 percent of GDP. Special consumption taxes and the license tax followed the same situation as the profit tax; both were stable over the 1990–99 period.

As shown in Figure 18.2, social expenditures increased considerably in the 1991–98 period. In 1991, social expenditures made up 4.36 percent of GDP. This ratio peaked in 1995 at 7.95 percent and in 1998, it was 7 percent. In contrast, ordinary expenditures as a share of GDP was 38, 46 and 50 percent, in these respective years. Thus, in comparison with GDP, social expenditures reached the highest level in 1995, but in comparison with ordinary expenditure, social expenditure was highest in 1998.

The situation is somewhat different for expenditures on health care. In 1991, health care expenditures were 0.83 percent of GDP; in 1995, it was 1.04 percent and in 1998, 0.76 percent. That is, government expenditure on health care

*Table 18.3* Taxes on fiscal revenue, 1991–99 (as a % of GDP)

| | *1991* | *1992* | *1993* | *1994* | *1995* | *1996* | *1997* | *1998* | *1999* |
|---|---|---|---|---|---|---|---|---|---|
| Taxes in state budget | 10.926 | 13.675 | 17.473 | 18.807 | 19.086 | 19.582 | 17.690 | 17.010 | 15.200 |
| Taxes from SOEs | 7.257 | 8.718 | 9.619 | 9.371 | 8.874 | 9.137 | 8.662 | 7.550 | 6.820 |
| Tax from private sector | 1.227 | 1.647 | 2.147 | 2.216 | 2.314 | 2.339 | 2.273 | 2.530 | 2.230 |
| Agricultural tax | 0.922 | 1.171 | 0.963 | 0.620 | 0.678 | 0.699 | 0.541 | 0.540 | 0.460 |
| Income tax | 0.081 | 0.138 | 0.131 | 0.188 | 0.227 | 0.498 | 0.473 | 0.490 | 0.380 |
| Land and housing tax | 0.0065 | 0.0163 | 0.1283 | 0.1232 | 0.1367 | 0.1397 | 0.1062 | 0.080 | 0.080 |
| Import-export duties | 1.433 | 1.985 | 2.068 | 5.608 | 5.799 | 5.553 | 4.319 | 4.580 | 4.130 |
| Tax from joint venture enterprises | 0.000 | 0.000 | 0.277 | 0.681 | 0.931 | 1.100 | 1.211 | 1.230 | 1.110 |
| Transfer power of using land tax | 0.000 | 0.000 | 0.000 | 0.000 | 0.126 | 0.117 | 0.105 | 0.100 | 0.000 |

Source: Adapted from various version of GSO.

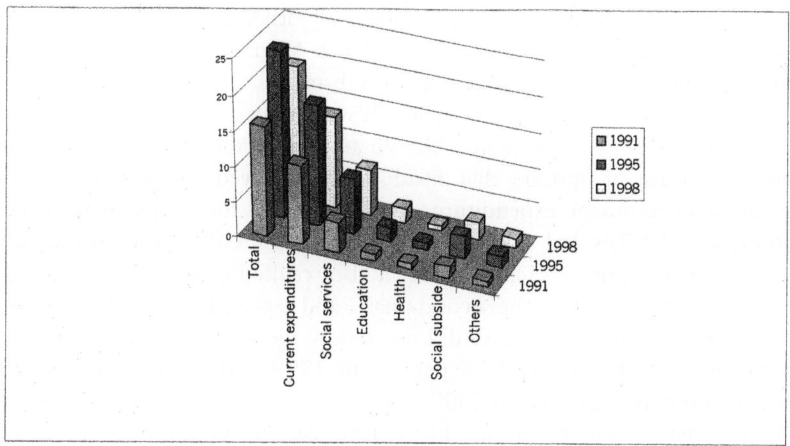


*Figure 18.2* Budget expenditure on social aspects, 1990 onward (as a % of GDP).

Source: Adapted from various issues of GSO.

continuously increased up to 1995, then declined. However, in comparison with ordinary expenditure, expenditure on health care made up 7.2 percent, 6.0 percent and 5.7 percent in those same three years.

Expenditure on social protection amounted to 1.67 percent of GDP in 1991, 3.23 percent in 1995 and 2.52 percent in 1998. Relative to ordinary expenditure, the share of social protection was 14.6 percent, 18.6 percent and 13.0 percent for those same three years. Thus, expenditure on social protection relative to ordinary expenditure was reduced in 1998.

Similarly, expenditure on education made up nearly 1 percent of GDP in 1991, slightly more than 2 percent in 1995 and 2.1 percent, the highest, in 1998. Naturally, in comparison with ordinary expenditure, expenditure on education was an even higher ratio in 1998. The respective rates for the same three years were 8.6 percent, 6.0 percent and 15.8 percent.

## Impacts of fiscal reform on economic development

### *Impacts on macroeconomic variables*

As can be seen from Table 18.4, GDP growth over the period 1990–2002 followed two distinct phases. In the first phase, from 1990–95, GDP growth continuously increased, with the highest growth occurring at 9.54 percent in 1995. The year 1997 represents the turning point, and the second phase takes place from 1996 onward. In this phase, GDP growth followed a declining trend, but began to recover in 2000.

In addition, in 1990–98 the interest rate generally followed the inflation rate. However, in 1999–2002, the interest rate had to decline even further as government expenditure increased to encourage domestic demand. Moreover, the exchange rate boomed in 1990–91 and it slowly increased to 2002. The trend in the Vietnam currency was different from almost all other currencies in the region. From 1997 onward, the exchange rate of the Vietnam dong versus the US$ changed somewhat, but the change was not substantial.

In general, there are two phases in which we can analyze government expenditure. The first phase takes place in 1990–96 and the second is from 1997 onward. In the first phase, it appears that fiscal policy followed the Keynesian model. Increases in government expenditure, such as salaries for people who work for government and SOEs, led to an increase in GDP, the CPI, and then the interest rate (Table 18.4, Figure 18.1). However, it also resulted in an increasing exchange rate in the first two years. In the second phase, and especially from 1999–2000, the effect of government expenditures did not follow the Keynesian model. Although government expenditure was 17.5 percent in 1999 and 15.0 percent in 2000, national income still increased in 2000.

One explanation for this is that, in the first years of the transition process, the market mechanism played its role in policing the economy. However, the market mechanism operates only in the goods market, but it does not work in the financial and property markets. Typically an increase in government expenditure would be associated with an increase in national income and household income and thus household consumption. However, in this case, household consumption did not increase as some of the household savings were placed in the property market. Especially after the financial crisis, people pulled their savings from gold and foreign currencies and placed it into the property market. But there is no channel to merge these markets so as to follow the Keynesian model. The reason behind this assessment lies in the transition process. Vietnam is undergoing the transition to a market economy, and the process that has been adopted is a gradual approach. As a result, the market mechanism first started in the goods and services market. Now it is starting to operate in the financial market as well (the stock market began operations in July 2000) but turnover of transactions remains very small. The property market and labor market are still under consideration. As such, the markets are still isolated, and there is no channel to move the resources between these markets.

### *Impact of fiscal management reform on poverty alleviation*

The achievement of poverty alleviation in Vietnam is clear. First, the overall poverty rate fell from 58 percent in 1993 to 37 percent in 1998 (General Statistic Office 1999). The food poverty rate was reduced from 25 percent in 1993 to 15 percent in 1998, an average reduction of 2 percent per year. In addition, micro data from the Ministry of Planning and Investment show that the number of food poverty households declined from 30 percent in 1992 to 17 percent in 1998 and 10–11 percent in 2000. Second, the living standards of those now living in poverty have improved compared to what they were five years ago. Third, the poverty rate has declined, but the drop has not been even among the different regions. The North Central Coast has the highest poverty rate reduction (26.4 percent), followed by the North Mountain and Midland (20.0 percent) and the Central

*Table 18.4* Main indicators of the Vietnam economy, 1990–2002

| | *1990* | *1991* | *1994* | *1995* | *1996* | *1997* | *1998* | *1999* | *2000* | *2001* | *2002* |
|---|---|---|---|---|---|---|---|---|---|---|---|
| GDP growth (%) | 5.10 | 5.96 | 8.84 | 9.54 | 9.34 | 8.15 | 5.83 | 4.8 | 6.8 | 6.9 | 7.1 |
| Inflation (CPI, %) | 67.5 | 67.4 | 14.4 | 12.7 | 4.5 | 3.6 | 9.2 | 0.1 | −0.6 | 0.8 | 4.0 |
| Government consumption (as a % of GDP) | 7.54 | 6.59 | 8.26 | 8.19 | 8.35 | 8.13 | 7.62 | 6.79 | 6.51 | 7.05 | 7.05 |
| Export growth (%) | 23.54 | 25.74 | 24.96 | 17.50 | 28.77 | 11.36 | 3.30 | 23.1 | 24.0 | 3.8 | 10.0 |
| Import growth (%) | 7.27 | 9.59 | 23.88 | 15.00 | 25.59 | 7.14 | −1.2 | 0.9 | 30.8 | 3.4 | 19.4 |
| Exchange rate (US$/VND) | 4,950 | 7,400 | 10,980 | 11,050 | 11,150 | 12,500 | 13,880 | 14,200 | 14,500 | 15,080 | 15,315 |
| Interest rate[a] (%/month) | 2.75 | 2.45 | 0.7 | 1.7 | 0.85 | 0.9 | 1.15 | 0.45 | 0.40 | 0.35 | 0.35 |
| Money supply (M2) | 27.2 | 26.4 | 29.6 | 22.5 | 23.7 | 26.0 | 27.5 | 33 | 38.9 | 23.3 | 27.5 |

Sources: Thanh (1996), Chung (1998), CIEM (2000, 2002).

Note

a 3-month deposit rate.

Highlands (17.6 percent). Fourth, the lives of the poor have become more equal between the two surveys (1994 vs. 1998). The square poverty gap index dropped from 7.87 percent to 3.55 percent. However, there is still a large difference between the lives of the urban poor and the rural poor. The two regions where the inequality among the poor people is highest are the Central Highlands (9.56 percent) and the North Mountain and Midland (6.48 percent). Fifth, the poor people are not located evenly between different regions. The North Mountain, Mekong Delta and North Midland have 70 percent of the total poor in Vietnam.

With respect to the five impact channels for poverty reduction (World Bank 1995),[1] spending on rural roads has all five, followed by family planning, maternity and child care and nutrition, which has four impact channels (except increased access to resources). Most other expenditures have three impact channels; these expenditures include the credit scheme of Women's Union, radio documentary for ethnic minorities, magazine for ethnic minorities, roads to schools, instruction for medicine use and better training. Expenditures with two impact channels include better medical services, safe water and sanitation, flexible teaching program, ethnic minority staff and disaster relief. Expenditure on the Credit of the Bank for Agriculture (now the Bank for the Poor) has one impact channel (increased access to resources).

Moreover, the results of the fiscal management reform process have shown positive impacts and led to achievements in poverty alleviation over the past years. First, fiscal management reform in Vietnam has had a positive impact on economic growth, and has therefore contributed to poverty alleviation. Second, fiscal management reform has gradually been oriented toward social issues, in general, and poverty alleviation, in particular. Though the rate of social expenditure in total government expenditure is not as high as required, the rate of expenditure on social issues and people as a share of total expenditure has increased as noted earlier. Third, expenditure on social issues, especially target programs, has contributed considerably to poverty alleviation. Target programs of government expenditure have directly contributed toward increasing jobs, improving rural infrastructure, improving health care services and promoting education. Therefore, poverty alleviation, which was originally an objective of the government, has become an objective of the people who implement the programs. Fourth, poverty alleviation has been targeted at the national level; therefore, government expenditure has widespread impacts and has attracted different resources to participate on this issue. Government expenditure has been the seed money to mobilize different resources in poverty alleviation in Vietnam.

Nevertheless, there are still limits and problems. Despite the progress that has been made, Vietnam is still one of the poorest countries in the world and the poverty rate in Vietnam, although considerably reduced, remains high. Although social expenditure has increased, this level of spending is not sustainable. If social expenditure does not continuously increase, this may affect the process of reducing the poverty rate. At the same time, demand for expenditures on investment is high, and as a result, expenditures on social issues cannot increase very much. Moreover, though fiscal management reform has had a positive impact on poverty alleviation, there have been problems with regards to the effectiveness.

## The road ahead: prospects, challenges and suggestions

### *Prospects*

With regard to fiscal management, the objectives have been clearly defined: the government must ensure transparency and equality in expenditure. Moreover, the prospects for Vietnam's economy look good in the coming years. First, the country's transition to a market-based economy has experienced long and stable steps. Vietnam has learned from successful and unsuccessful lessons of its own experiences as well as that of other countries. The coming steps will have more advantages, cost less and be more successful. Second, Vietnam now has more favorable external relations. Vietnam has established economic relationships with most countries in the world. Its participation in APEC, the signing of the Vietnam–United States Trade Agreement and the preparation process toward joining the WTO are major economic advantages for Vietnam. Fiscal management reform will be further supported as part of these efforts.

Following the fiscal management reform of the 1990s, Vietnam continues to take important steps. First, the taxation system will be continued to be reformed with further orientation toward the market. Income tax is being revised with a view to increasing the effectiveness of the taxation system. Second, public expenditures are being reviewed. With support from international financial institutions such as the World Bank and the International Monetary Fund, a public expenditure report is being synthesized.

### *Challenges*

However, there are still many challenges. First, there is only a limited possibility for increasing government revenue. It will be difficult to increase government revenue by adding new tax decrees, such as the income tax. In the short run, it will also be difficult to increase government revenue from state-owned enterprises. Moreover, in order to foster sources of income, it is a matter of fact that government revenue cannot be increased by raising trade taxes. In the integration into ASEAN and implementation of AFTA, Vietnam must reduce its tax to 0–5 percent in 2006. Therefore, tax revenue from imports from ASEAN countries will be reduced in the coming years. At the same time, government expenditure on social issues, including poverty alleviation, is always affected by the pressure to place a high priority on economic growth. Currently, the Vietnam economy is still at a low level compared to other countries in the world. As a result, government expenditure on social issues, in general, and poverty alleviation, in particular, is always in severe competition with spending on investment for growth. As far as GDP per capita is concerned, on the basis of either market price or PPP, Vietnam is still at very low level. This has posed large challenges of concentrating resources on investment for growth.

### *Suggestions for the future*

In general, planning and discipline should be strengthened in fiscal management. A realistic review of the government budget shows that government revenue and expenditure have not been completely stable, financial discipline has not been strictly followed, and inadequate attention has been paid to reporting, information sharing and processing. In addition, forecasting in fiscal management should be strengthened. Forecasting should be considered an important tool for improving the organization and implementation of ordinary fiscal management tasks. Accurate forecasts of government revenue are a decisive factor in allocating expenditure and balancing the budget. With regard to expenditure, apart from ordinary expenditure which is rather stable, the forecast should be based on the government's policies to reduce or increase socio-economic tasks. Moreover, transparency should be increased in fiscal operation and management. It is necessary to strengthen the fiscal system, thus ensuring transparency, equality and simplification in collecting and spending; and to further implement decentralization to increase the local government's responsibility in decisions on using revenue.

On the government revenue side, an accurate budget forecast is very important in budget management, especially in Vietnam where revenue sources as well as expenditures are not stable. A more accurate forecast that is closer to reality can be made by taking into account current government policy on financial mobilization, especially tax decrees and other nontax revenue regulations, adjusted and renewed policies on revenue, policies to encourage investment in each area and period of time, and number of years. In order to increase revenue collection, revenue policies should be simple and easy to understand and implement, but with adequate terms in order to manage all stages of the collection. In order to build a desirable taxation system and overcome existing matters, a restructuring of the system is needed with a view to ensuring government revenue, encouraging domestic competition and promoting integration. The personal income tax in Vietnam is now among the highest in the world (upward of 75 percent on the portion of incomes over $800 a month), and it discourages taxpayers from paying taxes. Thus, it should be revised to ensure equality for every citizen.

On the government expenditure side, in order to improve effectiveness of government expenditure which is oriented toward improving living standards of the people, especially given the current situation of financial constraint, government spending should be based with a development orientation. Priority should be given to outstanding domestic and foreign debt, with attention paid to possible negotiation to reschedule debt payments or borrowing to pay former debt. The number of core staff should be reduced. Law-based management requirements should be institutionalized by concrete and unified institutions. At the same time, there should be a clear expenditure model for infrastructure construction projects and target programs of the government. On one hand, the expenditure plan should be based on real spending demand to implement the tasks of branches and localities, as well as on the government's financial ability. On the other hand, responsibilities of heads of units/branches should be clearly defined by regulations in preparing the expenditure budget.

## Conclusion

Vietnam is in transition toward a market economy. Fiscal policy is one of the important aspects that should be reformed to operate under a market mechanism. Fiscal policy has played an important role in reducing poverty. In the macro-economy, the Vietnam economy followed the Keynesian model for the period 1990–98. However, evidence from 1999–2000 suggests that the Vietnam economy was not following the Keynesian model and not fully operating under a market mechanism. For further reform in fiscal policy and management, Vietnam should continue its market orientation with the goal of greater government transparency and effectiveness.

## Acknowledgments

We are grateful to Ms. Duong Thanh Mai and Dr. Tran Tho Dat from the National Economic University (Viet Nam) for providing us with substantial advice while we were conducting this study. We would also express our special thanks to Mr. Daniel Van Houte from the University Libral of Bruxell for his valuable comments.

## Note

1 These five channels include: (i) reduced differentiation; (ii) better management of risk; (iii) increased access to different resources; (iv) increased sustainability; and (v) increased participation (World Bank 1995).

## References

Ba, Le Xuan (2002) "The role of the People Council Committee in decisions on decentralized budget," paper presented at a seminar on Capacity Strengthening of the Standing Committees and Committees of People Council Committee, Can Tho, December.

Central Institute for Economic Management (CIEM) (1997) "Some measurement to increase domestic saving," unpublished paper, Hanoi. (In Vietnamese.)

Central Institute for Economic Management (CIEM) (2000) *Viet Nam's Economy in 1999*, Hanoi: Statistical Publishing House.

Central Institute for Economic Management (CIEM) (2002) *Viet Nam's Economy in 2000*, Hanoi: National Political Publishers.

Chung, T.K. (1998) "Vietnam economy in 1997–early 1998 and forecast summary," paper presented at Project LINK Fall Meeting, Rio de Janeiro, 14–18 September.

General Statistic Office (GSO) (1999) *Vietnam Living Standard Survey 1997–1998*, Hanoi: GSO.

Ministry of Planning and Investment (MPI) (2000). *Socio-Economic Report, no. 671*, 20 October, Hanoi: MPI.

Overseas Economic Cooperation Fund (OECF) (1996) *Fiscal and Financial Reforms in Vietnam: Economic Development and Transition to a Market Economy*, Tokyo: OECF.

Socialist Republic of Vietnam (SRV) (1997) *Law on the State Budget*, Hanoi: National Political Publishing House.

Tanzi, V. (1995) *Transition to Market: Studies in Fiscal* Reform, Washington, DC: International Monetary Fund.

Thanh, V.T. (1996) "The underlying determinants of inflation in Vietnam since 1989," paper presented at the workshop AusAid/NCDS Vietnam Economic Research Project, Ho Chi Minh City, 11–12 July.

Thin, Do Thi (1999) "Tax and tax reform in Vietnam," in *Reform on Economic, Finance: Achievements and Prospects*, Hanoi: Finance Publishing House. (In Vietnamese.)

United Nations Development Program (UNDP) (1998) *Human Development Report*, New York: Oxford University Press.

World Bank (1995) *Vietnam Poverty Assessment and Strategy*, Hanoi: World Bank.

World Bank (1996) *Vietnam Fiscal Decentralization and the Delivery of Rural Services*, Country Operation Division, Country Department I, East Asia and Pacific Region, Washington, DC: World Bank.

World Bank (1998) *The State in a Changing World: A Report on World Development*, Hanoi: National Political Publishing House. (In Vietnamese.)

World Bank and the International Monetary Fund (2000) *Vietnam Public Expenditure Review*, mimeo, Hanoi.

# Index

Italics are used to indicate information presented as a table (*T*) or figure (*F*).

For Product Safety Concerns and Information please contact our EU representative GPSR@taylorandfrancis.com Taylor & Francis Verlag GmbH, Kaufingerstraße 24, 80331 München, Germany

Printed and bound by CPI Group (UK) Ltd, Croydon, CR0 4YY
11/04/2025
01843977-0008